The Carrot or the Stick?

Towards Effective Practice with Involuntary Clients in Safeguarding Children Work

Edited by
Martin C. Calder

RHP

Russell House Publishing

First published in 2008 by:
Russell House Publishing Ltd.
4 St. George's House
Uplyme Road
Lyme Regis
Dorset DT7 3LS

Tel: 01297-443948
Fax: 01297-442722
e-mail: help@russellhouse.co.uk
www.russellhouse.co.uk

British Library Cataloguing-in-publication Data:
A catalogue record for this book is available from the British Library.

ISBN: 978-1-905541-22-5

Typeset by TW Typesetting, Plymouth, Devon

Front cover artwork by Stacey Laura Calder

Printed and bound in Great Britain by
CPI Antony Rowe, Chippenham and Eastbourne

Russell House Publishing

Russell House Publishing aims to publish innovative and valuable materials to help managers, practitioners, trainers, educators and students.

Our full catalogue covers: social policy, working with young people, helping children and families, care of older people, social care, combating social exclusion, revitalising communities and working with offenders.

Full details can be found at www.russellhouse.co.uk and we are pleased to send out information to you by post. Our contact details are on this page.

We are always keen to receive feedback on publications and new ideas for future projects.

If you are going through hell, keep going

Winston Churchill (1874–1965)

This book is dedicated with much admiration, affection and love to my parents.

To Janet, Stacey and Emma: everything I do is inspired by you

Martin C. Calder

Contents

Working with Specific Client Groups

Preface

It is a fact of everyday work across the whole area of safeguarding children that many practitioners and managers struggle to engage clients who resist getting involved with services that the clients either need or have offered to them.

Yet, although there is clearly a need to improve concepts and strategies in work with such involuntary clients, insufficient attention has been paid in recent years to systematically developing innovations in working with them; and there has been very little theoretical and practice research activity geared to this end. This book has been written to make it easier for a wide range of people to take steps towards addressing this shortcoming.

Who this book is for

This book is for all practitioners and managers – whether their expertise lies in care, welfare, education, justice, health or mental health – from any of the agencies involved in the wide spectrum of safeguarding children work, which includes child protection, children in need, domestic abuse and youth offending/justice.

It will also be useful for students on many courses – especially social work training at degree and PQ levels – and for Safeguarding Board trainers. It should also be appealing to government staff with responsibility for policy development or review.

Their clients

For convenience, the term 'clients' is used here to describe the full range of all of the people, of all ages, with whom this full spectrum of safeguarding children agencies work.

This could include:

- **Children and young people** who have been abused or neglected.
- Those who could be at risk of abuse or neglect.
- Those whose behaviour may already be a concern because of its impact on others.
- Those whose behaviour is judged to be at risk of becoming so.
- Caring **parents** of children in any of the above circumstances.
- Abusive parents.
- Parents who are neglectful, for whatever reason, potentially including substance misuse or inexperience in the skills of parenting.
- Parents who are caring to their children but who are nevertheless violent to each other.
- Those who are victims of such domestic violence.

- **Foster or residential carers** who are in place of parents in any of the above circumstances.
- **Anyone else who abuses or neglects to safeguard a child or young person**. This could be another family member, someone working in a school or club, a neighbour, or even a complete stranger.

Voluntary and involuntary clients

All of these clients range along a continuum from voluntary to involuntary.

At one end of the continuum are those **voluntary clients** who believe in the value and efficacy of professional services such as counselling, and who actively seek help in solving their problems and in achieving their personal goals. For example, parents may ask for assistance in dealing with tensions to avoid abusing their children; and substance abusers may voluntarily participate in counselling to reduce the frequency of their undesirable behaviours.

At the other end are those **involuntary clients** who not only are legally mandated to receive services but also do not wish to receive them. Those who are legally mandated include prisoners and other institutionalised clients in correctional and mental health settings. Other clients may be legally mandated by the courts to receive services but not be institutionalised.

In between the examples used above to illustrate these two clear-cut sets of circumstances, whether a client is voluntary or involuntary may vary:

- In relation to the **make-up of the client unit**. A worker's 'client' might be an individual, couple, family, or group. When there are two or more individuals in the client unit, one may be mandated to receive services and, thus or otherwise, be receiving services involuntarily; while the other person or people in the client unit may be receiving the same or other services entirely voluntarily. This difference depends on the degree to which they wish to participate in services provided. For example, in a family where sexual abuse or domestic violence is an issue, one or more family members may be mandated to receive services to help them stop their abusive behaviour; while others may voluntarily seek services, for example ones that help them to continue to provide care despite being badly affected by abuse themselves.
- **Over time**: a voluntary client may be involuntary on another day.
- **Depending on the service offered**: the same client may be 'voluntary' about some services that they consider desirable and 'involuntary' about others, which they consider undesirable, even from the same worker.

How this book can help

The carefully selected and edited chapters in this book offer systematic and evidence-based approaches to the critical areas in work with all of these clients in the full range of these circumstances. They are 'no-nonsense' approaches that will fit with practice wisdom and practice realities.

By exploring the range of problems facing professionals, coupled with frameworks and suggested strategies to attain better outcomes, they offer what for many readers will be innovative ways of enhancing their clients' motivation and helping them to change, not only in how they respond to services, but also in what they had been doing that caused the services to need to be delivered or offered.

Special attention is devoted to:

- Strategies for making and maintaining working relationships to achieve practice objectives with these clients.
- Examining the contemporary context of safeguarding children and the new considerations this brings.
- Links between risk assessment and involuntary clients as they are seen as two sides of the same coin.
- Examination of the emerging research and theoretical evidence-base in relation to this work linked to developing practice wisdom.
- Considering issues for the engagement of children as well as adults in the safeguarding process.
- Examining the importance of consent and coercion.
- Frameworks for understanding and working with motivation as well as resistance and change.
- Considering new approaches to working with involuntary clients across a range of settings.
- The risks to staff when clients respond to their involuntary status.
- The need to shift toward the engagement of men/fathers as well as women/mothers in the intervention process.

Experience, understanding and experimentation

The authors of this book's chapters are drawn from a wide range of disciplines; practitioners and researchers; in different countries with different systems. Whilst their descriptions derive from their own practice base, workers will find many of the messages and suggestions transferable.

The aspirations of this book

Many professional staff face a daily wall of resistance and barrage of uncaring feedback in the course of going about their work across the whole area of safeguarding children as well as their carers. It can become wearying and dispiriting.

If managers, trainers and lecturers have had to work as hard as was necessary to pull this book together, then they may also have become weary and dispirited when asked for help that they may not have been sure how to provide.

It is hoped that the encouragement that I, as the editor of this book, have received from the chapters that are presented here – all of which I have certainly found to be essential reading for my own practice, training and consultancy – will:

- Help everyone in training to enter the workplace to do so with a sense that they can succeed, not only when their assistance is sought, but also when others do not want to engage with their help.
- Rekindle the confidence and enthusiasm of those who have shared first-hand, sometimes for a long time, in the experience of trying to address entrenched client resistance without adequate help or guidance on how to do so.

About the Contributors

Ken Barter is a Professor with the School of Social Work, Memorial University of Newfoundland. He has a BA degree from Memorial University, a Masters degree in Social Work from the University of Calgary, Alberta, and a PhD degree in Social Work from Wilfred Laurier University, Waterloo, Ontario. His PhD is in the field of public child welfare and administration. Ken worked for 30 years in public child welfare systems in Newfoundland, Northwest Territories, and Prince Edward Island before entering academia in 1995. During these years he held positions in the front line, supervision, management, and social policy areas. Ken has published extensively in the form of book chapters, journal articles, research reports, and conference proceedings. He has presented to audiences at provincial, national and international conferences. His publications, presentations, teaching, and research are in the field of child protection and social work. Ken is a Board member with the Child Welfare League of Canada and a Board member with the Canadian Association of Schools of Social Work. He also serves on several community boards. From September 1998 until the end of funding in April 2003, Ken held the research position of Chair in Child Protection at the School of Social Work.

Calvin Bell is Director of *Ahimsa* (Safer Families) Ltd and an international consultant in the field of domestic violence. He has extensive clinical experience of working with men with histories of violent and abusive behaviours. His practice has involved supporting both male and female victims of domestic abuse. He has wide experience of carrying out adult family assessments where domestic abuse is a concern, and has acted as an expert witness in family law proceedings for over 10 years. Calvin has received numerous commissions to design and deliver training in various aspects of domestic violence from a number of UK and overseas organisations; has been commissioned to write domestic violence training manuals; and has published in the field. Having trained in teaching, community work and psychotherapy, he is currently undertaking PhD research at the Centre for Forensic and Family Psychology (Birmingham University).

Christine Bidmead MSc, RGN, RHV is an experienced health visitor working in both urban and rural communities. She has undertaken training in counselling with the Herts and Beds Pastoral Foundation and since 2001 has worked for the South London and Maudsley NHS Foundation Trust as a training facilitator of the Family Partnership Model. She is a visiting research fellow of King's College, London, Chair of the health visitor's forum of the Community Practitioners and Health Visitors Association and serves on the committee of the Association for Infant Mental Health.

Judith Bula Wise PhD (Bryn Mawr College) Professor Emerita, has held academic positions at Columbia University and the University of Denver. She is the author of *Empowerment Practice with Families in Distress* and co-editor (with Marian Bussey) of *Trauma Transformed: An Empowerment Response,* forthcoming in November 2007. Dr. Wise also developed and served as the first Coordinator of the Trauma Response Certificate Program at the University of Denver. She lives in Boulder, Colorado with her husband and two Labrador retrievers.

Martin C. Calder established Calder Training and Consultancy in 2005 after 20 years in frontline child protection practice. His aim has been to generate and collate the available and necessary assessment tools for frontline staff, especially in times of massive change. He also critiques central government guidance and attempts to provide remedial materials to help fill the gap left between aspiration and reality. He is contactable through his website at www.caldertrainingandconsultancy.co.uk

Mark S. Carich, PhD is the coordinator of the Sexually Dangerous Persons (SDP) program at the Illinois Department of Corrections, Big Muddy Correctional Center. He has been working with SDPs since 1989 and has coordinated this program since 1990 and is also on the teaching and dissertation staff of the Adler School of Professional Psychology in Chicago. Dr Carich has published extensively in the field of psychology and treatment of sex offenders. His most recent publications include *Contemporary Treatment of Adult Male Sex Offenders* (with M. Calder, 2003) *Adult Sex Offender Report* (with D. Adkerson, 2003) and *Handbook of Sexual Abuser Assessment and Treatment* (co-edited with S. Mussack, 2001). Dr Carich conducts sex offender training at an international level. He recently conducted six days of training in Taiwan on key points in contemporary treatment of sex offenders. When he isn't teaching, training, or testifying in court, Mark lives in Illinois with his family.

Sarah Cowley BA, PhD, PGDE, RGN, RHV, HVT, after 25 years as a practitioner, became interested in how organisations help or hinder practice. That curiosity led her into research; first a PhD focusing on how to account for health visiting practice, then to an academic post at King's College, London. She was appointed as Professor of Community Practice Development in 1997. She has published widely, mainly to report research projects that reflect her professional background in health visiting and interest in public health and positive health, especially in relation to needs assessment, families and the social environment. She has edited three books and co-authored three others, including a recent update of the *Principles of Health Visiting* in 2006.

Scott Curran is a child protection social worker on the long-term high risk team at Olmsted County Child and Family Services in Rochester, Minnesota and is currently completing a masters of social work degree at the University of Minnesota in St Paul. Scott is contactable at: curran.scott@co.olmsted.mn.us

Gerry Dobkowski MA LPC is a sex offender treatment counsellor working with Dr. Carich in the Sexually Dangerous Persons Program at Big Muddy River Correctional Center, part of the Illinois Department of Corrections.

Toby Fattore is a research scholar in the school of Political Economy, University of Sydney. His current research includes examining children's subjective assessments of well-being and developing a framework of children's economic agency by investigating children's work. Some of his other work includes developing modes of child-centred citizenship, examining the impact of administrative structures on child protection practice, developing practice guidelines for children's participation in research and an assessment of the impacts of economic reform on middle class Australians.

Erica Flegg is a risk assessor and psychotherapist working in the field of family violence. She has a wide experience in carrying out risk assessments in disputed contact and child protection cases where abuse within the family is a concern, and she has acted as an expert witness in both family law and criminal proceedings. She has a particular clinical interest in the dynamics of violent relationships and the psychology of gender, and she has helped to develop AHISMA's risk assessment model as it applies to mothers and the understanding of relationship risk factors. She trained at the Institute of Psychotherapy and Social Studies from 1988–1991, and subsequently helped to set up the East Oxford Women's Counselling Service where she saw clients and ran supervision groups, deepening a prior interest in women's therapy. She holds degrees from the University of Sussex and the London School of Oriental and African Studies, doing post-graduate research for two years at the University of Edinburgh on theories of the subordination of women, and she holds a post-graduate Certificate in Violence in the Home (University of Westminster).

Eileen Gambrill, PhD, is Hutto Patterson Professor of Child and Family Studies in the School of Social Welfare at the University of California, Berkeley. She is the author of a number of books, articles and chapters on the intersection between critical thinking and clinical practice, between ethical and evidentiary concerns.

Phil Harris is an independent writer who has worked in drug services for over fifteen years. He has designed and delivered internationally recognised treatment programmes and accredited training courses throughout the UK and Europe. Having worked as a treatment advisor to DSTs, criminal justice services and youth services, he has also managed several organisations and implemented innovative, practical and effective approaches to addressing people's problems with misuse of drugs and alcohol. He has published two books; *Drug Induced: Addiction and Treatment in Perspective* (Russell House Publishing, 2005) and *Empathy for the Devil: How to Help People Overcome Drugs and Alcohol Problems* (Russell House Publishing, 2007). A consultant lecturer to Bristol University's Social Policy Unit, he continues to practice in the South West of England and Wales.

Michelle Lefevre is a lecturer in social work and social care at the University of Sussex (M.Lefevre@sussex.ac.uk). Her research and teaching interests include child protection, direct work with children and therapeutic interventions. She also has a small private practice as a psychotherapist and independent social worker. Recent publications include: *Knowledge Review: The Social Care Needs of Children with Complex Health Care Needs and their Families; Knowledge Review on Teaching, Learning and Assessing Communication Skills With Children and Young People in Social Work Education; Ethical Considerations in Psychotherapy with Children; Facilitating Practice Learning and Assessment: The Influence of Relationship; Finding the Key: Containing and Processing Traumatic Sexual Abuse;* and *Playing with Sound: The Therapeutic Use of Music in Direct Work with Children.*

Brian Littlechild is Professor of Social Work at the University of Hertfordshire. He has published widely on issues of aggression and violence against social workers, and on conflict resolution approaches. He has presented papers at national and international conferences on these areas for a number of years, and has been providing consultancy and training to a variety of social work and criminal justice agencies for over 20 years.

Susan Lohrbach is supervisor of family group decision making and the long-term high risk team at Olmsted County Child and Family Services in Rochester, Minnesota and is currently completing her social work PhD at the University of Minnesota in St Paul. Sue is contactable at: lohrbach.sue@co.olmsted.mn.us

Peter Marsh is Dean of Social Sciences at the University of Sheffield. He is a social worker and Professor of Child and Family. He spent ten years as a lecturer/social worker in a joint post between the University and a community-based team, and is currently working on evidence-based and participative social work, focusing on family group conferences, task-centred practice, and the development of practice-based research. He is professional advisor to the Research in Practice evidence-based services initiative, and heads up the resources team for the national social work research strategy.

Lynda Regan has worked with children and families in various settings for over 20 years. She was a social worker on a busy area team for eleven years before moving into therapeutic work at Salford Cornerstone Project in 1997. She manages a growing team of staff who are committed to supporting children, and their families to move forward from sexual or domestic abuse, as well as helping to develop skills of other professionals in relation to working with children and families.

Phil Rich holds a doctorate in applied behavioural and organisational studies and a master's degree in social work, and has practiced as a licensed independent clinical social worker for over 28 years. Phil is the Clinical Director of the Stetson School, a 111-bed long-term residential treatment programme for sexually reactive children and juvenile sexual offenders in Massachusetts, where he supervises a clinical team consisting of 18 clinicians and 8 case managers. He is the author of *Understanding Juvenile Sexual Offenders: Assessment, Treatment, and Rehabilitation* and *Attachment and Sexual Offending: Understanding and Applying Attachment Theory to the Treatment of Juvenile Sexual Offenders*, and is currently writing a book on assessing risk in sexually abusive youth.

Ronald Rooney is a Professor at the School of Social Work, University of Minnesota. He is the author of *Strategies for Work with Involuntary Clients* and *Direct Social Work Practice*. Dr Rooney has over 25 years experience in practice, training, consultation and research with involuntary clients in varied populations with special expertise in child welfare.

Trevor Spratt is a senior lecturer in social work at Queen's University Belfast. He previously worked as a social worker, team leader and manager within social services departments in Northern Ireland. His research interests, which include translation of policy into practice and the effect this may have upon service users, have largely come about as a result of his experience of work with children and families. He is currently involved in an international comparison of service approaches to families with long term and complex needs.

Dr Chris Trotter worked for almost 20 years as a social worker and a regional manager in child protection and corrections prior to his appointment to Monash University in 1991. He has published widely on the subject of 'effective social work' particularly in public welfare settings. His research on the relationship between worker intervention styles and client outcome has achieved international recognition and the intervention model developed in his research is being used in several countries. He has two commercial books, *Working with Involuntary Clients* and *Helping Abused Children and their Families* published by Allen and Unwin in Australia and by Sage internationally.

Nick Turnbull is a lecturer in social policy at the University of Manchester. He researches and teaches about political conflicts around social policy problems. He is currently researching how households cope with high levels of debt. He also writes on the philosophy of social science and is developing an interpretative theory of policy and politics based on the concept of questioning.

Andrew Turnell is an independent social worker with Resolutions Consultancy from Perth, West Australia. Andrew works as a child protection consultant with social services agencies in Europe, Australasia and North America. More information about his work is available and he is contactable at: www.signofsafety.net

Professor Diane Yatchmenoff is Assistant Director at the Regional Research Institute in Human Services (RRI) at the School of Social Work at Portland State University. She is one of the faculty members at RRI who provides essential research and evaluation services for local organisations and agencies that serve children and families. Yatchmenoff is one of the University's leading researchers at the Regional Research Institute (RRI). The RRI's goal is to improve the manner in which social services and service delivery systems are designed, managed and evaluated.

Introduction

The seeds of this book were sown when developing materials to assist frontline practitioners in their risk assessment practice. It became clear that the provision of evidence-based materials was of little value out of the context of working with involuntary clients in the child protection field. It was for this reason that I set about the task of trying to track down the best available materials to address this point and I was fortunate enough to elicit the cooperation of many leading writers in this area to assemble this exciting and groundbreaking book. It goes to press at the same time as my work on contemporary risk assessment (Calder, 2008) so these should sit together neatly for workers.

The book is broken down into three sections:

- Understanding the Current Context
- Introducing Broad Frameworks
- Working With Specific Client Groups

In the contextual opening section, **Chris Trotter** starts off by laying down the foundations for the book with an overview of the literature.

This is followed by **Trevor Spratt** examining the implications of the social care landscape for this area of work. He examines three identified themes of *prevention*, *pathology* and *partnership* and shows how they have largely been re-conceptualised within the ideological framework of the social investment state. This has given rise to a much greater number of parents becoming, by virtue of the way the state has become concerned with regard to their children, involuntary clients of the state. This has come about as a result of the redrawing of the relationship between the family and the state. In this new understanding, *partnership* with families has become subsumed within a more general concern for the safeguarding of children and recast in the contractual terms of rights and responsibilities. *Prevention* has come to the fore as the defining theme of the social investment state. No longer is the concept of prevention limited to small populations such as children in the state care system but is broadened to include a wide range of vulnerable children who require early intervention if they are to meet acceptable norms of progress toward an independent and productive future. Notions of *pathology* have become reserved for those groups who, whilst small in number, require the punitive attentions of the state to ensure they either undertake the parenting role or become excluded from it altogether.

In Chapter 3, **Turnbull and Fattore** consider the current political context of engaging with children. They argue that developing a system of service provision which engages positively with children requires effort at the level of practice, administration and the political will of policymakers to support it. Working with children should not be coercive but should engage positively with them and accord them some measure of agency within a supportive relationship so that the child and the worker might develop a shared perspective and, in so doing, enact a sincere communicative process which also attends to outcomes.

In Chapter 4, **Eileen Gambrill** examines informed consent. She notes that Professional Codes of Ethics require practitioners to honour informed consent guidelines. However, there remains considerable confusion in the field about issues of consent as well as confidentiality. Although written from her experience within the US system, the messages are equally relevant here. Informed consent requirements, gaps in honouring them, related ethical principles and the contentious nature of informed consent are discussed in this chapter. Options for informed consent in involuntary settings are suggested and obstacles reviewed as well as discussing trends forwarding informed consent. She suggests that informed consent is especially vital in coercive situations and describes opportunities to honour related obligations in settings such as protective services for children and mental health services. Both clients and professionals have choices in such settings in relation to informed consent issues that have both legal and ethical implications.

In the second section, **Diane Yatchmenoff** starts off by presenting findings from two studies of client engagement embedded in a five-year evaluation of child protective service practice in Oregon. The findings generate thought and dialogue about how we might guide and supervise workers to think more systematically about engagement – both what they might observe in the clients and how their practice might influence the client's feeling state.

Relationship is considered the most fundamental tool in social work practice. **Michelle Lefevre** moves us on to consider relationship-based considerations within child protection practice. The type of relationship formed between social workers and families who are subject to child protection assessments can be the key to both engagement and to whether family members feel sufficiently safe to explore the kind of sensitive areas that the assessment demands. This promotes decisions being based on the fullest knowledge possible, because parents and children have been able to contribute. Where trust is felt, family members are more likely to let down their barriers, to acknowledge difficulties and to begin to work on themselves. This makes for a more dynamic assessment, where change and development become part of the process.

In Chapter 7 **Ken Barter** also examines the challenges, principles and practice considerations of building relationships with clients in the field of child protection drawing upon the Canadian experience. He notes that the investigative role in child protection has placed workers in positions of doing more judging than helping, more investigation than relationship building, more following rules and protocols than creative intervention and risk taking, more relying on tools and instruments than professional integrity and assessments, more attending to the needs of the organisation than to the needs of families and children, and more reacting after family breakdowns than interventions to prevent breakdowns. These practice realities represent fundamental barriers in engaging in relationships with families in order to realise desirable outcomes for children. He reviews some of the literature in relation to relationship building and makes some recommendations for practice. Children and families who come to the attention of or require services from child protection organisations are struggling with fundamental challenges associated with poverty, discrimination, injustices, lack of opportunity, and health issues. They require interventions in their lives that create opportunities for them to engage in a process of healing and change whereby they discover their personal power to make a difference in their lives. This engagement has to extend beyond child welfare systems to include mental health, schools, community resource centres, justice, and community. Currently, child protection systems tend to be alone for much of this engagement, particularly from a protection perspective. It is for this reason that he proposes a community dimension to our interventions.

Turnell, Lohrbach and Curran demonstrate that child protection work and the professional-service recipient relationships are best thought about more in terms of their effectiveness in creating safety for children than whether they are voluntary or involuntary. By building and maintaining a professional system to family network focus, exercising and using authority skilfully alongside equal measures of empathy and honouring the strengths and humanity of the parents, thereby drawing upon a naturally occurring network surrounding the child, and through organisational and supervisory structures focus, the whole voluntary/involuntary nature can be de-emphasised and its negative consequences inoculated. This professional system to family network focus enables child protection work to be seen through a more constructive and purposive lens than simply the 'myopia' of individual change.

Ronald Rooney in his chapter presents guidelines for initial contact, assessment, and contracting based on normalising perspectives of strategic self-determination and reactance theory.

In Chapter 10, I move on to present a conceptual framework for understanding resistance, motivation and change and then offer some practical materials to equip it for operational practice.

Brian Littlechild examines the important elements for social workers and social work agencies to consider in an area which is often ignored in the literature and research; the effects of stress and violence on social workers and their professional practice when this is perpetrated against them when they are working with clients who are receiving their services involuntarily. He also examines the evidence concerning the effect on child protection work and child protection workers of violence from clients, responses to perpetrators, and responses to the workers affected by aggression from involuntary clients in child protection work.

Judith Bula Wise introduces us to a framework for family empowerment. She argues that the integration of supportive, caring family members and empowerment-based principles for treatment with involuntary clients offers many possibilities for enhancing a client's (individual or family) motivation to make choices for change that leads toward greater health and well-being. The tools presented in her chapter offer possibilities for transforming realities at the beginning of work with involuntary clients to an empowering result, one that integrates the power of family dynamics to enhance the outcome for the well-being of the clients.

Peter Marsh covers some of the history and current development of Family Group Conferences (FGCs), outlines the basic model, concentrating on the major area of child welfare, before going on to draw out some key lessons for user engagement from the substantial FGC experience that is now available.

Bidmead and Cowley examine the key relationship between health visitors and parents. They trace the development of policies affecting health visiting, to explain the principles underpinning the work and how the service came to be organised in its current, universal form. The present formulation of 'progressive universalism' is outlined to explain how the service retains some involuntary elements, requiring health visitors to engage their clients as a prelude to any meaningful work. They provide an integrative literature review to show how health visiting works in practice, with a particular focus on research that illuminates processes involved in gaining access, engaging and developing a continuing relationship based on a genuine partnership between health visitors and their clients. They conclude by noting that the growth in understanding of processes required to engage clients has not necessarily been translated into practice, partly because service organisation does not always take this evidence into account. They explore barriers and facilitators in supporting partnership working between health visitors and their clients, concluding with a critical analysis of the evidence and current issues.

In the final section there are a number of chapters addressing issues with particular client problem behaviour. **Mark Carich and his colleagues** consider engagement and motivation issues with sex offenders. As sex offenders are often involuntarily placed in treatment by the legal system, they present unique challenges that have the potential to create barriers to their recovery. Front line staff witness resistance in various forms, expressions of which include non-compliance with directives, defiance, some form of denial, defensiveness, hostility, and cognitive distortions. Quite often, initially, the offender's motivation to change is largely external; that is, a vague attempt to satisfy court-mandated treatment. In their chapter they examine how to motivate resistant sex offenders and even though the focus of the chapter is on sex offenders, the ideas, perspectives, and methods apply to most therapeutic perspectives and can be utilised with most clients. In fact, the ideas presented have direct applications to hostage negotiations, crisis intervention, along with less urgent communication or interactional processes.

Phil Rich examines how to engage young people who sexually abuse in the treatment work. He notes that working with young people who engage in sexually abusive behaviour, or, more specifically, *engaging* such youth in treatment, is straightforward to the degree that the work is no different than therapeutic work with any other client population. That is, the workbooks, the relapse prevention plans, and the interventions targeted specifically towards sexually aggressive and inappropriate behaviour are interwoven into a larger treatment programme that is no different than any other kind of broad treatment programme addressed towards troubling and troubled adolescent behaviour. However, the individual practitioner has to decide which model is the most appropriate, both from a philosophical perspective about treatment and with regard to what constitutes necessary and effective treatment. He introduces us to two models. Model one is constituted by the 'one-size-fits-all' approach that is technique and technically driven. Conversely, model two recognises that our capacity as trained, experienced, and knowledgeable clinicians is central to the work. In this model, it's clear that who the client is, what the client brings into treatment, and the client's attitudes and perspectives about treatment are very much influenced by the therapeutic relationship, which, in turn, has an impact upon the expectancy effect, or the client's belief that things can and will improve through therapy. Accordingly, outcome variables are chiefly moulded by client expectations, therapeutic alliance, and placebo effect that work together. The argument here is straightforward; it's the therapeutic relationship that makes the difference in the capacity to engage the client in treatment. From this perspective, engaging involuntary young people who sexually abuse in treatment is a matter of therapeutic practice and skill, transforming involuntary participants into voluntary participants through not technique, but clinical skill.

Flegg and Bell move on to consider domestic violence situations. Their work comprises risk assessment and treatment in two family law contexts: private lay (disputed child contact/residence cases) and public law (child protection proceedings). They examine some of the issues arising from their experience of assessing parents for treatment suitability and delivering treatment in public law cases.

Continuing with the issue of domestic violence, **Lynda Regan and myself** examine the impact of misdirected professional interventions with mothers living in situations of either sexual abuse or domestic violence. We consider the similarities of the professional approaches and mistakes and offer some suggestions on how this can be modified to be more constructive. One of the recurring themes in professional responses to domestic violence and sexual abuse is that mothers are unfairly dealt with by the professional systems, thus compounding the harm they have already experienced within their adult relationships. Given that most children stay with their mothers after parents separate, it is vital that we rapidly develop a system that allows for the mother's experience and the impact of the abuse to be resolved in a safe way for the children. Mothers have needs and are better able to provide for their children if those needs are acknowledged and built into the systems of response. Regrettably, this is sometimes considered a luxury given the increasing pressures on agencies and the deficits in resources that threaten to dismantle even the existing systems of inter-agency working.

In the final chapter **Phil Harris** examines treatment issues for substance using clients, many of whom are there through court mandate or 'threatment' as he calls it. The formalisation and expansion of criminal justice responses demands that substance misuse services revise their assumptions of both addiction and the delivery of treatment. Treatment outcomes will only endure if services can not only bond with the most excluded users, but capture their individual aspirations and cultivate their resources to achieve them. Likewise, informal relationships should be recognised as an unmet need and as a potent resource for change. This potential should not be therapised with unsubstantiated judgments but supported in the attainment of mutually shared goals of restoring cherished relationships. This means that in both the formal and informal domains, coercion should not replace engagement as the central force in change. Problematic users should not reframe from consumption simply because to do so has become entirely hostile, but because they have come to value a new life more highly. Coercion may provide the means but it can never be the end.

References

Calder, M.C. (Ed.) (2008) *Contemporary Risk Assessment in Safeguarding Children.* Lyme Regis: Russell House Publishing.

Understanding the Current Context

CHAPTER 1

Involuntary Clients: A Review of the Literature

Chris Trotter

The literature on involuntary clients is in one sense limited and in another sense expansive. Three books published in English include the term 'Involuntary Clients' in the title: *Strategies for Work with Involuntary Clients* by Ronald Rooney (1992) *Involuntary Clients in Social Work Practice* by Andre Ivanoff, Betty Blythe and Tony Tripodi (1994) and my book, now in its second edition, *Working with Involuntary Clients* (2006). On the other hand there are too many books to mention, let alone articles and reports, which focus at least in part on involuntary clients.

These publications focus on involuntary clients in criminal justice, in child protection, in mental health, in drug and alcohol treatment and sometimes in school welfare. There are multiple publications in these fields. To take the criminal justice example, there are individual texts and articles focusing on particular types of offenders, for example sex offenders, young offenders, female offenders, domestic violence perpetrators and drug addicted offenders. There are also publications on particular methods of dealing with offenders such as restorative justice, motivational interviewing, cognitive behavioural programmes, pro-social modelling or relapse prevention approaches.

This literature review cannot cover all of the literature published on involuntary clients. I have, however, attempted to identify the key themes which run through many of the publications on the topic. First, a brief discussion is offered about how different authors define involuntary clients. I have then discussed a set of core skills for workers with involuntary clients which the research suggests are related to positive outcomes. I have also discussed risk assessment about which much has been written in recent years. I have then discussed some of the intervention models which in most cases are based on the research about effective practice. I have also highlighted the concept of case management that provides the overarching model for work with involuntary clients in most settings around the world. Finally, I have considered some of the theories that have influenced the development of the practice models, in particular critical theory which questions the validity of some of the current research and practice.

Definitions of involuntary clients

Ronald Rooney (1992: 6) in his book *Strategies for Work with Involuntary Clients* suggests that the involuntary client is 'forced to seek or feels pressure to accept contact with a helping professional'. He goes on to define two types of involuntary clients, mandated and non-voluntary. A mandated client 'must work with a practitioner because of a legal mandate or court order', and a non-voluntary client 'has contact with helping professionals through pressure from agencies, referral sources, other persons, family members, and outside events'.

Andre Ivanoff, Betty Blythe and Tony Tripodi (1994: 20) also provide a definition of involuntary clients:

> In involuntary treatment settings the recipients of direct service do not ask or apply for service, may not willingly accept service and may not see the need or any possible gain from service. Yet those recipients must be regarded as clients.

I have referred to involuntary clients in *Working with Involuntary Clients* in terms of a continuum, with clients on parole or a court order at one end of the continuum, to clients who are entirely voluntary, for example marriage counselling, at the other end. Nevertheless, even on this continuum the distinctions may not be clear-cut. Offenders on parole have a choice in terms of whether or not and how they engage with a parole officer, and they may even visit their parole officer on a voluntary basis to seek help with issues which are worrying them. On the other hand, one party who presents for marriage counselling may do so under some pressure and may not be entirely voluntary.

Core skills in work with involuntary clients

There are a number of core worker skills highlighted in the literature which appear to relate to effective work with a wide range of involuntary clients. These skills can be summarised under the following headings:

- role clarification
- collaborative problem-solving
- pro-social modelling
- the client worker relationship

The practice of identifying and focusing on high-risk clients is sometimes defined as another important skill. These skills are discussed in some detail in *Working with Involuntary Clients* (Trotter, 2006) and they are summarised below.

These concepts are not new. It is perhaps self-evident that outcomes are likely to be good when clients and workers understand the purpose of the intervention, when problems which have led the client to become a client are addressed, when an effort is made by the worker to change the clients self-defeating ways of thinking, when the worker has a positive relationship with the client and when resources are devoted to clients who are high risk. Nevertheless, focus of much of the literature is on these issues and there is some complexity in their definition and application.

Role clarification

Work with involuntary clients is more likely to be effective if the worker and the client have a common understanding of the role of the worker and the role of the client in the process of the intervention which is offered. A number of authors have argued this from different perspectives. Lawrence Shulman (1991), in a child protection study in Canada found that outcomes for clients were better if the worker attempted to clarify their purpose and role and seek client feedback on how they understood this. Jones and Alcabes (1993) argue that client socialisation is a key to effective work with involuntary clients including offenders, families where there has been abuse and in mental health settings. They argue that until the client accepts that the worker can help them with their problems then effective work cannot take place. Ronald Rooney, in his book *Strategies for Work with Involuntary Clients*,

also identifies socialisation as a key for effective practice. He talks about the importance of motivational congruence and refers to the need to talk to clients about rights and negotiable and non-negotiable aspects of the intervention.

While role clarification or client socialisation has received less attention in the literature in recent years some studies have continued to show its importance. A study that I undertook in child protection (Trotter, 2004) found that clients tended to be confused about the role of their workers. When asked to identify characteristics of their workers they tended to either see them as friends and helpers or as supervisors and investigators. In the small number of cases when they saw their workers as both a helper and supervisor they progressed better in both their own and their worker's estimation. In other words, clients did better when they were clear about the workers dual role. Similarly, in a study focusing on women exiting prison in Australia (Trotter and Sheehan, 2005), the women were less likely to return to prison and more satisfied with the intervention if their supervisor indicated that: 'their worker knew what I wanted from the service'; if the 'purpose of service and what worker aimed to achieve was clear'; and if 'the authority worker had and how it might be used was clear'.

Collaborative problem-solving

The literature suggests that helping clients with issues which have led them to become involuntary clients is likely to relate to good outcomes. In the field of corrections it is argued that a focus by workers on the clients' criminogenic needs relates to reduced re-offending (Andrews and Bonta, 2006). Criminogenic needs include factors which can be changed, such as peer group associations, family issues or employment. Non-criminogenic needs refer to more intra-psychic needs such as self-esteem. Helping clients to address problems that appear to relate to their involuntary status has also been seen to relate to improved outcomes in child protection.

Cognitive behavioural interventions commonly include a problem-solving component along with strategies to address distorted and unproductive thinking. They have proved in recent years to be effective in work in corrections, child protection, mental health and treatment for addictions. (Barber, 2002; Corcoran, 2000; Kolko, 2002; Polkki et al., 2004; Wilson et al., 2005.)

Much of the literature suggests, however, that it is insufficient to focus on the problems that may have contributed to the client becoming an involuntary client and that problem-solving approaches are only likely to be successful if the worker uses a collaborative approach. This argument is presented in a number of social work texts (Compton and Galaway, 2005; Hepworth et al., 2002). This has certainly been evident in the studies I have undertaken in corrections and child protection settings (Trotter, 1996, 2004, 2006). For example, when child protection clients indicated that they defined, decided on, or named the problem, the client was more than twice as likely to be satisfied with the outcome and the workers were also more likely to report that the clients were progressing well. The same positive outcomes were apparent when we asked the clients if the worker discussed 'your real problems as you define them'.

Pro-social modelling and reinforcement

The third core skill in work with involuntary clients relates to the worker modelling pro-social values and reinforcing pro-social comments and actions. A number of studies and reviews in corrections settings including meta-analysis have pointed to the value of this approach (Andrews et al., 1979; Trotter, 1990, 1996, 2006; Rex and Gelsthorpe, 2002; Dowden and Andrews, 2004). There is support for these approaches also in child protection (Gough, 1993; Letendre, 1999; Trotter, 2004) and in treatment of drug users (Acierno et al., 1994; Barber, 1995).

This approach has similarities with strengths-based work (Saleebey, 2001), but rather than focusing on the clients general strengths it focuses purposefully on pro-social strengths. For example, the support of a peer group may be a strength for some clients. However, if members of that peer group have pro-criminal values, the worker would not seek to build on this aspect of the client's life. The worker would instead seek to identify and build on more pro-social aspects of the client's life such as a relationship with a non-criminal friend or family member.

The concept of modelling pro-social values is important in work with involuntary clients. Our child protection study found that when clients reported that their workers responded to phone calls, kept appointments and did the things they said they would do, the outcomes were better – workers and clients reported that the clients were progressing well, cases were closed earlier and children were less likely to be removed from their families (Trotter, 2004). These are easily practiced examples of pro-social modelling and they seem to make a real difference to client outcomes.

Challenge and confrontation

A number of corrections programmes focus on challenging clients. The most extreme examples of this include programmes such as 'scared straight' where young people are placed in prison for a period of time to warn them of the dangers of embarking on a criminal career. There seems little doubt that such programmes are unhelpful. One meta-analysis suggested that such programmes contribute to an increase in re-offending of around 25 per cent (Andrews and Bonta, 2006).

Unfortunately, the research on confrontation with involuntary clients is limited. The research is also complicated by the different definitions of confrontation and the different forms of confrontation. Perhaps because of this it is difficult to say when and how confrontation should be used with involuntary clients. A review by Polcin et al. (2003) of confrontation in recovery from addiction found that confrontation by professional staff with drug users was often counter-productive, although they suggest some positive benefit of confrontation from significant others. Silvergleid and Mankowski (2006) point to the importance of an emotionally safe treatment environment in batterer programmes with the need to balance support and confrontation. Nevertheless, they argue on the basis of a qualitative study that support alone is insufficient and challenging is a necessary part of the learning process.

Our studies in child protection (Trotter, 2004) and the study of women exiting prison (Trotter and Sheehan, 2005) were also equivocal about confrontation. In both cases, the outcomes were better when the clients believed that their workers were clear about their authority and how it might be used. However, the outcomes were poorer when clients believed that their workers criticised them or focused on what they had done wrong.

It certainly appears that some level of challenging is appropriate in work with involuntary clients. However, this is likely to work better if it is part of a collaborative relationship. Andrews and Bonta (2006) refer to effective disapproval in work with offenders. Effective disapproval, they argue, based on their meta-analyses, works best if it is within an open and warm worker–client relationship and if it is based on the four to one rule, that is, four positive supportive statements for every confrontation or challenge.

Worker client relationship

The practice skills I have referred to in this chapter work best in the context of a warm and open worker client relationship (Shulman, 1991; Trotter, 2004; Andrews and Bonta, 2006; Trotter and Sheehan, 2006). They also work better if the worker is optimistic about the potential of the client to change (Kirk and Koeske, 1995; Hodges et al., 2003; Majer et al., 2003; Ryan et al., 2004; Trotter, 2004).

There is a vast literature on the nature of the helping relationship in work with both voluntary and involuntary clients (e.g. Hepworth et al., 2006). Those texts also discuss ways in which workers can let clients know that they understand their situation and communicate their belief in the client's capacity to change. In particular, they highlight the micro-skills of empathy, reflective listening and paraphrasing of clients' comments (e.g. Compton and Galaway, 2005; Hepworth et al., 2006).

While there is little argument about the importance of the worker client relationship, the process by which workers foster this relationship is often difficult to determine. The research on the effectiveness of the micro-skills is limited and again somewhat equivocal. For example, I found in a study undertaken with volunteer probation officers that levels of empathy of the probation officers made no difference to the re-offending of their clients (Trotter, 1991). A review of studies on this issue by Ivanoff et al. (1993) found that some involuntary clients found genuineness and empathy overwhelming and even aversive. Nugent and Halvorson (1995) found in role-play situations that inappropriate paraphrasing of client comments by workers could make some clients angry.

Studies in probation and child protection involving observations of interviews suggest that workers often make minimal use of the micro-skills set out in text books and that the successful development of the client worker relationship may be a more informal and conversational process than some textbooks

suggest (Trotter, 2004; Bonta and Rugge, 2004). More work needs to be done on this topic.

Other skills

There are a number of other approaches to work with specific groups of involuntary clients that the research suggests are effective. For example, relapse prevention techniques (identifying and avoiding precursors to offending) are widely in use for the treatment of drug users and sex offenders. A meta-analysis by Dowden and Andrews (2003) found these approaches to be generally effective in reducing re-offending particularly when used in combination with other effective practice principles.

There is also support for working with the families of involuntary clients. There have been a number of different family therapy models developed for use with involuntary clients; for example, multi-systemic therapy, functional family therapy (Sexton and Alexander, 2002) and collaborative family therapy (Trotter, 2006). These models are less psycho-dynamic and more behavioural than traditional family therapy models and may be particularly appropriate for work with involuntary clients. The research relating to multi-systemic family therapy, for example, has shown significant improvements in problems relating to school attendance, offending, drug use maltreatment and rates of institutionalisation (Perkins-Dock, 2001; Sexton and Alexander, 2002). A recent review of research on functional family therapy points to improvements for young people facing problems with substance abuse, mental health, maltreatment and offending, including sex offences. There is also some support for collaborative family therapy with involuntary clients (Trotter, 2006).

Another factor that is important in work with involuntary clients is that of peer group association. The importance of targeting peer group influence in work with young offenders in particular has been shown on a number of occasions (Trotter, 1995; Andrews and Bonta, 2006). A recent qualitative study found that the effectiveness of work done by professionals in a family welfare setting was also often dependent on peer group influence. If significant others (friends, neighbours, relatives) were supportive of the advice received by clients from their workers interventions were more successful (Walker, 2007).

Focus on high-risk clients

Much of the literature about involuntary clients talks about the importance of focusing on high-risk clients rather than low-risk clients. This has led to the development of risk assessment profiles and processes being adopted in work with a range of involuntary clients including offenders, child protection clients and clients in the mental health system (Schwalbe, 2004). In the field of corrections in particular, risk assessment has become increasingly prevalent in the last decade (Robinson, 2003). It is argued that there is a relatively large group of offenders who are unlikely to re-offend and are unlikely to benefit from intensive intervention, whereas there is a smaller group of medium to high-risk offenders who are more likely to re-offend and more likely to benefit from supervision (see for example Gendreau, 1996; Andrews and Bonta, 2006). For this reason it is important to assess risk levels and to focus resources on medium to high-risk offenders.

The issue of risk assessment is a complex one and it has its critics (see Robinson, 2003 for a discussion about the issues). The primary criticism is that in corrections settings risk levels are often used as part of a sentencing process and as part of a post-sentencing method to provide for varying levels of supervision. This can lead to offenders who are already disadvantaged getting harsher penalties. An offender who is homeless, without family support, with a drug or alcohol addiction, and without employment might receive a harsher sentence or intervention than someone else who does not have these problems, but has committed a similar offence. A further criticism is that risk assessment diverts workers from therapeutic work with clients. For example, one study in child protection in the UK found that in case planning meetings only 15 per cent of the discussion was focused on treatment with most of the rest of the time spent on risk assessment (Farmer, 1999).

Nevertheless, there is research support for the benefit of concentrating welfare or human service resources on higher risk individuals at least in corrections settings. Andrews and Bonta (2006) cite several studies which found that high-risk offenders had lower recidivism rates following intensive supervision or support, whereas low-risk offenders had higher recidivism if they received intensive services.

Following on from this research a range of risk assessment profiles have been developed in corrections, child protection and mental health with the aim of identifying high-risk clients. These profiles generally provide a numerical risk score or at least a categorisation into low, medium and high risk. The evidence suggests that these risk assessment profiles are more accurate in assessing the risk of recidivism than clinical judgement, including recidivism relating to offending, child abuse or hospitalisation (Schwalbe, 2004).

Intervention models

The literature on work with involuntary clients often focuses on direct practice skills as outlined above. A number of specific intervention models are also discussed in the literature. These models generally include some or most of the skills referred to above, however, they are organised into specific models of intervention.

Four examples of the numerous models include motivational interviewing, solution-focused therapy, pro-social modelling and relapse prevention. Motivational interviewing was initially developed in work with addictions and has a particular focus on helping clients to develop their motivation to change. It focuses on understanding the client's point of view, developing goals, accepting the client's autonomy, working with the client's definition of the problem and encouraging the client towards change (Moyers and Rollnick, 2002).

Solution-focused therapy is based on the notion that change is most likely to occur if the focus of the intervention is on solutions rather than discussion of problems. The model offers particular techniques to encourage hope and optimism; it searches for occasions when the problem was not present; it encourages clients to picture the way things could be rather than they are; and it encourages clients to identify things that help with the problem and to do more of them (Baker and Steiner, 1995).

Pro-social modelling is based on the effective practice principles outlined above. It focuses particularly on the worker skills of role clarification, collaborative problem-solving, modelling and reinforcing clients' pro-social behaviours and actions. Two studies in particular have indicated that offenders and child protection clients benefit greatly from workers who use these skills with consequent reductions in offending or abuse (Trotter, 2004; Trotter, 2006).

Case management

Professionals who work with involuntary clients for the most part do so using a case management model. The issue of case management receives some attention in the literature. Gursansky and colleagues (2003) in their book on case management point to difficulties in defining the term. The direct practice or supervisory process in work with involuntary clients may include several functions. These include assessment and the development of a case plan or intervention plan; therapeutic work or problem-solving with clients; referral to other agencies; and co-ordination and monitoring of work done by other agencies. Case management can be defined narrowly to include only the co-ordination role. The case manager arranges for an assessment, arranges for treatment to be provided and monitors and co-ordinates the treatment process. Under this definition of case management it would be possible for the case manager to not even meet the client. On the other hand, case management can be defined more broadly with the case managers carrying out each of these functions themselves. The common factor in definitions of case management is, however, the co-ordination and planning function and the involvement of specialist workers as appropriate.

There is a lot of criticism of the concept of case management in the literature. The criticisms focus on the lack of continuity for clients who may be asked to see several different specialist workers, the de-skilling of case managers whose primary function is to refer and monitor rather than provide therapeutic services, the overlap and consequent inefficiency of clients seeing several workers, and the inappropriateness of having several specialist workers when the research suggests that effective workers use core skills and practices regardless of clients problems (Ife, 1997; McMahon, 1998; Searing, 2003; Slawinski, 2004; Steib and Blome, 2004). There is, however, little research on the way in which clients experience case management and how the shortcomings described above can be avoided.

Therapeutic Integrity

There is increasing knowledge about what works and what doesn't in work with involuntary clients. There is less known about how to translate this knowledge into the day-to-day practice of workers with involuntary clients. The research can show that when workers use the core skills referred to in this chapter the outcomes for clients will generally be positive. There is, however, some research that suggests workers in their day-to-day practice with involuntary clients may not use these skills.

Andrews and Dowden (2005) have referred to the concept of therapeutic integrity. This concept refers to the extent to which programmes or interventions are delivered in a manner which is consistent with the way in which they are intended. Andrews and Dowden (2005) undertook a meta-analysis of therapeutic integrity in correctional treatment. Their results from 273 studies suggest that often interventions were not implemented as planned and that treatment effectiveness was subsequently compromised.

Bonta et al. (in press) found in a study of probation officers in Manitoba, Canada, that even though discussion of criminogenic needs was related to reduced offending, criminogenic needs were not discussed with clients in the majority of cases. This was similar to the findings in our child protection study (Trotter, 2004). We found, for example, that when workers talked with clients about their dual helping social control role the outcomes were better; however, there were few discussions between clients and workers about the dual role. This might explain why research on the overall effectiveness of interventions in areas such as child protection and corrections suggests minimal impact (Gough, 1993; Bonta et al. in press).

With increasing knowledge that work with involuntary clients can be effective, the new challenge is how to ensure that the knowledge is translated into practice. This is a complex issue because it involves changing established habits of workers and it involves knowledge about effective practice being accepted by policy makers and organisational managers to whom workers are ultimately responsible.

Theories relevant to work with involuntary clients

In this chapter I have focused on literature which describes research about effective practice with involuntary clients. I have also commented on the literature that describes specific models of intervention. The literature also refers to theories that help to explain why involuntary clients behave in particular ways and why some methods of intervention help them to change. The theories relating to involuntary clients can help to explain some of the research outcomes – why some things work and some things don't – and in turn also help to guide practice. It is not possible to do justice to the range of theories which are relevant to work with involuntary clients, however, a few key theories are highlighted here. More information is available in a number of general texts (e.g. Hepworth et al., 2006).

Ecological systems theory highlights the importance of holistic approaches to interventions with involuntary clients. Behaviourist and cognitive behavioural theories highlight the importance of working with clients' distorted ways of thinking as well as the importance of reinforcing positive behaviours. Feminist theories highlight the economic and social disadvantage faced by women.

Critical theory places the research based literature in a different context and for this reason it is worth highlighting in this chapter. Critical theory is based on a premise that social problems are in large part socially constructed. It accepts some of the traditional Marxist views that client problems are often related to socio-economic or structural factors such as class and role expectations, inequality, poverty, poor housing, unemployment and inadequate social security systems. It encourages consciousness raising, advocacy and social action.

Critical theory also points to the role that recent political and economic activity has played in the escalation of social problems, in particular globalisation, economic rationalism, managerialism, corporatism, privatisation and the accompanying erosion of public services (Morley, 2003). Critical theory emphasises that the oppression of many groups in society, including the involuntary clients discussed in this book, is sustained by adherence to the dominant discourses of economic rationalism and corporatisation. Critical theory is concerned about the oppression of groups on the basis of race, gender, age, disability, illness and poverty.

It is argued that critical theory has implications for day-to-day work with involuntary clients. Spratt and Houston (1999) refer, in an article about developing critical social work in child protection, to a number of implications for practice. They suggest that child protection workers can see their work from a number of ideologies, for example, a penal ideology which views child abuse as a deliberate act; a blaming, 'protect your back' ideology; a medical ideology which views child abuse as a disease; a bureaucratic or a humanist ideology. They suggest that the critical practitioner would take as a starting point a humanist ideology; 'that structural processes produce inequalities that generate (unfortunate) responses to these conditions which are best explained by social context rather than individual pathology' (Spratt and Houston, 1999: 5). In other words they need resources not therapy.

In practical terms, this involves constructing the client's situation in terms of needs/problems rather than risk, focusing on family group conferencing, for example, rather than the more impersonal case conferences and providing practical help and supports rather than therapy.

Critical theory questions the paradigms of the 'what works' research discussed earlier in this chapter. To perhaps oversimplify the discussion – research on involuntary clients generally focuses on how to change people, whereas critical theory is interested in how to change society. The discussions within these paradigms often run in parallel with little reference to each other. Nevertheless both points of view are represented in the involuntary clients' literature, and while this chapter is primarily concerned with literature from a research based perspective, it is important to acknowledge that there is a body of literature which takes a different approach.

Conclusion

This literature review could not hope to cover the vast literature on involuntary clients. I have, however, tried to identify the key themes which run through many of the publications on the topic. The difficulties inherent in defining involuntary clients have been discussed and it has been pointed out that voluntary and involuntary clients can be seen more in terms of a continuum rather than a dichotomy. Core skills, including risk assessment, have been highlighted. The research suggests these worker skills are related to positive outcomes for involuntary clients. Some specific intervention models have also been discussed. The concept of case management was raised which provides the framework for work with involuntary clients in most settings around the world. The chapter then commented on the notion of therapeutic integrity and the difficulties highlighted in the literature in relation to implementing effective practice skills in the workplace. Finally, I have considered some of the theories that have influenced the development of the practice models, in particular critical theory, which questions and places in context some of the current practices in work with involuntary clients.

References

Acierno, R., Donohue, B. and Kogan, E. (1994) Psychological Interventions for Drug Abuse: A Critique and Summation of Controlled Studies. *Clinical Psychology Review*, 14: 417–42.

Andrews, D.A. and Bonta, J. (2006) *The Psychology of Criminal Conduct*. Cincinnati: Anderson.

Andrews, D.A. et al. (1979) *Volunteers and the One-to-One Supervision of Adult Probationers*. Toronto: Ontario Ministry of Correctional Services.

Baker, M. and Steiner, J. (1995) Solution Focused Work. *Social Work*, 40: 2, 225–32.

Barber, J. (1995) Working with Resistant Drug Abusers. *Social Work*, 40: 1, 17–23.

Barber, J. (2002) *Social Work with Addictions*. Basingstoke: Palgrave Macmillan.

Bonta, J. et al. (in press) *Exploring the Black Box of Community Supervision*. Ottawa: Public Safety and Emergency Preparedness.

Compton, B. and Galaway, B. (2005) *Social Work Processes*. 6th edn, Homewood: Dorsey.

Corcoran, J. (2000) Family Interventions with Child Physical Abuse and Neglect: A Critical Review. *Children and Youth Services Review*, 22: 7, 563–91.

Dowden, C. and Andrews, D.A. (2004) The Importance of Staff Practice in Delivering Effective Correctional Treatment: A Meta-Analytic Review of the Literature. *International Journal of Offender Therapy and Comparative Criminology*, 48: 2.

French, S. and Gendreau, P. (2006) Reducing Prison Misconduct: What Works. *Criminal Justice and Behaviour*, 33: 2, 185–218.

Gendreau, P. (1996) The Principles of Effective Intervention with Offenders. In Harland, A.T. (Ed.) *Choosing Correctional Options that Work*. Newbury Park, CA: Sage.

Gough, D. (1993) *Child Abuse Interventions: A Review of the Research Literature*. London: Public Health Research Unit, University of Glasgow, HMSO.

Gursansky, D., Harvey, J. and Kennedy, R. (2003) *Case Management: Policy, Practice and Professional Business*. Sydney: Allen and Unwin.

Hepworth, D.H., Rooney, R.R. and Larson, J.A. (2002) *Direct Social Work Practice*. Pacific Grove, CA: Brooks Cole.

Hodges, J., Hardiman, E. and Segal, S. (2003) Predictors of Hope among Members of Mental Health Self-Help Agencies. *Social Work in Mental Health*, 2: 1, 1–16.

Ife, J. (1997) *Rethinking Social Work*. Melbourne: Longman.

Ivanoff, A., Blythe, B. and Tripodi, T. (1994) *Involuntary Clients in Social Work Practice*. New York: Aldine de Gruyter.

Jones, J.A. and Alcabes, A. (1993) *Client Socialisation: The Achilles Heel of the Helping Professions*. Wesport, CT: Auburn House.

Kirk, S.A. and Koeske, G.F. (1995) The Fate of Optimism: A Longitudinal Study of Case Managers' Hopefulness and Subsequent Morale. *Research on Social Work Practice*, 5: 1, 47–61.

Kolko, D. (2002) Child Physical Abuse. In Myers, J. et al. *The APSAC Handbook on Child Maltreatment*. 2nd edn. Thousand Oaks: Sage.

Letendre, J. (1999) Lender and Therapeutic Influences on Aggressive Behaviours and Pro-Social Skills in Groups with Children. *Dissertation Abstracts International A: The Humanities and Social Sciences*, 60: 6, 2228.

Majer, J. et al. (2003) Is Self-Mastery always a Helpful Resource? *American Journal of Drug and Addictive Behaviours*, May.

Morley, C. (2003) Critical Reflection in Social Work: A Response to Globalisation. *International Journal of Social Welfare*, 13: 297–303.

Moyers, T. and Rollnick, S. (2002) A Motivational Interviewing Perspective on Resistance to Therapy. *JCLP/In Session: Psychotherapy in Practice*, 58: 2, 185–93.

Perkins-Dock, R. (2001) Family Interventions with Incarcerated Youth: A Review of the Literature. *International Journal of Offender Therapy and Comparative Criminology*, 45: 5, 606–25.

Perkins, D. and Jones, K. (2004) Risk Behaviours and Resiliency within Physically Abused Adolescents. *Child Abuse and Neglect*, 28: 5, 547–63.

Polki, O., Ervast, S. and Huupponen, M. (2004) Coping and Resilience of Children of a Mentally Ill Parent. *Social Work in Health Care*, 39: 1–2, 151–63.

Polcin, D. (2003) Rethinking Confrontation in Alcohol and Drug Treatment: Consideration of the Clinical Context. *Substance Abuse and Misuse*, 38: 2, 165–84.

Rex, S. and Gelsthorpe, L. (2002) The Role of Community Service in Reducing Offending: Evaluating Pathfinder Projects in the UK. *The Howard Journal*, 41: 4, 311–25.

Robinson, G. (2003) Risk and Risk Assessment. In Wing, H.C. and Nellis, M. *Moving Probation Forward*. Pearson Longman.

Rooney, R. (1992) *Strategies for Work with Involuntary Clients*. New York: Columbia University Press.

Ryan, M., Fook, J. and Hawkins, L. (1995) From Beginner to Graduate Social Worker: Preliminary Findings of an Australian Longitudinal Study. *British Journal of Social Work*, 25: 1, 17–35.

Saleebey, D. (2001) Practicing the Strengths Perspective: Everyday Tools and Resources. *Families in Society*, 82: 3.

Schwalbe, C. (2004) Re-visioning Risk Assessment for Human Service Decision Making. *Children and Youth Services Review*, 26: 6, 561–76.

Searing, H. (2003) The Continuing Relevance of Casework Ideas to Long Term Child Protection Work. *Child and Family Social Work*, 8: 311–20.

Sexton, T. and Alexander, J. (2002) Family Based Empirically Supported Interventions. *The Counseling Psychologist*, 30: 2, 238–61.

Silvergleid, C. and Mankowski, E. (2006) How Batterer Intervention Programs Work. *Journal of Interpersonal Violence*, 21, 139–59.

Shulman, L. (1991) *Interactional Social Work Practice: Toward an Empirical Theory*. Itasca, IL: F.E. Peacock.

Siporin, M. (1984) Have You Heard the One about Social Work Humour? *Social Casework*, 68: 8, 459–64.

Slawinski, T. (2004) The Intensive Case Manager/Client Relationship: Understanding and Influencing Boundary Development and Compliance. *Dissertation Abstracts International A The Humanities and Social Sciences*. 64: 9.

Spratt, T. and Houston, S. (1999) Developing Critical Social Work in Theory and in Practice: Child Protection and Communicative Reason. *Child and Family Social Work*, 4: 4, 315–24.

Steib, S. and Blome, W. (2004) Fatal Error: The Missing Ingredient in Child Welfare Reform Part 2. *Child Welfare*, 83: 1, 101–4.

Trotter, C. (1990) Probation Can Work: A Research Study Using Volunteers. *Australian Journal of Social Work*, 43: 2, 13–18.

Trotter, C. (1995) Contamination Theory and Unpaid Community Work. *Australian and New Zealand Journal of Criminology*, 28: 2, 163–75.

Trotter, C. (1996) The Impact of Different Supervision Practices in Community Corrections. *Australian and New Zealand Journal of Criminology*, 29: 1, 29–46.

Trotter, C. (2004) *Helping Abused Children and their Families*. Sydney: Allen and Unwin.

Trotter, C. (2006) *Working with Involuntary Clients*. Sydney: Allen and Unwin.

Trotter, C. and Sheehan, R. (2005) *Women's Access to Welfare After Prison*. Conference paper presented to *What Works with Women Offenders*. Monash University, Prato, Italy.

Walker, S. (2007) *Clients Use of Therapy in The Extra-Therapeutic Environment*. PhD Thesis Monash University Melbourne.

White, M. and Epston, D. (1989) *Narrative Means to Therapeutic Ends*. Adelaide: Dulwich Centre Publications.

Wilson, D., Bouffard, L. and Mackenzie, D. (2005) The Quantitative Review of Structured Group Oriented Cognitive Behavioural Programs for Offenders. *Criminal Justice and Behaviour*, 32: 2, 172–204.

Wing, H.C. and Nellis, M. (Eds.) (2003) *Moving Probation Forward: Evidence, Arguments and Practice*. Essex: Pearson Longman.

CHAPTER 2

The Changing Landscape of Social Care: Implications for Working with Involuntary Clients

Trevor Spratt

Introduction

In surveying the current landscape of social care only two things are perhaps certain; the present is different from the past and the present is concerned with the future. In this chapter I will argue that whilst in the recent past the relationship between the state and its citizens has been variously characterised by themes of *prevention*, *pathology* and *partnership*, the prevalent theme of the present is a modern interpretation of *prevention* within an overarching strategy of state investment in the future social and economic wellbeing of its citizenry. Whilst these analyses will refer to families with children, much of the social policy trends identified also apply to other client groups.

Defining the involuntary client

However, before we undertake our survey of shifting social policy and its manufacture and management of involuntary clients, it is necessary to define how one may become an involuntary client of the state. The first thing to say here is that it is more helpful to think of the relationship between the state and the individual as representing a complex series of benefits and obligations or, in the terminology of New Labour, *rights* and *responsibilities*. So whilst as citizens we receive a range of benefits from the state we also have responsibilities to the state which, if unfulfilled, will result in the attentions of its agents, who may apply to the courts for restrictions on our liberty. For example, if we fail to renew our television licence we may be sent reminder letters, receive visits from government inspectors and appear before magistrates. Ultimately, if fines are not paid, we may be sent to jail. Our liberty, then, is only guaranteed as long as we remain compliant in our responses to the laws of the state. The degree of liberty we enjoy being retained for as long as we remain up to date with our taxes and observant of a

multiplicity of rules and regulations. Our freedom to act and choose as citizens is thus limited. Whilst we all understand this to be true, most of us choose to challenge such restrictions either via the ballet box or through special interest or pressure groups to achieve changes in our conditions of governance. These are the prescribed routes for achieving rule change within democratic states. It is left to a minority of citizens to challenge authority through non-prescribed routes such as the breaking of laws.

In many ways the relationship between the citizen and the state is replicated in the relationship clients have with providers of social care services. Whilst the use of the term *client* has been superseded in recent years by *service user* in the United Kingdom, the latter term is misleading in that it obscures the power relationship between parties, offering the illusion that the user of social care services is a consumer exercising choice in a market where providers are competing for their custom. As long as the client consumes services in ways acceptable to the social care provider the illusion of this being a voluntary arrangement is maintained. It is only when the client does exercise choice in relation to such services that the less than voluntary nature of the arrangement may become apparent. So the family who spurn the offers of post-natal midwifery, decide they do not require visits from the health visitor and demure when offered infant immunisations by their GP, may find that their exercise of choice in such matters attracts the attention of social workers who may make them offers which are more difficult to refuse. Such offers may be initially couched within general terms of enquiry to establish if the child in question might be deemed a 'child in need' within the definition contained in s.17 of the 1989 Children Act. If the social workers, however, are politely thanked for their interest but turned away at the door, they may interpret this response as signalling that the family have something to hide and later return, this time mandated by the duty to enquire where they have reasonable cause to suspect that the child may be at risk of suffering significant harm, under s.47 of the 1989 Children Act. If the social workers are not given access to the child on this occasion they may apply to the court for an Emergency Protection Order on the grounds that they have been denied access to a child whom they believe may be at risk of suffering significant harm. If the Order were granted, social workers could then remove the child from the care of its parents.

The chain of events described above demonstrates how failure to take up services may lead to a family having their preferences perceived as signifying that they have something to hide, triggering in turn interventions invoking the courts and mandating social workers to act, as agents of the state, to intervene in family life. Such a sequence of events illustrates the point that it is not possible therefore to simply classify some clients as voluntary and others as involuntary. It may be more helpful to think of the in/voluntary relationship between client and state as being one of degree rather than type – not as polarities, but as a continuum (Trotter, 2006). On such a continuum those fully compliant may appear to be without restriction with regard to their individual freedoms; however, when they choose to ignore or reject state sponsored services they may provoke reactions by the state which serve to illustrate the true limits of individual choice.

Constructing the involuntary client

At the one end of the in/voluntary continuum are clients whose potential to harm themselves or others results in their incarceration, populating the secure units within residential homes, prisons and hospital lock-up wards. An understanding of such clients is often underpinned by notions of *pathology* i.e. the reasons for their dangerous presentation may be located in the things done to them which have become internalised (the sexually abused child who goes on to sexually abuse children in adult life) or as a result of an organic illness or condition (the severely mentally ill person whose distorted perception of the world causes them to act towards self or others in harmful ways). A pathological construction of an individual's presentation or actions can, however, extend to other populations. When this occurs the

state will become concerned with identifying those who potentially might endanger others (in the case of families, usually the parents) and protecting potential victims (the children). A counterweight to this pathologising tendency may be found in understandings informed by the concept of *partnership*. Here, state intervention in family life is premised on the idea that families have the best interests of their members at heart, but may from time to time require the help of the state in the provision of resources and services and in support from professionals. A third way of understanding the needs of clients has been through the concept of *prevention.* Prevention has, in the past, been understood in both a negative and limited sense. Essentially this has been to do with the prevention of bad things occurring or reoccurring, that is, preventing the dangerous individual harming another or alleviating conditions known to be associated with harmful outcomes. As we shall observe, social policy in relation to families has historically been informed by, and oscillated between, these pathological, partnership and prevention constructions. In more recent times, however, the anticipation of future harms has led to the development of policies designed to measure the present performance of populations against a range of norms in order to predict and affect future outcomes, preventing negative ones and ensuring positive ones. It is this shift towards what is, essentially, an investment strategy based on the concept of *prevention* that has come to dominate the landscape of social policy in respect of social care in the United Kingdom in the early years of the new millennium and is the main conceptual tool for understanding the development of social policy under the New Labour Government.

A short history of pathology, partnership and prevention themes in social work with children and families in the United Kingdom

It would be a mistake to suggest that there has been a straightforward and linear progression from policies reflecting pathological, partnership and prevention themes in relation to children and families (Hendrick, 1994). Rather, it may be more helpful to think of these themes as individual strands in a three-ply rope. At any given time one strand may be thicker and stronger than the others and bear more of the weight of current polices. But all strands are nevertheless present at any one time. So, whilst successive policy initiatives may privilege or emphasise one particular strand, the weaker strands do not disappear altogether.

If we apply this model, for example, to the 1950s and 1960s, we might argue that in that era the dominant concern was for social workers to work in partnership with families to help alleviate some of the effects of social conditions. Corby observes that: 'the period between 1945 and 1970 was one in which family policy in general and the response to neglectful families in particular was relatively benign' (2006: 35). During this period any pathologising tendency was expressed in social workers viewing the troubles of some clients as indicative of deeper, unresolved psychological problems. Concerns regarding prevention tended to cluster around the need to identify families whose children were likely to come into care, to prevent negative outcomes associated with experience of the care system, to reduce costs to the state and support the idea of family life (Tunstill, 1997).

With the publication by Henry Kempe and his colleagues of their seminal paper on *The Battered Child Syndrome* (Kempe et al., 1962) the foundations for a medical model of child abuse were laid, with the causes located within the psychological make-up of some parents. Such foundations were built upon in the 1970s as widespread public disquiet, fuelled by public inquiries into the death of children at the hands of their caregivers, led to the establishment of the child protection system within the United Kingdom (Parton, 1991). As social workers colonised child protection work, their new expert status sat uncomfortably with ideas of partnership with families, with professional distance becoming necessary in which to refine diagnostic skills and operationalise a systemic response. Social workers who continued to seek to develop partnerships with families were variously accused of being 'naive beyond belief' (a comment made by the judge at the trial of Morris Beckford in relation to the attitude of Jasmine Beckford's social worker (Brent, 1985) and succumbing to a 'rule of optimism' (Dingwall et al., 1983). During this period, the concept of prevention became informed by a need to identify those pathological parents who had the potential to abuse their children. This resulted in the surveillance of the performance of those

parents in order to detect errant signals likely to indicate any abuse potential. It is unsurprising then, that the numbers of involuntary clients, as measured by families having their children taken into the care of the state, increased greatly through the 1970s and early 1980s, peaking at over 100,000 children in state care in 1982, with the use of statutory orders increasingly preferred over voluntary arrangements (Parton, 1985).

During the 1980s the apparatus designed to manage the phenomenon of child abuse at a community level continued to develop. The system of Area Child Protection Committees, case conferences and at-risk registers was to create, in one sense, its own market, drawing in large numbers of families whose children were either considered to have been abused or to be at risk of abuse. The system represented an essentially bureaucratic response to the management of child abuse. Whilst parents could not be compelled to co-operate with the systems requirements as it did not have legislative status; to describe the status of families caught up in it as voluntary would be misleading. The tacit threat underpinning the operation of the system lay in the understanding, sometimes stated, that non-compliance on the part of families could result in their case being brought before a court. As well as unmasking the power differential in the relationship between social workers and their clients, the child protection system also provides a good illustration of the ways in which pathology and prevention themes become subject to the control of experts who benchmark present performance against specified norms of behaviour. At its most straightforward this involves such experts defining certain actions on the part of parents as constituting child abuse. If such actions are not repeated, as measured over a specified time period, usually the periods between review case conferences, then, in the meeting of such performance targets, the family are judged to be no longer abusive. Whilst the genesis of this system may be located in a pathological understanding of parental behaviour this view became challenged by a broader, essentially ecological theory of causation (Jack, 2000). With the notable exception of child sexual abuse, abusive behaviour on the part of parents came to be understood as an essentially maladaptive response on the part of parents to stress, often within the contexts of poverty and poor social support. With much of the causation located outside the locus of the individual's control, intervention strategies which enhanced partnership perspectives became possible, at least theoretically. So, whilst the 1980s witnessed the highpoint of the pathologising tendency there remained awareness that good outcomes for children might be achieved, at least in some cases, by social workers working with families in a form of partnership.

If we were to locate a date to signify this shift in understanding it would probably be in 1988 when the publication of the *Cleveland Inquiry Report* (Butler-Sloss, 1988) marked the high-water mark of compulsory state interference in family life (Myers, 1994). Public disquiet with regard to the actions of police, social workers and doctors who were involved in removing 121 children, for reasons of suspected sexual abuse, from their families over a six-month period was to influence the final drafting of the 1989 Children Act to reflect new balances between the state and the family (Parton, 1991). The partnership theme was to be given a significant boost as it became one of the key principles underpinning the legislation. With the raising of the threshold for state intervention in family life to the standard of suspected or actual significant harm, alongside new duties regarding provision of support for families by local authorities, it was anticipated that there would be a realigning of the relationship between the state and the family. In fact this did not occur; at least to the degree it had been anticipated. The overview of government commissioned research, *Child Protection: Messages from Research* (DoH, 1995) portrayed a reactive social work system still preoccupied with the investigation of possible child abuse, with consequently little attention paid to the wider needs of children and families and restricted development of family support services.

The failure to realise the intentions of the 1989 Children Act was more to do with a robustness of the inherited child protection system and continued preoccupation with the management of risk rather than any ideological resistance on the part of social workers, who generally welcomed a partnership approach to practice (Spratt, 2000, 2001). During the 1990s, constructions of pathology became increasingly restricted to a small sub-set of parents and caregivers. Conceptually diverse, they included sexual abusers, the mentally ill, the violent, the alcohol and substance addicted and those with profound disabilities. These populations were not generally amenable to interventions made on the basis of supportive partnership, at least not within timeframes necessary to protect their children. As a result, much greater emphasis was made on placing their children in permanent placements within timescales which respected their developmental requirements and allowed them to make successful attachments with substitute carers (Sinclair, 2005). There was also considerable promotion of adoption as the preferred option for such children, with concurrent planning strategies encouraged to avoid undue delay in making decisions with regard to permanent placement. Parents at this end of the in/voluntary continuum found their own interests and rights becoming of secondary consideration in comparison with those of their children. By contrast, general pessimism with regard to the more impermanent nature of much of public care provision had helped create a situation wherein many of the children who would have been received into care in a previous generation were now remaining at home (DoH, 1991). This was part of a strategy designed to prevent children undertaking a care career with all the perceived dangers (an echo here of the interpretation of prevention prevalent in the 1950s and 1960s). This had the effect of increasing the number of families with complex needs receiving services within the community, with such families having their needs addressed within child protection and/or family support systems.

Through the later half of the 1990s, in part as a response to the publication of *Child Protection: Messages from Research* (DoH, 1995), there was a concentration of effort on the part of government to promote the policy of a greater proportion of families having their circumstances understood as requiring family support services as opposed to more narrow child protection interventions. This became known as the 're-focusing debate'. Whilst the initial drivers for this policy included the Social Services Inspectorate (Rose, 1994) local authorities continued to find it difficult to achieve this new balance in their interventions with families (DoH, 2001). There was, however, empirical support for the possibility of a shift from child protection to family support practice. A number of researchers reported positive findings in relation to attempts by social work services both in the United Kingdom and in Australia to reduce child protection activity and promote family support interventions (see Spratt, 2001 for a summary of this research). Despite this, in reviewing the evidence since the introduction of the 1989 Children Act, Jane Aldgate was forced to conclude that: 'it was also difficult to shift the attitudes of local authorities to the broader perspective of family support' (Aldgate, 2002: 165).

As part of their modernising agenda the New Labour government became more explicit in how they saw such balances being achieved (DoH, 1998a). Much of this involved the establishment of performance measures designed to track the response of local authorities against prescribed targets. For example, the reduction of numbers of children on the 'at risk' register; the use of the Social Services Inspectorate to reinforce good practice, often through public dissemination of exemplars of good practice such as local authorities who met or exceeded performance targets; and the award of stars to denote local authority performance standards, as well as the option of calling in three star generals (bosses from high achieving local authorities) to help 'failing' local authorities (SSI and Audit Commission, 2002). A third approach was to use commissioned research in ways designed to bolster policies. For example, in *The Children Act Now: Messages from Research* publication (DoH, 2001) eighteen of the summaries of the twenty-four research studies carried editorial comment expressing support for, or relationship with, current government policies and initiatives. In retrospect, such a crude behavioural approach to governance of local authorities may be seen to be a precursor to more sophisticated strategies employed to identify and 'encourage' change in under-performing parents in the latest dispensation of New Labour policy with respect to children and families.

In terms of practice, whilst social workers aspired to work with clients in partnership, the risks attendant to work with children and families led to difficulties in making the intentions of the policy drive real. Where social workers were able to move away from such constraints and seek to promote partnerships with parents within the context of family support work, usually within the context of supportive managerial arrangements (Spratt, 2001), there remained suspicion on the part of some parents as to their motivations and intentions. My own work in this area illustrates something of the difficulties in making policy intentions real in situations where social workers are trying to meet competing agendas to both protect children and build their supportive role where parents remain keenly aware of the social workers' powers and the limits of their own ability to enter into a truly voluntary partnership with them (Spratt and Callan, 2004). The next section elaborates on this research and provides a bridge between the outline of the recent history of social work with children and families and a discussion of the present policy context.

The experiences of 'voluntary' clients

One of the implicit assumptions of the re-focusing debate was that the movement to a more partnership-based approach, wherein the majority of family difficulties might be understood within a framework of supportive intervention, was that families had different experiences of child protection and family support interventions. The evidence was certainly strong that families viewed child protection interventions, with their forensic focus, as a traumatic and invasive process (Howitt, 1992; Bell, 1995; Cleaver and Freeman, 1995), but it was assumed that families receiving alternative responses would both view and experience these as essentially benign. My own research with social workers, however, indicated that they had difficulty in determining which cases should receive a child protection and which cases a family support response. Able to discern actual or potential risks to children within a majority of referrals, their first stated priority involved dealing with such risks, whether or not cases were categorised as child protection (Spratt and Callan, 2004). This was what the Department of Health somewhat coyly described as, 'keeping a watchful eye on children who *might be* [their emphasis] at risk of significant harm' (2001: 46) within cases categorised as family support. When we interviewed parents who received a family support response from social workers we wanted to ascertain how those social workers' preoccupation with possible child protection risks might be made manifest in their contacts with parents. Even though a number of parents in the study had self-referred, the majority of them exhibited some degree of apprehension in relation to social work contact. This ranged from a degree of trepidation illustrated by one parent, who had 'feelings of stigma . . . there's our name on a file . . . [this] assumes our child needs protection from us', to more pronounced fears like: 'My nerves, I didn't know whether to laugh or cry . . . I was worried that the social worker would be calling every day – checking up on me. I really don't want a social worker.' Whilst in the course of their contact with social workers most parents came to view them as helpful and understanding, they nevertheless felt it difficult to challenge their perspectives. This was particularly evident with parents who considered continued social work visiting, and in most cases 'service provision' was synonymous with such visiting, as neither necessary or appropriate, but felt it difficult to challenge their social worker. 'It's ongoing, but I really don't know what the "ongoing" is about . . . the social worker said she needed to speak to the senior social worker – there is obviously something in the pipeline. You're left in a state of doubt because you need to be told it's finished or let us know that it is.' The experiences of the parents in the study help illuminate the twilight world which exists somewhere between being a voluntary and an involuntary client of the state. None of the parents in the study were, in terms of the legislation, compelled to co-operate with social workers. Nevertheless, they were apprehensive as to the range of powers social workers possessed and wary of questioning their continued attentions. Families such as those in the study do not usually have knowledge of the law, are unaware of what is normal social work practice, since none of the parents in our own study had previously been referred to social services, and must rely on a media influenced stereotype to inform their views. Arguably, that stereotypical social worker is at least, in part, well-intentioned but powerful, and, in bringing the authority of the state into the living room, to be placated rather than challenged.

The social investment state

To appreciate why it is likely that many more families will share the experience of those occupying the twilight world of family support interventions it is necessary to locate the ideological underpinnings of social work with children and families. A number of social work academics have located much of current social policy with respect to children and families within the theoretical framework of the social investment state (Fawcett et al., 2004; Parton, 2006; Featherstone, 2006). Derived from a term used by Anthony Giddens in developing his 'third way' thesis, it is conceived to be an

'investment in *human capital* wherever possible, rather than the direct provision of economic maintenance. In place of the welfare state we should put in the *social investment state*, operating in the context of a positive welfare society' (Giddens, 1998: 117). At its heart, this represents a linkage of social and economic projects (Featherstone, 2006). Essentially, this means a shift from investment in the demand side of the economy (the Keynesian economic approach) to the supply side. This involves creating a workforce ready for participation in a global economy characterised by fluctuating markets, rapid relocation of capital and a demand for workers prepared and able to adapt to changing conditions and requirements. With the state unable to control the global economy, the best it can do for its citizens is to prepare them for participation in the new marketplace. 'Whilst the old welfare state sought to protect people from the market, a social investment state seeks to facilitate the integration of people into the market' (Fawcett et al., 2004: 41). In the 'third way' the task is therefore to prepare people for the market and not simply protect them from its vagaries. Central to this is a realignment of the relationship between the state and its citizens reflecting 'no rights without responsibilities' (Giddens, 1998: 65). Within this notion of conditional entitlement is the idea that citizens need to be proactive in their preparation for and participation in employment. The role of government is to help and enable citizens to do so through a series of investment strategies, whilst reducing the welfare functions of the state from the meeting of needs to the more limited management of risks (Giddens, 1994). Central to this have been changes to the tax and benefits systems designed to 'make work pay' whilst ensuring that citizens receive 'lifelong' education and training opportunities to enhance their employability in the changing marketplace.

It is recognised, however, that some groups within society, often referred to as the 'socially excluded', are restricted in their ability to utilise such opportunities. Consequently, much of New Labour policy has concentrated on particular investments in socially excluded populations. With regard to children, much of the early focus through *The Quality Protects Programme* (DoH, 1998b) was to identify those children already known to local authorities and develop performance targets against which to measure the impact of investment. For example, reductions in the numbers of children having their names added to the child protection register for a second time. Whilst such targets have often proved difficult to achieve, this has only served to redouble efforts. For example, one of the key projects under New Labour has been to improve the educational outcomes for children in care. Whilst this issue has received considerable investment, levels of qualification achievement amongst children in the care of the state have remained stubbornly static (DoH, 2003) causing the Government to seek to address the issue again within the 2006 Green Paper, *Care Matters*. Such particular investments, however, need to be seen within a much broader strategy designed to reduce social exclusion and eliminate child poverty and within which we may identify three levels of support for families with children (Parton, 2006: 95). These range from general support for all parents with children through changes in the tax and benefits system, specific and targeted help for poorer families to enable their participation in the labour market, and special initiatives targeted at disadvantaged children who are at particular risk of social exclusion. The later group of children have been in receipt of a number of service initiatives designed to offer particular help at different stages of the developmental cycle. Principle amongst these has been the Surestart programme designed to offer extra help to children prior to them starting school, the Children Fund targeted at specific, community-based initiatives designed to help children in the 5–13 age range and Youth Connexions to help with the transition from education to work. These developments reflect a recognition of . . .'the consequences of social exclusion for children including poor educational attainment, poor health, increased risk of criminal behaviour, increased risk of unemployment in the future, and economic deprivation' (Mason et al., 2005: 132). As Esping-Anderson (2003) has observed, such investments are central to an investment state strategy, with an increasing concentration on targeting investment in children's early years seen as particularly important. The reasons for this are that, in a model shaped as much by economic as social considerations, return on investments is crucial to the calculation. Investments made in the present may only be realised in the future (Jensen and Saint-Martin, 2001). Consequently, investment in children today becomes central as they are our future. Holtermann identifies (see refs) the

essential duality of such policy, designed to produce mutual benefits. 'Today's children . . . are tomorrow's adults, and investment in our children is an investment in our future as well as theirs. Investment in children will determine the shape of Britain's future society and economy' (1996: 4, 9). Children thus become the primary investment site as the benefits of such investment are repaid over an extended time in enhancement of their economic productivity and reduction in their cost to society through demands upon a range of services, including health, social security and criminal justice. Consequently, identifying which children need extra help becomes an imperative. Not simply because such children will need extra investment to become productive low cost workers of the future, but more negatively, to prevent them becoming citizens who disproportionately demand much of the share of future service provision.

The concept of the social investment state therefore introduces us to a much different notion of prevention. Whilst ideas of prevention in the past were largely concerned with small specified populations such as children who might enter the state care system or children who were at risk of suffering abuse, preventative strategies are now targeted at a much broader range of children. In fact, every child matters.

Every child matters

As Nigel Parton has observed '. . . the central principle which lies at the core of all recent policy developments in improving the safe-guarding of children is the importance of prevention and early intervention' (2006: 164). The Green Paper, *Every Child Matters*, was published by the Government in 2003 (subsequently to become the 2004 Children Act). Whilst in part it was a response to the recommendations set out in Lord Laming's Report into the circumstances surrounding the death of Victoria Climbié (2003), it also represented an attempt to connect an understanding of individual tragedies with the experiences of a much broader group of children, making it clear that, 'child protection could not be separated from policies to improve children's lives as a whole' (2003: 5). Essentially this reinterpreted the 1989 Children Act to emphasise the requirement for Local Authorities to 'safeguard and promote the welfare of the child'. As Axford and Little observe, the legislation 'gives greater stress to providing services for *all* [their emphasis] children (rather than services for the poor) and with orientating provision towards improved outcomes measured in terms of children's health, safety, enjoyment and achievement, ability to contribute to society and social and economic well-being' (2006: 301). This represents a practical and conceptual paradigm shift for providers of social work services, a far distance from the narrow concerns with pathology informed views of abusing families, characteristic of the 1980s, and a step further than the refocusing of children's services which began in the 1990s in response to the publication of *Child Protection: Messages from Research* (1995). The effect of this shift has greatly increased the number of children that local authorities need to be concerned about. Rather than prioritising children who might be at risk of significant harm or imposing narrow service led interpretations of children in need, their remit has become much broader. So whilst local authorities are responsible for some 32,000 children whose names are on the 'at risk' register, look after some 53,000 children and provide services to between 300,000 and 400,000 children in need, it is estimated that there are 4 million vulnerable children (requiring extra help) who may be joined at any time and for various reasons by others from the total population of 11 million children in England (DoH et al., 2000). Responses to the needs of such children is further characterised by a requirement to gear responses built on prediction rather than crisis. As Nigel Parton has observed of the policy context, '[an] emphasis in early intervention, family support and a focus on vulnerable children was being developed. Concerns about children not fulfilling their potential and becoming social problems in the future were the driving force for change as much as children being at risk of parental abuse' (2006: 166). So, if *every child matters* in a social investment state, how then do we decide which children need what kinds of help? The answers to these questions have wide ranging implications for how we address the issue of how and under what circumstances one becomes an involuntary client of the state.

The preventative state

Brid Featherstone has noted, 'whilst New Labour have, in the main, desisted from imposing a

particular family form, there is considerable concern that their explicitly normalising project in relation to parents' responsibilities rides roughshod over what people themselves feel is the right thing to do' (2006: 16). There is no doubt that at the heart of New Labour policies are a concern that children should be at the centre of family policies, with a particular emphasis on how they are parented. Whilst not being prescriptive on family form, the message of the 1989 Children Act that parents, whether absent or present, have responsibilities towards their children, receives a new emphasis across a range of policies. If families are to be supported by the state this is on the clear contractual understanding that such support is consequent on a proper discharge of parental responsibilities, with the joint project designed to ensure optimal outcomes for children through their developmental years and beyond. The framework for realising such policy ambitions has been set out in the Children Act 2004 and include new duties for agencies to cooperate to improve the well-being of children, the setting up of electronic databases where information about children can be collated and concerns 'flagged' when professionals have concerns with regard to individual children, and the establishing of Children's' Trusts to allow further integration of health, education and social care professionals. As Parton argues, the net effect of such changes has been to make the United Kingdom a *preventative state*, with policy developments having broadened and enlarged the population of children who are of potential interest to the state. 'In the process, the priority is not only that children are protected from significant harm but that the welfare of as many children as possible is safeguarded and promoted' (2006: 169).

The range of policy initiatives flowing from this shift to a preventative state may be bewildering, but at heart they position the state as an expert partner in its relationship with families. The former Prime Minister Tony Blair (2006a) made this position clear in a recent speech to the Rowntree Foundation. Locating the boundary between the state and the family he said that he was:

. . . not talking about . . . interfering with normal family life. I am saying that where it is clear, as it very often is, at young age, that children are at risk of being brought up in a dysfunctional home where there are multiple problems, say of drug abuse or offending, then instead of

waiting until the child goes off the rails, we should act early enough, with the right help, support and disciplined framework for the family to prevent it ... You can detect and predict the children and families likely to go wrong. The vast majority offered help, take it ... [However] about 2.5 per cent of every generation seem to be stuck in a life-time of disadvantage and amongst them are the excluded, the deeply excluded ... The new approach involves complex and variegated decision-making ... We should test it in critical areas, where specific problems exist and build our own clear evidence base for future work ... We have identified four groups [one of these are] families with complex problems – the Respect Task Force identified 7,500 such families.

It is instructive to examine the Respect agenda which, in keeping with the, 'something for something' ethos of 'no rights without responsibilities', has as its catchphrase, 'Give respect get respect' (Respect Task Force, 2006a). Whilst overall the Respect agenda is aimed at tackling anti-social behaviour, it identifies one of the key target groups as the small number of households responsible for a high proportion of such behaviour. It evokes the support of the general population for a series of measures to address the problems caused by poor parenting, quoting: '85 per cent of people in the UK think that parents not bringing up their children properly is the biggest reason for the perceived rise in anti-social behaviour' (Respect Task Force, 2006b: 18). Whilst much of this involves extending the provision of Children's Centres and Extended Schools, together with the establishment of Pathfinders to deliver integrated support service packages to families with children at risk, the 'new approach to the most challenging families' (2006a: 20), involves a more coercive series of measures. Described as 'families who have severe problems and are damaging themselves and their children, as well as those around them', the proposed solution is to 'grip' such families with the objective being to change their behaviour. 'Gripping' includes 'great persistence and assertiveness by project workers to ensure families stick to agreements and changes in behaviour [and] ensuring the adherence to a contract between the household and agencies involved in their case' (Respect Task Force, 2006: 22). The strategy envisages targeted service provision involving intensive outreach to families in their own homes or in supervised accommodation with a particular focus on the delivery of parenting programmes. Where there is non-compliance, 'the threat of sanctions or use of sanctions provides both a way of curbing bad behaviour and also helps persuade people to accept and co-operate fully with offers of support' (Respect Task Force, 2006c). Aside from the provisions for compulsory intervention in family life set out in the 1989 *Children Act*, on the basis of likely or actual significant harm, a new statutory instrument is to be made available. The Parenting Order is designed to secure the co-operation of parents who are not willing to take help voluntarily. Orders can be made in the criminal court, family court or magistrates' court acting under civil jurisdiction. Such Orders will normally include requirements to attend parenting courses, with fines up to a maximum of £1000 payable for non-compliance.

Reconstructing the involuntary client – the role of the state

It is important to note that the Respect Agenda's focus on families with more severe problems is merely a starting point in a larger project to identify problematic families with vulnerable children who require the attentions of the state. Writing in the Sun Newspaper on 21 November 2006, announcing a new national network of parenting experts *who will help mums and dads raise their children* (emphasis added), Tony Blair hinted at a broadening of scope. 'There are some families who can't cope ... It doesn't much matter whether it's their fault or not. The fact is when they don't cope, the children suffer ... No one's talking here about interfering with normal family life. But life isn't normal if you've got 12-year-olds out every night, drinking and creating a nuisance on the street, with their parents either not knowing or not caring. In these circumstances, a bit of nannying, with stick and carrots, is what the local community needs, let alone the child' (2006b). The Respect Task Force are more explicit with regard to their intention to widen the net. 'We need to deal with problem families now through the dedicated projects already described, but the aim must be over the long term to mainstream these approaches' (2006b: 23). This is a strategy described as 'progressive universalism' in a recent speech by Beverley Hughes (2006).

Such families are, of course, the province of social workers who have traditionally sought to provide support to them in the recognition that much of the difficulties visible to communities, as represented by the behaviour or presentation of their children, were often symptomatic of a range of complex problems, including mental illness, drug and alcohol addiction and experience of abuse or violence. Whilst powers of coercion have always been located within the framework of the *1989 Children Act*, the principle of partnership and the attempt to refocus practice away from narrow child protection concerns to include a broader understanding of children's circumstances within a more developmentally orientated child in need perspective, has led social workers to attempt to work in ways more understanding of family perspectives. Yet, as the Respect Task Force make clear, this traditional form of family support has been called into question and to some extent superseded by more modern notions of 'what works'. 'It is important to make clear that effective parenting programmes are not the same thing as parenting support . . . schemes such as Home Start uses volunteers to befriend and support parents but does not improve parenting skills and does not have measurable effects on children's behaviour' (2006d).

These new initiatives, then, represent an intense interest in children as sites for investment, wherein new technologies are used to locate such children (Munro, 2004), new administrative arrangements are set up to ensure integrated and multi-professional ways of working, new-evidence based programmes are applied and new penalties are visited on the non-compliant. Because these new understandings are based on future orientated economic calculation as well as social considerations they are likely to have a much longer shelf life than has historically been the case with family policies, which were characterised by a concern to balance the implementation of legislation to delineate the partnership between the state and the family and adjust the system of social care provision to reflect this. Consequently, modern investment policies are unlikely to be reversed or unpicked as they represent an experimental future orientated project. The effects of present policies may only be measured over a long time span within which investment may be tracked against outcomes, initially in relation to compliance to norms of behaviour, but later against developmental targets and beyond this in use of health and welfare services as well as in economic contribution. And, if such an enterprise requires 'a bit of nannying', then the cost of damaging the

partnership with the family is small when compared with future benefits realised by investment returns. After all, we're not talking here about 'normal family life'.

Reconstructing the involuntary client – the role of social work

In some ways, the targeting of a small number of multi-problem families, as a beginning, appears to signal a return to a previous time, but there are important differences. Whilst in a previous generation our understanding of child abuse was influenced by psychological theorising which located the problem in the inherent make-up of the person (the abuser), the present conceptualisation of child welfare is more complex, drawing, for example, on ecological perspectives (Jack, 2000) to present a relocated and multi-faceted picture of the child and family experience. This new paradigm renders the old limited aims of child and family social work redundant. No longer is it acceptable to aim to merely protect children from harm, the new priority is to ensure that children are helped to meet normal milestones of health and development, the focus being not on events but on environments, and, most importantly, the parenting environment.

Social work consequently becomes centrally concerned, not with monitoring families to ensure that child abuse does not occur or reoccur, or the provision of support to ameliorate difficulties for the family (although both these activities do remain), but rather with the new technologies of welfare, that is, empirically validated parenting programmes, to change patterns of parenting. At least, that is where social work should be positioned if it were to take advantage of a rising tide of concern for the safeguarding of children. Given, however, continued concern to prioritise risks associated with child protection work, it is unlikely that social workers will become central to this new direction in policy in the way they were once able to be so in relation to the phenomenon of child abuse. Various commentators, including Jordan with Jordan (2000) Garrett (2002), and Fawcett et al. (2004), have noted a tendency under New Labour to franchise social work out to a much wider range of social care, education, youth justice and employment workers. However, Fawcett et al. argue that 'it is possible to see more recent developments as New Labour quietly giving up the ghost on social services departments and transferring the mandate for supportive and preventative work to various 'new' initiatives' (2004: 67). The Children Act 2004 provides an opportunity for social work to take a central role in the planning and management of service provision. The 'lead professional', identified as responsible for co-ordinating cases where there is more than one professional involved, may likely be a social worker. Similarly, responsibilities for following up 'flagged' children on the new Identification, Referral and Tracking (IRT) system will, in all probability, fall to social workers. As we have noted above, it is also likely that the market for such services will greatly increase as a much wider population will be introduced to the gaze of social workers. As Fawcett et al. observe, 'children's needs cannot be categorised simply in terms of either protection or support and there are real dangers in encouraging such binary thinking' (2004: 68).

In widening prevention orientated investment strategies and introducing social workers to a new market there are, of course, risks associated with a blurring of the threshold for state intervention in family life. Parton notes that in requiring professionals to share information with regard to children where they had 'any cause for concern', that this was a lower threshold than 'significant harm or the likelihood of significant harm' or 'a child in need' (2006: 163). If we return to the issue of how an involuntary client came to be defined under the previously binary interpretation of the 1989 Children Act, we have observed that non-compliance with social workers could lead to clients being routed from family support to child protection interventions. And, even in cases where such shifts along the in/voluntary continuum did not occur, the perspectives of parents whose children were considered to be in need and who consequently experienced interventions of a more benign nature, betrayed a reflexive apprehension with regard to their involvement with representatives of the state. We should expect the population of this twilight world to increase as more are ushered into it on the basis of 'concern' for their children. And, whilst the entry points to this world will be many, those seeking exits will have aspirations to leave measured against the developmental progress of their children. Such progress may be monitored over increasing timescales as investors will want to see gains

consolidated and returns on their money. Exiting may consequently be rather difficult.

Conclusion

In relation to our three identified themes of *prevention, pathology* and *partnership* we have observed that they have largely been reconceptualised within the ideological framework of the social investment state. This has given rise to a much greater number of parents becoming, by virtue of the way the state has become concerned with regard to their children, involuntary clients of the state. This has come about as a result of the redrawing of the relationship between the family and the state. In this new understanding, *partnership* with families has become subsumed within a more general concern for the safeguarding of children and recast in the contractual terms of rights and responsibilities. *Prevention* has come to the fore as the defining theme of the social investment state. No longer is the concept of prevention limited to small populations, such as children in the state care system, but is broadened to include a wide range of vulnerable children who require early intervention if they are to meet acceptable norms of progress to an independent and productive future. Notions of *pathology* have become reserved for those groups who, whilst small in number, require the punitive attentions of the state to ensure they either undertake the parenting role or become excluded from it altogether.

References

Aldgate, J. (2002) Evolution Not Revolution: Family Support Services and the Children Act 1989. In Ward, H. and Rose, W. (Eds.) *Approaches to Needs Assessment in Children's Services*. London: Jessica Kingsley.

Axford, N. and Little, M. (2006) Refocusing Children's Services Towards Prevention: Lessons from the Literature. *Children & Society*, 20, 299–312.

Bell, M. (1995) *Child Protection: Families and the Conference Process*. Aldershot: Ashgate.

Blair, T. (2006a) *Our Sovereign Value: Fairness*. Speech given to the Rowntree Foundation, York, 5 September, http://www.number10. gov.uk/CareMattersoutput/Page100037.asp

Blair, T. (2006b) *Parenting*. Article for The Sun Newspaper, 22 November, http://www.number10.gov.uk/output/Page10448.asp

Brent, London Borough of (1985) *A Child in Trust: A Report of the Panel of Inquiry into the Circumstances Surrounding the Death of Jasmine Beckford*. London: London Borough of Brent.

Butler-Sloss, Lord Justice E. (1988) *Report of the Inquiry into Child Abuse in Cleveland 1987*. Cmnd 412, London: HMSO.

Cleaver, H. and Freeman, P. (1995) *Parental Perspectives in Cases of Suspected Child Abuse*. London: HMSO.

Corby, B. (2006) *Child Abuse: Towards a Knowledge Base*. 3rd edn. Maidenhead: Open University Press.

Dingwall, R., Eekelaar, J. and Murray, T. (1983) *The Protection of Children: State Intervention and Family Life*. Oxford: Blackwell.

DoH (1991) *Patterns and Outcomes in Child Placement: Messages from Research and their Implications*. London: HMSO.

DoH (1995) *Child Protection: Messages from Research*. London: HMSO.

DoH (1998a) *Social Care White Paper. Modernising Social Services. Promoting Independence, Improving Protection, Raising Standards*. London: HMSO.

DoH (1998b) *The Quality Protects Programme: Transforming Children's Services*, London: HMSO.

DoH (2001) *The Children Act Now: Messages from Research*. London: HMSO.

DoH (2003) *Care Leavers, Year Ending 31 March 2002, England*. London: HMSO.

Esping-Anderson, G. (2003) Against Social Inheritance. In Brown, M., Thompson, P. and Sainsbury, F. (Eds.) *Progressive Futures: New Ideas for the Centre Left*. London: Policy Network.

Fawcett, B., Featherstone, B. and Goddard, J. (2004) *Contemporary Child Care Policy and Practice*. London: Palgrave Macmillan.

Featherstone, B. (2006) Rethinking Family Support in the Current Policy Context. *British Journal of Social Work*, 36, 5–19.

Garrett, P. (2002) Encounters in the New Welfare Domains of the Third Way: Social Work, The Connexions Agency and Personal Advisers. *Critical Social Policy*, 22: 4, 596–619.

Giddens, A. (1994) *Beyond Left and Right: The Future of Radical Politics*. Cambridge: Polity Press.

Giddens, A. (1998) *The Third Way: The Renewal of Social Democracy*. Cambridge: Polity Press.

Hendrick, H. (1994) *Child Welfare: England 1872–1989*. London: Routledge.

Holtermann, S. (1996) *All Our Futures*. London: Barnardo's.

Howitt, D. (1992) *Child Abuse Errors: When Good Intentions Go Wrong*. Hemel Hempstead: Harvester Wheatsheaf.

Hughes, B. (2006) *Safeguarding Children: Everybody's Responsibility*. Keynote speech for ISPCAN conference, York, 5 September.

Jack, G. (2000) Ecological Influences on Parenting and the Child Environment. *British Journal of Social Work*, 30, 703–20.

Jensen, J. and Saint-Martin, D. (2001) Changing Citizenship Regimes: Social Policy Strategies in the Social Investment State. Workshop on Fostering Social Cohesion: A Comparison of New Political Strategies, University of Montreal, 21–22 June.

Jordan, B. with Jordan, C. (2000) *Social Work and the Third Way: Tough Love as Social Policy*. London: Sage.

Kempe, C.H. et al. (1962) The Battered Child Syndrome. *Journal of the American Medical Association*, 181, 17–24.

Laming, Lord. (2003) *The Victoria Climbie Inquiry Report*. London: The Stationery Office.

Mason, P., Morris, K. and Smith, P. (2005) A Complex Solution to a Complicated Problem? Early Messages from the National Evaluation of the Children's Fund Prevention Programme, *Children & Society*, 19, 131–43.

Munro, E. (2004) State Regulation of Parenting. *The Political Quarterly*, 180–4.

Myers, J. (1994) *The Backlash: Child Protection under Fire*. Thousand Oaks, CA: Sage.

Parton, N. (1985) *The Politics of Child Abuse*. Basingstoke: Macmillan.

Parton, N. (1991) *Governing the Family: Child Care, Child Protection and the State*. Basingstoke: Macmillan.

Parton, N. (2006) *Safeguarding Childhood: Early Intervention and Surveillance in a Late Modern Society*. Basingstoke: Palgrave Macmillan.

Respect Task Force (2006a) *Give Respect Get Respect*. London: Home Office.

Respect Task Force (2006b) *Respect Action Plan*. London: Home Office.

Respect Task Force (2006c) *Respect: Family Intervention* http://respect.gov.uk/article.aspx?id=9072&terms=domestic+violence&searchty

Respect Task Force (2006d) *Respect: Supporting Families*. London: Home Office.

Rose, W. (1994) *An Overview of the Development of Services: The Relationship Between Protection and Family Support and the Intentions of the Children Act 1989*. Sieff Conference, 5 Sept. Cumberland Lodge.

Sinclair, I. (2005) *Fostering Now: Messages from Research*. London: Jessica Kingsley.

Social Services Inspectorate and the Audit Commission (2002) *Model of Child Concern*, http//www.doh.gov/uk/qualityprotects/ . . .abase/northern/word_submission_139.html

Spratt, T. (2000) Decision Making by Senior Social Workers at Point of First Referral. *British Journal of Social Work*, 30, 597–618.

Spratt, T. (2001) The Influence of Child Protection Practice on Child Welfare Practice, *British Journal of Social Work*, 31, 933–54.

Spratt, T. and Callan, J. (2004) Parents' Views on Social Work Interventions in Child Welfare Cases. *British Journal of Social Work*, 34, 199–224.

Trotter, C. (2006) *Working with Involuntary Clients: A Guide to Practice*. 2nd edn. London: Sage.

Tunstill, J. (1997) Implementing the Family Support Clauses of the 1989 Children Act: Legislative, Professional and Organisational Obstacles. In Parton, N. (Ed.) *Child Protection and Family Support: Tensions, Contradictions and Possibilities*. London: Routledge.

CHAPTER 3

Engaging with Children: The Political Dimension

Nick Turnbull and Toby Fattore

Introduction

In some circumstances the state is mandated to act on behalf of children. It acts on behalf of individual children in certain therapeutic settings and also for children generally, for example by providing education and child protection services. These collective acts are decided without children's participation and in so doing also mark out norms about the appropriate boundaries of childhood. In this chapter we address the terms of this engagement, in particular political dimension which arises when the state acts for children it takes as involuntary clients. Involuntary clients are an ideal-type example of the issue of authority versus freedom in a liberal democracy. This is made more problematic where children are involved for three reasons:

1. Adults assume children lack capacity for autonomous action.
2. Children are largely absent from political theory.
3. Children's diminished legal status.

At each of these three levels, engaging with children as involuntary clients raises the question of the political dimension of that engagement. We consider this question in the broader context of the social construction of childhood itself, which is produced through the interaction in practice of children and the state.

Exploring the theme of the politics of working with children means that we must think through ideas about children and childhood and the nature of politics itself. While the political dimension of adult-child interaction is well established in the new sociology of childhood literature, the politics of engaging with children does pose difficult questions for both theory and practice. We discuss both of these themes. Regarding the former, theorising politics is complex and requires that we think carefully

about understanding the complexity of political relations; and whatever the theoretical intricacies, certainly in *practice* the political nature of professional-child interaction is expressed in the endless variety of situations encountered in the field. In practice we experience politics in the relationship between professional and child, between professional and family, and between the state and civil society. This inquiry will lead us from theory to practice and finally to consider the administrative procedures of the state which concern children.

Theorising the political dimension of engaging with children

Very often, children have been construed in social and political theory as apolitical beings. This has followed from two main presuppositions. Firstly, children have not been credited with active subjectivity, or at least not at a level sufficient for them to engage in political debates about serious problems. Politics has been defined in terms of competence to think about and discuss political questions using appeals to reason. Children have been thought incapable of attaining the necessary level of reasoning capacities until they reach adulthood, that is, until they achieve status as full beings. Political practice has therefore been reserved for those considered competent in particular ways of thinking and reasoning, namely that of adults. Many critics have argued against this, particularly in the new childhood studies and those working from a children's rights perspective (Freeman, 1983; James and Prout, 1990; Jenks, 1996; Qvortrup, 1994). This presupposition is expressed in institutional forms which aim to progress children through developmental stages towards full adult competence (Alanen, 1988). The attainment of developmental milestones is the objective of these institutions and sets the terms of engagement with children at the level of service delivery, for example. Only at the end of this process are children deemed fit to engage in the full spectrum

* Many thanks to Karen Clarke, whose helpful comments much improved our chapter.

of adult life, including politics. The second major argument for rejecting children as political beings arises from the idea that childhood is a time of innocence and that politics is a complex, contaminated mode of life to which children should not be exposed. Hence we often hear of calls for childhood to be protected from adult concerns, to remain a time of 'freedom' in which they can follow their desires freely and without worry. Certainly adults have an interest in advocating on behalf of children, but this should acknowledge that children themselves have their own interests and opinions, are part of the community and have a right to be involved in such debates.

Related to these norms about the developmental status of children are underlying norms about how we conceive of politics. In general, we can distinguish between individualist and collectivist conceptions of politics. Difficulties arise for understanding political engagement with children if we presuppose a uniquely individualistic view. Many political theories implicitly adopt the view that society is composed of atomised individuals, including children, rather than as individuals who are also social beings existing within, and identifying with, a network of social relationships. Western society makes a virtue of individuality and separateness, a value that is found even more strongly in the most liberal states. The Western ideal of the citizen as rational man has been extensively criticised by feminist scholars for excluding women from full political rights. Children are also excluded from the ideal for not meeting the implicit adult standards of agency, autonomy, and rationality. We disagree with the individualistic view and argue instead that our sense of ourselves as individuals emerges from collective identifications rather than the other way around (Fattore and Turnbull, 2005; based on Merleau-Ponty, 1964). The inadequacy of the individualistic view is particularly apparent in the case of children, for whom identity is shaped through their strong emotionally secured ties to others, especially immediate family but also to other family members and adult friends, and to other children. This means that the political must commence from the idea that – at the level of identity and reasoning, for both children and adults – the individual is *socially constituted*. For children this means that the sites of their identity formation include a political dimension. The family is crucial for children because ideally it provides a collective identity, strong emotional attachments and a supportive and nurturing environment, not simply because it is a social institution which contains the child until she emerges into adulthood. Our criteria for understanding children should work from their existence as individuals born from and identified by their social ties.

The individualistic view produces problems for conceptualising how we engage with children and also for theorising politics itself. If we conceive of politics as relationships between entirely autonomous individuals then children are excluded from politics on the grounds that in the dominant ideology they are deemed not fully mature individuals and therefore excluded from public life. Restricting our definition of politics to relationships between atomised individuals also casts politics itself as an undesirable intervention in the life of the individual rather than something which helps us negotiate shared problems between people who, at least to some degree, share a collective identity and interests. Nor should we accept the child liberationist view that children are individuals and therefore equivalent to adults, entitling them to full access to all the things enjoyed by adults. Adults enter into a relationship with a child as an adult and we cannot escape from that. Such individualised politics abrogates forms of social responsibility for others, especially children. It is an empirical fiction anyway because parents do show responsibility for children. More significant is how that responsibility is conceptualised and enacted within the complex relationships between adults and children.

The individualistic view errs because it fails to see that social life is composed of communications and collective identifications and processes between people which are equally as important as their choices made as individuals. This communication is *intersubjective*, grounded in social interaction and gaining meaning because of it. As long as adults are willing to engage in genuine ways with children, communication can proceed and the child's perspectives and needs can be given expression and represented by an adult, on behalf of, or with the child. That is, we need not define adult-child relations as a trade-off between absolute parental authority and absolute child autonomy, leaving us no realistic ground in between. An adult working in a professional capacity operates from the position of accepting the necessity of the state to represent the child's interests. The question is their ability to do so in a way that is not authoritarian. Open communication, which accepts the validity of each party's views and interests, regardless of age, is the starting point. The politics of working with children, therefore, should be conceptualised around the characteristics of the communicative process as much as the outcome of that process. Both are important, but it is the process of deliberation (the communicative process) that offers the best opportunities for children to express their interests and to reach a shared view about what children's needs and interests are. This then provides a communicative procedure upon which a worker can advocate with and for the child. From this we can derive a conception of politics fully capable of engaging with children as political actors, as individuals and as members of social groups, not as individuals who only become political beings once they are no longer children.

Liberal political theory simply cannot deal with the complex reality that children should have citizenship rights but that we should also tolerate the authority of the family and other caring adults (Elshtain, 1989). As Elshtain points out, this demonstrates the flaws in considering theory separately from practical reality. 'Equality between individuals' is not a political understanding but one which 'a priori' removes the political dimension of social interaction between different types of people. If we commence from an understanding of individuals as rights-holders regardless of their social situation we easily progress to apolitical views at either extreme: children are either apolitical in having no rights or politically equal to adults. Neither of these views is acceptable because they both fail to theorise the social construction of childhood, its specificity, and children's position within it in relation to each other and to adults. When it comes to children, we must conceptualise politics in a different way, one which acknowledges protection, participation and provision rights that are both similar to and different from those of adults, largely because of the social positioning of childhood and the specific needs of children for care. The precise content of these rights and needs for care should be negotiated over time through processes of deliberation, to take account of the transitions undergone by individual children. While research on children's development is useful here, adherence to strict developmentalism prevents an

understanding of children's individual needs and restricts the scope of what children's needs are.

At the same time the similarity of adults and children in the provision of rights includes freedom from exploitation and freedom from the abuse and neglect of all human beings. Children are citizens who are entitled to protection from the law and have their interests represented by agents appointed to them. The question of politics, therefore, is not simply whether children are political actors or not, but traverses the much more subtle territory of the political mediation of children's individual and collective interests and the procedures by which such a mediation takes place.

Intersubjective Communication Between Adults and Children

There is a vast literature in political theory that we could use to consider the question of the politics of working with children. One key strand of this field is normative theory, which attempts to develop base values from which we can derive guidelines for political practice. Another stream has been poststructuralism or 'antifoundationalism', which has argued that the idea of grounding normative principles is theoretically unsustainable and politically authoritarian. The former seeks a set of principles for politics while the latter argues for 'the political' itself as an element of fundamental problematicity that lies outside traditional conceptions of rationality. We cannot resolve these epistemologically opposed positions here but if we examine politics in practice then perhaps we can situate politics somewhere in between the two. The former idea expresses what we all desire, which is a principled way to operate in public life and principles, which guarantee individual rights to freedom of expression and the right to organise collectively to deal with public problems. The latter position affirms that politics is neither fixed nor predictable. We can always question political norms and so be open towards a future that we might change through political action. So, if we concede that children have political interests and the legitimate right to question, then engaging with children should support their questioning and not unilaterally impose solutions upon them, especially in terms of adult presuppositions about childhood.

Children, as questioners, are legitimate entrants to the political sphere. They are able to ask about the world and express their opinions. Children can negotiate from their own point of view and, if we concede their right to question, then we must also concede that we must enter into some form of discussion with them when we are called upon to implement policy on their behalf. We would not say that politics is not normative, however. Any action by a professional acting on behalf of collective interests mandated by the state is either explicitly normative or contains a normative view, even if it is only implicit. What this means is that the normative question always remains a live one, such that principles to guide practical action cannot be derived for every case because the question will appear different in each context. While we strive to have consistent, non-arbitrary and even-handed guidelines for policy implementation, in reality practitioners experience conflicts everyday in making choices on behalf of, and with, children. Perfect action from principles is not possible so the aim should be to establish the right procedures to deal with vexing normative questions so that we can act in a legitimate way.

This conception of politics has several advantages. First, it rejects liberal views based on autonomy and competence and includes children within the political dimension of public life (and it does not depend on a definition of politics in terms of individual voting rights). Secondly, and conversely, because it does not define politics in terms of individual freedom it does not suggest that children should have the same autonomy as adults, leading to support for highly undesirable assertions about children being able to operate in public life without regulation. Thirdly, it supports a view of politics situated in the context of real problems, hence it is not incompatible with practice. This reflects the reality that social norms are generated as much through practice as they are through abstract discussion. In the case of children, we would like to guarantee each child's right to a certain level of wellbeing and social conditions in which they will thrive. When professionals engage with children they implicitly give expression to public norms defined by adults. Furthermore, this opens the possibility of contributing to public norms through dialogue with children. This highlights that claiming normative support for one's work and even the creation of norms themselves cannot

be established beyond question: all social engagement is problematic and thus involves a political dimension.

What form does communication with children take? Previously, we have argued for an intersubjective view of communication to promote the formulation of children's political will (Fattore and Turnbull, 2005). We drew on the sociologist Habermas who points out that political discourse does not originate in elite state or private interests but in the ordinary language of public life (Habermas, 1996). Ordinary language is oriented towards others and seeks their understanding and opinion. The intersubjective view acknowledges that people's identity is formed through their interaction with others. This communication can be either monological, a one-way discourse of authority which dictates to the other, or dialogical, a two-way exchange of views which allows both parties the opportunity to speak and to develop a synthesis of views. The forms of communication which arise out of civil society become institutionalised in and mediated through the political public sphere. Politics arises from communication between individuals, including children, so we can develop processes which include children's perspectives in public deliberation and allow them to contribute to the formation of the general will. The right social conditions for effective deliberation must exist and these are outlined in the United Nations Convention on the Rights of the Child. These rights provide the baseline conditions for the participation of children in public life – rights to cultural identity, to freedom of expression and association, to economic security, health and education, freedom from exploitation and abuse, and to participation. This takes us beyond issues of voting and formal political institutions to a broader public sphere which includes children as well as adults. The public sphere provides a model of political participation that can be inclusive of children's points of view and ways of acting. But even deliberative forms might exclude children on the grounds that they have not attained sufficient competence to participate. However, scholars such as the philosopher Merleau-Ponty reject the idea of a developmental separation between childhood and adulthood (Lefort, 1990; O'Neill, 1973). Indeed, a child's sense of self arises from communicating with others, that is, it is intersubjective and develops from a very early age, such that children can make themselves understood and we can understand them. Here, individuality is not the defining criterion for rationality but something that evolves with rationality as children communicate with others: 'If I am consciousness turned toward things, I can meet in things the actions of another and find in them a meaning' (Merleau-Ponty, 1964: 71). Conceived intersubjectively, communication between adults and children can proceed without one-way coercion of children by adults, taking the form of a dialogue rather than unilateral instruction. Research into imitation (Meltzoff and Moore, 1991) by infants points out that children do actively interpret and construct their world even while their experiences are strongly influenced and directed by adults. They show that infants are not simply passive but active participants in social relationships and imitate adult practices to learn complex social interactions. The child's identity develops through being experienced *by* others and seeing how that is reflected back. Therefore the nature of those experiences is essential to the child's sense of self development. The experience of recognition can be positive if it is affirming but damaging if it is objectifying. Therefore when children experience being objectified it can impact negatively upon their sense of self and close off avenues for free expression and engagement in public life. So, rather than formulating contemporary concerns about the loss of childhood resulting from the intrusion of political concerns from which children should be 'freed', we would reframe this question as being about social processes which objectify and individualise children, for example, in individualistic educational testing regimes and as individualised consumers of products. So, we face a general question about the effects of objectification and rationalisation which do not offer children the right to participate in the construction of their lives. It is because the child is social first and foremost that the key question for child development concerns the characteristics of their engagement with others, which can either promote trust, autonomy, love, and inner worth or mistrust, doubt, shame, inferiority and isolation (Elshtain, 1982: 293).

So, we can evaluate the professional engagement with children in terms of process. Does the process give autonomy to the child, recognise their worth as an individual and positively engage them in interaction with adults? Or does it fail to take the child's

subjectivity into account, enforcing pre-established instrumentalising and objectivising standards upon them, leading them to doubt themselves? Here, communication and the recognition of self are intertwined. Honneth (1995) defines three forms of recognition which seem particularly pertinent to the case of engaging with children: loving relationships, social and political rights, and the social recognition of individuals' achievements and abilities. In the absence of recognition an individual might be led to react in a negative way towards the person or institutions that deny that recognition. Hence social arrangements which criticise, condemn, or shame children should be understood for their negative and authoritarian (monological) procedures.

This relationship need not be founded upon an idea of reaching agreement. Differences exist between adults and children but the individualistic view attempts to rule them out and thereby abolish them, or fix them by the developmental criterion which justifies denying political difference and implementing unilateral action. The intersubjective view offers space for disagreement and therefore makes politics a normal element of adult-child engagement. Not all political questions will be solved in these interactions, which makes life more complex. However, giving space for political expression is important because it is an element of sincere communication that affirms the child's worth. And, if we are flexible and adapt to children's mode of communication we can include the voices of children in public sphere deliberations regardless of adult-defined competence. In particular, such a framework offers the potential to represent the voices of marginalised children and, more importantly, offer them a positive experience of recognition. For those children encountered by professionals in the course of their work, it is the experience of positive recognition, which has most likely been denied to these children, therefore the question of process lies at the heart of redressing their social and political exclusion. We can think of children in these circumstances as a subordinated group experiencing misrecognition resulting from authoritarian communicative social relations which cast them as non-autonomous objects rather than engaging with them sincerely (Honneth, 1995). Mirowsky and Ross (1989) have argued that authoritarian political conditions and social inequity are sources of individual psychological distress. To work towards redressing the experience of children who have suffered the distress of misrecognition, professional engagement with children should be founded on a positive, intersubjective model. This model includes children actively participating in political processes and also adults acting with and on their behalf. It emphasises that responsible adults can translate children's perspectives into public discourse without making simplistic demands for children to be involved in public life in a way equivalent to adults.

The politics of child-professional relationships

The political dimension of child-professional relationships should be understood along two simultaneous axes. The first is the relationship between individuals around a problem. The second is the social positioning of the pair within the larger social system. The first axis concerns the ethics of communication and procedure, with the child approaching from a particular context involving a problem which has drawn professional scrutiny and the adult from a position as a professional with specific duties and standards to uphold. The second axis, the context through which the primary relationship takes place, concerns the broader collective identification and interests of the child and the worker as members of social groups of children and adults. Also at this level is the relationship between state and society, with the state regulating the encounter through policy. At the interpersonal level this is experienced as a 'client-worker' relationship. Jan Fook (2002) provides an excellent conception of how social work should combine a radical view oriented towards understanding and reforming oppressive social structures with a firm consideration of the individual's particular circumstances. She explains that social work has a tradition of seeing the individual in context but that social work can also work towards eliminating oppressive and exploitative social relations. It draws from social theory but is always oriented towards acting in context and working for change through practice, which helps individuals as well. To do this, social workers should adopt a critical outlook on the relationship

between individuals and society, informed through an inclusive dialogue with clients and ongoing critical reflection upon their own practice (2002: 18). In our case, particularly important is the child's position in relation to other children. A service provider working with a child is not simply dealing with an individual but an individual positioned in a social construction, childhood, which is also positioned in relation to another social structure, adulthood.

Regarding the first axis, the politics of the one-to-one relationship between adult and child, much work has already been done in the area of research ethics. As academics have begun to conduct more research on children and childhood they have dealt with difficult ethical questions arising from their recognition of children as social actors (Christensen and Prout, 2002). Christensen and Prout consider how changes in social structures have led to a 'personalisation of ethics' in which those undertaking research with children should not take responsibility away from them, as though they were passive, but rather take responsibility 'with' and 'for' them in the research by entering into a dialogue with child research subjects which 'recognises commonality but also honours difference' (2002: 480). Such attention to process requires researchers to consider the ethics of communication and the power differences involved between researcher and child. It turns attention back upon the researcher in how they deal with these differences. When we acknowledge that such differences exist and cannot be eliminated by a pre-established ethical norm – but must rather be continually mediated through communicative processes – we make explicit the political dimension of the research process. So, at this level we have the ethical and political relations in the intersubjective communication between researcher and child. An analogous issue arises in the relationship between adults and children in other professional contexts in which we find the contrasting characteristics of engagement described above, from open communication which recognises the child as a co-participant to a closed and inflexible monological discourse in which the adult asserts definitional authority over the child.

However, beyond this attention to the ethics of individual exchanges we must be careful to avoid tacitly creating an asociological conception of society by implying that society is composed of isolated individuals. Whatever the fragmentation of traditional social structures in postmodernity, society is still composed of related social systems and somewhat cohesive social groups. Each individual engagement between adults and children also works from, and contributes to, a second axis of larger social structural relations. Indeed, reconsidering research ethics brings to light implicit power relations between adults and children arising from the social context (Christensen and Prout, 2002; Mayall, 2000). Professionals approach their work in the context of a set of social values, including the intergenerational relationship of adulthood-childhood. Professionals must reflect upon their position as adults and upon social norms about childhood in order to see beyond pre-figured conceptions of childhood as an apolitical stage of life and children as less than competent. By being reflective within their practice they can try to understand the particular child's interests and the child's position within the larger social system. This should also involve considering whether automatic, bureaucratic responses to children's problems adequately reflect children's interests or whether they reinforce dominant conceptions of childhood, which take away the capacity for children to express their own opinions and have their political interests represented.

Political will formation is not restricted to children expressing their interests in the public realm and having professionals take up these interests on their behalf. To be complete, practice should also be able to challenge conventional definitions of childhood itself. This also pertains to the second axis of the working relationship, made possible when a supportive, dialogical relationship is built between worker and child. This is where the working relationship can open up the possibility for political change. Definitions of childhood are culturally constructed and it is these underlying norms of social relations which most strongly pre-figure social interaction. Such norms become entrenched in practice which, when established rules are implemented rigidly, can be most politically oppressive for children who might have needs which run contrary to such normative structures and cannot question them because they are denied the opportunity to do so. This is not to say that professionals oppress children. Rather, they will encounter children and young people who have been denied recognition in some form (love, rights, solidarity). In these cases it is not always clear that adults' opinions about ideal social institutions (for example, the middle class family) are what is required for the individual.

The reflective practitioner can work with the child to voice ideas otherwise implicit within children's discourse. The very process of thinking about such choices is a creative synthesis of worker and child perspectives. This process also helps make children autonomous by assisting them to transform a problem situation in which their self-worth has been harmed, to a positive relationship with an adult who recognises their value and represents their interests. Actively involving the child in the process is more persuasive and therefore it is more likely that they will be satisfied with the decision, even where that decision is legitimated through the authority of the state. Furthermore, this can only improve implementation. Of course, no worker is in a position to revolutionise society nor violate institutional rules, (we address the capacity of institutions to support or restrict dialogue between workers and children in the last section). However, by supporting the child to question and not constraining dialogue through blind adherence to cultural norms of childhood, workers can engage more effectively with the child and better represent the child as an individual, as a political being, and as a member of a social group.

Because we adopt a sociological conception of adulthood and childhood we include engagement between adults and young people as well as young children. As much as we have reconsidered childhood, adulthood today is also a problematic concept given changes to the labour market and living circumstances which make the transition from childhood to adulthood unclear. And it is engagements with young people in which we find paradigmatic examples of the new paternalism, which offers monological interaction as a necessary palliative for 'problem teenagers'. An example of non-dialogical communication is the contemporary form of contractualism between the state or its agencies and young people. Welfare-to-work programmes for unemployed young people impose punitive sanctions against those who do not fulfil the conditions stipulated in the contract they are forced to enter into with the state in order to secure welfare benefits. These contractual forms have been widely employed in liberal welfare states such as the UK, Australia and the US. They are credited with creating an 'active' welfare state and with providing necessary incentives to take up training and to seek work. However, such contracts often offer the young person little or no opportunity to set the terms and conditions of these arrangements. Without the right to communicate their interests and to develop a shared set of goals, such *quid pro quo* contracts are politically oppressive. What is considered best for the young person is decided by others and unilaterally enforced, regardless of the former's views on the subject. Such arrangements deliberately stigmatise the benefit recipient as being of poor character and not meeting moral standards. These stigmatising mechanisms, which are characteristic of social policy in liberal welfare states (Esping-Anderson, 1990) are the 'stick' which is supposed to help the marginalised to lift themselves out of their moral inadequacy to a decent, working life. However, this represents an example of an instrumental, authoritarian system which does not recognise the intrinsic value of the young person, instead using coercion and moral condemnation. These forms of misrecognition respond to the needs of a young person whose worth has been socially devalued by replicating precisely the same kind of condemnatory interaction.

While these policy mechanisms claim to promote 'active' rather than passive welfare, the political dimension of engagement is characterised by the exertion of authority from above. The only choice a person has is to meekly comply and accept the instrumental priorities of the state or to rebel against them. They are then punished by withdrawal of benefit or some other sanction. Thus, such mechanisms often exacerbate problem behaviours rather than providing an avenue beyond them. In such cases we see the symbolic demonisation of children institutionalised in forms which presuppose that children possess more agency than they have and which ignore the social context of their behaviour (Goldson, 2001: 40). We question whether such arrangements can effectively dictate norms of behaviour. These procedures do not engage with children by devolving some power to them so that they might really be given some leeway to take responsibility and be rewarded for their choices. Marginalised children and young people must be offered more caring relationships within which they might articulate their own needs as well as take on values which we think will help them. While many problems of social exclusion stem from structural causes that are difficult to address, more positive, dialogical processes might promote a sense of control by children and young people over their lives and make them better placed to deal with problems. The issue here is not the welfare state as such or insufficient intervention by the state. Rather, it is the processes of engagement that are problematic. Children and young people who find themselves marginalised by civil society must be supported to express their concerns in the public sphere and receive just recognition in response, whether by the state, private sector or not-for-profit organisations.

Politics in practice: children's wellbeing and caring relationships

For practice to be based on criteria other than the output rationality of the neo-liberal state, we must establish child-oriented criteria of well-being. We can already draw on research in this area. For instance Gilman, Huebner and Laughlin (2000) found that 'life satisfaction' amongst a sample of American young people emphasised family relationships, self–image, living environment, relationships with friends and success at school. These corresponded with Cummins' (1995) domains of life satisfaction for the general population: material well-being, health, safety, productive activity, place in community, and emotional well-being. Similar findings were obtained in consultations with children informing the Every Child Matters programme in the UK. Fattore, Mason and Watson (2006) asked children what was important to them to inform child-centred measures of well-being. While they identified domains such as activity, social responsibility and health, children also emphasised *agency* (having some capacity to act independently in everyday life), *security* (having a sense of security to be able to engage fully in life), and *positive sense of self* (seeing yourself as a good or okay person and having this recognised by those around you). These aspects of well-being suggest alternatives to contemporary objectifying testing regimes which push children into competitive rather than solidaristic relations with each other. These concepts are not familising but they do show the importance of family relationships for children. They are not economically-reductive but provide a basis for social policy and practice which is child-oriented because it has been drawn from children's own experiences and concerns.

The question of family is central to working with children but this raises important issues for practice. Professionals working for public institutions with or on behalf of child clients are often in the uncomfortable position of mediating a larger institutional conflict between the state and the family. They must not only consider the ethico-political dimension of their individual relationship with the child but also deal with the frustration and anger of families who may resent state intervention or conversely demand support from the state, which it cannot give. Despite the extensive statutory provisions guiding work with children there is always some leeway in practice, so the worker then faces difficult choices. Procedures cannot be rigidly prescribed but must always adapt to the context at hand by attempting to establish a process with all the parties. There are also times that each adult working with children will experience the anguish of balancing service provision with the constraints of their organisational life, such as the demands of a large workload and limited resources. They also face choices about whether to advocate more strongly to superior officers for more support for the child, and they feel the weight of personal responsibility about their choices. There are no easy solutions to these issues. Our suggestion here is that whatever solution is pursued, it needs to be informed by genuine engagement with the child, something increasingly acknowledged in child protection legislation and casework. The strong case for reforming the management of many areas of public policy involving the care of children is best found in the many reforms to the substitute care system in the UK and Australia in recent years. Even simple but effective changes to procedure can make for much more compassionate and effective relationships and casework outcomes for children in substitute care. For example, in NSW (Australia) researchers found that children in care felt unsupported and depersonalised by the continual change in personnel of their caseworkers (Cashmore, Dolby and Brennan, 1994; Mason and Gibson 2004). Allowing them to access their case files and to add personal material to the case file gave them a way to build up a narrative of their life and so gain control over it. The case file then served to stabilise children's relationships with an otherwise impersonal state and led them to feel more recognised and valued.

In another study of an Australian child protection government department (Fattore et al., 2000) managerialist responses to the problem of child protection produced many problems for workers and their child clients. The department had been under pressure to deal with huge increases in the number of notifications of children at risk of abuse and neglect, particularly in response to sensationalised reporting in the media. The department instituted many managerialist reforms aimed at suppressing damaging information for fear of receiving negative media coverage. This involved increasing controls on child protection workers, surveillance of their activities, and containing costs, all of which constituted a general attack on the autonomy of workers who reported to us in interviews that this often led to poor services for their child clients. For example, workers were unable to act quickly due to administrative restrictions on procuring resources, and many types of notifications were re-classified as non-urgent to reduce the number of active cases on the books. The changes produced an organisational culture of fear in which it was impossible for workers to advocate on behalf of their clients and to transmit their concerns upwards to their superiors. Work processes were defined in terms of outputs rather than the quality of their casework and the relationships they established with children in their care. Many of the department's problems have been addressed since with large amounts of new funding to restore its organisational culture to health. But whatever the levels of funding we think that, in general, certain forms of administrative operations can be problematic for work with children. Rationalised administrative procedures are rightly aimed at accountability and efficiency. However, this can transform the nature of work with children to the point where it becomes damaging for practice because it is not child-centred. Adams and Balfour describe how 'the values of procedural correctness and efficiency contribute to a blindness to the context in which they are applied and to the human consequences of administrative action' (1998: 135).

When the autonomy of workers is curtailed by a purely output-focused administration they are unable to represent their child client's needs on their own terms, i.e. in terms of child-centred criteria of well-being. Such procedures individualise children and result in workers suffering stress as they straddle two forms of life, the child's world and the administrative world. An alternative would be to develop administrative procedures which evaluate practice in terms of an ethic of care (see for example, Sevenhuijsen, Bozalek, Gouws and Minnaar-McDonald, 2003). Instead of judging casework by removing children from the state's ledger as quickly as possible, casework should be based on measures of process: positive, open engagement with the child; establishing a joint plan of action based on the child's needs; and providing ongoing support for the child, with the same caseworker wherever possible to sustain a more caring rather than impersonal relationship. In short, the reciprocity of the relationship between worker and child client would be the criterion for engagement. At an organisational level, workers must be allowed space to advocate on behalf of the child even where this might run against established policy. This political space can be uncomfortable for organisations but workers would at least be able to give children a voice and better represent their interests, which would in turn foster more reciprocity and trust in relationships between worker and child. This emphasises practical social work and social care skills over administrative operations and would go a small way to establishing positive state-child interactions. This need not interfere with accountability, indeed it should improve it because it would operationalise the idea that the state and its agencies have a responsibility to respond to the needs of their clients.

While we have positive guidelines for evaluating the process of engaging with children, child-centred criteria of well-being can be difficult to promote within contemporary administrative systems. Developing positive relationships with children is very difficult if policy does not support it. The many organisational reforms of the last two decades – particularly the performance management systems employed within state agencies and stipulated in contracts between non-government agencies and the state – have placed significant time and resource pressures upon professionals working with children, undermining the legislative changes aimed at promoting participatory relationships with children. This has produced an environment in which cost pressures are intense and performance-management regimes are oriented towards legitimation of the neo-liberal state rather than child well-being. Professionals need

autonomy to respond to the child's needs and to advocate on behalf of the child but the professional working with children cannot simply step outside the institutional context. Practitioners must be overseen and regulated in order to guarantee good practice and ensure that professional autonomy supports open, dialogical engagement with child clients. What is important is that 'reflective practitioners' (Schön, 1995) are supported to question their own professional practice and to engage in productive, politically constructive relationships with children. Within the new, partially devolved social policy systems it has been recognised that there are many opportunities to find space for developing new forms of interaction between providers and clients. If the criteria for good service provision can incorporate evaluations of process as well as outcomes, advances might well be achieved.

Conclusion

Developing a system of service provision which engages positively with children requires effort at the level of practice, administration and the political will of policymakers to support it. Working with children should not be coercive but should engage positively with them and accord them some measure of agency within a supportive relationship so that the child and the worker might develop a shared perspective and, in so doing, enact a sincere communicative process which also attends to outcomes. Child-centred criteria of well-being indicate that children experience greater levels of well-being through being able to assert agency, but also require positive recognition and collective support for this to be valuable. To facilitate such positive engagements, administrative systems must allow professionals the autonomy and space to advocate on behalf of the child. By allowing a measure of autonomy to the worker, they could then be supported to engage with the child and respond by advocating on their behalf, even if this means speaking against measures of performance defined by the state. If a supportive process became the standard for adult-child interaction, then an ethic of care could inform practice which would make children's experiences of the state positive, offering them affirmative recognition rather than objectifying them and subjecting them to top-down control mechanisms. Similarly, the state must be prepared to represent the child as an individual citizen through an open, communicative process. Caring relationships are dialogical and generate mutual respect, a respect built from collective security which might then generate the individual responsibility so desired by contemporary governments in policy concerning children and young people.

References

Adams, G.B. and Balfour, D.L. (1998) *Unmasking Administrative Evil*. Thousand Oaks: Sage.

Alanen, L. (1988) Rethinking Childhood. *Acta Sociologica*. 31: 1, 53–67.

Cashmore, J., Dolby, R. and Brennan, R. (1994) *Systems Abuse: Problems and Solutions*. Sydney: New South Wales Child Protection Council.

Christensen, P. and Prout, A. (2002) Working with Ethical Symmetry in Social Research with Children. *Childhood*, 9: 4, 477–97.

Cummins, R. (1995) The Comprehensive Quality of Life Scale: Theory and Development. *Health Outcomes and Quality of Life Measurement*. Canberra, Institute of Health and Welfare.

Elshtain, J.B. (1982) 'Thank Heaven for Little Girls': The Dialectics of Development. In Elshtain, J.B. (Ed.) *The Family in Political Thought*. Amherst: University of Massachusetts Press.

Elshtain, J.B. (1989) The Family, Democratic Politics and the Question of Authority. In Scarre, G. (Ed.) *Children, Parents and Politics*. Cambridge: Cambridge University Press.

Esping-Anderson, G. (1990) *The Three Worlds of Welfare Capitalism*. Cambridge: Polity Press.

Fattore, T. and Turnbull, N. (2005) Theorising Representation of and Engagement with Children: The Political Dimension of Child-Oriented Communication. In Mason, J. and Fattore, T. (Eds.) *Children Taken Seriously: In Theory, Policy and Practice*. London: Jessica Kingsley.

Fattore, T., Galloway Smith, M. and Turnbull, N. (2000) Managerialism Meets Human Rights: The Consequences for Children. In Rees, S. and Wright, S. (Eds.) *Human Rights and Corporate Responsibility: A Dialogue*. Sydney: Pluto Press.

Fattore, T., Mason, J. and Watson, E. (2006) *Overview of Children's Understandings of Well-being*. Sydney: New South Wales Commission for Children and Young People.

Fook, J. (2002) *Social Work: Critical Theory and Practice*. London: Sage.

Freeman, M.D.A. (1983) *The Rights and Wrongs of Children*. London: Pinter.

Gilman, R., Huebner, E.S. and Laughlin, J. (2000) A First Study of the Multidimensional Students' Life Scale With Adolescents. *Social Indicators Research*. 52, 135–60.

Goldson, B. (2001) The Demonisation of Children: From the Symbolic to the Institutional. In Foley, P., Roche, J. and Tucker, S. (Eds.) *Children in Society: Contemporary Theory, Policy and Practice*. Basingstoke: Palgrave.

Habermas, J. (1996) *Between Facts and Norms: Contributions to a Discourse Theory of Law and Democracy*. Cambridge: Polity Press.

Honneth, A. (1995) *The Struggle for Recognition: The Moral Grammar of Social Conflicts*. Cambridge: Polity Press.

James, A. and Prout, A. (Eds.) (1990) *Constructing and Reconstructing Childhood: Contemporary Issues in the Sociological Study of Childhood*. London: The Falmer Press.

Jenks, C. (1996) *Childhood*. London: Routledge.

Lefort, C. (1990) Flesh and Otherness. In Johnson, G. and Smith, M. (Eds.) *Ontology and Alterity in Merleau-Ponty*. Illinois: Northwestern University Press.

Mason, J. and Gibson, C. (2004) *The Needs of Children in Care*. Sydney: Social Justice and Social Change Research Centre, University of Western Sydney and UnitingCare Burnside.

Mayall, B. (2000) Conversations with Children: Working with Generational Issues. In Christensen, P. and James, A. (Eds.) *Research with Children: Perspectives and Practices*. London: Falmer Press.

Meltzoff, A. and Moore, M. (1991) Cognitive Foundations and Social Foundations of Imitation, and Intermodal Representation in Infancy. In Woodhead, M., Carr, R. and Light, P. (Eds.) *Becoming a Person*. London: Routledge.

Merleau-Ponty, M. (1964) *The Primacy of Perception, and Other Essays on Phenomenological Psychology, the Philosophy of Art, History and Politics*. Evanston: Northwestern University Press.

Mirowsky, J. and Ross, C.E. (1989) *The Social Causes of Psychological Distress*. New York: de Gruyter.

O'Neill, J. (1973) Embodiment and Child Development: A Phenomenological Approach. In Dreitzel, H.P. (Ed.) *Childhood and*

Socialisation: Recent Sociology Number 5. New York: Macmillan.

Qvortrup, J. et al. (1994) *Childhood Matters: Social Theory, Practice and Politics*. Avebury: Aldershot.

Schön, D.A. (1995) *Reflective Practitioner: How Professionals Think in Action*. 2nd edn. Aldershot: Arena.

Sevenhuijsen, S. et al. (2003) South African Social Welfare Policy: An Analysis Using the Ethic of Care. *Critical Social Policy*. 23: 3, 299–321.

CHAPTER 4

Informed Consent: Options and Challenges

Eileen Gambrill

Abstract

Potentials for informed consent in coercive contexts such as protective services for children and some adult mental health services are suggested as well as obstacles. Honouring the relationship between ethical and evidentiary issues is highlighted as key to informed consent (accurately describing the evidentiary status of recommended and alternative services) and as a key reason related obligations are ignored. Current developments encouraging client-informed decisions are described including the process and philosophy of evidence-informed practice.

Professional Codes of Ethics require practitioners to honour informed consent guidelines. Intimately related to informed consent is the issue of 'a proper authority' (Faden and Beauchamp, 1986: 13). That is, to whom does the proper authority for certain decisions lie? Who ought to serve as a legitimate authority and in what circumstances . . . and to what degree? Informed consent is also related to questions about the nature of practice knowledge; whether professionals are obligated to be familiar with this and to share it with clients; the basis on which policy and practice recommendations should be made; the degree of discretion of professionals and the responsibilities of clients. It is directly related to revealing the criteria on which decisions are made. Although the topic of informed consent has received greater attention in modern times, related obligations are usually ignored. An analysis of 1,057 taped exchanges between 124 physicians and patients regarding 3,552 clinical decisions revealed that typically (91 per cent of the time) informed consent requirements such as description of alternatives and their risk and benefits were not met (Braddock et al. 1999). Quotes from centuries ago ('Do not tell the patient anything') and in some cases, not so many years ago, caution professionals not to share information with clients.

Informed consent requirements, gaps in honouring them, related ethical principles and the contentious nature of informed consent are discussed in this chapter. Options for informed consent in involuntary settings are suggested and obstacles reviewed. Lastly, trends forwarding informed consent are discussed. The close connection between ethical and evidentiary issues is emphasised throughout. I suggest that informed consent is especially vital in coercive situations and describe opportunities to honour related obligations in settings such as protective services for children and mental health services. Both clients and professionals have choices in such settings in relation to informed consent issues that have both legal and ethical implications. Examples include whether to involve clients in a participatory discussion regarding decisions, by inviting clients to ask questions, and whether to accurately inform clients about the evidentiary status of recommended services and alternatives.

Requirements for informed consent

The right to informed consent was one of the 12 rights described in the American Hospital Association patients' 'Bill of Rights' announced in 1973. Faden and Beauchamp link the increased interest in informed consent and other ethical questions in health care to the US civil rights movements of the 1960s and 1970s:

> *Medical codes and didactic writings had traditionally emphasised the physician's obligations or virtues. Trust rather than commerce was the theme of the relationship. A paternalistic or authoritarian ethics easily flowed from this approach in the context of medicine. But the language of rights abruptly turned the focus in a different . . . direction.*
> (Faden and Beauchamp, 1986: 94)

Requirements suggested include:

- Lack of coercion.
- Competence to give consent.

---

*This chapter is based in part on a presentation at the International Conference on Mental Health and the Law, Amsterdam, July 2002.

- Description of recommended services and their risks and benefits, as well as description of alternatives (including the alternative of doing nothing) and their risks and benefits in relation to hoped-for outcomes.
- Description of potential consequences of not participating in recommended services.

(Appelbaum, Lidz and Meisel, 1987; Cannell, Hudson and Pope, 2001)

Examples of requirements in the Code of Ethics of the National Association of Social Workers (1996) include the following:

- *Social workers should provide services to clients only in the context of a professional relationship based, when appropriate, on valid informed consent. Social workers should use clear and understandable language to inform clients of the purpose of the services, risks related to the services, limits to services because of the requirements of a third-party payer, relevant costs, reasonable alternatives, clients' right to refuse or withdraw consent, and the time frame covered by the consent. Social workers should provide clients with an opportunity to ask questions.*
- *In instances when clients are receiving services involuntarily, social workers should provide information about the nature and extent of services and about the extent of clients' rights to refuse service.*

Legal requirements include disclosure of any personal interests unrelated to client well-being that may influence the helper's decision. Recommendations given in *Professional Liability and Risk Management* (Bennett, Bryant, Vandenbos and Greenwood, 1990: 49) published by the American Psychological Association include the following:

- *Do you describe the treatment approach and its risks and benefits as well as possible alternatives (including no treatment) and their risks and benefits, in sufficient detail to ensure that the client understands the procedures?*
- *Do you use an educative approach by inviting questions, testing the client's understanding, and providing appropriate feedback (and reinforcement as treatment proceeds)?*

In 1957 it was ruled that: 'A physician violates his duty to his patient and subjects himself to liability if he withholds any facts which are necessary to form the basis of an intelligent consent by the patient to the proposed treatment' (Handler, 1986: 273). This was changed later under the law of negligence: 'Physicians would be liable only if they failed to disclose what a reasonable physician would have revealed under the circumstances. Furthermore, there is a therapeutic privilege: the physician can withhold information that would seriously jeopardise the well-being of the patient' (p. 273).

A later court ruling further restricted patients' interests. A jury would have to consider what a reasonably prudent person would have decided, not what this particular patient would have done. Handler (1986: 273) notes that: 'this objective standard conflicts with the idea of self-determination which is supposed to protect individual choice, even if idiosyncratic'. Conditions described by Faden and Beauchamp (1986) for informed consent are:

- *A person must **agree** to an intervention based on an **understanding** of (usually disclosed) related **information**.*
- *Consent must **not be controlled** by influences that would engineer the outcome.*
- *The consent must involve the intentional giving of **permission** for an intervention. Intentional action is described as 'action ruled in accordance with a plan, whether the act is wanted or not'.*

They argue that (362–3):

> . . . *substantial understanding in the context of informed consent requires that a person satisfy both an objective criterion – generally based on some core disclosure made by the professional – and a subjective criterion composed of all the relevant beliefs that are material to the patient's or subject's evaluation whether to authorise a particular arrangement.*

Given these requirements, we can examine the following to review the extent to which informed consent requirements are implemented (Lidz et al., 1984: 5; Braddock et al., 1999):

1. *Information*: What was disclosed, how, when, and by whom? Was information tailored to the individuals' ability to understand it? Was there:
   – A clear and complete description in the client's native language and at their level of comprehension of hoped-for benefits and services including their evidentiary status as

well as a description of possible discomforts and risks of participation in services (including effects on the client's job, family, independence).

– A description of alternative options and their potential costs and benefits (e.g., the extent to which each has been critically tested and found to be useful, ineffective, or harmful in relation to pursuit of hoped-for outcomes, including the alternative of doing nothing, or 'watchful waiting').

– An offer to answer any questions.

2. *Assessment of degree of understanding*: What does the client understand about key issues and related decisions and their consequences?

3. *Competency*: If the client did not understand content provided, does he or she have the capacity to do so? Are alternative steps taken to make up for a lack of competence such as involving significant others who will guard the client's interests?

4. *Voluntariness*: Was the client free to choose? Was he or she subject to coercion or undue influence such as manipulation using social psychological persuasion strategies? Were clients informed that they are free to withdraw their consent and discontinue their participation at any time and were the potential consequences of different choices clearly described?

5. *Decision making process*: Was there a discussion and consideration of the client's role in decision making, the central issues and nature of the decision, alternatives, courses of action and their risks and benefits, uncertainties associated with decisions, and client values and preferences?

Thus, integral to informed consent is the competence to offer it and the extent to which it is offered voluntarily and is informed. Being informed requires accurate information concerning alternatives and their risks and benefits.

Informed consent as a process

Consideration of informed consent issues is a key part of the decision making process involved in helping clients. It is closely related to freedom (options for choice) provided to clients at different points and the discretion of the helper to offer them (or not). It is neither an 'either-or' matter nor an event that occurs at only one time

in working with clients although this is typically how it is handled, for example by asking a client to sign an informed consent form at the beginning of or prior to contact. This position has been argued by many (e.g. Appelbaum, Lidz and Meisel, 1987; Faden and Beauchamp, 1986; Sharpe and Faden, 1998). It involves a process in which there are many opportunities to honour related actions even within settings in which some or many client choices are constrained as discussed later. We can identify decisions made in the process of working with clients when they occur, and actions helpers can take to maximise client-informed participation. This allows us to identify options for autonomy within coercive contexts. Faden and Beauchamp (1986: 239) suggest that 'The more information the person understands, the more enhanced are the possibilities for autonomy of action'.

Ethical principles related to informed consent

Informed consent requires the balancing of four principles: autonomy, beneficence, non-malfeasance, and justice. It involves issues about the equitable distribution of knowledge.

Autonomy

The principle of respect for autonomy is that: 'Persons should be free to choose and act without controlling constraints imposed by others. This principle provides the justificatory basis for the right to make autonomous decisions, which in turn, takes the form of specific autonomy-related rights' (Faden and Beauchamp, 1986: 8–9). Katz (2002) distinguishes between self-determination and autonomy or 'psychological autonomy'. He denotes by the latter: 'the capacities of persons to exercise the right to self-determination'. Faden and Beauchamp (1986: 238) distinguish between the following:

- *Autonomous persons and autonomous actions.*
- *Substantially autonomous actions and those that are less than substantially autonomous (p. 235) and argue that a person can perform autonomous actions even in a coercive situation.*

They suggest that a person acts autonomously only if they act intentionally and with understanding and without controlling influences.

They illustrate that someone can satisfy one or more of these three conditions while not satisfying another. That is, they suggest that there are degrees of autonomy of intentional actions ranging from fully autonomous, fully understood, completely non-controlled through to the other end of the continuum which include fully non-autonomous decisions in which there is full ignorance and they are completely controlled. They argue that '. . . actions are autonomous by degrees, rather than categorically autonomous or non-autonomous . . .' (p. 239). They suggest the example of a robber who demands your wallet or he will harm you. This is a coercive situation but we do have a choice of whether or not to hand over our wallets. Thus, they suggest that autonomous actions can be performed by non-autonomous (individuals in a coercive situation) as well as autonomous individuals.

> *The **capacity** to act autonomously is distinct from **acting** autonomously, and possession of the capacity is no guarantee that an autonomous choice has been or will be made . . . An autonomous person who signs a consent form without reading or understanding it is **qualified** to give an informed consent, but has failed to do so . . . The autonomous person may fail to act autonomously in a specific situation if ill in a hospital, overwhelmed by new information, ignorant, manipulated by a clever presentation of data and so on.*
>
> (p. 237)

Many issues remain unsettled including the exact demands the principle of autonomy makes in specific contexts (e.g. what information should be disclosed) and the restrictions which society places on client choices when these conflict with other values.

Beneficence

Beneficence is a second major principle related to informed consent. The three elements in this obligation are:

- *One ought to prevent evil or harm.*
- *One ought to remove evil or harm.*
- *One ought to do or promote good.*
                (Beauchamp and Childress, 1994;
                          Sharpe and Faden, 1998: 86

Complexities include imbalances between obligations related to non-malfeasance (see next section) and those related to beneficence. Questions arise such as 'Whose interests count?'

and 'Whose interests count the most?' Faden and Beauchamp (1986: 11) suggest that: '. . . the principle of beneficence should not, as a *principle*, be restricted to single parties even in special contexts such as the [client-helper] relationship. Thus, the principle itself leaves open the question as to whom one's beneficence should be directed'. This point is important in situations such as child welfare in which staff have duties to their employers.

Non-malfeasance (The obligation to do no harm)

This obligation requires professionals not to inflict evil or harm and not to impose unnecessary or unreasonable risks of harm (Beauchamp and Childress, 1994). Sharpe and Faden (1998: 85) suggest that: '. . . the moral obligation to do no harm can be justifiably overridden but it can never be erased'. Non-malfeasance specifically involves refraining from an action whereas beneficence involves positive actions (Beauchamp and Childress, 1994). Non-malfeasance and beneficence are overlapping principles and some authors combine them into one category of beneficence. For example, we may be able to prevent harm by actively benefiting a client.

Justice

Justice is a fourth moral foundation of informed consent.

> *A person has been treated in accordance with the principle of justice if treated according to what is fair, due, or owed . . . Any denial of a good, service, or piece of information to which a person has a right or entitlement based in justice is an injustice. It is also an injustice to place an undue burden on the exercise of a right, for example, to make a piece of information owed to a person unreasonably difficult to obtain.*
>
> (Faden and Beauchamp, 1986: 14)

A question here is: 'Are the reasons related to honouring autonomous consent sufficient to override reservations based on justice?' (p. 15). Justice-based problems include allocating scarce resources and evaluating claims to services. For example, child welfare agencies purchase services (e.g. parent training and substance programmes) from a variety of agencies. What is valued for a population may not be by an individual. However, we cannot escape our responsibility to critically examine the purchase of services in its larger context; that is, money spent on ineffective and harmful services limits opportunities to purchase services that have been found via critical testing to be effective (Gray, 2001). Failure to use evidence-informed purchasing may result in an inequitable distribution of services. This refers to purchasing services based on evidentiary criteria, methods that have been found via rigorous appraisal, to do more good than harm.

Lack of informed consent

Informed consent involves ethical issues regarding the distribution of knowledge (information that decreases uncertainty about how or if a certain outcome can be attained) (Nickerson, 1986). Currently there is an uneven distribution. Katz (1984: 26) argues that: '... disclosure and consent in physician/patient interactions is largely an unwitting attempt by physicians to shape the disclosure process so that patients will comply with their recommendations'. Clients are often not informed regarding what knowledge helpers have in relation to key decisions that affect their lives nor how much they share. They typically do not know the competency levels of professionals they see. Although knowledge may not always be power in the sense that it provides opportunities that result in greater freedom of choice, it may, or, if it does not currently, it may in the future.

Comparison of current practices and policies regarding informed consent shows that helpers take advantage of only a small percentage of opportunities available as illustrated by the study by Braddock et al. (1999) described earlier. Although statutory and regulatory policy require psychiatrists to disclose the risks of neuroleptic medication (e.g. of tardive dyskinesia) a study of 540 psychiatrists from 94 state and county mental hospitals in 35 states found that only 54 per cent of psychiatrists told their patients about the possibility (Kennedy and Sanborn, 1992). (Tardive dyskinesia is an irreversible neurological condition characterised by involuntary muscular movements.) Work setting, helpers' values and theoretical orientation influence practices regarding informed consent (Somberg, Stone and Claiborn, 1993).

Deceptive practices include 'intentional strategies (such as) lying, withholding of information, true assertion that omits a vital

qualification, and misleading exaggeration in order to cause persons to believe what is false' (Faden and Beauchamp, 1986: 363). Faden and Beauchamp suggest that showing potential clients before and after pictures is a common deceptive tactic. The authors note that '... there is a venerable tradition in medicine of intentionally withholding information from patients.' Not informing clients 'has traditionally been defended as a way to make the patient take an optimistic attitude of hope rather than as a way to manipulate consent. Such practices certainly can manipulate consent decisions, but the kind of manipulation in clinical practice that is probably most difficult to discover, pinpoint, and describe is the subtle slanting, misrepresentation, or omission of information that leaves a patient critically ignorant (sometimes, but not always, intentionally)' (p. 364).

I was struck by the failure to provide critical information regarding potential consequences to parents alleged to have abused or neglected their children when I first became interested in decision-making in child welfare. Parents were told that if things went well, the worker would recommend that the child be returned for a trial visit. There was silence in relation to what would occur if objectives were not met (e.g., the worker would recommend termination of parental rights). This failure to disclose deprives clients of information that may influence their decisions. In spite of models of written agreements including disclosure of possible consequences for different degrees of participation and success in achieving clearly described outcomes published almost a quarter of a century ago (Stein, Gambrill, and Wiltse, 1978), such disclosure typically does not occur. Studies such as the Mercer County Study (Pelton, 1989: 119), showed that: 'Many parents who had had children in placement did not even have clear conceptions of why the agency had sought the placement of their children to begin with, and that many had faulty or vague conceptions of when and under what conditions their children would be returned'.

Informed consent as a contentious issue

Informed consent has been a contentious issue in the helping professions since their birth. As today, many people in the past were sceptical of the idea of informed consent (e.g. Fellner and

Marshal, 1970), and there were parodies of it. Related legal regulations attest to the struggle over this issue, which reflects a clash among client, agency and professional interests as well as different definitions of 'evidence' and different opinions about the value of self-determination and what this entails. The medical profession has been opposed to informed consent throughout most of its recorded history. Physicians have not only routinely withheld information from clients, they have defended the wisdom of so doing (see Katz, 1984; 2002). Reasons given against informed consent include concerns such as time. Katz argues that: 'The time costs of conversation may turn out to be much less than the costs of intervention' (2002: 228).

Some suggest harms such as not taking the necessary steps to attain desired outcomes as a result of a description of risks; the client may not choose the rational option. Arguments used to support the view that informed consent is: 'ineffective in achieving its primary goals' (Appelbaum, Lidz and Meisel, 1987: 138), are that many clients do not want to be informed, are unable to understand the information provided, do not use the information in decision making, or are dependent on the helper and, regardless of what information they are given, place decisions in the helper's hands. Research suggests that these arguments are not accurate. Consider the increasing use of the Internet to acquire information (Cullen, 2006).

When clients were asked what criteria they would like helpers to use to select methods, they mentioned the helper's track record of success in using a method successfully and related research evidence (O'Donohue, Fisher, and Plaud, 1989). Also, the fact that information is not used does not remove the obligation to provide it. Katz (2002: 228) doubts that patients don't want to share the burdens of decisions and suggests that we won't know this until professionals 'are willing to make a good faith effort to invite [clients'] participation. This would obligate physicians to reassure [clients] that they will take the time to talk with them, that [clients'] doubts and questions will be given a respectful hearing, and that they are prepared to provide [clients] with sufficient information so that [clients] can formulate their questions in a meaningful fashion'. And who is to say what is rational for an individual? Many decisions we make may not appear rational to others. We each may weigh the advantages and disadvantages of given options

in different ways because we assign different utilities to different options. The greater the cultural differences, the greater the possibility that a professional may consider a client's choice irrational.

Another objection is that clients often want reassurance. But are not clients obligated to share the burden of making decisions, especially when children are involved as in protective services? Acknowledging uncertainties will encourage more realistic expectations and perhaps contribute to a collaborative working relationship. Recognising the inherent uncertainty in providing services to clients and getting rid of 'the ethos of infallibility' (McIntyre and Popper, 1983), highlights the vital role of attending carefully to the consequences of decisions and making them transparent. Yet another argument against informed consent is that accurately informing clients will compromise healing sources of trust and hope. A counterargument is that involving clients as informed participants will contribute to a collaborative working relationship in which the burdens of uncertainty are shared (Gutheil et al., 1991; Katz, 2002). Some argue that informed consent will be carried out in a pro forma or 'manipulative' manner. Some argue that informing clients will decrease placebo effects. However, potential negative consequences of relying on placebo effects should be considered, such as increasing or maintaining dependency on unneeded services (Jarvis, 1990). Another objection to informed consent is the view that if there is any coercion, there can be no informed consent. Government mandated child welfare services occur within a coercive umbrella that compromises the informed consent requirement of freedom to withdraw without negative consequences, such as the removal of children. This does not take away the fact that many autonomous actions are possible in this context as discussed in the section that follows.

Some objections are pseudo-issues; they readily fall away when closely examined. Consider the objection that some clients are not competent. Child welfare staff may argue that because a parent is a drug addict they are not competent to make informed decisions. No one claims that all clients are competent and, competence is not an either/or matter. There are degrees of competency and procedures for protecting clients who lack certain degrees. Faden and Beauchamp (1986: 240) suggest that: '. . . many people's

1. Internet sources critically appraising research related to specific practice/policy questions such as the Cochrane and Campbell databases of systematic reviews.
2. User-friendly programmes designed to enhance critical appraisal skills such as the Critical Appraisal Skills Program (CASP).
3. User-friendly brochures accurately describing the evidentiary status of services related to particular desired outcomes.
4. User-friendly brochures available in waiting rooms describing informed consent requirements.
5. Required use of written agreements clearly describing agreed-on outcomes and consequences that may occur depending on participation and progress (See Stein, Gambrill and Wiltse, 1978).
6. Routine use of evidence-informed client choice forms describing the evidentiary status of services offered as well as alternatives and agency and staff success in using programmes.
7. Access to user-friendly computer decision-aids in waiting rooms.
8. User-friendly books describing the evidentiary status of procedures/services (see Enkin et al., 1995).
9. Client advocates who help to inform clients.
10. Creation of advocacy groups that promote access to information needed for informed decisions.
11. A client accessible agency library that provides relevant information including reprints of Carl Sagan's *Baloney Detection Kit.*

Figure 4.1   Options for informing clients

assumptions about informed consent are expressions of ideal rather than normal or adequate degrees of autonomy'. They argue that falling short of the ideal is an inevitable reality. 'To chain informed consent *to fully or completely* autonomous decision making stacks the deck of the argument and strips informed consent of any meaningful place in the practical world, where people's actions are rarely, if ever, fully autonomous'.

Options for informed consent in involuntary settings

Faden and Beauchamp (1986: 371) suggest that: '. . . from the undisputed fact that the patient role has inherent constraints, it would be absurd to suggest that every decision a person makes while in that role is non-autonomous, or even that the person's actions are *necessarily* rendered less autonomous by the patient role'. 'In both coercion and coercive situations the person does not act freely . . . It does not follow, however, that persons in such coercive situations do not act autonomously' (p. 344). That is 'loss of freedom cannot be equated with a loss of autonomy' (p. 345). Nowhere in the Code of Ethics of the National Association of Social Workers does it say: 'When clients are coerced to participate, it is not necessary to inform them about the risks and benefits of recommended services and alternatives, and it is not necessary to establish that clients understand information provided.'

There are many opportunities to honour informed consent requirements in coercive settings such as protective services for children and mental health services (see Figure 4. 1). Both clients and professionals have choices in such settings in relation to informed consent issues that have legal and ethical implications. Examples include inviting clients to ask questions, informing clients about the evidentiary status of recommended services and alternatives and avoiding manipulative ploys. Clients should be informed about the consequences that may occur depending on the degree of participation in services and/or attainment of certain objectives. They should be informed about the evidentiary status of assessment, intervention, and evaluation methods as well as risks and benefits of alternative methods (e.g., see Eddy, 1990). Let us say that a social worker is working with a parent whom they believe lacks parenting skills and they refer this client to a parent training programme. Informed consent calls for a clear description of the benefits and risks of this particular programme and the benefits and risks of other parent training programmes. Professional codes of ethics call on practitioners to draw on practice-related research to discover the evidentiary status of practices and policies. Some programmes have been critically tested and found to be helpful. Most have not been rigorously tested. Some have been critically tested and found to be harmful (see Evans, Thornton and Chalmers, 2006). If a social worker does not know whether a programme has been critically

Professionals should:
- Clearly identify the agency they represent (for example by alerting the client that you are present as an agent of the state).
- Accurately describe the reasons for your meeting.
- Describe the process that will occur.
- Involve the client in a participatory dialogue in making decisions including sharing uncertainties.
- Inform clients about choices they will and will not have.
- Find out what clients would like.
- Describe what will be done with information gathered and the limits of confidentiality.
- Inform clients that other records that pertain to them may be examined.
- Agree on clearly described hoped-for outcomes and the rationale for selecting them.
- Accurately describe the evidentiary status of practices recommended.
- Clearly describe recommended services, the rationale for selecting them and their risks and benefits.
- Clearly describe risks and benefits of alternatives.
- Prepare a written service agreement clearly describing hoped-for outcomes as well as possible consequences depending on degree of participation and outcomes attained.
- Clearly describe how progress will be monitored and the potential of each measure to accurately reflect progress.
- Invite the client to ask questions.

Figure 4.2   Professional ethics

tested and found to be effective, they should inform the client about this, seek related information and share what is found with clients. Informed consent requires sharing ignorance as well as knowledge.

In child protective settings, even if parents are told that service X is unlikely to be helpful, they may have to participate in this or their children will be removed from their care or will not be returned. This does not remove the obligation to inform them regarding the evidentiary status of recommended services. Indeed, it could be argued that informed consent (for example about the potential consequences of different degrees of participation and the track record of the success of programmes to which clients are referred) in a context of participatory decision making in which all adult parties shoulder their share of responsibility, is of special importance in involuntary settings in which children are involved. Those who are least powerful, i.e. children, may be those who are most harmed by lack of informed consent. (See later description of evidence informed client choice.) Clients should also be informed regarding the evidentiary status of assessment methods used. If social workers depend on the self-report of parents regarding their parenting skills and do not take advantage of observation of parent-child interaction that provides important information, clients should be so informed (Budd et al., 2001). In addition, clients should be informed about the likely accuracy of methods used to evaluate outcome;

for example that process measures, such as the number of parent-training classes attended, may not accurately reflect the attainment of hoped-for outcomes.

Balancing conflicting principles

The principle of respect for autonomy essentially argues that: 'Persons should be free to choose and act without control and constraints imposed by others.' The principles of beneficence and non-malfeasance urge professionals to do good and avoid harm, and the principle of justice urges that: '. . . a person is treated according to what is fair, due or owed.' How do we handle situations that pose conflicts among the principles of autonomy, justice, beneficence and non-malfeasance? Faden and Beauchamp (1986: 18) suggest that: 'Neither respect for autonomy nor any moral principle has an absolute standing that allows it on every occasion to override conflicting moral claims (for example, the autonomy of a parent and the protection of a child from risk)'. 'Moral dilemmas require a balancing of competing claims in untidy circumstances . . .' (p. 20). The aim of a process 'of specification and balancing' (Beachamp and Childress, 1994) is to provide a way by which conflicts among principles can be resolved '. . . to provide a coherent account of a moral problem and, if the problem has not been 'dissolved' by specification, a justification of its resolution one way or another' (Sharpe and Faden, 1998: 85). This process of balancing conflicts among principles provides an alternative to basing decisions on a single principle such as '. . . paternalistic prioritisation of a [social worker] knows-best beneficence or the libertarian prioritisation of respect for autonomy'.

'Practical judgement involving specification and balancing assumes that decisional complexities cannot be satisfactorily resolved by the rigid application of rules. Neither moral nor medical problems are, in other words, solved at the level of theory. They are resolved by individuals deliberating together about the values that they bring to the particular context of decision making' (Sharpe and Faden, 1998: 85).

One criterion that has been proposed as a guide to disclosure is the reasonable person standard. This standard requires a professional to provide the amount and type of information 'a reasonable person' would want to know before consenting, or withholding consent, with regard to participation in a programme. This criteria is not satisfactory because the essence of self-determination and autonomy is that an individual's unique situation and unique reasoning pattern is honoured (Sharpe and Faden, 1998). Standards of due care are appealed to, when they exist, to determine if a risk was justified by the anticipated benefits of a particular service. Did the helper follow standards of due care in an effort to prevent adverse consequences? Here, evidentiary questions are key, such as: 'On what criteria should standards of care be based?' 'What is valid health care research?' 'What are the "best" findings from this research?' 'When is practice/policy related research ready for application?' (Haynes, 2002). Controversies regarding the quality of evidence required to describe a service as effective are common (for instance, see differing views of the effectiveness of multi-systemic therapy) (Hengeller et al., 2006; Littell, 2006).

Obstacles to informed consent

A variety of factors contribute to the gap between rhetoric in professional codes of ethics regarding informed consent and what occurs when there is a lack of informed consent. Obstacles suggested by Sharpe and Faden (1998) include self interest, psychological factors, attitudes towards patients, training, the need to maintain the image of

authority, [and] problems of uncertainty. The perceptive writings by sociologists of the professions such as Abbott (1988) Friedson (1994) and Larson (1977) suggest obstacles, as does Katz (2002) in his eloquent plea for participatory decision making. The former bring to our attention the origins of the professions, including unfounded claims of special expertise and the creation of esoteric knowledge and procedures designed to offer the impression of expertise. Katz (1984, 2002) highlights the reliance on hope and trust in professional-client encounters, emphasised for centuries.

1. The politics and economics of knowledge distribution

The issue of informed consent is related to fundamental conflicts about who should have access to what information and who should make what decisions and what criteria should be used to make recommendations. Thus, it is closely related to power in exactly who should have what discretion about what and when. Obligations to, and interests of, clients, agencies and professions often conflict. Clients in social work settings are often among the most disadvantaged and dependent in society, especially those involved in the public social services. Informed consent can be viewed as a power struggle among professionals who claim they withhold information from clients for their [the clients'] own good, those interested in influencing the behaviour of professionals such as pharmaceutical companies and professional organisations such as the American Psychiatric Association, clients who are typically unaware of the information they are deprived of and how it may affect their decisions, and those who wish to inform them. Professionals may be indoctrinated into views of problems as psychiatric disorders which require coercive interventions when indeed such constructions are controversial (Moynihan, Heath and Henry, 2002; Rogers, 1999; Szasz, 1994, 2002). Millions of dollars may be at stake depending on the explanations favoured. Consider interventions recommended to alter behaviours viewed as indicators of Attention Deficit Hyperactivity Disorder (ADHD). Reliance on medication has increased dramatically. There is a spirited debate concerning the wisdom of placing so many children on medication to alter related behaviours (see *American Psychological Association*, 2006). Hiding information about possible harms of medication and the potential effectiveness of non-medical alternatives for altering behaviour allows medical options to flourish and grow (see Moynihan and Cassells, 2005).

Obstacles include political, social and economic influences forwarding secrecy; for example, concerning the evidentiary status of services and the fact that helpers themselves are uninformed, and so cannot inform clients, (see Figure 4.2). Maintaining power often requires secrecy. As Bobbio (1996: 137) suggests, 'There is no politics without the use of secrecy'. Secrecy serves to obscure self-interest and conflict, for example, between different views of problems and preferred remedies and their different consequences for involved participants. Describing options and their risks and benefits would reveal conflict among alternatives and the use of ineffective methods. The transparency required in informed consent will often reveal that 'the emperor has no clothes', that there is no special expertise or, even worse, that those who claim to be professionals with special expertise are recommending ineffective or harmful services because of avoidable ignorance regarding practice-related research. Not only are they not experts, they may be frauds and quacks. A quack is defined as someone who uses services known to be ineffective or of unknown effectiveness, for a profit (Young, 1992). Honouring informed consent obligations would reveal the questionable evidentiary status of most services and enhance clients' discretionary power, changes not valued by many professionals. It is hard to see how there could be a more threatening change to the helping professions than honouring informed consent obligations.

2. Paternalism

Some arguments against informed consent can be reduced to: 'We are doing it for you' (e.g. see Thompson, 1980). Faden and Beauchamp (1986: 13) suggest that:

> The issue of paternalism is at the core of many discussions of informed consent. Much of the literature in the field focuses on such fundamental moral questions as when consent need not be obtained and when refusals need not be honoured. Paternalism and anti-paternalism hide in every corridor of these discussions.

Professionals throughout time have appealed to their devotion to service and altruism as reasons. If we did inform you:

- *You might not participate in programmes we think you should participate in.*
- *You might not reap the full benefits from them.*
- *You might not make a rational choice.*
- *You may do something which limits your freedom in the future.*

(Scull, 2005; Valenstein, 1986)

The history of the helping professions shows that we cannot depend on good intentions to protect clients from harm.

Katz argues for a 'radically different climate of physician-patient decision making' (p. 228). He urges us to:

> . . . discard the dangerous notion that the complexities of physician-patient interactions can be resolved solely by trust in physicians' integrity, their compassion, and their commitment to the Golden Rule. The complexities inherent in the practice of medicine, in the conflicting motivations that physicians bring to their interactions with patients, and in the conflicting needs that patients bring to their interactions with physicians defy such appealing but simplistic notions
>
> (p. 229)

He argues that patients and physicians must talk more with one another, to participate more fully in the decisions that affect their well-being. He is not arguing that trust is not important. He is arguing for a different kind of trust: 'the confident and trusting expectations that physicians will assist patients to make their own decisions . . . [those] *they* deem to be in their best interest' (p. 101–2). Assumptions he notes as key to this model of trust are:

- *There is no one right decision.*
- *Physicians and patients bring their own vulnerabilities to their decision making process.*
- *Both parties need to relate to one another as equals. Their equalities and inequalities complement one another. Physicians know more about disease. Patients know more about their own needs. Neither knows at the outset what each can do for the other.*
- *All human conduct is influenced by rational and irrational expectations.*

Halpern (2001) argues that clients may not possess psychological autonomy in very difficult circumstances such as severe injury because of temporary misjudgements of their future. She suggests that in such situations empathy for clients may require temporarily overriding their wishes (e.g. to end their lives) by engaging them in a dialogue to more realistically appraise possible futures.

3. Reluctance to admit surveillance and coercion, resulting in conflicts of interest

Staff in government mandated child welfare agencies have dual roles:

- To investigate and evaluate and if necessary take actions that are against the wishes of clients.
- To help and support clients. They have considerable discretion in carrying out their jobs which may work for or against client interests.

Margolin (1997) argues that social workers routinely manipulate clients and hide their judgmental and evaluation role. Pelton (1989: 118) suggests that:

> In most child protection cases, it is the investigative regulator/coercive role with which the parents are first confronted ... Yet the agency is also charged with the task of attempting to help to preserve families, by offering treatment and services. These dual functions constitute different modes of influence, each of which tends to obstruct the other at certain points of intervention. They entail a juxtaposition of persuasion and coercion, assistance and control, advocacy for and advocacy against, and firmness and conciliation, which might often work at odds with each other.

This dual role encourages social workers to hide the coercive aspects of their investigation such as consequences that will occur contingent on the degree of participation. Indeed, as mentioned earlier, written agreements that clearly describe potential consequences contingent on participation and outcomes attained are still not used. Clearly separating legal/criminal issues from service issues, that is, separating the dual function of child welfare staff into legal and helping issues, would make related conflicts of interest more obvious. In a legal context, clients could be Mirandised, informed that anything they say may be used against them.

4. Expectations and relationship factors

Services are offered in an interpersonal context in which characteristics such as the warmth and charisma of the practitioner influence the client, for example by creating trust in the helper which

may influence what clients disclose and if and how they participate (Norcross, 2002). A positive relationship may increase trust and decrease clients' attention to their lack of knowledge about what will transpire and why. Regehr and Antle (1997: 301) suggest that '. . . the therapeutic alliance may not always serve the best interests of the client . . .' This is especially true in coercive contexts in which power differentials between clients and professionals are strong.

Faden and Beauchamp (1986) argue that professionals should avoid manipulative strategies and instead rely on reasoned persuasion. They define manipulation: 'as any intentional and successful influence of a person by non-coercively altering the actual choices available to a person or by non-persuasively altering the other's perception of those choices' (p. 354). They consider persuasion to be 'the model form of influence in informed consent and contexts: It can enable and even facilitate substantially autonomous authorisations' (p. 346). The authors define persuasion: 'as the intentional and successful attempt to induce a person through appeals to reason, to freely accept – as their own – the beliefs, attitudes, values, intentions, or actions advocated by the persuader . . . In persuasion, the influence agent must bring to the persuadee's attention **reasons** for acceptance of the desired perspective' (p. 348).

5. Professionals themselves are uninformed

Professionals' knowledge about the evidentiary status of services limits the extent to which they can provide informed consent. Although professional codes of ethics obligate practitioners to draw on practice-related knowledge, they typically do not do so. A key reason for the development of evidence-informed practice is that professionals do not keep up with practice and policy related research findings (Sackett et al., 1997, 2000). Only if helpers themselves are able to locate and critically appraise research regarding the evidentiary status of assessment, intervention and evaluation methods can they then accurately inform their clients. Only if they are aware of the play of social psychological persuasion strategies in their work with clients, can they identify and minimise manipulative strategies. Practitioners themselves must be informed about the uncertainties involved in decisions to help clients understand them.

6. Ignoring the close relationship between ethical and evidentiary issues

Informed consent requirements highlight the close relationship between evidentiary issues and ethical obligations. Lack of informed consent requires ignoring related requirements described in professional codes of ethics to draw on practice-related research. Our research suggests that professionals do not ignore this close relationship when their own health is at issue; social workers want their physicians to base recommendations for treatment on criteria such as the results of randomised controlled trials, but rely on questionable criteria such as tradition when making decisions regarding their clients (Gambrill and Gibbs, 2002). If child maltreatment is related to poverty and associated environmental conditions such as poor quality housing containing hazards to children, and most services offered are individually focused, such as parent training and substance abuse treatment, something is amiss.

7. A reluctance to recognise uncertainty

Informed consent requires a recognition of the uncertainties involved in making decisions. Discovering uncertainty may be frightening and there are many defences against it (Marris, 1996). Fox and Swazey (1974) suggest three major sources of uncertainty:

1. Lack of information concerning a problem.
2. Failure to get what is available.
3. Failure to recognise our own ignorance.

Clients often do not know what they want and stated preferences often do not match their actions (Haynes, Devereaux and Guyatt, 2002). Asking questions such as 'Is there a more effective programme?' and 'Is there evidence that this programme will help me?' will reveal competing options. Without acknowledging uncertainty in helping clients we are less likely to discover ways to decrease it, for example by identifying avoidable mistakes and learning how to minimise them. As McIntyre and Popper (1983) suggest, knowledge develops through error and correction rather than through accumulation. The discussion of conflicts among options is often critical for communication. 'A genuine dialogue involves questioning, listening, and openness' (Handler, 1992: 349) (see also Katz,

2002). Recognising uncertainty highlights mutual responsibilities for grappling with it (Dowrick, 1999). Related changes will require a shift in organisational and professional cultures.

Students are often taught to '. . . hide ignorance rather than regard it as a basis for learning' (Sharpe and Faden, 1998: 233). Only if we increase self-criticism within the professions and teach students to do this are things likely to change. 'Clinical education that is oriented to self-criticism and to uncertainty would also emphasise the centrality of informing patients about the nature and likelihood of the harms associated with clinical care' (Sharpe and Faden, 1998: 233). In continuous quality improvement programmes (self-learning organisations), there is an effort to maximise the quality of services and this is the spirit in which auditing and feedback occurs. 'Under a socialisation process that emphasises perfectability and infallibility, mistakes are viewed as unusual, unacceptable, and indicative of flawed character' (Sharpe and Faden, 1998: 137). Under a quality improvement programme '. . . everyone who had an opportunity to prevent the error is responsible' (p.139).

8. Cognitive biases

Research illustrates our capacity to deceive ourselves (Dunning, Heath and Suls, 2004). Kruger and Dunning (1999) found that those who are least competent are least likely to recognise their incompetence and least likely to learn from social comparison (watching others). Confirmation biases are robust (Nickerson, 1998). We tend to jump to conclusions, for example about the effectiveness of a practice or policy and search for instances that confirm our view; we selectively search for supporting information. We are subject to wishful thinking, confuse correlation and causation, and are influenced by vivid case examples (Gambrill, 2005; Hastie and Dawes, 2001). Such biases may compromise informed consent.

9. Organisational obstacles

Administrative and policy decisions influence staff behaviour, including the information they gather, what they share with clients, what alternatives are available and which are favoured (e.g., see Hasenfeld, 1987). Paternalistic attitudes and management practices and the ideology that supports them (e.g. 'We know best') will have to change as well as professional education cultures. (See later discussion of evidence-informed practice.) Handler (1992) suggests that even under benign circumstances, the bureaucracy will slip into dominating practices. He argues that only if we arrange incentives that encourage client involvement as informed participants will current circumstances change.

Strategies at the worker level include increasing information and knowledge, [and] assertion training . . . At the organisational level, clients have to become a more important interest group. Workers can help by adopting empowerment-based practice technologies and press for the adoption of different kinds of accountability measures . . . for example . . . client freedom of choice, the mobilisation of resources, client feedback and evaluation . . . At the policy level, there has to be an increase in client control over resources, for example vouchers, and the availability of alternative services (pp. 357–8).

10. Other obstacles

Professionals are held to typical standards of care. If these are poor, for example regarding informed consent, clients may have little or no legal recourse.

Emerging options for and trends encouraging informed consent

I don't think professionals will honour requirements for informed consent described in professional codes of ethics given current social, political and economic contingencies (see section on obstacles). There is another route we can take. We can inform clients and significant others of their right to informed consent (for example, via brochures in waiting rooms) and provide them with the resources needed to acquire related information (see e.g. Sievert, Cuvo and Davis, 1988). Many professionals have taken an active role in encouraging informed consent. Publications such as *Reforming Health Care by Consent: Involving Those Who Matter* by Ling (1999) *Evidence-based Patient Choice* by Edwards and Elwyn (2001) and *Ethical Child Welfare Practice* by Leever et al. (2002) emphasise involvement of clients as informed participants. This thrust is accompanied by increasing access to information on the Internet (Cullen, 2006). We

can critically appraise the effectiveness of different ways to increase informed consent such as user-friendly decision aides (e.g. see O'Conner et al., 2003; Stapleton, Kirkham and Thomas, 2002). Interactive computer programmes allow clients to educate themselves about alternative methods and their risks and benefits related to specific concerns (e.g., see Graham et al., 2000). Access to needed information should be available in agency waiting rooms and neighbourhood centres. Guidelines have been developed to review the quality of information provided to clients including readability, currency, and accuracy, and to make information readily available to clients (Coulter, Entwistle and Gilbert, 1998).

The Critical Appraisal Skills Program (CASP) offers training to both professionals and others in how to critically appraise research reports. The National Health Service in Britain has developed an Internet site to provide citizens with health care information. Client participation is actively encouraged in evidence-informed practice (Straus et al., 2005) and related developments such as the Cochrane and Campbell Collaborations (Chalmers, Sackett and Silagy, 1995; Davies and Boruch, 2001). Evidence-informed practice represents a shift in the basis on which decisions are made and the extent to which criteria relied on to select services are shared with clients (are transparent) (Gambrill, 2006). Rather than relying on authority-based criteria such as status or tradition, the professional poses well-structured questions related to life-affecting decisions, searches for external research, critically appraises what is found, shares what is found with clients, and considers client characteristics and circumstances including their values and preferences as well as available resources in making decisions together with clients (Haynes, Devereaux and Guyatt, 2002; Straus et al., 2005). The process and philosophy of evidence-informed practice calls on professionals to be honest brokers of knowledge and ignorance – to accurately inform clients. Reasons for its development included increased attention to the gap between practice/policy related research and what is drawn on by helpers – the realisation that many professionals are themselves not informed d (e.g. Sackett et al., 1997, 2000) and increased attention to harming in the name of helping.

We can prepare and disseminate accurate brochures describing potential risks and benefits of various alternatives. Reviews of 'educational' materials in brochures and on websites show that key information such as describing absolute as well as relative risk is often omitted (e.g. Jørgensen and Gøtzsche, 2004). Related material could include discussion of possible means of action, evidence of efficacy, description of adverse effects and accurate descriptions of the current evidentiary status of particular practices and policies. This should be available on user-friendly websites available in waiting rooms and include examples of questions clients could ask about services in easy to understand language. A brochure could be prepared for each kind of outcome pursued, such as decreasing alcohol use that describes major controversies (Is alcoholism a disease?) and provides accurate, up-to-date summaries of related research regarding the effectiveness of different programmes. Client oriented books should be written in other areas such as substance abuse programmes and parenting programmes similar to the book prepared by Enkin and his colleagues (1995) on peri-natal care and childbirth in which each method is described in relation to its evidentiary status using the following list:

1. Beneficial forms of care demonstrated by clear evidence from controlled trials.
2. Forms of care likely to be beneficial. (The evidence in favour of these forms of care is not as firm as for those in category 1.)
3. Forms of care with a trade-off between beneficial and adverse effects. (Clients should weigh these effects according to individual circumstances and priorities.)
4. Forms of care of unknown effectiveness. (There are insufficient or inadequate quality data upon which to base a recommendation.)
5. Forms of care unlikely to be beneficial. (The evidence against these forms of care is not as firm as for those in category 6.)
6. Forms of care likely to be ineffective or harmful. (Ineffectiveness or harm demonstrated by clear evidence.)

(Enkin et al., 1995)

Such books will reveal that most services are of unknown effectiveness. They will also reveal that well-tested programmes that maximise the likelihood of hoped-for outcomes may not be offered to clients.

We can provide accountable complaint systems that encourage informed consent. We can encourage clients to request information regarding the effectiveness of recommended services from professional helpers. Staff should be required to provide information to clients regarding the evidentiary status of each service to which a client is referred as well as the track record of success of the agency to which they are referred in offering such services and the success of the staff person in this agency who will offer this service (Entwistle et al., 1998, 1996). They should receive a written document describing such information for each programme to which they are referred. Informed consent should be made an agreed-on agency policy that is expected to be implemented by all staff. Its implementation should be carefully monitored and corrective feedback provided as needed. This expectation should be widely advertised to both clients and staff. We can distribute informed consent forms related to medication similar to the one suggested by Cohen and Jacobs (1998). Such forms could be examined at regular intervals by a disinterested party to explore gaps between informed consent requirements and what is suggested by a review of these forms.

Other options are to arrange for client advocates and to help clients to create effective advocacy groups (e.g. see Bastien, 1998; Handler, 1992; Taylor, 2000). Such groups could lobby for change, prepare informative brochures, and set up websites as needed in cooperation with professionals who value informed consent. Increased attention to propaganda in the helping professions will help to sensitise both clients and professionals to bogus claims that misinform rather than inform (Jacobson, Foxx and Mulick, 2005; Lilienfeld, Lynn and Lohr, 2003; Moynihan and Cassells, 2005). If enough practitioners and clients become aware that clients are being asked to participate in services that provide no benefit, they might form advocacy groups to press for services that have been critically tested and found to maximise the likelihood of success (e.g. Domenighetti, Grilli and Liberati, 1998). Informing those involved in making decisions would reveal changes required at other system levels. For example, it may become obvious that teachers who are not trained in contingency management skills and/or how to design individualised curricular programmes that maximise each child's potential to learn, cannot effectively manage behaviour and encourage learning in their classrooms. Clients could advocate for programmes that train teachers in such skills. We should establish peer review committees to monitor protection of clients' rights including informed consent (e.g., see Sheldon and Risley, 1990).

Conclusion

There is a gap between rhetoric and reality regarding informed consent – what professional codes of ethics call for and what is advocated in the professional literature and what occurs in everyday practice regarding lack of informed consent and lack of autonomy. The contingencies related to current practices and policies suggest that honouring informed consent obligations will be an ongoing challenge. Doing so will decrease decision making discretion of professionals; conflicts and uncertainties now hidden will be revealed by sharing ignorance as well as knowledge. The topic of informed consent highlights the close connection between ethical and evidentiary issues. Currently there is an inequitable distribution of knowledge among researchers, helpers and clients. Clients usually do not know what knowledge a professional has compared to what is available. Honouring informed consent obligations is one way that decision making power can be rebalanced in the direction of clients. Benefits of honouring informed consent obligations include no longer placing professionals in the position of violating their ethical codes and sharing the burdens of uncertainty. Neither professionals or clients would have to deceive themselves that certain services are likely to be effective. Better use could be made of scarce funds by not purchasing ineffective or harmful services and using the money saved to purchase services that have been critically tested and found to help clients (Gray, 2001).

There are many opportunities to honour informed consent obligations even in coercive settings. Informed consent requirements highlight the need for professionals to be informed about the evidentiary status of current practices and policies and, if they are found wanting (e.g., only ineffective programmes are available), to advocate for those that maximise the likelihood of success. Increased accessibility of information on the Internet and increased concern about the lack of informed consent encourage attention to this issue. Staff and client access to the Cochrane and Campbell databases of reviews describing the evidentiary status

regarding specific practice/policy questions will help staff and clients to make informed decisions.

Ethical codes call for providing information to clients that allows them to arrive at an informed estimate of the uncertainty related to different courses of action. If clients and significant others are accurately appraised of the evidentiary status of recommended services and alternatives, they may take a more active role in requesting programmes found to be effective.

References

Abbott, A. (1988) *The System of Professions: An Essay on the Division of Expert Labor*. Chicago: University of Chicago Press.

American Psychological Association (2002) *Ethical Principles of Psychologists and Code of Conduct*. Draft 7.

American Psychological Association (2006) Report of the Working Group on Psychotropic Medications for Children and Adolescents. *Psychopharmacological, Psychosocial, and Combined Interventions for Childhood Disorders: Evidence Base, Contextual Factors, and Future Directions*. Washington, DC: APA.

Appelbaum, P.S., Lidz, C.W. and Meisel, A. (1987) *Informed Consent: Legal Theory and Clinical Practice*. New York: Oxford University Press.

Bastian, H. (1994) Finding Out What Health Care Works: Consumer Involvement in Research and The Cochrane Collaboration. *Health Forum*, 32, 15–16.

Bastian, H. (1998) Speaking Up for Ourselves: The Evolution of Consumer Advocacy. *Health Care, International Journal of Technology Assessment in Health*, 14, 3–23.

Beauchamp, T.L. and Childress, J.F. (1994) *Principles of Biomedical Ethics*. 4th edn. New York: Oxford University Press.

Bennett, B.E. et al. (1990) *Professional Liability and Risk Management*. Washington, D.C.: American Psychological Association.

BMA (2001) *Consent, Rights and Choices in Health Care for Children and Young People*. London: British Medical Association.

Bobbio, N. (1996) Politics and Morality. In Gellner, E. and Cansino, C. (Eds.) *Liberalism in Modern Times: Essays in Honor of Jose G. Merquior*. New York: Central European University Press.

Braddock, C.H. (1999) Informed Decision Making in Outpatient Practice: Time to Get Back to

Basics. *Journal of The American Medical Association*, 282, 2313–20.

Budd, K.S. (2001) Clinical Assessment of Parents in Child Protection Cases: An Empirical Analysis. *Law and Human Behavior*, 25, 93–108.

Cannell, J., Hudson, J.I. and Pope, H.G. (2001) Standards for Informed Consent in Recovered Memory Therapy. *Journal of the American Academy of Psychiatry and the Law*, 29: 2, 138–47.

Chalmers, I., Sackett, D. and Silagy, C. (1997) The Cochrane Collaboration. In Maynard, A. and Chalmers, I. (Eds.) *Non-Random Reflections on Health Services Research: on the 25th Anniversary of Archie Cochrane's Effectiveness and Efficiency*. London: BMJ Publishing Group.

Cohen, D. and Jacobs, D. (1998) A Model Consent Form for Psychiatric Drug Treatment. *International Journal of Risk and Safety in Medicine*, 11, 161–4.

Coulter, A., Entwistle, V. and Gilbert, D. (1998) *Informing Patients: An Assessment of the Quality of Patient Information Materials*. London: King's Fund.

Cullen, R. (2006) *Health Information on the Internet: A Study of Providers, Quality and Users*. Westport, CT: Praeger.

Davies, P. and Boruch, R. (2001) The Campbell Collaboration: Does for Public Policy What Cochrane Does for Health. *British Medical Journal*, 325, 294–5.

Davis, P.K. and Peck, C. (1996) Increasing Self-Determination: Teaching People with Mental Retardation to Evaluate Residential Options. *Journal of Applied Behavior Analysis*, 29, 173–88.

Dicenso, A. et al. (2002) Interventions to Reduce Unintended Pregnancies Among Adolescents: Systematic Review of Randomised Controlled Trials. *British Medical Journal*, 324, 1426.

Domenighetti, G., Grilli, R. and Liberati, A. (1998) Promoting Consumers' Demand for Evidence-Based Medicine. *International Journal of Technology Assessment in Health Care*, 14: 1, 97–105.

Dowrick, C. (1999) Uncertainty and Responsibility. In Dowrick, C. and Frith, L. (Eds.) *General Practice and Ethics: Uncertainty and Responsibility*. New York: Routledge.

Dunning, D., Heath, C. and Suls, J.M. (2004) Flawed Self-Assessment: Implications for Health, Education and the Work Place. *Psychology of Science in the Public Interest*, 5, 69–106.

Eddy, D. (1990) Comparing Benefits and Harms: The Balance Sheet. *Journal of the American Medical Association*, 263.

Edwards, A. and Elwyn, G. (2001) *Evidence-Based Patient Choice: Inevitable or Impossible*. New York: Oxford.

Enkin, M. et al. (2006) *A Guide to Effective Care in Pregnancy and Childbirth*. 3rd edn. New York: Oxford University Press.

Entwistle, V.A. et al. (1996) Supporting Consumer Involvement in Decision Making: What Constitutes Quality in Consumer Health Information? *International Journal of Quality Health Care*, 8, 425–37.

Entwistle, V.A. et al. (1998) Evidence-Informed Patient Choice. *International Journal of Technology Assessment in Health Care*, 14, 212–15.

Evans, I., Thornton, H. and Chalmers, I. (2006) *Testing Treatments: Better Research for Better Health Care*. London: The British Library.

Faden, R.R. et al. (1986) *A History and Theory of Informed Consent*. Oxford: Oxford University Press.

Fellner, C.H. and Marshall, J.R. (1970) The Myth of Informed Consent. *American Journal of Psychiatry*, 126, 1245–50.

Fox, R.C. and Swazey, J.P. (1974) *The Courage to Fail: A Social View of Organ Transplants and Dialysis*. Chicago, IL: University of Chicago Press.

Friedson, E. (1994) *Professionalism Reborn: Theory, Prophecy, and Policy*. Chicago: University of Chicago Press.

Gambrill, E. (2005) *Critical Thinking in Clinical Practice: Improving the Quality of Judgements and Decisions*. 2nd edn. New York: Wiley.

Gambrill, E. (2006) Evidence-Based Practice and Policy: Choices Ahead. *Research on Social Work Practice*, 16, 338–57.

Gambrill, E. and Gibbs, L. (2002) Making Practice Decisions: Is What's Good for the Goose Good for the Gander? *Ethical Human Sciences and Services*, 4: 1, 31–46.

Gibbs, L. and Gambrill, E. (1999) *Critical Thinking for Social Workers: Exercises for the Helping Professions*. 2nd edn. Thousand Oaks, CA: Pine Forge Press.

Graham, W. et al. (2000) Randomised Controlled Trial Comparing Effectiveness of Touch Screen System with Leaflet for Providing Women with Information on Prenatal Tests. *British Medical Journal*, 320, 155–60.

Gray, J.A. (2001) *Evidence-Based Health Care: How to Make Health Policy and Management Decisions.* 2nd edn. New York: Churchill Livingstone.

Greenhalgh, T. et al. (2002) A Comparative Case Study of Two Models of a Clinical Informaticist Service. *British Medical Journal*, 324, 524–9.

Gutheil, T.G. et al. (1991) *Decision Making in Psychiatry and the Law.* Baltimore, MD: Williams and Wilkins.

Haas, L.J. (1991) Hide and Seek or Show and Tell? Emerging Issues of Informed Consent. *Ethics and Behavior*, 1: 3, 175–89.

Halpern, J. (2001) *From Detached Concern to Empathy: Humanising Medical Practice.* New York: Oxford University Press.

Handler, J.F. (1986) *The Conditions of Discretion: Autonomy, Community, Bureaucracy.* New York: Russell Sage Foundation.

Handler, J.F. (1992) Discretion: Power, Quiescence and Trust. In Hawkins, K. (Ed.) *The Uses of Discretion.* Oxford: Clarendon Press.

Hasenfeld, Y. (1987) Power in Social Work Practice. *Social Service Review*, 61, 469–83.

Hastie, R. and Dawes, R.M. (2001) *Rational Choice in an Uncertain World.* Thousand Oaks, CA: Sage.

Haynes, R. (2002) What Kind of Evidence is it that Evidence-Based Medicine Advocates want Health Care Providers and Consumers to Pay Attention To? *BMC Health Services Research*, 2:3. www.Biomedcentral.Com/1472–6963/2/3

Haynes, R.B., Devereaux, P.J. and Gyatt, G.H. (2002) Editorial. Clinical Expertise in the Era of Evidence-based Medicine and Patient Choice. *ACP Journal Club*, 136(A 11).

Henggeler, S.W. et al. (2006) Methodological Critique and Meta-analysis as Trojan Horse. *Children and Youth Services Review*, 28, 447–57

Jarvis, W.T. (1990) *Dubious Dentistry: A Dental Continuing Education Course.* Loma Linda, CA: Loma Linda University School of Dentistry.

Jacobson, J.W., Foxx, R.M. and Mulick, T.A. (2005) *Controversial Therapies for Developmental Disabilities: Fad, Fashion, and Science in Professional Practice.* Mahwah, NJ: Erlbaum.

Jørgensen, K.J. and Gøtzsche, P.C. (2004) Presentation on Websites of Possible Benefits and Harms from Screening for Breast Cancer: Cross Sectional Study. *British Medical Journal*, 328, 148–55.

Katz, J. (1984) Why Doctors Don't Disclose Uncertainty. *The Hastings Center Report*, 14: 1, 35–44.

Katz, J. (2002) *The Silent World of Doctor and Patient.* 2nd edn. Baltimore, MD: John Hopkins Press.

Kennedy, N.J. and Sanborn, J.S. (1992) Disclosure of Tardive Dyskinesia: Effect of Written Policy on Risk Disclosure. *Pharmacology Bulletin*, 28: 1, 93–100.

Kruger, J. and Dunning, D. (1999) Unskilled and Unaware of It: How Difficulties in Recognising One's Own Incompetence Lead to Inflated Self-Assessments. *Journal of Personality and Social Psychology*, 77: 6, 1121–34.

Larson, M.S. (1977) *The Rise of Professionalism: A Sociological Analysis.* Berkeley: University of California Press.

Leever, M. et al. (2002) *Ethical Child Welfare Practice.* Washington, DC: Child Welfare League of America.

Lidz, C.W. et al. (1984) *Informed Consent: A Study of Decision Making in Psychiatry.* New York: Guilford.

Lilienfeld, S.O., Lynn, S.J. and Lohr, J.M. (2003) *Science and Pseudoscience in Clinical Psychology.* New York: Guilford.

Lindsey, D. (2004) *The Welfare of Children.* 2nd edn. New York: Oxford University Press.

Ling, T. (Ed.) (1999) *Reforming Health Care by Consent: Involving those who Matter.* Abingdon: Radcliff.

Littell, J.H. (2006) The Case for Multisystemic Therapy: Evidence or Orthodoxy? *Children and Youth Services Review*, 28, 458–72.

Margolin, L. (1997) *Under the Cover of Kindness: The Invention of Social Work.* Charlottesville, VI: University Press of Virginia.

Marris, P. (1996) *The Politics of Uncertainty: Attachment in Private and Public Life.* New York: Routledge.

McIntyre, N. and Popper, K. (1983) The Critical Attitude in Medicine: The Need for a New Ethics. *British Medical Journal*, 287, 1919–23.

Moynihan, R. and Cassells, A. (2005) *Selling Sickness: How the World's Biggest Pharmaceutical Companies are Turning us all into Patients.* New York: Nation.

Moynihan, R., Heath, I. and Henry, D. (2002) Selling Sickness: The Pharmaceutical Industry and Disease Mongering. *British Medical Journal*, 324, 886–90.

National Association of Social Workers. (1996) *Code of Ethics* (Revised, 1999). Washington, DC: Author.

Nickerson, R.S. (1986) *Reflections on Reasoning.* Hillsdale, NJ: Lawrence Erlbaum.

Nickerson, R.S. (1998) Confirmation Bias: A Ubiquitous Phenomenon in many Guises. *Review of General Psychology*, 2: 2, 175–220.

Norcross, J.C. (2002) *Psychotherapy Relationships That Work: Therapists Contributions and Responsibilities to Patients.* New York: Oxford.

O'Connor, A.M. et al. (2003) *Decision Aids for People Facing Health Treatment or Screening Decisions.* The Cochcrane Database System.

O'Donohue, W., Fisher, J.E. and Plaud, J.J. (1989) What is Good Treatment Decision: The Client's Perspective. *Professional Psychology: Research and Practice.* 20, 404–7.

Oxman, A.D. and Guyatt, G.H. (1993) The Science of Reviewing Research. In Warren, K.S. and Mosteller, F. (Eds.) *Doing More Good Than Harm: The Evaluation of Health Care Interventions.* New York Academy of Sciences.

Pelton, L. (1989) *For Reasons of Poverty: A Critical Analysis of the Public Child Welfare System in The United States.* New York: Praeger.

Pope, K. and Vasquez, M.J. (1998) *Ethics in Psychology and Counselling: A Practical Guide.* San Francisco: Jossey-Bass.

Reason, J. (2001) Understanding Adverse Events: Human Factors. In Vincent, C. (Ed.) *Clinical Risk Management: Enhancing Patient Safety.* 2nd edn. . London: BMJ.

Regehr, C. and Antle, B. (1997) Coercive Influences: Informed Consent in Court-Mandated Social Work Practice. *Social Work*, 42: 3, 300–6.

Robinson, A. and Thomson, R. (2001) Variability in Patient Preferences for Participating in Medical Decision Making: Implication for the Use of Decision Support Tools. *Quality in Health Care*, 10, 134–8.

Rogers, A. (1999) Broadening the Agenda in Coercion Research: Addressing The Sociopolitical Context of Risk, Violence and Mental Disorder. In Morrissey, J.P. and Monahan, J. (Eds.) *Coercion in Mental Health Services: International Perspectives.* Stamford, CT: JAI Press.

Sackett, D.L. et al. (1997) *Evidence-Based Medicine: How to Teach and Practice EBM.* New York: Churchill Livingstone.

Sackett, D.L. et al. (2000) *Evidence-Based Medicine: How to Teach and Practice EBM.* 2nd. edn. New York: Churchill Livingstone.

Schwartz, I.S. and Baer, D.M. (1991) Social Validity Assessments: Is Current Practice State of the Art? *Journal of Applied Behavior Analysis*, 24, 189–204.

Scull, A. (2005) *Madhouse: A Tragic Tale of Megalomania and Modern Medicine.* New Haven, CT: Yale University Press.

Sharpe, V.A. and Faden, A.I. (1998) *Medical Harm: Historical, Conceptual, and Ethical Dimensions of Iatrogenic Illness.* New York: Cambridge University Press.

Sheldon, J.B. and Risley, T.R. (1990) Balancing Clients' Rights. The Establishment of Human Rights and Peer Review Committees. In Bellack, A.S., Hersen, M. and Kazdin, A.E. (Eds.) *International Handbook of Behavior Modification and Therapy.* 2nd edn. New York: Plenum.

Sievert, A.L., Cuvo, A.J. and Davis, P.K. (1988) Training Self-Advocacy Skills to Adults with Mild Handicaps. *Journal of Applied Behavior Analysis*, 21, 299–309.

Skene, L. and Smallwood, R. (2002) Informed Consent: Lessons from Australia. *British Medical Journal*, 324, 39–41.

Skrabanek, P. and Mccormick, J. (1998) *Follies and Fallacies in Medicine.* 3rd edn. Whithorn: Tarragon Press.

Smith, T.S. et al. (1991) Clinical Ethical Decision Making: An Investigation of the Rationales Used to Justify Doing Less than One Believes One Should. *Professional Psychology: Research and Practice*, 22, 235–9.

Somberg, D.R., Stone, G.L., and Claiborn, C.D. (1993) Informed Consent: Therapists' Beliefs and Practices. *Professional Psychology: Research and Practice*, 24: 2, 153–9.

Stapleton, H., Kirkham, M. and Thomas, G. (2002) Qualitative Study of Evidence Based Leaflets in Maternity Care. *British Medical Journal*, 324, 639.

Stein, T.J., Gambrill, E.D. and Wiltse, K.T. (1978) *Children in Foster Homes: Achieving Continuity of Care.* New York: Praeger.

Straus, E.S. et al. (2005) *Evidence-Based Medicine: How to Teach Our Practice.* 3rd edn. New York: Churchill Livingstone.

Szasz, T. (1994) *Cruel Compassion: Psychiatric Control of Society's Unwanted.* New York: John Wiley.

Szasz, T. (2002) *Liberation by Oppression: A Comparative Study of Slavery and Psychiatry.* New Brunswick, NJ: Transaction.

Taylor, M. (2000) Patient Care (Empowerment): A Local View. *British Medical Journal*, 320, 1663–4.

Thompson, D.F. (1980) Paternalism in Medicine, Law and Public Policy. In Callahan, D. and Bok, S. (Eds.) *Ethics Teaching in Higher Education.* New York: Plenum.

Valenstein, E.S. (1986) *Great and Desperate Cures: The Rise and Decline of Psychosurgery and Other Medical Treatments for Mental Illness.* New York: Basic Books.

Veatch, R.M. (2000) Doctor Does not Know Best: Why in the New Century Physicians must Stop Trying to Benefit Patients. *Journal of Medicine and Philosophy,* 25, 701–21.

Young, J.H. (1992) *American Health Quackery.* Princeton: Princeton University Press.

Introducing Broad Frameworks

A Closer Look at Client Engagement: Understanding and Assessing Engagement from the Perspectives of Workers and Clients in Non-voluntary Child Protective Service Cases

Diane Yatchmenoff

This chapter presents findings from two studies of client engagement embedded in a five-year evaluation of child protective service practice in Oregon. A theoretical perspective is provided regarding the definition, role and importance of engagement as a feeling state rather than a set of behaviours that may reflect *compliance* among non-voluntary clients but not necessarily *positive involvement in a helping process*, as engagement is defined here. Data from CPS clients suggested four dimensions of engagement that could be assessed by self-report. Findings also illustrated a wide range of ways that workers define engagement and the cues they use to 'know' whether or not clients are positively involved in a helping process. Data from a subset of cases reflected moderate convergence between workers' and clients' ratings of client engagement in individual cases, but a tendency for workers to rate engagement higher than their clients, particularly when compliance was high. Clients reported respect, concrete assistance, and personal support from the worker as important in achieving engagement. Implications for training, supervision, and research are discussed.

The engagement challenge

Engaging difficult or hard to reach clients in a helping process through the child protective service system continues to be one of the major challenges in the public child welfare field. Although service outcomes have received the larger share of attention at the policy level in recent years, at the practice level workers struggle daily with this challenge. Imagine for example:

Shawna, a 23-year-old African American mother of three children, all under 10 years old, lives in a housing project along with her children and boyfriend, Ralph, who is father of two of the children. Recently two neighbours

called the child abuse hotline to report that Shawna and Ralph fight frequently and loudly. The reports mentioned loud music playing in the middle of the night, trash in the yard, children crying constantly. One neighbour said 'I think they brawl in there', the kids are 'wandering all over the place, dirty and hungry.' The other said she suspected drug use. The school also called during this same month to report concerns about the 2nd grader, who frequently arrives late to school or not at all, appears dirty and tired, and is often hungry. A worker is assigned to respond to these reports and goes out to the housing project to determine whether the children are in danger of imminent harm and should be removed or – if removal is not indicated – whether services could help improve the quality of care and reduce the likelihood of harm. Finding evidence of drug use, little food in the home, and a young child with soiled diapers alone in a crib in an unheated room, all three children are removed and the mother is instructed to report to court 48 hours later for a preliminary hearing. After the hearing, during which the judge orders that the children will remain in care during an assessment or investigation period, the 'social work' phase begins, and Shawna becomes one of 14 families on the worker's caseload.

For the parent, Shawna, this is without question a traumatic event. Although there is no single or predictable way that a parent would react, Shawna's emotional state might well include rage at the idea that a stranger has the right to take her children from her, anger at others for their role in putting her in this position, fear that she has lost her children forever, fear about where they are being taken and what will happen to them, fear about repercussions in her personal life (maybe from the boyfriend, maybe from family members), fear about other damaging information the worker may uncover, potentially placing her in greater jeopardy, shame that she has failed to care for her children, shame that her life is out of control, helplessness that her life is out of control, anticipation of embarrassment when her friends, family and neighbours learn what has happened, anguish, despair, righteous indignation, and a host of other feelings. If her state is complicated by underlying mental, emotional or behavioural health challenges, she may be deeply depressed, cognitively impaired (temporarily or more permanently) – in one way or another unable to fully think, listen, or learn and probably not able to be judicious with her behaviour either. If she or others in her close network of family and friends have had prior negative experiences with child protective services, she may be deeply mistrustful of anyone from the state who is assigned to her case.

The child protective service worker also has an initial set of reactions, formed by what they have seen firsthand as well as what they bring to the situation from their past experience, personal history, and their particular values and belief system. In the initial encounter, the worker may be anxious approaching a situation with many unknowns. They may react with anger at the sight of children who are cold, dirty, hungry, appearing to be poorly nurtured, possibly at risk of harm. The caseworker may feel frustration or despair at the dreary sameness of scarcity, child neglect, impoverished lives that constrain the possibilities for young children. The worker may feel pity for the mother, or anger, or disgust, disdain or empathy. The worker may have seen so many similar situations that they are cynical and cannot begin to imagine a more hopeful future for this family. Moreover, the worker also is under pressure, constrained by tight timelines, paperwork requirements, court appearances, the next referral that will land shortly on their desk, and above all the ever-present underlying anxiety in a field where workers daily encounter trauma to children and occasionally, and unpredictably, child fatality.

In this highly charged context, workers are expected to establish a working relationship with the parents, determine service needs, make referrals for services, find and maintain out-of-home placements, make recommendations to the court, and above all, see that the parents begin to engage in a helping process that will reduce the potential for harm to the child and make it possible for the family to be reunited (or

remain together if the child has not been removed).

While the legal and custodial functions of the child welfare system often appear to govern practice, the role of child protection in providing an effective point of entry to formal and informal support services in the community may be the single most important ingredient in achieving long-term positive outcomes for children and their families (Videka-Sherman, 1991). Despite the importance of this aspect of practice, however, little work has been done to articulate either a theoretical or practice model for working with non-voluntary clients in child welfare generally (Bricker-Jenkins, 1992; National Research Council, 1993) or more specifically to understand the processes by which the protective service system is or is not successful in engaging families at the critical entry point of practice.

Current political and ideological directions in child welfare have shifted sharply over the past decade from an emphasis on maintaining children in their homes and preserving attachments between parents, children and siblings, to a heightened emphasis on safety (Morton and Salovitz, 2006) along with accelerated procedures to provide permanent adoptive placements when reunification is not possible (Bartholet, 1999; Rittner, 1995).

At the level of practice, however, an equally compelling ideology exists, based on tenaciously held social work values combined with practice wisdom. This ideology suggests that family-centred services will continue to be the best way to meet the critical needs of children, including safety (Wells and Tracy, 1996). Training for social workers continues to emphasise focusing on strengths and capacities rather than deficits, respecting clients' values, cultural and individual beliefs, and providing services in a way that is as respectful and de-stigmatising as possible. And practice models such as family decision meetings or family group conferences (Burford et al., 1996; Ryburn, 1993), solution focused intervention (Kim-Berg and Kelly, 2000; Rymarchyk, 2000), signs of safety (Turnell and Edwards, 1999), strengths/needs based services (Judge, 1998) and others have been built around these values, most recently including the adoption of 'Systems of Care' principles in child welfare from the children's mental health field (Nelson, Yatchmenoff and Cahn, in press). All of these approaches share common underpinnings that either explicitly or implicitly are aimed at increasing the system's capacity to engage caregivers to secure the future safety and wellbeing of the children.

What is missing, however, are theories of practice or intervention against which to examine specific initiatives and their outcomes and empirical evidence to either support or challenge the underlying assumptions. Instead, we are most often limited to judging effectiveness by distal outcomes that are based on shifting and problematic indicators such as reunification, re-entry, or the indefinable construct 'permanency'. Although considerable work has been done over the past decade to strengthen outcome data in child welfare (Barth and Johnson-Reid, 2000; Poertner, McDonald and Murray, 2000; Waldfogel, 2000) these measures continue to be weak. Results of outcome studies are generally mixed at best and fail to tell us what worked and did not – neither helping us to improve these emerging models nor to strengthen core casework practice through evidence-informed training and supervision.

The Oregon client engagement study described in the following pages was designed to contribute to a more theoretically sound and empirically based conceptual framework for thinking about and talking about client engagement and the application of theory to practice. Its overarching purpose was to stimulate critical thinking and ideas about how training and supervision of child protective service caseworkers could more effectively strengthen practice.

Theoretical background: a closer look at engagement

Engagement is a central concept in social work practice. In virtually every major text used to educate professionals over the last four decades, the concept appears frequently in references to interactions with clients or service consumers in the early phase of work (see, for example, Compton and Galaway, 1994; Hepworth and Larsen, 1993; Kadushin and Kadushin, 1997). However, although this 'engagement phase' is recognised to be extremely important, the *goal* of the engagement process (that is, the state of positive engagement) has been left to the imagination: 'we know it when we see it'.

In part, this is because the answer for most community-based social work programmes is obvious: the client is 'engaged' if they enrol, comes back, shows up, completes services etc. (see, for example, McKay, 1996). Enrolment and attendance have been used as synonymous terms with engagement in this context although more recently attention has turned to the nature and quality of participation as well (Littell, Alexander and Reynolds, 2001; Plasse, 2000).

For reluctant or 'hard to reach' but technically voluntary clients, service utilisation is likewise generally considered a sufficient indicator of engagement, indicated by enrolment in programmes, attendance, retention, or continuous contact with programme staff. If adults with serious and persistent mental illness or homeless teens stay in contact with case managers, attend group sessions or show up at drop-in centres, come in for medication or comply with other treatment protocols, come in for showers or a place to sleep, or in other ways participate in programmes that are made available to them, they are assumed to be 'engaged' (Rife et al. 1991).

Compliance and engagement

In non-voluntary settings such as child protective services, however, the picture is more complex. With sufficient legal threat or the fear of losing their children permanently, parents can frequently be coerced into attending parenting classes, enrolling in substance abuse treatment programmes, receiving mental health services, or attending anger management classes. Indeed, effectiveness research on court ordered clients, although mixed, appears to suggest that legal leverage does indeed promote enrolment and attendance, and can reduce drop-out rates from services such as substance abuse treatment (Anglin and Maugh, 1992). For at least for some populations, this approach has been considered necessary and relatively successful. For example, evidence is strong and mounting that the now-popular drug courts reduce the likelihood of re-arrest for substance abuse-related offences and furthermore may increase the length of time in treatment and the likelihood of abstinence following treatment (Huddleston, 2000, 2005; Satel, 1999). Overall, findings suggest that a legal mandate is not an impediment to positive outcomes and, when warranted, may serve as a necessary first step.

But mandates do not always produce desired longer-term results, and this is especially true in the child welfare setting, where the issues in families are often complex and a single service is not likely to resolve all of the problems. Instead, families may need to work through a range of problems and challenges over time, and sometimes fundamental changes in their circumstances, life styles and parenting practices may be required in order to safeguard their children's wellbeing.

It is a central tenet of this chapter that compliant behaviours are not a substitute for an internal state of engagement (that is, a *feeling state of positive involvement in a helping process*) and that this feeling state is one of the determinants of whether or not positive outcomes are achieved, along with other factors such as service fit and service quality (Altman, 2003). Caseworkers know this intuitively as do parents in the system (Yatchmenoff, 2005). In one worker's words: 'If the client is not on board, you have nothing'.

But what does this mean and how might it work?

The logic of practice

Figure 5.1 below depicts in a simplified way a model of the child protective service process and the role that a feeling state of engagement might play in what happens. The left column (Inputs) is a reminder that upstream variables to a CPS intervention make a difference to what happens:

- The characteristics, circumstances, history, and capacities of the family (that is, parents or other caregivers, children, extended family, social network) will partly – maybe largely – determine the course of events.
- The incident: something happens (or a series of things happen); a referral is made to child protective services; possibly there are multiple referrals.
- The service system (child welfare as well as related systems) has characteristics, capacities, ways of doing business; these will all influence the CPS response and subsequent events.
- The community is a factor as well. Community expectations, history, values, and resources – all these will play into the CPS response.

Once a referral is made (or multiple referrals are made), the child protective service system responds (the second column). This includes everything that happens at the front end: the assignment to a worker who will 'go-out' to begin the investigation, the immediate decisions (removal or not, court involvement or not, etc.), interviewing of the family and the investigation into the allegations, the disposition, and – possibly most important – needs assessment and service planning.

The intended results of the CPS intervention are presented in the third column (Proximal Outcomes). As a result of the immediate response, we hope at a minimum the children will be safe. Ideally also, the risk factors in the family are clearer and the needs of the children and caregivers are evident and a plan can be made. Ideally also, the client is 'on board', and resources (formal and informal supports) are mobilised to address needs in the family. Finally, court involvement and the use of mandates, as well as referrals, may be employed to 'encourage' or coerce the family to utilise services or to make specific changes in circumstances or behaviours.

If this process works as intended, the plan for the family will be based on actual service needs that have been identified; those services will be utilised and effective (supported by client engagement as well as mandates), leading to the longer term positive outcomes of child and family safety and wellbeing (the last column) that we all would like to see occur.

The role of engagement

From both theoretical and practical perspectives engagement – 'getting the client on board' – is likely to affect child welfare outcomes in a number of important ways, reflected by some of the arrows in the diagram. In the simplest terms, achieving engagement with non-voluntary clients should at a minimum:

- Increase the quality of needs identification and service planning. The parent who has engaged in a helping process is more likely to participate in planning and more likely to share their perception of the families' needs. Thus service fit is likely to be strengthened.
- Increase the support from community and kin. The parent who has positively engaged will be more able to enlist the support of others and the worker's assistance in generating that support.
- Increase the utilisation of services. The client who is engaged has helped in the planning process and is now receiving services that they

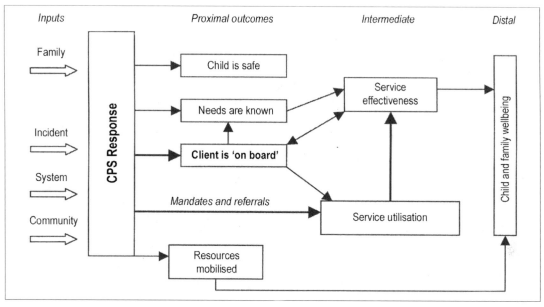

Figure 5.1 The logic of practice

recognise to be needed and potentially of benefit. As noted above, evidence is fairly strong that court mandates and the threat of losing children permanently increases service utilisation. However, in the presence of positive engagement, service utilisation should be easier to achieve, potentially requiring less court involvement and fostering utilisation of services that may not be mandated but potentially beneficial, such as use of natural support systems in the community.

- Increase the likelihood of benefit from services, because the parent is 'on board' and has 'bought-in' to the service plan.

From core social work perspectives: what does it mean to have the client 'on board'?

In a series of papers describing the major streams of practice as the field developed up through the 1960s, the editors (Roberts and Nee, 1974: ix) asked contributing authors to include eight common central points in their discussion, one of which was 'a discussion of how professional workers engage clients in treatment.' The major perspectives presented in this series including psychosocial (or diagnostic) social work, the problem solving approach, functional casework,

and the behavioural approach. Over the succeeding decades, the evolution of social work has contributed new perspectives and principles for practice such as task-centred social work, crisis theory, the life model approach, radical behaviourism, empowerment practice, competence and strengths-based practice, structural and systems theories, and more. Together they represent a mix of explanatory theory, practice theory, practice models, and practice principles or perspectives that are overlapping and interwoven, frequently commingled in the literature (see for example, Turner and Jaco, 1996).

Each perspective provides a lens through which it is possible to infer the goals of the engagement process. For example, psychosocial casework (Hollis, 1964; Woods and Robinson, 1996) focuses on building *motivation* (and reducing resistance) and the client's recognition of the *expertise of the practitioner*. The functional approach (Smalley, 1970) emphasised creating *hope, sense of choice*, and *goal ownership* on the part of the client. Problem-solving casework (Perlman, 1970; Turner and Jaco, 1996) added a focus on promoting a *sense of capacity* and *opportunity* and the client's *felt competence*. Task-centred approaches (Reid, 1996) emphasised finding an *agreed-upon problem focus* and establishing *accountability*. Crisis theory (Rapoport, 1970;

Parad and Parad, 1968) capitalises on the presumed greater availability for intervention that clients may demonstrate during periods of extreme duress, and as such would lead to increased *perception of need, acceptance of help*. Behavioural approaches (Thyer, 1988; Thomas, 1970) emphasise *adherence to a treatment plan* (this may be more in line with compliance than with an underlying feeling state), while competence-oriented practice or strengths-based casework describe approaches aimed at generating a *sense of personal competence*, a sense of *mutuality* with the worker, and a sense of *comfort* or *trust in the helping process and in the worker* (Maluccio, 1981).

More recently, in the field of psychotherapy, engagement has been defined as the *relationship* or *alliance* between therapist and client (Horvath and Greenburg, 1994) and in social work practice; the *helping relationship* has also sometimes been used as a proxy for engagement (Poulin and Young, 1996). Moreover, the concept of *motivation* has been reframed in recent years as a fluctuating state of *readiness to change* (Miller and Rollnick, 1991) that is accessible to intervention by a worker through specific interviewing techniques. Strategies to help increase clients' *readiness*, based on this earlier work, have been developed for child welfare as well (see, for example, Littell and Girvin, 2004), though there is as yet limited information available about the implementation or outcomes of this approach.

All of these different perspectives reflect feeling states that are related to a client's positive involvement in a helping process in the broad social work arena. However, there are challenges in applying these concepts to child protective service work. First, caseworkers are not therapists in that often they do not provide services directly and sometimes have quite limited contact with families, as well as limited training in relationship-based work. In fact, the focus of services is often not on the adult client at all, but rather on ensuring that the needs of the children are met. Moreover, the difficulties that families present are only sometimes amenable to intervention targeted at change in the individual client or family unit, as is implied with the *readiness to change* approach. In many instances, families' problems reflect multi-level, multi-faceted conditions such as poverty, mental or physical disorders of children or adults, domestic violence, unemployment, homelessness, and other circumstances that have overwhelmed

families' capacities to cope. Approaches that focus on a change process within the individual are less useful than those that can accommodate other points of intervention as well. And finally, of course, clients in the child protective service system have not sought out assistance and may have very different ideas about what they need than does the worker. To be useful for our purposes, a conceptual framework for client engagement needs to be broad rather than narrow and needs to reflect the special circumstances of the non-voluntary child protective service context as well.

The Oregon studies

The study of client engagement as an intermediate goal of intervention grew out of a series of projects in the Oregon child welfare system, the first of which was a federal funded demonstration project in the mid-1990s to more effectively serve multi-need families referred for child maltreatment for whom substance abuse was a significant concern (Shireman, Feyerherm and Yatchmenoff, 1996). Our interest was initially driven by the observation that parents, chiefly mothers with open cases as a result of alleged maltreatment, varied greatly in their engagement in a helping process through the intervention of the child welfare system. The level of engagement among these clients appeared to the research team to have little to do with the seriousness of the circumstances. Engagement didn't seem to be determined by the presence of substance abuse, mental health issues, domestic violence, criminal history, or other challenges that often seriously undermine families. Families with all kinds of challenges appeared to us to be highly engaged, while some families who seemed to have fewer barriers were resistant or disengaged. We wondered what made the difference. We wondered especially about the relationship of engagement to the skill set, attitudes, and capacities of the caseworker and potentially to certain other characteristics of the service system as well, for example the use of family unity meetings (later appearing as family decision meetings) or the availability of flexible funds to address immediate concrete needs. We also thought we 'knew' which clients were engaged and which were not – in part because respondents in the study saw the research team as friendly neutrals, sometimes as allies, not connected with the child welfare agency and were often surprisingly frank about their feelings as well as their circumstances and behaviours.

However, our capacity to study systematically the phenomenon of engagement was curtailed by the lack of a clear definition of the construct or a way to assess it outside of the notion from psychotherapy of a helping relationship or therapeutic alliance (Horvath and Greenburg, 1994; Poulin and Young, 1996), which seemed to be related but different constructs.

In a subsequent five-year study of a state-wide initiative to improve child protective service practice in Oregon, client engagement became a critical focal point for understanding casework practice, client experiences, and outcomes for children and families. The evaluation focused on the implementation of a state-wide initiative to improve practice. The initiative, known as Strengths/Needs Based service delivery, emphasised:

> *Using a strengths perspective in working with families.*
>   *Collaborating with parents or other caregivers in ident-*
> *ifying their children's needs.*
> (Shireman, Yatchmenoff, Wilson
> and Sussex, 1997)

Including extended families, foster parents, and community partners in identifying children's needs and creating service plans.

Using flexible funds as necessary to craft individualised services to meet children's needs.

One of the underlying assumptions of the strengths/needs based approach was that it would increase the child welfare agency's capacity to positively engage parents who had been referred for maltreatment, resulting in greater follow through on service plans and recommendations.

Two waves of data, approximately 100 cases per year from 6–8 different field offices around the state, were used for the engagement study, which focused on clients who were in the CPS phase (in the first 60 days of service) as well as those who had been involved for longer periods based on our observation that engagement sometimes increased dramatically over time (especially if a new worker came on board) and sometimes drastically dropped and *in any case* needed to be sustained or strengthened throughout the life of a case. It was not simply the early phase of work that mattered.

Defining client engagement in the non-voluntary child protective service context

In focusing on client engagement, our first objective was to more clearly articulate what we meant by the construct in this setting. We began with a series of discussions with caseworkers, supervisors and other direct service workers in which we elicited ideas and perceptions about the concept of engagement, its role in the helping process with child welfare clients, and how its presence or absence is observed in practice. As these discussions proceeded, the central question became 'how do you know the difference between a client who is just 'going through the motions' and one who is positively involved in a helping process?' Answers varied widely, leading us to develop the study on worker perceptions that is discussed later in this chapter. However, workers who focused on a feeling state pointed to changes in affect and expression as well as behaviour that were perceived by the workers ('the client begins to call me to tell me how things are going'; 'the client asks, starts to ask, for services'; 'the clients starts to take responsibility'; 'the client takes the initiative in making use of services'; 'the client is glad to see me when I come out to the house').

An evaluation advisory group of biological or adoptive parents who were or had been clients of the child welfare protective service system also helped us think about what engagement means. This group was vehement about the difference between compliance and engagement, noting 'parents who are just taking up chair space,' versus those were who were 'really working their programme' or otherwise actively engaged in making changes in their lives. In fact, the themes that parents suggested were similar to those we heard from professionals. Themes centred around clients' acknowledging rather than denying circumstances that threatened their children's safety and actively working to make changes in their lives. The input we got from parents as well as workers corresponded well to dimensions that had emerged from the review of social work literature.

We also embedded a mix of open-ended and structured questions in the caseworker interview. Questions to workers included: 'What does the term 'engagement' mean to you?' 'How do you know when a family is engaged?' as well as case specific questions such as 'What evidence indicates to you that this particular family is engaged or not engaged in a helping process?' Questions to the CPS client (a parent or other caregiver) encouraged them to talk about how they felt about being involved with the child welfare system, how they felt about the allegations against them, what kind of impact the agency was having on their lives, and so on. Study interviews in 1998–99 also included a preliminary set of close-ended questions for clients and workers, based on our early thinking about theoretical dimensions (Shireman, Yatchmenoff and Wilson, 1999; Shireman, Yatchmenoff, Wilson and Sussex, 1998).

This process resulted in clarification and refinement of these early dimensions and the identification of an additional aspect, drawn directly from worker and client data. This was a negative dimension, quite specific to the non-voluntary context. It reflected the expressions on the part of some clients of extreme lack of trust in the intentions of the agency and agency personnel; the sense that there was a hidden agenda, that the client was being lied to or manipulated, with an intention of harm. The anti-engagement dimension was labelled *mistrust* and defined in the negative because it did not represent the lack of a positive feeling but rather the presence of a pervasive negative feeling. The working definition of engagement that resulted from this preliminary work contained the following five aspects of engagement:

- **Receptivity:** openness to receiving help, characterised by recognition of problems or circumstances that resulted in agency intervention and by a perceived need for help.
- **Expectancy:** the perception of benefit; a sense of being helped or the expectation of receiving help through the agency's involvement; a feeling that things are changing (or will change) for the better.
- **Investment:** commitment to the helping process, characterised by active participation in planning or services, goal ownership, and initiative in seeking and utilising help.
- **Working Relationship:** interpersonal relationship with worker characterised by a sense of reciprocity or mutuality and good communication.
- **Mistrust:** the belief that the agency and/or worker is manipulative, malicious or capricious, with intent to harm the service recipient.

The *Client Engagement in Child Protective Services* (CECPS) questionnaire was subsequently developed to capture these dimensions. Transcripts from the evaluation study provided source material for generating a large pool of items, many of which were drawn directly from the responses of caregivers and workers. Several procedures helped to reduce this large item pool to a manageable set. First, in keeping with conventional scale construction procedures, we eliminated those items that were redundant, poorly worded, or obviously confusing, and any that contained multiple constructs (DeVellis, 1991). We then examined the face and construct validity (Nunnally and Bernstein, 1994) with the help of three expert panels. The first panel, a diverse group of social work scholars, practitioners, and research methodologists, considered the concept of engagement and our definition of it, reviewed and provided feedback on the five dimensions and then each member independently sorted the items into our constructs so that we could examine the level of agreement among panel members about how individual items matched our hypothesised framework. This entire process resulted in the elimination of some items, the modification of others, and the addition of several extra items.

The resulting 37-item measure was tested on a sample of 287 parents, primarily mothers, who had open child protective service cases because of child maltreatment. Results of this study have been reported elsewhere (Yatchmenoff, 2005) but in brief, confirmatory factor analytic procedures were used to examine the fit of the data to the hypothesised model and to examine the utility of individual items to achieve the best fit with the greatest parsimony. The 19-item final instrument (included in the Appendix to this chapter) reflected four dimensions (two of our initial dimensions, *Expectancy* and *Investment*, although conceptually distinct, empirically combined into a single dimension we named *Buy-in*). Each subscale had strong reliability (alpha coefficients ranged from .81 to .91) as did the overall measure (alpha .95), allowing us to combine individual items into computed subscale scores and to have confidence in the total score as well.

Correlations among the subscales were significant (ranging from $r = .49$ to $r = .89$, $p < .001$). However, Receptivity (the parent's acknowledgement of the need for help) correlated only moderately with Working Relationship ($r = .49$) and Mistrust ($r = -.60$) whereas the relationships among the other three factors were high. Tentatively, this suggested that Receptivity was present in some cases independent of other dimensions of engagement, a finding consistent with the impression of our interviewers in the field. That is, many parents who expressed a need for help were not positively involved in a helping process: they were mistrustful of the agency; they felt judged rather than helped by their worker; they did not feel heard; they felt no ownership or expected benefit from the service plan. Nonetheless, they recognised that they and their children needed help.

In fact, *most* families that we interviewed acknowledged problems and a need for assistance. This finding contrasts sharply with the common perception that parents who abuse or neglect their children are difficult to help because they are *in denial* or *unmotivated*. Although this purported denial or lack of motivation has frequently been used to explain negative outcomes (Faver, Crawford and Combs-Orme, 1999), other investigators (Janko, 1994) have described similar findings:

- Counter to my expectations when I began this study, every parent [I interviewed] believed that CPS should have intervened in their parenting on behalf of their children (p. 66).
- [Respondent name] . . . said she knew from the outset why CPS intervened . . . Although one can never be absolutely certain of the sincerity of another person, I believed that [respondent names] recognised that the parenting they provided their children was inadequate (p. 106).
- If these findings have merit, it would appear that we need to encourage workers to enter new CPS cases with a somewhat different set of assumptions than is often the case, and moreover, we need to shape practice specifically to build a working relationship with parents, to reduce mistrust and to enhance their sense of *hopefulness about* and *investment in* the service plan (Buy-In).

Worker perceptions and worker judgments

The logic model in Figure 5.1 presented a set of assumptions about how the client's level of engagement may affect the client's progress through the system and the resulting outcomes

for children and families. Worker characteristics or values may also affect the outcomes (Barnes, 2000; Ryan et al., 2006) and *the perception on the part of the worker of the client's engagement*, may be critical. In child protective services, workers are called upon to make judgments and decisions daily, frequently with limited information and in an atmosphere of uncertainty:

- Will Shawna's child be safe if returned home?
- Does Shawna's explanation for her situation hold water?
- Will she do as she says she will do?
- Is she really committed to her child or will her relationship with an abusive boyfriend turn out to be more important to her?
- Can her mother, who has offered to watch the child while Shawna goes to treatment, be trusted?
- Is Shawna telling the truth when she says she has stopped using drugs?
- Should we give her the 'benefit of the doubt?

Worker judgments and expectations determine how case notes are written up, the kinds of recommendations that are made to the court, the types of services that are offered to the family, the goal of those services, which may be to assist the family but is sometimes aimed at demonstrating that the family 'can't make it', and the level of attention or effort that the worker puts into this case on a day-to-day basis:

- How do workers make these judgments?
- What criteria do they use to decide which parents are engaged in a helping process and which are merely 'going through the motions?'
- To what extent would worker and client reports of engagement converge or diverge on individual cases?
- To what extent do workers equate compliance with engagement?
- And how do workers' perceptions affect case process and/or outcomes?

These were the questions that drove the second study of client engagement in the Oregon child welfare system. To answer the first of these questions, we returned to the qualitative data, drawn from transcripts of interviews with workers and focusing on the two key questions: What does the term *engagement* mean to you? How can you tell when a client is engaged rather than just 'going through the motions?'

We analysed a subset of worker transcripts (n = 40) using open coding by a team of three research assistants and Ethnograph software (Qualis Research Associates, 1998). A second level axial coding process (Denzin and Lincoln, 2000) helped us collapse preliminary codes into broader categories, generating themes through a process that was iterative in nature, using consensus to resolve differences of opinion. Subsequent cross-coding on an additional sub-sample of transcripts also increased our confidence in the trustworthiness of how we chose to organise the responses.

Worker descriptions of engagement

There were three domains into which workers' responses fell: observations about the *behaviour* of the client, observations about the *affect* of the client, and observations about their *interactions with* the client. Strikingly, virtually all of the caseworkers we interviewed limited their responses to observations about only one of these dimensions; almost none incorporated elements of all three in their responses.

Client behaviour

More than a third of the workers in the sample seemed to focus almost exclusively on client behaviours, emphasising what we called *Participation* or a related but different aspect of behaviour that we termed *Initiative*.

Responses that we grouped under Participation ranged from workers noting that they look for evidence of active participation in classes or other services to a much narrower focus on compliance with the mandatory service plan. For example, some workers commented primarily on the importance of clients simply showing up, following through on service plans, enrolling in services, attending, doing what they were 'supposed to do':

- *It's what they do that counts . . . how they feel about me doesn't matter.*
- *When they are following through with their service plan.*
- *When they take, start taking, actions and when they start participating in services.*
- *When they do what I tell them to.*

Others told us they looked for evidence of more active participation, as evidenced by observable

behaviours in the service setting (e.g., in parenting class).

- *When they are participating in their service, not just going, but getting feedback from the parenting classes that there is cooperation in class rather than just going to go.*

On the other hand there were workers who also focused on behaviour but were looking for clients to demonstrate more *Initiative* or ownership of the helping process. Responses that we clustered into this category reflected workers observations that when clients 'engage' there is a shift in their behaviour from recipients of services to initiators of services.

- *When it turns the corner from 'I am not setting up appointments and I am not making decisions for them' . . . they take over all that themselves. They are making the appointments, they are seeing what the next step is and they are doing it and they are telling me what they are doing.*
- *She went out and hooked herself up with all of her services.*
- *Asking for help. When they call concerned about the child . . . asking what shall I do.*
- *When I have someone call me or check in when they don't have to.*

Client affect

A second set of workers in our sample, when asked about their understanding of engagement, talked about affect, or the observable expression of an underlying feeling state. In many cases, they spoke about a shift in affect from hostility to receptivity, from resistance to cooperation, or from 'denial' to acknowledging responsibility for the experience of their children and the harm that may have been inflicted. We grouped these answers into expressions about *responsibility*, *cooperation* and *ownership*.

Caseworkers who focused on what we termed *responsibility* were looking for evidence that clients acknowledged their responsibility for what had happened to their child and responsibility as well for their child's future wellbeing. Whether 'confession' is necessary to move cases forward in child welfare has been a source of debate but in our sample there were definitely adherents to this notion:

- *She has been able to be honest and tell me about the abuse.*

- *When they start opening up.*
- *Taking responsibility for what happened.*
- *Hearing what the concerns are, not denying them.*

Other workers looked for *cooperation* or what appeared to be a 'cooperative attitude.'

- *Ready to take that step forward and work with us.*
- *She was very cooperative. She really wanted to work to keep her kids at home.*

Others looked for manifestations of the clients' sense of ownership for the changes that needed to happen in their lives to safeguard themselves and their children:

- *When there is some ownership. She feels in charge.*
- *They felt they had the same concern I did.*
- *Beginning to set goals for herself. Realising what she needs.*

Client interactions

Lastly, some workers focused most on the quality of interactions they had with clients and the relationship they perceived they had or would have with the client. In some instances, workers seemed to judge this relationship by the style of communication:

- *Easy to talk to, accepting my suggestions . . . I was like right on, this is going to be a great client.*
- *The way they are talking to you. Body language and tone.*
- *I knew I was going to have a wonderful relationship with this woman up front.*

In other instances, workers noted a reciprocity or capacity to work together:

- *They are hearing what the concerns are and the worker is hearing what the family issues are.*
- *Just the way that everything is being reciprocated. If they are not going to put as much effort to getting their family back together . . . then I am not going to either.*
- *We just felt like we had a working situation here. It felt very good.*

Finally, for others, a sense of trust or openness in the relationship was the deciding factor:

- *A trusting relationship between us.*
- *When the client shows a willingness to trust.*

Many of these observations, though certainly not all, were consistent with the conceptual framework we had constructed for client engagement. We noted also, however, that underneath some statements lay the workers' own comfort level, when, for example, there is a reduction in apparent hostility on the part of the client, and a reliance on the social cues the client provides that are reassuring, i.e. how pleasant they are to be around. We wondered whether social skills were a valid proxy for engagement, and whether there were considerations here that should potentially be addressed in training or supervision.

The role of culture and class

In particular, it may be important to examine the degree to which perceptions of clients are governed by expectations that are bound by culture and class. The construct of engagement, for example, may or may not be meaningful across diverse populations in the way that it resonates for European-Americans in the mainstream of the middle class. When perceptions of engagement depend on social forms and norms such as modulated tone of voice, 'acceptable: verbal expressions, eye-contact, etc., we may need to think more deeply about what we are looking for. What does *positively engaged in a helping process* mean and how would it manifest for the Shawna in our example or for a mother from Somalia or a father from Mexico? On the other hand, workers who are basing their judgments about engagement strictly on client behaviours like attending parenting classes, for example, run the risk of never looking beyond compliance, which would also likely be affected by cultural norms, to determine if we have indeed initiated an intervention that has meaning and potential for the caregiver whose progress is so vitally important to the wellbeing of the child and family. This is particularly important since 'overly compliant' behaviour may represent a protection again intrusion or loss of freedom as much as more overt forms of resistance or reactance (Ivanoff, Blythe and Tripodi, 1994; Rooney, 1992).

The impact on practice

In the Oregon study, we also asked workers to talk with us about how their practice and the decisions they made were affected by their perceptions about whether the parent was positively engaged in a helping process, just 'going through the motions' or refusing outright.

Some workers spoke of making early judgments about how cases would go:

• *I just got a feeling from the get-go that it wasn't going to be cooperative. I never went back to the home.*

Others talked about how their perception that the parent was positively engaged shaped significant decisions or recommendations to the court:

• *. . . Not wanting to make the wrong decision, jeopardising the kids' safety, but respecting the family's cooperation . . . really going out on a limb for them.*

Still others spoke about how their perceptions of the family influenced the level of effort they put into cases:

• *When you get that case when you know that you are going to be a help . . . those are the ones you go out of your way . . . providing even more services than normal.*

Our findings were limited to a relatively small sample and an exploratory set of questions, and there is nothing in the published literature to date that addresses this issue in any rigorous way. Nonetheless, even these early findings confirm what is intuitively obvious: workers' perceptions make a difference in what happens. In light of this, we wanted to examine the congruence of worker and client reports of engagement.

The convergence of caseworker judgment and client reports

To look at congruence, we examined a sample of 135 cases from one wave of data collected in the Oregon study during 2000–2001. These cases were drawn at random from all cases that had opened because of a referral for child maltreatment. In 70 per cent of the cases, one or more children had been removed from the home at the time of the referral or shortly thereafter. Abuse types were split between physical abuse (20 per cent), neglect (24 per cent), and 'threat of harm' (47 per cent), which at that time in Oregon included cases where children were at risk

because of domestic violence, substance abuse, the presence of a prior abuse perpetrator, or any number of other factors. Most of the clients were women (87 per cent), and half had prior open cases with the child welfare system. Domestic violence was reported in 55 per cent of the cases, substance abuse in 56 per cent, and mental health issues in 44 per cent.

The parents we interviewed completed the 19-item Client Engagement in Child Protective Services (CECPS) instrument, described earlier in this chapter. Caseworkers answered 13 questions to capture the worker's view of client engagement. Items on this measure reflected much the same dimensions as on the CECPS, with questions on Buy-In ('This client feels ownership over the case plans and goals,' 'This client wants the same things for her/himself and the family as the agency wants'), questions on Receptivity/Investment ('This client is ready to make some changes to safeguard his/her children'), Expectancy ('I think this client believes we can help her/him,' 'I think this client feels hopeful about the outcome of [the agency's] involvement'), as well as questions about mistrust, openness or honesty ('I believe this client is fairly open with me about what goes on in the family,' 'I believe this client is honest with me about her/his feelings.'). We also asked workers a global question about engagement based on their level of agreement with the statement: 'In my opinion, this client is positively engaged with [the CPS intervention].' The 13-item Worker's View showed strong internal consistency (alpha .93) and also correlated strongly with the global measure ($r = .78$, $p < .001$). The full set of items in the Worker's View measure is included in the Appendix.

Our primary interest was in whether the Workers' Views aligned with what their clients told us, which our interviewers impressionistically reported to be sometimes the same and sometimes quite divergent. These impressions proved accurate. Data on both measures had fairly good distribution. Scores on the Worker's View ranged from 13 to 65, with a mean of 48 and a median of 50 (sd 12). The CECPS had a positively skewed distribution, with scores ranging from 25 to 95, a mean of 66 and a median of 70. There was moderate congruence between the CECPS scores and the summary score on the Worker's View ($r = .58$). The worker's global rating was also linked with the client's CECPS scores ($r = .52$). Taken together, these

Table 5.1 Worker/client agreement on engagement (n = 135)

	Worker rates high	Worker rates medium	Worker rates low
Client reports high	n = 57 (42%)	n = 11 (8%)	n = 5 (4%)
Client reports medium	n = 11 (8%)	n = 14 (11%)	n = 4 (3%)
Client reports low	n = 12 (9%)	n = 9 (7%)	n = 11 (8%)

findings support the contention that when workers assessed client engagement to be high, clients were also likely to report their engagement to be high. But these correlations are far from perfect, and certainly there is room for improvement.

To understand this a bit more clearly, we used the high, medium and low categories of both global measures and looked to see the extent to which workers and clients placed the client in the same category. Again, we found that in the majority of cases (about 60 per cent), there was agreement. If workers said engagement was high, so did clients. If workers said it was medium, so did clients. And in these cases, both parties agreed when engagement was low (see Table 5.1 below).

In about 40 per cent of the cases, however, there was disagreement. Either the worker rated engagement high but the client family told us otherwise, or alternatively the clients told us they were highly engaged, while the worker perceived a different picture.

We also wanted to know whether workers tended to assess clients as engaged when they were merely 'compliant', that is, following through in their behaviour with case plans, such as attending classes, for example. We wondered whether some workers were looking only at compliant behaviour rather than considering the feeling state of the client they were working with, since we knew from clients, and from at least some workers, that attending did not always signify positive involvement.

We used a 5-item measure of compliance, which workers completed, with questions focusing on behaviours ('This client is following through on what we've agreed she/he would do.' 'This client is following through on service referrals.' 'This client shows up for scheduled appointments.'). Internal consistency reliability was good with an alpha of .85. The client self-report measure consisted of four parallel items and also had acceptable reliability (alpha = .78).

We recognised the limitations of these data, knowing that in particular clients, whether engaged or not, would be likely to tell us they were 'doing everything [they were] supposed to, and in fact most parents reported themselves to be compliant. Workers, likewise, may have inaccurate observations or skewed perceptions in some instances. So these data were treated with caution as a way to stimulate thinking and conversation about the ideas rather than as providing definitive answers.

Indeed, the strongest correlation in the study was between workers' ratings of compliance and their global rating of the clients' level of engagement (r = .66, p < .01). This finding cuts two ways. From our logic model for practice (Figure 5.1), we would expect that greater engagement would lead to greater utilisation of, and benefit from, services. So the relationship here is an expected and promising one. However, the relationship between CECPS scores, the clients' self-reports of their engagement, and caseworker ratings of compliance was, although significant, more modest (r = .33, p < .01). What this implied to us was that sometimes workers were rating clients as engaged merely because they were compliant.

Worker and client ratings of the client's compliance also aligned modestly (r = .35, p < .01). Parents who said they were more compliant also tended to report greater levels of engagement (r = .20, p < .05 on the global rating) but this finding is relatively weak in comparison to others in the study. However, overall, there was not as much variance in clients' responses as we would have liked to see to be comfortable with the data, so these findings are merely suggestive of the need for further study.

What made the difference for clients?

We asked parents what workers did that made the difference in how they felt about their involvement with the child protective service system. We asked parents who reported high levels of engagement and families who did not. When families were engaged they felt:

Treated with respect

- *'She asked me what I needed instead of ordering me around.'*
- *'He offered me options, choices . . .'*
- *'Gave me power in the situation.'*

Helped

- *'He kept my child safe.'*
- *'Saved my son.'*
- *'Made a really good placement decision for my son.'*
- *'Took care of my son and made him safe.'*
- *'My worker had the best interests of my children in mind.'*
- *'Picked me up from prison.'*
- *'Showed me how to manage my ADD son.'*
- *'Got an interpreter to help with communication.'*
- *'Cared about me and my job.'*
- *'Took personal time to drive me to appointments.'*

Supported, listened to, rather than judged

- *'Gave me a chance.'*
- *'Saw my strengths.'*
- *'Took time to listen.'*
- *'My caseworker saw both sides . . . listened to me also.'*
- *'Non-judgmental'*
- *'Very supportive of me.'*
- *'Caring, understanding . . . has feelings.'*
- *'Gave me support I don't get from my family.'*
- *'Very patient . . . didn't rush me.'*

Conversely, when parents were clearly not engaged in a helping process, their reflections on what went wrong also focused on their workers' attitudes and behaviours, although there are some systemic issues implied as well. When we asked parents what would have made it better, by and large their answers reflected:

Feeling judged and treated poorly

- *'He never gave me a chance.'*
- *'They need to see families as real people.'*
- *'The worker had a judgmental attitude.'*
- *'Treated me like trash.'*
- *'I needed the worker to listen to me and quit assuming.'*

- *'The workers need to see your strengths.'*
- *'They just looked at the negative stuff.'*
- *'If they would be more fair to families . . . and not just see me as the bad guy.'*

Feeling frustrated by the quality of service

- *'The worker wasn't paying any attention to my case at all.'*
- *'If he had just returned my phone calls once in a while.'*
- *'I needed more communication . . . more home visits.'*
- *'They make promises they don't keep.'*
- *'There was really poor follow through after the family meeting.'*
- *'Slowness . . . nothing got done when it was supposed to.'*
- *'I had no contact with the worker.'*
- *'I needed the worker to follow up on what he said he would do.'*
- *'I needed more frequent contact.'*
- *'Some workers should not be doing this kind of work.'*

Feeling powerless, abused, mistrustful

- *'They should investigate the truth before taking your kid away.'*
- *'He misrepresented me in court.'*
- *'Caseworkers do black market adoptions.'*

Discussion

For every frustration on the part of an angry or fearful parent with an open child protective service case, there are a multitude of frustrations that workers experience as well. The challenge of engagement is not a simple one nor is there a simple solution – indeed it is not something the worker can create single-handedly without the parent coming forward as well. But we also know that it happens – sometimes against all odds.

Findings from the Oregon study and other related research are useful primarily to generate thought and dialogue about how we might guide and supervise workers to think more systematically about engagement – both what they might observe in the clients and how their practice might influence the client's feeling state. We know from the data that multi-dimensional feeling state of engagement can be assessed with some reliability by client self-report, at least if the questions are asked by independent researchers. We know that workers form impressions of engagement and that they were moderately accurate, at least in this study, relative to what families said. We also know something about the bases for their impressions and that they varied considerably in what mattered most in their impression-formation. It is important in training that these processes be explored and illuminated so that workers are aware at a conscious level of how they are forming impressions and making judgments as well as how those judgments may affect outcomes.

It might also be possible in training and supervision to explore ways that workers could address what we learned about engagement from the clients themselves, so, for example, we might consider some of the following questions:

Is this family feeling *receptive* to our services?
- Does the family recognise problems?
- Are they the same problems that the agency sees?
- Does the family express a need for help?
- What kind of help?
- Can we supply what the family seems to want and need while simultaneously attending to the safety issues?
- What could we do to increase the family's receptivity? ·
- Could we ask the family that question?

Does this parent feel *hopeful* about how their case will come out?
- About the benefit they or their child will get?
- Is there something we can do to help this parent feel hopeful about the future – to feel that things will get better?
- What would it take?
- Can we ask the parent that question?

Does this parent *buy-in* to the case plan?
- Is the parent invested in making changes?
- Does the parent feel ownership over the plans and really want the services we are providing?
- Is there something we could do to increase that feeling, such as offering choices, options?
- Could we ask the parent that question?

Does this parent feel reciprocity in the *working relationship* with the caseworker?
- Do they feel that we can communicate, that they feel heard and that there is give and take?
- What might it take to create that sense of reciprocity?
- Would the client have any ideas about that?

Do we need to address a deep-set fundamental *mistrust* in the agency?
- Is this a parent who fears that anything they say will be used against them?
- That the agency is simply out to steal their child?
- That 'they' have a hidden agenda and are 'out to get her'?
- If that is in fact the case, is there something we could do to reduce that mistrust?
- What would it take?
- Could we ask the client that question?

Future research needs to address some of the important limitations in the studies presented here. Samples were drawn from one child welfare system in one state at a particular juncture in time. Moreover, this is a state without a substantially diverse population, hampering our ability to generalise findings widely or understand their applicability beyond this context. Much more work is needed to understand how engagement manifests across race and culture.

Research also is needed to understand the processes by which families engage in a helping process and how worker behaviours, practice approaches or system characteristics play into this process. Our ongoing study of the child welfare system in Oregon pointed to collaborative practices on the part of the worker, in particular, as enhancing engagement and to certain other worker characteristics as well (Yatchmenoff, 2001). Others have also focused on the role of worker characteristics and behaviours (Lee and Ayon, 2004; Dumbrill, 2006) but all these findings need replication and more rigorous study. In particular, it is difficult to draw conclusions about the causal direction when workers and clients both enter the situation with a set of prior experiences, habits, feelings, etc. that are mutually influential.

Finally, we need empirical evidence to support the intuitive understanding and practice wisdom that the feeling state of engagement is critical to child and family outcomes. Currently workers, and their supervisors and frequently the courts, struggle to know how to handle cases in which parents have completed service agreements by doing everything they were told, and yet no one is comfortable returning the child to their care. At present, we have no well-articulated perspective to respond to these situations and so we 'move the bar' and require further services, frequently without a sound rationale.

We need better assessment procedures, observational as well as self-report tools that are guided by sound and testable theory, to provide simpler but effective ways to examine client engagement. In the last analysis, our capacity to help vulnerable children and families in the complex and challenging child protective service context may well depend – not on the provision of individual services – but on engaging families in the helping process itself, for which the child protective service system is a critical gateway.

References

Altman, J.C. (2003) A Qualitative Examination of Client Participation in Agency-Initiated Services. *Families in Society*, 84: 4, 471–9.

Anglin, M.D. and Maugh, T.H. (1992) Overturning Myths About Coerced Drug Treatment. *California Psychologist*, 19–22.

Barnes, V. (2000) Initial Assessments in Child Protection: The Reality of Practice. *Practice*, 12: 4, 5.

Barth, R.P. and Jonson-Reid, M. (2000) Outcomes After Child Welfare Services: Implications for the Design of Performance Measures. *Children and Youth Services Review*, 22: 9–10, 763–87.

Bartholet, E. (1999) *Nobody's Children*. Boston, MA: Beacon Press.

Bricker-Jenkins, M. (1992) Building a Strengths Model of Practice in the Public Social Services. In Saleebey, D. (Ed.) *The Strengths Perspective in Social Work Practice*. White Plains, NY: Longman.

Burford, G. et al. (1996) Reunification as an Extended Family Matter. *Community Alternatives: International Journal of Family Care*, 8: 2, 33–55.

Compton, B.R. and Galaway, B. (1994) *Social Work Processes*. Pacific Grove, CA: Brooks/Cole.

Denzin, N.K., and Lincoln, Y.S. (2000) *Handbook of Qualitative Research*. 2nd edn. Newbury Park: Sage.

DeVellis, R.F. (1991) *Scale Development*. (Vol. 26) Newbury Park, CA: Sage.

Dumbrill, G. (2006) Parental Experience of Child Protection Intervention: A Qualitative Study. *Child Abuse and Neglect*, 30: 1, 27–37.

Faver, C.A., Crawford, S.L. and Combs-Orme, T. (1999) Services for Child Maltreatment: Challenges for Research and Practice. *Children and Youth Services Review*, 21: 2, 89–109.

Hepworth, D.H. and Larsen, J.A. (1993) *Direct Social Work Practice: Theory and Skills*. 4th edn. Pacific Grove, CA: Brooks/Cole.

Hollis, F. (1964) *Casework: A Psychosocial Therapy*. New York: Random House.

Hollis, F. (1970) The Psychosocial Approach to the Practice of Casework. In Roberts, R.W. and Nee, R. (Eds.) *Theories of Social Casework* 4th edn. Chicago: University of Chicago Press.

Horvath, A.O. and Greenburg, L.S. (Eds.) (1994) *The Working Alliance: Theory, Research, and Practice*. New York: John Wiley and Sons.

Huddleston, C.W. (2000) *The Promise of Drug Courts: The Philosophy and History*. National; Drug Court Institute Training Presentation.

Huddleston, C.W. (2005) Drug Courts: An Effective Strategy for Communities Facing Methamphetamine. *Bureau of Justice Assistance Bulletin*, May. US Department of Justice.

Ivanoff, A., Blythe, B.J. and Tripodi, T. (1994) *Involuntary Clients in Social Work Practice*. New York: Aldine De Gruyter.

Janko, S. (1994) *Vulnerable Children, Vulnerable Families: The Social Construction of Child Abuse*. New York, NY: Teachers College Press.

Judge, D.L. (1998) *Making Child Welfare Work*. Washington DC: Bazelon Center for Mental Health Law.

Kadushin, A. and Kadushin, G. (1997) *The Social Work Interview: A Guide for Human Service Professionals*. 4th edn. New York: Columbia University Press.

Kim-Berg, I, and Kelly, S. (2000) *Building Solutions in Child Protective Services*. NY: WW Norton.

Lee, C.D. and Ayon, C. (2004) Is the Client-Worker Relationship Associated with Better Outcomes in Mandated Child Abuse Cases? *Research on Social Work Practice*, 14: 5, 351–7.

Littell, J.H. and Girvin, H. (2004) Ready or Not: Uses of the Stages of Change Model in Child Welfare. *Child Welfare Journal*, 83: 4, 341–66.

Littell, J.H., Alexander, L.B. and Reynolds, W.W. (2001) Central and Underinvestigated Elements of Intervention. *Social Service Review*, 75: 1.

Maluccio, A.N. (1981) Competence-Oriented Social Work Practice: an Ecological Approach. In Maluccio, A.N. (Ed.) *Promoting Competence in Clients: A New/Old Approach to Social Work Practice*. New York: The Free Press.

McKay, M.M. and Nudelman, R. (1996) Evaluating a Social Work Engagement Approach to Involving Inner-city Children and Their Families in Mental Health Care. *Research on Social Work Practice*, 6: 4, 462–73.

Miller, W.R., and Rollnick, S. (1991) *Motivational Interviewing: Preparing People to Change Addictive Behavior*. New York: The Guilford Press.

Morton, T.D., and Salovitz, B. (2006) Evolving a Theoretical Model of Child Safety in Maltreating Families. *Child Abuse and Neglect*, 30: 12, 1317–27.

National Research Council (1993) *Understanding Child Abuse and Neglect*. Washington, DC: National Academy Press.

Nelson, K., Yatchmenoff, D. and Cahn, K. (In Press) Can Child Protective Services Be Reformed? In Karger, H., Midgley, J., Kindle, P, and Brown, B. *Controversial Issues in Social Policy*. 3rd edn. Boston: Allyn and Bacon.

Nunnally, J.C. and Bernstein, I.H. (1994) *Psychometric Theory*. New York: Mcgraw-Hill.

Parad, H.J., and Parad, L.G. (1968) Study of Crisis-Oriented Planned Short-Term Treatment. *Social Casework: The Journal of Contemporary Social Work*, 46, 346–55.

Perlman, H.H. (1970) The Problem-Solving Approach to Casework Practice. In Roberts, R.W. and Nee, R. (Eds.) *Theories of Social Casework*. 4th edn. Chicago: University of Chicago Press.

Plasse, B.R. (2000) Components of Engagement: Women in A Psychoeducational Parenting Skills Group in Substance Abuse Treatment. *Social Work With Groups*, 22: 4, 33–51.

Poertner, J., McDonald, T.P. and Murray, C. (2000) Child Welfare Outcomes Revisited. *Children and Youth Services Review*, 22: 9–10, 789–810.

Poulin, J. and Young, T. (1997) Development of a Helping Relationship Inventory for Social Work Practice. *Research on Social Work Practice*, 7: 4, 463–89.

Qualis Research Associates (1998) *The Ethnograph V5.0*. Colorado Springs, CO: QRA.

Rapoport, L. (1970) Crisis Intervention as a Mode of Brief Treatment. In Roberts, R.W. and Nee, R. (Eds.) *Theories of Social Casework*. 4th edn. Chicago: University of Chicago Press.

Reid, W.J. (1996) Task-Centered Social Work. In Turner, F.J. (Ed.) *Social Work Treatment: Interlocking Theoretical Approaches*. New York: Simon and Schuster.

Rife, J.C. et al. (1991) Case Management with Homeless Mentally Ill People. *Health and Social Work*, 16: 1, 58–67.

Rittner, B. (1995) Children on the Move: Placement Patterns in Children's Protective Services. *Families in Society: The Journal of Contemporary Human Services*, 75, 469–77.

Roberts, R.W. and Nee, R.H. (Eds.) (1974) *Theories of Social Casework*. 4th edn. Chicago: University of Chicago.

Rooney, R.H. (1992) *Strategies for Work With Involuntary Clients*. New York: Columbia University Press.

Ryan, J.P. et al. (2006) Investigating the Effects of Caseworker Characteristics in Child Welfare. *Children and Youth Services Review*, 28: 9, 993–1006.

Ryburn, M. (1993) A New Model for Family Decision Making in Child Care and Protection. *Early Child Development and Care*, 86, 1–10.

Rymarchyk, G.K. (2000) Solution-Focused Interventions in Child Protective Investigation: A Promising Alternative for Working with Families. *Dissertation Abstracts International*, 61, 2469-A.

Satel, S.L. (1999) *Drug Treatment: The Case for Coercion*. Washington, DC: American Institute Press.

Shireman, C., Feyerherm, W. and Yatchmenoff, D. (1996) *Evaluation of Project Team Final Report*. Regional Research Institute in Human Services. Portland, OR: Portland State University.

Shireman, J., Yatchmenoff, D., Wilson, B. and Sussex, B. (1997) *Strengths/Needs Based Services Evaluation Year End Report*. Regional Research Institute in Human Services. Portland, OR: Portland State University.

Shireman, J., Yatchmenoff, D., Wilson, B. et al. (1998) *Strengths/Needs Based Services Evaluation Interim Report*. Regional Research Institute in Human Services. Portland, OR: Portland State University.

Shireman, J., Yatchmenoff, D., Wilson, B. et al. (1999) *Strengths/Needs Based Services Evaluation Year End Report*. Regional Research Institute in Human Services. Portland, OR: Portland State University.

Smalley, R.E. (1970) The Functional Approach to Casework Practice. In Roberts, R.W. and Nee, R. (Eds.) *Theories of Social Casework*. 4th edn. Chicago: University of Chicago Press.

Thomas, E.J. (1970) Behavioral Modification and Casework. In Roberts, R.W. and Nee, R. (Eds.) *Theories of Social Casework*. 4th edn. Chicago: University of Chicago Press.

Thyer, B.A. (1988) Radical Behaviorism and Clinical Social Work. In Dorfman, R.A. (Ed.) *Paradigms of Clinical Social Work*. New York: Brunner/Mazel.

Turnell, A. and Edwards, S. (1999) *Signs of Safety: A Solution and Safety Oriented Approach to Child Protection*. New York, NY: WW Norton.

Turner, J. and Jaco, R.M. (1996) Problem-Solving Theory and Social Work Treatment. In Turner,

F.J. (Ed.) *Social Work Treatment: Interlocking Theoretical Approaches.* New York: Simon and Schuster.

Videka-Sherman, L. (1991) Child Abuse and Neglect. In Gitterman, A. (Ed.) *Handbook of Social Work Practice With Vulnerable Populations.* New York: Columbia University Press.

Waldfogel, J. (2000) Child Welfare Research: How Adequate Are The Data? *Children and Youth Services Review* 22: 9–10, 705–41.

Wells, K. and Tracy, E. (1996) Reorienting Intensive Family Preservation Services in Relation to Public Child Welfare Practice. *Child Welfare*, 75: 6, 667–92.

Woods, M.E. and Robinson, H. (1996) Psychosocial Theory and Social Work Treatment. In Turner, F.J. (Ed.) *Social Work Treatment: Interlocking Theoretical Approaches.* New York: Simon and Schuster.

Yatchmenoff, D. (2001) Measuring Client Engagement in Non-voluntary Child Protective Services. Doctoral Dissertation, Portland State University, *Dissertation Abstracts International*, 63/02.AAT3043087.

Yatchmenoff, D. (2005) Measuring Client Engagement From The Client's Perspective in Non-voluntary Child Protective Services. *Research on Social Work Practice*, 15: 2, 84–96.

Appendix

Client engagement in child protective services (B19)

We're interested in your feelings about your involvement with child welfare. There are no right or wrong answers to any of our questions. Please answer as honestly and openly as you can. Your answers will be kept absolutely confidential.

Here are some of the ways families may feel about having child welfare in their lives. Some are positive and some are negative. You may have both positive and negative feelings at the same time. Please read (listen to) the following statements carefully. Then, thinking about how you feel *right now* about your involvement with child welfare, please indicate how much you agree or disagree with each. Thank you!

	Strongly agree	Agree	Not sure	Disagree	Strongly disagree
1. I believe my family will get help we really need from child welfare.	5	4	3	2	1
2. I realise I need some help to make sure my kids have what they need.	5	4	3	2	1
3. I was fine before child welfare got involved. The problem is theirs, not mine.	5	4	3	2	1
4. I really want to make use of the services (help) child welfare is providing me.	5	4	3	2	1
5. It's hard for me to work with the caseworker I've been assigned.	5	4	3	2	1
6. Anything I say, they're going to turn it around to make me look bad.	5	4	3	2	1
7. There's a good reason why child welfare is involved in my family.	5	4	3	2	1
8. Working with child welfare has given me more hope about how my life is going to go in the future.	5	4	3	2	1
9. I think my caseworker and I respect each other.	5	4	3	2	1
10. I'm not just going through the motions. I'm really involved in working with child welfare.	5	4	3	2	1
11. My worker and I agree about what's best for my child.	5	4	3	2	1
12. I feel like I can trust child welfare to be fair and to see my side of things.	5	4	3	2	1

	Strongly agree	Agree	Not sure	Disagree	Strongly disagree
13. I think things will get better for my children because child welfare is involved.	5	4	3	2	1
14. What child welfare wants me to do is the same as what I want.	5	4	3	2	1
15. There were definitely some problems in my family that child welfare saw.	5	4	3	2	1
16. My worker doesn't understand where I'm coming from at all.	5	4	3	2	1
17. Child welfare is helping me take care of some problems in our lives.	5	4	3	2	1
18 I believe child welfare is helping my family get stronger.	5	4	3	2	1
19. Child welfare is not out to get me.	5	4	3	2	1

Worker's view of case

With respect to the primary adult client, and thinking about how things are going at this point in time in the case . . .

	None or almost none of the time	A little of the time	Some of the time	A lot of the time	All or nearly all of the time
1. I believe this client is fairly open with me about what goes on in the family.	1	2	3	4	5
2. This client wants the same things for themselves and the family as the agency wants.	1	2	3	4	5
3. This client is in a real battle with the agency, not working with us.	1	2	3	4	5
4. I think this client is overwhelmed by [agency name] involvement and is feeling pretty helpless.	1	2	3	4	5
5. This client is ready to make some changes in behaviour or lifestyle to safeguard their children.	1	2	3	4	5
6. In my opinion, this client feels genuine ownership over the case plans and goals.	1	2	3	4	5
7. I'm not particularly confident that this client is telling me the truth. I feel this way . . .	1	2	3	4	5
8. I think this client believes we can help them.	1	2	3	4	5
9. I believe this client is honest with me about their feelings.	1	2	3	4	5
10. This client has a completely different agenda than the agency.	1	2	3	4	5
11. I think this client feels hopeful about the outcome of [agency name] involvement.	1	2	3	4	5
12. This client denies any responsibility for the circumstances that got the agency involved.	1	2	3	4	5
13. This client is able to focus on the needs of their child.	1	2	3	4	5

Assessment and Decision-Making in Child Protection: Relationship-Based Considerations

Michelle Lefevre

Introduction

Child protection concerns can generate some very difficult decisions for families and professionals. Abusing parents and carers need to decide whether to face up to their behaviour and take steps towards change. Non-abusing parents may be faced with excruciating choices between remaining with their partner or keeping their children. Professionals must assess the current and future risk of significant harm and to determine what kind of actions might best promote positive outcomes for children. Families frequently experience their involvement in such assessments as conflictual and stressful. Dumbrill (2006) notes that a number of in-depth qualitative studies of parental experience reveal that parents view child protection services as powerful, inhumane and fear-provoking. Some feel angry or misunderstood about negative judgements being made about their lifestyle and parenting capacity. They feel unable to correct these misunderstandings because their views are not taken into account and so they experience themselves as excluded from decisions and powerless to prevent professional intrusion into their lives. In Dumbrill's own study some parents described workers actions as using power over them in a way that felt absolute, tyrannical or frightening.

Parents felt they were given little opportunity to challenge or even dialogue with workers regarding the interpretation given to events or to discuss the plans workers formulated for their families.

(Dumbrill, 2006: 30)

Many parents find it extremely difficult to engage in working constructively with professionals about the risks to their children when feeling disempowered and helpless in situations that they cannot control. Instead of being able to participate actively in the assessment process, some exhibit open hostility towards professionals and resistance to working co-operatively. Alternatively, they may be wary of the consequences of such direct action and be tempted towards superficial compliance through 'playing the game', and feigning co-operation (Dumbrill, 2006). This can mask their anger and distress but it may prevent them from actively engaging with professionals towards recognising or addressing the issues that are of concern to others. This can lead the child protection system to assume that they are unable to create a safer home environment or that they are less committed to their children (Holland, 2000).

Children and young people should equally be active participants in the assessment process (DoH et al., 2000; DoH, 2001). However, their feelings and experiences may similarly interrupt them from engaging with the worker carrying out the assessment. Previous difficult experiences with adults, such as abuse, may have eroded their trust in others and cause them to feel unsafe (Cleaver, 1996; Prior et al., 1999; Ruch, 1998; Schofield and Brown, 1999). The assessment may be imposed or mandated by parents, professionals or the courts leaving them feeling particularly powerless in the interaction; fear, suspicion and hostility can result (Cooper, 1994; Kroll, 1995; Head, 1998; Ruegger, 2001). Some children are influenced by their parents' negative perceptions about the situation. Feelings of confusion, powerlessness and fear of consequences about what they say are common (Bell, 2002; Cleaver, 1996). Externally imposed deadlines such as looked-after children reviews (Francis, 2002) and guidance under the Department of Health Assessment Framework add further pressure.

These factors inhibit authentic engagement and open communication between children and professionals. Like their parents, they may refuse to directly contribute to the assessment process by avoiding contact altogether, withholding their views and accounts of their situation, or, more subtly, deflecting questions which they suspect (often accurately) disguise a hidden agenda (Thomas and O'Kane, 2000). By so doing, though, they may often communicate much information indirectly and non-verbally about their wishes and experiences, if workers are attuned to these.

For both parents and children, then, participation in assessment and decision-making is fraught with difficulties and pressures. If they are not enabled to participate, their views are lost and the picture formed by professionals is consequently incomplete. This does not facilitate good, or ethically-based, decision-making. As families are in the less powerful position, it is incumbent upon professionals to find ways of engaging all family members so that they are able to contribute as fully as possible. This chapter considers the importance of the working relationship between families and professionals in facilitating this. A range of individual and interpersonal factors are explored here in order to consider how workers may be able to develop and build upon the relationships formed to promote collaborative and effective decision-making.

The importance of the relationship built between service users and professionals

Traditional approaches to assessment in child protection situations were influenced strongly by psychodynamic and quasi-therapeutic models. Within these the nature of the relationship between 'clients' and professionals was considered to be central to the success of the work (see, for example, Biestek, 1961; Mattinson, 1975). These approaches fell out of favour in the latter part of the 20th Century, though, being criticised for their long-termness of approach, lack of evidence regarding outcomes, positioning of worker as 'expert' and, as structural analyses of power and oppression moved centre stage, failure to acknowledge the social situation (Cooper et al., 2003; Payne, 2005; Ruch, 2005). The individual and psychological emphasis of these perspectives was felt to potentially pathologise individuals by viewing their problems as solely resulting from personal difficulties rather than considering additionally or alternatively any wider social or political influences such as poverty, racism or homophobia (Trevithick, 2003).

More recently, though, there has been a renewed interest in relationship-based practice, with a view that, whatever the setting, aim and

task, the engagement between worker and family member is the crucible within which the ingredients of personality, history, context, and interpersonal relating come together (Howe, 1998; Schofield, 1998; Trevithick, 2003; Ruch, 2005). This builds on research findings that the helping relationship is one of the most significant components of successful therapeutic intervention, being more influential than the method chosen (Norcross, 1986; Marziali and Alexander, 1991; Bogo, 1993; Clarkson, 1993).

Whilst contemporary relationship-based approaches continue to have roots in psychodynamic perspectives, many frame themselves 'psychosocial', as they additionally emphasise the importance of recognising the person-in-context and the impact of structural dynamics such as oppression by integrating empowerment and anti-oppressive perspectives (Howe, 1997, 1998, 2002; Gordon, 2000; Turney and Tanner, 2001; Trevithick, 2003; Payne, 2005; Ruch, 2005). The practical is attended to alongside the emotional to ensure that the relationship is purposeful, goal-oriented and interactive (Saari, 1986). In this way relational working can be seen as a relevant tool for practitioners in a resource-scarce environment (Schofield, 1998).

Its utility was demonstrated in a recent study of family support interventions with families who were thought to be potentially difficult to engage. Where practitioners attended to building rapport, showed empathy and worked in partnership, families felt safer and developed trust in their worker. This meant they were more likely to participate in interventions which promoted positive outcomes for their children. Conversely, workers' poor interpersonal skills and a patronising, judgmental manner were (unsurprisingly) off-putting and made parents feel inexpert, belittled, hostile and disaffected (Moran et al., 2004).

A number of skills, attitudes and attributes are needed to work in a relationship-based way. This chapter will draw upon Clarkson's (1993) 'multiplicity of psychotherapeutic relationships' model to outline these. Clarkson suggests that these different kinds of relationship may all potentially be present within any one set of interactions between a worker and service user, although not necessarily to the same degree or at the same time.

Engaging families in a working alliance

As mentioned above, many parents feel hostile or unhappy about participating in assessments regarding the safety and wellbeing of their children.

> Rose, a 31-year-old woman, has an 8-year-old daughter, Anna. Jenny is assessing the situation because it has been discovered that Rose's new partner, Fred, has a conviction for sexual abuse of a previous partner's child. Fred has told Rose that his ex-wife fabricated the story to cause trouble for him. He is not prepared to engage in any treatment work. Rose accepts his story and is reluctant to explore this further. She is openly hostile when Jenny meets with her, stating she will not comply with the child protection plan.

Engaging family members in a constructive working alliance is often the first step towards eliciting the co-operation necessary to their participation in such assessments. This requires the worker to establish the kind of facilitative conditions necessary for family members to begin to lower some of the barriers that they feel protect them (Bogo, 1993).

Firstly, they need to feel they are treated with the dignity and respect accorded to them as human beings. The worker needs to be reliable and committed to promoting families' welfare and to be accountable and transparent about their intentions and goals (Compton and Galloway 1984; Clarkson, 1993). Some messages relevant to this are found in an analysis of recent research studies (DoH, 2001). Negotiation skills are needed to be able to convey to families the tensions and dilemmas inherent in a situation where the needs and wishes of parents and children may conflict with each other and with the views of professionals. Families who were given information, time to think, time for questions and reassurance about their anxieties felt relieved when their stress was recognised and understood and were able to participate more fully in decision-making. Where parents felt workers were being open and honest with them, they were in turn more confident about providing vital information about their child, themselves and their circumstances. Such participation is associated with improved welfare outcomes for children (ibid).

Secondly, families need to feel that a real concern for their needs is demonstrated by the worker. This requires not just professional skills but personal qualities such as empathy, acceptance, unconditional positive regard, non-possessive warmth, congruence or genuineness, approachability, sensitivity, humour, and commitment. These attributes can demonstrate caring and concern, and enable liking and trust to develop, which are associated with positive outcomes for the work (Rogers, 1951; Compton and Galloway, 1984; Egan, 2002; Biestek, 1961; Truax and Carkhuff, 1967; Bogo, 1993; DoH, 2001).

Thirdly, a collaborative approach which shares power as much as possible needs to be taken. Here the practitioner needs to acknowledge and respect the client's own expertise in the situation rather than being driven solely by their own perceptions, as 'expert' (Turney and Tanner, 2001; Turnell and Edwards, 1997). This is confirmed by Dumbrill's (2006) study. Parents who felt that professionals shared power with them tended to engage in the work, rather than fighting workers by openly opposing them, or 'playing the game' by feigning co-operation:

> *For parents who experience themselves as powerless and their workers as powerful, small words of encouragement by workers took on enormous proportions. Trivial comments can enable . . . or disable.*
>
> (Dumbrill, 2006: 31)

It seems that workers need to begin where parents are 'at' and acknowledge parents' real fears in a situation of unbalanced power. Using advocacy and offering practical assistance are recommended as concrete ways of using power with and for parents, rather than over them (Dumbrill, 2006).

Sharing power in child protection situations is not the same as workers denying the reality of their own authority. Not only would this be dangerous in terms of protecting children, but it seems tokenistic or patronising to parents who may feel coerced into 'sham' or 'enforced' partnerships, being threatened with court action if they do not comply (DoH, 2001). Instead, what is proposed is a partnership approach, which is characterised by the following qualities:

- A shared commitment to negotiation and actions about how best to safeguard and promote children's welfare.
- Mutual respect for the other's point of view.

- Recognising the unequal nature of power between parents and professionals.
- Recognising parents have their own needs which should be addressed.
- Good communication skills by professionals.
- The establishment of trust between all parties.
- Integrity and accountability on the part of both parents and professionals.
- Shared decision-making.
- Joint recognition of constraints on services offered.
- Recognition that partnership is not an end in itself.

(DoH, 2001: 67)

In aiming to build a working alliance relationship, Jenny acknowledges to Rose the shock she must have felt about being told about Fred's conviction and having child protection professionals enter into her life unasked and unwanted. Jenny gives space for her to express her feelings and anxieties about this. Jenny offers her perception that although she and Rose may have differing views about the risks of the situation, that they are essentially both engaged on the same task – of wanting Anna to be safe and well. Jenny gives information to Rose about how and why professionals have developed concerns and about what their expectations are in respect of the child protection plan so that Rose can make informed choices. This enables Rose to accept the reasons for the enforced involvement of professionals, even though she is unhappy about it. She agrees to comply with assessments and child protection visiting as a way of getting done what needs to be done.

This working alliance, then, is the first stage in the assessment process. Clarkson (1993) sees it as the bedrock of the work and considers it necessary for worker and client to frequently revisit these conditions when matters become difficult to ensure that sufficient working engagement is re-established to enable the work to progress again.

The real or person-to-person relationship

As could be seen with the second set of conditions in the working alliance, families in crisis need to feel that their worker is concerned about them at a real and human level. They need to feel that they are met not by a professional persona but by a real person-to-person response (Clarkson, 1993). Buber (1970) termed this an 'I-thou' form of relating, where the other is treated as a subject, a whole being, rather than an 'I-it' interaction, where the other is seen only as an object, a part-being, someone who meets a need or performs a function. Working intersubjectively as a whole person rather than being restricted to role and professional identity, can enable workers to operate more holistically at a real and authentic level (Biestek, 1961; Folgheraiter, 2004). Allowing the worker their own humanity, history and emotionality in the work alongside that of family members arguably allows for mutuality of engagement, empathy, empowerment and self-development, and may give added vitality to the work (Miller and Stiver, 1997; Gordon, 2000; Spencer, 2000).

On one occasion, frustrated with Jenny's involvement, Rose hurls the accusation that Jenny has no idea what it is like to be asked to choose between your partner and your children. Jenny recognises that this is true. As a way of helping herself to empathise with Rose's experience Jenny reconnects with the feelings of loss and fear which emerged when she separated from a previous partner. Her tone of voice, choice of words and expression change as she remembers what has been painful to her and caused her to feel vulnerable. This conveys to Rose that Jenny is deeply touched by what she has said and is beginning to appreciate the depths of her despair. What Rose begins to experience here is Jenny's real felt sense of how difficult this must be for her. Jenny is still asking her to make difficult decisions, but she feels that Jenny understands, at a real human level, how appalling this must be. She feels less alone and less judged.

Not all practitioners may agree that they should meet their clients at a personal as well as a professional level. Some may be concerned that workers who do so are perhaps meeting their own personal and relational needs. Indeed, Clarkson (1993: 34) cautions against this, advising that this approach 'does not include transforming the professional relationship into a social one, nor seeking extraneous personal gratification from the dialogue with the [client]'. It is not an excuse for workers to get their own needs met. In fact, it probably requires the 'most skills, the most self-knowledge and the greatest care because its potential for careless or destructive use is so great' (ibid: 35).

Other workers may view themselves as an objective outsider when working with families, someone who can observe situations dispassionately and form disinterested judgements more safely through so doing. They may even view those who experience feelings about those with whom they are working as overly subjective and even dangerous. However, it is argued that this objective armour is a fiction as:

> *Whether or not it is acknowledged or utilised we ... bring all of us to each encounter and aspects of our personal selves inevitably leak into our professional activities ... our feelings ... resonate in every present interaction, however 'professional' its context. 'Objective professional' and 'subjective personal' constantly overlap and the less aware we are of this the less effective we are in practice.*
> (Ash 1995: 25)

Research evidence supports this assertion, observing how subjectivity and bias have been found to continually undermine the quality of assessment and decision-making (Munro, 1999; Holland, 2000; MacDonald, 2000). Munro's scrutiny of child abuse inquiry reports published in Britain between 1973 and 1994 found that professionals made recurrent common errors of reasoning which related to their feelings, perceptions and cognitive processes. Practitioners were less likely to employ analytic reasoning, a more logical, transparent and rigorous process, as it did not sit comfortably with the need to rapidly sift through large amounts of information in emotionally charged situations. Many became too reliant on empathic and intuitive processes as an alternative. Whilst workers experienced these as more creative and empathic and so appropriate for complex situations involving human interactions and a rapid digest of numerous factors, they did not always recognise their own tendency towards bias and how it influenced their practice. Some, for example, were overly influenced by their first impression of a family (either positive or negative). This affected the way they interpreted new information and they were slow to revise their judgements despite a mounting body of evidence contradicting them. Some workers even went as far as selectively reporting or omitting information from their reports if it conflicted with the view they had formed. Because of the sheer volume of material they uncovered in assessments, workers often took heuristic shortcuts in selecting information to attend to. These were biased towards the facts that come most readily to mind, i.e. those which were vivid, concrete, aroused emotion and were either the first or most recent.

Munro advises that these kind of errors in reasoning can be minimised by bringing them into our awareness and striving consciously to avoid them. This suggests the need for both enhanced self-awareness and for rigorous self-reflection. Both are demanding intellectually and emotionally and will require not only the commitment of the individual practitioner but a context for practice which supports, validates and encourages the worker in recognising and reflecting on the role their emotions and subjective selves play in understanding their intra-psychic, cognitive and inter-personal processes.

Holland (2000) similarly found that worker self-awareness was essential. Her study found that the nature of the relationship formed between social workers and parents during assessments seemed to have some influence over decisions made:

> *... the ability of the parent to enter into a constructive working relationship with the assessing social worker was seen as an indication of the personality of the parent and ultimately perhaps their ability to care for their child.*
> (Holland, 2000: 52)

Whereas parents who could work well within the relationship and be co-operative at a verbal level were seen as motivated and plausible, those who did not were viewed more negatively as inconsistent and passive. Practitioners struggled to form relationships with parents who seemed passive and inarticulate. Such parents were far less likely to have their children returned to them following the assessment and it seems that the parent's capacity to form the working alliance with the professional was being judged as a central indicator, although this was not always within the worker's awareness.

Some social workers seemed somewhat reluctant to accept the extent to which they might affect this process. Others used compensatory tactics to try to minimise the impact of their self on their practice. Holland felt this was a futile aim. Instead she suggests that workers should attempt to disentangle the interpersonal processes and dynamics within assessments in order to be more aware of the contribution both they and families make to the forming of the relationship. Such reflection is good modelling for families, given that the development of an individual's reflective capacity, understanding, and self-awareness are good indicators for future change (Saari, 1986).

Working at a depth level

These findings, then, suggest that even where practitioners would prefer to manage their work at a 'surface' level, i.e. being rational, objective and procedural, interactions and dynamics occur additionally at a 'depth' level, where personal feelings and processes related to both the worker and the client, which are unprocessed and out-of-conscious awareness, additionally come into play and require attending to (Howe, 1996). Psychodynamic theories provide a range of ways of thinking about some of the ways in which people perceive and respond to their situations and each other which appear to have less to do with reason and choice and more to do with the impact of previous experiences and unconscious processes.

One example of this is the way that families' opposition to assessment and intervention may be thought about. Consideration from a humanistic perspective might emphasise the normative nature of the hostility families feel about enforced professional intrusion into their lives. A structural analysis would be concerned with families' powerlessness in such situations and see opposition as a constructive challenge and evidence of a more empowered stance. Both of these perspectives are, of course, very much valid, and receive important attention elsewhere in this chapter and in the book as a whole. However, psychodynamic reflection on possible 'resistance' adds a further useful window into understanding. Resistance, from this perspective, is seen as a psychological defence mechanism protecting the individual from overwhelming feelings, primitive terrors or unpalatable realities which cannot be recognised and managed more overtly due to previous experiences, particularly from early childhood, which have meant the individual has not been able to internalise a capacity to contain and process powerful

emotions (Bion, 1962; Winniccott, 1965; Bow, 1988; Mitchell et al., 1989). Resistance is construed as an unconscious process, with the individual compelled to act from outside of their awareness in ways that serve archaic needs and fears rather than promote progress in the current situation. Individuals might be thought to be projecting thoughts and feelings onto the worker, which are based on characters from their internal world. These 'internal objects' are not literal, based on actual persons. Rather they are representations – internal mental structures formed during early development through a series of experiences with significant others and internalised through a process of introjection. How these processes impact upon relationships can be understood through the concepts of transference and counter-transference.

Transference

In the concept of 'transference', an individual's patterns of relating, based on earlier relationships, emerge in the here-and-now through an unusual, unexpected or particularly intense reaction to another person:

> . . . the experiencing of feelings, drives, attitudes, fantasies and defences towards a person in the present which do not befit that person but are a repetition of reactions originating in regard to significant persons of early childhood, unconsciously displaced on to figures in the present.
> (Mattinson 1992: 33)

An individual may treat a professional as if they were someone other than who they are, transferring onto the worker the characteristics of a figure from their internal world. The real person that is the worker can become obscured. This happens with a real sense of immediacy in the interpersonal relating and, as the worker, it may feel at times as if there is a real dissonance between who you are intending to be and how the client experiences you to be.

A new worker, Sam, takes over working with Rose. He feels great sympathy for Rose in her difficult situation and wishes to work supportively with her in the assessment. He uses all his interpersonal skills in attempting to engage her and to demonstrate he cares about her concerns and wants to hear them. However, Rose persists in treating him as if he is hostile. She becomes angry and upset when they meet. She interprets his eye contact with her as intrusive staring, as a way of trying to intimidate her. She hears his attempts to explore the situation and elicit her views as attempts to control and break her.

In other situations, there may be less of a dissonance and it is more that the client's feelings are an extreme or intense version of what might be expected.

These relational templates were formed through the individual's contact with the world in early childhood, particularly in the relationships with the parents or parent figures. They were a way of helping the psyche make sense of and predict the world and had a purpose in helping the infant and young child survive and adapt to less-than-optimal circumstances. In these ways transference can be seen as an out-of-date way of relating (belonging to the past not the present) which is often unhelpful in current relationships. Reder and Duncan (1999) in their analysis of factors leading to abuse-related deaths of infants note how the parents implicated in these circumstances often have 'unresolved care or control issues' due to their own inadequate or abusive parenting as children. Not only may these emerge in the parents' relationships with each other and their children, but also in the relationships with professionals, e.g. some parents will view all professionals in authority as necessarily hostile as a result of an inner world which is peopled by critical, harsh and punitive 'objects'. This might cause them to feel frightened, angry, bitter or resentful and their reactions to the worker will be based on these feelings rather than the way the worker is attempting to interact.

Workers may often be alert to where the transference is negative but, where the internal world additionally has benign figures, transference may also be positive. The worker may be idealised, imbued with a range of attributes which offer hope to the client. These positive projections may be very helpful at the start of a working relationship in engaging the client. However, they can become problematic when the worker's 'feet of clay' become apparent and the idealised image shatters. Idealisation can quickly then become denigration.

Not all practitioners will feel comfortable with the concept of transference, citing the way that some psychoanalysts have abused it to negate the very real impact of their own behaviour upon the client (Masson, 1988). I am here, though,

presenting it as part of an integrative, intersubjective and anti-oppressive model in which the worker additionally is aware of and attuned to how their own self, power and actions influence the client's experience. It is essential for the worker to consider first if the client is simply reacting to the stimulus they are providing, e.g. their own warmth, coldness, unreliability, lateness, uncertainty, hostility, etc., before they begin to consider the possibility of transference (Rowan, 1998). Similarly, it is essential to recognise the normative nature of the fear and powerlessness many families will feel during mandatory assessments that might determine the future of their family life. Families need the stresses they are under to be recognised and their own emotional needs and circumstances to be given some focus (DoH, 2001). This does not mean minimising parents limitations in parenting skills or the very real risks some pose to their children but recognising that parents will feel blamed and threatened in these circumstances and will become hostile or withdrawn if the approach is not sensitive to this.

Given these caveats, though, should the worker fail to consider the possibility of transference there may be a danger of them 'grossly underestimating' how the client's reactions, feelings and fantasies may be distorting their present reactions (Mattinson, 1992: 34). Without this, the worker is arguably less able to recognise and understand the range of communications from families. Working collaboratively with parents on being able to understand the possible meanings of their behaviour also offers them the possibility of developing ways to control their own behaviour better, as it becomes more within their conscious awareness.

Counter-transference

In the simplest terms 'counter-transference' covers the range of emotional and psychological responses the worker has to the client. It may be quite tricky to un-pick which of these reactions would be provoked in most workers by the client's behaviour or transference and which 'belong' to the worker. The latter may be termed 'proactive' counter-transference, defined more as material brought to the interpersonal relationship as an artefact from the worker's own history and internal world (Mackewn, 1997). This can be noticed as patterns in the practitioner's relational style. For example, some workers may often find themselves wanting to rescue or nurture their clients, whilst others might secretly experience positive feelings from being in a powerful position when assessing families in child protection situations.

'Reactive' counter-transference, by contrast, is where the worker may feel their response to have been almost conjured out of them, induced by the client's behaviour (Mackewn, 1997). It may feel rather alien and unlike what the worker might normally expect of themselves. A worker who is normally warm and empathic with clients, for example, might find him/herself 'irrationally' provoked by a mother who is behaving more like a rebellious teenager, and want to punish or control them. Reactive counter-transference can provide useful information about the client's patterns of relating and their internal world. It can give a window into understanding not only how a parent might feel towards their children but how it may feel to be a child being parented by them.

Where feelings seem unbearable or parts of the self unwelcome, they may need to be denied or rejected by being 'split off' from conscious awareness and acceptance. They may then be repressed into the unconscious and/or projected into someone else without being recognised at a conscious level. Here the worker may begin to experience and enact feelings which do not belong to them.

> Rose grew up with a physically and emotionally abusive father who constantly criticised her and undermined her. She felt useless and worthless. The social work assessment has caused similar feelings to be awoken in her at an unconscious level, particularly as Sam is male. These feelings are unbearable to Rose and need to be 'split off', and projected into Sam.
>
> Sam begins to feel rejected and undermined, that nothing that he does will work. He worries that his lack of success in engaging Rose will cause other professionals to question his capabilities. This causes him to feel angry with Rose and determined to make sure she complies with the child protection plan. He is determined she will not see his vulnerability and becomes critical and controlling in his interactions with her. In this way he could be seen as having both experienced Rose's split off feelings of denigration and as having identified with her transference of him as her father and enacted this.

Rowan (1998) offers a useful summary of different counter-transference positions that can assist practitioners in analysing their responses.

Attachment

Attachment theory can be used as a tool for reflecting on the dyad of self and other in the work. Using the categories identified through the adult attachment interview (George et al., 1996), it is possible to see which pattern or strategy you and/or the client most seem to enact. Individuals who are thought to be 'secure-autonomous' will either have developed a secure internal working model in childhood, based on consistently available, safe and attuned parenting, or will have resolved that insecurity at a later stage through reparative experiences (Crittenden, 2000). They are able to draw on both cognition and effect to respond to situations and are able to empathise with both their own and other people's perspectives. Secure-autonomous workers are thought to be able to show self-awareness, emotional and psychological strength and flexibility, have realistic expectations of the work, hold appropriate professional boundaries, and be able to work in a supportive manner (Morrison and Baim, 2002). This is clearly an ideal to be aimed for, with practitioners aiming for a resolved-secure position through self-work where they have not been gifted this through childhood experience.

Individuals classed as having a dismissive attachment style are thought to be cognitively-rather than emotionally-organised in their functioning. They tend to dismiss negative feelings in themselves and interpersonal problems or omit them from their discussions. This will have resulted from developing an avoidant attachment during childhood in response to a parenting environment that was consistently hostile, neglectful or rejecting (Schofield, 2002). During assessments they often distance themselves from the past or idealise it, e.g. 'I can't really remember very much about my childhood' or 'Things were absolutely fine when I was growing up, my father was a good man, a strong man' (from someone who grew up in a family where the father regularly beat the children and their mother). What the worker may notice in an assessment is that their attempts to expand and explore are met with a thin, minimal narrative. For example, when asking a parent to complete a 'life river', an exercise to map out the client's history chronologically, it is completed very quickly and there is minimal detail. Clients may simply look at you blankly when you invite them to fill in the gaps. It is important to be aware of the spectrum of behaviours that may fall into this category (Crittenden, 2002). Whereas some people may just seem careful in their interactions, thinking before speaking, others may appear quite 'cut-off' from 'expected effect' regarding matters of significance. Some individuals may attempt to soothe or please you as a worker, others may be quite controlling in the interaction.

A spectrum of behaviours can also be seen in those people who are classed as 'preoccupied' in their attachment style. These individuals are affectively-rather than cognitively-organised, so that their own feelings and perspective dominates for them and the experience of others can be dismissed. They were likely to have grown up in a parenting environment that was inconsistent and developed either an insecure-ambivalent or a disorganised attachment as a response to their childhood. What may be noticeable in the assessment is that the parent has become preoccupied by negative emotions and their own experiences to the exclusion of everything else, including the experience of their children. The narrative will be overflowing so that the worker can hardly get a word in, follow a theme or make sense of the whole. The parent will speak first, interrupt, wander and elaborate. The past seems alive in the present and traumas and difficulties remain unresolved. Individuals seem unable to make sense of their own lives or the behaviour of others and they seem unable to believe they can have control over their own future as a result of their behaviour.

As a worker, it can be useful to think of how we react to the client's way of being and which of these three attachment styles we feel most comfortable working with. How do we feel when working with a preoccupied client, for example? Are we able to maintain a secure-autonomous position, enabling the client to slow down the narrative and bring some cognition in to mediate the overwhelming effect? Or does it evoke our own attachment insecurity, perhaps provoking a dismissive response, where we are irritated by the flood of feelings, attempt to control the situation, and categorise the parent negatively in our assessment for not being able to think more constructively about their situation? (Morrison and Baim, 2002).

Developing a reflexive stance

In all of these cases it is crucial for workers to develop their own reflexivity. This can be defined as a critically reflective capacity which enables the worker to untangle where the material originates from, to be able to make sense of what the client may be communicating through their behaviour, and to have an awareness of their own patterns in order to recognise their impact and challenge them (D'Cruz, 2006). Reflexivity demands a capacity to process and work at both a cognitive and emotional level and to move back and forth between your own and your client's past and present. In this way it invokes both reflection-on-action and reflection-in-action (Schön, 1983) from the worker in order for both worker and client to learn and develop through the interaction.

Supervision will be an essential tool here to make sense of how our personal selves relate to our experiences with clients but it needs to be of the right kind if it is not to be counter-productive (Yip, 2006). It should provide safety and containment in order for the worker to be able to experience sufficient trust and safety to negotiate and work with such personal and emotive processes (Ruch, 2005). The organisation as a whole, not just the individual supervisor, has a role here, in terms of setting an overall context where emotional processes are recognised and valued. Arguably, families can only be 'held' and attuned to if the worker's own needs for holding, security, safety and attunement are met by 'congenial' working arrangements (Heard and Lake, 1997: 169).

Ultimately, though, whatever the role of the agency, I would suggest that workers must take their own responsibility for developing self-awareness and ensuring their own emotional availability in the work. It may be useful for the worker to re-consider how and why they chose this area of work. Ash (1995:26) suggests that: 'we tend to get drawn into either work or life experiences that relate to our individual internal issues', and that we are: 'influenced by, often unacknowledged, forces springing from our personal/individual experience'. It may be helpful to question whether there is a pay-off in working with people who may be vulnerable, in crisis or in despair. Perhaps we feel powerful or in control by comparison? Our desire to feel needed or to rescue may be met. We may feel enlivened by the high emotions and rapidly changing context of a crisis situation.

Some workers will have their own reasons for not engaging in this self-examination and guarding themselves against feeling the distress of the people with whom they are working. A rich resource is then lost and the worker may become rather one-dimensional (Ruch, 1998). For some workers, individual counselling or therapy may be needed where such unresolved issues prevent the worker from expanding their emotional availability and repertoire in their practice.

The reparative relationship

The previous section discussed how parents may expect workers to act into the role their transference has assigned them. When this is not enacted, this can be a novel experience for the parent, which can contribute to the development of new patterns of relating to others.

> In supervision Sam begins to reflect on his reactions to Rose and recognises how he had become the harsh and punitive figure she was expecting him to be. Reflecting on how the interaction with Rose caused him to feel enables him to empathise with her position rather than continuing to act in the way she was provoking and expecting from him. Rather than being controlling and critical he becomes warmer and more understanding in his approach to her, whilst still being able to maintain the boundaries his role demands. He asks Rose to explain to him how he makes her feel and helps her begin to make connections between the way she expects him to be and the powerlessness, fear and anger she felt towards her abusive father whilst growing up. Rose is pleasantly surprised to find that Sam is now not reacting towards her in the negative way she is used to and instead is prepared to help her understand herself. She feels met and cared for. This is a new experience for her and begins to challenge her pre-existing views of the world.

In therapeutic work the goals of the intervention might specifically include an intention that the worker provide an experience for the client which allows there to be some repair towards the damage caused when the original parenting experience was deficient, abusive, over-protective, absent or traumatic (Clarkson,

1993). Within child protection assessments this is unlikely to be a goal but it may be something that can be promoted along the way. What makes this relevant to assessment is the recognition that it is these deficiencies that lead to the kind of unresolved care and control conflicts which Reder and Duncan (1999) have identified as contributing to unsafe home environments for children. So, a mother who was ignored and not attuned to in childhood is likely to benefit from a worker who is able to show good attention to her needs. Not only might this be likely to increase her engagement in the assessment but it may help to repair the internal lacuna that meant she had been unable to attend to her children's needs in the first place. Winnicott's (1965) suggestions about how a practitioner may replicate the early parental 'holding environment', Bion's (1962) capacity of the worker to act as 'container' and Kohut's (1977) empathic attunement are useful models for the worker to follow here. Trust can be built up for the client as they experience the worker as a steady, safe and containing presence who is able to hear and recognise their feelings and needs without being fearful, rejecting or denigrating.

Working in this way requires emotional strength and humility on the part of the worker to acknowledge what they may have done to provoke a negative response in the client, whether this is at a real or transference level. Doing so may powerfully challenge the client's expectations and can demonstrate that relationships can be worked on and improved.

> *I do not think clients are helped in acquiring a better sense of reality if the worker is too superior a being – one who believes that he does not collude at times, that he cannot or should not be influenced, and that he sometimes does not walk into traps which the clients set for him. A worker who has walked into a trap and can then do something about it – can resolve something, can relinquish some aspect of his behaviour – is not only providing a more realistic model, but gives the client hope that he can do likewise.*
>
> (Mattinson 1992: 41)

Working with children and young people in assessments

The children in the family where there have been concerns are even closer to the source of these developmental needs having not been met. Even in a short interaction the worker may be able to reparatively offer a different model to the child of how adults may be with them. This can challenge the child's perception of him/herself and of the world. They may be able then to internalise a benign internal 'object' and a sense of being worthy of love and care, before lifelong patterns are set-up. Such interactions, however brief, can help provide a foundation for the development of resilience (Iwaniec et al., 2006). This does not suggest that workers should be attempting to set themselves up as primary attachment figures to children in these circumstances, or taking sole responsibility for repairing the previous deficient or abusive parenting experiences, but rather to embody some aspects of good parenting, such as warmth, interest, and guidance, in the relationships which they form with their child clients. By drawing on therapeutic principles in assessments workers may 'effect change, . . . enable children to be in touch with their wishes and feelings, and can facilitate their means of expressing these' (Bell, 2002: 7). If they provide consistency, boundaries and attunement,workers may become secondary attachment figures for children; this will be particularly crucial for those children who have previously lacked a 'secure base' (Bowlby, 1988) and are in deep shock in the midst of child protection investigations (Bell, op. cit.).

Current legislation, policy and practice guidance such as the Assessment Framework (DoH, 2000), emphasise children's right to be consulted and to have their wishes and feelings taken into account, with due consideration to their age and understanding, when decisions are being made which concern them. The importance of this in being able to fully assess children's needs in order to protect them has been emphasised in inspections (e.g. Joint Chief Inspectors, 2005) and Inquiry reports (e.g. Laming, 2003). Children and young people themselves testify to the significance of this in a number of research studies (e.g. Bell, 2002). I would suggest that the relational considerations discussed elsewhere in this chapter are as pertinent to children as they are to adults. What will be emphasised here are some relational factors identified by research as particularly facilitating or hindering of children's contributions to assessment and decision-making.

One study (Bell, 2002) highlighted how children are likely to feel frightened about the accuracy of information collected about them and the potential consequences of what they had shared during the assessment, e.g. whether or not they might be removed from home. They wanted to be involved in decisions about them but, unsurprisingly, felt intimidated by the size and formality of decision-making forums such as case conferences. Some remained wary and distrustful throughout the work. Children often felt powerless and that they lacked choice about what was happening to them; some, though, were able to exercise control within the interaction in more subversive ways through not communicating with the worker, perhaps by changing the subject.

It was notable that many of the children in Bell's study had experienced a particular worker to be helpful and significant in their lives. In fact, the quality of the relationships they formed with their social workers was found to be by far the most important aspect of the service for them. Research studies (e.g. Cleaver, 1996; Triseliotis et al., 1998; Hill, 1999; Prior et al., 1999; de Winter and Noom, 2003; Cleaver, Walker and Meadows, 2004) identify a number of qualities that children require social workers to demonstrate in order for this trusting relationship to form; they need workers to be available, open, supportive, consistent, and reliable; to listen to them, and take what they say seriously; to treat them with respect and non-judgementalism; to provide boundaries which evoke safety rather than control; to show human aspects such as concern, friendliness, kindness and humour. These are qualities which reflect a range of personal and emotional qualities as well as ethical commitments and professional skills in the individual social worker which are then enacted within the interpersonal relationship.

Conversely, children report feeling marginalised and dismissed in decision-making when they feel patronised, controlled, insufficiently listened to and involved or consulted with (Biehal et al., 1995; Williamson and Butler, 1995; Selwyn, 1996; Dearden and Becker, 2000; Bell, 2002). Many, too, feel disempowered, betrayed and unsafe rather than protected when workers share information, which they would prefer to be confidential, with other professionals 'for their own good' (Berman-Rossi and Rossi, 1990; Ryan et al., 1995; Daniels and Jenkins, 2000; van Rooyen and Engelbrecht, 2001; Dalrymple, 2001).

Children's demands of their relationships with their social workers are often not met. The current context of child protection work has been criticised as service- rather than child-led, with onerous administrative demands causing case management and routinised practice to dominate (Schofield and Brown, 1999; Leveridge, 2002; Garrett, 2003). Social workers are said to be 'diverting time and attention away from personal contact and towards filling in forms and making telephone calls' (Leveridge, 2002: 22). The direct work with children so valued by children has dwindled with many workers feeling that they lack the time, skills, confidence or mandate to work directly with children or even feel that it is not part of their role (Biehal, 1995; Sinclair et al., 1995; Triseliotis et al., 1995; Schofield, 1998). This is not welcomed by children who feel that 'too many social workers remain behind their desks' and that there is 'too little personal involvement' (de Winter and Noom, 2003: 326).

Individual children's voices will not be heard and their rights and needs will be compromised unless such bureaucratic structures shift to enable workers to prioritise more direct and relational practice with children, based on therapeutic and ethical principles (Bell, 2002). Rather than workers feeling constrained to meet externally set deadlines (e.g. those of the Assessment Framework), workers need to feel they have the time and environment available to carry out the kind of open-ended work which is most effective in engaging children to express their wishes and feelings in assessments (Thomas and O'Kane, 2000). It is essential for workers, and organisations, to appreciate how children communicate differently to adults. They need a communicative environment which is child-centred which uses creative, playful, open-ended and active methods, rather than just talking or invasive questions which close them down, making them feel suspicious and/or uncomfortable (Luckock, Lefevre and Orr et al., 2006).

Conclusion

The type of relationship formed between social workers and families who are subject to child protection assessments can be the key to both engagement and to whether family members feel sufficiently safe to explore the kind of sensitive areas that the assessment demands. This promotes decisions being based on the fullest knowledge possible, because parents and children have been able to contribute. Where trust is felt, family members are more likely to let

down their barriers, to acknowledge difficulties and to begin to work on themselves. This makes for a more dynamic assessment, where change and development become part of the process.

Much is required from workers in order to achieve this. They need to be not only knowledgeable, skilled, and ethically committed to principles of anti-oppressive practice, but able and prepared to use themselves fully, having developed their emotional capacity through self-awareness. They cannot do this alone – organisations must play their part through offering a context which facilitates the worker providing the conditions for practice outlined in this chapter and containing process-informed supervision in which the worker feels safe to explore these issues. Nests of containing relational contexts can then be observed: as the organisation provides a 'holding' environment for the worker, they can 'hold' the parents who, in their turn, are able to provide a safe, facilitating and nurturing environment within which the children can flourish.

References

Ash, E. (1995) Supervision: Taking Account of Feelings. In Pritchard, J. (Ed.) *Good Practice in Supervision: Statutory and Voluntary Organisations.* London, Jessica Kingsley.

Bell, M. (2002) Promoting Children's Rights through the Use of Relationship. *Child and Family Social Work.* 7: 1, 1–11.

Berman-Rossi, T. and Rossi, P. (1990) Confidentiality and Informed Consent in School Social Work. *Social Work in Education,* 12: 3, 195–207.

Biehal, N. et al. (1995) *Moving on: Young People and Leaving Care Schemes.* London: HMSO.

Biestek, F. (1961) *The Casework Relationship.* London: Allen and Unwin.

Bion, W.R. (1962) *Learning from Experience.* London: Maresfield.

Bogo, M. (1993) The Student/Field Instructor Relationship: The Critical Factor in Field Education. *The Clinical Supervisor.* 11: 2, 23–36.

Bow, J. (1988) Treating Resistant Children. *Child and Adolescent Social Work.* 5: 1, 3–15.

Bowlby, J. (1988) *A Secure Base: Clinical Applications of Attachment Theory.* London: Routledge.

Buber, M. (1970) *I and Thou.* New York: Simon and Schuster.

Clarkson, C. (1993) A Multiplicity of Psychotherapeutic Relationships. In Clarkson, P. and Pokorny, M. *On Psychotherapy.* London: Whurr.

Cleaver, H. (1996) *Focus on Teenagers.* London: HMSO.

Cleaver, H., Walker, S. and Meadows, P. (2004) *Assessing Children's Needs and Circumstances: The Impact of The Assessment Framework.* London: Jessica Kingsley.

Compton, B. and Galloway, B. (Eds.) (1984) *Social Work Processes.* 3rd edn. Illinois: The Dorsey Press.

Cooper, A., Hetherington, R. and Katz, I. (2003) *The Risk Factor: Making the Child Protection System Work for Children.* London: Demos.

Cooper, R. (1994) *The Voice of the Child: Piaget and the Children Act Interpreted.* Norwich: University of East Anglia, Social work monographs no. 126.

Crittenden, P. (2000) A Dynamic-Maturational Approach to Continuity and Change in Pattern of Attachment. In Crittenden, P. and Claussen, A. *The Organisation of Attachment Relationships: Maturation Culture and Context.* Cambridge: Cambridge University Press.

Dalrymple, J. (2001) Safeguarding Young People through Confidential Advocacy Services. *Child and Family Social Work.* 6: 2, 149–60.

Daniels, D. and Jenkins, P. (2000) *Therapy with Children: Children's Rights, Confidentiality and the Law.* London: Sage.

D'Cruz, H., Gillingham, P. and Melendez, S. (2006) Reflexivity, its Meanings and Relevance for Social Work: A Critical Review of the Literature. *British Journal of Social Work,* Feb.

de Winter, M. and Noom, M. (2003) Someone who Treats You as an Ordinary Human Being . . . Homeless Youth Examine the Quality of Professional Care. *British Journal of Social Work.* 33: 3, 325–37.

Dearden, C. and Becker, S. (2000) Listening to Children: Meeting the Needs of Young Carers. In: Kemshall, H. and Littlechild, R. (Eds.) *User Involvement and Participation in Social Care.* London: Jessica Kingsley.

DoH, DfEE and Home Office (2000) *Framework for the Assessment of Children in Need and their Families.* London: HMSO.

DoH (2001) *The Children Act Now: Messages from Research.* London: HMSO.

Dumbrill, G.C. (2006) Parental Experience of Child Protection: A Qualitative Study. *Child Abuse and Neglect.* 30, 27–37.

Egan, G. (2002) *The Skilled Helper: A Problem-Management and Opportunity-Development Approach to Helping,* 7th edn. Pacific Grove, CA: Brooks/Cole.

Folgheraiter, F. (2004) *Relational Social Work: Toward Networking and Societal Practices.* London: Jessica Kingsley.

Francis, J. (2002) Implementing the 'Looking after Children in Scotland' Materials: Panacea or Stepping-Stone? *Social Work Education.* 21: 4, 449–60.

Garrett, P.M. (2003) Swimming with Dolphins: The Assessment Framework, New Labour and New Tools for Social Work with Children and Families. *British Journal of Social Work.* 33:b 4, 441–63.

George, C., Kaplan, N. and Main, M. (1996) *The Adult Attachment Interview.* Unpublished manuscript. Berkeley, Department of Psychology, University of California, 3rd Edition.

Gordon, W. (2000) The Relational Paradigm In Contemporary Psychoanalysis: Towards a Psychodynamically Informed Social Work Perspective. *Social Service Review.* 74, 352–79.

Head, A. (1998) The Child's Voice in Child and Family Social Work Decision Making: The Perspective of a Guardian ad Litem. *Child and Family Social Work.* 3: 3, 189–96.

Heard, D. and Lake, B. (1997) *The Challenge of Attachment for Caregiving.* London: Routledge.

Hill, M. (1999) What's The Problem? Who Can Help? The Perspectives of Children and Young People on Their Well-Being and on Helping Professionals. *Journal of Social Work Practice.* 13: 2, 135–45.

Holland, S. (2000) The Assessment Relationship: Interactions Between Social Workers and Parents. *British Journal of Social Work.* 30, 149–63.

Howe, D. (1996) Surface and Depth in Social Work Practice. In Parton, N. (Ed.) *Social Theory, Social Change and Social Work.* London: Routledge.

Howe, D. (1997) Psychosocial and Relationship-Based Theories for Child and Family Social Work: Politics, Philosophy, Psychology and Welfare Practice. *Child and Family Social Work.* 2, 162–9.

Howe, D. (1998) Relationship-based Thinking and Practice in Social Work. *Journal of Social Work Practice.* 12, 45–56.

Howe, D. (2002) *Psychosocial Work, in Social Work: Themes, Issues and Critical Debates.* In Adams, R.,

Dominelli, L. and Payne, M., 2nd edn. Basingstoke, Macmillan.

Iwaniec, D., Larkin, E and Higgins, S. (2006) Research Review: Risk and Resilience in Cases of Emotional Abuse. *Child and Family Social Work*, 11, 73–82.

Joint Chief Inspectors (2005) *Safeguarding Children: a Joint Chief Inspectors Report on Arrangements to Safeguard Children*. London: The Stationery Office.

Kohut, H. (1977) *The Restoration of the Self*. Connecticut, International Universities Press.

Kroll, B. (1995) Working with Children. In Kaganas, F., King, M. and Piper, C. (Eds.) *Legislating for Harmony: Partnership under the Children Act 1989*. London: Jessica Kingsley.

Laming, L. (2003) *The Victoria Climbié Inquiry: Report of an Inquiry*. http://www.victoria-climbie-inquiry.org.uk/finreport/finreport.htm.

Leveridge, M. (2002) Mac-Social Work: The Routinisation of Professional Activity. *Maatskaplike Werk/Social Work*. 38: 4, 354–62.

Luckock, B., Lefevre, M. and Orr, D. et al. (2006) *Knowledge Review on Teaching, Learning and Assessing Communication Skills With Children and Young People in Social Work Education*. London: Social Care Institute for Excellence.

MacDonald, G. (2000) *Effective Interventions for Child Abuse and Neglect: An Evidence Based Approach to Evaluating and Planning Interventions*. Chichester: Wiley.

Mackewn, J. (1997) *Developing Gestalt Counselling*. London: Sage.

Marziali, E. and Alexander, L (1991) 'The Power of the Therapeutic Relationship'. *American Journal of Orthopsychiatry*, 61: 3, 383–91.

Masson, J. (1988) *Against Therapy: Emotional Tyranny and the Myth of Psychological Healing*. New York: Atheneum.

Mattinson, J. (1975/1992) *The Reflective Process in Social Work Supervision*. London: Tavistock.

Miller, J.B. and Stiver, I. (1997) *The Healing Connection*. Boston: Beacon Press.

Mitchell, S. et al. (1989) Counselling Troubled Adolescents: An Evaluation of a Statewide Training Program. *Journal of Sociology and Social Welfare*. 16: 3, 95–108.

Moran, P., Ghate, D. and van der Merwe, A. (2004) *What Works in Parenting Support? A Review of the International Evidence*. London: HMSO.

Morrison, T. and Baim, C. (2002) *Attachment-Based Interviewing*, unpublished course handouts.

Munro, E. (1999) Common Errors of Reasoning. *Child Abuse and Neglect*. 23: 8, 745–58.

Norcross, J.C. (1986) Eclectic Psychotherapy: An Introduction and Overview. In Norcross, J.C. (Ed.) *Handbook of Eclectic Psychotherapy*. New York: Brunner/Mazel.

Payne, M. (2005) *Modern Social Work Theory*. 3rd edn. Basingstoke: Palgrave Macmillan.

Prior, V., Lynch, M.A. and Glaser, D. (1999) Responding to Child Sexual Abuse: An Evaluation of Social Work by Children and Their Carers. *Child and Family Social Work*. 4: 2, 131–43.

Reder, P. and Duncan, S. (1999) *Lost Innocents: A Follow-up Study of Fatal Child Abuse*. London: Routledge.

Rogers, C.R. (1951) *Client-centered Therapy: Its Current Practice, Implications and Theory*. London: Constable.

Rowan, J. (1998) *The Reality Game: A Guide to Humanistic Counselling and Psychotherapy*, 2nd edn. London: Routledge.

Ruch, G. (1998) Direct Work With Children: The Practitioner's Perspective. *Practice*. 10: 1, 37–44.

Ruch, G. (2005) Relationship-based Practice and Reflective Practice: Holistic Approaches to Contemporary Child Care Social Work. *Child and Family Social Work*. 10, 111–23.

Ruegger, M. (2001) Seen and Heard But How Well Informed? Children's Perceptions of the Guardian ad Litem Service. *Children and Society*. 15: 3, 133–45.

Ryan, V., Wilson, K. and Fisher, T. (1995) Developing Partnerships in Therapeutic Work with Children. *Journal of Social Work Practice*. 9: 2, 131–40.

Saari, C. (1986) The Created Relationship: Transference, Countertransference and the Therapeutic Culture. *Clinical Social Work Journal*. 14: 1, 39–51.

Schofield, G. (1998) Inner and Outer Worlds: A Psychosocial Framework for Child and Family Social Work. *Child and Family Social Work*. 3, 57–67.

Schofield, G. and Brown, K. (1999) Being There: A Family Centre Worker's Role as a Secure Base for Adolescent Girls in Crisis. *Child and Family Social Work*. 4: 1, 21–31.

Schofield, G (2002) *Attachment Theory: An Introduction for Social Workers*. Norwich: University of East Anglia: School of Social Work and Psychosocial Studies.

Schön, D.A. (1983) *The Reflective Practitioner: How Professionals Think in Action*. New York: Basic Books.

Selwyn, J. (1996) Ascertaining Children's Wishes and Feelings in Relation to Adoption. *Adoption and Fostering*. 20: 3, 14–20.

Sinclair, R., Garnett, L. and Berridge, D. (1995) *Social Work and Assessment with Adolescents*. London: National Children's Bureau.

Spencer, R. (2000) A Comparison of Relational Psychologies. *Stone Center Working Paper*, No. 5.

Thomas, N. and O'Kane, C. (2000) Discovering What Children Think: Connections between Research and Practice. *British Journal of Social Work*. 30: 6, 819–35.

Trevithick. P. (2003) Effective Relationship-Based Practice: A Theoretical Exploration. *Journal of Social Work Practice*. 17: 2, 163–76.

Triseliotis, J. et al. (1995) *Teenagers and the Social Work Services*. London: DoH.

Truax, C.B. and Carkhuff, R.R. (1967) *Toward Effective Counselling and Psychotherapy*. New Jersey: Aldine.

Turnell, A. and Edwards, S. (1997) Aspiring to Partnership: The Signs of Safety Approach to Child Protection. *Child Abuse Review*. 6, 179–190

Turney, D. and Tanner, K. (2001) Working with Neglected Children and Their Families. *Journal of Social Work Practice*. 15, 193–220.

van Rooyen, C. and Engelbrecht, A.N. (2001) Confidentiality: Investigating the Impact of Breaches of Confidentiality on Teenage Children in Care. *Maatskaplike Werk/Social Work*. 37: 1, 84–97.

Williamson, H. and Butler, I. (1995) No One Ever Listens to Us: Interviewing Children and Young People. In Cloke, C. and Davies, M. (Eds.) *Participation and Empowerment in Child Protection*. London: Pitman.

Winnicott, D. (1965) *The Maturational Process and the Facilitating Environment*. London, Hogarth Press.

Yip, K. (2006) Self-reflection in Reflective Practice: A Note of Caution. *British Journal of Social Work* 36, 777–88.

CHAPTER 7

Building Relationships with Involuntary Clients in Child Protection: Lessons from Successful Practice

Ken Barter

Introduction

Building reciprocal helping relationships is considered to be the core of social work practice. Many challenges and tensions are associated with making this core a central tenet in child protection. It is a field of practice well acknowledged to be fraught with crises (Swift and Callaghan, 2006; CASW, 2003, 2005; Kufeldt and McKenzie, 2003; Wharf, 2002, 2003; Barter, 2000, 2001a,b, 2002, 2003, 2004, 2005; Berg and Kelly, 2000; Prilleltensky, Nelson and Peirson, 2001; Schorr, 1998; Waldfogel, 1998). These crises are associated with social injustices attached to the continuing critical problem of child and family poverty; the pervasiveness of child maltreatment; the increasing numbers of children coming into the care of the state; the continuing crises in foster care; the increase in the use of food banks by families with children; the continuing absence of investments in prevention and early intervention; the increase in violence within families, schools, and communities; and the ever continuing negative public attitudes towards poor and disadvantaged citizens (Campaign, 2000, 2006; Trocmé et al., 2001, 2005; Lundy, 2004; Kufeldt and McKenzie, 2003; Willms, 2002; Barter, 2002, 2003; Conway, 2001; Prilleltensky et al., 2001; Pulkington and Ternowetsky, 1997; Ross, Shillington and Lochhead, 1994).

Child protection organisations and social work, as the predominate profession within child protection (Callahan, 1993) are in a difficult bind in the midst of these social injustices as they endeavour to manage and deliver complex and competing statutory obligations. Mandatory and risk assessment policies and procedures have created within the general public and with child serving professionals the idea that child protection consists of reporting and investigation, being *'forensic'* units with a blaming dimension attached and establishing who is accountable (Lindsey, 2004; Melton, 2003; Wharf, 2003; Roberts, 1991). As a result, child welfare agencies are coerced into devoting the majority of

resources to these activities. Evidence gathering and preparation of actual or potential court action have taken significant human and fiscal resources from other essential activities such as prevention, early intervention, and family support initiatives in terms of community capacity building and resource development to respond to environmental concerns affecting families.

The investigative role in child protection has placed workers in positions of doing more judging than helping, more investigation than relationship building, more following rules and protocols than creative intervention and risk taking, more relying on tools and instruments than professional integrity and assessments, more attending to the needs of the organisation than to the needs of families and children, and more reacting after family breakdowns than interventions to prevent breakdowns. These practice realities represent fundamental barriers in engaging in relationships with families in order to realise desirable outcomes for children (Barter, 2005; Lindsey, 2004; Wharf, 2003; Turnell and Edwards, 1999; Berg and Kelly, 2000; Prilleltensky et al., 2001). The report entitled *Child Welfare Project: Creating Conditions for Good Practice* produced by the Canadian Association of Social Workers (CASW, 2003) acknowledge the presence of these barriers. Data collected across Canada from over one thousand social workers involved in child protection identify other barriers such as low worker morale, fears of liability and prosecution, lack of experienced and trained social workers, inadequate financial and human resources to respond to demand, the adversarial process of investigation, and the overall residual approach to child protection work. A quote from this report captures the essence of what is taking place in practice:

In the meantime, in many parts of the country practitioner morale is poor. Caseloads are heavy, there is a shortage of qualified social workers, practitioners are poorly paid, the attrition rate is high, and there is a major 'image' problem in many communities. Child protection work is always stressful and is sometimes high profile, and social workers who do this work often feel they are 'damned if they do and damned if they don't'. Many social workers in child protection feel their role is misunderstood in their communities and that the organisations who employ them do not provide the supports they need in order to do their work well. A major issue for some practitioners is the discrepancy between the demands of the work place and their own allegiance to ethical social work practice. As well, many practitioners carry with them the chronic sense of being unable to influence the system that employs them because of the layers of bureaucracy between the client and the child welfare system.

(CASW, 2003: 3)

According to the report: 'The most powerful messages from all the data are that the demands of the work environment overwhelmingly impede the use of relationship as a catalyst for change, and that social workers feel keenly the lack of visible and public support for good practice' (CASW, 2003: 21). Of equal significance in the report is the statement suggesting: 'There is a sense that many of these practitioners feel lonely and isolated, and that there is a pervasive sense of powerlessness and fear'. The irony is that the sense of powerlessness, fear, and frustration being felt by social workers are the same feelings as being experienced by the parents and families who require or need protective intervention services. How can those who feel unsupported, powerless and hopeless engage in building helping relationships with others who need support, encouragement and hope in order to appreciate their strengths and discover their personal power to address and problem-solve issues related to their oppression and poverty? This chapter explores the challenges and tensions, as well as practice considerations, associated with this question.

Relationship building in child protection: challenges and practice tensions

Work in statutory settings has always caused considerable difficulties for social workers in terms of practice and relationship building. Values of social justice, self-determination, and empowerment place social workers in positions where they have to carefully negotiate through a minefield of moral and ethical dilemmas (Dominelli, 2000). Social work values often challenge the rigidity attached to bureaucracies

where there is an emphasis on efficiency, consistency, accountability through extensive paper work, and the surveillance/supervision tasks associated with risk assessment and risk management. These emphases tend not to be balanced with professional principles and expectations. Child protection social workers are in positions of authority and they are often viewed as being authoritarian as they struggle to represent the best interests of society and the bests interests of children. This struggle makes it difficult for them to relinquish power. Any attempts on their part to do so tend to be experienced by parents as a tokenistic display of rhetoric in action as opposed to being real and genuine (Dominelli, 2000).

The statutory obligation attached to investigating alleged maltreatment of children is seen by parents as something to avoid wherever possible. The work is associated with such failure, stigma, suspicion and low regard (Jones, 2002) that parents resist voluntarily coming forward for services unless it is absolutely necessary and there are no other alternatives.

Lafrance (2003) captures the reality of child protection work under three categories of practice tensions. The first is what he refers to as a 'process versus task' tension. Even though relationship building is one of the best attributes for good child protection work, the over-emphasis on rules and procedures interfere with this being done and de-humanises the interaction between workers and clients. The second is that of 'creativity versus prescription' meaning that the application of prescribed rigid procedures stifles worker discretion, creativity, flexibility, and professional practice. The final tension, 'community partnership versus isolation', indicates failure on the part of child welfare organisations to support advocacy, educate the public, and to be involved in building community capacities in terms of informal support networks for children and families. As stated by Lafrance: 'The overall paradigm in child protection agencies seems to be moving toward increasing power and control over clients and away from interpersonal elements necessary for the achievement of child welfare activities and which are central to agency goals' (2003: 151). Tensions such as these have created work environments that are hostile toward child protection workers and the parents and families in need of services. Social workers within these systems find themselves more and more into being managers of scarce resources, co-ordinators of services, and assessors of risk. They are confined to being more office bound, rule driven and kept at arms length (Wharf, 2002; Jordan, 2000).

Is it possible to develop a collaborative relationship with parents when the involvement is precipitated by a third party referral, where the investigation carries with it a legislative authority to intervene, and there is an expectation that if child maltreatment is substantiated the parents must engage in a supportive, helping relationship for the purposes of bringing about change? How do you begin to help someone who would prefer you not to be intervening in their lives? How do you engage in a helping relationship with someone when, in attempts to help, you are also collecting information that may subsequently be used in court against them? How do you work with someone in a collaborative manner but also be in a position to make authoritative decisions about their lives? How do social workers play the dual role of being investigators of alleged maltreatment and yet work collaboratively with parents and families on issues which caused the maltreatment in the first place? These are fundamental questions in terms of relationship building and practice.

Not surprisingly, people will have a difficult time trusting someone who has the authority to intrusively intervene in their lives and make decisions and assessments based on legislation and procedures. They do not actively seek out the intervention. If through the intervention process maltreatment is substantiated they become involuntary clients. Rooney (1992) suggests that involuntary clients can be divided into two categories, mandated and non-voluntary. The mandated status suggests court ordered participation where the non-voluntary suggests pressure to participate under the threat of court action or apprehension of children.

The terms non-voluntary or mandated evoke strong and predictable reactions from social workers and are often associated with such words as 'difficult', 'uncooperative' 'negative', 'hostile', and 'resistant' (De Jong and Kim Berg, 2001). Engaging clients through active listening, empathy, trust, caring, and reciprocity, all critical relationship building dimensions, become critical challenges when endeavouring to engage with someone who does not believe they need help or refuses the help being offered because of the social control role being carried out by the worker. The legalistic role tends to emerge more so than relationship building.

Relationship building in child protection: suggestions from the literature

Goldstein and Noonan (1999) suggest that workers must be aware of and be prepared to address common characteristics displayed by involuntary clients. For example:

- Often parents do not want to be involved in, or have difficulties making use of, the interventive process because they fear the loss of self-determination and seeming control, intrusion, exposure, feelings of being powerless, and negative repercussions.
- Parents may have limited expectations that anything positive can be done to help them because of prior disappointments or the overwhelming nature of their problems.
- Parents tend to distrust authority figures based on their past experiences.
- Frequently, parents involved with child protection lack material resources and social supports for even minimal subsistence and well-being.
- Parents will often demonstrate angry and provocative behaviour or apathy and indifference in order to protect themselves.
- Many parents may be survivors of extreme childhood and adult trauma in which they have been exploited, abused, and not protected by others, even those closest to them.
- Many parents involved in child protection have born the brunt of dislocation, racism, discrimination, and other forms of societal neglect and oppression that contribute to their feelings of rage, alienation, and despair.
- Parents may not be verbal and able to articulate their thoughts and feelings easily.
- Often parents will tend to act out their feelings rather than talk about them.
- Many parents involved with child protection become easily frustrated, argumentative, or demanding when their needs are not met immediately because of their history of deprivation.

What protection workers experience with many families who come to their attention are situations where there is chaos instead of stability, neglect instead of love, abuse instead of discipline, and where there is despair instead of hope. Engaging and building relationships with parents who are living in these situations demands a full understanding by social workers to explain what underpins the resistance, reluctance, hurt, and anger often displayed by involuntary clients.

According to Rooney (2002) there are several themes from research on effective practice with involuntary clients:

- Court-ordered clients can experience gains from required participation in helping programmes.
- Changes that result from self-attribution (or client acknowledgement that changes are in their own best interest) tend to be more long lasting than those based on punishment, avoidance or the desire to attain rewards.
- Social workers cannot predict level of motivation for change entirely by the presence or absence of a legal mandate.
- Role socialisation whereby involuntary clients understand what is expected of them from social workers and from the helping process, results in improved outcomes.
- Involuntary clients are more likely to be invested in treatment alternatives when they have participated in the construction of the treatment plan that includes choices between alternatives, even when those choices are constrained.

Juxtaposed to these themes is the importance of social work values of dignity, respect, and client self-determination. The literature suggests that in working with involuntary clients it is important for social workers to be proactive and tell the truth about why they are intervening in their lives; for them to identify potential risks, including that not all risks can be anticipated; they should clearly outline time lines and potential consequences; that it is important to explain the limits of confidentiality; and that they need to discuss divided obligations and responsibilities (Rooney, 1992; Ivanoff, Blythe and Tripodi, 1994; Turnell and Edwards, 1999). Ivanoff, Blythe and Tripodi (1994) suggest the importance of being clear, honest, and direct as well as acknowledging the involuntary nature of the relationship. Once acknowledged, discussions can centre around removing some of the barriers toward making the relationship less involuntary.

According to Turnell and Edwards (1999) parents are able to detect if social workers have a genuine interest in and respect for their views. These authors suggest that a more positive relationship is likely to emerge if the focus of intervention is concerned about the safety of children in collaboration with the parents rather than their safety in opposition to them. If the intervention is geared toward gathering evidence for the courts the parents feel they are being dealt with 'by the book' as 'cases' as opposed to being treated as people. Another major factor for the parents is the emphasis on identifying deficits in family functioning and parenting. As such, parents feel they are being viewed as 'abusive' and not seen as individuals with strengths and capacities. Risk assessment procedures have met with the same concern from parents in that the assessment tends to focus on deficits, blame them for things beyond their control, and forces them to answer questions posed by people with different values and expectations (Callahan, 2001). The process places parents in positions of not wanting to be open and honest about their situation for fear of losing their children. This fear underpins why parents tend to be overly cautious. They do not feel permission to challenge social workers or to advocate for themselves and their children with respect to any services. If parents feel judged or blamed in any way, according to Trotter (2004), the relationship is doomed for failure.

Turnell and Edwards (1999) and Hutchison (1987) suggest several principles that help build cooperative relationships in child protection work:

- Parents and children want to be cared about as individuals and to have their strengths acknowledged as well as their not so strong attributes understood. Parents have articulated the importance of not being treated as another 'case'.
- Parents want to know that their story and their perspective regarding the allegations are heard and understood. Their story must be understood and respected in the context of their culture, beliefs, assumptions and values.
- Families respond better if there is recognition and sensitivity expressed about the turmoil and stress associated with an investigation of child maltreatment.
- The interface with parents and social workers must be based on honesty with as much information given to the parents about the

allegations and the process of investigation to be fully explained in terms of roles, responsibilities and expectations. This open communication is important during all interactions.

- Opportunities for parents to be involved in influencing decisions and planning are essential. Parents can be informed of what decisions are within their authority and which decisions within the authority of the agency. They need to have possible alternatives about which they can make self-determined decisions and choices. Parents need to be heard regarding their wishes and their ideas on how to improve the situation.

These principles capture what Trotter (2004) puts forth as suggestions for effective interventions with involuntary clients:

- Clear, honest and frequent discussions about the role of the worker and the role of the client in the relationship.
- The worker focusing on modelling and encouraging pro-social expressions and actions by the client.
- The use of collaborative problem-solving which focuses on the client's definition of problems and goals.

According to Trotter (2004), to apply any one or two without attention to the third will not work. Of significance for the social worker in the relationship building process is having an optimistic view about the client's capacity to change and a genuine belief in their own capacity to help. Trotter's (2002) research with respect to worker skill and client outcomes in child protection discovered that effective practice emerged when there was sufficient investment in helping clients understand and be clear on the role of the protection worker; working through a problem-solving process which focuses on the client's definition of the problems; reinforcing client strengths and capacities; making appropriate use of confrontation; and engaging in a collaborative worker-client relationship.

Suggestions for improvement and change in working with involuntary clients in child protection

It is well recognised that interventions with children and families who come to the attention of child protection are philosophically grounded in the best interests of children and their health and well-being. The needs of children are widely known and accepted in society. These needs begin before birth, with a healthy, knowledgeable mother who has the personal and environmental resources that facilitate caring, love, support, encouragement, and health. Following birth, children need attachment, love, continuity of care, acceptance, relationships, safe environments, education, health care, and resources to ensure their basic needs are met, all of which make significant contributions to their maximum physical, emotional, social, and psychological development (Barter, 2001b). There is a consensus on these needs as well as the rights of children as outlined in the United Nations Convention on the Rights of the Child. However, the practice realities suggest there is an over-concentration on needs with less emphasis on rights. It is paramount to make the rights of children front and centre in child protection practice and policy. Mitchell (2003) puts forth a valid argument that the Convention can be a viable framework from which to base theory and practice in working with children and families. Bringing the Convention into social work practice is critical and would be fundamentally important for parents as they engage with child protection authorities. Operating from a rights perspective gives the parents and social workers a common ground on which to commence and build a working relationship.

Child protection is not only an issue of rights but also of health. Protection is one key determinant of the health and well-being of children. According to Guy (1997) there are three other determinants of equal importance: relationships, hope and opportunity, and community:

- Relationships: human beings need other people to thrive and survive. Caring and supportive relationships with parents, relatives, neighbours, teachers and others are critical to healthy development.
- Hope and opportunity: children and parents need opportunities to explore, to love, to learn, to listen, to be heard, to work, to take and to give back. These opportunities enable them to build self-esteem and sustain hope for the future.
- Community: children, youth and families require a strong sense of community and social cohesion.

All four determinants are intricately associated with other fundamental determinants such as income and social status, social support networks, education, employment, social environments, physical environments, and personal health practices and coping skills.

Current practices and policies in child welfare work emphasise protection with little emphasis on the other three health determinants. The complex needs of children and families involved with child protection are not likely to be effectively met by a concentration on one health determinant independent of the others (Fallon, 1999). Concern with all four determinants of health and well-being would suggest the need to extend interventions beyond the family and individual levels to include interventions at the professional, organisational, and community/ societal levels. These interventions are necessary in order to not only support children and youth in their own families but to equally influence the social, economic, and political forces that affect families and communities (Swift, 1993). Expanding interventions beyond the four walls of parenting and moving into the public issues arena recognises, as suggested by Gil (1998), that the abuse inflicted upon children by society exceeds in scope and destructive consequences the neglect and abuse by parents. It also recognises Seita's (2000) suggestion that a major shift in child welfare practices would occur with the adoption of four key principles:

- Connectedness – promoting close, positive relationships.
- Dignity – courtesy, respect, and safety.
- Continuity – continuous belonging to a group, family or community.
- Opportunity – capitalising on one's strengths, and forming a personal vision.

A determinant of health focus in child protection supports what Cameron (2003) and Cameron and Vanderwoerd (1997) suggest are fundamental principles in working with children and families that would be beneficial in realising positive outcomes:

- Working holistically with children and families due to multiple factors impacting on parents and families. All factors have to be considered.
- Having specialised services and information readily available to families.

- High levels of personal contact with children and families, contact that is individualised, flexible, responsive to the needs and continues over time.
- Having crisis supports in place that are readily available.
- Linking children and families to informal support networks and parental involvement in programming.
- A conscious investment in reducing concrete, psychological and social obstacles to consistent participation.
- Creating opportunities for parents to build their own support and service networks whereby there is less reliance on professionals.
- Ensuring programmes and services are actively involving parents, are sensitive to the developmental needs of children and youth, and are responsive to culture and community.

These principles sound the call for a more collaborative and comprehensive approach to child protection that goes well beyond current practices. 'The dominant emphases of current Canadian child protection systems are overly restrictive. In particular, the increased reliance on a common bureaucratic organisational framework for service delivery, standard operating procedures for front-line services, and the gathering of formal legal evidence about parental adequacy has drawn a lot of criticism. Many argue that a more inclusive concern with child and welfare is needed' (Cameron, 2003: 94). Taking a more inclusive approach within determinants of a health framework as well as acknowledging the principles associated with positive outcomes will greatly facilitate reducing tensions and barriers that interfere with relationship building.

Child protection organisations tend to be politicised, bureaucratised, and hierarchical systems (Wharf, 2002). There is evidence to suggest that bureaucracies are not necessarily the right environment for creating opportunities where relationships, caring, investment in people, and compassion take place. Instead, it is an environment that is governed by policies and procedures; where power remains with high-level bureaucrats who are isolated from the grass roots; where thinking is compartmentalised and often re-active in attempts to fix things; where, at times, there is unwarranted political involvement; and where those who seek services or provide services are not seen as equal partners in the decisions. Contemporary child protection organisations were never designed to appropriately respond to the complex issues, crises, and current realities facing children, families and communities. Their endeavours to do so suggest an attempt to try and reduce the complexities and uncertainty that permeate child protection to issues of bureaucratic administration. There is a requirement to move from the professional/ bureaucratic paradigm to the parent/community paradigm. Making this move requires re-thinking and moving away from past practices and policies. Expectations associated with partnership, inter-professional team work, client participation and involvement, staff empowerment, user-friendly services, primary prevention and promotion, community development, seamless systems of delivery, integrated programmes and services, and community decision-making and governance align with the community/parent paradigm as well as with social work principles and values. The community/ parent paradigm creates a more conducive environment for relationship building and supports the principles involved in working with involuntary clients.

Community-based systems are ideal environments for social work, given its commitment and interest in connecting personal troubles and public issues. The community paradigm creates opportunities for people to be empowered, to work together, and to begin renegotiating relationships between social workers, professionals, organisations, and citizens. The community paradigm is about caring, respect, acceptance, personal and social power, and community capacity building. Assuming a community approach to child protection is an important consideration in terms of building working relationships with parents. As pointed out by Trocmé and Chamberland (2003), the families and children who come to the attention of child protection agencies are neglected by communities, institutions label them and society rejects them. To counter this, it is important to embrace community as an essential part of service delivery. Working with parents at the community level creates opportunities for relationship building, networking, self-help initiatives, and building community capacity for the health and well-being of children.

A community capacity building approach suggests re-thinking the concept of relationship building with parents. Although relationship is acknowledged as critical, it is not exactly clear how this is interpreted by social workers. There is a consensus that more time is required in the intervention to develop more trusting relationships. However, if this time was available, what would social workers do? Would it be more individual counselling time with parents, more monitoring and supervision, or spending more time with children? What would parents suggest be done with this time? What would foster parents suggest? What would be considered reasonable outcomes if there was the time to build relationships? How would this time help to address many of the current tensions for parents and social workers with respect to relationship building?

The ultimate challenge is to invest the time in realising desirable outcomes for children, parents and families. Ernst (2003) puts forth the following outcome statements:

- Increased safety or reduced high risk.
- Increased client functioning in terms of competencies with respect to parenting, personal functioning and increased self-sufficiency and independence.
- Increased social support in terms of relationships with family, community, culture, spirituality, social supports and with peers.
- Increased knowledge in access to and use of resources.
- Increased learning and participation in employment or education.

Investment of time in realising these outcomes is essential in the relationship building process. Current language being used in child protection also creates tensions in relationship building. For example, child protection families are most commonly referred to as 'cases'. 'Treating people as cases dehumanises them' (Wharf, 2000: 132). The term represents classification and categorisation for purposes of management control and administration. It does little to place children, parents and families as citizens who have rights to services and basic needs. Categorising children and parents as a 'case' presents the same disrespect as the term 'client'. Rather than being seen as an equal person, 'client' denotes someone of concern and requiring professional attention rather than someone who can make a contribution. The word implies that a person has less knowledge, information, expertise, or resources than the professional.

Social work education tends to promote 'clientism' (Parsloe, 1990) or 'clientise' people (Smale, 1995). Doing so shares with racism, sexism, ageism in that it is devaluing a particular group of people by those with power. Parents requiring or needing services, as well as workers providing services, come to the relationship with each having their own skills, resources, experiences, strengths and vulnerabilities. Viewing parents from this perspective will enhance the relationship building process and facilitate partnerships.

Another language issue is the term 'at risk'. Swadener and Lubeck (1995) promote the term 'at promise'. The notion of children and families being 'at risk' promotes deficit model assumptions and discourse which tend to locate problems or pathologies in individuals and families rather than in institutional structures that create and maintain inequality. 'At promise' conveys the importance of locating many problems faced by parents and children outside the family. It focuses attention on the larger contexts within which families struggle and where change is required both individually and structurally. Viewing children and families as 'at promise' enhances the possibilities of constructing authentic relations where active listening and learning from one another takes place (Muluccio and Anderson, 2000; Waldfogel, 1998).

The use of the word 'protection' also needs to be reconsidered in terms of the messages implied. It presupposes that children need to be protected from their parents. 'The concept of child protection automatically pits the child against the parent, since a child cannot exist without a parent, and one ceases to be a parent without a child' (Turnell and Edwards, 1999: ix). The child protection investigation process often place parents in the position of advocating to protect their children from being controlled by the child protection system. Building supportive relationships becomes very difficult in these circumstances. Any language that diminishes the current fears of parents, provides a better understanding of the importance of collaboration, and supports relationship building needs to be considered.

Abandoning 'clinical' labels is equally important. Terms such as 'behaviour disorder', 'dysfunctional', 'disruptive', 'disturbed' remain a part of practice language. According to Seita (2000: 80) 'These terms border on the derisive, are disrespectful of our children, focus on so-called weaknesses, fail to recognise the social context, and may contribute to negative, judgmental, and punitive practices by those in the child welfare field and by society in general'. Promoting different and more positive language will influence the relationship building process.

Finally, it is important in the relationship building process to not only acknowledge that children and families requiring or needing protective interventions face significant barriers, but to equally acknowledge that those with the mandate to intervene are also faced with significant barriers. There is a sense of powerlessness felt by all. As pointed out by Smale: 'Social workers power over resources is actually very limited indeed, and social workers do themselves and their clients no favour by pretending that it is more or less than it actually is' (1988: 131). Parsloe equally suggests that: 'Social workers are in fact powerless to meet most of their clients' needs directly except those which require their time, which they can personally provide' (1990: 19). Most needs that clients have, according to Parsloe, have to be obtained from services controlled by others. The Directors of Child Welfare across Canada acknowledge that many of the services required to support children and families are under separate government structures making it difficult for child welfare workers to access them in an efficient manner (Rodgers, 2003). This is an important dimension of child protection work that requires public acknowledgement. Failure to not make this public only perpetuates the belief within clients and the community that the professional and the bureaucracy do in fact have the necessary power and resources to make a difference. Promoting this false belief only exacerbates a sense of powerlessness. Education around the realities of child protection practices is perhaps the single most important consideration in promoting change in practices, working conditions, and building relationships with parents and in communities in order to bring about desirable outcomes for children and families.

Moves to have these suggestions applied in practice would take child protection from its current residual approach (Lindsey and Henly, 1997) and create opportunities for thinking 'outside the box' (Kim Berg and Kelly, 2000) and challenge current tensions that exist between parents and social workers as well as a beginning to do things differently.

Conclusion

This chapter captures many of the critical realities with respect to relationship building in child protection work. Children and families who come to the attention of, or require services from, child protection organisations are struggling with fundamental challenges associated with poverty, discrimination, injustices, lack of opportunity, and health issues. They require interventions in their lives that create opportunities for them to engage in a process of healing and change whereby they discover their personal power to make a difference in their lives. This engagement has to extend beyond child welfare systems to include mental health, schools, community resource centres, justice, and community. Currently, child protection systems tend to be alone for much of this engagement, particularly from a protection perspective. Social workers also feel alone. They face phenomenal barriers within their systems, barriers that interfere with engaging in relationships with children and families. This chapter identifies many of these barriers and how they impact on developing helping and supportive relationships with parents. Child protection workers are also working in less than ideal conditions and child protection practices are fraught with many tensions and challenges. Current outcomes for children and families are also less than ideal.

Relationship is considered the most fundamental tool in social work practice. The Canadian Association of Social Workers publication *Child Welfare Project: Creating Conditions for Good Practice* (CASW, 2003), recognises the importance of relationship as a catalyst for change in the child welfare system. It is acknowledged in social work literature and practice that it is the power of relationship that brings about change, not programmes and services. Changes are required at many levels if the issues identified in this chapter are to be addressed. Of significance is for all the key players, be they families, professionals, organisations, and communities, to come together to renegotiate relationships whereby interventions with children and families who come to the attention of child protection systems are indeed interventions that are helpful and will bring about desirable outcomes. Society has sanctioned the social control function associated with child protection and recognises social work as the predominant profession. The profession cannot take a stance to retreat from this authority as it did in the past within social welfare institutions (Hutchison, 1987). For example, the profession moved itself significantly from social welfare programmes such as welfare assistance only now to find this important role has been taken over by others. Yet, in child protection, many of the direct needs of parents and families require these very services (Parsloe, 1990). The challenge for the profession is to embrace the many complexities and dilemmas associated with the child protection role and balance the dual role associated with linking the personal and the political. Social work is perhaps the only profession that can claim a mandate to pursue this linking. It is also the profession to work with and build relationships, even with the involuntary client.

References

Barter, K. (2000) Renegotiating Relationships in Child Protection. *Canada's Children*. Summer, 35–8.

Barter, K. (2001a) Building Community: A Conceptual Framework for Child Protection. *Child Abuse Review*, 10: 4, 262–78.

Barter, K. (2001b) Services for Vulnerable Children: A Conceptualisation. In Turner, J.C. and Turner, F.J. (Eds.) *Canadian Social Welfare*. 4th edn. Toronto: Pearson Education Canada.

Barter, K. (2002) Enough is Enough: Renegotiating Relationships to Create a Conceptual Revolution in Community and Children's Protection. *Canada's Children*, Spring, 28–9.

Barter, K. (2003) Strengthening Community Capacity: Expanding the Vision. *Relational Child and Youth Care Journal*, 16: 2, 24–32.

Barter, K. (2004) A Community Approach to Child Protection. *Perspectives*, 1: 1, 27–32.

Barter, K. (2005) Re-conceptualising Services for the Protection of Children. In Turner, J. and Turner, F. (Eds.) *Canadian Social Welfare*. 5th edn. Toronto: Pearson Education Canada.

Berg, I.K. and Kelly, S. (2000) *Building Solutions in Child Protective Services*. New York: WW Norton.

Callahan, M. (1993) Feminist Approaches: Women Recreate Child Welfare. In Wharf, B. (Ed.) *Rethinking Child Welfare in Canada*. Toronto: McClelland and Stewart.

Callahan, M. (2001) Risk Assessment in Child Protection Services: No: 'These tools . . . do not

Reduce Risk for Children'. *Canadian Social Work Review*, 18: 1, 157–62.

Cameron, G. (2003) Promoting Positive Child and Family Welfare. In Kufeldt, K. and McKenzie, B. (Eds.) *Child Welfare: Connecting Research, Policy, and Practice.* Waterloo, Ontario: Wilfred Laurier University Press.

Cameron, G. and Vanderwoerd, J. (1997) *Protecting Children and Supporting Families.* New York: Aldine De Gruyter.

Campaign 2000 (2006) *Child Poverty in Canada: Report Card 2005.* Toronto: Child Poverty Action Group.

Canadian Association of Social Workers (2003) *Child Welfare Project: Creating Conditions for Good Practice.* Ottawa: Canadian Association of Social Workers.

Canadian Association of Social Workers (2005) *Working Conditions for Social Workers and Linkages to Client Outcomes in Child Welfare: A Literature Review 2005.* Ottawa: Canadian Association of Social Workers.

Conway, J.F. (2001) *The Canadian Family in Crisis.* 4th edn. Toronto: James Lorimer.

De Jong, P. and Berg, K. (2001) Co-constructing Cooperation with Mandated Clients. *Social Work*, 26: 4, 361–74.

Dominelli, L. (2000) Introducing International Perspectives in Child Welfare. In Dominelli, L. (Ed.) *Community Approaches to Child Welfare: International Perspectives.* Aldershot: Ashgate.

Ernst, K. (2003) *Toward the Development of an Outcome Evaluation Model: Formative and Organisational Requirements in Outcome Evaluation.* Paper presented at the Canadian Symposium of Child and Family Services Outcomes. Calgary, Alberta: Canadian Outcomes Institute.

Fallon, B. (1999) Outcomes Literature Survey: A Preliminary Review for the Client Outcomes in Child Welfare Project. In Thompson, J. and Fallon, B. (Eds.) *The First Canadian Roundtable on Child Welfare Outcomes.* Toronto: University of Toronto Press.

Gil, D.G. (1998) *Confronting Injustice and Oppression: Concepts and Strategies for Social Workers.* New York: Columbia University Press.

Goldstein, E.G. and Noonan, M. (1999) *Short Term Treatment and Social Work Practice.* New York: The Free Press.

Guy, K.A. (Ed.) (1997) *Our Promise to our Children.* Ottawa: Canadian Institute of Child Health.

Hutchison, E.D. (1987) Use of Authority in Direct Social Work Practice with Mandated Clients. *Social Service Review*, Dec. 581–98.

Ivanoff, A., Blythe, B.J. and Tripodi, T. (1994) *Involuntary Clients in Social Work Practice: A Research-based Approach.* New York: Aldine De Gruyter.

Jones, C. (2002) Social Work and Society. In Adams, R., Dominelli, L. and Payne, M. (Eds.) *Social Work: Themes, Issues and Critical Debates.* 2nd edn. New York, NY: Palgrave.

Jordan, B. (2000) Conclusion: Tough Love: Social Work Practice in UK Society. In Stepney, P. and Ford, D. (Eds.) *Social Work Models, Methods and Theories.* Lyme Regis: Russell House Publishing.

Kufeldt, K. and McKenzie, B. (2003) (Eds.) *Child Welfare: Connecting Research, Policy, and Practice.* Waterloo, Ontario: Wilfred Laurier University Press.

Lafrance, J. (2003) *Social Work Practice and Child Welfare-Paradox and Possibility.* Paper presented at the Canadian Symposium of Child and Family Services Outcomes. Calgary, Alberta: Canadian Outcomes Institute.

Lindsey, D. (2004) *The Welfare of Children.* New York: Oxford University Press.

Lindsey, D. and Henly, J.R. (1997) The Future of Child Welfare. In Reisch, M. and Gambrill, E. (Eds.) *Social Work in the 21st Century.* London: Pine Forge Press.

Lundy, C. (2004) *Social Work and Social Justice: A Structural Approach to Practice.* Peterborough, Ontario: Broadview Press.

Melton, G.B. (2003) *Mandatory Reporting: A Policy without Reason.* Commentary prepared for virtual discussion sponsored by the International Society for Prevention of Child Abuse and Neglect.

Mitchell, R.C. (2003) *Ideological Reflections on the DSM IV-R.* Paper presented at the 7th International Child and Youth Conference, University of Victoria, BC, August 20–23.

Muluccio, A. and Anderson, G.R. (2000) (Eds.) Future Challenges and Opportunities in Child Welfare. *Child Welfare*, 1, Jan./Feb.

Parsloe, P. (1990) Social Work Education in the Year 2000. *International Social Work.* 33, 13–25.

Prilleltensky, I., Peirson, L. and Nelson, G. (2001) Mapping the Terrain: Framework for Promoting Family Wellness and Preventing Child Maltreatment. In Prilleltensky, I., Nelson, G. and Peirson, L. (Eds.) *Promoting Family Wellness and Preventing Child Maltreatment: Fundamentals for Thinking and Action.* Toronto: University of Toronto Press.

Pulkingham, J. and Ternowetsky, G. (1997) The Changing Context of Child and Family Policies.

In Pulkingham, J. and Ternowetsky, G. (Eds.) *Child and Family Policies: Struggles, Strategies, and Options*. Halifax: Fernwood.

Roberts, D. (1991) Child Protection in the 21st Century. *Child Abuse and Neglect*, 15: 1, 25–30.

Rodgers, J. (2003) New Directions in Child Welfare: Provincial and Territorial Directors of Child Welfare. In Trocmé, N., Knoke, D. and Roy, C. (Eds.) *Community Collaboration and Differential Response: Canadian and International Research and Emerging Models of Practice*. Ottawa: Child Welfare League of Canada.

Rooney, R.H. (1992) *Strategies for Work with Involuntary Clients*. New York: Columbia University Press.

Rooney, R. (2002) Working with Involuntary Clients. In Roberts, A.R. and Greene, G.J. (Eds.) *Social Workers Desk Reference*. New York: Oxford University Press.

Ross, D.P., Shillington, R.E. and Lochhead, C. (1994) *The Canadian Fact Book on Poverty*. Ottawa: Canadian Council on Social Development.

Schorr, L.B. (1988) *Within our Reach: Breaking the Cycle of Disadvantage*. Toronto: Doubleday.

Schram, B. and Mandell, B.R. (1997) *An Introduction to Human Services: Policy and Practice*. 3rd edn. Toronto: Allyn and Bacon.

Seita, J.R. (2000) In our Best Interest: Three Necessary Shifts for Child Welfare Workers and Children. *Child Welfare*, 1, 77–92.

Smale, G.G. (1995) Integrating Community and Individual Practice: A New Paradigm for Practice. In Adams, P. and Nelson, K. (Eds.) *Reinventing Human Services: Community-and Family-centred Practice*. New York: Aldine De Gruyter.

Smale, G.G. (1998) *Managing Change Through Innovation*. London: National Institute for Social Work.

Swadener, B.B. and Lubeck, S. (1995) *Children and Families 'At Promise'*. Albany: State University of New York Press.

Swift, K. and Callahan, M. (2006) Problems and Potential of Canadian Child Welfare. In Freymond, N. and Cameron, G. (Eds.) *Towards Positive Systems of Child and Family Welfare: International Comparisons of Child Protection, Family Service, and Community Caring Systems*. Toronto: University of Toronto Press.

Swift, K. (1993) Contradictions in Child Welfare: Neglect and Responsibility. In Baines, C., Evans, P. and Neysmith, S. (Eds.) *Women's Caring: Feminist Perspectives on Social Welfare*. Toronto: McClelland and Stewart.

Turnell, A. and Edwards, S. (1999) *Signs of Safety: A Solution and Safety Oriented Approach to Child Protection Casework*. New York: WW Norton.

Trocmé, N. and Chamberland, C. (2003) Re-involving the Community: The Need for a Differential Response to Rising Child Welfare Caseloads in Canada. In Trocmé, N., Knoke, D. and Roy, C. (Eds.) *Community Collaboration and Differential Response: Canadian and International Research and Emerging Models of Practice*. Ottawa: Child Welfare League of Canada.

Trocmé, N. et al. (2005) *Canadian Incidence Study of Reported Child Abuse and Neglect – 2003*. Ottawa: Minister of Public Works and Government Services Canada.

Trocmé, N. et al. (2001) *Canadian Incidence Study of Reported Child Abuse and Neglect*. Ottawa: Health Canada, Government of Canada.

Trotter, C. (2004) *Working with the Involuntary Client: A Guide to Practice*. London: Sage Publications.

Trotter, C. (2002) Worker Skill and Client Outcome in Child Protection. *Child Abuse Review*, 11: 38–50.

Waldfogel, J. (1998) *The Future of Child Protection: How to Break the Cycle of Abuse and Neglect*. Cambridge, MA: Harvard University Press.

Wharf, B. (2003) Addressing Public Issues in Child Welfare. In Kufeldt, K. and McKenzie, B. (Eds.) *Child Welfare: Connecting Research, Policy, and Practice*. Waterloo, Ontario: Wilfred Laurier University Press.

Wharf, B. (Ed.) (2002) *Community Work Approaches to Child Welfare*. Peterborough, ON: Broadview Press.

Wharf, B. (2000) Cases or Citizens: Viewing Child Welfare Through a Different Lens. *Canadian Social Work*, 2: 2, 132–9.

Willms, J.D. (Ed.) (2002) *Vulnerable Children: Findings from Canada's National Longitudinal Survey of Children and Youth*. Edmonton, Alberta: University of Alberta Press.

CHAPTER 8

Working with Involuntary Clients in Child Protection: Lessons from Successful Practice

Andrew Turnell, Sue Lohrbach and Scott Curran

Introduction

An English social services worker, who we will call 'Miriam', was required to undertake a 4.30 p.m. Friday afternoon home visit interview with the father of an eight-year-old girl who had bruises on her arms. The girl had earlier in the day talked about the bruising, first to the school nurse and then Miriam, telling them that her father had caused the bruises. After introducing herself to the father, who lived on the 17th floor of a housing estate block of flats, the man began to yell at Miriam, finishing by screaming at her that she should 'f*** off!' Miriam paused for a moment and replied 'okay I can f*** off, but we have to talk, so when can I f*** back?' The man was momentarily taken aback but then laughed. 'Ah well,' he said, 'you'd better come in luv'. When Miriam began to introduce herself to the man her attention had immediately been drawn to the fact that he had at some stage lost most of his left ear and all that remained was part of the earlobe and a considerable amount of scar tissue. As they sat down at the kitchen table, Miriam said, 'We have to talk about your daughter, but you know I couldn't help notice the fact you hardly have a left ear, and if you don't tell me how that happened I don't think I'll be able to concentrate on what we have to talk about'. Again the man laughed and told Miriam a story of getting into a fight in a pub when he was a young man, and having his ear sliced off by his opponent who was wielding a machete. He finished by saying 'But don't worry though, I may have lost my ear, but I still won the fight'. As a result of this first few minutes of contact Miriam was quickly able to build a good working relationship with the father so that during the first interview and the following few weeks they were able together to focus on creating safety commensurate to the problem.

What is happening here? This man for a brief moment was clearly not only an 'involuntary client', he was a personification of a child protection worker's worst fears of the worst type of involuntary client. It is easy to imagine, given a different response from Miriam, that things between Miriam and the father could have gone from bad to worse very quickly, and as a consequence the eight-year-old probably would have been removed into care and the next contact with this man would have been in a court setting. By then the perception of him as an involuntary client would probably have hardened considerably and he would likely have also begun to be framed as resistant and possibly 'untreatable'.

Building ideas from practice

Most social work and helping relationships are framed around the idea of the voluntary client, which often leaves a conceptual and skills vacuum for practitioners faced with clients who do not want the helping service being offered. In the child protection arena the majority of service recipients are involuntary in that they do not choose to enter the relationship with a child protection worker and they certainly do not, nor should they in our view, control the decision that determines when the relationship is deemed to be concluded. Thus much of the helping professions' literature that presumes a voluntary relationship between helper and client do not address many of the challenges that face a statutory practitioner. Even the descriptor 'client' does not reflect very well the identity and experience of people caught up in the child protection system. Our practice experience and our reading of research with people who are involved with child protection services (for example, see Aubrey and Dahl, 2006; Cashmore, 2002; Cleaver and Freeman, 1995; Dale, 2004; Dumbrill, 2006; Farmer and Owen, 1995; Fergurson and O'Reilly, 2001; MacKinnon, 1998; Teoh et al., 2003; Thoburn et al., 1995; Thomas and O'Kane, 1999; Westcott, 1995) suggests that they do not see themselves as a 'client' or even 'service user' of the professionals involved. Since people involved in the child protection area see themselves as on the receiving end of services which they did not choose, we prefer to speak of 'service recipients' as a more transparent representation of parents' and childrens' experience and of the power dynamics within the child protection helping relationship.

Fortunately, there is a small but growing body of literature, which now includes this book, regarding working with involuntary clients (Barber, 1991; De Jong and Berg, 2001, 2002; Lohrbach, 2003; Lohrbach and Sawyer, 2004; Rooney, 1992, 1998; Tripodi and Blythe, 1994; Trotter, 2006; Turnell and Edwards, 1999; Turnell and Essex, 2006), that in Karen Healy's words point toward: 'the emergence of critical practice theories that are responsive to social work practices in statutory settings and other settings involving overt use of authority (Healy, 2000: 77). Theorising about working with involuntary clients is challenging, particularly in such a highly scrutinised and highly anxious practice arena as child protection, because there is a strong proclivity to describe practices that are seen to conform to ideals that are often far removed from the realities of everyday practice. As Canadian child protection worker Gerald de Montigney observes about his own and his colleagues front-line work:

> . . . *our practice did not conform to the idealisations in the texts. Yet, we did our best inside the reality of the organisation. It is this reality that must serve as the beginning for inquiry – and not the idealised fantasies of social work educators about what good social work should look like.*
>
> (de Montigney, 1995: 131)

One of the strengths of the involuntary client literature lies in the fact that the ideas and practices suggested therein are in the main derived from on-the-ground practice experience. Chris Trotter (2002, 2006) for example, creates his ideas for working with involuntary clients from research he has undertaken with direct service practitioners. Seeking to follow in this tradition we will ground our ideas in the direct work we are involved in. Our aim in this chapter is to describe our best understanding of statutory child protection work that engages involuntary child protection service recipients and maximises their involvement while maintaining a rigorous focus on child safety. To achieve this aim we will describe a case example that we believe enacts these practice aspirations and then we will draw

upon this example to suggest the themes and practice issues we consider are at the heart of working constructively and purposively with involuntary child protection service recipients.

Case example

The case example we will consider here involves a couple we will call 'Hazel' and 'Harry' who were involved with Olmsted County Child and Family Services (OCCFS). This case example was prepared through a collaborative, appreciative inquiry writing process (Ludema, Cooperrider and Barrett, 2006; Turnell, in press). Andrew interviewed Scott and Sue (they being respectively social worker and supervisor in the OCCFS high-risk long-term team) about the casework, and following this we have prepared both the example and the themes we draw from it in a successive drafting, reviewing and editing process. Some details of this case have been altered to protect the family's privacy and the publication of this example is undertaken with the full support of the parents and OCCFS.

Harry and Hazel's baby son David was three months old at the time of the initial contact with OCCFS. Hazel and Harry had previous contact with the child protection authorities, with each parent having had a child from a previous relationship permanently removed from their care. This history meant that when a report was made to Olmsted county regarding David the current situation was automatically treated as a high-risk case. Hazel suffered from a chronic degenerative disease that severely limited her physical capacity to care for David, leaving her completely incapacitated for up to thirty minutes at a time and often also leaving her depressed and withdrawn. The report alleged that Hazel had left David crying for extended periods of time and was not responding to his needs and also that there were times when Hazel became very frustrated and verbally abusive toward the baby.

Initial contact

When investigator Shani Green first contacted Hazel by phone, Hazel was very agitated and distressed. Hazel refused to talk to Shani and in short order hung up on the child protection worker. Shani took some time to reflect on the first call and then rang back. Shani began the second call by telling Hazel that she had been thinking about the last conversation ever since she got off the phone and didn't want to leave things with Hazel feeling so distressed and perhaps afraid that Olmsted was going to turn up on her doorstep to remove David. In response, Hazel thanked Shani for phoning back, and said she had begun to feel terrified that CPS would be coming to get her son. Shani asked to meet with Hazel and Harry, but Hazel stated she didn't want to do this and that there was no need for Shani to worry since David was fine. Shani reiterated that this must be very distressing for Hazel but added that she (Shani) had no option, since the requirements of her job meant she had to meet with the couple about the concerns. By moving backwards and forwards between empathy for Hazel's fears about child protection involvement while also calmly spelling out her statutory obligation to meet with the parents, Shani was able to negotiate a meeting with Hazel and Harry. In this initial conversation Hazel had been determined that Shani could not come to her home, so they negotiated that the meeting would occur at Olmsted county offices.

In this initial meeting with Hazel and Harry, Shani continued this mix of empathy and a careful articulation of OCCFS's bottom line requirements. Shani emphasised that both she and the county wanted Hazel and Harry to have David, and continually underlined that for the couple to get the CPS out of their life, the county needed to be involved with the family for a period of time and would need to come and work with the family in their home. In this context, Shani introduced the fact that a long-term worker, Scott Curran would be contacting them, introducing him as a good man and someone who could help them. Through this skillful blending of empathy and authority, Shani was able to get Hazel and Harry to sign a voluntary contract that they were willing to work with Olmsted County.

Scott made the first phone call to the home the following day, and when Hazel answered the phone it was clear to Scott that she was very anxious. Scott was very conscious of acknowledging that Hazel must be feeling very worried about allowing him as a child protection worker into her family's life. Hazel responded quietly and put Harry on the phone. Scott reiterated to Harry who he was and the things he was concerned about, emphasising that from what Shani had told him, he believed he and they

could work through the concerns about David. Previous professionals that had been involved with Harry, together with reports that Scott had read, suggested that Harry was very disinterested and disengaged, and that he was limited in his capacity as a father and as Hazel's partner to deal with the issues the child protection professionals were worried about. What attracted Scott's immediate attention on this phone call was that Harry was acting very calmly and purposively, talking first to Scott then taking time to talk to Hazel, brokering an agreement with Hazel for Scott to visit the couple. Scott could hear that Hazel was listening to the phone conversation and that she was expressing her anxieties in the background. Harry would take time to hold up the conversation with Scott to help calm Hazel's anxieties and explain what Scott was saying and what he wanted. To facilitate these negotiations, Scott was very mindful of not speaking definitively as if he was the expert in what the problems were or what should be done. Instead, Scott repeatedly emphasised that he needed to meet with Harry and Hazel to be able to understand their situation and figure out the best plan of action together. In this way, Scott's first home visit was set up and Scott viewed this as a big step forward.

First home visit

As Scott sat down in the couples' living room on that first home visit he was conscious that for Harry and Hazel it was a 'big deal' to let him visit their home. Scott therefore made a point of thanking them for being willing to allow him into their home, particularly given their past experiences with child protection services. When Andrew asked Scott what he thought made the difference to enable this first meeting to go well, Scott commented that:

> Had I made up my mind that Harry had limited capacity like I was told and read, I probably would have seen everything he was doing in that light. In fact what I saw was him demonstrating a quiet vigilance to Hazel's anxiety and emotional state and I witnessed Harry continuing to help create a context where we could talk about the issues around David's care.

Scott also commented that continually acknowledging the couple's fears about the child protection authorities removing David was important, as was asking a lot of open-ended questions while sustaining a clear and calm articulation of the agency's bottom-line requirements.

One of the key bottom-line issues Scott needed to explore with Harry and Hazel concerned the nature and extent of Scott's involvement with the family and there was a lot of discussion and negotiation about this at the first meeting. Shani had told Harry and Hazel that given the couple's past history and the allegations, Scott would have to see the couple at least three times each month. Hazel immediately stated that she did not want Scott coming to the home. Rather than get into a fight with Hazel about this, Scott responded by asking 'Well, what shall we do? What are your ideas about us working together?' In the discussions that followed it was agreed that Scott would only come to the house once a month and the other meetings would be elsewhere. This was important for Hazel and seemed to give her a greater sense of control of the process which in turn led to Hazel shifting from being opposed to any home visits to agreeing to one each month. Nevertheless, the home visits were important for many reasons, including giving Scott the opportunity to observe David in his home environment.

Hazel was also very worried about how long Scott would be involved with the family – the voluntary written agreement that the parents prepared with Shani spoke of a minimum of three months involvement, and Hazel was keen to have a commitment from Scott that his involvement would conclude after that time. Scott had to carefully but clearly communicate to the couple that they might be able to get the job done in three months, but he wasn't able to make any promises in that regard.

Scott was conscious that above all else it was vital that he was 'able to keep his foot in the door'. To facilitate the working relationship with Hazel and Harry he was very mindful of offering the couple choices at every opportunity and as much control over the process as possible. Thus he spent a lot of time in this meeting exploring how, where and when they would meet.

To more fully understand the couples' position about child protection services, Scott spent a considerable period of time in this meeting asking the couple to tell him about their experience of working with CPS in the past. It seemed clear to Scott that without understanding the couple's previous experiences he would be limited in his capacity to work with them in the current situation.

After the best part of two hours, in which Scott asked about and listened to the couples previous experiences Scott then moved the conversation on to focus on the question, 'How can you show me and the county that David is okay all the time?' Hazel and Harry were quick to say that David was fine, which enabled Scott to continually reiterate that therefore, 'What we have to do is set things up so I can be confident that that's the case and I can convince my supervisor that everything is fine for David'. In this process, Scott introduced the idea of involving others in helping Hazel and Harry to show Olmsted that David was safe. Scott explained that as far as Olmsted was concerned, 'The best way to shut us up and get us out of your life' was for the couple to have other people – friends and family members who knew about the worries and that Olmsted had confidence in – who would be involved in working with the couple on the problems and helping out with David. Scott explained that the more people the couple had involved with them, the more confident Olmsted would be. Scott asked the couple who they thought they could involve that could help them out like this? In this way Scott was able to lay the groundwork for the first Family Group Decision Making conference (FGDM) to be held.

The first FGDM

The use of family group decision-making conferences are a well-established child protection approach in enacting the old maxim 'it takes a village to raise a child'. The FGDM process draws upon a naturally occurring network of friends and extended family that are connected to the immediate family and is designed to privilege the family and network's ideas and solutions to address the child protection concerns. The FGDM conference is essentially the US name for the Family Group Conference approach that was developed in New Zealand in the late 1980s (Burford and Hudson, 2000; Hudson et al., 1996). OCCFS was one of the first US jurisdictions to adopt the approach and has been utilising the FGDM approach since the mid 1990s. The agency has a team of five conference conveners and has evolved a comprehensive ongoing approach to the use of family network conferencing, most particularly for its high-risk cases, that goes well beyond an emphasis on a single set-piece conference (see Lohrbach and Sawyer, 2003, 2004; Christiansen and Maloney, 2006).

Following on from Scott's first home visit one of Olmsted county's FGDM conveners, Amy Oian, contacted Harry and Hazel and set up the first Family Group Decision Making conference. Harry and Hazel had asked that two of their friends, Harry's parents and Hazel's mother be present at the conference. The conference focused on ensuring that everyone present understood the concerns that Olmsted held about David's care and then moved on to create a plan in which everyone involved could be confident that David would be safe and well cared for. Out of the 'family-alone-time' of this conference Hazel, Harry and their support people created the following plan:

- David would go to one of the friend's home each weekend, and at other times as the parents and network felt was needed.
- Three people were identified who were willing to come to the home at any time, '24/7', to help with, or take David.
- Harry's job involved working night shifts and it was agreed Harry would call Hazel four or five times each night to check in with her and see that everything was okay.
- One of the friends and Harry's mother agreed that they would check in with Hazel every day by phone or in person.

In creating this plan there was extensive discussion about how the network people would know Hazel needed help. After considerable discussion, it was agreed that all of the support people needed to be alert for times when Hazel was very quiet and said very little, especially when people were trying to get her to speak, whether on the phone or in person. It was clear that Harry was particularly attuned to times when Hazel was in this withdrawn place. When Harry was asked what he would do if he rang from work and was worried that Hazel wasn't coping, but she was not able to acknowledge it, Harry was clear that he would phone one of the network people to immediately go to the house.

The conference also spent time discussing how Hazel could manage the times when she was feeling frustrated. This led into an extended conversation between Hazel and Harry which in turn lead to an agreement between all present that when Hazel became frustrated, the best thing she could do was to put David in his cot and call either Harry or one of the safety network. In and around this, an important extended conversation

also evolved, focused on David's needs for attention, nurturance and physical contact, his crying and how David communicated his needs and how the caregivers were able to recognise that communication.

When Andrew asked Scott what enabled both himself and Amy to work at this level of detail with the couple and the network he stated:

> We had a young vulnerable child and the parents had a lot of history with CPS so we had to get down to this level so we could be satisfied the problems were being addressed. Having said that, it was also out of respect for them, they had every reason not to show up, but here they were and we owed it to them to make sure we got down to specifics to help them have the best chance of keeping David. We didn't know the answers to their problems, so we had to keep getting at their positioning on relationships, family dynamics, grief and loss of previous children, and capacity to provide/create safety. It was very clear that they had been emotionally hurt from their previous experience with child protection, and we needed to go forward carefully not only to build safety, but also to honour them as human beings. In order for movement to occur, it was essential for all of us from the county to demonstrate a commitment to caring about their spirit, and create a context in which Harry and Hazel could maintain their dignity in the midst of their intense fear of the potential for yet another loss of a child.

As a result of his involvement in the first FGDM, Scott became very aware that he knew very little about the disease that Hazel suffered from, so he spent time reading up on the illness and its effects. Taking time to do this enabled Scott to have a better understanding of the consequences for Hazel in terms of her care of David. This knowledge created a firmer footing for Scott to ask better questions of Hazel and Harry about their experience of the disease and what needed to happen to ensure David was always well cared for. Scott commented that: 'Even though I did that reading I knew I didn't have the disease so I really couldn't understand its effects on their lives, so I told them that and kept asking questions'.

Two more reports

At about this time two more reports came in to the county regarding Hazel's care of David, and these were brought forward at the next conference with the parents and their support people. With Amy again facilitating this conference, Scott laid out the concerns raised in the reports and sought to link these issues with

Hazel's struggles to manage the effects of her disease. Hazel, however, refuted both the concerns and that the disease was inhibiting her capacity to look after David and told the meeting she didn't want to have any more discussion about the allegations or her illness.

At this point, Scott and Amy redirected the conversation by engaging Hazel's mother, saying, 'It seems like this disease has been a huge thing for your family since other members of your family have the illness and with your husband dying of it so recently. Since so many members of your family have had to live and struggle with it, you must know an enormous amount about this disease and how to cope with it. What thoughts do you have about Hazel's situation?' This led Hazel's mother to say that she felt that Hazel was exactly like her father and was not really facing up to the disease and, just like her father, was resisting seeking out medical treatment. Hazel's mother was very direct in telling Hazel she needed to seek medical help. Scott felt the conversations that followed were crucial in helping the family address the county's concerns for David's safety. He stated:

It was a tricky conversation for the family and Amy did a magnificent job of letting the family talk things out. When the family would get off topic Amy would get them back on track with gentle reminders and reframing of their conversation to make it apply to the agenda items. I know Amy found it difficult and frustrating at times to bring them back on topic but Amy didn't show her frustration at all. Amy kept a high level of focus, and often found the exact right times to step into the family's conversation without cutting them off, or making them feel like they weren't being heard.

Scott stepped back into these discussions by asking Hazel a series of open-ended questions about how she thought her father coped with the disease, what helped him deal with it and whether she saw herself as similar or different to him. Out of these discussions a plan began to be formulated in which Hazel committed herself to getting the medical care she needed, including seeing a specialist and receiving physiotherapy. The couple also agreed that Harry would help Hazel with some of the treatment. After the conference, Hazel followed through on all of the medical treatment commitments she had made.

In this same conference, and flowing on from the discussions of the effects of Hazel's disease, with Amy continuing to act as facilitator to the conversations, Scott was able to ask more detailed questions about Hazel's daily care of David. In this way Hazel, Harry and the network were able to agree to more specific plans about David's daily and nightly care. These included:

- Hazel would take naps at the same time that David would nap.
- If Hazel needed to take a nap when David was not going to sleep, Hazel would ring one of the others to come over to look after David.
- David's crib would be placed alongside Hazel's bed so that David would be within reach of Hazel even if she was unable to get up (at times after waking it would take up to 30 minutes for Hazel's body strength to return so that she could be active). In this way, Hazel would at least be able to rock David's crib even if she couldn't pick David up.
- As part of these arrangements things would also be set up so that the phone, pacifier and toys were also within Hazel's easy reach.

As the conference drew to a close Amy formalised an agreement with Harry, Hazel and their support people that documented the planning around Hazel's medical needs and the care arrangements for David, incorporating these as part of the wider safety planning.

This case description represents only a portion of the work that was undertaken with this case. However, the part reflects the whole in that the example captures the safety-organised approach OCCFS seeks to bring to working with its child protection cases and in responding to involuntary recipients of child protection services.

Good practice with involuntary child protection service recipients

We want now to draw on the case example to point to the aspects and themes of the practice we think are crucial in working constructively with involuntary 'clients'.

The fine details of lived life

The influential interpretive anthropologist Clifford Geertz (2000: xi) writes: 'The answers to our most general questions – why? how? what? whither? – to the degree that they have answers, are to be found in the fine detail of lived life'. The child protection field has been influenced by many grand theories, protocols, models and frameworks. At the end of the day for these ideas to make any difference in the lives of at-risk children they have to be brought down to the level of life as it is lived for the families and social networks within which vulnerable children exist. To the extent that child protection social workers are able to protect and enhance the life circumstances of vulnerable children, that protection comes about in the relationships, and day-to-day encounters between the social worker and the child, their family and their social network, and between the social worker and other professionals.

In preparing this case study we have deliberately focused on the minutia of the human interactions between the professionals, the family members and the extended network since this is where the most significant action happens and where the most substantial practice wisdom is to be found. In listening to and writing up many workers and service recipients' stories we are often struck by the contrast between the seeming complexity of a professionally rendered and dramatised problem, alongside the everyday dignity and humanity of the endeavour that brings about a solution or way forward to that problem. Serious cases are usually talked and written about in complex professionalised ways, very often layered in descriptions of dysfunction, cycles of abuse, grief and loss, denial and multi-generational, multi-problem families. Solutions described by workers and service recipients, however, come layered in the textures of everyday life, involving the vulnerability of people working together in the face of anxiety, talking straight, facing challenges, building opportunity, distilling common goals, attending to detail and seeing the task through. In thinking about the best ways for helping professionals to make a difference in working with involuntary 'clients' in child protection settings we believe it is vital that more attention be paid to particularities of how practitioners are able to achieve on-the-ground success with these sorts of situations.

Inquiry that makes frontline success notable and uses this as a foundation to envision constructive practice has, we believe, the potential to create significant news of difference and reinvigorate child protection practice and organisation. Anne Weick (2000), writing specifically to a social work audience suggests that the social work profession has two voices; a dominant, professionalised, scientised second voice of assessments and interventions, policy and procedure, and a mostly hidden first voice of everyday caring, solution-building and compassionate action. Weick's paper gives an important insight into one of the dynamics that leads the caring professions to overlook the richness of everyday good child protection practice.

An important part of paying attention to the fine details of lived child protection practice is that it slows the impulse to try and find the 'quick fix' or the 'magic bullet' that so often bedevils high-risk child protection work. Complex problems such as child abuse or neglect are not solved in one fell swoop, solutions require time and sustained purposive focus within a context of honest relationships. Working constructively with involuntary 'clients' is a step-by-step process and this in our view cannot be said often enough. It is not a particular model, strategy or technique that delivers a positive outcome, though these may help. Rather a way forward is most often found through purposive sustained relationships that involves as many people as possible who have a stake in the child's life brought together with the focus on building future safety for the child (Turnell and Essex, 2006).

The supervisory relationship behind the practice

To get at more of the richness and detail of the practice and to draw together the themes regarding the notion of the involuntary client we see as critical within the case example, we want to reflect on Scott and Sue's experience of the supervisory relationship.

Scott's experience

The following comments provide some of Scott's thoughts about the context that Sue's supervision creates that that sets the scene for how he was able to manage this case.

What's most important for me about how Sue supports me in the work is that she models with me what she wants me to do with the family. She helps me and prompts me to get out the dilemmas I am struggling with in the case – she doesn't give me the answer and she let's me know its okay to work a case without necessarily knowing what the answer is. Time and again Sue will help me clarify what the child safety issues are that we have to get dealt with in the family but then she doesn't ask for absolutes, instead she'll ask questions that make me struggle with what is the best thing to do. One of the things Sue constantly asks me to see is that this work is not about it being solely my professional responsibility but rather that I and the parents and whoever is around them are a group of people doing our best to struggle with difficult human issues. She demonstrates to me an appreciation of the humanness of the problems and that this is about human beings struggling with problems of everyday living. Because Sue does this for me it means I can go into the family's life and be a social worker who doesn't have to play the expert and that means I'm not trying to tell them what to do but can hand the dilemmas over to them so they struggle with the issues and decisions.

There are times when I felt very frustrated with how things were proceeding in this case, even feeling like we had to remove the baby. I was able to go to Sue and get my frustrations out, I knew that was okay and that I didn't have to come up with the perfect solution. On one of these occasions, after the second set of reports came in and just before we had the conference where we looked at those issues I had a 'rant and rave session' with Sue. It was really important for me, it probably only lasted 10 minutes and after I calmed down Sue helped me focus by asking me to list out the things I was most worried about from the phone reports. She stayed with where I was at with the case and then pushed me to be clear – I needed that to be able to go into the conference knowing what I needed to focus on with the family and network.

I have worked in other statutory contexts and the most important thing about Olmsted for me is that I know I am one component of a system looking at issues of very serious child abuse. Its not for me to fix it, that's not my burden. My job is to facilitate interactions and relationships between all the players, parents, children, extended family and friends and other professionals for all of us to look at and address the issues together. But in other places I've worked in its like the case problem is my problem which makes you want to cover your own arse. Here at OCCFS I don't have to play

out that sort of defensive practice drama. What this does for me as a practitioner working with the families is that I don't have to turn it into a power struggle between me and the client – I've learnt to present the issues to the family and their network in a way that says look, here's the issues I see, here's the questions we need to answer (like how can you show me, the agency and my supervisor that your child is safe?) and then we struggle together with trying to figure out the answers.

We repeatedly get the message in our agency from the Director and our supervisors that we need to explore these issues with the family, and that these are complex human problems. Sue has a saying that sort of sums this up. She says 'its important to not land on something as an absolute'. I've learnt that not having to play the expert with the big answers means that I can actually do my job better. I can say something to the family like 'I have to know the child is safe and I can't leave any unanswered questions'. I don't know the answers, so then I have to set about asking the family all the hard questions. Not having to pretend to have the answers helps me to ask questions and to help them to focus, to formulate and demonstrate their answers.

Sue's perspective

I endeavour to maintain an overview of the cases that come through my team, most particularly the high-risk cases. Any child protection worker responsible for a high-risk case will inevitably become anxious about the situation they are facing and I endeavour to help them to slow down, and step away from anxiety and reactivity. In this particular situation I was aware of this case coming into our team through processes we have in place to track cases. Before the case is assigned I make a point of undertaking my own overview assessment of the situation so I feel settled in my sense of the case. In this case it seemed clear to me that the concerns focused on deprivation or neglect due to the mother's disability, there was no active harm being directed at the child and this gave me confidence that we had space to work things through with the family.

At the outset I sat with Scott and helped him think himself through the concerns and the bottom lines the county would require so that he was settled in approaching the family. I also seek to ensure the worker focuses on essential things such as a medical screening so we can have a clear, independent line through the developmental and medical situation for the child. After this, I also sought to help Scott think through the issue that is almost always at the forefront of a worker's mind, namely, whether a removal is or may be necessary. It is important to assist the worker to get their concerns out in the open in this regard; if the worker keeps this worry to themselves they are likely to act it out and take actions that diminishes the working relationship with the family. My aim is to enable the worker to be settled with their analysis of the situation so they can set about exploring the issues calmly and overtly with the family.

There are many ways that a child protection system can intervene in family life where a child is vulnerable, ranging from stranger care through to kinship care or involving relatives and friends to ensure the child's wellbeing in the home. The best course of action can only be determined when the worker has built relationships with the family and the network of people that surrounds the family. In this way by dealing with the worker's anxieties in the office they are more able to work constructively and purposively with the family and the naturally occurring network and do this in a thoughtful, structured way rather than work in a reactive manner.

Helping the worker to focus on the specific details of the risk to the child helps them put these issues on the table for the family. Most often child protection work can be carried out calmly and thoughtfully and my role in this is to help the worker manage their anxiety and be clear in their thinking. As statutory child protection professionals we always have the capacity to remove the child and this actually means we can afford to go slowly and carefully. Knowing we have that capacity in my view means we can be more confident in providing an opportunity to the parents and their own network to see if they can provide for the child but if not we can always step in if needs be.

I am not sure that the notion of the involuntary client is something that makes best sense of the child protection task. I tend to frame the work in terms of our workers making an involuntary entrance into the

family's life but that then our task is to do everything we can to create voluntary and participative spaces in our relationship with the family and their network. We do this by using our authority skillfully and responsibly, being clear about our bottom lines, giving the family choices wherever possible, treating them as human beings and honouring their experiences and their strengths. Critical to this is that we ask the parents to involve as many people as possible around the child as a way of demonstrating to us that the child will be well cared for.

Our work often involves what I call offering the family the 'rock and hard place' choice. The 'rock' choice involves letting the parents know that we the child protection professionals can take over the decision-making for them. The 'hard place' choice involves the family and their network of people working with us to figure out together a way of moving forward where we can be confident that the wellbeing and safety of the child is ensured. If we are to create the sort of voluntary and participative spaces between the child protection professionals and the family network it is crucial to be straightforward with the family about our professional authority and our requirements.

One of the biggest issues in building a system in Olmsted county that can consistently deliver a collaborative service response to families and their networks has been to address the parts of the system that push the relationship back toward adversarial and expert driven relations. For example, in the past, we were frustrated in our attempts to partner with the family and their network when their case came before the court, and we would find out collaborative work would be overtaken by the decisions of attorneys, judges and expert testimony. In this context, the families would be alienated from the decision-making. This led us to be involved in rethinking the way our courts responded to high-risk child protection cases and led to establishing participatory processes when cases are before the courts (see Lohrbach and Sawyer, 2004).

Thinking systemically: beyond privatising the problem

Helping professionals have a proclivity to focus on the individual worker-client relationship, seeing this as the key location in which change arises. Chris Clark calls this proclivity to privatise human problems the 'characteristic myopia' (2000: 92) of the social work profession. Eileen Munro, looking specifically at child protection practice, believes that helping professionals' preference for the personal and private is a major obstacle for 'changing their use of theory and evaluating practice' (2002: 89). Reducing a problem like child maltreatment to a privatised problem inevitably makes the issue of involuntariness of individual parents into a bigger issue than it deserves and the role of the worker tends to become focused on getting the involuntary client to change.

In our view it is important to frame the 'involuntary' problem in interactional terms (de Shazar, 1991). The issue of involuntariness is not simply a characteristic of any particular client. It is also all about the fact that the child protection system identifies not only a problem in the parenting of those clients, but also defines what must change. More than this, we regard child protection issues as best addressed in the relationships between the professional child protection system and the network of parents, extended family and friends that surround the child in question. Thinking about the problem of child protection in this way defocuses the involuntariness of any particular individual and locates the issues as something to be addressed through a consistent system-wide child protection response in working with all of the people that have a stake in that child's life.

These are very aspirational ideas, but the case example demonstrates our thinking. As a result of Olmsted county approaching the work in this way, the professionals moved very quickly to involve as many people around the immediate family as possible, and used the conferencing processes to locate the responsibility for David's care with the network of people that attended these conferences. The professionals created a context where the network then started to hold Hazel and Harry accountable to the tasks of caring for David, and Hazel's mother challenged Hazel about facing the disease and doing more about this problem for herself. It would have been very easy to focus this case around Hazel's difficulties and the opposition to child protection involvement. This is also the sort of focus that has been shown to lead child protection professionals down a mother blaming track (Allan, 2004; Scourfield, 2001, 2003).

Conclusion: beyond changing the light globe

The notion of the involuntary client is an important issue for helping professions whose theorising and practice models mostly focus on voluntary helping relationships. Within statutory child protection where the professional holds all the aces as to when a relationship begins and ends there is a very important sense in which all clients are involuntary. Families, parents and children simply do not come to child protection agencies saying 'You did such a great job with our next door neighbours, please come and do that for us too, but we want the deluxe service with all the trimmings, so please make sure you bring the police too so we are fully prosecuted for our failings!'

The notion of the involuntary client, therefore, is immediately relevant since almost all child protection clients are involuntary. It is vital for statutory helping professionals to think through how they operate in this territory, especially when most of their training prepares them for voluntary professional-client relationships. In another way though we believe the issue of the involuntary client can be easily over-emphasised and skews the professional toward focusing on trying to change the individual involuntary client. The discourse of the involuntary client, it seems to us, is informed primarily around the almost sacred status attributed by helping professionals to the individual professional-individual client relationship. The 'I-thou' relationship is a dominating, mostly unquestioned motif of the helping professions. The well known joke; 'How many social workers does it take to change a light globe?' and its answer, 'Only one, but the light globe has to want to change', speaks in everyday language about the priority the helping professionals tend to place on their capacity to motivate the problematic, resistant client. This is the language of therapy and individualised change informed by the privatisation of problems so embedded in the western psyche (Turnell and Essex, 2006).

The child protection task is first and foremost about protecting the vulnerable and in this context the work is most effective when the practitioner is grounded in and comfortable with the knowledge that they are the agent of social and legal structures and organisation to ensure that vulnerable children are as safe and as well cared for as possible. In this context we have tried to de-emphasise the 'I-thou' individual worker-client relationship and argue that working with 'involuntary clients', especially in a child protection context, is better framed in terms of a professional system to family/extended family system interaction. This is another way of honouring the old wisdom that it takes a village to raise a child (whether or not particular parents participate voluntarily). This can also be explained in the words of a colleague Susie Essex: 'I'm not so worried about whether the light globe (the supposedly involuntary parent) changes or not, I'm more interested in installing a whole new lighting system' (Turnell and Essex, 2006).

We have tried to demonstrate in this paper that child protection work and the professional-service recipient relationships are best thought about more in terms of their effectiveness in creating safety for children than whether they are voluntary or involuntary. We have tried to demonstrate through the work of OCCFS and the case of Harry and Hazel that if in this case Scott had become focused on the nature of the involuntariness of the parents, and particularly Hazel's opposition toward child protection services, the case would have probably become irretrievably bogged down. Instead, by building and maintaining a professional system to family network focus, exercising and using authority skilfully alongside equal measures of empathy and honouring the strengths and humanity of the parents, and by drawing upon a naturally occurring network surrounding the child, and through organisational and supervisory structures that supported this practice focus, the whole voluntary/involuntary nature of the mother to worker relationship was de-emphasised and its negative consequences inoculated. This professional system to family network focus enables child protection work to be seen through a more constructive and purposive lens than simply the 'myopia' of individual change.

References

Aubrey, C. and Dahl, S. (2006) Children's Voices: The Views of Vulnerable Children on their Service Providers and the Relevance of Services they Receive. *British Journal of Social Work*, 36: 21–39.

Barber, J. (1991) *Beyond Casework*. London: Macmillan.

Burford, G. and Hudson, J. (2000) *Family Group Conferencing: New Directions in Community-Centred Child and Family Practice*. New York: Aldine de Gruyter.

Cashmore, J. (2002) Promoting the Participation of Children and Young People in Care. *Child Abuse and Neglect*, 26: 837–47.

Christianson, B. and Maloney, S. (2006) One Family's Journey: A Case Study Utilising Complementary Conferencing Processes. *Protecting Children*, 21: 31–7.

Clark, C. (2000) *Social Work Ethics: Politics, Principles and Practice*. London: Macmillan.

Cleaver, H. and Freeman, P. (1995) *Parental Perspectives in Cases of Suspected Child Abuse*. London: HSMO.

Dale P. (2004) 'Like a Fish in a Bowl': Parents' Perceptions of Child Protection Services. *Child Abuse Review*, 13: 137–57.

De Jong, P. and Berg, I.K. (2001) Co-constructing Cooperation with Mandated Clients. *Social Work*, 46: 4, 361–75.

De Jong, P. and Berg, I.K. (2002) *Solution-focused Interviewing*. 2nd edn. San Francisco: Brooks-Cole.

Dumbrill, G. (2006) Parental Perceptions of Child Protection Intervention: A Qualitative Study. *Child Abuse and Neglect*. 30: 27–37.

Farmer, E. and Owen, M. (1995) *Child Protection Practice: Private Risks and Public Remedies*. London: HSMO.

Fergurson, H. and O'Reilly, M. (2001) *Keeping Children Safe: Child Abuse, Child Protection and the Promotion of Welfare*. Dublin: A and A Farmar.

Geertz, C. (2000) *Available Light: Anthropological Reflections on Philosophical Topics*. Princeton: Princeton University Press.

Healy, K. (2000) *Social Work Practices: Contemporary Perspectives on Change*. London: Sage.

Hudson, J. et al. (1996) *Family Group Conferences*. Monsey: Willow Tree Press.

Lohrbach, S. (2003) Family Group Decision Making: A Process Reflecting Partnership-Based Practice. *Protecting Children*, 18: 2, 12–15.

Lohrbach, S. and Sawyer, R. (2004) Creating a Constructive Practice: Family and Professional Partnership in High-Risk Child Protection Case Conferences. *Protecting Children*, 19: 2, 26–35.

Ludema, J., Cooperrider, D. and Barrett, F. (2006) *Appreciative Inquiry: The Power of the Unconditional Positive Question*. In Reason, P and Bradbury, H. (Ed.) *Handbook of Action Research*. London: Sage.

MacKinnon, L. (1998) *Trust and Betrayal in the Treatment of Child Abuse.* New York: Guildford Press.

Montigny, J., de (1995) *Social Working: An Ethnography of Front-line Practice.* Toronto: University of Toronto Press.

Munro, E. (2002) *Effective Child Protection.* London: Sage.

Rooney, R. (1992) *Strategies for Work with Involuntary Clients.* New York: Columbia University Press.

Rooney, R. (1998) Socialisation Strategies for Involuntary Clients. *Social Casework,* March: 131–40.

Teoh, A., Laffer J., Parton, N. and Turnell, A. (2003) Trafficking in Meaning: Constructive Social Work in Child Protection Practice. In Hall, C., Juhila, K., Parton, N. and Pösö, T. (Eds.) *Client as Practice.* London: Jessica Kingsley.

Thoburn, J., Lewis, A. and Shemmings, D. (1995) *Paternalism or Partnership? Family Involvement in the Child Protection Process.* London: HMSO.

Thomas, N. and O'Kane, C. (1999) Children's Participation in Reviews and Planning Meetings when they are Looked After in Mid-Childhood. *Child and Family Social Work,* 4: 221–30.

Tripodi, T. and Blythe, B. (1994) *Involuntary Clients in Social Work Practice: A Research-Based Approach.* New York: Aldine de Gruyter.

Trotter, C. (2002) Worker Skill and Client Outcome in Child Protection. *Child Abuse Review,* 11: 38–50.

Trotter, C. (2006) *Working with Involuntary Clients: A Guide to Practice.* 2nd edn. London: Sage.

Turnell, A. and Edwards, S. (1999) *Signs of Safety: A Solution and Safety Oriented Approach to Child Protection Casework.* New York: Norton.

Turnell, A. and Essex, S. (2006) *Working with Denied Child Abuse: The Resolutions Approach.* Buckingham: Open University Press.

Turnell, A. (In press) *Building Safety in Child Protection Services: Making a Strengths and Solution Focus Stick.* London Palgrave.

Westcott, H. (1995) Perceptions of Child Protection Casework: Views from Children, Parents and Practitioners. In Cloke, C. and Davies, M. (Eds.) *Participation and Empowerment in Child Protection.* London: Longman.

Weick, A. (2000) Hidden Voices. *Social Work,* 45, 395–402.

CHAPTER 9

Contracting Strategies for Working with Involuntary Clients

Ronald H. Rooney

Initial contacts between involuntary clients and helping practitioners are often disagreeable to both. Involuntary clients include both persons pressured to work with a helping practitioner under a legal mandate and non-voluntary clients who experience significant, but not legally mandated pressure (Rooney, 1992). For example, reluctant spouses brought to marital counselling and adolescents referred for school problems are often non-voluntary. Helping professionals, trained to assume that clients seek assistance on their own, wanting to know 'who am I', often encounter reluctant clients who want to know 'who are you and when will you leave? 'The social work profession's commitment to values supporting client self-determination, enhancement of strengths and client empowerment seems to presume that social clients are the vulnerable voluntary, in needs of advocacy and protection from persons and forces that might harm them (Hepworth et al., 2005). Such values create dissonance in work with involuntary clients who may have acted to endanger themselves or others (Ryder and Tepley, 1993). Does a helping professional seek to use techniques that would empower a terrorist or paedophile?

At the root of this provocative question are assumptions about who are clients, what is owed them, and the roles of helping professionals. Involuntary clients frequently contain disproportionate representation of members of oppressed groups lacking equal access to resources (Dewberry-Rooney, in press). Practitioners working with involuntary clients frequently perform social control roles aimed in part at protecting society (Trotter, 2006). Such practitioners require guidelines about how to perform those roles in ways that both protect society and support feasible client self-determination (Regehr and Antle, 1997). This chapter presents guidelines for initial contact, assessment, and contracting based on normalising perspectives of strategic self-determination and reactance theory.

Initial involuntary encounters

Involuntary practitioners present themselves to carry out unwanted assessments and perform unrequested duties to involuntary clients. As such, they often represent an unwanted intrusion in an involuntary client's ability to live their lives as they wish. Involuntary clients often respond by denying harm or guilt, affixing blame on others, and acknowledging no problems. This interaction has been characterised in the substance abuse field as a confrontation-denial cycle whereby allegations of wrong-doing or improper behaviour are met by assertions that deny harm to others or self (Miller and Rollnick, 2002). These denials are often then interpreted as reinforcing the view that the client lacks motivation or insight into their concerns, calling for yet more confrontation. Proponents of the motivational interviewing approach suggest that such clients may not perceive their concerns as do others and might better be considered to be in a state of pre-contemplation or contemplation in which action to address the issues seen by others is not imminent (Prochaska and DiClemente, 1984). Involuntary clients who wish that involuntary practitioners could be convinced to avoid their legal responsibilities and not enforce laws, might be accused of magical thinking. So, too, involuntary practitioners may be thinking magically if they wish for involuntary clients to quickly and genuinely acknowledge the error of their ways, and espouse rapid, genuine insight into the harm their behaviour has caused themselves and others. Rather than label such involuntary clients as unmotivated, it may be more useful to view them as not sharing the same motivation as those putting pressure on them. In the task centred approach, this distinction is drawn between attributed problems which are concerns identified and labelled by others and acknowledged problems which are concerns that an individual owns as his or her own (Reid, 2000).

Strategic self-presentation is a social psychological theory that seeks to explain how people respond when they perceive that others control their desired outcomes (Jones and Pittman, 1982). If a person is not confident that a simple request for the desired outcome will be sufficient (i.e. can you help me finish my sentence early?), several types of less candid responses can be predicted. For example, a person might selectively confess to part of a problem, acknowledging some of what is attributed by others, without owning all of it (Kelly, 2000). Clients may choose to ingratiate the practitioner, flattering him or her on a level of competence and caring not experienced with earlier helping professionals, in hopes that compliments might influence a favourable recommendation. On the other hand, some clients may choose to attempt to intimidate the practitioner, frightening him or her away from performing duties. Other clients may throw themselves at the practitioner's mercy, soliciting guidance. Additional strategies include self-promotion or exemplification whereby accounts of one's own behaviour are shared in such a way as to paint one's own motives and actions in the most positive, ethical light (Schlenker and Wowra, 2003).

Rather than label the involuntary client who uses a self-presentation strategy as resistant, dishonest, or deviant, it is more useful to interpret the behaviour as predictable in circumstances in which the client wants something that they believe the practitioner can provide such as a favourable recommendation. The practitioner can thank the involuntary client for the compliment or interpret the self-serving story as an indication of client strengths and proceed to clarify the basis of the recommendation that he or she must write and how the client can influence that (Rooney, 1992).

Reactance theory seeks to explain how people act to protect valued freedoms (Shoham et al., 2004; Brehm, 1966, 1976). Those responses include attempting to restore a freedom directly by refusing to comply, or restoring the freedom by implication or 'finding the loophole' by complying superficially while undercutting the spirit of the requirement. For example, some clients may attend a parenting class as a requirement but pay little attention, arrive late and leave early. Practitioners may find themselves acting similarly in compliance with required training. Technical compliance with a requirement that violates the spirit is often labelled as manipulative by practitioners. Hostility may be expressed toward the source of

the threat and forbidden behaviour may become more desirable than before. As with strategic self-presentation, reactance is a normalising theory that lends itself to practical guidelines to reduce the hostile response. Avoiding giving directives, emphasising choices, and contracting to restore freedom are among the ways reactance theory can be used to enhance cooperation (Brehm, 1976).

Insights from strategic self-presentation and reactance theory can be usefully applied to methods used to prepare for initial contact with involuntary clients. The practitioner is advised to review available background information for facts about law violations or behaviour that led to contact. Being able to describe what was observed rather than focusing on deviant labels should reduce reactance during intake sessions. Second, the practitioner should review available client choices and seek to expand them. For example, a client may have a limited choice between incarceration and participation in a domestic violence treatment programme. Further, however, the client may be able to exert constrained choices in choosing among available treatment alternatives.

Contracting with involuntary clients

The practitioner can prepare for contact by examining legal requirements facing mandated clients, potential pressures facing non-voluntary clients, and considering constrained choices available to both. The practitioner can then explain in a matter of fact, non-blaming way, the reason for initiating contact and seek the involuntary client's view of what led to the contact. Motivational congruence or a fit between the client's view of the problem and that of the agency and practitioner has been associated with better treatment outcomes (Videka-Sherman, 1988). The practitioner can explore for motivational congruence by attempting to find a fit between the client's view and the legal requirement facing mandated clients and pressures facing the non-voluntary client. Hence, the practitioner may find a way of looking at the problem that might influence the client to work on a problem for his or her own reasons. For example, parents who are alleged to have abused or neglected their children rarely acknowledge such behaviours, but readily see the problem as risking the loss of custody of their children

(Rooney, 1992). Under an *agreeable mandate* contracting strategy, the practitioner can seek motivational congruence by contracting around maintaining or regaining custody of their children. In other cases, a client can *make a deal* such that they accept an inducement for participating in a programme. For example, disgruntled spouses brought unwillingly to marital therapy can be assured that their own concerns and solutions will be considered in contracting as well as those of the more voluntary spouse. A third strategy is one that addresses the concerns of those clients who perceive their problem as pressure from legal authorities, parents, and other sources of non-legal pressure. Rather than accusing them of failure to acknowledge their own responsibility for their difficulties, lacking insight and motivation, the practitioner can take advantage of their motivation to *get rid of the pressure* (ibid.). With each of these contracting strategies, the practitioner can identify and enhance motivation by linking with current concerns and seeking motivational congruence. Finally, with those clients who acknowledge no concerns of any kind, an *informed consent* option can be explored in which they consider their choices of allowing the practitioner to establish the contract unilaterally, in the case of mandated clients, or choose not to work on the problems attributed to them by others in the case of non-voluntary clients and take the consequences from those persons exerting pressure and refuse further contact. Some involuntary clients, faced with these options, will select one of the earlier options as a better alternative.

Conclusion

The contracting guidelines suggested above are designed to enhance engagement and agreement. The practitioner can capitalise on available motivation instead of judging it as inadequate. Rather than insist on total personal responsibility for actions and consequences, the practitioner can ask the client to identify on a scale of 1 to 10 what proportion of responsibility they now acknowledge (Chovanec, in press).

These strategies consider persons in involuntary situations as potential clients rather than simply as subjects whose behaviours are the targets for involuntary change. To what extent is society justified in involuntarily attempting to

modify the behaviour of those who have harmed others and broken laws? In particular, those who have perpetrated sexual abuse or violence on others raise these questions. This chapter does not propose an answer to this question but suggests ways to enhance their voluntarism.

References

Brehm, S. (1976) *The Application of Social Psychology to Clinical Practice*. New York: John Wiley.

Brehm, J. (1966) *A Theory of Psychological Reactance*. New York: Academic Press.

Chovanec, M. (in press) Work with Men in Domestic Abuse Treatment. In Rooney, R.H. (Ed.) *Strategies for Work with Involuntary Clients*. 2nd edn. New York: Columbia University Press.

Dewberry-Rooney, G. (in press) Members of Oppressed Groups as Involuntary Clients. In Rooney, R.H. (Ed.) *Strategies for Work with Involuntary Clients*. 2nd edn. New York: Columbia University Press.

Hepworth, D., Rooney, R., Dewberry-Rooney, G. and Strom-Gottfried, K. (2005) *Direct Social Work Practice*. 7th edn. Pacific Grove, CA: Brooks-Cole.

Kelly, A. (2000) Helping Construct Desirable Identities: A Self-Presentational View of Psychotherapy. *Psychological Bulletin*, 126, 475–94.

Miller, W. and Rollnick, S. (2002) *Motivational Interviewing: Preparing People to Change Addictive Behaviour*. 2nd edn. New York: Guilford.

Pittman, T. (1982) Toward a General Theory of Strategic Self-Presentation. In Suls, J. (Ed.) *Psychological Perspectives on the Self*. Hillsdale, NJ: Erlbaum.

Prochaska, J. and DiClemente, C. (1984) *The Transtheoretical Approach: Crossing Traditional Boundaries of Therapy*. Homewood, Il: Dow Jones/Irwin.

Regehr, C. and Antle, B. (1997) Coercive Influences: Informed Consent in Court-Mandated Social Work Practice. *Social Work*. 42: 3, 300–6.

Reid, W.J. (2000) *The Task Planner: An Intervention Resource for Human Service Professionals*. New York: Columbia University Press.

Rooney, R.H. (1992) *Strategies for Work with Involuntary Clients*. New York: Columbia University Press.

Ryder, R. and Tepley, R. (1993) No More Mr. Nice Guy: Informed Consent and Benevolence in Marital Family Therapy. *Family Relations*, 42, 145–7.

Schlenker, B. and Wowra, S. (2003) Carryover Effects of Being Socially Transparent or Impenetrable on Strategic Self-Presentation. *Journal of Personality and Social Psychology*, 85: 5, 871–80.

Shoham, V., Trost, S. and Rohrbaugh, M.J. (2004) From State to Trait and Back Again: Reactance Theory Goes Clinical. In Wright, R.A., Greenberg, J. and Brehm, S.S. (Eds.) *Motivation and Emotion in Social Contexts*. NJ: Lawrence Erlbaum Associates.

Videka-Sherman, L. (1988) Meta-analysis of Research on Social Work Practice in Mental Health. *Social Work*, 33: 4, 325–37.

CHAPTER 10

A Framework for Working with Resistance, Motivation and Change

Martin C. Calder

Introduction

This chapter attempts to provide a conceptual and practical framework for working with resistance, motivation and change. It selectively reviews the available literature and combines this with practice wisdom to furnish workers with an evidence-based toolkit.

I have argued previously (Calder, 2003) that the interactive nature of engagement, resistance and motivation (see Figure 10.1) between the worker and the client is an important consideration that is not represented pictorially within the new assessment framework. The triangle does not have any interactive dimensions suggesting it is a static model, and the worker does not appear. This is a significant and worrying omission that needs to be redressed if we are to engage with the clients with whom we work.

Defining involuntary clients

The definition of mandated clients refer to legally mandated clients as clients who make use of social work services because they are under compulsion to do so as a result or requirement of a court order, for example a person who is on probation, the parents of a child following child abuse, a drug user who is required to receive treatment, or a perpetrator of domestic violence who is ordered by a court to attend a treatment group.

Both Rooney (1992) and Ivanoff et al. (1994) distinguish mandated clients from other involuntary clients who are focused to receive services through some other circumstance such as poverty or illness or due to some psychological rather than legal pressure, for example, a perpetrator of domestic violence who attends counselling because his wife and family pressure him to do so.

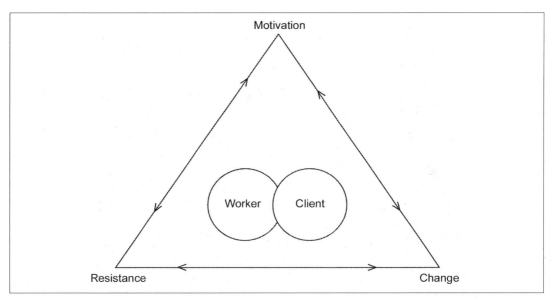

Figure 10.1 The engagement triangle (Calder, 2003)

The nature of casework services to mandated clients can be distinguished from casework services to clients who are more voluntary. One of the differences relates to the goals of the social worker. The social worker's goals in relation to mandated clients may not be consistent with the client's goals. The social worker may have a commitment to goals that are not necessarily the expressed or primary goals of the client. In fact, the goals may be set by the state or by the employing organisation (see Calder, 2003 for a detailed examination of this point).

Additionally, there are particular issues of authority that are present in work with mandated clients. Even in work with entirely voluntary clients there is likely to be a level of psychological authority by virtue of the workers ability to influence the decisions of the client. However, in relation to mandated clients there are particular issues relating to the authority contained in a court order. The worker may, for example, have to remove children or return clients to court.

Some factors appear to be more important in work with involuntary clients, Rooney (1992: 80), and that the following particular factors are related to positive outcomes for involuntary clients:

- Enhancing client choices and sense of personal control.
- Enhancing socialisation into appropriate roles.
- Use of behavioural contracting.
- Facilitating treatment adherence through client commitment to goals and participation in task design and selection.

(Rooney, 1992: 80)

Rooney (1992) also refers to the capacity of the worker to influence client behaviours and attitudes. It is suggested that a client's behaviour can be influenced even by non-verbal clues from the worker. He refers to compliance-oriented methods that 'directly punish or reward certain behaviours' and to persuasion methods which 'influence actions and attitudes by providing information rather than manipulating rewards and constraints' (Rooney 1992: 91). Rooney points to research which suggests that whilst the use of punishments is often unsuccessful in changing attitudes and behaviour in the long term, inducement or the provision of rewards may be more successful. He also suggests that clients are more likely to be persuaded by people who they like and trust.

Engagement

There are a number of tasks involved in engagement with clients and these include inviting participation, since partnership is one of the underlying principles of social work practice. Engagement lays the groundwork for all future work and establishes the partnership essential for effective social work practice (see Calder, 2008). Understanding the presenting problem from the client's point of view requires interviewing and communication skills and empathy. Where many problems exist, some agreement is needed on which ones to address and why, thus creating the potential for focus and common ground. We might need to suggest options to those who lack any potential motivation, as it is impossible to proceed in the absence of some agreement. Understanding what the client wants is crucial, as many clients want help in implementing some already-decided solution rather than in examining alternatives. Workers are often on 'auto-pilot' and seek to resolve the problem from their perspective, so it is hardly surprising when resistance emerges from the client to our fixed ideas. We need to explore what the client wants done and what solutions they can propose, and clarifying expectations and the preliminary agreement is the final stage of the engagement process and sets out how people will work together and to what end.

Seabury (1985) identified engagement as the basic task of the social worker as it forms the basis of a working relationship. This can never be taken for granted and the worker must make a conscious, persistent and skilful intervention in order to facilitate relationship development. In some circumstances, a short encounter between a social worker and a family may in itself be a problem-solving experience. However, if a working relationship cannot be developed, then it is unlikely that there will be any agreement on the child protection plan. In child protection services, the target population is often the 'hard core' families where the initial relationship is usually characterised by a guardedness or reluctance to share information, avoidance and a desire to leave the relationship, or strong negative feelings such as anxiety, anger, suspicion, guilt or despair. Sharland et al. (1995) identified that workers often misinterpret or underestimate the release of mixed emotions, particularly in cases of child sexual abuse. We need to accept that the best we can achieve is honesty rather than positive feelings and a high degree of mutuality. Conflict and disagreement are not something that should be avoided, but as realities that must be explored and understood. Whilst they are not easily overcome, it is possible to engage people from a position of tension and maybe even declared initial distrust (Davies, 1995: 12).

This crucial area is often overlooked in our work, yet it can be essential to the outcome of any assessment work. Many of our child protection clients are involuntary and this leaves an uphill challenge for the workers whose initial task is to convert them to accept the planned work. Denial and the projection of responsibility are likely to become more entrenched in the mother in the face of immediate confrontation. It is clear, therefore, some degree of flexibility and creativity will be needed from the workers when attempting to engage the resistant client. In order to start the process, workers do need to consider where the client is starting from, as there is frequently a discrepancy between the professional and client starting points, which contributes to the problem, rather than serving to address and resolve it (see later model of change section). The focus on strengths (Calder, 1999), as well as weaknesses, should encourage greater parental participation as they do not feel labelled as failed parents.

Workers clearly need to reserve the right to use authority and statutory powers where necessary, but only to the extent that it provides a mandate for the work. Punishment is not a feature that encourages family co-operation. This is particularly important as we usually start with a reluctance by the family to share information and with them portraying strong negative feelings such as anxiety, anger, suspicion, guilt or despair. In sexual abuse work, great care needs to be taken in interpreting the cause of any such emotions, as misinterpretation can aggravate the tensions or conflict. It is possible to engage families from such positions, but this will need careful, considered interventions on the part of the workers.

Preparing for engagement

This stage is often overlooked by workers. Beginnings are important and establish the pattern of ongoing relationships, so we need to do everything possible to reduce unnecessary obstacles to communication.

Compton and Galaway (1999) explored the issues of engaging potential clients in some detail. They describe engagement as the first phase of the problem-solving process. It begins as we establish communication with an applicant, respondent or prospect, and ends when we have a preliminary agreement to work together. Here, an 'applicant' is defined as someone who is seeking help from the agency. A 'respondent' is defined as a person who has been referred to you because someone else has identified a problem and either asked you to intervene or required the client to seek a service from you. A 'prospect' is defined as someone who you are reaching out to offer a service to, but they may not want it.

This agreement should include tentative objectives. Engagement is a process, not a set period of time. It may take only a few minutes for applicants, but a full interview for others, especially for respondents and prospects, which may spread over several weeks or months and involve multiple contacts. The engagement process will differ depending on whether you are engaging an applicant, a respondent, or a prospect. For applicants, since they are seeking help from you and your agency, we can start with a relatively brief exploration of the presenting problem and by starting where the applicant is. Open-ended questions such as 'Could you tell me what brings you to see us?' are useful.

Engaging prospects will be different from engaging applicants, where the roles seem to be reversed. We will be reaching out to them with the offer of a service. They may not want it and are often unaware about the potential usefulness of the service. We thus need to act as a salesperson. There may be an historical dimension to the situation if they found a previous contact demeaning or a service was offered to them in terms that were not acceptable to them. This group thus requires considerable communication skills, patience and persistence, and often requires the worker to be accessible.

Engaging respondents happens because someone else recognises a problem and asks you to intervene or requires the respondent to seek a service from you. The worker needs to be clear with the referrer about their perception of the problem, any contextual considerations, the possibility of change and their expectations from you.

Engagement is a process of communication: an interactive process that gives, receives, and checks out meaning. We can never completely understand what another person is saying, thinking and feeling, and we should not try and pretend otherwise. However, we have a responsibility to improve clarity and understanding in our communications. As Bloom (1980: 337) argues: 'Communications to clients ought to be simple, clear, accurate, and direct. Social workers should choose words that are precise and cannot be misunderstood, words that are not evasive or vague'.

Worker selection

Adcock (2000) suggested that consideration be given to the selection of an appropriate social worker by asking the following questions:

- Is the worker the right person to complete the assessment in terms of race, gender and class? Are they able to work in an anti-oppressive manner while recognising child welfare concerns?
- Does the worker have the appropriate knowledge and understanding for making a core assessment of the child and family?
- What has been the family's previous involvement and experience of social services? How will it affect their ability to participate in an assessment?
- Can the worker be open and honest and work with this family, sharing concerns, goals and expectations?

Assessment should not be seen as a means of the worker gaining information. Family members should be able to derive a benefit from the process. Rose (1994) stated that a task for social workers is to identify ways in which they can provide acceptable and non-stigmatising services, which safeguard children and promote their welfare by:

- Working alongside families rather than dis-empowering them.
- Raising the self-esteem of parents rather than provoking a defensive or angry response.
- Promoting family relationships enabling parents to safeguard and promote the well-being of their children whenever possible.
- Focusing on the overall developmental needs of children rather than on an overly narrow concentration on the alleged incident of abuse.

Cleaver and Freeman (1995) found that families wanted to be kept fully informed, treated with courtesy and involved in all stages of the social work process (the procedural aspects of empowerment). Shemmings and Shemmings (2000: 93) observed that sensitivity is an essential 'envelope to contain the other three'. They also noted that for trust to develop, family members wanted all four conditions to be demonstrated, typically by being invited to meetings, seeing records and being informed of their rights and options. As such, family members require both the procedural and the relational aspects of empowerment to be demonstrated – typically, developing trust, being transparent, genuine and even-handed, and being direct yet sensitive (p92).

Rose and Aldgate (2000) identified several parental worries associated with their contact with child welfare professionals:

- Being vulnerable to child protection enquiries and being afraid of losing their children.
- Being perceived as failed parents.
- The impact of losing control and forfeiting their parenting responsibilities.

They identified various areas valued by parents:

- Communication that is open, honest, timely and informative.
- Social work time with someone who listens, gives feedback, information, reassurance and advice, and is reliable.
- Services that are practical, tailored to particular needs and accessible.
- An approach that reinforces and does not undermine their parenting capacity.

Model of change

In order to start the engagement process, workers need to consider where the client is starting from, as there is frequently a discrepancy between professional and client starting points, which contribute to the problem, rather than serving to address and resolve it. This point can be made more clearly when looking at the model of change. This model (see Figure 10.2) is very useful for setting out realistic plans of work at the outset, for setting attainable targets, and for reviewing what progress, if any, has been made. The model of change shows just how important it is for the professional to allow the client to move

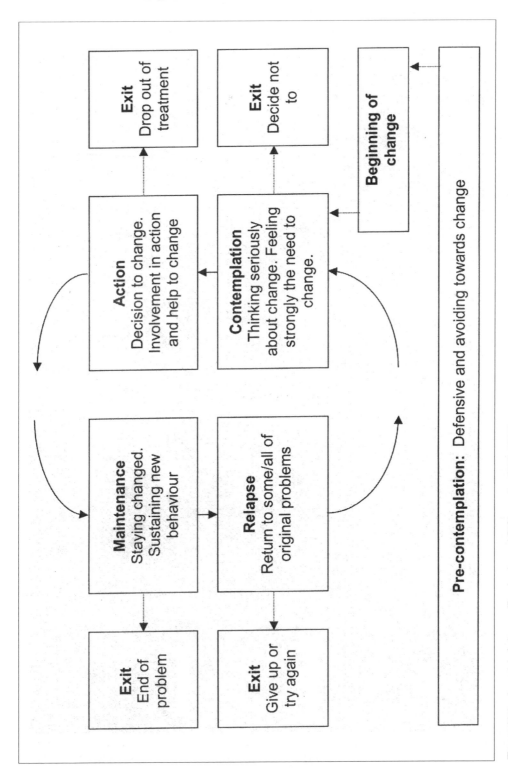

Figure 10.2 A model of change (Prochaska and DiClemente, 1982, 1986)

from pre-contemplation through to action if there is to be any professional-family congruence about what needs to happen. Any failure to allow for this (and this is a very real issue with the timescales set down) sets the worker and the family up to fail. Given the worker should allow sufficient time in their assessment schedule to negotiate and hopefully create the necessary conditions for the client to engage in the work and effect some of the mutually agreed areas requiring change, workers do need to have some understanding of the important initial steps in the model of change. These are described below.

Pre-contemplation: This is where the individual is considering change far less than the professionals, who are often reacting to the presenting situation. Morrison (1995) pointed out that this phase is characterised by blaming others, denying responsibility, or simply being unaware of the need to change, e.g. depression. Whilst in this stage no change is possible. Individuals thus require information and feedback in order that they can raise their awareness of the problem and the possibility of change (Miller and Rollnick, 1991: 16). Pre-contemplation is the point at which the initial assessment takes place in order to ascertain, and hopefully enhance, motivation to at least consider and contemplate the need for change. Whilst the professionals enter the work at the action stage, the involuntary client is probably only in the pre-contemplation change. Such a combination cannot succeed as the two groups are at incongruent stages of change. There may also be a very different definition of the problem between the two groups. For the client, they are unlikely to be in a position to meaningfully engage in the proposed assessment work and a legal mandate often has to be sought.

DiClemente (1991: 192–3) identified four categories of pre-contemplation. Reluctant pre-contemplators are those who through lack of knowledge or inertia do not want to consider change. Rebellious pre-contemplators have a heavy investment in the problem behaviour and in making their own decisions. The resigned pre-contemplator has given up on the possibility of change and seems overwhelmed by the problem. The rationalising pre-contemplator has all the answers but has discounted change as they have figured out the odds of personal risk, or they have plenty of reasons why the problem is not a problem or is a problem for others but not for them.

Contemplation: Clients in this stage are most open to consciousness-raising interventions, such as observations, confrontations, and interpretations (Prochaska and DiClemente, 1986: 9). Through this process, their awareness of the problem increases, and they are then free to reject or adopt to change. The worker's aim is to tip the balance in favour of change (Miller and Rollnick, 1991: 16–17). Contemplation is often a very paradoxical stage of change. The fact that the client is willing to consider the problem and the possibility of change offers hope for change. However, the fact that ambivalence can make it a chronic condition can be very frustrating. It is the stage where many clients will be waiting for the one final piece of information that will compel them to change. The hope is that the information makes the decision for them. Failing this, we need to offer them incentives to change by looking at past changes and by accentuating the positives (DiClemente, 1991: 194–6). It is only after such contemplation that a viable contract for work can be made. There are six steps to the contemplation stage before we can move into the action stage and attempt change. They are:

1. I accept that there is a problem.
2. I have some responsibility for the problem.
3. I have some discomfort about the problem and my part in it.
4. I believe that things must change.
5. I can see that I can be part of the solution.
6. I can see the first steps towards change.

Determination: In the determination stage, the client may now accept that something has to change although they may be unsure how it can be achieved. The task for workers is to remove any barriers to change, and create an environment where change is a realistic possibility. Change remains a very painful process.

Action: Is the stage where the client engages in structured work to bring about a change, in a way that they believe they have determined. Such a tactic avoids dependency on the workers. Yet action is a potentially stressful stage of change as they can fail and feel that they have failed or been rejected. We need to plan for relapse and involve the wider family and the community networks, for it is they who are most likely both to spot the early signs of lapse, and who will provide the most day-to-day support (Morrison, 1995). This stage is where the individual is seen 'in action', implementing the plan. It is where they feel able to make a public commitment to action; to get some external confirmation of the plan; to seek support; to gain greater self-efficacy; and finally to create artificial, external monitors of their activity (DiClemente, 1991: 198–9). For the worker, they should focus on successful activity and reaffirm the client's decisions. They should point out that change is predictable where a person adheres to advice and the plan. The focus should be on learning, exploring and rehearsing ways of relating, thinking, behaving and feeling. All change is essentially a combination of these four basic human processes. This stage may take several months as new behaviour takes time to become established. At the end of the initial planning stage, the aim is to produce a longer-term plan of work.

Maintenance: Is about sustaining and consolidating change and preventing relapse. This is the real test. It occurs when the new ways of relating and behaving become internalised and generalised across different situations. They do not now depend on the presence of the workers, but become consolidated and owned by the individual/family as part of themselves. It is through this process that the client's sense of self-efficacy has been increased (Morrison, 1995). Successful maintenance builds on each of the processes that have come before, as well as an open assessment of the conditions under which a person is likely to relapse (Prochaska and DiClemente, 1986: 10). Stability and support will be essential to sustaining change, especially with the many families who have such poor experience of problem solving (Morrison, 1991: 96).

Relapse: The cyclical model of change allows for the reality that few people succeed first time round. Change comes from repeated efforts, re-evaluation, renewing of commitment, and incremental success. Relapse is thus part of, rather than necessarily hostile to, change. Change is a battle between the powerful forces that want us to stay the same, and our wish to be different (Morrison, 1991: 96). It usually occurs gradually after an initial slip (often due to unexpected stress) rather than occurring spontaneously (DiClemente, 1991: 200). It can lead to a loss of all or most of the gains, resulting in a giving-up and a return to pre-contemplation. This can be counteracted by the worker, giving feedback, on how long it takes to accomplish sustained change. They should aim to keep the change effort going rather than becoming disengaged and stuck. Morrison (1995) reported that where it is noted quickly enough, and help is urgently sought and

available from friends, family or professionals, all is by no means lost. This may lead to further work through the contemplation stage.

The assessment of change is a very uncertain process, and is often very fragile where it is achieved. It is important that we acknowledge that change is very slow and, as such, workers need to set realistic expectations of involuntary clients.

There are a number of useful principles which workers can adopt when considering their role in encouraging change and these include:

- Change is possible.
- Change comes through supportive relationships.
- Change comes through new ways of thinking about problems and possibilities.
- Changes can sometimes come from little things.
- Change can grow from the ordinary and the everyday.
- Change may come from a single opportunity or positive turning point that leads on to other good things.
- Changes comes from tapping into strengths in a child's circumstances.
- Change may sometimes come through chance – experiences or contacts – which if allowed may lead to positive outcomes.
- Getting even some things right may be the best place to start.
- Look for strengths and possibilities.
- Relatives and other people in their informal social networks are likely to be around longest for a child.
- The child can be one of the agents of change and development in their own lives.
- Complex problems rarely have single answers – small steps may interact in positive and unforeseen ways.
- Big plans have a habit of coming unstuck – it may be best not to have all the planning eggs in one basket.
- 'One size fits all' solutions are unlikely to work.
- 'The best may be the enemy of the good' – waiting to achieve the elusive best possible solution may mean missing the potential good of valuable intermediate steps.

Cautionary notes

Parental motivation and readiness for change are of considerable interest to child welfare workers.

Readiness for change is a central component of the stages of change model. In the past, researchers have viewed readiness for change as 'a dichotomous phenomenon, a presence or absence of motivation' (DiClemente and Hughes, 1990: 218). Clients were either ready or they were not. Similarly, behaviour change has been described as 'a one-step process – one simply changes from one form of behaviour to another' (Gelles, 1995: 4). The change model is thought to have considerable heuristic value for practitioners (Sutton, 1996) because it portrays readiness for change and behaviour change as phenomena that develop over time.

By suggesting that many behavioural problems are not quickly or easily remedied, the change model may encourage greater patience and persistence in change efforts. The model may promote less pejorative views of clients who are not ready for change and of those who relapse (Davidson, 1992). Indeed, problem denial (pre-contemplation) can be seen as a common state and a potential starting point in the change process.

Stage-matched interventions are said to be more effective than interventions that are not matched to the stages (Prochaska, 1995) but there is limited empirical support for this assertion (Littell and Girvin, 2002). In sum, the weight of the empirical evidence does not confirm the existence of discrete stages, orderly progression through a sequence of stages, or the benefits of stage-matched interventions. Critics suggest that, like all stage theories, the change model imposes artificial categories on continuous processes (Bandura, 1997; Davidson, 1998; Sutton, 1996). 'Debate has emerged as to whether the descriptive aspects of the model over-simplify or even misrepresent the more complex reality of human change' (Miller and Heather, 1998: 1).

Stage classification is not straightforward in child maltreatment cases. As the developers of the model observed, rarely is there 'a single, well-defined problem . . . reality is not so accommodating and human behaviour is not so simple . . . Although we can isolate certain symptoms and syndromes, these occur in the context of complex, interrelated levels of human functioning' (Prochaska and Norcross, 1994: 470). A parent can be 'pre-contemplating' (not thinking about) one issue, contemplating change in another, and making change in a third area related to child maltreatment. People can be simultaneously involved in multiple stages in relation to a single behaviour and that single-stage classifications are not accurate (Sutton, 1996). Even if we could classify individuals according to change stages, the stage categories have multiple meanings and, hence, would include dissimilar cases. For example, the pre-contemplation category includes clients who deny they have a particular behaviour problem, along with those who acknowledge the problem but are not ready to work on it; these are different issues that call for different intervention strategies. Contemplation covers a wide range of thoughts and intentions, from wishful thinking that things were different to the serious

Genuine commitment	Tokenism
Parent recognises the need to change and makes real efforts to bring about these changes.	Parent will agree with the professionals regarding the required changes but will put little effort into making change work. While some changes may occur they will not have required any effort from the parent.
Compliance/approval seeking	**Dissent/avoidance**
Parents will do what is expected of them because they have been told to 'do it'. Change may occur but has not been internalised because the parents are doing without having gone through the process of thinking and responding emotionally to the need for change.	Dissent can range from proactively sabotaging efforts to bring about change to passively disengaging from the process. The most difficult parents are those who do not admit their lack of commitment to change but work subversively to undermine the process (i.e. sexual abuse perpetrators or perpetrators of Munchausen Syndrome by proxy).

Figure 10.3 Potential responses to change efforts (from Horwath and Morrison, 2000)

consideration of alternatives. Among clients in the action category are those who are making real behavioural changes and those who only say that they are working on their problems.

It is useful to have a framework for gauging the parental response to change efforts and Figure 10.3 provides us with one useful option.

Barriers to engagement

Compton and Galaway (1999) offered us five barriers to engagement:

1. Anticipating the other: we do not listen carefully if we believe we know what the other person is going to say, as we are anticipating the message.
2. Failure to make the purpose explicit: if we fail to make the purpose of the contact explicit, then the worker and the client may have different, even contradictory ideas of what the purpose is and will interpret each other's communications in the light of different ideas. As the subtle distortions continue, the two will be heading in entirely different directions.
3. Premature change activities: efforts to effect change will fail where the worker attempts change efforts without clearly understanding what the client wants and whether that change is feasible. Change efforts should be based on the client's understanding of the problem and what they want done about it. To urge change prematurely may create a barrier to communication and can lead to directive approaches that are often ineffective in the absence of trust.
4. Inattentiveness: if our mind wanders during the contact, then the communication process is compromised.
5. Client resistance: The barriers that clients create can be thought of as forms of resistance against entering into a problem-solving process. They identify three sources of resistance: that which stems from the usual discomfort and anxiety involved in dealing with a strange person and a new situation; from cultural or sub-cultural norms regarding involvement with service agencies and asking for help; and some clients may be securing a degree of satisfaction from their problems or from the attention that the problems earn for them.

Ivanoff et al. (1994) articulated obstacles to engagement at four different levels:

Practitioner-centred obstacles: including problem orientation and worldview, professional expectations, and inadequate training. Research indicates that what the worker and client think, feel and assume about each other may be at least as important as the intervention techniques per se. Problem orientation and worldview variables may decrease a worker's ability to engage involuntary clients. Indeed, ingrained biases inbreed over time, combined with misinformation (e.g. such as misconceptions about the lives of economically disadvantaged people). Workers thus need to examine carefully assumptions based on such client characteristics as ethnicity, gender, sexual orientation, or economic status that may affect their work with clients. Workers need to set realistic expectations of involuntary clients so as not to personalise disappointment, experience frustration, impatience and feelings of failure. Few workers are effectively trained to deal with negatively charged emotional material, reluctance, or non-compliant behaviour.

Client-centred obstacles: including reluctance, unwillingness, and non-compliant behaviour, over-agreeable or compliant behaviour. Even where clients are mandated to attend, to admit this is too close to admitting that the workers are right and that a problem exists. Some clients have a history of fighting the system, and sometimes even winning. They may have their own agenda about fighting the system. Conversely, workers should be aware of extremely co-operative, compliant, or agreeable behaviour, as this may also indicate a lack of successful engagement and contribute to later difficulties.

Environmentally-centred obstacles: including the socio-political bases of mandated treatment and the agency and setting demands. For example, the mandated treatment of sex offenders in today's climate could reflect social definitions of problems. Thus involuntary treatment may be regarded as a political process that involves the socially sanctioned use of power in a context of conflicting interests between the client and some part of the social environment, or as a moral interference in the life of the client.

Client environment-centred obstacles: such as malingering and deception. Malingering is the voluntary production of false or grossly exaggerated physical or psychological symptoms. These symptoms are produced in pursuit of a goal that is easily recognisable within an understanding of the individual's current circumstances rather than of his or her own psychology. Such goals may include evading criminal prosecution. Most workers should see this as a problem-solving strategy that the client uses as a method of coping with adverse circumstances.

Shemmings and Shemmings (2000) noted that agency policies could also obstruct openness in assessment. For example, workers trying to empower families whose first language is not English will find it virtually impossible if interpreting facilities are difficult to access. These authors also note that empowerment is difficult to achieve during the initial assessment as the time available for assessment may be limited and the client may not have met the worker before. It is important for workers to prepare for meetings and to have a framework to guide the conversation, rather than using a set formula. It is also important to try and avoid assumptions as these may be incongruent with research findings and can often act as a barrier to participatory practice (though this is different in work with sex offenders – see Calder, 1999b).

Strategies for enhancing engagement with involuntary clients (Ivanoff et al., 1994)

1. *Prior to client contact*
   – *Problem orientation and worldview check –* workers need to identify, acknowledge and examine their negative biases and assumptions about clients as these can be dangerous and compromise effective practice.
   – *Developing realistic expectations for practice –* many workers coming from academia are prepared for ideal, not real clients, and thus can become easily disappointed. The following self-statements can be helpful when beginning work with involuntary clients:
   - It is reasonable that involuntary clients resent being forced to participate.
   - Because they are forced to participate, hostility, silence and non-compliance are common responses that do not reflect my skills as a worker.
   - Due to the barriers created by the practice situation, clients may have little opportunity to discover if they like me.

- Lack of client co-operation is due to the practice situation, not to my specific actions and activities.
2. *During initial contacts with the client*
   – *General guidelines –* start by adopting a general, non-defensive stance. Be clear, honest and direct, and acknowledge the involuntary nature of the arrangement. Clarify the role of the workers and the expected role of the client; the activity necessary to achieve mandated compliance; the structure and format of contacts; how the worker can be expected to respond to non-compliance; and the possibilities or options for rewards, incentives, early discharge etc.
   – *Motivational congruence between worker and client –* is important to successful outcomes. This often involves preparing the client for their role, and can include some choices about selecting an intervention to promote their adherence to the plans.
   – *Conversational responses –* for the worker to avoid. Common examples include:
   - Avoid expressions of over-concern.
   - Avoid moralistic judgements.
   - Avoid criticising the client.
   - Avoid making false promises.
   - Avoid displays of impatience.
   - Avoid ridiculing the client.
   - Avoid blaming the client for his or her failures.
   - Avoid dogmatic utterances.
   - Respect the right of the client to express different values and preferences from yours.

As Horwath and Morrison (2000: 83) have pointed out: 'Engaging with the change process involves positively weighting, increasing or establishing motivators for change, whether these are material, psychological, individual or environmental. This can be understood only by recognising that motivation is an interactive phenomenon in which professionals are highly significant figures . . .'

Resistance

There have been many definitions of resistance that highlight three key points:

- It is a behaviour aimed at maintaining present behaviours.

- It is about not participating.
- Refusing to change.

It is clear that resistance arises, to a significant extent, from the interpersonal interaction of the worker and the client (Miller and Rollnick, 1991: 101). This will occur whoever the worker is, and may occur when we try to use strategies which are inappropriate to the client's readiness or attitude to change, or where the views and judgements of the workers are rejected by the family. Resistance is frequently dependent upon the posture or style adopted by the workers. Whilst resistance can be seen as functional to the family, it can work either way for the worker.

Professionals need to acknowledge that resistance may peak during the assessment and planning phase of their intervention. For women, they are often either treated as mothers with no regard to their own needs as adults, or as a secondary perpetrator. A determination not to be overwhelmed, distracted, or immobilised by the parents' initial response is essential in establishing genuine emotional contact. Hostility can be diminished by being clear about tasks to be done and demonstrating a willingness to be flexible about matters that are negotiable.

Resistance can take a variety of forms, and there are a number of different categorisations to draw from:

The four categories of resistance (Dale et al., 1986)

1. Hostile resistance – shown through overt anger, threats, physical intimidation and shouting.
2. Passive-aggressive resistance – conveyed under a guise of niceness or obsequiousness, with overt compliance on top of covert antagonism, anger and the suppression of explosive behaviours.
3. Passive-hopeless resistance – a more overt presentation demonstrated by tearfulness, immobility, and an attitude of despair towards any help that is offered.
4. Challenging resistance – which is manipulative behaviour along the lines of 'cure me if you can'.

The origins of resistant behaviour

Research (such as Cleaver and Freeman, 1995) stresses the need for workers to begin by considering why the family member appears resistant. It may simply be that the worker and the client are in the early stages of their relationship and insufficient trust has developed, or that the family perceives the process as challenging and anxiety-provoking. Egan (1994) reminded us that 'involuntary clients' are much more likely to be reluctant or resistant. He provided some practical tips for managing the problem:

1. How might resistance show itself?
- By only being prepared to consider 'safe' or low priority areas for discussion.
- By not turning up for appointments or by being overly co-operative with professionals.
- By being verbally/and or physically aggressive.
- By minimising the issues.

2. When might resistance show itself?
- When there is fear of intensity and high levels of empathy being expressed by the child or family.
- In situations in which lack of trust or fear of betrayal are present.
- When the family member feels s/he has no choice but to take part.
- When there is resentment of third-party referrers (such as other family members).
- When the goals of both parties are different.
- With people who have negative experiences or images of social services departments.
- When people feel that to ask for help is an admission of failure.
- When people feel that their rights are not respected.
- When people feel they are not participants in the process.
- If the worker is disliked.

3. What might we be doing or have done already to make matters worse?
- Becoming impatient and hostile.
- Doing nothing, hoping the resistance will go away.
- Lowering expectations or blaming the family member.
- Absorbing the family member's anger.
- Allowing the family member to inappropriately control the assessment.
- Becoming unrealistic.
- Believing that family members must like and trust us before assessment can proceed.

- By ignoring the enforcing role of some aspects of child protection work and hence refusing to place any demands on family members.

4. Are there productive approaches to working with 'reluctant and resistant' people during assessment?

- Give practical, emotional support – especially by being available, predictable and consistent, thus modelling a secure attachment style.
- By seeing some resistance and reluctance as normal.
- By exploring our own resistance to change and by examining the quality of our own interventions and communication style.
- Establishing a strong and well-articulated relationship by clarifying all the rules of sharing records, by inviting people to meetings, by sharing with them how and why you have to make decisions and explaining the complaints procedure.
- Helping family members to identify incentives for moving beyond resistance.
- Tapping the potential of other people who are respected as partners by the family member.
- By understanding that reluctance and resistance may be avoidance or a signal that we are not doing our job very well (pp.147–53).

Strategies for reducing resistance

Resistance is a natural response to the fear of change. A worker who understands that resistance is part of the dynamics of a helping relationship will be able to help the client in the process of making the desire to change their own behaviour. Even initially hostile and uncooperative clients prefer openness and honesty and a social worker who shows concern and listens to their point of view. There will always be some families that do not wish to work in partnership with the statutory agencies because they believe they have no problem or because of their hostility towards such bodies. Even with the most resistant of families it should be possible to engage some members in the child protection process and at the very least keep them informed about what is happening and how they could participate more fully. The guiding principle for work that encourages the involvement of and partnership with families must be that the welfare of the child is of paramount importance. Low levels of client

resistance are not only easier for the worker but it is also associated with longer-term change. By re-framing resistance as a feature of motivated behaviour, the workers can unlock an opportunity to help the client's change. It is important to identify the individual features of resistance to select a commensurate strategy of intervention, which may include:

Interviewing strategies:

- Simple reflection – and acknowledgement that the disagreement, emotion, or perception can permit further exploration rather than defensiveness.
- Amplified reflection – or exaggeration can encourage them to back off a bit and reflect.
- Double-sided reflection – acknowledges what they have said and we then add it to the other side of their ambivalence.
- Shifting focus – away from the stumbling block by bypassing them.
- Agreement with a twist – offer initial agreement, but with a slight change of emphasis that can influence the direction and momentum of change.
- Emphasising personal choice and control – in the end, even where the current freedom of choice is threatened.
- Re-framing – information they offer so you acknowledge it but offer a new meaning of it or an interpretation for them.
- Therapeutic paradox – where the resistance is designed with the hope of movement by the client in a beneficial direction.
- Handling missed appointments – seek them out and offer them a new appointment, regardless of the reasons (adapted from Miller and Rollnick, 1991, pp.104–11).
- Change the style of the worker to either increase or decrease the level of resistance.
- Where the family dispute the findings of the investigation, suggest that a fuller assessment would give them the opportunity to demonstrate evidence for their claims. It is important that any evidence parents produce to support claims or demonstrate strengths and positive qualities is taken seriously and looked at together with evidence that demonstrates problems or confirms concerns, and use any high levels of anxiety to reduce any resistance to any ongoing work, e.g., where clients see their situation as beyond their control. Here, we can often get them to consider alternatives to their resistant behaviour or situation as a prelude to change.

Structural strategies:

- Co-work to provide strength in numbers.
- The use of a consultant or 'expert' to emphasise the authority held by the workers. This needs to be done with care as otherwise it can become just an exercise in power.
- Promote effective inter-agency perspective to resist any transference of family anxieties onto the workers.
- Good intercommunication between the different professionals involved.

These need to be applied after careful consideration, particularly where the potential dis-empowerment may have a long-term impact on the recipient families. It is important for the workers to try and bring the family anxieties within working limits, and this can be achieved by getting them to list their anxieties. We can then agree goals that are likely to reward the client and act as a source of motivation to them. We need to be aware that motivation may fluctuate between real optimism and scepticism that change may create more problems than it resolves. It is the responsibility of core group members to persuade them that it is worthwhile, and this can be encouraged by clarifying the goals, spelling them out clearly, and collectively working towards the same outcomes.

Small changes can be used to demonstrate that change is possible and rewarding, thus offering some pay off that will exceed the costs of change. Where the family does not accept that the benefits outweigh the costs, the worker can ask them not to change but to consider what changes would be desirable if and when they decided to change. This may activate their self-determination and the initiation of change internally. For any child protection plan or assessment to have any chance of success, there must be at least some motivation within the family.

Motivation and change

Motivation is defined as 'the probability that a person will enter into, continue, and adhere to a specific change strategy' (Miller and Rollnick, 1991: 19). It is about a state of readiness or eagerness to change, which may fluctuate from one time or situation to another. Moore-Kirkland (1981: 28) argued that motivation is not an attribute of the client but a product of the interaction of client, worker and environment. It

is not a characteristic of the client's personality structure or psychological functioning. She argues that by viewing motivation as a transactional concept and a process rather than a trait, we are free to mobilise motivation in such a way as to build on and enhance the competencies of clients in their life experiences.

A transactional model of motivation enables us to assess several factors in relation to the change effort:

- Affective arousal – the level of emotional arousal related to the change.
- Directionality – the goals or direction of change/movement.
- The environment – as each person in the change effort perceives it.

None of these factors individually can explain or predict the level of motivation available for accomplishing a given task or for initiating change. Each of the components are interacting, interdependent forces affected and being affected by the others. As such, all components must be considered in assessing the motivation of a system, and each is necessary but not sufficient to explain motivation or to predict if change will occur. If we can identify the reluctant or disabling component, this can become the target for the initial intervention.

Morrison (1991: 93) has argued that motivation comes from the interplay of internal and external factors and it is rarely the case that real change is accomplished only on the basis of personal motivation without the assistance of external reinforcement.

An alternative way of assessing the parent's motivation for problem solving is to locate them on the following scale. We need to be aware that many parents will not share the same views or the same level of motivation to change, and this should not be overlooked.

A scale for assessing the parent's motivation for problem-solving

1. Shows concern and has realistic confidence
- Parent is concerned about children's welfare; wants to meet their physical, social, and emotional needs to the extent he/she understands them.
- Parent is determined to act in best interests of children.

- Has realistic confidence that he/she can overcome problems and is willing to ask for help when needed.
- Is prepared to make sacrifices for children.

2. Shows concern, but lacks confidence

- Parent is concerned about children's welfare and wants to meet their needs, but lacks confidence that problems can be overcome.
- May be unwilling for some reason to ask for help when needed. Feels unsure of own abilities or is embarrassed.
- But uses good judgement whenever he/she takes some action to solve problems.

3. Seems concerned, but impulsive or careless

- Parent seems concerned about children's welfare and claims he/she wants to meet their needs, but has problems with carelessness, mistakes and accidents. Professed concern is often not translated into effective action.
- May be disorganised, not take enough time, or pays insufficient attention; may misread 'signals' from children; may exercise poor judgement.
- But does not seem to intentionally violate proper parental role; shows remorse.

4. Indifferent or apathetic about problems

- Parent is not concerned enough about children's needs to resist 'temptations', eg competing demands on time and money. This leads to one or more of the children's needs not being met.
- Parent does not have the right 'priorities' when it comes to child care; may take a 'cavalier' or indifferent attitude. There may be a lack of interest in the children and in their welfare and development.
- But parent does not actively reject the parental role.

5. Rejection of parental role

- Parent actively rejects parental role, taking a hostile attitude toward child care responsibilities.
- Believes that child care is an 'imposition', and may ask to be relieved of that responsibility. May take the attitude that it isn't his or her 'job'.
- May seek to give up the responsibility for children.

(Magura et al.,1987: 25)

It is now clear that an assessment must include a family's motivation to change. Workers need to be careful not to label all involuntary clients as unmotivated. It is wrong to believe that work can only be accomplished with motivated clients, as there are strategies available to professionals to help tap motivational elements in the family's social and extended family network. Workers need to believe that they can motivate the client and accept that this is more important than the client's pre-existing level of motivation.

Strategies for enhancing motivation for change

Change has been defined as' the elimination or substantial modification of the presenting problem' (Papp, 1983: 215). One of the principal tasks for the professional is to reach some agreement about what will count as change in a particular case – when it starts, how it progresses and where it ends. In order to fulfil this task, the professional has to have some understanding of what conditions facilitate change, what barriers restrict change, and how we can measure change. If we are unable to set realistic targets we end up with shifting goalposts that often inflame families who are unable to project forward with any certainty. Any failure to individually negotiate the projected outcomes will also lead to professional dysfunction, which may mirror the family dynamics (see Calder, 2008).

Adopting useful theories to guide our interventions

Empowerment in child protection work

Jack (1995: 11) distinguishes between two different meanings of empowerment. The first is enablement 'which, being about the development of another's capabilities, is a professional skill . . .' whereas empowerment '. . . being about the struggle for power and control, is essentially a political activity'. As such, most workers tend to see empowerment as 'enablement'.

Empowerment represents recognition of client strengths. Child protection, based on anti-oppressive premises, needs to believe that families have the ability to define their own problems, set their own goals and take their own action for change; a commitment to basing this change on a broader social analysis than is commonly the case, with most professional intervention; and a style of working in partnership with people which facilitates and empowers them to move in the direction they choose.

Boushel and Lebacq (1992: 45–6) identified certain elements required of a model of empowerment for child protection work:

- Support the right of service users to choose the social roles they wish to fulfil (e.g. mother, daughter, carer, or partner).
- Support the right of service users to undertake those roles in ways that do not jeopardise the welfare of others.
- Facilitate an awareness of the ways in which the dynamics of structural and inter-personal oppression operate in the service-users situation.
- Acknowledge, and where possible, build upon service user's previous attempts to protect themselves and/or others from child protection work.
- Provide information on the range of resources and options available to service users and their possible consequences.
- Support and facilitate service users in their expression of equivocal feelings about interventions, issues and problems.
- Generate an awareness in service users of the power exercised by welfare professionals on behalf of the state and their rights of redress.
- Facilitate service users in challenging paternalistic or discriminatory welfare provision.

Social work practice based on empowerment assumes that client power is achieved when clients make choices that give them more control over their presenting problem situations and, in turn, their own lives. In addition, it has to assume that people have choices available to them to make. This leads workers to attend to the dynamics of personal power, the social power endemic to the client's environment, and the relationship between the two. For workers, promoting empowerment means believing that people are capable of making their own choices and decisions. Their role is 'to nourish, encourage, assist, enable, support, stimulate, and unleash the strengths within people . . . [by helping] clients articulate the nature of their situations, identify what they want, explore alternatives, for achieving those wants, and achieve them' (Cowger, 1994: 264). The role of the social worker is not, however, to empower

people. They do not possess power that they can distribute at will. They are resources for enabling client empowerment.

Barriers to empowerment

The retention of a blinkered view of the problem supports the omission of class, gender, race and ability inequalities in child protection work. It gives workers considerable social control over the clients they have to work with. It places clients at a disadvantage in terms of interpersonal power, and supports a paternalistic approach to the problem. The concern in this approach is that the professional agenda prevails and sets a series of obstacles that the client has to overcome. Many exit from any attempt to engage or discuss the need for change. We should not expect the client to admit their powerlessness before any real progress can be made, but we could use the power inherent in the relationship as a lever to induce change.

It is very important that we differentiate between childcare (voluntary clients) and child protection (involuntary clients) before looking at strategies for engaging families. Where the client is involuntary, the aim of our intervention initially is to try to convert them into being able to accept the services on offer to protect the child. The protective agencies clearly have to reserve the right to use the authority invested in them where the need arises, e.g., a refusal to co-operate with the work and the risks to the children are believed to be too high in the absence of any willingness to discuss areas of change required. We can use the feelings brought by the family to create a mandate to work with the problems they have and which can lead to a relationship based on mutual respect. Social workers will find that it is always more difficult to make good working relationships when they have the ultimate responsibility in law to act to protect. In this situation, they must remain involved until the child has been protected.

We need to acknowledge and work with strong parental reactions without becoming defensive about the proper exercise of our professional responsibility and without endorsing or colluding with them. Workers need to be alert to the reasons why families resist their interventions. We know that the child protection system as a whole operates against a background of conflict and uncertainty. The process of investigation initiates a traumatic sequence of events in the lives of family members and which encroaches on the family's privacy, and this is frequently more acute where statutory powers are invoked. Thoburn et al. (1995) found that parents do understand the professional need to discharge their duties, but strongly objected to those who did things by the book, without any warmth or concern, and who didn't listen. The DoH research (1995) found that post-registration poor case supervision can induce hostility and anger from the parents to the point that they are unable to accept, even consider the help on offer (p49). Workers need to be aware that they should listen to the family views and take them into account, but should never amend the assessment to the point that any of the key issues are overlooked (DoH, 1988: 23).

The strengths of families

Consumers of social work services are often oppressed by society and abused by other people. Keeping in mind the strengths necessary to struggle against oppression offers clues about client capabilities that the social worker should validate and build on.

(Early and Glenmaye, 2000)

The strengths' perspective argues that client empowerment is central to social work practice and client strengths provide the fuel and energy for that empowerment. Client empowerment is characterised by two interdependent and interactive dynamics: personal empowerment and social empowerment. The personal empowerment dynamic is where clients give direction to the helping process, take charge and control of their personal lives, get their 'heads straight', learn new ways to think about their situations, and adopt new behaviours that give them more satisfying and rewarding outcomes. The social empowerment dynamic recognises that client definitions and characteristics cannot be separated from their context and that personal empowerment is related to opportunity.

The strength approach is one model which has proved useful in engaging resistant families. Understanding how to assess strengths and intervene in ways that strengthen and support family functioning is of particular importance in child protection work. It can help us work effectively with families in a way that protects the child, but does not oppress the family:

To assess the power of the individual to create change, it is necessary to focus on their strengths as well as the problems. This focus can lead to interpretations of behaviour as coping abilities or survival strategies.

(Rodwell and Blankebaker, 1992: 159)

The proposition that client strengths are central to the helping relationship should not be a controversial statement, but it often is (Cowger, 1994). Maluccio (1979) found that social workers repeatedly underestimate client strengths and view clients as reactive organisms with continuing problems, underlying weaknesses, and limited potential. He also found that social workers had more negative perceptions of clients than clients had of themselves. If this is true then one must look to a cause. One possibility is that workers do not have a helpful guidebook to help them understand and then deploy strengths-based thinking.

The strengths perspective clearly demands that we adopt a different way of looking at individuals, families and communities. All must be seen in the light of their capacity, talents, competencies, possibilities, visions, values and hopes, however dashed and distorted these may have become through circumstance, oppression and trauma. Personal qualities and strengths are often forged in the face of abuse and oppression (Saleebey, 1996). Figure 10.4 usefully contrasts the strengths approach with conventional, pathology-based approaches.

Any deficit-based assessment targets the individual as 'the problem' and this often leads to a reinforcement for the client of their powerlessness as well as reinforcing the social structures that generate unequal power. It often acts as a self-fulfilling prophecy.

The strengths perspective is rooted in the belief that people can continue to grow and change; that many of the barriers that people labelled as belonging to 'disadvantaged groups' face in meeting basic needs for shelter, food and positive community participation, tend to come from educational, political and economic exclusion based on demographic rather than individual characteristics.

Working with strengths has considerable advantages, not least that it is consistent with the values underpinning the social work profession. Other advantages include:

- It takes cognisance of the power relationship between social workers and clients. Clients

Pathology	Strengths
Person is defined as a 'case'; symptoms add up to a diagnosis.	Person is defined as unique; traits, talents, resources add up to strengths.
Therapy is problem focused.	Therapy is possibility focused.
Personal accounts aid in the evocation of a diagnosis through reinterpretation by an expert.	Personal accounts are the essential route to knowing and appreciating the person.
Practitioner is sceptical of personal stories, rationalisations.	Practitioner knows the person from the inside out.
Childhood trauma is the precursor or predictor of adult pathology.	Childhood trauma is not predictive; it may weaken or strengthen the individual.
Centrepiece of therapeutic work is the treatment plan devised by practitioner.	Centrepiece of work are the aspirations of family, individual or community.
Practitioner is the expert on clients' lives.	Individuals, family or community are the experts.
Possibilities for choice, control, commitment and personal development are limited by pathology.	Possibilities for choice, control, commitment and personal development are open.
Resources for work are the knowledge and skills of the professional.	Resources for work are the strengths, capacities and adaptive skills of the individual, family or community.
Help is centred on reducing the effects of symptoms and the negative personal and social consequences of actions, emotions, thoughts, or relationships.	Help is centred on getting on with one's life, affirming and developing values and commitments and making and finding membership in or as a community.
	Reprinted with the permission of the author

Figure 10.4   Comparison of pathology and strengths (Saleebey, 1996: 298)

enter into the relationship in a vulnerable position and with comparatively little power. A strengths perspective reinforces client competence and thus mitigates the significance of unequal power between the client and the worker.

- It provides a structure and content for an examination of realisable alternatives, for the mobilisation of competencies that can make things different, and for the building of self-confidence that stimulates hope.
- By combining personal and environmental resources creates situations for goal achievement.

(adapted from Cowger, 1994)

The strengths' perspective is particularly important for mandated or involuntary clients because of the powerlessness implicit in the involuntary nature of the client-worker relationship. For social workers to shift towards the strengths approach they need to have some understanding of its underlying beliefs. They must also not lose sight of the need to take appropriate action to protect children whenever

necessary. The following summary is offered to workers in this context, as the strengths approach cannot be adopted on a blanket basis without reference to individual circumstances. The social worker doesn't change people, but aims to act as a catalyst for clients' discovering and using their resources, to accomplish their goals (Saleebey, 1992). This makes it less likely that workers will 'rescue' clients and more likely to reinforce their strengths, even in a crisis.

Any proactive approach to child protection focuses on family strengths and capability in a way that supports and strengthens family functioning. All families have strengths and capabilities. If we take the time to identify these qualities and build on them rather than focusing on correcting deficits or weaknesses, families are not only more likely to respond favourably to interventions, but the chances of making a significant impact on the family unit will be enhanced considerably. A major consideration as part of strengthening families, is promoting their abilities to use existing strengths for meeting needs in a way that produces positive changes in family functioning. This can be achieved by using empathy or attempting to promote some mutual agreement between each other.

Using the principles of the strengths perspective with abusing families may be the only chance to empower families to change their behaviour. Yet uncovering strengths cannot be accomplished in a simplistic manner, as they 'are not isolated variables, but form clusters and constellations which are dynamic, fluid inter-related and inter-acting' (Otto, 1963: 80). Developing a strengths-based practice involves a paradigm shift from a deficit approach to a positive partnership with the family, and will involve:

- The relationship between a worker and a family must be re-framed from an adversarial one to a helping alliance and partnership with the family. This suggests a major emphasis on the engagement phase.
- Empowering individuals and families to discover and use the resources and tools within and around them.
- Integrating knowledge of resilience in workers as it may be crucial to families in overcoming future risks.

(DePanfalis and Wilson, 1996)

Although the child abuse field has just begun to apply the strengths perspective to its repertoire, there is a catalogue of documented benefits to date:

- An emphasis on strengths as well as on risks increases the opportunity for developing a helping alliance – a crucial element in achieving positive treatment outcome and risk reduction.
- Positive reinforcement for positive conditions and behaviours is more effective than trying to convince or coerce individuals to alter negative conditions or behaviours.
- Cultivating strengths offers the opportunity for more permanent change.
- Emphasising strengths helps family members build in successes in their lives, which in turn should help them more effectively manage crises and stress.
- Helping families through short-term positive steps empowers families to take control of their lives.
- Celebrating successes changes the tone of treatment, for both client and helper.

- Communicating a true belief that a family can change destructive patterns helps to promote more long-lasting change.

(DePanfalis and Wilson, 1996)

It is important to give the families the confidence to believe they can change, and this may be partly achieved by considering some of their behaviours as survival strategies or coping mechanisms in an oppressive environment. Leung et al. (1994) identified a set of guiding values for workers within the strengths perspective:

- Children should grow up in their own families.
- People can change.
- People can do their best when empowered.
- Instilling hope is a central part of the child protection remit.

The strength approach gives the worker a systematic way to identify and utilise the ability, talent, potential and resources of the client system. It becomes a strategy of empowerment through which clients recognise their competencies and strengths.

There are several components of a strength approach:

- Developing positive attitudes towards clients.
- Focusing on family strengths and not problems.
- Encouraging them to engage in effective behaviours.
- Challenging clients to appreciate their own ethnic and cultural backgrounds.
- Encouraging clients to locate their own resources (e.g. Family group conferences).

Identifying family strengths creates a non-threatening atmosphere in which the client-worker relationships can be established. It also helps workers to determine interventions that will build on client strengths. It can help the workers operationalise the basic social work values such as self-determination. In order to maximise the opportunities available to families, the workers need to identify and utilise the formal and the informal networks. The worker's use of language is very important: if they refer to clients as 'manipulative' it focuses on their pathology, compared to seeing them as 'resourceful' which focuses on their strengths. It is important to search for strengths, even when it is like searching for a needle in the haystack with some abusive families. The strengths approach is built upon a simple belief – the power is in the hands of the clients.

Some practitioners value strengths more than risks as a foundation for practice (Kwang and Cowger, 1998), particularly since social work researchers have pointed out the debilitating effects of the stigmatisation that deficit-based thinking has on clients. The current problem is that workers lack the tools that support a strengths-based approach. This is particularly true in the sexual abuse arena, and most definitely in the material relating to work with mothers. Strengths-based practice not only promotes more comprehensive, balanced, and optimistic views of clients and their situations than deficit-based treatment, but such a positive emphasis also is one of several factors associated with treatment effectiveness. Strengths-based practice also builds upon the observation that people can overcome even substantial risks if they are able to mobilise resources that help them cope with, adapt to, or overcome the risks.

Conclusions

In this chapter I have attempted to pull together some of the key issues in relation to motivation, resistance and change and link these with strengths-based and empowerment practice to provide a template for evidence-based practice.

References

Adcock, M. (2000) The Core Assessment Process: How to Synthesise Information and Make Judgements. In Horwath, J. (Ed.) *The Child's World: Assessing Children in Need.* London: NSPCC.

Bandura, A. (1997) *Self Efficacy: The Exercise of Control.* NY: WH Freeman.

Boushel, M. and Lebacq, M. (1992) Towards Empowerment in Child Protection Work. *Children and Society,* 6: 1, 38–50.

Calder, M.C. (1999) Towards Anti-Oppressive Practice with Ethnic Minority Groups. In Calder, M.C. and Horwath, J. (Eds.) *Working for Children on the Child Protection Register: An Inter-Agency Practice Guide.* Aldershot: Arena.

Calder, M.C. (1999b) *Assessing Risk in Adult Males who Sexually Abuse Children: A Practitioners Guide.* Lyme Regis: Russell House Publishing.

Calder M.C. (2003) The Assessment Framework: A Critique and Reformulation. In Calder, M.C. and Hackett, S. (Eds.) *Assessments in Childcare: Using and Developing Frameworks for Practice.* Lyme Regis: Russell House Publishing.

Calder, M.C. (2008) Involuntary Clients and Risk Assessment: Philosophical, Policy and Practice Considerations. In Calder, M.C. (Ed.) *Contemporary Risk Assessment.* Lyme Regis: Russell House Publishing (In Press).

Calder, M.C. (2008) A Contemporary Framework for Understanding Organisational and Professional Dangerousness. In Calder, M.C. (Ed.) *Contemporary Risk Assessment.* Lyme Regis: Russell House Publishing.

Cleaver, H. and Freeman, P. (1995) *Parental Perspectives in Cases of Suspected Child Abuse.* London: HMSO.

Compton, B.R. and Galaway, B. (1999) *Social Work Processes.* 6th edn. Pacific Grove, CA: Brooks/Cole.

Cowger, C.D. (1992) Assessment of Client Strengths. In Saleebey, D. (Ed.) *The Strengths Perspective in Social Work Practice.* NY: Longman.

Cowger, C.D. (1994) Assessing Client Strengths: Clinical Assessment for Client Empowerment. *Social Work,* 39: 3, 262–8.

Dale, P. et al. (1986) The Towers of Silence: Creative and Destructive Issues for Therapeutic Teams Dealing with Sexual Abuse. *Journal of Family Therapy,* 8: 1–25.

Davidson, R. (1998) The Transtheoretical Model: A Critical Overview. In Miller, W.R. and Heather, N. (Eds.) *Treating Addictive Behaviours.* NY: Plenum Press.

Davies, M.G. (1995) Parental Distress and Ability to Cope Following Disclosure of Extra-Familial Child Sexual Abuse. *Child Abuse and Neglect,* 19: 4, 399–408.

DePanfilis, D. and Wilson, C. (1996) Applying the Strengths Perspective with Maltreating Families. *The Apsac Advisor,* 9: 3, 15–20.

DiClemente, C. (1991) Motivational Interviewing and the Stages of Change. In Miller, W. and Rollnick, S. (Eds.) *Motivational Interviewing.* London: Guilford Press.

DiClemente, C.C. and Hughes, S.O. (1990) Stages of Change Profiles on Outpatient Alcoholism Treatment. *Journal of Substance Abuse,* 2: 217–35.

DoH (1988) *Protecting Children: A Guide for Social Workers Undertaking a Comprehensive Assessment.* London: HMSO.

DoH (1995) *Child Protection: Messages From Research.* London: HMSO.

Early, T.J. and Glenmaye, L.F. (2000) Valuing Families: Social Work Practice with Families from a Strengths Perspective. *Social Work,* 45: 2, 118–30.

Egan, G. (1994) *The Skilled Helper.* 5th edn. Monterey: Brooks/Cole.

Gelles, R.J. (1995) *Using the Transtheoretical Model of Change to Improve Risk Assessment in Cases of Child Abuse and Neglect.* Paper Presented at The 4th International Family Violence Research Conference, University of New Hampshire (22.7.1995).

Horwath, J. and Morrison, T. (2000) Assessment of Parental Motivation to Change. In Horwath, J. (Ed.) *The Child's World: Assessing Children in Need.* London: NSPCC.

Ivanoff, A., Blythe, B. and Tripodi, T. (1994) *Involuntary Clients in Social Work Practice.* NY: Aldine De Gruyter.

Jack, R. (Ed.) (1995) *Empowerment in Community Care.* London: Chapman and Hall.

Kwang, S.C. and Cowger, C.D. (1998) Utilising Strengths in Assessment. *Families in Society,* 79: 25–31.

Littell J.H. and Girvin, H. (2002) Stages of Change: A Critique. *Behaviour Modification,* 26: 223–73.

Littell, J.H. and Girvin, H. (2004) Ready or Not: Uses of the Stages of Change Model in Child Welfare. *Child Welfare,* 83: 4, 341–66.

Magura, S., Moses, B.S. and Jones, M.A. (1987) *The Family Risk Scales.* Washington,DC: Child Welfare League of America.

Maluccio, A. (1979) The Influence of the Agency Environment on Clinical Practice. *Journal of Sociology and Social Welfare,* 6: 734–55.

Miller, W. and Rollnick, S. (1991) *Motivational Interviewing: Preparing People to Change Addictive Behaviour.* NY: Guilford Press.

Miller, W.R. and Heather, N. (1998) The Transtheoretical Model of Change. In Miller, W.R. and Heather, N. (Eds.) *Treating Addictive Behaviours.* NY: Plenum Press.

Moore, B. (1996) *Risk Assessment: A Practitioner's Guide to Predicting Harmful Behaviour.* London: Whiting and Birch.

Moore, K.L (1981) The Use of Orientation Groups to Engage Hard-To-Reach Clients: Model,

Method and Evaluation. *Social Work With Groups,* 12: 2.

Morrison, T. (1991) Change, Control and the Legal Framework. In Adcock, M., White, R. and Hollows, A. (Eds.) *Significant Harm: Its Management and Outcome.* Croydon: Significant Publications.

Morrison, T. (1995) *Learning, Training and Change in Child Protection Organisations.* Keynote Presentation to The National Child Protection Trainers Conference, 15 March.

Otto, H.A. (1963) Criteria for Assessing Family Strengths. *Family Process,* 2: 329–37.

Prochaska, J.O. and DiClemente, C.C. (1982) Transtheoretical Therapy: Toward a more Integrative Model of Change. *Psychotherapy, Theory, Research and Practice,* 19: 276–88.

Prochaska, J.O. and DiClemente, C.C. (1986) Towards a Comprehensive Model of Change. In Miller, W.N. and Heather, N. (Eds.) *Treating Addictive Behaviours: Processes of Change.* NY: Plenum Press.

Prochaska, J.O. and Norcross, J.C. (1994) *Systems of Psychotherapy: A Transtheoretical Analysis.* 3rd edn. Pacific Grove, CA: Brooks/Cole.

Rooney, R. (1992) *Strategies for Work with Involuntary Clients.* NY: Columbia University Press.

Rose, W. (1994) *An Overview of the Developments of Services: The Relationship between Protection and Family Support and the Intentions of The Children Act 1989.* SIEF Conference, September.

Rose, W. and Aldgate, J. (2000) Knowledge Underpinning The Assessment Framework. In DoH *Assessing Children in Need and Their Families: Practice Guidance.* London: HMSO.

Saleebey, D. (1996) The Strengths Perspective in Social Work Perspective: Extensions and Cautions. *Social Work,* 41: 3, 296–305.

Saleebey, D. (Ed.) (1992) *The Strengths Perspective in Social Work Practice.* New York: Longman.

Seabury, B.A. (1985) The Beginning Phase: Engagement, Initial Assessment and Contracting. In Laird, J. and Hartman, A. (Eds.) *A Handbook of Child Welfare: Context, Knowledge and Practice.* NY: Free Press.

Sharland, E. et al. (1995) *Professional Intervention and Child Sexual Abuse.* London: HMSO.

Shemmings, Y. and Shemmings, D. (2000) Empowering Children and Family Members to Participate in the Assessment Process. In Horwath, J. (Ed.) *The Child's World: Assessing Children in Need.* London: NSPCC.

Sutton, S. (1996) Can 'Stages of Change' Provide Guidance in the Treatment of Addictions? A Critical Examination of Prochaska and Diclemente's Model. In Edwards, G. and Dare, C. (Eds.) *Psychotherapy, Psychological Treatments and the Addictions*. Cambridge: Cambridge University Press.

Thoburn, J., Lewis, A. and Shemmings, D. (1995) *Paternalism or Partnership? Family Involvement in The Child Protection Process.* London: HMSO.

CHAPTER 11

Social Work with Involuntary Clients in Child Protection Work

Brian Littlechild

Introduction

Families who are subject to child protection inquiries from statutory agencies are more often than not involuntary clients. One implication of this, from a small minority of clients, is the use of aggression and violence against social workers. This can be seen to be in response to the statutory agency's – as it is perceived by parents and carers – accusations of their having abused their children, and challenging what is seen by many families as their right to privacy in the family, and to bring up their children as they see fit.

This chapter examines the important elements for social workers and social work agencies to consider in an area that is often ignored in the literature and research; the effects of stress and violence on social workers and their professional practice when this is perpetrated against them when they are working with clients who are receiving their services involuntarily. The chapter will go on to examine the evidence concerning the effect on child protection work and child protection workers of violence from clients, responses to perpetrators, and responses to the workers affected by aggression from involuntary clients in child protection work.

Violence against social workers is a feature of the professional lives of social workers, as evidenced by the work of Pahl (1999) and NISW (1999) amongst others. The UK British Crime Survey is a large scale survey of people's experiences of victimisation of crime and violence carried out by the Government's Home Office every few years. One set of data from this research addressed experiences of violence and aggression at work and demonstrates that social workers are at particular risk. Against an average of 1.2 per cent of all occupational groups reporting assaults, 9.4 per cent of social workers and probation officers reported assaults, the highest of any of the groups apart from the police. Against an average of 1.5 per cent of all occupational groups reporting threats, 9.5 per cent of social workers and probation officers reported such threats, the highest of any of the groups (Budd, 1999). The level and effects of such violence was illustrated by the work of Balloch et al. (1995, 1998) on stress in workers in Social Services Departments. Their research discovered that violence and threats of violence to social workers were major areas of stress for childcare and child protection staff.

Concerns about how violence from service users can negatively affect both the workers themselves and child protection assessments and decision making processes have been raised by a number of authors and researchers (Reder et al., 1993; Farmer and Owen, 1995, 1998; Stanley and Goddard, 2002). Whilst such violence may not be present in the responses of parents and carers in the great majority of child protection work, it is a significant feature in a number of the most serious cases. The evidence from public inquiries into child abuse deaths concerning violence from clients, and the fear engendered by it, is frequently present within the sets of relationships surrounding these situations (Bridge Child Care Development Service, 1997; Dingwall, Eekelaar and Murray, 1983; Guardian, 2002; Newham Area Child Protection Committee, 2002; O'Hagan and Dillenburger, 1995).

Dingwall et al. noted as long ago as 1983 how:

> ... a violent man may sufficiently intimidate (the predominately female) front line staff in health visiting and social work to prevent them from discovering maltreatment (e.g. of father of Stephen Menheniott 1979, who instilled fear in the whole of his small island community).
> (p.107)

The Kimberly Carlisle child abuse death inquiry team recommended that:

> Every effort must be made to make sure that the social worker's assessment, on which might hinge the safety of a child, is not disarmed by the possibility of violence, or the fear of its possibility.
> (DoH, 1991: 71)

The Bridge Child Care Development Service report (1997) into the circumstances surrounding the death of Rikki Neave in Cambridgeshire suggested that there are often links between violence towards staff and others in a family's network, which were not taken into account in this situation.

The child abuse death inquiry report into the death of Ainlee Walker found that workers from the different agencies were intimidated by the parents to such an extent that it affected the assessment and intervention concerning the visiting of the family. Threats of violence to staff were judged to have contributed to the elaborate concealment of Ainlee's abuse from the workers and agencies by the parents (Newham Area Child Protection Committee, 2002).

Dennis Henry was sentenced to 12 years imprisonment, and Leanne Labonte was sentenced to 10 years imprisonment, for the manslaughter of their 2-year-old daughter, Ainlee Walker, after having 'paralysed by fear' the social workers and health visitors involved in the child protection inquiries (*Guardian*, 2002).

Such aggression has been shown to significantly affect workers' well being, and their commitment to that work (Norris, 1990; Littlechild, 2000; Brockmann, 2002). Lord Laming, in his child abuse death inquiry report into the death of Victoria Climbié stated that:

> I recognise that those who take on the work of protecting children at risk of deliberate harm face a tough and challenging task. Staff doing this work need a combination of professional skills and personal qualities, not least of which are persistence and courage. Adults who deliberately exploit the vulnerability of children can behave in devious and menacing ways. Staff often have to cope with the unpredictable behaviour of people in the parental role.
> (Lord Laming, 2003: 3)

O'Hagan and Dillenburger (1995: 145–6) in their analysis of child abuse death inquiry reports, and the factors which contributed to these children's deaths, found that workers' avoidance of aggressive and violent men is a feature in a number of them:

> Violent men consistently dominate the 35 inquiry reports produced since 1974, and have, with few exceptions, been responsible for the deaths of the children in those reports . . .

and that:

> . . . avoidance . . . seriously exacerbates the paramount task of protecting the child.

Child abuse death inquiry reports have, in a number of situations, demonstrated the ways in which assessment and decision making in child protection can be negatively influenced by workers' reactions to client's aggression (DoH, 1991).

If these issues of aggression and violence against child protection staff are not addressed more systematically in assessment and child protection plans, the fear, distress and dangers for workers – and the children they are charged with protecting – will persist.

Why does violence from clients in child protection work occur?

Brown, Bute and Ford found in their study (1986) that issues of power, authority and control appear to be key factors in violence against social workers. The changing nature of assessment and interventions in childcare and child protection work, evident since the last few decades of the 20th century, means that these issues are important features of social work intervention from clients' perspectives.

Child protection interventions can impinge upon the power and control dynamics within the family situation which are often a feature of child abuse (Reder et al., 1993; O'Hagan and Dillenburger, 1995; Littlechild and Bourke, 2006; Stanley and Goddard, 2002), causing clients to use aggression, threats and violence against the worker.

While similarities in the means by which such fear is induced in mothers and children has been recognised within inquiries into child deaths (DoH, 1991, 1995; O'Hagan and Dillenburger, 1995), these types of behaviour have not been given attention within policies or priorities in policies or supervision when such aggression is employed against child protection workers as a means of gaining power and control over such workers in order to intimidate them, and which can make them desist from inquiring into, or working effectively with, the family concerning the abuse of the child.

The power/control dynamics which produce fear of violent parents or carers – normally exhibited by a man – can be the same for abused children, other abused family members (particularly women), and the child protection workers involved (Littlechild and Bourke, 2006; O'Hagan and Dillenburger, 1995).

The situations where violence is most likely to occur are when the power, authority and control elements in the social work role are most clearly present, for example in situations where decisions are being made concerning parents' control over, and retention of, their children. Such situations include involvement before, during or immediately after child protection conferences or court hearings where care orders are applied for, or when parents are told of recommendations for care orders in court reports. Supervised contact sessions are also times of increased risk for those supervising such sessions (Littlechild, 2002).

Issues of dual role

Social workers in child protection work have a dual role; not only do they have to try to engage with families to help improve the health and well-being of the children involved in an abusive situation, but they also have to act as agents of social control if the abuse is so severe that action has to be taken – immediately in the most severe situations, or in the longer term if there is neglect or abuse which is continuing after intervention. Howe states that the 'welter of procedures and guidelines' has led to the social worker becoming an *'investigator, reporter and gatherer of evidence'* (Howe, 1992: 502).

This dual role, or double mandate, in social work, appears to have a significant bearing on the causes of such violence. Social workers are expected to support, but then also control and judge parents in the area of child protection. This then relates to the effects of power, authority, and control in the social work role, and the parent's views – in relation to their children, and the workers involved. This role ambiguity is one of the reasons for aggression towards workers from parents when carrying out the dual role which contains both supportive and investigative functions; an element of the work which official guidance tends to ignore – see the section later in this chapter on 'official' government agency guidance and requirements. Such conflicts have significant effects upon how social workers and parent service users view each other, the effectiveness of engagement, assessment and interventions, and the well-being of workers, as well as on their professional practice.

The nature of state defined social work interventions in child care work within the social services departments of England and Wales has changed significantly since the 1980s, with an increasing curtailment of social workers' ability to undertake preventive work, and an increased emphasis on investigative risk assessment focused work within what can often become situations of conflict (Parton and Small, 1989; Otway, 1996; Parton, 1998). In the few pieces of work that take account of violence against staff within child protection work, the effects of such situations are not addressed (e.g. Parton and Small, 1989). These interventions impinge upon the power and control dynamics within the care situation, which are often a feature of child abuse, and produce problematic areas for child protection workers and their agencies to address (Hearn, 1998; Briere, 1992; O'Hagan and Dillenburger, 1995; Humphreys, 1999). Clients' perceptions of social workers in the child protection role, then, can have a very real effect on their use of aggression and violence.

Hetherington et al. (1997) and Corby (2000) have questioned the viability of social workers being able to carry out these functions simultaneously and the effect of such a 'virtual role' in helping parents to understand and respond to this ambiguous relationship. Parents often experience social workers' child protection role as judgemental and controlling (NISW, 1999). Pahl (1999: 91) notes the importance of the 'very real power' in the role, 'which can provoke service users and their relatives to abuse, but which also protects them from more serious physical attack'.

Acknowledging the effects of aggression and violence in assessments

However, despite such evidence as presented so far in this chapter, the experiences and views of the professionals who attempt to operate child protection work go unacknowledged in official policy guidelines; nor is there recognition of the nature or meaning of the aggression against workers in official reviews of research of relationships which can affect such interventions. *Child Protection: Messages from Research* was a review and analysis of research commissioned by the Department of Health, and had a major impact on policy and practice in the UK (DoH,

1995). The overview of lessons to be learnt from the studies emphasised the need for social services departments in England and Wales to deal with a greater number of abusive situations within a 'children in need' framework of section 17 of the Children Act 1989, designed to keep such children in their families of origin, rather than use the full-blown child protection system – a family support model rather than an investigatory model. However, this can bring greater uncertainty for workers and their managers, particularly where there is violence involved in the situation.

The lack of attention in the *Child Protection: Messages from Research* document (DoH, 1995) to the problems as they may be experienced by workers who are victims of violence, and the possible effects on risk assessment and subsequent interventions, are explored by Littlechild (1998). The assumption within such official guidance appears to be that all families co-operate with child protection services; a wrong and dangerous assumption. The same is true for the effects of violence within the family; non-abusing women carers in particular may fear violence from male partners who abuse them if they were to inform agencies of the abuse (O'Hagan and Dillenburger, 1995; Mullender and Debbonaire, 2000), or give details of it during agency interventions. It appears that policy makers are unable to process and operationalise knowledge from the evidence of such violence, and the key part it has to play in a small but significantly dangerous number of abusing families.

The UK government's *Framework for the Assessment of Children in Need and Their Families* (DoH et al., 2000), and the associated *Family Pack of Questionnaires and Scales* (Cox and Bentovim, 2000), omit to address this issue, despite James in 1994 in a Department of Health report (James, 1994) recommending incorporating assessment of parental violence and how it may affect interventions. These recommendations were never acted upon, although the previous Department of Health guidance, *Protecting Children* (DoH, 1988: 12) considered that professional dangerousness is possible when 'a social worker is allowed to avoid contact with the child or family due to unacknowledged fears for personal safety'. Even this one isolated reference to the damaging effects of violence does not appear in the Framework or its associated materials.

Such fear of aggression and violence can affect the confidence and actions of those caught up in the threats and power and control dynamics, which are components of violent relationships and attitudes, be they victims within the family, or workers. Workers experiencing such violence and threats can have similar feelings of fear and powerlessness as the many clients who have to face such violence, even if less severe and pervasive than for those more intimately involved in the family violence.

The effects of violence from involuntary clients in child protection work

Balloch et al. (1998) examined social workers' experiences of stress, which found that violence from service users was a particular cause of stress for them, a finding which was also evident in the research findings of Smith and Nursten (1998).

Littlechild's research (2000, 2002) suggests that physical violence from adult clients in child protection work is comparatively rare, but other forms of aggression – such as intimidating abuse and threats – occur frequently, and the effects of such violence can be significant.

Stanley and Goddard (1997) suggest that abusive families can use tactics to draw the worker into the role of victim. One particularly severe form of such dynamics, they suggest, is the Stockholm syndrome (Wardlaw, 1982), concerning the relationship which can develop between hostages and terrorists, which may also apply to relationships in and surrounding abusing families – including the relationship with the child protection worker. They suggest that this complex set of dynamics can draw the worker into becoming a victim of these abusing/controlling dynamics, which means they are unable to challenge the abuse, or utilise procedures properly. They also suggest that at times, workers appear to indulge in self-deception and denial of violence. The Kimberley Carlisle child abuse death inquiry concluded that social services and school staff found a father in a child protection situation intimidating, and that:

> *The effects of fear of violence are likely very hard to identify . . . if, as is the case, some social workers are too ashamed after being attacked to report the incident and are even then inclined to blame themselves, how much more*

unlikely must it be that they will admit to the feeling of uneasiness before any violence has occurred. It is not easy to admit to being afraid; social workers must, for their sake and their clients' sake . . . it is only too easy to find other reasons for doing something, or not doing something, when the real reason is that we are afraid to do it.

(DoH, 1991: 71)

The report stated that efforts must be made to make sure that the social workers' assessment is not affected by fear. The report encouraged:

. . . social workers to be straight, open and frank with their clients when investigating possible cases of child abuse . . . and to speak out if they are fearful for their own safety or if they consider their performance as a social worker is being handicapped by fear of violence.

(DoH, 1991: 71)

The Cleveland inquiry noted that anger, aggressive and destructive behaviour and the possibility of violent impulsive reactions from parents being investigated for potential child abuse should be faced up to by workers and agencies. The social worker needs to maintain an open, structured relationship with the family (DoH, 1991).

Research (Littlechild, 2000, 2002) into the effects of aggression and violence from clients found a number of examples of the effects of such experiences:

- One worker's family *'(was) concerned about the nature of my work and risks involved'*.
- (Worker who lives in same geographical area as that of her work): *'I am more wary about going to the shops and I am concerned about meeting this man'.*
- (Worker who lives in the same area as that of her work, threatened by what several families said they would do to her in her private life): *'Reduced visits to town with husband and teenage children – not wanting to put them at risk'.* *'Watching back mirror when driving home, stopping en route to ensure not being followed. Disturbed sleep and dreams'.*
- *'Repercussions for my functioning as a wife, mother, etc.'*
- *'My husband gets angry that I have to put up with such behaviour and suffer the effects in my private life'.*
- *'Anxieties spill over into home time. I find I am emotionally drained which gives rise to physical exhaustion – possibly ill-health'.*

A number of workers specifically mentioned effects on their practice. These effects appear to depend upon the assessment the worker makes of the situation, their attributions towards clients behaviour and motives and how similar the family/situation is to previous experiences of aggression and violence.

One worker reported 'General reluctance to visit. Difficulty being positive with the client. My anxiety and anger prevent me being positive with the family.'

Another worker had received 'a serious threat to kill us from someone who had been seriously violent in the past and killed a child', which led to an injunction being given by a court to keep the client away from their office. The worker was concerned about having been followed, and receiving threats in their personal and family life outside of work.

One other worker was subject to threats to shoot her, from a client whose past history demonstrated was capable of such behaviour. In another situation where a worker's life was threatened, the worker went on long-term sick leave, and eventually resigned.

One service user in another situation was extremely verbally threatening to the workers, and damaged their cars. The service user also threatened to harm the children, the foster carers and the foster carers' children.

Some of the most severe effects on workers are where there are personalised threats against their family; these are the most difficult for workers and managers to manage and overcome – such as 'I know where you live', or 'I know where your children go to school'.

Threats from clients had the greatest effects, especially when this appeared to the worker to be focused individually against her/himself and sometimes on their family, rather than on their role as an agency representative. The effects were largely psychological, with fear having the most serious effects on themselves and their behaviour. Such findings are consistent with those of Smith and Nursten (1998).

Whilst mothers are the most frequent perpetrators of physical violence against workers, men are the most frequent perpetrators of threatening behaviour. This behaviour constitutes such actions as personalised verbal abuse and threats, following workers in their cars or whilst walking, and threatening violence to the worker's family, producing significant fearful effects on workers (Brockmann and McLean, 2000; NISW,

1999; Stanley and Goddard, 2002). Littlechild (2000, 2002) found that these types of situations were usually not one-off incidents, but part of a set of dynamics and threats that built up over time, and which can best be described as 'developing violent scenarios'; which are hard to identify and deal with until late in the process, producing dangers of non-recognition and lack of objectivity.

One particular issue which can affect workers relates to ethnicity. Balloch et al.'s (1998) research into the social work and social care work force in England and Wales found that 75 per cent of black staff had experienced racial abuse. Racism can also affect child protection interventions and decision-making. One child abuse death considered by a public inquiry report team found that the social workers feared the 'aggressive, overtly racist and hostile' parents, which meant that in thirty visits the child was seen only eight times. In this situation, the workers in the authority had not felt able to tell their managers of their concerns, and the Director of Social Services in that local authority commented that 'It's a question of changing the whole ethos of social work in general so that people report openly what they feel' (Mason, 1992).

However, the full extent and effects of such aggression and violence are not fully known, as under-reporting presents a problem for dealing with the problem that the research evidence clearly informs us is there (Norris, 1990; NISW, 1999).

Workers may believe their experiences will not be believed or taken seriously; that they are expected to just cope; that it is to be expected as part of the job (Norris, 1990; UNISON/BASW, 1996). This needs to be addressed so that workers regard reporting aggression and violence as an important element in protecting not only themselves, but also as an element in child protection assessments in order to ensure the proper protection of the child. Several pieces of research have underlined how workers do not report aggression and violence because they fear being seen as 'weak' or incompetent workers, fear that they will somehow be blamed for the aggression and violence directed against them, or that they believe it is part of the work and should be just accepted (Norris, 1990; Rowett, 1986: NISW, 1999). If staff are not encouraged to report by way of a culture of support within agencies, rather than denial and at times, exasperation with workers' fears, then researchers and agencies will

not be able to know the true extent, nature or causes of violence against child protection staff dealing with these issues, and then collate, analyse and act upon as required by the Management of Health and Safety at Work Regulations 1992.

Responses to violence

There is little evidence of knowledge of the effects of such violence having been incorporated into social work assessments or interventions, agency policies, supervisory practices, or child protection plans (Littlechild, 2005a, 2005b; Stanley and Goddard, 2002). The dynamics created by the maintenance of power, control and abuse by certain abusers is more complex than commonly supposed in most social work and research literature, and are often ignored altogether. There is now a good deal of evidence, as outlined above, to demonstrate that in a significant number of the most serious situations of child abuse, there is an inherent conflict caused by the role of the protection agency, and the small number of clients who are, however, real threats to the protection workers and the children they are trying to protect.

A head teacher was intimidated by Richard Fraser's stepmother and concerned that an external examination of Richard would provoke a strong adverse reaction from the stepmother, and so a proper examination never took place. The social worker was attempting to give support but found this very difficult because of a fear of an atmosphere of antagonism towards her. She felt herself to be at risk, and expressed her anxiety to a child protection conference, where it was agreed that she would continue on the case on the basis of 'low profile' visits of a routine nature. The inquiry notes that the social worker 'clearly wasn't safe with Richard's family and asked to be taken off the case' (Richard Fraser inquiry, DoH, 1991: 62).

Social workers and their employing agencies often fail to recognise the types of threat present within parents or carers power/control patterns that can disempower and intimidate both them and other family members. Male abusers in particular may make use of controlling threats of violence or other forms of threat if other family members were to reveal the secret of the abuse to any agency. If their power and control within the family is threatened by the scrutiny of outside statutory agencies, abusers can equally attempt to maintain control by intimidating workers in order to keep them at bay. While the precise mechanisms may vary, the use of power/control mechanisms to intimidate others can be a key feature of the behaviour of violent and controlling males (Littlechild and Bourke, 2006). In addition, child protection managers have expressed concerns that child protection interventions can sometimes impinge upon the power and control dynamics within the family situation, which are often a feature of child abuse. Research findings have shown that social work child protection workers believe service users who are aggressive and violent need to have improved responses to their behaviour, whilst risk assessments do not always consider the possible effects of violence and aggression towards staff on the assessment and intervention process. Set within more general concerns about non-reporting and workers' accommodation of the aggression, the lack of appropriate responses by a number of individual workers, and ineffective agency procedures, demonstrates a need to improve understanding and assessment processes (Littlechild, 2005a, 2005b).

Legal and professional requirements on work and agencies

There are various Acts of the UK Parliament relating to staff safety at work, including the Health and Safety Work Act 1974. The General Social Care Council (GSCC) (2002) Codes of Conduct and Practice for Social Care Workers and Employers of Social Care Workers also have effects on issues of support and safety for child protection workers.

Injunctions are available where serious threats have been made against workers, which keep people from being within a certain distance of an office, for example. Again, under the provisions of the Protection from Harassment Act, 1997, where someone – including a social worker – experiences violence or threat (including psychological threat) from someone else on at least two occasions, an application for an injunction can be made under either the civil law, or, in addition, the police can take the matter forward under the criminal law. Such knowledge of possible responses available under the law for social workers where they are experiencing involuntary clients as being threatening,

intimidating or seriously abusive can be extremely valuable.

The GSCC requirements in their Codes for employing agencies state that they must regularly supervise and effectively manage staff to support good practice and professional development and to address any deficiencies in their performance, and make it clear to service users and carers that violence, threats or abuse to staff are not acceptable. Agencies are also advised to have clear policies and procedures for preventing violence and managing violent incidents.

The nature of the duty of care on employers towards staff who are stressed was examined in courts of law in 1987, as in the case of John Walker, a child protection manager, who was experiencing severe pressure at work because of the number of cases he was responsible for. He had very few social workers to allocate them to, and the resulting stress later led to him going on sick leave with mental health problems. He returned to work with nothing having changed in the situation, and eventually he went on sick leave again, not to return. The case was taken to the High Court, and he was awarded substantial damages because the court took the view that the employer had not exercised a proper duty of care in relation to him and his problems at work. This has been an important case in clarifying under law the responsibilities which employers have to support staff, which has implications for support for workers severely stressed by threats and violence.

The Health and Safety at Work Act 1974 provides the main piece of legislation concerning the safety of staff. The Act requires employers to take reasonable steps to protect staff from health and safety risks, including mental health and stress related issues. On the other hand, under the Act, employees also have a duty not to put themselves into situations of risk.

There are also duties not only on employers, but also on individual workers, under the GSCC Codes. Social workers must follow 'practice and procedures designed to keep you (the social worker) and other people safe from violent and abusive behaviour at work'. They must also take necessary steps to prevent service users from doing actual or potential harm to themselves or other people (including the worker); challenge dangerous, abusive, discriminatory or exploitative behaviour, and use established processes and procedures to report it. They also require workers to inform their employer or the appropriate authority about any physical, mental, emotional or legal difficulties that might affect their ability to do their job competently and safely; to inform their employer or the appropriate authority if they do not feel competent to carry out any aspect of their work; and to seek necessary supervision and training. Social workers are required not to 'put themselves or other people at unnecessary risk'. All of these provide guidance for, and place requirements on, social workers reporting aggression and violence, and demand responses from employers, concerning the safety of staff where clients use aggressive, intimidating or other violent behaviour.

Supervision and support for staff

It is important for child protection supervisors and managers to be sensitive, open, and honest in acknowledging workers' fears where they are carrying out child protection inquiries in situations where there is – or maybe – violence and threats against them. A key element here is for the worker to feel able to say they do feel capable to challenge the service user or to carry out a piece of work – an issue addressed in the GSCC Codes as outlined earlier.

Dale et al. (1986) and Reder et al. (1993) note the potential danger for workers who are not supervised or supported properly. Stanley and Goddard (1997) identified how some workers have accommodated service user aggression as part of their defence mechanisms. If this happens, the worker can find it difficult to challenge abusive and aggressive parents. Two groups of workers in my research were seen as being particularly vulnerable; those who were inexperienced, and those who did not feel they have the right and/or the confidence to carry out the control elements that have to be utilised in protection work.

Lord Laming in his report on the death of Victoria Climbié states that:

> Supervision is the cornerstone of good social work practice and should be seen to operate effectively at all levels of the organisation. In Haringey, the provision of supervision may have looked good on paper, but in practice it was woefully inadequate for many front-line staff. This must change.

(Lord Laming, 2003: 14)

Bell's (1999) research findings demonstrated that one third of respondents said that the reasons for not being able to undertake a thorough child protection investigation were not through the lack of time, but due to the characteristics of the family which the social workers experienced as lack of co-operation. She found that the workers' supervision did not focus on this, but consisted of management of the investigation, and dealing with particular problems concerning tasks.

However, in recent years supervision in England has tended to concentrate on supervisors'/managers' monitoring of their supervisees' work to ensure that performance indicators are being met, rather than dealing with the complex difficulties and stresses workers face in child protection work. Gibbs (2001) proposes that supervision is a vital element in the workers' ability to maintain their own health and well-being whilst dealing with these stresses, but also, crucially for the children, to sustain the focus of their work. She also argues that a lack of attention to the often unconscious defence mechanisms adopted by individuals to survive in the face of high levels of anxiety and distress become dangerous to them. In her study of anxiety in child protection workers in Australia, physical or verbal violence were mentioned as major sources of such stress.

In summary, supervision skills are important to support the worker, to assess over time if role conflict, ambiguity and aggression are affecting the protection work, and to ensure that the worker is not becoming potentially endangered by putting themselves or the children at risk by avoiding – consciously or unconsciously – the effect of threat, psychologically or physically, in their work with a family.

Developing guidance and policies

Supervision and support from managers is a key factor in reducing stress for workers in their work with involuntary and threatening clients (Gibbs, 2001; Jones, Fletcher and Ibbetson, 1991) and in dealing with issues of aggression and violence within families, and against workers (Stanley and Goddard, 2002). If workers experience supportive reactions from managers and employing agencies, this helps and encourages staff to report intimidation and violence. Such positive experiences will also change workers' views that some forms of violence are not sufficiently serious to report, or that clients have justifications for being violent. Supportive responses from senior staff can provide clear messages that acceptance of violence is not 'part of the job', and should dispel concerns that managers will not fully support the worker or take actions to deal with the behaviour from clients (Norris, 1990).

Agency policies for dealing with the different factors which may affect the safety and well-being of staff, and of children, when dealing with violent clients, and for the reasons set out in this chapter, need to take into account the following elements:

(a) There needs to be recognition that a small but potentially dangerous number of parent/carer clients use threats or physical violence to prevent social workers from intervening effectively in the protection of children.

(b) The supportive and informed reactions of managers and employing agencies are vital in order to:
   - Increase reporting, monitoring and review of safety for staff.
   - Provide clear messages that acceptance of violence is not 'part of the job'.

(c) Supervisors need to have an awareness of how to assess and deal with situations when workers are becoming potentially endangered in their avoidance of confronting the abuse due to the abusive and controlling dynamics within the family.

(d) Agencies need to ensure that effective strategies are in place to support threatened workers and appropriately confront violent service users, and work on their violence prevention for the safety of workers, but also for the safety of the children being investigated.

(e) It is essential the worker is clear about the nature of the job and the role they are undertaking with the parents/carers and the children, and the nature of their powers and decision-making processes.

(f) Provide greater impetus to formulate child protection plans which assess and address directly abusers' power/control strategies.

(g) Put clear procedures in place establishing who will deal with the perpetrator, how, and with what involvement from the victim.

(h) Agencies can ask of themselves, and workers should ask of their agencies:
   - Are there clear risk assessment procedures in place which take into account actual and potential aggression from clients as part of the systematic planning and reviewing of the assessment and interventions over time, not just at initial referral?
   - How are limits and boundaries on different types of behaviour agreed, set, and maintained?
   - How clear are these to workers and clients, and how are they best spelt out and maintained over time?

Conclusion

It has been argued in this chapter that, from the evidence concerning work with involuntary clients who use violence and aggression against social workers, much greater emphasis has to be placed upon an understanding of interpersonal conflict and power relationships within a small minority of child protection situations where clients are involuntary. There is a need for agencies, managers and workers to understand and respond more effectively to such violence, aggression and power dynamics, and the meaning of such matters in relation to the experiences of clients and of workers. Strategies need to be in place for social work agencies, supervisors, managers and social workers to deal effectively with the effects of such interpersonal violence both for the clients – especially children and non-abusing partners – and themselves.

Denial of the actions of some involuntary clients in child protection work by workers, agencies, and government guidance can lead to dangerous situations for workers and children who may be living in fear and are being damaged by the abusive situations in which they are living. Such denial can be worked with, with strategies to recognise and support workers, children, and the parents/carers as well, by use of child protection plans which make clear, and then work with, the effects of such aggression and violence.

References

Balloch, S. et al. (1995) *Working in the Social Services*. London: NISW.

Balloch, S., Pahl J. and McLean, J. (1998) Working in the Social Services: Job Satisfaction, Stress and Violence. *British Journal of Social Work*, 28, 329–50.

Bell, M. (1999) Working in Partnership in Child Protection: The Conflicts. *British Journal of Social Work*, 437–55.

Bridge Child Care Development Service (1997) *Report on Behalf of Cambridgeshire County Council Social Services Department.* Cambridge: Cambridgeshire County Council.

Briere, J. (1992) *Child Abuse Trauma: Theory and Treatment of the Lasting Effects.* Thousand Oaks, CA: Sage Publications.

Brockmann, M. (2002) New Perspectives on Violence in Social Care. *Journal of Social Work, 2: 1,* 29–44.

Brockman, M. and McLean, J. (2000) *Review Paper for National Task Force on Violence against Social Care Staff.* London: National Institute for Social Work.

Brown, R., Bute S. and Ford P. (1986) *Social Workers at Risk: The Prevention and Management of Violence.* Basingstoke: Macmillan.

Budd, T. (1999) *Violence at Work: Findings from the British Crime Survey.* London: Home Office/Health and Safety Executive.

Corby, B. (2000) *Child Abuse: Towards a Knowledge Base.* Buckingham: Open University Press.

Cox, A. and Bentovim, A. (2000) *The Family Pack of Questionnaires and Scales.* London: DoH.

Dale, P., Davies, M., Morrison, T. and Waters, J. (1986) *Dangerous Families.* London: Tavistock.

Dingwall, R., Eekelaar, J. and Murray, T. (1983) *The Protection of Children: State Intervention and Family Life.* Oxford: Basil Blackwell.

DoH (1991) *Child Abuse Deaths: A Study of Inquiry Reports 1980–1989.* London: HMSO.

DoH (1995) *Child Protection: Messages from Research.* London: HMSO.

DoH (2000) *Framework for the Assessment of Children in Need and Their Families.* London: HMSO.

Farmer, E. and Owen, M. (1995) *Child Protection Practice: Private Risks and Public Remedies.* London: HMSO.

Farmer, E. and Owen, M. (1998) Gender and the Child Protection Process. *British Journal of Social Work.* 28, 545–64.

General Social Care Council (2002) *Codes of Conduct and Practice for Social Care Workers and Employers of Social Care Workers.* London: GSCC.

Guardian (2002) *Ainlee Walker inquiry.* 19 December.

Gibbs, J.A. (2001) Maintaining Front-Line Workers in Child Protection: A Case for Refocusing Supervision. *Child Abuse Review,* 323–35.

Hearn, J. (1998) *The Violences of Men.* London: Sage Publications.

Hetherington. R., Cooper, A., Smith, P. and Wilford, G. (Eds.) (1997) *Protecting Children:* *Messages from Europe.* Lyme Regis: Russell House Publishing.

Humphreys, C. (1999) Avoidance and Confrontation: The Practice of Social Workers in Relation to Domestic Violence and Child Abuse. *Child and Family Social Work,* 4, 77–87.

Howe, D. (1992) Child Abuse and the Bureaucratisation of Social Work. *The Sociological Review,* 40: 3, 491–508.

James, G. (1994*) Study of Working Together 'Part 8' Reports.* London: DoH.

Jones, F., Fletcher, B.C. and Ibbetson, K. (1991) Stressors and Strains Amongst Social Workers. *British Journal of Social Work,* 21: 5, 443–70.

Lord Laming (2003) *The Victoria Climbié Inquiry: Summary Report.* Norwich: HMSO.

Littlechild, B. (1998) Does Family Support Ensure the Protection of Children? Messages From Child Protection Support. *Child Abuse Review,* 7, 116–28.

Littlechild, B. (2000) *I Know Where You Live: How Child Protection Social Workers are Affected by Threats and Aggression. A Study into the Stresses Faced by Child Protection Workers in Hertfordshire: with Notes on Research into Finnish Social Workers' Experiences.* Hatfield: Centre for Community Studies, University of Hertfordshire.

Littlechild, B. (2002) *The Management of Conflict and Service User Violence Against Staff in Child Protection work.* Centre for Community Research, University of Hertfordshire, Hatfield.

Littlechild, B. (2003) Working With Aggressive and Violent Parents in Child Protection Social Work. *Practice,* 15: 1, 33–44.

Littlechild, B. (2005a) The Stresses Arising from Violence, Threats and Aggression Against Child Protection Social Workers. *Journal of Social Work,* 5: 61–82.

Littlechild, B. (2005b) The Nature and Effects of Violence against Child-Protection Social Workers: Providing Effective Support. *British Journal of Social Work,* 35: 387–401.

Littlechild, B. and Bourke, C. (2006) Men's Use of Violence and Intimidation Against Family Members and Child Protection Workers. In Humphreys, C. and Stanley, N. (Eds.) *Domestic Violence and Child Protection: Directions for Good Practice.* London: Jessica Kingsley.

Mason, P. (1992) Working in Fear. *Social Work Today,* 9 January, 14.

Mullender, A. and Debbonaire, T. (2000) *Child Protection and Domestic Violence.* Birmingham: Venture Press.

NISW (1999) *Violence Against Social Workers. Briefing Paper 26*. London: NISW.

Newham Area Child Protection Committee (2002) *AINLEE: Born 24.06.1999 Died: 07.01.2002, Chapter 8 Review*. London: Newham Council.

Norris, D. (1990) *Violence Against Social Workers*, London: Jessica Kingsley.

O'Hagan, K. and Dillenburger, K. (1995) *The Abuse of Women within Child Care Work*. Buckingham: Open University Press.

Otway, O. (1996) Social Work With Children and Families: From Child Welfare to Child Protection. In Parton, N. (Ed.) *Social Theory, Social Change and Social Work*. London: Routledge.

Pahl, J. (1999) Coping With Physical Violence and Verbal Abuse. In Balloch, S., McLean, J. and Fisher, M. (Eds.) *Social Services: Working Under Pressure*. Bristol: Policy Press.

Parton, N. (1998) Risk, Advanced Liberalism and Child Welfare: The Need to Rediscover Uncertainty and Ambiguity. *British Journal of Social Work*, 5–27.

Parton, N. and Small, N. (1989) Violence, Social Work and the Emergence of Dangerousness. In Langan, M. and Lee, P. (Eds.) *Radical Social Work Today*. London: Unwin Hyman.

Reder, P., Duncan, S. and Gray, M. (1993) *Beyond Blame: Child Abuse Tragedies Revisited*. London: Routledge.

Rowett, C. (1986) *Violence in Social Work*. Institute of Criminology, Cambridge University.

Smith, M. and Nursten, J. (1998) Social Workers' Experiences of Distress: Moving Towards Change? *British Journal of Social Work*, 351–68.

Stanley, J. and Goddard, C. (1997) Failures in Child Protection: A Case Study. *Child Abuse Review*, 6: 1, 46–54.

Stanley, J. and Goddard, C. (2002) In the Firing Line: Violence and Power in Child Protection Work. Chichester: Wiley.

UNISON/British Association of Social Workers (1996) *Dealing with Violence and Stress in Social Services*. Birmingham: UNISON/BASW.

Wardlaw, G. (1982) *Political Terrorism: Theory, Tactics and Counter-Measures*. Cambridge University Press.

CHAPTER 12

A Framework for Family Empowerment: Tools for Working with Involuntary Clients

Judith Bula Wise

Introduction

The purpose of this chapter is to consider what a framework for family empowerment can offer practitioners who work with involuntary, or mandated, clients. The integration of supportive, caring family members and empowerment-based principles for treatment with involuntary clients offer many possibilities for enhancing a client's (individual or family) motivation to make choices for change that leads toward greater health and well-being. The realities that lead to a mandate for services, however, often include exactly the opposite, i.e. family members lacking in their ability to support, perhaps even abusive or absent, and previous helping attempts that may have been experienced as pathology-based, coercive, or punitive. The process occurring before the mandate is put in place and the process shaping the response to that mandate are two quite different entities. The tools presented in this chapter offer possibilities for transforming realities at the beginning of work with involuntary clients to an empowering result, one that integrates the power of family dynamics to enhance the outcome for the well-being of the clients.

To maximise the potential for a framework for family empowerment to work effectively with involuntary clients, several important differentials are worth considering:

- Treatment approaches that work with voluntary family clients are not necessarily the most effective with involuntary family clients.
- Treatment choices that work effectively with the individual involuntary client may not be effective with a family mandated for services.
- Family members may be supportive and help anchor the changes that occur as a response to the mandate or they may sabotage the work.

In the discussions to follow, the empowerment framework is used to offer methods to assess the presence or absence of these differentials at

personal, interpersonal, and social/community levels. Guidelines for interactions at the beginning, middle, and ending phases of work are also considered. Seven practice principles are offered for shaping the transactions that occur between client families and helping professionals. Readers are also invited to consider three practice directions effective in promoting change that is do-able and that lasts over extended periods of time. Brief practice illustrations will be used for clarification. For more extended examples of practice, readers are referred to chapters in this book related to child protection practice. For additional perspectives on work with families mandated to services, readers are also encouraged to turn to the works of Trotter, 1999; Rooney, 1992; O'Hare, 1996; De Jong and Berg, 2001 and Wise, 2005.

A family empowerment framework

(Parts of the following discussions have been previously published in Wise (2005) *Empowerment Practice with Families in Distress*.)

Empowering approaches have played a major role in the helping professions for over a century. Highly versatile and easily grasped as a concept, the pervasiveness of empowerment thinking has reached nearly every aspect of human activity, growth, and possibility. This same quality has also been questioned as its possible demise (Weissberg, 1999). If 'empowerment' can be applied everywhere, then what unique meaning can be derived from such an inclusive term? This is an important question, one that helps refine the use of this term and its accompanying practices. Clarifications about what an empowerment approach can and cannot accomplish strengthen the accountability of practicing professionals who use it and promote realistic expectations for its application with clients. With this in mind, the definition of 'empowerment' as it is used here is the freedom to make choices that strengthen and enhance one's ability to move forward in life with a sense that an ongoing context of choice, well-being, and growth is possible. When working with the complex dynamic interactions in a family, this definition applies equally to the individual members of the family and to the family as a unit.

The framework for family empowerment is grounded in an understanding of simultaneous thought and action at three different, yet constantly intertwined, levels of empowerment: personal, interpersonal, and social/community. From that base, seven practice principles are then discussed:

- Building on individual and family strengths while simultaneously diminishing oppressive factors.
- Enacting multicultural respect.
- Building the work on an awareness of individual and family needs.
- Gathering sufficient resources from which family members can make choices and reach self-defined goals toward their own sense of well-being.
- Integrating the support of their own family and extended family members and the support of others.
- Equalising power differentials.
- Using cooperative and collaborative roles.

(Wise, 2005; Lee, 2001)

Guidelines for each phase of the work – beginning, middle, and ending – are then identified and, within the middle phase of work, three specific practice directions – providing information about what is happening, helping to increase skills to cope with the situations being faced, and integrating support from others who have experienced similar challenges – are discussed as essential steps in shaping the course of the work with families and their individual members.

Levels of empowerment: personal, interpersonal, and social/community

All three levels of empowerment are in a continual dynamic flux that affects each family member and the family as a whole. These three levels of activity are inseparable in the day-to-day life of a family. When one member (personal) of a family is mandated to counselling or to receive services (social/community) all members of the

family are affected (interpersonal) in some way. Likewise, when the whole family is required to participate (interpersonal) involuntarily to meet the requirements of a mandate (social/community), each individual member (personal) is affected.

Personal empowerment includes self-esteem, self-respect, self-worth, and self-efficacy (Gutierrez and Lewis, 1999; Lee, 2001). Personal empowerment can originate within the person, from family members, or from those in the wider social context. One indication that a person is living from a position of personal empowerment is the refusal to accept or tolerate devaluation of themselves or of others (Evans, 1992). Personal empowerment is evidenced through connection, through mutually empathic and mutually empowering relationships, through *interpersonal* transactions.

Interpersonal empowerment mobilises 'the energies, resources, strengths, or powers of each person through a mutual, relational process' (Surrey, 1987) through relationships that build connection and enhance personal power, everyone's personal power. The relationships among and between the members of a family are an essential element in understanding empowerment within the family system. When an assessment of the family of an individual involuntary client is made, the practitioner gains valuable knowledge about family messages regarding how to be in the world and how to respond to perceived authority, about the supports or barriers present from family members, about any developmental needs that have been met or unmet within the context of the family, and, perhaps, about the neglect or abuse suffered as part of the family.

When the entire family is mandated to receive services, again the relationships among and between family members is a key element for assessment before implementing service. Identifying strengths in the parental or partnership relationship, in the relationships between parents and children, and among and between siblings is an essential first step so that, when enacting the empowerment principles – i.e. building on strengths, the practitioner will have that information available. Likewise, assessing the areas of conflict, biased and stereotypic attitudes (such as gender role stereotyping) and the oppressive forces that exist within the family unit will help the practitioner's understanding of characteristics requiring efforts that will decrease their negative impact on the family members. Working with these family dynamics can make the difference between a family that participates in service and one that places barriers against complying with the requirements of the mandate.

One way empowerment is recognised at the *social/community* level is through the availability of a wide variety of resources to the families in that community. Empowerment practice is not complete without attention to matching the needs of families with the available community and social network resources as well as identifying their needs that remain unmet due to resources that are either inadequate or lacking. Professionals practicing at the community-based level recognise how environments shape families. When the temporary contact with a helping professional comes to an end for a family mandated to service, that family's need for community and social support continues. The social dimensions of poverty, violence, addictions, and discrimination, for example, are evident in inadequate housing and health care, malnutrition, unemployment and underemployment. Practitioners using an empowerment framework to shape the directions of their work will integrate a family's reality at personal, interpersonal, and social/community levels to determine intervention choices that will have a strengthening effect at all three levels simultaneously. Those intervention choices are also guided by seven empowerment principles for practice.

Empowerment principles for practice with families

We do not 'empower' other people nor do we have the capacity to 'empower' their families; personal and collective power is already theirs. As helping professionals, we can, however, help families gain access to their power. 'The concept of empowerment is the cornerstone of all family-based programmes. Empowerment encompasses a way of thinking about families. It's a conviction that families deserve respect, have strengths, *can* make changes in their lives, and are resilient, and it means helping families gain *access* to their power, not giving them power' (Kaplan and Girard, 1994: 40). Family members deserve respect from those who serve them in every phase of the work in a mandated environment, but initially, in making clear that

the helper sees beyond the label of the mandate to the wholeness of the family. All families have strengths; all families are capable of change toward growth and greater well-being; and all families are resilient, capable of bouncing back after (or in the middle of) major life stressors and disruptions. An empowerment thinker avoids using any label that places the family at a distance, such as 'resistant' or 'uncooperative,' and instead considers her or his own role in the process when clients are not making use of the services offered.

Client families, and perhaps especially families mandated to service, do not necessarily know that the helper believes in their strength and resilience. Their capacities need to be acknowledged in concrete and specific ways. An empowerment approach includes the assumption that facing life stressors is common to all families. The perceived degree of stress at any moment will be different for each family, and for each family member, but distress is a universal experience. This commonality builds mutuality and credibility in the helping context.

Seven principles for empowering practice with families have been identified:

1. Identify and build on strengths and resources while simultaneously identifying and diminishing oppressive factors.
2. Establish a relationship of mutual, multicultural respect with all client families, supporting all ethnicities, ages, genders, sexual orientations, differing abilities, languages, religions/spiritual beliefs, developmental stages, socio-economic strata, geographic backgrounds, levels of education, and family structures.
3. Include an awareness of individual, interpersonal, and community needs as well as the transactional needs between these three levels and the impact of those needs on the family system.
4. Work from the premise that, with sufficient resources, family members have the capacity to empower themselves (Lee, 1994).
5. Recognise that family members need each other and the support of other families and community organisations to find empowerment as a family.
6. Establish and maintain a 'power with' relationship to equalise the power differential between client family members and practitioner.

7. Serve families through roles that support and assist family members and reflect these empowering principles.

Principle 1: Build on strengths; diminish oppressions

Beginning with strengths is especially important with an involuntary family (or individual), because the reason for the mandate – i.e. violence, abuse, substance use – may carry the greater weight in the description of the client as it appears in intake information and in the recommendations for specific treatment. To begin with and to build on a family's strengths requires, first of all, a mindset that allows us to come to our work believing that it is more beneficial to see this family and each of its members, and for them to see themselves, as persons with much more to their lives than the distress and pain they are facing in the moment. It is exactly the 'much more,' the strength and capacity for resilience, that helps them through that distress. By no means are the stressors and oppressions ignored, but are rather 'put in their place' (Weick and Chamberlain, 1997) where they will not be a barrier to the well-being of the family.

   Identification of strengths is one way empowerment thinking is operationalised and it occurs from the very first moments of contact. Three methods of discovering strengths are recommended: using highly tuned-in observation skills; listening carefully and empathetically to client stories; and letting them know of our interest in their capacities, talents, hopes and dreams (Saleebey, 1999: 19–20). Strengths already present can be applied to help manage the current stressors. If information and skills to manage those stressors appear lacking, professionals can implement the core practice directions of the empowerment framework (discussed below in greater detail): gaining information, learning additional coping skills, and potentially integrating the support of others such as extended family members, support group members, or those who participate in social or community organisations with services that are relevant to the family's needs. The ongoing use of these three practice directions helps to create strengths where they did not previously exist.

   The second aspect of this first empowerment principle, envisioned as occurring simultaneously with building on strengths, is that of diminishing oppressions. As strengths are applied and created, oppressive forces – i.e. violence, addictions, prejudice and discrimination – are often no longer needed to maintain a shaky balance in the family dynamic. At other times, however, the patterns of these behaviours that threaten and destroy a family's integrity, may not respond to increased strengths. When oppressive forces are this overbearing, the core practice directions – providing relevant information, strengthening coping skills, and including the support of others – offer focus and direction with specific actions for helpers and family members to address each family's needs at personal, interpersonal, and social/community (including political) levels. Oppressions that are forms of social abuse, poverty for example, may lead to the need to confront the oppressors face-to-face, holding them accountable and seeking reparative actions, ones that repair the damage suffered. Four families, for example, living in an apartment building that had become increasingly dangerous because of faulty electrical connections joined together, with the help of a social advocate, to confront their landlord about the unrealistic increase in rent when the building was in drastic need of repair. Not only was their landlord given a timeline to make the needed repairs, but these tenants were assured that there would be no rise in their rent payment for at least one year after the repairs were in place. In addition, each family was awarded payment in an amount equivalent to the rent they had paid when their apartment building was in severe disrepair.

   Confronting the oppressor in work with families who have been ordered to receive mandated services may also mean that the oppressor is a member of the family, such as in instances of domestic partner abuse, elder abuse, and child abuse. Such a confrontation is a viable option in many situations but not necessarily in all situations and it is definitely not a choice to be taken lightly. It is an intervention choice that requires careful assessment for effectiveness and for potential outcomes for everyone involved.

   Awareness of strengths and oppressions is a key factor in all phases of work with mandated clients. Those who physically and emotionally abuse their family members, for example, are known to show a charming exterior and to minimise the abuse when in the presence of someone in a position of perceived authority. Professionals who are unaware of these dynamics may unintentionally support unrecognised oppressive forces in the family or inadvertently contribute to the perpetuation of the abuse rather than work effectively to end those behaviours. Building on each family's strengths and diminishing or ending oppressive behaviours shape the structure and purpose of subsequent work.

Principle 2: Enact multicultural respect

Multicultural factors include ethnicity, gender, age, socioeconomic class, religion/spiritual belief, sexual orientation, differing abilities, and language (Schniedewind and Davidson, 1997):

- *Ethnicity*: Connectedness based on commonalities (such as religion, nationality, and region) where specific cultural patterns and a common history are shared (Pinderhughes, 1989).
- *Gender*: 'A social, not a psychological, concept denoted by the terms "femininity" and "masculinity," which refer to a complex set of characteristics and behaviours prescribed for a particular sex by society and learned through the socialisation experience' (Ruth, 1990: 14).
- *Age*: Number of years since birth or conception, noting that some ethnic and religious groups begin counting at the time of conception rather than at the time of birth.
- *Socioeconomic class*: 'Class is more than just the amount of money you have; it's also the presence of economic security' (Langston, 1995: 101).
- *Religion/spiritual belief*: 'In most societies it is the basis for morality and for all human relationships, especially where it is believed that there is divine law controlling all things, and it gives meaning to life' (Allen et al. 1993: 626).
- *Sexual orientation*: One's feeling of sexual attraction to people of the same sex, to people of the opposite sex, or to people of both sexes (Marcus, 1993).
- *Differing abilities*: Having abilities that differ from the established social norm, some of which may include living with impaired sight or hearing, needing to use a wheelchair, having intellectual capacity that exceeds that of one's peers, or utilising different patterns of learning and processing information.
- *Language*: Includes one's first and primary language as well as later learned language, not necessarily spoken (i.e., sign language) with emphasis on bilingual and multilingual skills as definite strengths.

These eight do not constitute an exhaustive list of possible factors, but they do reflect ones currently and consistently appearing in the literature (National Association for Multicultural Education). Multicultural awareness is accessed through family stories of survival and coping, through the narratives of ancestors, and through the history of a family's major transitions, crises, rituals, and celebrations. Multicultural counselling competencies include: counsellor awareness of his or her own assumptions, values, and biases; an understanding of the worldview of the culturally different client; and development of appropriate intervention strategies and techniques (Sue, Arredondo and McDavis, 1995).

A 'lack of cultural congruence that affects the communication process' (Leigh, 1998: 39) has been identified as the major barrier in forming a relationship across cultures. To address this lack, the ethnographic approach is a very helpful tool for working with families from a position of multicultural respect. Its main objective is 'to learn about cultural behaviour, values, language, and worldviews of the person who is representative of the cultural group' (p. 79). Ethnographic information is used to determine directions for practice that are 'congruent with the cultural demands of the person' (p.79). Steps to the ethnographic interview are: tuning in with cultural empathy before contact with the family; setting the stage through friendly conversation; explaining the model by expressing ignorance of their culture and inviting them to be the worker's 'cultural guide'; assessment of the situation using global questions (broad questions leading to cultural understanding), descriptive questions, and reaching for explanation of cover terms (words that cover a range of ideas and meanings, often symbolic meaning); reaching consensus through negotiation for plans about how to address, for purposes of this chapter, the mandated situation; selecting interventions that are culturally relevant; and ending the interview in a manner respectful of the family's cultural patterns regarding endings.

Empowering practice with families using multicultural respect through the steps of the ethnographic interview requires that the helping professional let go of expectations that a client family will learn the culture of the helping process. Instead, the helper must be willing to take on the role of learning from the family members.

Principle 3: Recognise needs at the three levels of empowerment (personal, interpersonal, social/community)

Families know what they need. Listening to the narratives of the family members, both involuntary and voluntary, and responding with sensitivity to timing and cultural influences are key to empowerment practice. Families report that when professionals respond first to concrete and immediate needs and follow this with responses to ongoing needs, the family members are more likely to feel that they have been helped. Kaplan and Girard (1994) specifically identify concrete needs as the professional helper's first priority with client families. Clients tend to be more open in allowing a helper to assist with concrete needs, needs that we all share, in the earlier phases of the relationship. As such, these responses can serve as an important entry point into developing levels of trust required for later interactions between clients and helpers.

Simultaneous occurrence of concrete and immediate needs at personal, interpersonal, and social/community levels can be observed in the following illustration. When the Ramirez family stood on the lawn of their burning apartment building, each expressed the need for support at personal and interpersonal levels. Mrs. Ramirez anxiously watched for her husband's van. Her teenage daughter asked the social worker if she could borrow a cell phone to call her best friend to come be with her. The four-year-old son just needed to be held by his mother. A short time later, a staff member from an emergency aid organisation in the community brought information about a temporary shelter for the family, an ongoing need.

Responses to ongoing needs that have been reported by families as most helpful are information about what is happening, help with increasing skills to cope with the situations they face on a day-to-day basis, and support from others who have faced similar experiences. These coincide directly with the core practices at the centre of the framework for empowerment practice. Each will be considered in greater depth below in the discussion of the middle phase of work.

Principle 4: With sufficient resources, families can empower themselves

Assessment of a family's personal, interpersonal, and social/community resources is an ongoing process throughout every phase of the work, not only at the time of intake or during the introductory work with the family. Every decision about which interventions will be chosen and how they will be implemented will include the use of these resources. Interventions that integrate resources that are already familiar to the clients tend to result in longer lasting outcomes than interventions that require previously unknown behaviours or interactions. Known resources, for example, may be extended family members, peers or colleagues in a job setting, neighbours, teachers, or support groups in the community. They may include financial resources; access to jobs, job training, or job interviews; assistance in applying to educational programmes; or enhancing resources related to food, clothing, shelter, and recreation.

Determining when the number and quality of resources is sufficient to move forward can only happen through close collaboration with the members of the family. Identifying verbal and nonverbal indicators that clients are not yet ready to move forward is a skill of equal importance. Such indicators include their statements of wishing to maintain behaviours and attitudes as they are or their actions of turning away from assistance to break cycles of addiction, abuse, or other repetitive actions. Other indicators may include isolation, loneliness, losing the will to live, clinging to a victim stance, or feeling immobilised by fear or depression. Some family members will be ready to move forward when others are not.

Principle 5: Integrate support needed from others

All people need the support of parents, siblings, and extended family members yet social workers often observe the opposite. For families facing the events prior to a mandate for involuntary services, showing support to each other may be overshadowed by extreme personal pain. Responses to stress and trauma often involve withdrawal or lashing out in flashes of emotion. At the times when family members need each other the most, they may have the least to give.

When working with involuntary clients, helping efforts that are empowering may include encouraging connections of support among and between family members. If one member of the family has been mandated to service and may be fearing the anger of other family members for her or his behaviors, for example, it can be important for that person to hear that she or he has the support of family members. If the entire family has been mandated to receive service, it is equally important that blame and accusations within the family be redirected, if possible, toward support and how to move forward.

The exception to reaching for support within the family is from individuals who are abusive and/or violent. Survivors in these families need love and support from others, just as all persons do, but for them these needs must be met where their safety is assured. Their needs for love and support may need to be met through other relationships and through supportive connections in the community. The first concern is always for the client's safety.

Families receiving services involuntarily also need the support of their communities and for their peers, colleagues, friends, co-workers, supervisors, and others to respond to their needs. Vulnerable families are alert to physical and social threats in the community that present barriers. Especially poor families, families that are living with violence, those who are controlled by addictions, and those who face discrimination on a daily basis, the neighbourhood and community may not be helpful or healthy places to live. Extended family networks, natural helpers or non-kinship networks, and religious and work or educational institutions often serve as resources for these families.

Principle 6: Establish and maintain a 'power with' relationship

The family members who receive involuntary services need to be assured that they have an active role to play in determining what will happen to them in the relationship with the social worker and the institution delivering the mandated services. Workers come to the practice setting with three kinds of power: power from their expertise, power from their interpersonal skills, and power related to the resources to which they have access and that the clients need (Hasenfeld, 1987). Client families come with these three kinds of power as well. However, it may be exactly at the time of the initial meeting with the social worker that involuntary families have their greatest sense of powerlessness. The requirements of the mandate are likely to have been explained to them shortly before that meeting. When the social worker begins with

their strengths and resources (Principle 1), this step assures them that their power, their ability to influence how the requirements of the mandate are met, is recognised from the outset.

Yet, even with this assurance, families enter the helping relationship with ambivalence. From the position of their involuntary status, they may also be highly suspicious about a relationship that may either enable or frustrate them in their process of moving toward their goals. Before a 'power with' relationship can be explained and demonstrated, clients view their social workers as only extensions of the institution. They may have experienced 'power over' and 'power under' relationships in other institutions and, at least initially, they may see no reason to believe that there would be any difference with this person.

The steps and skills of the empowerment framework offer ways to address these challenges. From the family's initial narrative, clues about previous experiences can lead to helpful interactions for the present working relationship. Those earlier efforts are respected and, at the same time, a picture develops of what specific needs, resources, information, skills, support, and interactions may need to occur with the family at this time.

Principle 7: Using cooperative roles to support and assist family members

In empowering practice, the use of cooperative roles means role sharing. No role works in only one direction. Any role assumed by the worker to assist the client may, at another time, be a role assumed by the client to assist the worker's understanding. Any role can be filled by family members and by workers. Individual skills and experience, as well as specific contexts and needs, determine when different people fill different roles and when one role is more appropriate than another.

The workers and family members serve as *co-consultants* for each other. They seek to *collaborate* with each other. The family members sometimes *guide* the worker and sometimes the worker serves as a guide. The worker may assume a *teaching* role at times and, equally important, is in a *learning* role when the client family is teaching the worker about their history and their other experiences, talents, and skills. *Co-investigators* and *co-creators* are the final two roles considered here. The prefix 'co-' identifies many of these roles as shared and makes explicit the cooperative and mutual nature of roles congruent with empowerment thinking. 'Role sharing is a coping device well suited to the complexity of modern family pressures' (Lee, 2001: 171–2). Role sharing can also be modelled as an effective coping skill for the family once the work in the social work setting has been completed.

Co-consultants

As co-consultants 'workers and clients confer and deliberate together to develop plans for change.' Co-consultants acknowledge 'that both social workers and client systems bring information and resources, actual and potential, which are vital for resolving the issue at hand' (Miley, O'Melia and DuBois, 2001: 14).

Collaborators

As collaborators, workers using the empowerment perspective function as team players, working together in a way that the strengths of family members and workers alike are called out to be used for the actions related to planning, setting goals, and taking steps to reach those goals.

Guides

Family members guide the worker to know who they are individually and together, how they face challenges, what works and does not work for them. Social workers guide family members by clarifying the conditions and requirements of the mandate, where the family can make choices, and where the requirements must remain firmly in place. Social workers can also serve as guides about available services and how to access them. The balance and the equal distribution of opportunities to serve as guides to each other become the focus of an empowering process, each family member and each worker serving as guide where she or he has the information and experience to do so.

Co-teachers and co-learners

In any process of teaching, one is also learning. It is impossible to separate these two. Accepting them as integrated cooperative roles in the empowering process of practice interaction between client families and their social workers is also reflected in the major practice direction of providing relevant information, discussed further below.

Co-investigators

Investigation for additional information or facts is required when there is a gap in information, when there is a contradiction in facts or perceptions, or when the worker and the family seem to be stuck in their process. Certain members of the family are likely to have easier access to the needed information, or to the people with the answers being sought, than other family members or the social worker. Social workers often invite family members to participate in the search for information that will help the family reach their goals, adding valuable interpersonal time that helps strengthen the working relationship between clients and workers.

Co-creators

Family members have a long history together, usually, before they come to the attention of helping professionals. Patterns developed over time, unique to each family, play a key role in responding to the restrictions and requirements of a mandate to involuntary service. These patterns can help inform the social worker about how the family copes with stress. Each family member contributes to the creation of the family as a unit and also creates herself or himself as an individual within the context of that particular family. The creative process is a key component of the purpose of empowerment practice: to help sustain, enhance, and create family well-being.

Guidelines for the beginning, middle, and ending phases of the work

The three phases of helping – beginning, middle, and ending – assist in shaping the progression of the work even though these phases may or may not occur in a linear fashion. Formal mandates, those coming from court-ordered and other institutional sources, and informal mandates, ones, for example that may come from within the family in the form of a 'have to' or a threat, have a marked influence on all three phases. Working from an empowerment framework requires engagement, assessment, and working together at each phase from a conscious use of personal, interpersonal, and social/community dynamics and resources while enacting the seven principles of empowerment practice.

The beginning phase of work

The first principle of empowerment practice clearly states the necessity of beginning with and building upon client strengths. Some practitioners, however, have assumed hostility, resistance, and lack of motivation on the part of involuntary clients (Miller and Rollnick, 1991; Rooney, 1992). Some have indiscriminately accepted the reports of referral sources, even though those reports may be based in pathology-oriented terminology rather than coming from a strengths-based approach. It has been found that involuntary clients do tend to view the mandate with ambivalence, minimise or deny their problems, see others as the cause of their difficulties, and feel coerced into treatment (McConnaughy et al., 1989) but they do not fit the stereotype of being unable or unwilling to change. In one study, over one-fourth (28.3 per cent) of the court-ordered clients were 'thinking about changing, actively engaged in doing something about the problem, or trying to maintain previous gains in dealing with a problem' (O'Hare, 1996: 420).

Empowering beginnings include the worker's awareness of family power dynamics in her or his own family that may influence the present work at hand. With involuntary families, and as well with voluntary families, the beginning contact sets the stage with a respectful greeting, conveys appreciation for strengths, and engages family members in friendly conversation that indicates the importance of building a relationship. The beginning also includes an open acknowledgement of the mandate, simultaneously maximising clients' sense of choice and control while being clear about any non-negotiable terms in the mandate (Rooney, 1992; De Jong and Berg, 2001). Acceptance of any reluctance, clarification of the practitioner's role, and providing a sense of choice about goals and methods in the work together (Behroozi, 1992; Rooney, 1992) are also important steps in the initial contact. 'Empowering approaches emphasise a variety of choices for meeting the requirements of the mandate and the client family's control over what those choices will be and how they would like to use them. Every family member is seen as important in fulfilling a role in the process' (Wise, 2005: 187).

In the beginning phase of the work, the practitioner attends to strengths-based versus deficit-based language while discovering the family's views about what help is desired, and then offers service and approaches that work through an empowering assessment, one that is based upon and inclusive of the family's perceptions. An empowering assessment is a competency-based assessment (Lee, 2001: 73). With involuntary clients, it may be especially significant to explore the effects of powerlessness as part of the assessment 'conveying a sense of respect for having the strength and resiliency to withstand' those effects (Robbins, Chatterjee and Canda, 1998: 109).

Six levels of family assessment for empowerment practice (Lee, 2001: 209) are:

1. Content – worldview, multicultural factors, stress as resource and/or oppression.
2. Family Process – communication, alliances, feelings, boundaries, conflict resolution, decision making as resource and/or oppression.
3. Family Structure – formal organisation, roles and rules, gender differences, authority seen as resource and/or oppression.
4. Family history including historical oppression.
5. Individuals' strengths and resources, stages of development, ways of coping, health status, stressors.
6. Environment – physical and social factors as manifestations of resource and/or oppression.

Concrete needs and understanding what the family has already done to address the issues at hand are additional assessment factors to raise in the beginning phase. An empowering context is characterised by staying connected with the family's goals in the present. Tools that reach into their past are helpful when relevant to the present and are part of developing the relationship during the beginning phase which, in turn, determines the quality of interactions in the middle and ending phases of work.

The middle phase of work

The foundation of empowering practice has always been shaped from careful, attentive, and empathic listening to the voices of our clients, working from the descriptions of their needs and requests for assistance in their own words.

Focusing on providing concrete assistance has been suggested as one avenue for increasing motivation of involuntary clients to engage in other aspects of change (O'Hare, 1996). Client families have identified three core actions helpful and empowering to them as they strive to move forward with their lives:

- To provide information relevant to the circumstances they are facing in the present.
- To assist them in strengthening their ability to cope.
- To integrate support from others who have faced similar challenges.

> (Gutierrez and Lewis, 1999; Lee, 2001;
> Wise, 2005)

These three actions define the purpose, structure, and direction of the work during the middle phase.

Providing information

Offering relevant information to client families in a manner consistent with empowering outcomes requires sensitivity to different learning styles and different ways of processing information for each person. Children learn differently than adults (Knowles, 1977; Brookfield, 1995). Women learn differently than men (Gilligan, 1977). People who have suffered oppression learn through a different lens than those who have lived as members of a dominant status (Ponterotto et al., 1995). Survivors of trauma process information differently than those who have not faced such experiences (Van der Kolk, McFarlane and Weisaeth, 1996). Diverse sensory preferences – auditory, visual, kinesthetic – also play a role in how people take in and comprehend information. Some are internal processors, doing a great deal of thinking before speaking about their thoughts. Others are external processors, needing to speak their thoughts first and hear the responses from others to help clarify what they are thinking.

Involuntary clients may face internal and external barriers to taking in and processing information. Internal barriers may result from the tendency to minimise, deny, or disagree with the need for services. They may see themselves in a position of powerlessness, assuming that they have no influence on how the requirements of the mandate can be met. Externally, they may have had earlier experiences with mandates imposed upon them with less than helpful outcomes and carry suspicions that the present mandate might repeat that experience. External events may reactivate internal trauma responses. Sensitivity to the involuntary nature of the relationship and use of the empowerment principles can maximise the possibility that information offered is perceived as accessible and useful in meeting the requirements of the mandate and moving forward with their lives.

Strengthening coping skills

The relationship between coping and empowerment is a tightly knit one, reciprocal in nature. Successful coping strengthens personal, interpersonal, and situational dimensions of empowerment, while commitment to an empowerment lens centres around the coping actions taken to address a family's distress. Effective coping in the short term diminishes immediate distress and, in the long term, contributes to the physical, emotional, and social well-being of the family.

Families often have a long history of coping with stressors and challenges before they come to the attention of the courts and justice systems and human service professionals. When they do come to the attention of public institutions, it may be because they have tried forms of coping that worked in the past yet nothing seems to work with their present difficulties. Acknowledging their earlier forms of coping as strengths and as possible resources in the present situation, plus assisting them in finding the forms of coping that are the best fit for their present challenges can serve as key empowering tasks when working with involuntary client families toward strengthening coping skills. Through the empowerment lens, an assessment is made as to whether each choice for coping will sustain, enhance, and create a sense of well-being for the family as a whole and for each member individually.

Several 'interlocking dimensions of empowerment' (Lee, 2001: 34) are coping behaviours that can add to the number of choices available to families and those helping them during the middle phase when work centres on strengthening coping skills. Those dimensions are:

- Developing a stronger and more positive sense of self.
- Building knowledge about the social and political realities of one's environment.

- Cultivating resources and strategies to attain personal and collective goals.

Integrating support from others

Support from others may come from within the family, from extended family, from friendship and peer networks, from co-workers, from mutual aid support groups, from community groups, and from participation with those identified by the social worker as ones who are facing similar challenges as the client family.

Family members provide one of the key supports for managing distress. 'The family and community are key structures that mediate against the effects of oppressions and enable people to cope' (Lee, 2001: 46). Individuals who have strong support from family members suffer fewer and less severe consequences following traumatic events. Their ability to recover is enhanced, and their capacity to cope with situations that cannot be changed increases. And yet the view is not one-sided but highly complex. Families and other members of the community can mediate and be supportive or they can be sources of stress and oppression. Accurate assessment to determine where resources exist is an essential step.

A further way of integrating support of others is for the social worker to remain alert to ways her or his relationship with the client family can be deepened through the use of empowerment principles. The worker's demonstration of *equalising power differentials* through *cooperative roles* enhances the environment for effective helping. The cooperative nature of being a consultant, collaborator, guide, co-learner, co-investigator, and co-creator potentially allow family members to interact with helpers in new ways. As families gain information, strengthen their coping skills, and make informed choices that help them move forward with their lives, they gain the understanding about empowering practice that is the most long-lasting.

The ending phase

Endings with families are also unique to each family. The helping professional who uses the empowerment framework at the ending phase will ask questions such as, 'What can make the quality of this ending one that *sustains* this family?' 'How can this final stage *enhance* the strengths already seen in the work we have done together?' 'How can this ending serve the family in the ways they are *creating* who they are and who they are becoming?'

Responses related to past, present, and future increase the likelihood of empowering endings. Issues pertinent to each dimension include:

- *Past*: personal histories of ending and loss for individual family members and for the family as a whole; the history of the helping relationship, including both its content and its process, its highlights and milestones, its frustrations, and its humour.
- *Present*: how to make this ending one that is empowering for each family member and family as a whole; talking openly about the tendency to avoid this ending; inviting feedback about what was helpful, what was not helpful, and any recommended changes.
- *Future*: how the gains from this experience can be carried forward into the family's future; imagining what skills they will use when faced with another challenge in the future; seeing the social worker in the future for follow-up or in more informal settings; if referral to another worker is part of the plan, introducing that worker to family members.

Five key tasks for endings in empowerment practice have been identified: dealing with feelings, inviting the family members to identify gains in their own words, consolidating those gains, reunifying with the community, and evaluation (Lee 2001: 253–8).

Dealing with feelings may occur as a result of memories related to earlier endings and loss. When unresolved, these memories can instil more powerful emotions onto the present ending with the social worker. When these feelings are acknowledged, respected, and brought from past to present, this part of the work in the ending phase can empower family members with understanding about the cumulative effects of endings and loss.

Identifying and consolidating gains in their own words from an empowerment perspective include gains at personal, interpersonal, and social/community levels. Gains in personal power are evident in self-efficacy and greater freedom to make choices. Interpersonal gains are observable in actions taken from a stance of 'power with' rather than 'power over' or 'power under.' Social/community gains are visible through networks that strengthen the family's ability to move forward with their lives. These gains come in direct response to challenges or oppressive factors, internal and external, that the family has faced and are in the process of overcoming. Gains are a result of claiming positions of justice and asserting one's right to respect and fairness. Gains from an empowerment framework are built on resilience and self-respect, from challenging stereotypes, managing feelings, and taking pride in one's cultural uniqueness.

Reunifying with the community may or may not be an essential part of the ending phase in the work with client families. Empowerment practice, by definition, includes maintaining connections with the community and social networks in the family's life throughout the work. For some families, however, the separation from community supports is very profound and the sense of disconnection can prevent empowering results. Approaches that respect the uniqueness of each family's situation, assess with responsive awareness, and make choices specific to the family's needs provide the most empowering context for the work.

Central to *evaluation* of empowering practice with families is what has been done to diminish the impact of oppressive forces upon the family's well-being. A social worker's assistance in helping family members meet the requirements of a mandate and to lift that mandate from their lives may be interpreted by involuntary families as diminishing an oppressive force. A simultaneous part of evaluation is identifying what factors have enhanced their individual and collective strengths. Increased skills to address needs also characterise an evaluation of empowering practice. The evaluation is 'ethnosensitive' (Lee, 2001: 255). It integrates cultural and ethnic standards for relationship and connection, for rituals of ending and going separate ways, for acknowledging the mutuality and universality of giving and receiving assistance.

Practice with involuntary client families is supported with time-honoured theories and perspectives. Guided by what is most responsive and effective with the families who open their lives to their social workers and other helping professionals, the contributions offered in this chapter are selected with those families and professionals in mind. The relationship of power among and between family members, as well as between the family and the wider community, is truly empowering only when all variations of

powerlessness have been transformed at personal, interpersonal, and social/community levels.

References

Allen, D.A. et al. (1993) Religion. In McLeish, K. (Ed.) *Key Ideas in Human Thought.* NY: Facts on File.

Behroozi, C.S. (1992) A Model for Social Work with Involuntary Applicants in Groups. *Social Work with Groups*, 15, 223–38.

Brookfield, S. (1995) *Becoming a Critically Reflective Teacher.* San Francisco: Jossey-Bass.

De Jong, P. and Berg, I.K. (2001) Co-Constructing Cooperation with Mandated Clients. *Social Work*, 46: 4, 361–74.

Evans, P. (1992) *The Verbally Abusive Relationship.* Holbrook, MA: Adams.

Gilligan, C. (1977) In a Different Voice: Women's Conceptions of Self and Morality. *Harvard Educational Review.* 47, 481–517.

Gutierrez, L.M. and Lewis, E. (1999) *Empowering Women of Color.* NY: Columbia University Press.

Hasenfeld, Y. (1987) Power in Social Work Practice. *Social Service Review.* 61, 469–83.

Kaplan, L. and Girard, J.L. (1994) *Strengthening High-Risk Families.* New York: Lexington Books.

Knowles, M.S. (1977) *The Adult Education Movement in the United States.* 2nd edn. Huntington, NY: Kreiger.

Langston, D. (1995) Tired of Playing Monopoly. In Anderson, M.L. and Collins, P.H. (Eds.) *Race, Class, and Gender: An Anthology.* San Francisco: Wadsworth.

Lee, J.A. (1994) *The Empowerment Approach to Social Work Practice.* New York: Columbia University Press.

Lee, J.A. (2001) *The Empowerment Approach to Social Work Practice: Building the Beloved Community.* 2nd edn. New York: Columbia University Press.

Leigh, J.W. (1998) *Communicating for Cultural Competence.* Boston: Allyn and Bacon.

Marcus, E. (1993) *Is It a Choice? Answers to 300 of the Most Frequently Asked Questions About Gays and Lesbians.* San Francisco: Harper.

McConnaughy, E.A. et al. (1989) Stages of Change in Psychotherapy: A Follow-Up Report. *Psychotherapy.* 26, 494–503.

Miley, K.K., O'Melia, M. and DuBois, B. (2001) *Generalist Social Work Practice: An Empowering Approach.* Boston: Allyn and Bacon.

Miller, W.R. and Rollnick, S. (1991) Dealing with Resistance. In Miller, W.R. and Rollnick, S. (Eds.) *Motivational Interviewing: Preparing People for Change.* New York: Guilford Press.

O'Hare, T. (1996) Court-Ordered versus Voluntary Clients: Problem Differences and Readiness for Change. *Social Work.* 41: 4, 417–22.

Pinderhughes, E. (1989) *Understanding Race, Ethnicity, and Power: The Key to Efficacy in Clinical Practice.* New York: Free Press.

Ponterotto, J.G. et al. (1995) *Handbook of Multicultural Counseling.* Thousand Oaks, CA: Sage.

Robbins, S.P., Chatterjee, P. and Canda, E.R. (1998) *Contemporary Human Behavior Theory.* Boston: Allyn and Bacon.

Rooney, R.H. (1992) *Strategies for Working with Involuntary Clients.* New York: Columbia University Press.

Ruth, S. (1990) *Issues in Feminism: An Introduction to Women's Studies.* Mountain View, CA: Mayfield.

Saleebey, D. (1999) The Strengths Perspective: Principles and Practice. In Compton, B.R. and Galaway, B. (Eds.) *Social Work Processes.* Pacific Grove, CA: Brooks/Cole.

Schniedewind, N. and Davidson, E. (1997) *Open Minds to Equality.* Des Moines, IA: Allyn and Bacon.

Sue, D.W., Arredondo, P. and McDavis, R.J. (1995) Multicultural Competencies and Standards: A Call to the Profession. *Journal of Counseling and Development.* 70, 477–86.

Surrey, J.L. (1987) *Relationship and Empowerment.* Wellesley, MA: Stone Center for Developmental Services and Studies.

Trotter, C. (1999) *Working with Involuntary Clients: A Guide to Practice.* London: Sage.

Van der Kolk, B., McFarlane, A.C. and Weisaeth, L. (1996) *Traumatic Stress: The Effects of Overwhelming Experience on Mind, Body, and Society.* New York: Guilford.

Weick, A. and Chamberlain, R. (1997) Putting Problems in Their Place: Further Explorations in the Strengths Perspective. In Saleebey, D. (Ed.) *The Strengths Perspective in Social Work Practice.* New York: Longman.

Weissberg, R. (1999) *The Politics of Empowerment.* Westport, CT: Praeger.

Wise, J.B. (2005) *Empowerment Practice with Families in Distress.* New York: Columbia University Press.

CHAPTER 13

Engaging Children, Young People and their Families via Family Group Conferences

Peter Marsh

A Family Group Conference (FGC) is a model of decision-making for serious social problems that has been remarkably successful in engaging service users.

The era of mandatory use of FGCs began in 1989 in New Zealand with the Children, Young Persons and their Families Act. In the same year in the UK the Children Act brought in many of the principles that underpin FGCs, such as a strong preference for family care if possible, and for negotiated rather than imposed help. In the following years there have been thousands of FGCs in New Zealand, and their substantial use in the UK, as well as in Scandinavia, the Netherlands, the US, Canada and many other countries throughout the world. This extraordinary growth shows the strength and importance of the FGC model, not least for the tens of thousands of service users who have been actively engaged when it has been used.

This chapter covers some of the history and current development of FGCs, and outlines the basic model, concentrating on the major area of child welfare. It then goes on to draw out some key lessons for user engagement from the substantial FGC experience that is now available.

Family group conferences: context and current development

In New Zealand, before 1989, there was a history of professional-led decision-making in child welfare and youth justice. There was a groundswell of opinion amongst many professionals that a more inclusive, and partnership based, model should replace this, but there were also strong views that professionally-led practice should be maintained. Alongside practitioner voices, there emerged a powerful user-based movement in the Maori community, whose children were in care in excessive numbers. These Maori children were looked after in large national childcare residences, and in mostly Pakeha (white settler) foster families, with a good number moving to Pakeha adoption. A strong cry went up from the Maori community to 'give us our children back' (Marsh and Allen, 1993).

In the UK there was also pressure for change, with a number of family-led organisations, such as the Family Rights Group and the Grandparents Federation, backed up by academics studying user views and professional child care processes, arguing for a more family based and more user friendly and responsive service (Marsh and Crow, 1998: 37–44). Family oriented services, based on professional partnerships with service users, were being actively promoted.

Strong user views lay behind the substantial changes that were to occur in legislation, and that were to underpin the development of FGCs. But listening to and respecting those views had been a major element of the best social work practice for decades, and indeed one of the most prominent practice models, task-centred social work, has developed with the idea of partnership between professionals and service users at its core (Marsh and Doel, 2005).

The combination of user push and professional pull was a powerful one. The pressure intensified with the notable success of FGCs, with the vast majority, in all countries and settings, producing agreed plans between professionals and families, and generating high satisfaction scores from all parties (American Humane Association, 1996; Hudson, Morris et al., 1996; Marsh and Crow, 1998, 1999; Lupton and Nixon, 1999).

Of course, there were circumstances where service users were not happy with the outcome, or where sheer complexity, or depth of problem, defeated the process, but they were very small in number. For the great majority of people the FGC did engage users despite the complex, fraught, and fragile circumstances that gave rise to it being held.

FGCs are a successful model that fits UK legislation, current policy developments (see for example Marsh and Walsh, 2007, for connections with the Every Child Matters programme from the Department for Education and Skills), and the UK professional code of conduct for social work (General Social Care Council, 2002). They now have many years of development and research behind them in many different areas of social work practice (Ashley, 2006).

Nonetheless, despite the rationale for widespread use, FGCs remain marginal in the UK (Brown, 2003: Doolan, 2003), and they are still, some many years after their initial development, an 'unfolding agenda' (Dignan and Marsh, 2001: 99). Perhaps this indicates the journey that professionals must make in order to take service user engagement seriously, because, as has been clearly shown, the users are clearly in favour and vote with their feet when FGCs are on offer. The struggle for better engagement for service users is clearly a continuing one, and given the substantial experience from FGCs it is opportune to note some of the lessons they can provide to help with this, and address the important wider agenda of user engagement and participation.

What are family group conferences?

FGCs are a decision-making process, and their lessons about service user engagement will be lessons about decision making. The process is more than just a 'Conference', more than a meeting, because the work before the Conference is a vital part of the FGC model.

FGCs are also about engaging families, so lessons are predominantly about family engagement, although many are perfectly appropriate for individuals or groups engaging in decision making.

FGCs are not tokenistic decision-making sessions, and they need to involve serious decisions about important social problems. They are relevant to the more difficult end of practice, and they therefore provide a particularly good example from which to learn lessons of user engagement.

FGCs take place where there are major child well-being concerns, or in similar serious social circumstances in other areas, such as youth justice, school problems, mental health problems and so on. They involve the family working in partnership with agencies.

The Conferences are convened by an independent co-ordinator, who arranges a

meeting of extended family and professionals in order to consider the needs of the child, young person, or adult, and agree a suitable plan to meet those needs.

Four key stages are involved.

1. Preparation before the meeting (invitation, discussion and briefing).
2. The first stage of the meeting (information giving by all parties who are there).
3. The second stage of the meeting (private family planning).
4. The third stage of the meeting (all parties agreeing on an acceptable plan of action).

The process has some key ingredients and principles:

- There needs to be clear jargon free information about concerns, and about resources available to help (the meeting will have many 'lay people' in it).
- The concept of 'family' needs to be a wide and inclusive one. All people who act as if they are family, and seem to be family from the point of view of the person at the heart of the Conference, are potential invitees.
- There must be an independent co-ordinator for the Conference, who is not directly engaged in the provision of services to the family.
- The decision of the Conference should be respected and supported unless there is risk of significant harm to a child or adult, so that all concerned are fully aware that this is serious decision making in action.
- The overall process should be built on family strengths, and negotiation of services, as the aim is to maximise resources and make the best fit between people and services that is possible.
- Finally, there should be maximum flexibility in setting and style for the Conference, within the overall model, to allow for different cultures and family approaches.

Conferences will typically take a few weeks to set up, and will run for about two hours. There may be around six to ten family members attending, and perhaps two or three professionals, although both time spans and attendance can show wide variations in different circumstances. Additionally, there might be some supporters or advocates for family members if they are needed. The Conference should be held in relatively neutral territory and very rarely in the professionals' office, and many take place outside of standard working hours. Efforts to fit the Conference to the family culture could include, for example, disability access, provision of relevant food, and holding the Conference in the preferred language of the family and providing interpreters for the professionals.

FGCs, based on the principles and ingredients outlined above, therefore involve the following themes:

- Preparation for decision-making, and gathering the family together.
- Active support for participation.
- Preparation of professionals for family led decision making.
- A meeting place and a meeting style.
- Information giving.
- Clarity about what can and cannot be decided: a bottom line.
- Private family time.
- A process to agree a plan.

We will cover each of these eight themes to see what lessons they might offer to help with the broader issues of user engagement in decision-making.

Family Group Conference Themes: Resistance to, and Engagement in, Decision-Making

Thousands of FGCs, hundreds of policy and practice documents, tens of research studies, and years of family and practitioner experience provide substantial lessons across all eight themes outlined above. The brief version below should ideally be built on by more thorough understanding of the FGC model, available in work that pulls together research and practice in detail (e.g. Ashley, 2006; Marsh and Crow, 1989).

Each of the eight key themes around engagement, beginning with who to engage, and then moving through to the final agreement about action, provides lessons about resistance and participation, and these are outlined below, with two or three central questions provided to help with the consideration of engagement in that particular area.

Preparation and gathering the family

Before an FGC can begin, the prospective participants need to be identified, and they need

to know about the FGC process and model. In short, for maximum engagement co-ordinators need to address the right people, and to make sure they understand the process that is beginning.

1. If the family are important for this particular decision, then who is 'family' from the point of view of the service users?

In order to engage the family we need to ask the question 'who is "family" in this particular circumstance?' This is to avoid slipping into any routinised ideas, for example about family just being the parents of the child or just being blood relatives, since uncles, aunts and grand parents are regularly key players in FGCs. For instance, very good friends, partners and others have often been willing to be asked to be, and to behave like, family for the purposes of the FGC. Co-ordinators will work 'outwards' from the child, young person, or adult who is the centre of the Conference to identify family members. Professional guesswork is not a good guide as to who is family.

2. Have there been multiple attempts to explain to service users, in the clearest way, the decision making processes that are going to occur?

FGCs have deliberately used multiple means to overcome the very difficult issue of the professional jargon that inevitably creeps into professional discussion, and the need to help people, who do not use this jargon everyday, to understand what it means. Leaflets about the Conferences, for example, have been designed in conjunction with service users themselves. Videos have been made to show the processes, and then these can be left in people's homes. Much work has been done on finding simple phrases, that do not simplify, to put over the key elements of the Conferences. Simply asking the question 'Am I using the simplest appropriate words?' is a key lesson from FGCs.

Questions of participation and support

Who can and should come to a decision-making meeting, and how can they best be helped to participate effectively? Addressing these issues correctly can be of central importance to engagement, and FGCs provide a number of lessons in how to do this.

3. Is there someone who should be pressed to be involved even if they are reluctant?

Experience with FGCs has shown that sometimes the issue of 'Who attends?' is also importantly an issue of 'Who would be very badly missed?' A key figure who is not present can make the decision making stall, and FGC experience shows that a repeat meeting can be needed in these circumstances, with every effort made to get the missing person there. Is there a key player (or key players) from the point of the central person in the Conference who really needs to attend?

4. Can you be creative about involvement?

Sometimes involvement may not mean physical attendance at the meeting. FGCs have learned that using a wide variety of other means of expression can be very effective, and can definitely be better than no involvement at all. People have asked others to speak for them as if 'delegates'. People have written letters, or recorded tapes, for the meeting. Phones have been used during the meetings to talk to people who were reluctant or unable to be present in person. Participation can take many forms.

5. Does involvement need support?

Allied to the point above it has been found that some people will need personal support if they are to be involved. It might be because they are worried about consequences that could follow on from them speaking, or because they feel relatively powerless, or for a wide variety of other reasons. FGC co-ordinators have taken this issue very seriously, and in particular they work on the principle of matching the support to the circumstance as far as possible. So, for example, it might be that another family member would be good for support, or support might need a particular type of advocate. The key lessons are both to be sensitive to the need for support *and* to match it to the person needing it and the reasons that it is needed.

Preparation of professionals

The professional task changes when engagement is at the centre of practice. Being both understood outside of your professional group, and helping others be understood, become key activities.

6. Is the professional language fully understandable by non-professionals?

For many decades this issue has been seen as important, and many examples exist of ways to avoid jargon as far as possible. In recent years in the UK it has also become clear that talking and writing in ways that service users can understand can have important benefits for better professional practice in its own right. Examples include the clearer policy documents that emerged from the UK Department for Education and Skills when they worked with a young people's group, the Children and Young Person's Unit, to improve the language, or the better research that can come from user involvement as shown in the UK Department of Health 'Involve' project. FGCs can add some lessons to this, as a review of the literature would show, but their main contribution is to reinforce the fact that clarifying language is not an added extra, but rather a central plank of good engagement practice.

7. Are the professional inputs to the decision making reasonably in tune with each other?

Most FGCs have more than one professional present, and they are often from different professional groups. As shown in many other settings as well, it is clear that these groups can themselves engage in misunderstandings, and they may need to spend time to sort this out, and to make sure they are not misinterpreting each other. Service users have found it particularly frustrating when this has occurred during the FGC itself, as they rightly feel that the work should be done in professional time and not take up the time of the family. The message is for the professionals to make sure that they are fully understanding of each other's views *before* they engage with the process of family led decision making.

The meeting place and style

Family Group Conferences are not professional meetings with a family added. When, where and how the meetings are carried out have been shown to be important issues.

8. What timing works best for the meeting?

Most professional meetings, unsurprisingly, are fitted around the needs of professionals. They generally take place during the week and during standard working hours. FGCs are designed to encourage engagement of service users, so these principles are turned on their head, with the best time for the family being the starting point. Often, but not always, this will be outside working hours, but it might need to fit in with child care (either pre-existing child care, or child care that needs to be provided), or with someone's frailty, for example, the need for a meeting that involves a decision with a very old person taking place in the morning. The attitudinal issue is to make sure that meeting timing works well for the family, with the professionals doing their best to accommodate this.

9. How will the place for the meeting affect attendance?

Clearly, there are practical reasons why the place of a meeting can affect attendance, if there are, for example, disability access issues. But FGCs have also shown that other practical issues can matter, like the need for a small area for children to play in, or an additional room that can hold the food and allow for a proper break in the meeting. Another important lesson has been around the emotional meaning of places. Avoiding professional offices is generally important, but it can also be important to avoid the house of a key family member who is regarded as far too domineering and whose ownership of the meeting space could affect outcome.

10. How can the style of the meeting reflect the aspects of family culture that matter the most?

Few professionals nowadays would not be sensitive to the need to respect a family culture as far as possible in their dealings with the family. The FGC lesson is that some aspects of that culture matter a great deal to families, and some they are much more happy to be relaxed about. As with 'Who is in the family?' professional guesswork about this is often not the best guide to what matters most. So for some families,

holding the meeting in the language they speak at home is vital, and for others it could take second place to the cumbersome element it brings of translation (for the professionals). Asking what matters to these people in these circumstances is the key.

The information giving

Decisions clearly need good information to underpin them, and there has been a great deal of experience of trying to provide this in the information giving period of FGCs. It has often been found that professionals new to FGCs are anxious about this stage, and two key lessons stand out as important.

11. Are all professionals genuinely motivated to share information?

Given the effort that needs to be put into providing information in 'lay friendly' form it is not surprising that professionals often worry if their effort in doing this is worthwhile. So the first lesson is that it is important to build up the motivation of professionals to supply good clear information to service users, not just as a piece of good ethical practice, but also because all the experience of FGC work shows that it makes for better and more accurate information. Service users rarely object strongly to particular pieces of information, which is a common professional worry, but they often do correct small, but potentially significant, errors. Shared information, in the experience of FGCs, is usually better quality information, and this is to the benefit of all.

12. Who will facilitate the questioning?

The co-ordinator of the FGC acts like the chair of the meeting during this stage, and experience shows that this is an important role. There will be less anxious professionals, and there will be better service user questions, if there is some form of appropriately active chairing during any participative session that involves information exchange.

The bottom line

Frustration builds up if people feel that they are engaged in coming to decisions only to be told that their decision is in some way 'wrong', and that they need to think again. FGCs try and avoid this problem by tackling openly the issue of what can and what cannot be negotiated.

13. Do service users know what is not negotiable?

If a meeting is, for example, about placement decisions for a child, then there may well be some placements that the professionals will not sanction because of clear concerns about safety. Not to know this at the start of the family discussions could lead to frustration about involvement on the part of the family. Some things may clearly not be negotiable, but some areas may simply need more detailed negotiation. In the spirit of providing the maximum user led negotiation the only areas that are non-negotiable should be those that really are 'off limits' because of proven safety and legal reasons. FGC experience shows that the exercise of working out what this involves is valuable in its own right, and can help best practice overall.

14. Are all professionals genuinely motivated to be open about the bottom line?

In common with providing clear and jargon free information, there is a real cost for professionals in working out carefully the nature of any bottom line. Building up the motivation to do this is important, and FGC co-ordinators use their experience of when it has really helped good decision-making to show the value of the effort. The FGC literature cited in this chapter can provide many such examples, with the clear message that it is well worth while and that professional anxiety is common, but at the end of the meeting professional satisfaction for the process is nearly always very high.

The private family time

All families will have different ways of holding their own discussions, based on history, culture, personality and so on. The private family time at the heart of the FGC provides the family with a period to hold discussions in their own way.

15. How can private time be built into participation models?

Private time provides a clear statement of trust in people to get on with sensible discussions on their own. FGCs show that this trust is nearly always well placed. A clear statement that private conversations are welcome may be possible in a number of different decision-making settings, and it should be explored. This private time also provides for different sorts of conversations, as discussions between service users and other service users are often different from discussions between professionals and service users. Any parent who has talked about their child's school with other parents, and then done so at a school parents evening, knows that difference quite well.

16. How can existing family processes be built into participation models?

If we want maximum engagement and participation then people need to have the skills to participate and engage. People do this 'naturally' in everyday life, but professional processes are often different from everyday life, and new ways of working and talking are likely to be needed. FGCs address this problem by providing time that is 'natural' via the private family session, but there may be ways that existing family processes could be built into other models, for example, noting during a meeting the ways that individuals are talking one to another and then using facilitation skills to build on these exchanges as a way of taking issues forward in the meeting. The principle of trying to encourage people to learn new skills in order to engage and participate is a good one.

17. What helps this family contribute?

A whole range of 'comfort' factors are important in helping people to engage. Worry, hunger, and other emotions can get in the way of engagement. Parents will worry if children are stressed, so crèches may be needed, and often food plays a role in keeping people going and also in breaking up time and providing more social space. FGC work has shown how important it is to work hard at providing a comfortable setting for participation, in the widest meaning of the word 'comfortable'. This is not an added extra, it is often a vital part of the work.

Agreeing the plan

In conversation we can think we understand, but when ideas are written down we may realise there are gaps in that understanding. Writing or recording in some way also means that we can share our understanding more widely and store and review the ideas. FGCs end with agreements on paper (or some equivalent record if needed) so that all are clear about what is agreed, and they can be committed to the agreement and in due course review it.

18. Is there a system to provide accurate and clear notes of what is agreed, check that everyone understands what words mean, and clarify if everyone knows what to do?

All good meetings will have this, but working on the principles of the FGC means that it is done in a way that helps the process then and there, for example, by the use of flip charts, and by quick recording at the end of the meeting, and that effort is put into double-checking that people really do understand what is meant.

19. Is there an explicit agreement to actions, specified in appropriate detail?

FGCs, in common with the task-centred model mentioned earlier, are built on the idea that action will motivate people to participate and that through actions new learning will occur. This is decision-making that is clearly about changed behaviours, and there needs to be a way of writing that down in ways that indicate just what the new behaviour is going to be. So 'providing some help with picking up Jim from school' is not as good as 'meeting Jim from school on Monday and Wednesday in order to help with picking him up'. Providing the appropriate level of detail in the actions that are specified in agreements is an important piece of work to help engagement.

20. Is there a system for reviewing what was agreed and how it is working out?

The best decision making may result in decisions which need changing in the light of experience. FGCs provide a mechanism to reconvene the FGC, and they may involve an agreed review FGC some months after the initial one. Being clear that decisions can and should be reviewed helps engagement, and is, of course, good practice.

Overall

This chapter has posed twenty questions that professionals who want to encourage family engagement in decision making could ask

themselves, based on the experience of a number of decades of Family Group Conferences. Any one may be useful; overall they should help to deliver more engagement and more participation, and build the ethical, efficient, and effective practice that this underpins.

References

American Humane Association (1996) The Practice and Promise of Family Group Decision Making. *Protecting Children*, 12: 3.

Ashley, C. (Ed.) (2006) *The Family Group Conference Toolkit: A Practical Guide for Setting up and Running a FGC Service.* London: Family Rights Group.

Brown, L. (2003) Mainstream or Margin? The Current Use of Family Group Conferences in Child Welfare Practice in the UK. *Child and Family Social Work*, 8: 331–40.

Dignan, J. and Marsh, P. (2001) Restorative Justice and Family Group Conferences in England: Current State and Future Prospects. In Morris, A. and Maxwell, G. *Restorative Justice for Juveniles*. Oxford: Hart Publishing.

Doolan, M. (2003) *Partnering with Families: A Study on Mandating the Use of Family Group Conferences in Services for Children and Their Families.* Maidstone: Kent County Council Social Services.

General Social Care Council (2002) *Code of Practice for Social Care Workers and for Employers of Social Care Workers.* London: GSCC.

Hudson, J. and Morris, A. et al. (Eds.) (1996) *Family Group Conferences: Perspectives on Policy and Practice.* Leichhardt: The Federation Press.

Lupton, C. and Nixon, P. (1999) *Empowering Practice? A Critical Appraisal of The Family Group Conference Approach.* Bristol: The Policy Press.

Marsh, P. and Allen, G. (1993) The Law, Prevention and Reunification: The New Zealand Development of Family Group Conferences. In Marsh, P. and Triseliotis, J. *Prevention and Reunification in Child Care.* London: Batsford.

Marsh, P. and Doel, M. (2005) *The Task-Centred Book.* London: Routledge.

Marsh, P. and Crow, G. (1998) *Family Group Conferences in Child Welfare.* Oxford: Blackwell Science.

Marsh, P. and Crow, G. (1999) Family Group Conferences. *Highlights*. 169. NCB.

Marsh, P. and Walsh, D. (2007) *Outcomes of Family Group Conferences: More Than Just the Plan.* Maidstone: Kent County Council.

CHAPTER 14

Partnership Working to Engage the Client and Health Visitor

Christine Bidmead and Sarah Cowley

Health visiting

Health visitors provide a service that originated in the 19th century philanthropic public health movement. Victorian society was very divided, both in terms of gender and social class, and various 'sanitary associations' developed, which largely aimed to solve the public health problems caused by rapid urbanisation, through either engineering and building solutions, or by the delivery of bibles and religious tracts to promote cleanliness and hygiene. In Salford, a Ladies branch of the local sanitary association was established; believing that health and hygiene needed to start in the home and family, they chose a different, more practical route. They employed a local woman to visit homes, offering both help and advice where it was acceptable:

> Whitewash pails and brushes were placed at her disposal to lend, and also chloride of lime for purification of the air in the rooms of those who were suffering from fever. She had not only given instruction in common sanitary rules, but would herself wash and make comfortable a sick person whom she might find neglected or dirty, thus encouraging those who were around to follow her example by showing people how to do what was needful in the best way.
>
> (Salford Ladies Sanitary Reform Association: Annual report 1868, cited by Dingwall, 1977: 294)

This idea spread rapidly, and by the end of the nineteenth century, this home health visiting service was mainly funded by the Metropolitan Boroughs (Dingwall, 1977). The Notification of Births Acts of 1907 and 1915 provided a basis for developing the profession as we know it today. It became a statutory requirement for local authorities to provide a health visiting service for all new mothers, offering at least a single visit after the birth of a baby. Mothers did not, however, ever have to allow the health visitors entry to their home, so health visitors needed to ensure their service was acceptable in order to gain access to the family. This was largely achieved by avoiding reference to official authority, relying instead on relationships and being seen as the 'mother's friend' (Davies, 1988).

Two issues from these early days remain. First, the activities stemmed from not only the philanthropic ideal of kindliness and charitable concern to reduce the suffering of individuals and families, but also from the public health need to reduce the spread of epidemics, which had begun to affect the middle and upper classes following the industrial revolution. Today's health visiting profession is, likewise, motivated by twin concerns. There is empathy towards parents and children who (in today's jargon) have health needs; also the early interventions and preventive care delivered by health visitors are intended to meet today's public health imperatives, which are to reduce health inequalities, and to tackle the spiralling cost of health care identified by Wanless (2002). Second, although the 'new birth health visit' is no longer a statutory requirement, the contradiction established a century ago still pertains. The NHS is expected to provide this preventive service to all expectant and new mothers, their babies and their families, but the health visitors have no legal right of access and their services may be rejected.

Another issue that is hotly contested at present concerns the legitimacy of the universal service. Debates centre on the meaning of the term, who is included and whether it is the best way of organising services, particularly in respect of prevention, public health and health inequalities. Provision of a service to everyone acknowledges the broad social gradient in health, and that there are a large number of people who are not formally regarded as socially excluded, but who are relatively disadvantaged in health terms (Graham and Kelly, 2004). A service that is universally available, even if not delivered in a uniform way, takes account of this gradient, and the fact is that 'the bulk of health and social problems occur in the large number of people who are not especially at risk, rather than in the few who are at high risk' (Elkan, 2001: 117). In addition, it is generally hailed as non-stigmatising, and the fact that everyone has access to a health visitor is used to promote identification and acceptance by the most needy families, who are often the most difficult to engage, because they feel they are being singled out in some way (Cowley and Frost, 2006).

A different policy approach to reducing health inequalities is to focus exclusively on these very needy groups: the most socially excluded and those with most risk factors, who are the most difficult to reach (Graham and Kelly, 2004). Policies pursued by the social exclusion unit (Cabinet Office, 2006) and the health visiting review (Lowe, 2007) strongly favour this more targeted approach. The universal health visiting service has not been formally disbanded, but a quote highlighted in the health visiting review summarises the approved belief, which is that:

Health visitors are skilled, experienced and expensive. They need to be directed to where they can have the most impact – needs assessments and vulnerable families.
(DoH, 2007: 23)

Officially, health visitors are encouraged to deliver their service through a process of 'progressive universalism,' one of three principles the government set for all policies affecting children and families (HM Treasury and DfES, 2005). These are:

- Rights and responsibilities: all families are entitled to high quality public services which complement the role of parents and the community in supporting children.
- Progressive universalism: government should provide support for all and more support for those with greater need, delivered through personalised, integrated services and a skilled workforce.
- Prevention: all universal services should have a strong preventative element and there also needs to be dedicated preventative services for specific groups.

However, the number of health visitors employed in England has fallen from 10,680 whole time equivalents in 1988 (Health Visitors Association, 1994) (citing parliamentary questions) to 9,056 in 2007 (The Information Centre, 2008), a drop of some 15.2 per cent in less than two decades. Whilst this scarcity of the health visiting resource is not fully acknowledged by government, it is used to justify the approach to focus primarily on disadvantaged groups in the health visiting review, which translates the idea of 'progressive universalism' into:

A universal service that is systematically planned and delivered to give a continuum of support according to need at neighbourhood and individual level in order to achieve greater equity of outcomes for all children. Those with greatest risks and needs receive more intensive support.
(DoH, 2007: 25)

This apparent disapproval of health visitors giving time to families from across the social spectrum sends a message (whether intended or not) to service users, who experience reduced input as judgmental and failing to meet their needs (Roche et al., 2005). In turn, reports of dissatisfaction with services are likely to encourage rejection by those who most need support and help; whether because of social exclusion and deprivation, or as a result of health needs that cross the social spectrum, like post-natal depression, domestic violence, or children who have complex needs or behavioural difficulties. Official perceptions about the legitimacy of a universal service, provided to all parents of newborn babies and pre-school children, inevitably affect the way health visiting is viewed by families being offered the service.

In practice, provision of a universal, proactive service means that health visitors arrange home visits not necessarily because the family have particular problems, but because the service is provided to carry out the child health promotion programme. Although health visitors do not have a statutory right of entry it is an expected norm that health visitors will be allowed into homes to carry out their functions of child health promotion, and the identification of family health needs. In some cases, the health visitor may receive a referral from a GP or other health professional, in which case the family are generally aware that the health visitor will be calling and will be pleased to see her as she will have come with the offer of a service to meet their needs. However, in many circumstances (e.g. the birth of a new baby, family moving into a new area), health visitors visit because it is their job to do so, not because they have been invited by the family. To this extent it may be considered that their clients are involuntary.

Collinson and Cowley (1998) found that clients welcomed the fact that the health visiting service is proactive and preventative with professionals contacting clients without them having to ask for help. Others have reported more negative perceptions, identifying concerns that health visitors are just there to check whether or not the child is being mistreated, or to establish whether the mothers are being sufficiently 'good' at child rearing (Abbott and Sapsford,1990). Dingwall and Robinson (1990), similarly explore the notion of health visitors 'policing the family,' stressing more positively that the service is society's way of ensuring that the more vulnerable members of society are given an opportunity to gain help in a non-stigmatising way, as well as providing affirmation and positive feedback for mothers. These mixed views inevitably lead to communication problems at times, necessitating skilled intervention to establish the kind of trusting relationship that will allow health visitors to achieve their purpose. To indicate what that relationship might look like and how health visitors might work to involve clients in it, the next section considers what might be termed the 'ideal' relationship.

The 'ideal' relationship

The work of health visiting is governed by the Nursing and Midwifery code of professional conduct (2002: 3) which suggests that all nurses should 'recognise and respect the role of patients and clients as partners in their care and the contribution they can make to it'. This partnership approach has been hailed as possibly more effective in improving child health than much of the routine work done by health visitors (Goodwin, 1991). However, in their systematic review of health visiting, Elkan et al. (2000) have suggested that management may not construe this way of working as being real 'work'. There therefore existed a need to demonstrate not only that working in partnership does indeed lead to healthy outcomes for families but also to detail what partnership actually entails in practice.

Bidmead and Cowley (2005) made some headway with this in outlining what the relationship might involve, defining it as follows:

> *Partnership with clients in health visiting may be defined as a respectful, negotiated way of working that enables choice, participation and equity, within an honest, trusting relationship that is based in empathy, support and reciprocity. It is best established within a model of health visiting that recognises partnership as a central notion. It requires a high level of interpersonal qualities and communication skills in staff who are, themselves, supported through a system of clinical supervision that operates within the same framework of partnership.*

This might be considered an 'ideal' relationship and is probably one to which most health visitors would aspire. Trying to attain this with clients is not an easy task and demands high levels of personal qualities such as respect, empathy, quiet enthusiasm, humility, personal integrity and genuineness (Davis et al., 2002). Along with these qualities, considerable expertise in skilled communication will also be necessary (e.g. active listening, exploring skills, negotiation, challenging skills etc.) plus knowledge of the helping process (see Figure 14.1). However, it is not only the skills of the health visitor which may be critical here. The engagement of the organisation and management is also important in supporting partnership working.

Although skilled health visitors may seek to work in this way not all clients engage with the service, but the majority do so. However, research shows that even when they do, some may be less inclined than others to allow the health visitor into their lives (Luker and Chalmers, 1990; Barlow, 2005). They have misperceptions about the purpose of the service, or have reasonable objections to accepting it if it seems unlikely to meet their legitimate needs. There are reports of clients clarifying issues, or accepting the service only on their own terms, as explained by this health visitor:

> *I remember when I worked in a poor inner-city area, and them opening the door to me, and I was new to the area, and they said 'Do you only visit people who are not married, who've got children?' and I said, 'No, I visit everyone' 'In that case, you can come in'.*
>
> (Cowley, 1991: 653)

Clients may not be emotionally ready to enter into the relationship and this leaves health visitors to offer whatever support they can, however briefly. There are a complexity of processes involved when two strangers meet for the first time to form a relationship of partnership and it is the level of the mutuality of their respective qualities and skills that dictates how the relationship will develop. It may, therefore, be helpful to consider why some women may choose not to engage with the service. A deeper understanding of the complexities and difficulties encountered in the relationship in the light of construct theory may be helpful here.

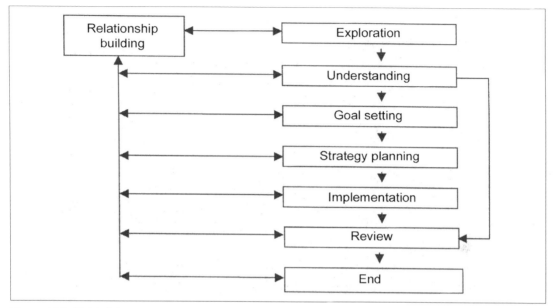

Figure 14.1   The helping process (Davis, Day and Bidmead, 2002)

The construing process

Fundamental to relationship building and to the whole of the helping process is the theory of personal constructs (Kelly, 1955). For the purposes of this chapter this may be briefly described as follows:

- *Everyone develops through their thought processes a picture, or set of constructions about their world.*
- *Through these processes they make sense of their world enabling them to predict and therefore to adapt to all aspects of it.*
- *Each person's constructions are unique to them, although they may overlap with those of others.*
- *Constructions are formulated by our experiences and therefore change over time to adjust to new events.*
- *Our social interactions are determined by our understanding of the constructions of those with whom we interact.*

(Bidmead and Davis, 2007)

These ideas may be very helpful in enabling an understanding of all the difficulties that are encountered in trying to establish partnership relationships with clients. For example, the health visitor-client relationship may be understood in terms of the constructions that each person has of the other. The client's previous good or bad experiences of professionals will colour their expectations and will affect the success of the whole process. The development of a partnership is a process in which the client begins to construe the practitioner as of value and to be trusted and they begin to make explicit and agreed constructions, or the rules, governing how they work together and why.

The practitioner also needs to construe the client as an expert on their children and family life, and able to change, if necessary. This enables the health visitor to approach the client with respect so that clients feel valued for the contribution that they are able to make to the helping process. The client is the 'senior partner' in the process without whom the health visitor's task of searching for health needs or promoting child health would not be possible.

Construct theory aids our understanding of the research literature that follows, which shows evidence that some families find it difficult to engage with the health visiting services.

Reasons why some families may not readily engage with the service

Over the last two and a half decades there has been an increasing amount of research literature which has examined the health visitor–client relationship. From this wealth of mainly qualitative work it is possible to discern the following causal components to provide an explanation of why some families may have difficulties in engaging with the service. We will examine each of these in turn and look at their implications for the health visitor–client relationship and the helping process:

- Difficulties in trusting.
- Differing perceptions or constructs of identification of client need.
- Differing constructs of health visitors and their service.
- Health visitor communication skills.

Difficulties in trusting

The ability of parents with young children to trust is essential to establishing a positive and productive relationship, without which the work of health visiting may not be able to proceed (Jansson et al., 2001). However, with the most vulnerable clients this ability to trust others may be lacking or compromised due to unconsciously remembered experiences, such as their construct of professionals or services or relationships in general, or they may be unwilling to participate due to recently remembered negative encounters with others.

Young teenage women in particular have found it difficult to trust professionals (Barlow et al., 2005; Kirkpatrick et al., 2007). There were difficulties even for a researcher with a warm and friendly approach in establishing a rapport and the women were perceived as antagonistic, anti-authoritarian and unwilling to consider the offer of support being made to them. They often reported receiving support from their mothers whom they experienced as authoritarian and may have construed the professional in a similar manner. Parents may come across as defensive and say that they 'trust no-one'. They view trust as something to be earned over time. Mothers who did not trust the nurse or home visitor either failed to disclose personal information, or, because they were fearful of being reported to social services, decided to 'play along with them' so that they would 'leave me alone' (Jack et al., 2005; Wilson, 2001). The power inequalities inherent in a relationship that masquerades as a 'friendship', but may in reality be one of surveillance and monitoring, leads mothers to

actively 'keep the peace' and not upset the relationship (Wilson, 2001). This lack of honesty which is manifest in some of these relationships with professionals highlights the lack of true partnership working in which neither mother nor health professional would feel the need to be anything but completely open with each other.

In an exploration of the views of health visitors and women who had suffered domestic violence there is some ambivalence about whether the health visitor is someone who can be trusted to be supportive or an authority figure who would be instrumental in having children taken into custody (Peckover, 2002). They feared the power of the state. This ambiguity leads to resistance to the service on offer and avoidance of the health visitor. Consideration of the ethical implications of relationships between public health nurses and child protection clients in Canada also suggests that the power differences between the nurse and the client puts vulnerable clients at risk of being exploited (Marcellus, 2005). Although public health nurses strive to establish collaborative partnerships with parents, a parent who feels threatened is likely to be uncooperative.

Many mothers are ambivalent about receiving public health nurse visits at home for fear that they will be judged as failing or inadequate mothers (Jack et al., 2005). They feel that they have to try to 'measure up' to the nurse's expectations and nurses were coming to 'check up on them.' The mothers' fear led to hesitancy in accepting support, not being at home when visits were scheduled and choosing not to disclose information (Chalmers, 1992; Jack et al., 2005). Thus those most in need of professional help become the least likely to access services (Atree, 2005).

Many of the women in the intensive home visiting study in Oxford (Kirkpatrick et al., 2007) found that it took time for their relationship with the home visitor to develop. The factors that were found to be helpful were the fact that the health visitor was friendly, non-judgemental, interested in the mother and not just the baby and made the mother feel comfortable and at ease.

Implications for health visitor relationship building

The above dilemma of providing a service which may not be accessed because of a perceived tendency of professionals to judge families has seemingly been overcome to some extent in health led local Sure Start Programmes. These were more effective in reaching the more vulnerable families as they provided a universal service to all families with children under four in a defined locality and were therefore more able to contact families (Melhuish et al., 2005). There is something of a paradox here. Although every parent has to be allocated a health visitor which renders clients 'involuntary,' a service that is available to all reduces the sense of being stigmatised as failing and allows easier access.

However, establishing a relationship of trust can be hard work where families are suspicious, fearful and defensive. It requires that some common ground is established from the beginning. Jack et al. (2005) found that parents sought to reduce the formality of visits by encouraging some brief social exchange and an offer of refreshments. They wanted to be treated as human beings, rather than cases, and to meet the human being that was the public health nurse. An important element here may be the willingness of the nurse to reveal something of herself to the client in order to establish this common ground. This was an important factor in reducing the power differential. Trust and mutuality were more likely to be established if 'conversations were filled with humour, caring and empathetic responses, respect and a mutual exchange of ideas' (Jack et al., 2005). The home visitor's body language was important too. They needed to nod their heads in encouragement, smile, and give them time thus beginning to create an atmosphere where both visitor and client could be completely open with each other. This mutual honesty is the hallmark of partnership and it seems that the mutuality of the relationship is paramount in health visiting.

Research studies have shown that health visitors and their clients establish this mutuality though what is described as a process of 'giving and receiving' (Luker and Chalmers, 1990; Chalmers, 1992), in order to facilitate their entry into the home. The health visitor provides a service that the client receives but the service provided is dependent upon the client giving information and allowing entry into her home and into her world, allowing the health visitor to identify needs and provide a service. As Jack et al.'s (2005) study shows this 'giving and receiving' may also extend to the health visitor being able to 'receive' the offer of refreshments from the client and also to 'give' something of

herself from the outset. This 'willingness to be known' is also a feature of some effective psychotherapeutic relationships where the quality of the relationship with the client has been shown to produce positive outcomes (Horvath and Bedi, 2002), especially where the client has difficulties in trusting the therapist (Hill and Knox, 2002).

At the heart of the health visiting process are the personal characteristics, qualities, skills, values and experiences of the health visitor and the parent. The speed with which a partnership relationship develops is dependent on the mutuality of respect and trust that exists in the interaction. Clearly, parents may feel vulnerable and powerless in the face of a state provided service intruding into the home, but parents themselves take steps to limit these feelings of vulnerability, often by having someone else present at the time of the visit e.g. a family member or a friend (Jack et al., 2005). This self-protective strategy helps the parent to feel safer and, because the nurse would be less likely to be judgemental, shifts the power balance in the parent's favour. There is also evidence to suggest that they may 'tidy up' and clean before a visit which ensures that parents feel they are 'measuring up' to the home visitor's expectations. The other strategy that may be used is that of 'hiding nothing' which entails allowing the nurse entry so that she can see for herself that all is well. It is clear that mothers in this Canadian study went to considerable lengths to overcome their fear of state intrusion (Jack et al., 2005).

Parental lack of trust may be demonstrated by checking out the reliability of information that they are given with secondary sources (Jack et al., 2005). Clearly, health visitors must have up-to-date professional and technical knowledge as there are many sources with which parents can verify the information that they are given (e.g. websites, other parents, their own parents, magazines). These may or may not give correct information, but health visitors need to be alert to the fact that parents seeking information may not just ask the visiting professional and so should be prepared to pre-empt conflicting advice by open discussion of the topic. This will require that they have the most up-to-date knowledge in the field, or if they do not know, to be prepared to admit this and find a reputable resource to access the information.

They may also 'test' the health visitor for trustworthiness by trying to see if she will divulge information about other clients. More 'gossipy' health visitors were viewed as untrustworthy and so would not gain access to the more sensitive information about clients' lives (Jack et al., 2005). The implication here is that trust will only be built if the health visitor is able to maintain confidentiality and is able to demonstrate this within the interaction. Confidentiality and its bounds need to be discussed during a first meeting so that the client is under no illusions about what this may mean for herself and for the health visitor.

Where health visitors work hard at establishing relationships with clients they appear to be determined to demonstrate their potential usefulness. De La Cuesta (1993) identified what she called 'Fringe work' as activities in which health visitors engaged which often met client needs for practical help and cemented relationships with them, although the work may not have been officially sanctioned. She found that it increased the reciprocity ('giving and receiving') within the relationship and helped to make health visiting services relevant to clients. It facilitated the entry work that Chalmers (1992) had identified. However, the propensities of this work to become paternalistic were also identified, with health visitors becoming the judges of who were and were not the 'deserving' poor. More recently, middle classes have been construed as 'undeserving' of support, so difficulties have been reported in the relationship between health visitors and these clients (Roche et al., 2005). Clearly, a non-judgemental attitude would be a required quality of health visitors seeking to establish trusting relationships with clients who may feel fearful of being judged as failing at the outset, whether failing to live up to some expected socio-economic criteria or falling below criteria for support services. However, the health visitor is required to 'search for health needs' with the client in order to agree with them the kind of service they might need.

The policy of 'progressive universalism' may affect how professional judgements are made and these will need to be explicitly negotiated with the client. Barlow et al. (2005) found that those clients whom health professionals deemed to be most in need did not feel themselves to be any different from the norm and therefore refused the service.

Differing perceptions or constructs of identification of client need

As noted above, health visitors search for health needs. It is intended that this search be carried out with the family so that the needs as expressed by the family themselves are identified. However, research studies carried out in this area suggest that health visitors and clients may well have divergent views of what constitutes their particular needs.

Pearson (1991) noted that there were differing perceptions of need between health visitors and their clients at three different stages in the first year of an infant's life. Interviews were carried out with parents during pregnancy (28–32 weeks, Stage 1), postpartum (8–10 weeks, Stage 2) and 7–8 months postpartum (Stage 3). At Stage 1, the health visitor's perceptions of health and/or problems are dissimilar to those of parents. At Stage 2 health visitors and parents views have drawn much closer and this has been achieved through a mutual focus on practical problems. The role of the health visitor in providing support and advice at this stage becomes more important and is valued by parents. At Stage 3 the perceptions of need compared with the actual help provided is divergent. The author suggests that this is in part due to the health visitor needing to become less involved with the family as the child grows older. The health visitor thus denies the existence of needs in order to avoid the requirement to offer a service beyond her capacity. This capacity to deliver a service is compromised where staffing levels are low as has been seen in recent years and noted at the beginning of this chapter. However, the value of the health visitor role is likely to be deemed acceptable where the views about need converge and a greater external control is accepted by the parent. As views diverge by Stage 3, and if a positive relationship has been achieved, then less external control is accepted.

Chalmers (1992) echoes some of the above findings when she identified that where the health visitor is unable to identify the client's need from the client's perspective then the offer of help may not be forthcoming or it may be an unhelpful solution. Clients who perceive the offer of a service or advice as unhelpful then control the health visitor's attempt to explore issues more fully and do not respond to the health visitor's invitation to 'open up'. They are more likely not to accept any advice the health visitor gives and may not attend appointments nor allow the health visitor into the home on rare occasions.

Jack et al.'s (2005) study of maternal engagement with family visitors and Canadian public health nurses demonstrated that mothers sought to create mutuality by creating alliances with their home visitors. Mutuality was reduced where the nurses failed to identify or ignored the mother's priority needs and instead established their own agendas for what should be discussed during a visit. Mothers who felt that their needs were not being met were most likely to resist help or withdraw from home visits. A study of British health visitors on the other hand showed that they could shift their policy related agendas to respond to the client's perceived need. The shift only tended to be temporary, however, as the health visitor hoped to be able to introduce her agenda at a later stage (De La Cuesta, 1992).

When health visitors follow their own agenda rather than that of the client they may give unsolicited advice which the client does not need and already may have knowledge about (Kendall, 1993; Mitcheson and Cowley, 2003). This means that they do not tailor the information that they give to the client but assume a need which they then proceed to meet with 'stereotyped advice' (Kendall, 1993). As a result, clients become passive as recipients of information and the health visitor uses valuable time with 'wasted' advice-giving and fails to build a relationship that should have involvement and participation at its core.

Implications for health visitor relationship building and the helping process

The research cited above clearly implies that the search for health needs must be client led if a useful service is to be provided for the benefit of families.

De La Cuesta (1994a) noted that health visitors have to sell themselves and their services, labelling this as a process of 'marketing' in order to convince families that they needed the service. She notes that health visitors often 'adjusted their approach, their physical appearance and language' in order to convey messages of being 'innocent and useful'.

Where health visitors are able to establish a partnership with the client the perceptions or constructs of need will be shared and negotiated between them so that relevant help can be made available to the family. With the most vulnerable families this will not be without difficulties and

may require time to be invested. To enable the family to move forward and to change, if this is necessary for their wellbeing, represents a considerable challenge to both the client and the health visitor.

It is not only at the micro level of individual family work that this challenge needs to be addressed but also at the macro or strategic level. The literature indicates that there is a clear requirement for services to be relevant to clients and that parents need to be involved in the planning and design of services (Ghate and Hazel, 2002; Atree, 2005). The impact of managerial constructs or perceptions of what the content of the service to be delivered should be may well constrain the ability of the practitioner to provide a relevant and flexible approach that really involves the family in identifying their needs that then generates a responsive and relevant service.

Nowhere was this more evident than in a study that considered the use of health needs assessment tools to help the practitioner discover the client health needs (Mitcheson and Cowley, 2003). The problems that were identified stemmed from the fact that they were structured with a pre-determined list of questions that assumed family health needs could be categorised and predicted in advance. This led to minimal parental involvement and a lack of emphasis on relationship building. The health visitors took control of the interaction in a way that emphasised their professional expertise and disempowered the client. This was found to be most noticeable where the health visitors were themselves more explicitly controlled by management organisation, structure and culture. The authors recommended an open style of needs assessment stemming from a trusting relationship built with skilled communication as the basis from which a successful needs assessment can be made. Interestingly, a study of American public health nurses found that they preferred not to use a structured questionnaire at the early stages of the relationship: 'the clients concerns must first be heard so that she will have a sense of control rather than intrusion' (Zerwekh, 1991: 32).

The sense of intrusion may well be aggravated by the giving of unsolicited advice. It may be more helpful for the health visitor to firstly enquire as to the clients existing knowledge of the subject area before launching into giving vast amounts of information. This may help to ensure that the client is fully involved and any information given is tailor-made to the client's particular circumstances, thus enhancing the relationship through a clear demonstration of respect for the client's contribution to the process.

Enabling the client to tell their story is essential to building their sense of self-efficacy, which in a health visiting context is crucial, as clients find the service more acceptable when health visitors are most responsive to client determined need and engage in a relevant discussion (Machen 1996; Normandale 2001)

Differing constructs of health visitors and their service.

A lack of explanation of the type of service that can be offered by health visitors leads to its under utilisation or inappropriate use (Collinson and Cowley, 1998). Some women may not be aware that health visitors are trained nurses (Kelly, 1996) and the name health 'visitor' may lead some clients to expect home visits more often than are provided. These unrealistic expectations are then connected with the client's perceptions of a service failing to meet their needs (Collinson and Cowley, 1998). This echoed the work of Pearson (1991) where there seemed to be a mismatch between what clients expected to receive in terms of help or advice and what the health visitor was actually able to offer. The requirement for clarity between the health visitor and the client about the health visitor role and the client expectations came to the fore when during the nineties there was an emphasis on 'marketing' health visiting and for health visitors to 'sell' their service in order that their services might be purchased. However, the wisdom of this approach was questioned as possibly inducing dependence in clients who come to view the service as one with which they cannot do without (De La Cuesta, 1994a).

One of the quotes used in the Barlow et al. (2005: 205) study shows a problem with the perception of health visitors as middle class and therefore unable to understand what life is like for some of the clients they visit. This quote is from an identified vulnerable mother, who has three children already and was being offered a weekly home visit by a health visitor:

People should not go around professionally asking people how they are to say 'there, there dear, I'm sorry you feel upset' – and they go back on with their smart life and their

nice car and their nice children, and their nice home, leaving me . . .

Peckover (2002: 374) also found similar problems:

The health visitor . . . was rather nice, but I think they live in a different world . . . They are more often than not married, they have got this comfortable job which is a job they want to do, and their husbands have got jobs, and it is all very comfy. They are not living on the breadline; they are not living like a lot of people are having to live. They are not scrimping and scraping, and they are not really with it. 'Oh yes, it's hard, we know'. But they don't know because they don't have to live like it . . .

However, there is evidence to suggest that some health visitors do not ignore altogether their client's material deprivation and engage in 'fringe work', giving out clothes and food to the most needy (De la Cuesta, 1993). However, this smacks of paternalism and of an earlier age when health visitors were recruited from middle and upper class women with important religious and philanthropic values and may serve to reinforce some of the negative perceptions of health visitors.

Health visitors may find it difficult to gain entry into the home because of the client's previous poor experience with professionals (Luker and Chalmers, 1990: 76). Here the constructs of the parent are formulated by their previous encounter, and expectant of the same experience, react negatively to the invitation to engage:

She sort of left me on the door step . . . She said, 'I'm not having a health visitor, I'm sorry but I don't want you to visit and I'm capable of bringing up my own children'. . . The last health visitor she had had rattled a pair of keys in her son's ears and made the child cry and so that was the basis for her not wanting another health visitor now. You know they remember such things; she had woken him up to weigh him and did other tests on him.

Health visitors may have to work hard to overcome such resistance in order to gain entry even on the doorstep! This will involve a process of challenging the client's constructs to help the client to see that not all health visitors are necessarily going to behave in the way that was previously experienced.

Implications for health visitor relationship building and the helping process

From the evidence presented above it appears that a potential interaction may mean one thing to a client, and another to the practitioner. The unsolicited and proactive nature of the work may require the health visitor to, somehow, convey her vision about the purpose of the work in a manner that takes on board the perceptions and expectations of the client, before any meaningful interaction can take place. Clients' views about health visiting in general, about how their particular service is being offered (through home visit or clinic attendance, for example, which relates to the way it is organised at national or local level), and the focus of the contact, will all affect the degree of acceptability. This process has been described as one or both 'getting to know' a client, at the same time as 'getting known' by them, in order to build a relationship based on openness and agreement about the purpose of the service, which would differ according to the perceived needs of each client (Cowley, 1991).

The first meeting between the health visitor and client is clearly crucial in the process of relationship building. The research quoted above would indicate the need to clarify roles at the beginning of the interaction and establish client expectations of the service to be of paramount importance to the successful development of the rapport necessary for continuing work. As Roche et al. (2005) point out: 'if parents know little of their role as 'partners' they will subsequently look to providers for a very different service'.

It is not only the first meeting however, where the relationship can run aground. Even prior to this, the way in which the health visitor telephones and involves the client in the setting of the time and date to meet appears to be of importance. An American study of home visiting public health nurses (Josten et al., 1999) found that where the nurse used a collaborative process with the client to set the appointment the client was more likely to keep the appointment.

Recently, there has been an interest in more intensive home visiting (Barlow et al., 2005; Cabinet Office, 2006) which has allowed more time for the development of the relationship with specially trained health visitors which has enabled clients to change their construct of health visitors:

Well from experience, like, my friend . . . had a kid and she like she wasn't looking after him properly and the health visitor come round the house and was pushing her . . . took her to court and stuff because he was underweight, and that is what I thought health visitors were for. Just to check that you are keeping your kid fed properly and stuff like that. Not to talk to you or none of that, they just come to

weigh, and go. But obviously I was proved wrong. She is there to talk to you.

(Kirkpatrick et al., 2007)

The ability to spend more time with clients who are most in need has developed in popularity since the publication of the work in America by Olds et al., 2007. The outcomes are extremely positive and cost-effective for families and children. There are now ten pilot sites in England in areas of deprivation, targeting mothers under the age of twenty years. Each health visitor has a caseload of 25, a far cry from the reported caseload of 1,422 reported in one London borough (Family and Parenting Institute, 2007). Young mothers in this pilot scheme will be visited by specially trained health visitors who may be perceived as 'middle class' but trusting relationships may develop with shared experiences, beliefs and values, it was not the helper's demographic background that was important but the 'skill and ability to develop rapport and mutuality' (Jack et al., 2005).

This section of the chapter has considered the evidence from research of what we know about the health visitor–client relationship. It identified a number of barriers and facilitators to partnership working on the part of the practitioner (see Table 14.1).

It is clear the 'ideal relationship' as defined by Bidmead and Cowley (2005) at the start of the chapter is one to which many health visitors aspire. However, there are also parental factors that impinge on the relationship and which may also facilitate or hinder the helping process (see Table 14.2).

Health visitor communication skills

The key to the health visitor's ability to build a productive partnership with the client is her skilled communication. There is much evidence of dissatisfaction with health visitor professional communication from research through the 1980s and 90s (Abbott and Sapsford,1990; Clark, 1984; Luker and Chalmers, 1990). However, there have also been some features that appear a little more positive, describing reciprocity (De La Cuesta, 1994b), and of mothers valuing the role of their health visitor and asking for more home visiting (Machen, 1996). Collinson and Cowley (1998) link this valuing of the health visiting service to women's knowledge of the role of the health visiting service and the extent to which it meets

Table 14.1 Practitioner barriers to, and facilitators of, partnership working

Barriers to partnership working	Facilitators of partnership working
Lack of time.	Ability to give clients time to build trusting relationships (Collinson and Cowley, 1998; Jack et al., 2005).
Agenda for needs assessment. Not listening (Mitcheson and Cowley, 2003; Cowley et al., 2004; Jack et al., 2005).	Open exploration and listening to client's perceived needs (Machen, 1996; Normandale, 2001).
An inability to share self and become involved.	'Willingness to be known' with a friendly approach (De La Cuesta, 1994b; Wensing et al., 1998; Hill and Knox, 2002; Horvath and Bedi, 2002; Jack et al., 2005).
Preconceived ideas (constructs) about the clients or their situation and the service they need.	Open to the situation and client's world. A non-judgmental attitude (Kirkpatrick et al., 2007).
Dominance of professional expertise (Mitcheson and Cowley, 2003).	Acknowledgement and respect for client as expert on their own lives and children.
Not listening to the client.	Actively listening (Zerwekh, 1991; Kirkpatrick, 2007).
Giving of unsolicited advice (Mitcheson and Cowley, 2003).	Giving appropriate information building on what the client already knows.
Goals of intervention determined by the professional.	Agreeing appropriate aims and goals of intervention.
No negotiation of roles or boundaries whilst working together (Collinson and Cowlely, 1998; Mitcheson and Cowley, 2003).	Negotiation of roles and appropriate boundaries at beginning of intervention.
Lack of interest and understanding, empathy.	Being prepared to really try to understand the other and their world (Jack et al., 2005; Coulter, 2005).
Closed body language.	Open body language, nodding, smiling etc. (Jack et al., 2005).
Lack of genuineness and honesty (Wilson, 2001).	Ability to be oneself, honest and sincere (Jack et al., 2005; Kirkpatrick, 2007).
Lack of up-to-date knowledge.	Up-to-date professional knowledge (Kirkpatrick, 2007).

Table 14.2 Client barriers to, and facilitators of, partnership working

Barriers	Facilitators
Inability to trust health professionals due to poor previous experiences (Luker and Chalmers, 1990; Jansson, 2001; Barlow et al., 2005).	Quickly builds trusting relationships with health professional based on previous good experiences.
Inability to build relationships generally due to own poor parenting (Barlow et al., 2005).	Ability to trust others and build relationships with good experiences of being parented.
Unrealistic expectations of the service (Collinson and Cowley, 1998).	Realistic and negotiated expectations of the practitioner.
Perceptions of class or cultural difference (Peckover, 2002; Barlow et al., 2005).	Open to the practitioner in spite of differences.
Inability to articulate problems.	Able to talk well and explain problems, situation, ask questions etc. (Kettunen et al., 2002).
Lack of motivation to change if this is necessary.	Motivated to change because of situation.
Inability to reflect on problems.	Ability to reflect on situation (Kettunen et al., 2002).
Lack of knowledge of health visitor role and service (Cowley, 1991; Collinson and Cowley, 1998; Kelly, 1996; Roche, 2005).	Knowledge of health visitor role and service.

their expectations. Health visitors were seen as approachable in one study (Cowpe et al., 1994). However, there have been renewed concerns regarding the communication and partnership working skills of health visitors more recently, particularly linked to changes in the organisational agenda. Mitcheson and Cowley (2003) found that using the health needs assessment tool required by their employers meant that client participation was reduced, and professional expertise emphasised in such a way as to disempower clients. Although there was evidence that some of the health visitors in the study resisted the organisational agenda to try and protect their clients and maintain control over their professional practice, they were not wholly successful and in some cases made matters worse (Cowley et al., 2004). This professional power exerted by health visitors may inhibit the exercise of their supportive role, particularly in the field of domestic violence (Peckover, 2002).

This raises concerns about how health visitors might maintain their collaborative working relationship when the professional construct of what is happening in the home with regard to child care or the parental relationship is contrary to that of the parent. How does the health visitor help the parent to move forward and to change when necessary for the child or parent's own sake? (McIntosh and Shute, 2006). This clearly requires advanced communication skills and a relationship that can be negotiated through these kinds of difficulties so that the parent does not feel alienated as in the example below:

> *I think you sort of get lulled into a false sense of security because you sort of think, after her coming round every week for nearly two years isn't it, you begin to look on her as a friend instead of a health visitor, but then she will do something and you will remember she is a health visitor she isn't your friend.*
>
> (Kirkpatrick et al., 2007: 40)

There is always present the propensity for the relationship to flounder where the mother perceives that there is less than open practice, with reports made to social services without prior discussion. Cowley's (1991) grounded theory study suggested that health visitors were acutely aware of the need to overcome suspicions, misunderstandings or just different perceptions. Strategies included an approach of showing care and concern for the client, respecting their

viewpoint and being open about their (the health visitors') perceptions. At times, either the client or the health visitor may avoid complete openness to avoid overt conflict, but this brings the risk of the parent becoming mistrustful once again and warns against any sense of collusion.

However, if the relationship is strong enough then even a referral to social services can be facilitated without compromising the relationship (Kirkpatrick et al., 2007). The parent may not like the fact that a referral has to be made but the sheer persistence in believing in the parent and continuing to visit may pay dividends:

> *And I really didn't like her then and at the next visit, the next couple of visits I wasn't horrible to her, but I don't think I was very nice to her ... which ... I am not usually like that. I mean, I am quite ashamed when I think about it. But I did say to her later on, when I started to get a bit better, 'you know, I really hated you, I didn't like you then'.*
>
> (Kirkpatrick et al., 2007: 39)

In spite of these problems this mother referred to the health visitor as her 'friend' and invited her to be godmother to her baby.

Evidence from this study shows that as well as seeing the health visiting service in a more favourable light there were positive consequences for the use of other health and social services. The constructs of professionals and the services they were able to offer had been changed. However, it is important to note here that the health visitors were all trained in skills of building partnership relationships and in listening and communicating with parents and were supported by fortnightly, good quality clinical supervision (Brocklehurst et al., 2004).

Implications for relationship building and the helping process

The evidence presented here appears to indicate that health visitors may need to be trained to a high level in relationship building and the helping process. Traditionally, health visitor education has not focused on these skills but much more on technical knowledge and academic achievement. However, although these things are important they should not negate the importance of the skills needed to engage families in facilitative interaction requiring their involvement and participation. Incorporation of these core skills into health visitor training may greatly enhance the experience of families.

The key to being able to build a relationship with a client is to be able to read their cues and to follow their lead. This sensitive attunement of the practitioner to the client that tries to understand the client's world is paramount. This requires in the first place that health visitors are selected for their qualities as well as their skills and knowledge. Individual characteristics of reliability, genuineness, warmth and the ability to be empathetic were found to make all the difference to clients in their ability to trust the home visitor (Jack et al., 2005). The ability to build trust and rapport is never more important than at the first meeting where the success of future work and contact is dependent on the qualities and skills of the nurse (Jansson et al., 2001).

An interesting study from Finland demonstrated how patients exercise their power over visiting public health nurses during home visits (Kettunen et al., 2002). They did so by asking direct questions of the nurse, keeping the lead for the conversation to meet their needs. They may also give information about themselves or what they know about the topic under discussion and sometimes interrupt the nurse. The point here is that patients (if given the chance) may use the very strategies that professionals use themselves to exert their power and professional expertise as seen in the study by Mitcheson and Cowley (2003). Even this ability of the patient, however, needs the public health nurse to allow some silence for the patient to ask the questions, give information and interruptions by the patient need to be tolerated, and not talked over. The nurse does not interrupt the patient during the conversation. When patients or clients ask questions they acknowledge the nurses' legitimate expertise but are able to maintain a sense of responsibility for themselves as co-equal experts or partners (Kettunen et al., 2002). In this study, although patients constructed the nurses as powerful experts, they also constructed a corresponding power of their own. This reinforces the notion found by McNaughton (2000) in her qualitative review of the literature surrounding public health nursing and health visiting that the aims of relationship building are the support it gives to the clients independence, decision making, self-efficacy and empowerment.

Listening

Active listening, where the health visitor not only hears what the client says but responds to the meaning, content and feelings expressed helps the client to feel valued and respected (Kirkpatrick, 2007). Not only does this facilitate the client's exploration of their health needs as they see them but has the added function of building a relationship based on trust and respect. It facilitates a deeper exploration of the client's world and means that there is more likelihood of developing a shared understanding of their problems, goals and aspirations.

Challenging constructs

Constructs may need to be challenged on the doorstep with the health visitor demonstrating respect for the family by the way in which she knocks on the door and introduces herself to the client. As discussed, if the client construes the service negatively, then the health visitor will have to work with a great deal of skill to be allowed access by the client and Chalmers (1992) and De la Cuesta (1993) have both illustrated how health visitors accomplish this task.

It is often the families who are most at risk who find it most difficult to trust and it is these very families for whom health visitors need to have the most respect and the greatest effort at making a connection (Marcellus, 2005). This needs time to find common ground and in working with other family members (Jack et al., 2002). It will also take time for these families to be ready to start to think about or see their circumstance differently where this is necessary, and this will rely on a relationship of trust with the worker before this can happen.

Organisational issues

It is clear from all the research cited above that there has been an indisputable growth in understanding of the processes involved in health visiting, and yet there seems to be real difficulties in translating this knowledge into practice, partly because service organisations fail to take this evidence into account.

Health visitors provide a potentially helpful, supportive promotional health service to all families with children under the age of five years. They have, through custom, access to all homes and are welcomed by the majority of parents. However, there are huge potential dangers to the acceptability of the service where staff are constrained by shortage of numbers, quality of

Table 14.3   Organisational barriers to and facilitators of partnership working

Barriers to partnership working	Facilitators of partnership working
Authoritarian management (Cowley et al., 2003).	Partnership working between management and practitioners.
Lack of skilled quality clinical supervision.	Clinical supervision in partnership with practitioners (Davis and Spurr, 1998; Brocklehurst et al., 2004).
Lack of experienced, well-trained staff.	Good education of adequate staff numbers in communication skills, partnership working and helping process (Davis and Spurr, 1998; Brocklehurst et al., 2004).
Lack of integrated multi-agency approach.	Recruitment of staff with appropriate qualities and skills (Davis and Spurr, 1998).
Inappropriate skill mix, inability to provide continuing care (Krikpatrick, 2007).	Appropriate skill mix to meet population needs.
Government policy that is reactive and fails to plan appropriately for the needs of all parents.	Government policy that pro-actively supports the development of a universal service.

training and organisational structures and demands that impinge on their ability to form meaningful and collaborative relationships with clients (see Table 14.3).

With recent cutbacks in health visiting services there has been an outcry from the Family and Parenting Institute who commissioned a YouGov poll of 5,000 parents to find out what they felt about health visitors and the services that they provide (FPI, 2007). It is clear from the quotes in this document that health visitors are unable to provide the sort of service that parents feel is needed, with health visitors being responsible for caseloads of between 160 to 1,142 pre-school children per health visitor. There is therefore little evidence to support the ideal way of working, or that managers recognise the importance of allowing home visitors flexibility in deciding how many visits are required in the early phase of engagement (Jack et al., 2005; McIntosh and Shute, 2006). Health visitors in today's NHS are very likely to be only able to manage one visit, due to time constraints, and then invite attendance at the clinic where time is very limited.

In the Scottish 'Starting Well' project, health visitors became overwhelmed as the intensive nature of the home visiting led to the identification of more needs with an attendant increase in the health visiting workload. New needs were uncovered for families as the work with some families intensified (McIntosh and Shute, 2006). So although targeting may be desirable, targeting too early in the health visitor/parent relationship could result in the

failure to identify and address important health needs. It takes considerable experience to be able to decide who may and may not need a service and requires time at the beginning of the relationship for trust to grow so that the parent feels comfortable enough to express the needs that they may have.

The recent health visiting review (Lowe, 2007) talks of 'progressive universalism' expounding the concept to encourage a universal service that targets the needy for more intensive services. However, what constitutes a universal service has yet to be clarified. Needs may arise at any time in the pre-school child's life and cannot necessarily be assessed at one visit in infancy.

Although there are moves afoot to target services at the most needy in society (Lowe, 2007) it may not be appropriate to only think of need in terms of the socio-economic circumstances of the family. Many needs, such as children with physical or intellectual disabilities, mental health problems like post-natal depression, domestic violence and child protection concerns and so on, are found in all sectors of the community.

Evidence from research about the health visitor–client relationship is increasingly clear, showing the part to be played by both practitioners and clients in establishing a relationship. Parents too may find that the communities in which they live make it either easier to find help or more difficult with a lack of support from informal systems e.g. family, friends, local volunteer schemes etc. (Bidmead and Whittaker, 2004). Importantly, the development of partnership working may be

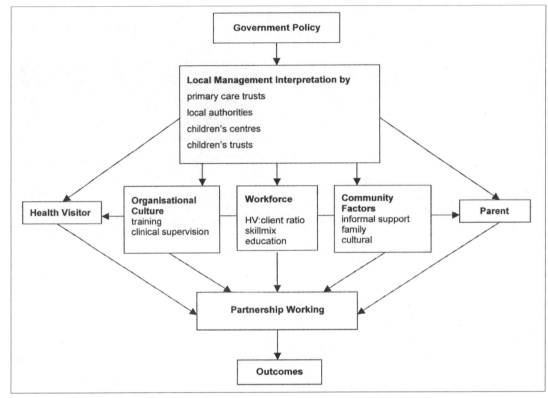

Figure 14.2   External factors impinging on the ability of parents and health visitors' ability to work in partnership

hindered or facilitated by organisational factors, including the management of services in which they work to provide the formal interventions of parenting support. In turn, the types of organisation that are considered acceptable for funding by public services are affected by wider policy issues, and the extent of government support for attitudes towards practitioner-client relationships (see Figure 14.2).

Conclusion

At the turn of the last century health and hygiene were the considered hazards to society, but in modern times it has been parenting practices that are impacting on society and have become one of the public health imperatives. Health visitors find themselves at the forefront of the battle to help parents by virtue of the fact that they visit all families with a newborn baby and continue their care for the whole of the pre-school period. As they cannot give equal time to each family by

virtue of the number involved, they target the time that they can give to those who are most needy. Who are deemed 'needy' is generally a question of directives from government policy, local interpretation of that policy and the managers of the health visiting service who decide how the needy will be identified through a set of criteria. It is difficult to see where the rhetoric of involving the public in choice and in the planning of delivery of services happens.

We know clearly what patients in primary care want. They want to be treated by health professionals who give them time, are interested, empathic, are knowledgeable and involve them in their care (Coulter, 2005). However, the most important factor is the 'humaneness' of the practitioner (Wensing et al., 1998). Parents want to be listened to and involved in the planning of services for them and their children so that services are relevant (Ghate and Hazel, 2002). Perhaps it is time for a truly evidence based approach that takes into account some of the messages presented in this chapter so that the voice of the client is really listened to at all levels of society.

Parents do not have to allow a health visitor access to their homes, but it has become a societal norm to grant this permission. In some respects, this norm is so strong that clients may feel 'involuntary' yet health visitors are often in a privileged position of being allowed, not just into homes, but into their clients' lives. It remains to be seen if the shortage of staff and restrictive interpretations of the present government policy of 'progressive universalism' culminates in providing a service that stigmatises the vulnerable and fails the majority. Rather than reducing health inequalities it may, in fact, lower the health status of the whole population of parents and children. Health visitors and parents are at the mercy of how services are organised and although both groups have been vocal in expressing their concerns it remains to be seen if changes proposed aid partnership working and increase the likelihood of positive outcomes.

References

Abbott, P. and Sapsford, R. (1990) Health Visiting: Policing the Family? In Abbot, P. and Wallace, C. (Eds.) *The Sociology of the Caring Professions*. Basingstoke: Farmer Press.

Atree, P. (2005) Parenting Support in the Context of Poverty: A Meta-Analysis of the Qualitative Evidence. *Health and Social Care in The Community*. 13: 4, 330–7.

Barlow, J. et al. (2005) Hard-To-Reach or Out-Of-Reach? Reasons why Women Refuse to Take Part in Early Interventions. *Children and Society*. 19,199–210.

Bidmead, C. and Davis, H. (2008) Partnership Working: The Key to Public Health. In Cowley, S. (Ed.) *Policy and Practice in Community Public Health: A Sourcebook*. 2nd edn. Edinburgh, Bailliere Tindall.

Bidmead, C. and Cowley, S. (2005) A Concept Analysis of Partnership with Clients. *Community Practitioner*. 78: 6, 203–8.

Bidmead, C. and Whittaker, K. (2004) *Positive Parenting A Public Health Priority*. London: CPHVA.

Brocklehurst, N. et al. (2004) The Contribution of Health Visitors to Supporting Vulnerable Children and Their Families at Home. *Community Practitioner*. 77, 175–9.

Cabinet Office. (2006) *Reaching Out: An Action Plan on Social Exclusion*. London: Cabinet Office.

Chalmers, K. (1992) Giving and Receiving: An Empirically Derived Theory on Health Visiting Practice. *Journal of Advanced Nursing*. 17, 1317–25.

Clark, J. (1984) Mothers Perceptions of Health Visiting. *Health Visitor*. 57, 265–8.

Collinson, S. and Cowley, S. (1998) An Exploratory Study of Demand for the Health Visiting Services within a Marketing Framework. *Journal of Advanced Nursing*. 28: 3, 499–507.

Coulter, A. (2005) The NHS Revolution: Health Care in the Market Place. What do Patients and the Public want from Primary Care? *British Medical Journal*, 331, 1199–201.

Cowley, S. and Frost, M. (2006) *The Principles of Health Visiting: Opening the Door to Public Health in the 21st Century*. London: CPHVA and UKSC.

Cowley, S. (1991) A Symbolic Awareness Context Identified through a Grounded Theory Study of Health Visiting. *Journal of Advanced Nursing*. 16, 648–56.

Cowley, S., Mitcheson, J. and Houston, A. (2004) Structuring Health Needs Assessment: The Medicalisation of Health Visiting. *Sociology of Health and Illness*. 26: 5, 503–26.

Cowpe, M., Maclachlan, A. and Baxter, E. (1994) Clients' Views of a Health Visiting Service. *Health Visitor*. 67: 11,1390–1.

Davies, C. (1988) The Health Visitor as Mother's Friend: A Woman's Place in Public Health, 1900–1914. *Social History Medicine*, 1.

Davis, H., Day, C. and Bidmead, C. (2002) *Working in Partnership with Parents: The Parent Adviser Model*. London: The Psychological Corporation.

Davis, H. and Spurr, P. (1998) Parent Counselling: an Evaluation of a Community Child Mental Health Service. *Journal of Child Psychology and Psychiatry*. 39, 365–76.

De La Cuesta, C. (1993) Fringe Work: Peripheral Work in Health Visiting, *Sociology of Health and Illness*. 15: 5, 665–81.

De La Cuesta, C. (1994a) Marketing: A Process in Health Visiting. *Journal of Advanced Nursing*. 19, 347–53.

De La Cuesta, C. (1994b) Relationships in Health Visiting. *International Journal of Nursing Studies*. 31: 5, 451–9.

Dingwall, R. (1977) Collectivism, Regionalism and Feminism: Health Visiting and British Social Policy. *Journal of Social Policy*. 6: 3, 291–315.

Dingwall, R. and Robinson, K. (1990) Policing the Family? Health Visiting and the Public Surveillance of Private Behaviour. In Guberium, G. and Sanhar, A. (Eds.) *The Home Care Experience: Ethnography and Policy.* Newbury Park, CA: Sage.

Elkan, R. (2001) *The Effectiveness of Domiciliary Health Visiting: A Systematic Review of International Studies and a Selective Review of the British Literature.* The Research Findings Register, 411.

Elkan, R. et al. (2000) The Effectiveness of Domiciliary Health Visiting: A Systematic Review of International Studies and a Selective Review of the British Literature. *Health Technology Assessment.* 4, 13.

Family and Parenting Institute (FPI) (2007) *Health Visitors: An Endangered Species.* London: FPI.

Ghate, D. and Hazel, N. (2002) *Parenting in Poor Environments: Stress and Coping.* London: Jessica Kingsley.

Goodwin, S. (1991) Breaking the Links Between Social Deprivation and Poor Child Health. *Health Visitor,* 64: 11, 376–80.

Graham, H. and Kelly, M.P. (2004) *Health Inequalities: Concepts, Frameworks and Policy.* London: NHS Development Agency.

Health Visitors Association (1994) *A Cause for Concern: Health Visitors' Association Citing Parliamentary Question 3966/1993/94 Written Answer 25th May 1994.* London: Health Visitors' Association.

Hill, C. and Knox, S. (2002) Self-Disclosure. In Norcross, J. (Ed.) *Psychotherapy Relationships that Work.* New York: Oxford University Press.

HM Treasury and DfES (2005) *Support for Parents, The Best Start for Children.* London: HM Treasury.

Horvath, A. and Bedi, R. (2002) The Alliance. In Norcross, J. (Ed.) *Psyhcotherapy Relationships that Work.* New York, Oxford University Press.

Jack, S., Dicenso, A. and Lohfield, L. (2002) Opening Doors: Factors Influencing the Establishment of a Working Relationship Between Paraprofessional Home Visitors and At-Risk Families. *Canadian Journal of Counselling.* 34, 59–69.

Jack, S., Dicenso, A. and Lohfield, L. (2005) A Theory of Maternal Engagement with Public Health Nurses and Family Visitors. *Journal of Advanced Nursing.* 49: 2, 182–90.

Jansson, A., Petersson, K. and Uden, G. (2001) Nurses' First Encounters with Parents of New-Born Children – Public Health Nurses' Views of a Good Meeting. *Journal of Clinical Nursing,* 10, 140–51.

Josten, L.V. et al. (1999) Factors Associated with Clients Not Keeping their Initial Home Health Visit. *Journal of Public Health Management Practice.* 5: 6, 70–80.

Kelly, C. (1996) Public Perceptions of a Health Visitor. *International Journal of Nursing Studies.* 33: 3, 285–96.

Kelly, G. (1955) *The Psychology of Personal Constructs.* New York: Norton.

Kendall, S. (1993) Do Health Visitors Promote Client Participation? An Analysis of the Health Visitor-Client Interaction. *Journal of Clinical Nursing.* 2, 103–9.

Kettunen, T., Poskiparta, M. and Gerlander, M. (2002) Nurse-Power Relationship: Preliminary Evidence of Patients' Power Messages. *Patient Education and Counseling.* 47: 2, 101–13.

Kirkpatrick, S., Barlow, J., Stewart-Brown, S. and Davis, H. (2007) Working in Partnership: User Perceptions of Intensive Home Visiting. *Child Abuse Review.*16, 32–46.

Lowe, R. (2007) *Facing the Future: A Review of the Role of the Health Visitor.* London: DoH.

Luker, K. and Chalmers, K. (1990) Gaining Access to Clients: The Case of Health Visiting. *Journal of Advanced Nursing.* 15, 74–82.

Machen, I. (1996) The Relevance of Health Visiting Policy to Contemporary Mothers. *Journal of Advanced Nursing.* 24, 350–6.

Marcellus, L. (2005) The Ethics of Relation: Public Health Nurses and Child Protection Clients. *Journal of Advanced Nursing.* 51: 4, 414–20.

McIntosh, J. and Shute, J. (2006) The Process of Health Visiting and its Contribution to Parental Support in the Starting Well Demonstration Project. *Health and Social Care in the Community.* 15: 1, 77–85.

McNaughton, D.B. (2000) A Synthesis of Qualitative Home Visiting Research. *Public Health Nursing.* 17: 6, 405–14.

Mitcheson, J. and Cowley, S. (2003) Empowerment or Control? An Analysis of the Extent to which Client Participation is Enabled During Health Visitor/Client Interactions using a Structured Health Needs Assessment Tool. *International Journal of Nursing Studies.* 40, 413–26.

Normandale, S. (2001) A Study of Mothers' Perceptions of the Health Visiting Role. *Community Practitioner.* 74: 4, 146–50.

Nursing and Midwifery Council (NMC) (2002) *Code of Professional Council.* London: NMC.

Olds, D.L., Sadler, L. and Kitzman, H. (2007) Programs for Parents of Infants and Toddlers: Recent Evidence from Randomized Trials. *Journal of Child Psychology and Psychiatry*. 48: 3–4, 355–91.

Pearson, P. (1991) Client's Perceptions: The Use of Case Studies in Developing Theory. *Journal of Advanced Nursing*. 16, 521–8.

Peckover, S. (2002) Supporting and Policing Mothers: An Analysis of the Disciplinary Practices of Health Visiting. *Journal of Advanced Nursing*. 38: 4, 369–77.

Roche, B. et al. (2005) Reassurance or Judgement? Parents' Views on the Delivery of Child Health Surveillance Programmes. *Family Practice*. 22, 507–12.

The Information Centre (2008) *NHS Hospital and Community Health Services Non-Medical Workforce Census, Detailed Results 2006*. London: The Information Centre.

Wanless, D. (2002) *Securing our Future Health: Taking a Long-Term View*. London: HM Treasury.

Wensing, M. et al. (1998) A Systematic Review of the Literature on Patient Priorities for General Practice Care. *Social Science and Medicine*. 47, 1573–88.

Wilson, H.V. (2001) Power and Partnership: A Critical Analysis of the Surveillance Discourses of Child Health Nurses. *Journal of Advanced Nursing*. 36: 2, 294–301.

Zerwekh, J.V. (1991) Tales from Public Health Nursing. True Detectives. *American Journal of Nursing*. 91: 10, 30–6.

Working with Specific Client Groups

CHAPTER 15

Treating Resistance in Sex Offenders: Enhancing Motivation

Mark Carich, Sarah Williamson and Gerry Dobkowski

Introduction

As sex offenders are often involuntarily placed in treatment by the legal system, they present unique challenges that have the potential to create barriers to their recovery. Front line staff witness resistance in various forms, expressions of which include non-compliance with directives, defiance, some form of denial, defensiveness, hostility, and cognitive distortions. Quite often, initially, the offender's motivation to change is largely external; that is, a vague attempt to satisfy court-mandated treatment.

The primary goal of treatment, usually externally imposed, is for the client convicted of a sexual offence to create no more victims, with a minimal expectation of harm reduction. To achieve this aim, providers realise that their treatment must enhance internal motivation at some level. They will often utilise external pressures to create a pathway to internal motivation, helping the client create an inner desire to reach a goal versus that of accomplishing a goal because an external entity requires it. Given that sex offenders typically enter treatment because of legal mandates or to avoid further legal repercussions, issues of motivation need to be addressed. The methodology of contemporary treatment in working with motivational issues often hinge on the therapist's perspective, knowledge, and skill level.

Current research by Marshall and colleagues demonstrates that effectiveness resides with the process variables or therapist characteristics and features therapeutic context along with perspective (Marshall et al., 2002, 2003a, 2003b) and is supported by post-modern perspectives. 'The model is not only a philosophy; it is also a perceptual in that it becomes a lens. This lens tells the practitioner what to look for and respond to in the therapeutic encounter-but it is a double-edged sword in that it focuses and limits viewing simultaneously. The therapist then passes on the lens to the patients' (Zeig and Munion, 1990: 8). The therapist cannot detach from his or her own perspective, the result being the therapist's perspective is superimposed onto the client. Indeed, this position is reflected throughout the history of sex offender treatment.

Historically in treating sex offenders, psychoanalytic or psychodynamic approaches were used without empirical support. It appears that Alfred Adler (1934, 1941, 1956) may have published the first sex offender case treatment from an individual psychology perspective that he had pioneered. Adler's approach involved a number of ideas and methods that were in the forefront of current treatment (i.e. group therapy, cognitive, cognitive–behavioural, strategic, etc.) emphasising self-determination, a cooperative relationship, responsibility and holism. Psychodynamic approaches were predominate, followed by behaviourism into the 1960s, 1970s and 1980s (Marshall and Laws, 2003). Behavioural treatment consisted of individualised aversive conditioning procedures often requiring booster sessions. The sensitivity-oriented group therapies, based on the Synanon approach of shame-based harsh confrontation, were adopted from alcohol and substance abuse treatment. Although the leaders in the field downplay such approaches, the shame-based groups are still common (Fernandez, 2006). By the early 1980s, Gene Abel emphasised combining cognitive therapy techniques, targeting or restructuring cognitive distortions, with behavioural therapy to modify deviant arousal patterns (Abel, 1989; Schwartz and Cellini, 1995, 1997).

Cognitive-behavioural group therapy coupled with relapse prevention (RP) is currently the predominant approach (Carich and Calder, 2003; Carich and Mussack, 2001; Marshall, 1996, 1999; Marshall, Anderson and Fernandez, 1999; Marshall et al., 2006). Many group therapists still use cognitive-behavioural RP with a shame-based confrontational approach. Research indicates that shame-based therapy is quite often anti-therapeutic, creating 'resistance' in accomplishing goals (Marshall et al., 2003). Resistance can be seen as stemming from the therapist's perspective and behaviour. As such, from a post-modern perspective, one might argue that the concept of resistance runs contrary to the current thinking that places responsibility on the treatment provider to meet the client's needs. Questions often arise as to what is 'resistance' and as to the best approach to effectively treat 'resistance' in order to produce the best results or outcomes.

The purposes of this chapter include the following:

- Review the concept of resistance and its various forms.
- Reframe resistance into a more conducive or user friendly concept.
- Provide a brief review or contemporary treatment related targets.
- Review of key process (therapist) variables and related therapeutic processes.
- Review of the therapeutic change process.
- Provide principles of interventions.
- Selected tactics to elicit cooperative responses.

The premise of this chapter rests with the post-modern constructivist/ social constructivist perspective in which one creates or generates his or her own worldview or constructs their own reality.

Therefore, the theme of this chapter hinges on a post-modern or a constructivist perspective in which the therapist is an active participant in co-creating the therapeutic context. The therapist's theoretical framework is the lens which is used to organise the client's problem issues, pathology, as well as the therapeutic strategy. Although, paradoxically, one cannot escape their own box, they can reshape it. The reader is challenged to assess his or her own box and shape it as needed to produce the desired results.

What is resistance in sex offender treatment?

Resistance can be defined a number of ways. Often confused with denial itself or any cognitive distortion, resistance is most usefully defined as *the creation of a barrier to accomplishing some designated goal.* Denial is a sub-category of resistance, where cognitive distortions are dysfunctional thought patterns rooted in any form of resistance. Even denial has been defined a number of ways and is often conceptualised as

cognitive distortion (Bays, 2001; Barbaree, 1991; Marshall et al., 2006).Therefore cognitive distortions are usually viewed as some form of resistance, further muddling conceptualisation. Denial can be viewed as a systems issue. Likewise, resistance (i.e. denial) is often conceptually confused with defence mechanisms. There are multiple reasons for denial:

- Masking the feeling like a bad person.
- Fear of legal consequences.
- Fear of social consequences.
- Shame or toxic shame.
- Guilt versus lack of guilt.
- Fear of rejection.

A sample of the different typologies of resistance, in particular denial, is shown below (see Table 15.1). Denial exists on a continuum ranging from categorical non-admission to partial admission. Though some denial (often in the form of minimisation) is expected, it remains a treatment target. As Table 15.1 illustrates, denial has been the subject of much research, and has been examined from diverse perspectives.

Features of denial and minimisation

1. Complete denial.
2. False accusation.
3. Partial denial.
4. Wasn't really sexual abuse.
5. Denial of a problem.
6. Minimising the offence.
7. Minimising responsibility.
8. Denying/minimising of harm.
9. Denying/minimising planning.
10. Denying/minimising fantasising.

Summary types (Marshall, 2006)

Complete denial

False accusation
- Police out to get me
- Victim hates me
- Victim trying to get financial compensation
- Victim's mother wants to deny access to children

Wrong person
- Victim mistakenly identified the client

Table 15.1 Types of denial

7 Types of denial (Winn, 1996)
1. Denial of facts as if nothing happened.
2. Denial of awareness that it is wrong.
3. Denial of impact – form of self-preservation.
4. Denial of responsibility/blame.
5. Denial of grooming, organising, setting up offence.
6. Denial of deviant arousal.
7. Denial of denial/meta denial that minimises and disqualifies as ways of protecting self.

7 Levels of denial (Freeman-Longo and Pithers, 1992) (also adapted from *A Structured Approach: Client's Manual.* Safer Society Press, 1992 with Permission.)
1. Responsibility – making excuses and justifications: 'I didn't do it'.
2. Intent – accidental offences: 'It just happened'.
3. Harm – minimise and deny any impact: 'I did it but it didn't harm them'.
4. Frequency – minimises number of assaults: 'I did it but only a few times'.
5. Intrusiveness – denial of penetration: 'I only fondled her'.
6. Fantasy – denial of deviant thoughts: 'I never get turned on when I think about it'.
7. Minimisation – making the offence less significant: 'I only touched them'.

12 Steps or types of denial (Happel and Auffrey, 1993)
1. Denial of crime.
2. Denial of responsibility.
3. Denial of intent and premeditation.
4. Denial of deviant arousal and fantasies.
5. Denial of deviant acts.
6. Denial of the intrusiveness of offending.
7. Denial of injury to victims.
8. Denial of sexual gratification from offending.
9. Denial of grooming behaviours.
10. Denial of risk management activities.
11. Denial of difficulties of change and need of help.
12. Denial of relapse potential.

Memory loss
- Cannot remember but client sure he did not do it

Partial denial

Memory loss
- Cannot remember but it probably happened

Was not abuse
- Victim consented
- They lied about their age
- It was only a massage
- It was done for educational/protective purposes
- It was love

Denies having a problem or that he needs treatment
- I did it but I am not a sexual offender
- I have no sexual interest in, or fantasies about children or rape

- I have learned my lesson so I know I will never do it again

Minimisations

Concerning offence
- Did not happen as often as victim claims
- No use of threats, coercion, or force
- Less sexually intrusive than victim claimed
- Only one victim

Concerning responsibility
- Victim was prostitute so how can it be rape
- Victim was seductive
- Victim's parents were neglectful
- I was intoxicated
- I was depressed/stressed/angry
- My partner was not sexually interested
- I have a high sex drive or I am a sex addict
- Victim said no but he or she clearly wanted it

Minimising harm
- Friends/family tell me victim is okay
- Victim's current problem not caused by me
- I was loving/affectionate so it was not harm
- I am was not forceful so no harm was done

Denies planning/fantasising
- It was a 'spur of the moment' thing
- It just happened
- Victim started it
- I have never had deviant sexual thoughts
- I did not think about it before it happened

Denial refers to any types of categorised omission, not acknowledging an offence, partial acknowledgement of the offence, or an unwillingness to take responsibility for an offence. As Table 15.1 reveals, it manifests itself in diverse ways, and is best viewed on a continuum ranging from total denial to near full admission and responsibility. For instance, minimisation is considered a form of denial that is a form of resistance, but at the same time, it could also be considered a cognitive distortion *along with denial.* Such distortions could promote a self-righteous, victim stance in sex offenders who believe themselves to be unjustly prosecuted or persecuted. Thus, cognitive distortions are often an integral part of treatment. They are identified and provide treatment targets for the therapist (Carich and Mussack, 2001; Carich and Calder, 2003; Marshall, Anderson and Fernandez, 1999).

Despite such minimisations, research indicates a provider can maximise efficacy by approaching sex offenders similarly as they would clients in the general population (Marshall, 2006). Marshall advocates avoiding hostility and harsh confrontation and providing an atmosphere of supportive challenge, recognising the unique challenges of the population and suggests the following *reasons for resistance* in sex offenders:

- Desire to continue behaviour for same reason it originally occurred.
- Protect view of self.
- Reaction to views of other, i.e. police, courts, assessments.
- Beliefs that change is not beneficial.
- Beliefs that change is too difficult or impossible.
- Beliefs about the efficacy of treatment (from media, other offenders, prison staff, friends, and relatives).
- Lack of hope for future.
- Previous bad experience with professionals.

- Denial of a problem: one-off event.
- Concern about feeling worse.
- Feeling alienated from others.
- Fearing animosity.
- Concern for loss of supports.
- Concern over having to talk about private issues in public.
- Hated school therefore will hate therapy.

The sex offender's knowledge and treatment beliefs, well founded or not, creates initial resistance to treatment. For instance, the potential client could doubt the effectiveness of treatment, perhaps due to misinformation propagated by the popular media. Side effects, such as toxic shame and decreased self-esteem ('Making me feel like a bad person') are potential by-products of treatment. There is also a fear of legal consequences and the fear of social consequences, as well as the possibility of experiencing rejection within the treatment process ('the therapist or group won't like me'). The stigma of defining oneself openly as a sex offender to the hostile general population is also worthy of note. Perhaps with all that in mind, over half of the refusers expressed a desire that has a broader aim than just addressing their criminal history (Mann, 2000).

As in most treatments, some element of denial is considered normal. Denial is actually a defence mechanism or self-strategy. The distortion is avoiding responsibility but not admitting to it. And though denial has often been the focus of treatment, empirical support is lacking to correlate denial to recidivism (Hanson and Morton-Bourgon, 2004).

Ruth Mann (2000) provides an interesting typology of resistance shown below. Mann's typology includes four basic strategies (see Table 15.2).

Resistance has also been explored from an *interpersonal* perspective, recognising the therapist's role in the creation of barriers. If one believes the plethora of evidence that therapeutic relationship in all forms of treatment is, in fact, a curative factor (Marziali and Alexander, 1991), the sex offender therapist must be hyperaware of behaviours that demonstrate the client is building resistance to the treatment process. The therapist-client relationship is a dynamic process that has the potential to transcend resistance, but within the context of this potentially shame provoking subject matter (incest, paedophilia, rape) it can increase or even create resistance (Marshall et al., 2003).

Table 15.2 Ruth Mann's types

Four types of resistance (the four R's) (Mann, 2000)
  − Reluctance − don't consider change because of lack of knowledge.
  − Rebellious − resists being told what to do (resent authority).
  − Resigned/resignation − overwhelmed with problems.
  − Rationalising − pre-contemplator has all the answers and reasons not to change.

Four Categories of Client Resistant Behaviour (Mann, 2000)
1. Arguing − the client contests the accuracy, expertise and integrity of the therapist:
  − Challenging directly challenges accuracy.
  − Discounting questions therapist's personal authority.
  − Hostility − client expresses direct hostility to therapist.
2. Interrupting − the client breaks in and interrupts in a defensive manner:
  − Taking over-speaking over the therapist.
  − Cutting off − client cuts therapist off.
3. Denying − unwillingness to recognise problems, cooperate, accept responsibility or take advice:
  − Blaming.
  − Disagreeing − client refuses to take suggestions, 'yes, but'.
  − Excusing − makes excuses.
  − Claiming impunity − claims not in danger.
  − Minimising − therapist exaggerating risks.
  − Pessimism − pessimistic, defeatist or negative tone.
  − Reluctance − expresses reservations and reluctance.
  − Unwillingness to change − lack of desire not to change.
4. Ignoring − client shows evidence of not following or ignoring the therapist:
  − Inattention − has not been following or attending to therapist.
  − Non-answer − response is not an answer.
  − No response − no verbal or nonverbal reply.
  − Sidetracking − changes the direction of the conversation.

For example, Miller and Rollnick (1991: 73) emphasise six traps that professionals get into:

1. The question/answer trap − elicits yes/no short answer responses.
2. The confrontational/denial trap − confronting denial, power struggles.
3. The expert trap − the professional has all the answers.
4. The labelling trap − labelling problems carry stigmas.
5. The premature focus trap − client/therapist focusing on different topics.
6. The blaming trap − blame as excuses as to why.

As the resulting roadblocks occur, a frustrated treatment professional could overreact from a defensive posture, thus further discounting the client and his struggles. In fact, Miller and Rollnick (1991, 2002) outline several types of roadblock responses:

- Ordering, directing, or commanding.
- Warning or threatening.
- Giving advice, making suggestions, providing solutions.
- Persuading with logic, arguing, lecturing.
- Moralising, preaching, telling clients what they should do.
- Disagreeing, judging, criticising, blaming.
- Agreeing, approving, praising.
- Shaming, ridiculing, labelling.
- Interpreting, analysing.
- Reassuring, sympathising, consoling.
- Questioning, probing.
- Withdrawing, distracting, humouring, changing the subject.

Miller and Rollnick's (1991, 2002) work applies to any therapeutic model or treatment process, and other areas of communication, such as negotiation, and including hostage negotiation. However, our current concern is sex offender treatment, and with this in mind, the next section is based on a snapshot of contemporary treatment for those that may be novices to the field.

Table 15.3   Summary of key elements of treatment

1. Offence disclosure/responsibility.
2. Offence specific cognitive restructuring.
3. Offence process (assault cycle/intervention (regulation) skills.
4. Victim empathy.
5. Arousal control or regulation skills.
6. Clinical core issue resolution.
7. Social skills and interpersonal issues/relationships and affective regulation skills.
8. Lifestyle restructuring.

Review of contemporary treatment

Contemporary sex offender treatment is based on a cognitive behavioural group approach. Given the range of potential and actual treatment targets, the term dynamic is added by the authors. In any effective treatment process, an array of experiential dimensions is in play. A simple rigid cognitive behavioural approach itself is limiting and may contribute to resistance.

Basic philosophy and generic goals

The overall philosophy is in the slogan: 'No more victims'. That said, any amount of harm reduction is preferable to the status quo and is thus, by some measure, successful treatment. The field's more innovative therapists are emphasising helping offenders to develop productive lifestyles, or a 'good life', by meeting needs appropriately (Ward, 2002; Ward and Stewart, 2003; Ward and Marshall, 2004). In doing so, harm is reduced and abstinence from offending is reaffirmed.

The theoretical philosophies and tenets of cognitive behavioural treatment rest on the following: self-determinism, learning process, holistic views, and responsibility (Carich and Mussack, 2001; Carich and Calder, 2003). Adler (1941, 1956) explained that people continuously make choices at all levels of awareness. It follows that offending requires a series of choices at multiple levels. *The locus of control* ultimately rests with the offender, although quite often the offender, as does most of society, places the locus of control on others. Therefore, responsibility, or accountability is emphasised. Although physiological processes play roles in causality at some level, the learning processes are emphasised (Ward, Polaschek and Beech, 2006). Offending is a learned choice at various levels.

Lastly, a holistic view has been emphasised (Longo, 2003; Carich and Calder, 2003). Holistic views are based on the whole being the sum of a synergistic process. The offender's entire self and context is emphasised; therefore, the treatment plan acknowledges a variety of the targets.

The hallmark and theme in sex offender treatment is to help the client make both internal and external changes, along with developing coping skills. In order to reduce harm, quite often a variety of treatment elements may be packaged into treatment goals. Therefore, treatment elements or targets are translated into goals and objectives. Treatment is based on the notion that there is not an acceptable cure; however, the offender can reduce deviancy significantly and manage behaviours indefinitely. Likewise, goals or treatment targets or elements are translated into treatment components or aspects of the programme developed to address concerns. The outcomes or results of interventions are referred to as recovery factors (Carich and Calder, 2003; Carich and Spilman, 2002) or dynamic risk factors (DRFs) (Hanson and Harris, 2001; Thorton, 2002).

These elements are packaged in 10 goals. For a more detailed list of goals and objectives, the reader is referred to Carich and Calder (2003); Metzger and Carich (1999).

These goals include:

1. Offence disclosure and responsibility
2. Motivation and commitment
3. Identify and restructure offence cognitive distortions and core schemas
4. Identify assault cycle and develop regulation skills
5. Develop victim empathy
6. Identify/reduce deviant arousal
7. Develop social skills and interpersonal issues
8. Identify and change dysfunctional lifestyle behaviours
9. Identify and resolve key core issues, beliefs
10. Develop appropriate self-concept

Table 15.4   Process variables

Therapist behaviours that enhance treatment effectiveness		
Empathic	warm	asks open-ended questions
Directive	genuine	asks open-minded questions
Confident	attentive	encourages participation
Rewarding	trustworthy	self-disclosing
Supportive	flexible	use of humour
Self-disclosing	respectful	emotionally responsive
Instils positive expectations		
		(Marshall et al., 2003: 209)
Therapist behaviours that reduce treatment effectiveness		
Aggressive	confrontation	judgmental authoritarian
Rejection	defensive	nervous
Manipulation of patient	rigidity	coldness
Low interest	dishonest	unresponsive
Critical	sarcastic	hostile/angry
Discomfort with silences	need to be liked	does not wait for answers
Boundary problems		
		(Marshall et al., 2003: 215)

To simplify the process, the key elements are presented in five components:

1. Clinical core issues
2. Victim empathy
3. Skill development
4. Offending process (cycle i.e. offence chain) and regulation skills or relapse prevention (RP)
5. Arousal control (sexual regulation skills)

Recovery outcomes

The goal in recovery is to reduce risks of re-offending. Recovery is defined as the capability of maintaining abstinence from offending (Carich, 1991; Carich and Spilman, 2002, Carich and Calder, 2003).These are outcome criteria from programmes across the spectrum intended to cover a wide range of variables.

Eight recovery factors include:

1. Motivation and commitment to recovery
2. Personal responsibility/ disowning
3. Social interest (victim empathy remorse)
4. Social-affective dimension
5. Assault cycle (offending process)/intervention (regulation) skills
6. Lifestyle behaviours and pyschopathology
7. Clinical core issue/needs resolution (shifting core schemas):
    – Identify and resolve motivating issues
    – Sexual identity Issues

   – Self-structure
8. Arousal control

As previously noted, the limited research available points to a consistent body of evidence which demonstrates that therapeutic techniques for the effective treatment of sex offenders mirror those used with the general population. Of course, the heinous details of sexual offences have the potential to elicit responses from therapists that reflect the shock and repulsion of the general population. Indeed, treatment providers are likely to be hyperaware of the potentially adverse consequences of inappropriate sexuality. Thus, being empathic to the victims' pain while at the same time attending to the interest of the perpetrators presents professional, emotional, and spiritual challenges. The hostility toward the offenders, so prevalent in the 1980s, is still evident in a number of treatment settings (Fernandez, 2006).

Citing current research that aggressive confrontation of client's defensiveness and deceits is often counterproductive, Fernandez advocates a strength-based approach that goes as far as to question the label 'Sex Offender' as anti-therapeutic and a remnant of an ineffective, shame-based treatment strategy that had been integrated into the treatment field.

The implications for sexual offender treatment are clear. The utilisation of cognitive-behavioural procedures does not preclude the importance of the therapist's method. The therapist's behaviour remains a key to the development and maintenance of the therapeutic alliance. Therapist features that influence this alliance include *empathy and warmth,* as well as *a rewarding style.* Effectiveness was heightened with both *directiveness* and the *asking of open-ended questions.* Utilisation of these contrary methods was explained as a need for flexibility in the treatment provider. The *ability to deal effectively with problems* demonstrated an ability to adjust to changing client responses and emotional states. Furthermore, with the therapist's coping skills and perspective-taking in accurately assessing and addressing client needs, the client is provided a role model for future interpersonal relationships.

Applied generic therapeutic processes and issues

Any therapeutic process is based on communication in a specialised context. The context is developed between a therapist system and a client system. The therapeutic context consists of patterns of interaction between the therapist and client, with the intent that the therapist helps the client make changes, resolve problems, enhance functioning capability, develop emotional growth process or at a minimum reduce stress and gain support (Rychlak, 1981; Corsini, 1979, Corsini and Wedding, 1995; Zeig and Munion, 1990). Although specific goals and themes vary depending upon the therapist, client, and therapeutic model, treatment is based upon communication and interactions, and thus forms a multi-level system (Keeney, 1983). Therefore, 'resistance' can be examined through the therapeutic processes.

Basic assumptions: developing and analysing the therapeutic process

Resistance and the therapeutic process can be analysed any number of ways, depending upon the lens used by the observer. The authors have chosen to review useful assumptions: the change process, assumptions of the communication process, therapist process variables, as applied to the offender and treatment, and client factors.

A therapeutic process is based on assumptions from the observer. The therapeutic process may be predicted upon any number of assumptions,

depending upon the client, therapist and therapeutic model. Generally, there are several useful ones which are presented below and fall in line with contemporary sex offender treatment.

These include post-modern views, self-determinism, multi-levels and systems learning, and holistic views.

The post-modern views encompass constructivism and social constructivism (Hansen, 2004; Mahoney, 2003; Niemeyer and Bridges, 2003). In essence, people subjectively create or construct their own worlds based on external reality and their own past or current reality. These views are based upon idealism and Kant's critical realism philosophy and more currently post-modern thinking (Adler, 1941, 1956; Kelly, 1955, Rychlak, 1981). Post-modern views are best summarised thus:

> Like existential philosophy, constructivism says that we humans are active participants in our own lives. We choose and our choices make important differences in our lives and in the lives of all with whom we are connected. We are often reactive and constructivism does not deny our capacity for unreflective reflex and conditioning . . . fundamentally proactive. We anticipate . . . we are moving in the midst of forces far greater than ourselves, yet we have a choice within those forces. The central point of this first theme is that humans are not passive pawns in the game of life.
>
> (Mahoney, 2003: 5)

In constructivism, 'the individual is an active agent in the process of experiencing. We need order. We organise our world in which we develop patterns and create meanings. We are creatures of habit' (Mahoney, 2003: 6).

In terms of changes, Mahoney (2003) states:

> There are, of course, biological structures and processes that shape any individual's experiencing in five themes, that is, that biochemically and neurologically humans are ever-active organisers whose biological patterns develop and change in ways that reflect an extensive network of dynamic relationships. When the many factors influencing any given life moment are taken into account . . . (genetic constraints and activations, cultural and developmental history, current health, skills development and life circumstances) each human being can be seen as doing and feeling what is natural for him or her. They are still responsible for their actions, and as an important part of that responsibility is engagement in the future development . . .'
>
> (Mahoney, 2003: 9)

Human development rarely follows a simple linear path. It is more often than not a zigzag course, with frequent striking points, repetitive cycles, occasional regressions, and few – leaps and falls. The particulars may seem dizzying in their diversity, yet these are patterns.

(Mahoney, 2003: 10)

Mahoney's point is that people are not robots that can be simply programmed. However, the individual interacts with external reality, the individual filters external reality through an internal lens.

Sex offenders create their own experiential reality, as do therapists. In treatment, they bring to the therapeutic table their own set of beliefs and perspectives at multiple levels. For example, some cognitive distortions (i.e. 'I educated the victim', 'They deserved it') are superficial beliefs. Deep seated core schemas or beliefs and perceptions, referred to as implied theories (ITs) by Ward and colleagues, are the most inner templates or blueprints out of which the offender operates from at all times. These ITs (i.e. 'Women are unknowable') are key guiding belief systems. Ultimately, for sufficient and deeply rooted change, these core schema or ITs need to change (Ward and Keenan, 1999; Polaschek and Ward, 2002; Mann and Shingler, 2006).

Constructivism

Constructivism implies self-determinism or choice. Adler (1941, 1956) has emphasised self-determinism for one hundred years (Dreikurs, 1950, 1967). In a more useful context, the person makes choices at multiple levels of awareness by definition. Offending is a complex series of choices at all levels of consequences and involving all experiential domains to some degree (Carich and Stone, 1996; Carich and Calder, 2003). In treatment, the offender will choose what to bring into therapy and ultimately make the decision about change. At the same time, the offender can be influenced to change and learn or incorporate new behaviours, while deleting or extinguishing other behaviour. The level of influence depends upon the receptiveness of the client and therapeutic process variables presented below.

Holistic view

The human condition and change process is best viewed *holistically* (Dreikurs, 1950, 1967). A *holistic view* is inner-connected in which the

whole equals more than the sum of its parts (Rychlak, 1981). In other words, all elements both within the context and outside of the context are inner-connected systems. The practical application includes looking at the client's context, change context, including the therapist's style, and involve all experiential domains in differing degrees. The focus varies: cognitive, behavioural, interpersonal, social, spiritual, bio-physiological, and environmental contexts, along with multiple levels of awareness, are all surveyed, rather than just one dominant area.

Therefore, learning occurs at multiple levels of awareness, and within those levels experiential domains vary. All of these domains are inner-connected with each other and is centrally connected with core perceptual belief systems portraying the mind-body connection. The mind-body connection is located in the hypothalamic limbic system of the brain (Rossi, 1993, 2002).

It is hypothesised that the experiential domains are part of the mind-body process known as SDML and B system (State Dependent Memory Learning and Behavioural System). Rossi applied the SDML and B system to sex offenders, speculating an internal switchbox in which the offender can turn on and off deviant states (Rossi, 1993, 2002; Carich and Parwatakar, 1992). The goal in treatment is enhancing and creating non-deviant states. However, a client has to be receptive to the therapeutic messages delivered via interventions. Receptivity involves an appropriate change context.

Change process

The change process is the context of generating or creating a difference. This difference occurs in the context of communication patterns of forming interactions. Therefore, therapeutic communication is the exchange of behaviours in a specified context. The change process is predicted on the assumptions in Table 15.5 (DiClemente, 1991, Mahoney, 2003; Rychlak, 1981; Becvar and Becvar, 1984).

There are multiple levels of meaning and communication

- One cannot direct at some level.
- Therapist always directs.
- Even the most non-directive are direct.
- Goal is to direct client toward change.
- Goal is to meet treatment goals by channelling therapeutic messages/interventions.

Table 15.5   Change process assumptions

One cannot NOT believe/perceive	One perceives continuously based on beliefs
One cannot NOT communicate	One always communicates in multiple contexts
In group, one cannot NOT participate	There is always a level of participation (interwoven), even if the client is silent
One cannot NOT choose	People always have choices at some level, (self-determination)
One cannot NOT influence at some level	Influence is inevitable to some degree. The key is to enhance client receptivity Influence best occurs if the client is receptive

- Influences exist at some level.
- Ultimately the client chooses to accept or reject influence.
- Any therapy session can be demarcated into interventions.
- All behaviours emitted from therapist are interventions.
- Therapists project attitudes and theories, both non-verbally and unconsciously.

There are levels of control and influence	(Control and influence are an illusion)
One cannot NOT construct realities	(One always constructs his or her own realities)
One cannot NOT avoid one's own reality	(People are plugged into life and can choose to accept or reject influence)

These assumptions are designed to influence the effect or change to some deeper level. Both the client and therapist have active roles in the process. Change can be viewed in terms of multiple levels. Watzlawick, Weakland and Fish (1974) outlined the classical view of changes, portrayed as orders of changes:

Levels of change

1. 1st order of change (i.e. linear oriented, surface or superficial change, not an extensive amount of change.
2. 2nd order of change (i.e. a major transformation of the system including core schemas/beliefs, worldviews, lifestyle).

A 3rd order of change was added by the authors, reflecting long-term changes, beyond system transformation; enduring and highly observable. In essence, the client and therapist form a close, non-sexual intimate relationship with specified boundaries and roles calibrated by patterns of behaviour (Keeney and Ross, 1983).

Cybernetics meta systemic view best captures the interactional dance or play between both parties and internal dynamics, referred to as socio-feedback (Keeney and Ross, 1983). The interactional system is mutually influenced, however, and both parties mutually produce feedback, calibrating the client's patterns of stability and change. Patterns of stability refer to patterns of sameness, while change is generating patterns of differences. The therapist calibrates his or her responses, in accordance to the client and vice versa. Both exchange information. Therefore, there are two levels of responsibility. The client is 100 per cent responsible for making the change, while the therapist is 100 per cent responsible for creating the effective context. This involves process variables or characteristics of the therapist.

Process variables

Though there were notable exceptions for thirty plus years (Blanchard, 1995), basic psychotherapeutic principles were abandoned in treating sexual offenders, as shame-based methods came into favour (Fernandez, Shingler and Marshall, 2006; Fernandez, 2006; Shingler and Mann, 2006). It was up to the client to 'shape up' or be terminated, if even accepted into treatment. As Marshall and Serran (2000) and Marshall (2005) point out, many offenders were left out, adding to the increased risk to society. Therefore, beginning with Marshall's (1996) keynote address and paper on best ways to view the offender, Marshall and colleagues landed an entire research project on process variables along with others (Drapeau, 2005; Fernandez, 2006; Fernandez, Shingler and Marshall, 2006; Shingler and Mann, 2006; Mann, 2000; Marshall, Anderson and Fernandez, 1999; Marshall et al., 2006).

Since the research is of high importance both to this chapter and the field, several points of it are noteworthy. Marshall and Serran (2000) emphasise developing approach-oriented RP or intervention strategies. Emphasis is also placed on enhancing self-esteem, perhaps reducing the dosage or length of treatment depending on the client's needs, treating offenders in denial, and developing a more positive approach to treatment.

The therapist's style and characteristics directly impact the treatment process. The moment the therapist meets the offender or enters the group, the 'therapeutic game' is on. The therapist's view partially relays a message to the client. Simple non-verbal behaviours can influence the process. For example, a simple handshake can convey quite a bit of information without saying a word. It indicates respect, confidence, or lack thereof from the therapist, as it helps facilitate rapport. In an extreme case, the senior author observed Milton H. Erickson's personal physician, Dr. Marion Moore, deliver a hypnotic trance via a simple handshake. Another example is silence, which can have a lot of meaning within a group, and can be a potent intervention if used correctly. Thus, non-verbal behaviour is an influential aspect of communication.

Both the therapist's verbal and non-verbal behaviours are interventions at multiple levels. Furthermore, any therapeutic session can be demarcated into segments of interactions defined as interventions. The therapeutic relationship is the hallmark of therapy, including offender treatment and management. The goal is to elicit client cooperation and responses. Historically, the roles in therapy were fairly delineated. The therapist was the power broker as the 'expert' or in a 'one up' position, while the client or offender was in the 'one down' position. Adler (1941, 1956) was one of the first to emphasise a cooperative therapeutic relationship (Dreikurs, 1987; Mosak, 1979, 1984). Although Milton H. Erickson, the famous psychiatrist and hypnotherapist, and particular colleagues and followers, emphasised eliciting cooperative responses, some other colleagues viewed Erickson as maintaining the 'one up' position through skilful manipulation (Haley, 1967, 1973, 1976, 1981; Havens, 1985; Lankton and Lankton, 1983; O'Hanlon, 1987; Erickson et al., 1976; Zeig, 1987). Erickson was famous for developing quick client rapport, eliciting change responses while respecting the client. He joined the client and utilised the client's

behaviour, while operating at multiple levels of awareness. Both Adler and Erickson avoided power struggles, as the goal was to elicit cooperative responses.

By definition, the contextual relationship with the offender is differentiated by unequal roles at multiple levels. At one level, the therapist is the expert or professional whose role is to affect change. At another level, a cooperative relationship is necessary. For years, Erickson had emphasised flexibility, as Marshall (2005) now emphasises, that structure and firmness can be achieved with a flexible approach.

Client factors

The client or offender comes to therapy with a variety of factors. They have varying perspectives with core beliefs, emotional responses, resources, non-deviant behaviours, deviancy or deviant patterns, other pathology, motivations to change and levels of discomfort with deviancy. Emphasis is placed on the therapist matching treatment responses to client needs.

Eliciting cooperative responses: breaking up resistance

The overall goal in any therapy or treatment is to help the client, that is, the offender, to manage or overcome various problems (i.e. sexual deviancy, along with directly and indirectly related factors). Client receptivity is key to effective treatment. A fundamental therapeutic issue is eliciting responsiveness or cooperative responses.

In this section, we explore specific principles, strategies, and interventions. One such approach is motivational interviewing (MI). MI is considered by many as a cognitive behavioural approach based on a trans-theoretical model, although the originators credit Carl Rogers as the primary influence, following nondirective, reflective, active listening skills (Miller and Rollnick 1991, 2002). Emphasis is on a non-confrontational approach, based on motivating the client towards change. The focus of this chapter is not only supportive of MI strategies, but also moving beyond. It is pointed out that MI has been applied to sex offenders (Mann, 2000).

Basic therapeutic principles

Carich and Spilman (2004) surveyed the literature on therapy and deduced basic principles of therapeutic intervention. The principles are summarised below:

- Respect and acknowledge client as a unique person – differentiate worth versus deviancy.
- Rapport, connection, psychological contact.
- Joining or identifying with client in his reality.
- Compassion/ empathetic understanding.
- Cooperation: client receptivity to therapeutic messages. The client completes the goal.
- Flexibility: pliability, ability to adapt.
- Utilisation Principle: utilise client's responses towards goals or change.
- Safety Principle: using both patterns of change (differentiates) and stability (sameness).
- Generative change: small changes create bigger changes.
- Metaphoric Principle: provide meaningful communication in form of useful packages.

Interestingly and similarly, Miller and Rollnick (1991, 2002) emphasise five basic principles of MI:

- Express empathy
- Develop discrepancies (confusion)
- Avoid argumentation
- Roll with resistance
- Support self-efficacy

The essence of these principles rest on the responsivity principle involving respect, rapport, empathy, compassion, flexibility, and utilisation, along with avoiding confrontation or staying with resistance. The central premise of the responsivity principle involves meeting the client's needs within a therapeutic relationship. It is important for the therapist to connect with the offender and thus develop rapport. This is based on being supportive, respectful, and empathetic with the client. The sexual offender has to be treated with respect, that is, an acknowledgement of him as an individual (Fernandez, 2006; Mann, 2000; Fernandez, Shingler and Marshall, 2006; Marshall, 1996, 2005; Marshall, Anderson and Fernandez, 1999; Carich and Calder, 2003). The shame-based confrontational approach has been deemed less effective and unwarranted. Miller and Rollnick (1991, 2002) emphasise developing discrepancies, thus inducing confusion states. In between, the MI oriented therapist plants seeds of change, initiating small changes and following them up with bigger changes, referred to by the Ericksonians as generative change (Lankton and Lankton, 1983; Zeig, 1987). This is done through

the utilisation principle (Erickson, Rossi and Rossi, 1976; Rossi, 1993). This is the hallmark of Milton H. Erickson's approach (Haley, 1967, 1973; Havens, 1985; Zeig, 1987). The client's behaviour is used to induce change or states of differences.

Miller and Rollnick (1991, 2002) outlined eight general motivational strategies and they are as follows:

1. Giving advice: clear, concise, and well-timed (client receptivity) with explanation of why change is important and specify why.
2. Removing barriers: practical problem solving strategies.
3. Providing choices allow offender to experience freedom of choice.
4. Decrease desirability: increase desirability for change, while making problem less desirable.
5. Practice empathy. Understand the other person.
6. Providing feedback.
7. Clarifying feedback: check perception of normal versus abnormal.
8. Actively helping: active with affirmative interest in change process.

Re-focus on process variables and intervention

As highlighted before, there is current interest and emphasis on process variables or variables related to the therapist (Marshall, 2005; Marshall et al., 2006; Fernandez, 2006; Fernandez, Shingler, and Marshall, 2006; Rich, 2003; Shingler and Mann, 2006). This includes style, interactional style, communication skills, perspective, therapeutic skills, therapeutic relationship, etc. Process variables relate to several therapy outcome studies (Rich, 2003).

Rich (2003) does an excellent job of translating basic findings from outcome studies (Lambert, 1992; Lambert and Bergin, 1993). Rich (2003) discerns the following percentages of variable categories determining successful outcomes in psychotherapy, based upon Lambert (1992). There are four elements:

- model/technique – 15 per cent
- client factors – 40 per cent
- therapeutic alliance – 30 per cent
- hope or expectancy effects – 15 per cent

Rich (2003) emphasised that 70 per cent of the results were due to interpersonal related factors of the therapist.

Paradoxically, one can make the point that any and all aspects of therapy involve interventions or techniques at some level. The mere fact of developing rapport or a therapeutic alliance requires interpersonal skills via interventions. The therapist intervenes or does something, i.e. emitting verbal and nonverbal behaviours, in the form of communication. Together, both therapist and client form a therapeutic system, each calibrating the others' behaviour (Keeney and Ross, 1983). The client responds to the therapist and the therapist to the client. By definition, the therapist participates within the process. There is always participation at some level. Simply accessing client resources requires intervention, as does facilitating offender receptiveness. Likewise, the therapist cannot detach from his or her therapeutic model. The model is projected onto the client.

The same applies to sex offender treatment. One of the issues commonly found is the lack of hope, therefore creating a failure expectation. A past issue of the field was total disregard of the process variables. Together, these key factors create barriers. Historically, effective models and responsivity factors were ignored in favour of shame-based driven treatment to change; *the resulting effects were referred to as resistance.*

The basic intervention process

Since the treatment process is contextually defined as a communication process in which the therapist helps the client change based on communication and interaction, any session can be subdivided, or segmented, into therapeutic interventions and techniques discerned from communication patterns. Techniques and interventions are differentiated in that a technique is the overall modality for delivering interventions. Interventions are specialised communications usually harbouring a therapeutic message aiming at intervening; therefore, creating change. Rich (2003) classifies interventions into targets, intensity, and form. Applied to groups, he identifies three targets: personal, interpersonal, and group. Interventions range in intensity from low, moderate, and high (strong). Different forms include: conceptual (verbal and interpersonal), experiential (evokes affective cognitive responses), and structured exercises.

There are literally thousands of therapy techniques that are documented throughout the

literature over the last 100 years. Several basic skills are briefly outlined below, and may be helpful in reducing barriers to reaching one's goals. Of course, it is appropriate to remove as many external barriers as and when possible.

Basic communication skills

Basic communication skills draw from Rogerian nondirective techniques and related Carkhuff dimensions. Together these include:

- reflective responses
- eye contact
- active listening (i.e. actively reflecting what the speaker says)
- double sided reflections (reflecting both sides of the issue)
- paraphrasing
- respect
- empathy
- immediacy
- appropriate confrontation
- concreteness or specificity
- warmth
- genuineness
- summarising
- mirroring
- 'I' messages

(Carkhuff, 1967; Miller and Rollnick, 1991, 2002)

When in doubt, the clinician can always fall back to the basic skills or the cornerstone of therapy.

Preparatory programmes

Added to the challenges of group therapy, a number of misconceptions surrounding sex offender treatment result in building resistance to the treatment process before it begins.

Noting this, Marshall and Moulden (2006) in their work with the Correctional Service of Canada, have developed a preparatory treatment plan hypothesised to address these concerns and increase the effectiveness of subsequent long-term sex offender therapy.

The Rockwood Psychological Services Preparatory Programme lasts from six to eight weeks, and consists of two, two and a half hour weekly group sessions with six to eight offenders participating. Clients appealing their conviction are not deemed suitable, though denial in itself does not eliminate one from eligibility. The cognitive-behavioural therapy utilises an open format to accommodate sometimes-unpredictable needs of a clientele subject to the demands of the penal system. Two sessions are provided as an adjustment period before the client is given an initial assignment. This task will typically focus on disclosure of their sexual offence, or offences, and will be utilised to facilitate client comfort with the challenges of the group process. To that end, expectations are minimal and most efforts are met with affirmations. During this period, the following treatment goals are clarified:

- Let the client know that treatment can be positive.
- Introduce the client to the group setting.
- Increase the comfort with disclosure.
- Identify victim harm.
- Explore core issues and reasons for the offence.
- Enhance motivation.

Consistent with the current trend, the programme utilises a positive strength-based philosophy, which is more approach than avoidant. Drawing from Hope Theory (Snyder, 2000), an attempt is made to increase the client's belief in his ability to meet treatment goals and more clearly define the client's therapeutic role. To that end, the aim is to reduce resistance by highlighting how the client will personally benefit besides the programme goal of No More Victims. Those benefits include but are not limited to personal growth, enhancing intimacy skills, and anger management.

Initial results have been promising. When compared to a similar population of non-participants, participants in the preparatory programme displayed greater treatment readiness and an increased likelihood of being accepted into subsequent lower intensity treatment. They received earlier parole and they were less likely to be returned into custody due to recidivism.

Paradoxical interventions

Paradoxical techniques were popular over the last thirty years. These tactics centre on a paradox. A paradox is communication in which a message is logical at one level and illogical at another level or a set of self-contradictory messages (Erickson, Rossi and Rossi, 1976; Haley, 1967, 1973, 1976, 1981; Havens, 1985; Lankton and Lankton, 1983; Weeks and L'Abate, 1983; Seltzer, 1986; Zeig, 1987). Although Milton H. Erickson and

colleagues have popularised the use of paradoxical interventions, Adler (1941, 1956) was one of the first to introduce rudimentary paradoxical tactics i.e. 'spitting in the client's soup' (Carich and Willingham, 1987; Carich, 1989, 1991). There are numerous versions and variations of paradoxical techniques including:

- parallel communication
- metaphors
- shock
- reframing
- implication
- suppositions
- confusion
- paradoxical prescription
- restraining

Given the limitations of this chapter, only a few are discussed in this text. The essence of these tactics is in line with the tenets of MI: rolling with the resistance and avoiding power struggles. More specifically, paradoxical tactics involve the following principles: rapport, respect, meaningful context, utilising the clients' behaviour, and flexibility. Paradoxical interventions move beyond MI, based upon Erickson's work.

Reframing

Reframing refers to changing or providing a new conceptual frame to an event or person that changes the perceptual view. One's frame of reference is altered (Haley, 1973, 1984, 1996; Lankton, 1990: Lankton and Lankton, 1983: Bandler and Grinder, 1979). Re-labelling is changing the label of a behaviour without re-conceptualisation. Examples of reframing include: normalising denial or different aspects or denial, denial into shame, denial into protection, anger into struggling, anger into caring, etc.

Parallel communication

Parallel communication refers to the use of metaphors, in which messages providing meaning at one level and at another level have a different meaning within the same contextual frame (Lankton, 1990; Lankton and Lankton, 1993: Havens, 1995; Zeig, 1997; O'Hanlon, 1987). Metaphors are symbolic communication, in which the meaning of one element is transferred to another through representation. It is a symbolic representation, in which messages reach unconscious levels. Metaphors include puns, jokes, stories, images, analogies, etc. For example, stories may represent the client's problems and solution. Typically, it is suggested not to directly reveal the therapeutic meaning of the metaphor and allow the client to engage in a trans-directional (unconscious) search for the actual meaning (Bandler and Grinder, 1979; Lankton, 1980).

An example may include telling a 'resistant' offender a story representing their dynamics, with a solution.

Paradoxical prescription

Paradoxical prescription is often referred to as symptom prescription. The symptom or problem behaviour is prescribed in a specific context, in order to elicit selected response (Erickson, Rossi and Rossi, 1976; Haley, 1973, 1976, 1981; Stricherz, 1984). For example, an offender entering treatment denies offences, can be told that it is OK, normal and may continue to deny as long as needed but perhaps you may deny not sooner or later, perhaps more sooner than later. This also reflects the use of double binds. A double bind is a linguistic pattern in which the individual is placed into a forced choice linguistic situation, from which there is no escape (Weeks and L'Abate, 1982; Haley, 1973, 1976). For instance, implying that whether you do this now or later, it will inevitably happen. As with any paradoxical tactic, rapport and respect are absolutely necessary. In this example, implication is built into the linguistic patterns, indicating that it is the offender's decision to deny or not and that is OK for now.

As with any paradoxical technique, the therapist needs to know what the expected targeted response will be as compared to the target goal of the interventions.

Face saving tactics

A related tactic often used in MI is face saving tactics, in which the offender is allowed to save face, which meets the goal. For example, the therapist could be empathic to a client's denial, framing it as an attempt to protect the client's family system. Of course, an awareness of group cohesion is imperative, and the therapist has to be mindful of the effect such tactics could have on other group members. Without skilful delivery, this could lead to a perception of enabling.

As if/what if

The 'as if' tactic is an old Adlerian tactic, in which the client is projected into the future (Carich, 1989, 1991; Mosak, 1979; Dinkmeyer, Dinkmeyer and Sperry, 1987). There are many variations (Carich, 1989).The Ericksonians use 'what if' while MI refers to it as a 'look forward. 'The offender is projected into his future, by asking him to look into his future by answering the questions of 'what if or as if. 'For example, this would include, 'How would it be as if you admitted to or took responsibility for X?' Another example is, 'What would it be like to, or what would happen,' or 'How would you feel if?' The clients' responses are then processed in the group.

Utilising reflections

Reflection in its simplest form refers to the Rogerian sense of mirroring what was said back to the client, which also includes nonverbal behaviours (Miller and Rollnick, 1991, 2002; Egan, 1995). An effective therapeutic relationship consists of reflection at multiple levels of awareness and at both verbal and nonverbal levels. Much of the mirroring process occurs at unconscious levels. Miller and Rollnick (1991, 2002) highlight three reflection interventions:

1. simple reflection
2. double sided reflection
3. amplified reflection

The latter two can be considered paradoxical in nature. Simple reflection is the acknowledgement and exploration of the client's disagreement and perception. Reflection coupled with basic active listening helps the client feel validated and understood. Double-sided reflection refers to acknowledging both sides of the offender's ambivalence to change.

Amplified reflection is reflection in an exaggerated form. For example, a group member saw no need to keep a journal. Journals are used as a basic tool to help offenders monitor and process behaviour. He was challenged to sell the programme his idea that journals are not useful. By being forced to list the pros and cons of keeping a journal, he convinced himself of the utility of journalling.

Utilising intervention

The delivery interventions require some thought in several different areas. The principles outlined earlier refer to guidelines enhancing the delivery of interventions. Other areas need to be taken into consideration, such as case conceptualisation and a basic delivery strategy. It is important to conceptualise the case in order to map out specific dynamics, problem areas, targets, and the use of effective interventions. A generic case conceptualisation strategy is provided below:

- Identify problems, patterns, and issues.
- Establish treatment philosophy and theory, which is usually in place.
- Develop a therapeutic contextual frame of reference of the problem based on theory, presenting issues, client system and philosophy.
- Outline dynamics.
- Select therapeutic messages.
- Select potential interventions via techniques.
- Review possible outcomes.
- Intervention delivery.
- Evaluate outcome.
- Prepare to utilise outcomes.

Likewise generic interventions delivery strategy is outlined below:

- Therapeutic goals.
- Establish rapport.
- Establish contextual frames.
- Select therapeutic messages.
- Select intervention options.
- Delivery of interventions.
- Utilise outcome.

Interventions are delivered through techniques. This strategy can be used with any intervention.This strategy can be helpful for the novice therapist, who might be advised to memorise the strategy, incorporating it as an automatic response.

Conclusion

Mental health practitioners view resistance as a common phenomenon that occurs with most clients, in particular those who enter treatment due to coercion. This category includes substance abusers, batterers, criminal offenders, and especially sex offenders.

The therapist's perspective of resistance and how to work with motivational issues is paramount to success. For example, resistance

was generically defined as barriers toward completing goals. A variety of typologies were provided, indicating conceptual problems between psychological defences, cognitive distortions versus core schemas (i.e. deep seeded blue prints, or ITs) and forms of resistance. It appears that defences protecting psychodynamics contain distorted ideas, which ultimately stem from core schemas held at unconscious levels. The mere labelling of resistance establishes the ground work or pathway of the therapeutic treatment targets and interventions. This applies to the therapist as well. The therapist has internal core beliefs, or maps.

The key points in working with resistance rest in several views and tenets:

- post-modernism
- holistic views
- social influence
- interpersonal communication principles
- responsivity

Post-modern viewpoints (i.e. constructivism or social constructivism) place emphasis on the individual actively participating in the contextual environment, constructing or creating his or her unique realities (Mahoney, 2003; Hansen, 2000, 2004). The client and therapist have their own realities, co-creating the therapeutic context. Hopefully, both collaborate to create a therapeutic reality system within the therapeutic context, based on interpersonal processes, involving mutual influences at one level, realising one may be more influenced than another. Therapeutic communication involves the therapist dispersing therapeutic messages in the forms of interventions, packaged in a useful metaphor. The elements of therapeutic influence include:

- Rapport.
- Alliance.
- Respect.
- Hope.
- Meaningful metaphors of therapeutic frames.
- Compassion.
- Established boundaries.
- Avoidance of shaming and power struggles.
- The flexibility to utilise a variety of interventions in conjunction with one's therapeutic perspectives, client's frame of reference, and client's needs.

The Responsivity Principle is central to success. The Responsivity Principle 'meets offender's needs or changing and matching the mode of treatment delivery depending on learning style and personality of the offender' (ATSA, 2005).

The client's perspective or multi-level reality needs to be respected and acknowledged. The sex offender is best viewed as a whole person, not just as a sex offender, with issues and patterns involving deviancy. Even though there may be common 'denominators' or issues, dynamics, and patterns, each offender is a unique individual who has different 'numerators'. The adage 'one size does not fit all' applies to sex offenders. Different interventions are effective with different clients. Clinical delivery is key.

The goal in treatment is to influence the client to complete treatment goals. This involves influencing the client via interventions, along with process variables. Social influence involves the use of social skills. Entering a therapeutic process, in itself, has impact and makes a statement. The degree of impact depends on the client. Therefore, social or interpersonal influence occurs in terms of communication skills. Within the therapeutic context, interpersonal skills involve the delivery of therapeutic messages through interventions. Each intervention is a demarcated communication. The skill and instinct of the therapist is key to effective situational implementation of the numerous interventions available.

The essence of any therapeutic endeavour is to help the client change or create differences within their functioning. In sex offender treatment, it involves creating and maintaining change in functioning at some levels, along with learning a variety of coping skills. In order to conduct effective work, it behoves the offender to be receptive to interventions. The ultimate goal or mechanism involves eliciting cooperative responses toward goals. Perceiving resistance merely as a barrier to treatment results in the treatment provider missing an opportunity to gain a fuller understanding of their client. Resistance must not be viewed only as a barrier to recovery, but also fully explored, as the pathway to discovery.

Even though the focus of this chapter is on sex offenders, the ideas, perspectives, and methods apply to most therapeutic perspectives and can be utilised with most clients. In fact, the ideas presented in this chapter have direct applications to hostage negotiations, crisis intervention, along with less urgent communication or interactional processes.

References

Abel, G. (1989) Behavioral Treatment of Child Molesters. In Strunkard, A.J. and Baum, A. (Eds.) *Perspectives on Behavioral Medicine*. NY: Lawrence Erbaum Associates.

Adler, A. (1934) Sexual Perversion. *Individual Psychology Pamphlets*, 13, 25–36.

Adler, A. (1941) *Understanding Human Nature*. (Trans Wolfe, W.B.) Cleveland, OH: World Publishing.

Adler, A. (1956) The Individual Psychology of Alfred Adler. In Ausbacher, H. and Ausbacher, R. (Eds.) New York: Basic Books.

ATSA (2005) *Practice Standards and Guidelines for Members of the Association for the Treatment of Sexual Abusers*. Beaverton, OR: ATSA.

Bandler, R. and Grinder, J. (1979) *Frogs Into Princes: Nuerolinguistic Programming*. Moab, UT: Real People Press.

Bays, L. (2001) Denial in Sex Offenders: Some Clinical Suggestions. In Carich, M.S. and Mussack, S.E. (Eds.) *A Handbook for Sexual Abuser Assessment and Treatment*. Brandon, VT: Safer Society Press.

Barbaree, H.E. (1991) Denial and Minimisation among Sexual Offenders: Assessment and Treatment Outcomes. *Forum on Corrections Research*, 3, 30–3.

Becvar, D.S. and Becvar, D.S. (1984) *Family Therapy: A Systematic Integration*. Boston: Allyn and Bacon.

Blanchard, G.T. (1995) *The Difficult Connection*. Brandon, VT: Safer Society Press.

Carich, M.S. (1989) Variations of the 'As If' Technique. *Individual Psychology*, 45: 4, 538–45.

Carich, M.S. (1991) The Hypnotic 'As If' Technique: An Example of Beyond Adler. *Individual Psychology*, 46: 4, 509–14.

Carich, M.S. and Calder, M.C. (2003) *Contemporary Treatment of Adult Male Sex Offenders*. Lyme Regis: Russell House Publishing.

Carich, M.S and Mussack, S.E. (2001) *Handbook for Assessment and Treatment of Sexual Abusers*. Brandon, VT: Safer Society Press.

Carich, M.S. and Parwatikar, S. (1995) Mind-Body Interaction: Theory and its Application to Sex Offenders. *Journal of Correctional Research*, 1.

Carich, M.S and Spilman, K. (2002) Can Guilty Sex Offenders Recover Part I: Criteria to

Evaluate Recovery. *The Forensic Therapist*. I: 1, 2–8.

Carich, M.S. and Spilman, K. (2004) Basis Principles of Intervention. *The Family Journal: Counselling and Therapy for Couples and Families*. 12: 4, 405–10.

Carich, M.S. and Stone, M. (1996) *Sex Offender Relapse Intervention Workbook*. Chicago, IL: Adler School of Professional Psychology.

Carich, M.S. and Willingham, W. (1987) The Roots of Family Systems in Individual Psychology. *Individual Psychology: The Journal of Adlerian Theory, Research and Practice*. 43: 1, 71–8.

Carkhuff, R.R. (1969) *Helping and Human Relations: A Primer for Lay and Professional Helpers, Volume I: Selection and Training*. NY: Holt, Rinehart, and Winston.

Corsini, R. (1979) *Current Psychotherapies*. Itasca, Il: FE Peacock.

Corsini, R. and Wedding (1995) *Current Psychotherapies*. 5th edn. Itasca, Il: FE Peacock.

DiClemente, C.C. (1991) Specific Tactics Involving the Wheel of Change. In Miller, W.R. and Rollnick, S. (Eds.) *Motivational Interviewing: Preparing People to Change Addictive Behavior*. NY: The Guilford Press.

Dinkmeyer, D.C. Sr., Dinkmeyer, D.C. Jr. and Sperry, L. (1987) *Adlerian Counseling and Psychology*. Columbus, OH: Merrill Publishing.

Drapeau, M. (2005) Research on the Processes Involved in Treating Sexual Offenders. *Sexual Abuse: A Journal of Research and Treatment*, 17: 2, 117–27.

Dreikurs, R. (1950) *Fundamentals of Adlerian Psychology*. Chicago, Il: Alfred Adler Institute.

Dreikurs, R. (1967) *Psychodynamics, Psychotherapy, and Counseling*. Chicago, Il: Alfred Adler Institute.

Egan, G. (1986) *The Skilled Helper: A Systematic Approach to Effective Helping*. Monterey, CA: Brooks/Cole.

Erickson, M.H., Rossi, E.L. and Rossi, S.I. (1976) *Hypnotic Realities: The Induction of Clinical Hypnosis and Forms of Indirect Suggestions*. NY: Irvington Publishers.

Fernandez, Y. (2006) Focusing on the Positive and Avoiding the Negativity in Sexual Offender Treatment. In Marshall, W.L. et al. (Eds.) *Sexual Offender Treatment: Controversial Issues*. W. Sussex, J. Wiley and Son.

Fernandez, Y., Shingler, J. and Marshall, W.L. (2006) Putting 'Behavior' Back into the Cognitive-Behavioral Treatment of Sexual Offenders. In Marshall, W.L. et al. (Eds.) *Sexual Offender Treatment: Controversial Issues*. J. Wiley and Son.

Freeman-Longo, R.E. and Pithers, W.D. (1992) *Client's Manual: A Structured Approach to Preventing Relapse. A Guide for Sex Offenders*. Brandon. VT. Safer Society Press.

Haley, J. (Ed.) (1967) *Advanced Technique of Hypnosis and Therapy*. NY: Grune and Stratton.

Haley, J. (1973) *Uncommon Therapy: The Psychiatric Technique of Milton H. Erickson*. NY: WW Norton.

Haley, J. (1976) *Problem Solving Therapy*. San Francisco: Jossey-Bass.

Haley, J. (1981) *Reflections on Therapy and Other Essays*. Chevy Chase, MD: The Family Therapy Institute of Washington, DC.

Haley, J. (1984) *Ordeal Therapy*. San, Francisco: Jossey Bass.

Hansen, J.T. (2000) Psychoanalysis and Humanism: A Review and Critical Examination of Integrationist Efforts with Some Proposed Resolutions. *Journal of Counseling and Development*. 80, 315–21.

Hansen, J.T. (2004) Thoughts on Knowing: Epistemic Implications of Counseling Practice. *Journal of Counseling and Development*, 82, 131–8.

Hanson, R.K. and Harris, A. (2001) A Structured Approach to Evaluating Change among Sexual Offenders. *Sexual Abuse: A Journal of Research and Treatment*, 13, 105–22.

Hanson, R.K. and Morton-Bourgon, K. (2004) *Predictors of Sexual Recidivism: An Updated Meta-Analysis*. Public Works and Government Services Canada.

Happel, R.M. and Auffrey, J.J. (1995) Sex Offender Assessment: Interrupting the Dance of Denial. *American Journal of Forensic Psychology*, 13: 2, 5–22.

Havens, R. (1985) *The Wisdom of Milton H. Erickson*. NY: Irvington Publisher.

Keeney, B.P. (1983) *Aesthetics of Change*. New York: Guilford Press.

Keeney, B.P. and Ross, J.M. (1983) Cybernetics of Brief Family Therapy. *Journal of Marital and Family Therapy*. 9, 375–82.

Kelly, G. (1955) *The Psychology of Personal Constructs*. New York: Norton.

Lambert, M.J. (1992) Implications of Outcome Research for Psychotherapy Integration. In Norcross, J.C. and Goldstein, M.R. (Eds.) *Handbook of Psychotherapy Integration*. New York: Basic Books.

Lambert, M.J., and Bergin, A.E. (1993) The Effectiveness of Psychotherapy. In Bergin, A.E. and Garfield, S.L. (Eds.) *Handbook of Psychotherapy and Behavioral Change.* 4th edn. New York: Wiley.

Lankton, S. (1980) *Practical Magic.* Cupertino, CA: Meta Publications.

Lankton, S. and Lankton, C. (1983) *The Answer Within: A Clinical Framework of Ericksonian Hypnotherapy.* New York: Bruner/Mazel.

Longo, R.E. (2002) A Holistic/Integrated Approach to Treating Sexual Offenders. In Schwartz, B.K. (Ed.) *The Sexual Offender: Current Treatment Modalities and Systems Issues, Volume IV.* Kingston, NJ: Civic Research Institute.

Mahoney, M.J. (2003) *Constructive Psychotherapy: A Practical Guide.* NY: Guilford Press.

Mann, R.E. (2000) Managing Resistance and Rebellion in Relapse Prevention Intervention. In Laws, D.R., Hudson, S.M. and Ward, T. (Eds.) *Remaking Relapse Prevention with Sex Offenders: A Sourcebook.* Thousand Oaks, CA: Sage.

Mann, R.E and Shingler, J. (2006) Schema-Driven Cognition in Sexual Offenders: Theory, Assessment and Treatment. In Marshall, W.L. et al. (Eds.) *Sexual Offender Treatment: Controversial Issues.* Chichester: J. Wiley and Son.

Marshall, L.Y. (2006) Powerpoint Presentation for Illinois Department of Corrections.

Marshall, L.E. and Moulden, W.L. (2006) Prepratory Programs for Sexual Offenders. In Marshall, W.L. et al. (Eds) *Sexual Offender Treatment: Controversial Issues.* Chichester: J. Wiley and Son.

Marshall, W.L (1996) Assessment, Treatment, and Theorising about Sexual Offenders: Developments over the Past 20 Years and Future Directions. *Criminal Justice and Behavior,* 23, 162–99.

Marshall, W.L. (1999) Current Status of North American Assessment and Treatment Programs for Sexual Offenders. *Journal of Interpersonal Violence,* 14, 221–39.

Marshall, W.L. (2005) Therapist Style in Sexual Offender Treatment: Influence on Indices of Change. *Sexual Abuse: A Journal of Research and Treatment,* 17: 2, 109–16.

Marshall, W.L., Anderson, D. and Fernandez (1999) Cognitive Behavioral Treatment of Sex Offenders. NY: J. Wiley and Son.

Marshall, W.L. et al. (2003a) Process Variables in the Treatment of Sexual Offenders: A Review of Literature. *Aggression and Violent Behavior,* 8 205–34.

Marshall, W.L. et al. (2003b) Therapist Characteristics in the Treatment of Sexual Offenders: Tentative Data on their Relationship with Indices of Behavioral Change. *Journal of Sexual Aggression,* 9, 25–30.

Marshall, W.L and Laws, D.R. (2003) A Brief History of Behavioral and Cognitive-Behavioral Approaches to Sex Offender Treatment: Part 2. The Modern Era. *Sexual Abuse: A Journal of Research and Treatment,* 15, 93–120.

Marshall, W.L. (2006) Appraising Treatment Outcome in Sexual Offenders. In Marshall, W.L. et al. (Eds.) *Sexual Offender Treatment: Controversial Issues.* Chichester: J. Wiley and Son.

Marshall, W.L, and Serran, G.A. (2000) Improving the Effectiveness of Sex Offender Treatment. *Trauma, Violence, and Abuse,* 1: 3, 203–22.

Marshall, W.L. et al. (2002) Therapist Features in Sexual Offender Treatment: Their Reliable Identification and Influence on Behavior Change. *Clinical Psychology and Psychotherapy,* 9, 395–405.

Marshall, W.L. et al. (2006) *Treating Sexual Offenders: An Integrated Approach.* NY: Routledge.

Marzialli, E. and Alexander, L. (1991) The Power of the Therapeutic Relationship. *American Journal of Orthopsychiatry,* 61: 3, 383–91.

Miller, W.R. and Rollnick, S. (1991) *Motivational Interviewing: Preparing People to Change Addictive Behaviour.* New York: Guilford Press.

Miller, W.R. and Rollnick, S. (2000) *Motivational Interviewing: Preparing People to Change Addictive Behaviour.* 2nd edn. New York: Guilford Press.

Mosak, H. (1979) Adlerian Psychotherapy. In Corsini, R. (Ed.) *Current Psychotherapies.* Itasca, Il: FE Peacock.

Mussack, S.E. and Carich, M.S. (2001) Sex Offender Assessment. In Carich, M. and Mussack, S.E. (Eds.) *A Handbook for Assessment and Treatment of Sexual Abusers.* Brandon, VT: Safer Society Press.

Niemeyer, M.A. and Bridges, S.K. (2003) Postmodern Approaches to Psychotherapy. In Gurman, A.S. and Messer, S.B. (Eds.) *Essential Pyschotherapies.* NY: Guilford Press.

O'Hanlon, W. (1987) *Tap Roots.* New York: WW Norton.

Polaschek, D.L. and Ward, T. (2002) The Implicit Theories of Potential Rapists. What Our Questionnaires Tell Us. *Aggression and Violent Behavior,* 7, 385–406.

Prochaska, J.O. and DiClemente, C.C. (1983) The Stages and Processes of Self-Change in Smoking: Toward an Integrative Model of Change. *Journal of Consulting and Individual Psychology*, 51, 390–5.

Rich, P. (2003) *Understanding, Assessing, and Rehabilitating Juvenile Sexual Offenders.* New York: J. Wiley and Son.

Rossi, E.L. (1993) *The Psychobiology of Mind-Body Healing: New Concepts of Therapeutic Hypnosis.* 2nd edn. NY: WW Norton.

Rossi, E.L. (2002) Expectancy and Surprise: A Conceptual Review of Stress and Psychosocial Genomics in Therapeutic Hypnosis. *American Journal of Clinical Hypnosis.* 45, 2.

Rychlak, J.F. (1981) *Introduction to Personality and Psychotherapy: A Theory Construction Approach.* Boston: Houghton-Mifflin.

Schwartz, B.K. and Cellini, H. (Eds.) (1997) *The Sex Offender: New Insights, Treatments and Legal Developments.* Kingston, NJ: Civic Research Institute.

Schwartz, B.K. and Cellini, H. (Eds.) (1995) *The Sex Offender: Corrections, Treatment, and Legal Developments.* Kingston, NJ: Civic Research Institute.

Seltzer, L. (1986) *Paradoxical Strategies in Psychotherapy: A Comprehensive Overview and Guidebook.* New York: Wiley.

Shingler, J. and Mann, R.E. (2006) Collaboration in Clinical Work with Sexual Offenders: Treatment and Risk Assessment. In Marshall, W.L. et al. (Eds.) *Sexual Offender Treatment: Controversial Issues.* W. Sussex: J. Wiley and Son.

Snyder, C.R. (2000) *Handbook of Hope: Theory, Measures and Applications.* New York: Academic Press.

Stricherz, M. (1984) Ericksonian Theories of Hypnosis and Induction. In Wester, W. and Smith, A.H. (Eds.) *Clinical Hypnosis: A Multidisciplinary Approach.* Philadelphia: Lippincott.

Thorton, D. (2002) Constructing and Testing a Framework for Dynamic Risk Assessment. *Sexual Abuse: A Journal of Research and Treatment*, 14: 2, 137–51.

Ward, T. (2002) Good Lives and the Rehabilitation of Sex Offenders: Promises and Problems. *Aggression and Violent Behavior: A Review Journal.* 7, 513–28.

Ward, T. and Keenan, T. (1999) Child Molesters: Implicit Theories. *Journal of Interpersonal Violence*, 14, 821–38.

Ward, T. and Marshall, W.L. (2004) The Role of the Good Lives Features in the Etiology of Sexual Offending. *Journal of Sexual Aggression.*

Ward, T., Polaschek, D.L. and Beech, A. (2006) *Theories of Sexual Offending.* London: J. Wiley and Son.

Ward, T. and Stewart, C.A. (2003) Good Lives and the Rehabilitation of Sexual Offenders. In Ward, T., Laws, D.R. and Hudson, S.M. (Eds.) *Sexual Deviance: Issues and Controversies.* Thousand Oaks, CA: Sage.

Watzlawick, P., Weakland, J. and Fisch, R. (1974) *Change: The Principles of Problem Formation and Problem Resolution.* New York: Garland Press.

Weeks, G. and L'Abate, L. (1982) *Paradoxical Psychotherapy: Theory and Practice with Individuals, Couples, and Families.* New York: Brunner Mazel.

Winn, M.E. (1996) The Strategic and Systematic Management of Denial in Cognitive/ Behavioral Treatment of Sex Offenders. *Sexual Abuse: A Journal of Research and Treatment*, 8: 1, 25–36.

Yalom, I.D. (1985) *The Theory and Practice of Group Psychotherapy.* NY: Basic Books.

Zeig, J.K. (1987) Therapeutic Patterns of Ericksonian Influence Communication. In Zeig, J.Z. (Ed.) *The Evolution of Psychotherapy.* New York: Brunner/Mazel.

Zeig, J.K. and Munion, W.M. (1990) What is Psychotherapy? In Zeig, J.K. and Munion, W.M. (Eds.) *What is Psychotherapy? Contemporary Perspectives.* San Francisco: Jossey Bass.

CHAPTER 16

Engaging Sexually Abusive Youth in Treatment

Phil Rich

Introduction

In many, if not most, significant ways, working with sexually abusive youth is no different than working therapeutically with any young person. A primary and obvious difference, of course, lies in the purpose of the treatment and the context within which sex offender specific treatment is embedded, as well as the specific tasks of the therapy. That is, sexually abusive youth enter treatment because they have engaged in sexually abusive behaviour, and because there are concerns about what they may do in the future.

In treating sexually abusive behaviour, we intend to ameliorate the possibility that such behaviour will occur again in the future, and here lies the crux of the treatment itself, as well as the question for treatment. How is it best to treat not past behaviours, but *current* attitudes, beliefs, and emotional needs, as well as co-existing psychiatric conditions and special educational needs, that contributed to the past behaviour and may also support future engagement in sexually abusive behaviour?

This has led to two models for the treatment of sexually abusive behaviour in children and adolescents. In one model, behaviour is considered the outcome of poorly constructed ideas; in the second, behaviour of all kinds, including sexually abusive behaviour, is seen as one possible product of a rich complex of ideas, emotions, social skills, and life history catalysed by social forces that act upon each individual.

In the first case, we treat just the sexually abusive behaviour and related cognitive processes, often through a mixture of mild cognitive-behavioural therapy and psycho-education (usually geared towards psycho-education). This model is fuelled by the assumption that it is enough to treat ideas, attitudes, and beliefs related to sexual behaviour and subsequently correct cognitions considered to be faulty, as well as providing treatment 'roadmaps.' These maps will help juveniles recognise problems with their thoughts and behaviours, develop alternatives to problematic

behaviours, and plan escape routes from inappropriate behaviours that utilise newly developed coping skills and support networks. This has been the 'standard' model for the treatment of both adult and juvenile sexual offenders, and is often referred to as the cognitive-behavioural or relapse prevention model. Its focus is on recognising problems and avoiding them, or, once a behavioural chain has been started, escaping the loop that forms in which problematic emotions, thoughts, or attitudes build upon one another and eventually result in inappropriate behaviour.

However, there is a danger if we come to think that this is the *only* focus in treatment, and that we may somehow treat the presenting condition (i.e. sexually abusive behaviour) without also treating the 'other' parts of the child. These include those aspects of the individual that have little to do with sexual behaviours, and which certainly in total add up to far more than just the sexually abusive behaviour alone. Indeed, the chances are that, although the sexually abusive behaviour is the behaviour of concern, for most children inappropriate and abusive sexualised behaviour is merely the tip of the iceberg, often reflecting many elements of their lives that are disturbing to them and to us. In this case, it is unlikely that we will be effective in fully understanding the aetiology or cause of the sexually abusive behaviour. Neither is it likely that we will be able to recognise the *meaning* of the behaviour and the needs it filled for the sexually abusive youth, or effectively treat the complex of treatment needs that came together to produce the behaviour.

For example, in addition to engaging in sexually abusive behaviour, the child entering treatment may be depressed. Although he has not come into treatment *because* he is depressed, the depression must nevertheless be treated if we are to provide effective and comprehensive treatment and we hope to improve the quality of the child's life, in addition to improving public safety as we reduce the likelihood of further sexually abusive behaviour. Indeed, it may not be *possible* to effectively treat sexually abusive behaviour without recognising and treating the depression, or whatever behavioural or psychiatric conditions may co-exist alongside the sexually abusive behaviour (including conduct, attention deficit, stress, anxiety, autistic spectrum, and substance abuse disorders, for instance), as attitudes, beliefs, social skills, and social forces are quite likely to have interacted with any co-existing conditions in the first place to produce or contribute to the sexually abusive behaviour that we seek to treat.

Accordingly, the second model, increasingly more commonplace in the treatment of sexually abusive youth, and inching its way into the world of adult treatment as well, embraces a far broader approach to treatment. Here, treatment is multi-dimensional, multi-faceted, and often pan-theoretical, blending ideas, structures, modes, and techniques of treatment together with a model that also recognises the client as multi-dimensioned and in which the juvenile is recognised as a 'whole' person with multiple personal and treatment needs. This is an integrated model of treatment in which we recognise that one-size-fits-all models of psycho-educationally-driven cognitive treatment cannot possibly meet the complex needs of individuals, nor even recognise those needs.

Under any circumstances, in the case of either model, the primary question is not just *how* to treat the sexually abusive behaviour that is ultimately the target of treatment, or identifying the elements of sexually abusive behaviour that must be treated, but what are the conditions that must be created in order to effectively treat the behaviour?

However, we frankly don't know enough about effective sex offender specific treatment to unequivocally define its essential elements, or best practice. We are still not clear about exactly what works in treatment, or how best to provide it. This is especially true because the base rate for sexual offence recidivism among adolescent sexual abusers (as reported by most studies) is so low that we can't easily discern patterns that predict recidivism, and we therefore can't easily identify elements of treatment that are or are not effective or crucial in treatment.

Rather than argue about which targets, methods, and techniques of treatment must be included and which are unnecessary, in this chapter we'll look at elements of treatment that seem universal to good practice and our ability to understand and engage our clients in treatment. That is, these elements seem pertinent unless one assumes that treatment can be effectively and satisfactorily provided through workbooks or limited protocols alone, with little psychotherapeutic interaction between the clinician and client.

Conceptualising treatment

In any well-reasoned treatment programme, several discernible elements are evident. Not only are these elements discrete from one another, in which their presence highlights the fact that 'sex offender specific' treatment is actually composed of different components, but they also illustrate that treatment proceeds in stages, in which one element of treatment follows and is built upon earlier elements, and in other cases treatment elements are linked to, but independent from, one another.

Because there are multiple elements involved in the treatment of sexually abusive youth, as well as multiple targets for treatment, it can be difficult to know where to start work, how to pace treatment with respect to introducing different elements of treatment at different points, and how to recognise expected treatment growth and progress. Without a model of some kind by which the work and process of treatment may be defined, the work of any individual clinician risks being idiosyncratic, shapeless, inconsistent, and arbitrary, leaving the clinician with few means by which to formulate what treatment should look like at any given point and how best to evaluate movement and progress in treatment.

With a model of treatment in place, the practitioner is able to conceive of the treatment process as a series of sequenced or overlapping tasks which, together, not only define the work to be accomplished in sex offender specific treatment, but also provide a roadmap of sorts to guide the practitioner through treatment. One option is for the practitioner to depend upon a prescribed manual for the provision of treatment. However, this is not only likely to lead to a cookbook approach to treatment (that is, one-size-fits-all), but is also likely to limit the capacity of the treatment to be individualised to meet the needs of any particular client. A second option is to define a framework (rather than a manual, or specific protocol) to define and shape the application and direction of treatment.

Obviously, these two approaches – manualised versus framework – reflect the two approaches to treatment described above. The former is rigid, shallow, and limited; the latter flexible, rich, and comprehensive.

I have previously described a treatment framework (Rich, 2003) in which treatment can be considered in terms of both phases and stages. Although in my earlier model I described three phases, I now conceptualise treatment occurring in four phases, each of which is built upon and incorporates the treatment tasks of the prior phase: *pre-treatment*, which involves understanding the case and preparing for treatment; *foundational treatment*, focusing on the development of the therapeutic climate; *offence-specific treatment* (formerly 'active treatment'), during which sex offender specific treatment activities occur, as well as the evaluation of treatment over time; and *post-treatment* involving the transition to an aftercare model of continued treatment or supervision.

Although there are any number of tasks or goals to be completed in treatment (specific treatment tasks are also suggested in Rich, 2003), treatment can nevertheless be considered to proceed in stages that describe the sequence of treatment activities that build upon and link to one another, and the focus of treatment at any given point. Such a model suggests that different treatment tasks are relevant at different points in treatment, tying specific tasks of treatment to

distinct stages, in which later treatment tasks build upon completion of earlier ones. In so doing, the model also describes treatment unfolding in a sequential order, suggesting that treatment tasks are not only relevant to different stages, but that their accomplishment is possible only during the appropriate stage.

Of course, any stage model offers a rough approximation of life only. In reality, the tasks of any given stage overlap with the tasks of each contiguous stage, and in a model that describes the unfolding of treatment we also must recognise that youths in treatment move back and forth through these stages, often *necessarily* regressing at times before moving ahead once again. Further, the model is conceptual only; in reality many of the treatment tasks linked to each of the stages described below occur throughout treatment, and are not limited to any one stage or period of time.

Figure 16.1 identifies ten stages of treatment (with one pre-stage) and shows how they may be folded into the three phases of foundational treatment, offence-specific treatment, and post-treatment. Space does not permit a more complete description of treatment stages, which are described in more detail elsewhere (Rich, 2003). However, briefly, these stages outline the development of treatment over time, identifying the work to be completed by sexually abusive youth, and the focus of the clinician's work, over the course of treatment.

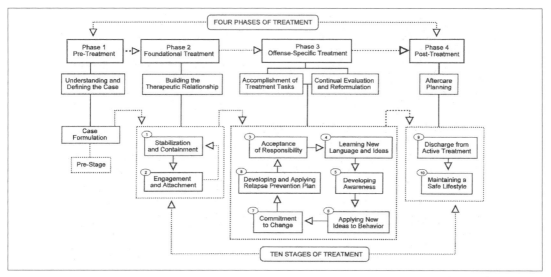

Figure 16.1   Stages of treatment incorporated into a four phase treatment model in the treatment of sexually abusive youth

1. *Stabilisation and containment,* in which the primary focus is on emotional and behavioural stability.
2. *Engagement and attachment,* involving the ability of clients to form attachments with the practitioner, or the development of the therapeutic alliance.
3. *Acceptance of responsibility,* moving through denial and beginning to acknowledge and accept personal responsibility.
4. *Learning new language and ideas,* focusing on helping clients recognise how ideas, attitudes, and beliefs affect and influence sexually aggressive and other antisocial and self-defeating behaviours.
5. *Developing awareness,* helping clients to become more aware of themselves, their motivations and their influences, the needs of others, and their impact on others.
6. *Applying new ideas to behaviour,* a more advanced stage during which clients demonstrate their ability to retain what they have learned and demonstrate changes in their behaviours and social interactions.
7. *Commitment to change,* in preparation for discharge, clients must recognise the necessity of change and demonstrate a commitment to such change.
8. *Development and application of a behavioural/relapse prevention plan,* involving the development of a refined and active behavioural safety plan.
9. *Discharge from active treatment,* during which aftercare plans are developed and during which it is critical that the client, family members, and outside agencies are fully committed to such plans.
10. *Maintaining a safe life style.* In this post-treatment stage, the life of the treated juvenile takes its next form, including behavioural monitoring and supervision, on-going therapy, and other forms of interventions designed to ensure a healthy and safe lifestyle in the post-treatment setting.

It is useful to visualise treatment occurring in phases and stages of treatment because this makes it clear that treatment doesn't happen all at once and instead passes through discrete periods, evolving over time. It also makes clear that the cognitive-behavioural portion of treatment that is central to effective sex offender treatment, involving much psycho-education as well as

application and practice, is built upon and nested within a framework that is relational. Referring to Figure 16.1, it is clear that the foundational phase of treatment is largely process-oriented and aimed at relationship-building, with the emerging therapeutic relationship setting the pace for and enabling the treatment that follows.

Case formulation

With respect to treatment phases and stages, the practitioner must first understand the case. However, this is less important, if important at all, in a one-size-fits-all approach. In this case, one might easily argue that juvenile sexual offenders are all alike and all require the same method of treatment, in which case neither elements specific to the actual sexually abusive behaviour nor the motivations and behaviour of the sexually abusive youth really matter. In such a limited model, the assumption is made that it is only the treatment that is important, and that treatment should and can be provided through a defined treatment protocol, regardless of dissimilarities among sexually abusive youth. In today's treatment environment, however, it is increasingly unlikely that we will find such a limited model.

Accordingly, for the most part, all treatment models are going to include a stage of treatment during which information is gathered about the youth, typically through the process of psychosocial assessment. Through this process, relevant information is gathered about the youth's life and, in the most comprehensive model, through multiple sources, including record reviews, interviews with the youth, and information gathered from collateral sources such as the parents, social service caseworkers, probation officers, teachers, former therapists, and others who know the case well and know the child's developmental history and current functioning. From the psychosocial history comes an understanding of the individual youth from a developmental perspective, including and recognising steps in the youth's personal development and the development of their emotional and behavioural makeup, resulting in a formulation of the case.

Case formulation, or conceptualisation, represents an understanding of the case that allows the practitioner to deduce how the client came to be, with respect to history and current functioning, including attitudes, expectations about the world, and functional social skills. The formulation represents the practitioner's theory about the case:

- Causes of, and precursors to, current functioning, or aetiology and ontogenesis.
- Explanation and understanding of current behaviour as outcome, or extension of prior development.
- Prediction or trending of likely future behaviour if things remain unchanged, or prognosis.
- Determination of treatment interventions, or those things to be applied to alter the projected trajectory of the case.

Case formulation hence allows the practitioner to approach the case from the vantage point offered by a detailed understanding of the individual client and the context of his or her life, and with a theory, at least, of why the client acted in the manner in which he or she did. From there, case formulation allows an individualised approach to treatment and the selection of treatment targets.

Pacing and building treatment

Conceptualising treatment occurring in sequential stages not only informs clinicians of work relevant to each stage, and thus helps set the pace for treatment, but also makes clear that treatment not only does not happen all 'at once,' but *cannot*. A stage model shows that treatment deepens over time, and that success in treatment builds upon the development of a foundation. In treatment, one cannot run before walking, and before that crawling. Pacing in the treatment of multiple areas means that treatment in one area may well be dependent upon treatment in another, and that one type of treatment target must precede another. In some cases, the provision of one type of treatment intervention may depend on work being done in other treatment areas, thus pacing always implies a sequence of treatment, although in some cases multiple treatment targets are being approached simultaneously. Above all, though, it means that treatment is progressive, developing and changing over time.

In many models of group treatment, for instance, we recognise that group therapy also proceeds in stages, in which more complex work is not possible until group members have successfully engaged in the earlier tasks of first becoming oriented to the group, building structure and becoming familiar with expectations, and recognising and addressing dissatisfaction in the group and resolving issues that interfere with a higher level of communication and group interaction. In a stage model of group work, we thus recognise that high functioning groups are possible only after a basic level of group work has been accomplished. Group members must learn earlier essential tasks in order to perform therapeutically later; in effect, group members first learn *how* to be group members.

The same is true for every aspect of treatment. In working on trauma issues, for example, it is important to first build a therapeutic foundation, including the establishment of at least a rudimentary therapeutic relationship, before trauma work is undertaken. Pacing treatment not only means identifying appropriate treatment targets, but also arriving at critical points in treatment at the right time, at the right speed, in the right order, in the right frame of mind for the client, and with the right foundation for the work.

Thus, although we'd like to accomplish all tasks of treatment in the shortest time possible, we recognise that treatment must be paced, building over time and accumulating depth and breadth, starting at the client's developmental and emotional level, and tracking and following that developmental level throughout treatment. Further, not only must treatment be geared to the individual client's needs, abilities, and capacities, but we must also be cognisant of the fact that changes in the client, including the acquisition and retention of new ideas and behaviours, take place only over time. Accordingly, although we wish to approach and tackle treatment issues as soon as possible, in reality treatment must be paced; addressing treatment issues prematurely may result in failure, at least in that treatment area. A youth may be willing to reveal or learn only so much at any given point in treatment, which is why it is essential to revisit the same ideas and situations over time. A later look at the same situation, event, behaviour, or relationship may reveal many more complex factors with the further development of the clinician-client relationship and as the youth himself has progressed in treatment.

Accordingly, treatment is serial and dynamic, rather than episodic and static. That is, treatment builds and feeds upon itself; earlier treatment experiences lead directly to later ones, and treatment episodes that occur later in treatment are the outcome of earlier treatment experiences. Because, through the many treatment sessions and experiences shared by the clinician and client, earlier treatment is connected to later treatment, all individual treatment events must be recognised as a single frame in a larger and connected treatment experience that unfolds and can be fully recognised only over time. Part of the work of the clinician is not only to pace treatment, ensuring that the 'right' treatment intervention is applied at the 'right' time, but also to serve as the conduit and link that connects and makes treatment continuous across time, building later treatment experiences upon earlier ones.

Pacing means making informed and reasonable decisions about what treatment goals are appropriate at any given moment in treatment, and how and in what order treatment interventions should be applied, including the intensity and depth of such interventions. Clients who are neither ready for nor willing to accept treatment must first be engaged at a level that prepares them for treatment (foundational treatment). Thus, before sexual offender treatment can be seriously considered the sexually abusive youth must demonstrate a level of behavioural and emotional control, a willingness and ability to work on sexual issues, and the sort of therapeutic engagement that is

necessary to take seriously the lessons and tasks of sex offender specific treatment. In the increasingly popular trans-theoretical model of change (often linked to motivational interviewing), this means that clients have reached at least the 'contemplation,' if not the 'preparation,' stage, in preparation for significant engagement in the abuse-specific aspects of treatment. In a traditional 12-step model of treatment, this is the equivalent to the first three steps, involving a willingness to accept that a problem exists and that help is needed to overcome the problem.

It happens that a modified version of the 12-step model is a useful means to describe pacing and sequencing in treatment for sexually abusive youth. For instance, in order to become honest with others (Step 5) clients must first become honest with themselves (Step 3). Before sexually abusive youth can meaningfully work on victim restitution (Step 9) they must first accomplish earlier treatment tasks that prepare them for meaningful engagement in this later treatment task. Figure 16.2 provides an overview of a 12 step model adapted for sex offender specific treatment, recognising that it is simply intended as a means to describe the sequential and paced quality of treatment, and that, in practice, many treatment tasks occur at the same moment, and in many cases treatment goes back-and-forth rather than striding forward in linear fashion.

1. *Overcoming denial.* In this first step, the individual is able to recognise and admit that they have a problem.
2. *Recognising need for help.* The individual recognises that they cannot handle or overcome this problem on their own.
3. *Accepting help.* Having accepted that help is required, the individual is ready to accept help and work with, and not against, helpers.
4. *Becoming honest with self.* The individual is able to engage in honest, and often painful, self-appraisal.
5. *Becoming honest with others.* The individual is able and willing to be honest and authentic with helpers.
6. *Willing to change.* The individual has reached a point where the need to change is apparent and has been internalised, and is willing, if not able, to change.
7. *Ready to change.* The individual is now willing *and* able to effect real change.
8. *Ready to explore the damage caused to others.* The individual begins to honestly appraise who has been damaged by his or her behaviour, and how.
9. *Willing to make restitution and seek forgiveness in the spirit of healing others and self.* The individual is willing and able to make amends and pay restitution to others as part of the spiritual healing process.
10. *Able to accept personal flaws and fully accept responsibility.* The individual demonstrates humility, recognises and acknowledges personal flaws and poor behaviours, and accepts personal responsibility.
11. *Building a life built on meaningful relationships, awareness of others, and self awareness.* The individual is aware of and considers their own actions, and are tuned into themselves and the impact of their behaviours on themselves and others.
12. *Living a changed life.* Individuals have changed in significant aspects of their lives.

Figure 16.2   Steps in the treatment of juvenile sexual offenders

The treatment relationship in the treatment experience

In fact, suggesting that treatment has a serial quality to it, progressing and deepening over time, is not to suggest that treatment is simply a linear process. In practice, treatment sometimes takes unexpected turns and corners, moving back and forth, but over time is more exponential or harmonic than linear.

That is, the treatment effect is more than the simple combining or accumulation of a specific number of treatment sessions, but increases in power because of the *combined* effect of treatment experiences in which exponential growth spurts are apparent, and in which treatment 'overtones' and 'undertones' appear, creating a rich treatment experience that is more than simply the linear sum of the parts. Much of this harmonic is evident in changes in the client, and many of those changes are the result of the therapeutic relationship that produces that harmonic.

This relationship is central to the process of personal change if such change is to be ascribed to the provision of therapy. This is because, regardless of theoretical focus or technique, therapy always occurs within the context of the therapeutic relationship, or the therapeutic alliance defined by Edward Bordin (1976) as the integration of the relationship bond, the working goals of the clinician and client, and the definition of tasks that must be accomplished in treatment. Dryden (1989) describes the relationship in terms of the emotional *bonds* of the relationship itself, shared *goals* which define the reasons for the relationship, and *tasks* which clarify the boundaries of the relationship and define the roles of both client and therapist.

In fact, the development of the therapeutic alliance is the first task in any form of treatment that recognises treatment as more than simply the application of technique or the unfolding of a treatment manual. Although we can conceive of it as an early step in a treatment sequence (as shown in Figure 16.1) the treatment relationship is not a chronological event but an evolving and living relationship that serves as the medium through which treatment is provided and the framework from which treatment techniques are applied, and itself is an integral part of the treatment process. The treatment relationship is alive, dynamic, and evolving throughout treatment, formed at the moment that treatment begins, and drawing to a close only at its conclusion.

Treatment as craft, not technique

We come back to the idea that there are two underlying ideas in the treatment of sexual offenders. In one case, there is a belief that treatment can and should be manualised, and is thus largely focused on the provision of treatment driven by technique (including treatment protocols) described and defined by the treatment manual. This does not mean that personal elements, such as the relationship between the client and clinician are unimportant, but it does mean that treatment can be fully defined and operationalised in writing, and, in effect, can be reduced to both a technical description and technique.

A second model asserts that successful treatment does not rest on the form or technique of therapy, but instead upon elements at play *behind*, and regardless of, technique. For instance, in studies designed to identify the relationship of treatment elements to treatment outcome, effective therapists used elements of both psychodynamic and cognitive-behavioural in their treatment (Ablon and Jones, 1998; Castonguay et al., 1996). Indeed, this second model purports that elements common to *both* forms of treatment are most responsible for efficacy in treatment, rather than technique or theory. In describing therapies that cut across and integrate therapeutic forms, Holmes and Bateman (2002: 8) write that 'common factors such as the therapeutic relationship, the creation of hope, explanations, a pathway to recovery, and opportunities for emotional release remain important explanatory variables for the similar outcomes of different therapies in the same conditions'.

The essential elements in these common factors are the interpersonal factors introduced by the therapist and the client together, embodied in the therapeutic alliance that forms between them and in which the work of treatment is accomplished. Indeed, John Norcross (2000) has written that the clinician-client relationship accounts for as much of treatment outcome than any particular treatment techniques, and Michael Lambert and associates (Asay and Lambert, 1999; Lambert, 1992; Lambert and Bergin, 1993) have written that *most* of what happens in successful treatment is unrelated to treatment model or technique, related instead to factors common to all therapy, accounting for 85 per cent of treatment outcome (Lambert, 1992). According to Lambert (1992) of the four elements most commonly associated with treatment outcome, technique accounts for only 15 per cent of the variance in treatment outcome, with most treatment success resulting from client factors (40 per cent), therapeutic alliance (30 per cent), and the self-healing placebo effects of expectancy and hope (15 per cent).

Of course, technique is very important, as is method. Although acquired through experience and training, effective skills are built upon technique, which is first learned. And, just as technique allows formalisation, method allows organisation and focus. Whether art, craft, or skill, therapy should not be practiced without first learning technique and developing method because without technique and method, skill is usually poorly developed, raw, naive, uncontained, or uncontrolled, and sometimes unfulfilled. Accordingly, technique and method are essential, and are skills in themselves. The risk, however, is that we may come to depend solely upon them, mistaking them for the final product, or believe that technique and method is enough or can replace the craft aspect of the skill. When technique defines treatment, we risk having treatment *become* technique. In the words of Salvador Minuchin: 'if the therapist becomes wedded to technique, remaining a craftsman . . . contact with patients will be objective, detached, and clean, but also superficial, manipulative . . . and ultimately not highly effective. Training . . . should therefore be a way of teaching technique whose essence is mastered then forgotten . . . Only a person who has mastered technique and then contrived to forget it can become an expert therapist (Minuchin and Fishman, 1981: 1).

The role and attributes of the therapist

Norcross (2000) and Blanchard (1998) have described the therapist as a central agent of change, and Bachelor and Horvath (1999) have written that the important therapeutic relationship is formed early in therapy, established through the climate of trust and safety fostered by the clinician through responsiveness, listening, and the communication of understanding, regard, and respect. In a similar vein, Keijsers, Schaap and Hoogduin (2000) write that the effective therapeutic relationship includes the client's perception of the therapist as self-confident, skilful, and active.

Lambert and Bergin (1993) describe reassurance, structure, advice, and modelling as important factors in the therapeutic alliance.

With this in mind, sexually abusive youth are not coerced, confronted, or even educated into improved attitudes, increased self-awareness and awareness and concern for others, greater emotional and behavioural control, and pro-social behaviour. It is through the therapeutic alliance that treatment becomes a joint venture into which the client willingly enters and engages in treatment. This relationship includes the fit between the emotional experiences of both clinician and youth, the effect of the clinician's attitudes on the client, and the youth's investment of trust, safety, and faith in the therapist as an agent of hope and change.

In fact, depending on how one defines the nature and goals of sex offender treatment, many of the tasks of therapy can be accomplished only through the development of a meaningful relationship between the clinician and youth. Such relationships can only be built over time, and are key to the pacing of treatment and what can be accomplished during any given period in the therapeutic relationship. An enriching therapeutic relationship can facilitate the youth's ability and willingness to explore difficult emotional areas, and become more self-expressive, as well as recognising and responding to the needs of other people. In this regard, it is the clinician's role to establish a climate that facilitates change and prepares the youth for emotionally uncomfortable experiences while changing, and provide a level of support for the client while working on difficult issues.

Ablon and Jones (1998) defined a prototype for both psychodynamic and cognitive-behavioural therapy that recognised essential differences between the two treatment models. A single combined prototype integrates the functions and approach of both models, and offers a view of the effective therapist as flexible, able to assume different styles to match the needs of the client and changing treatment circumstances, able to use and combine supportive and task-focused approaches, and capable of using the methods and approaches typically associated with both therapeutic forms. This prototype (Rich, 2003) describes 31 therapist characteristics organised into five categories reflecting the totality of an integrated prototype from which the clinician draws:

Therapeutic categories	Clinician attributes
Interactive style	1. Confident and self-assured. 2. Empathic and sensitive. 3. Emotionally neutral. 4. Supportive, non-judgmental, and accepting. 5. Informed by affective issues.
Use of therapy	6. Uses therapy to recognise cognitive framework. 7. Uses therapy to understand the client's phenomenological experience. 8. Uses therapy to understand the way that the client relates to others. 9. Uses therapy to re-frame client's experiences and events. 10. Uses therapy to instruct.
Therapeutic focus	11. Emotional experiences. 12. Cognitive themes, ideas, and beliefs. 13. Psychological defensiveness. 14. Avoidance of difficult feelings. 15. Recurrent themes in the client's experience. 16. Current and recent life experiences. 17. Connections between current and past experiences. 18. Insight or new understanding. 19. Meaning and clarification.
Executive function	20. Defines and controls structure, including content. 21. Ensures focused discussion. 22. Seeks clarification. 23. Sets therapeutic activities or tasks to be completed outside of the session.
Facilitative	24. Communicates clearly. 25. Facilitates the client's ability to speak freely. 26. Explains treatment rationale. 27. Discusses and defines treatment goals. 28. Ensures the client understands what is expected. 29. Ensures the client is committed to the work. 30. Gives explicit advice and direction. 31. Encourages the client to try or adopt new behaviors.

Figure 16.3   A prototype of clinician attributes, combining 31 elements common to cognitive-behavioral and psychodynamic treatment into an integrated prototype, grouped into five therapeutic categories (Rich, 2003)

- interactive style
- use of therapy
- therapeutic focus
- executive function
- facilitation

Figure 16.3 shows the 31 individual attributes grouped into an integrated prototype.

Drawn from this model, combined with a model of treatment influenced by attachment theory and an understanding of the youth's attachment needs in the therapeutic relationship, we can identify 14 aspects that drive the work of the attachment-informed clinician (Rich, 2006):

1. The therapist is experienced as dependable, reliable, consistent, emotionally responsive, and supportive.
2. The therapist fosters a meaningful relationship in which the client can feel secure, form a bond, and engage in self-expression.
3. The therapist encourages and allows both self-dependency and help-seeking in the client, recognising that although these behaviours may seem exclusive of one another they are, in fact, mutually compatible.
4. The therapist builds an environment in which the client feels secure, recognised, valued,

and connected, and in which the client may engage in exploration, expressing and working through problems.

5. The therapist recognises the client's attachment patterns, and uses these to individualise treatment interventions that fit the attachment needs of each client.

6. The therapist becomes attuned to the client's attachment-related needs, remaining aware of the need for emotional connection with the client.

7. The therapist helps the client to recognise and explore relationships and strategies for building and maintaining social connections.

8. The therapist helps the client recognise that relationships, ideas, and attitudes are related to and often the result of prior experiences, including early and on-going significant relationships.

9. The therapist challenges the client, offering opportunities for the client to stretch emotionally and cognitively, creating opportunities for new learning while remaining in the proximal learning zone. (The proximal learning zone is conceptualized by Vygotsky (1978) as the learning junction between the child's actual developmental level and the edge of the next developmental leap, at which point the potential for learning is immediately ahead. Treatment is ideally paced and on the boundary between the actual and proximal learning zones, never too far ahead or treatment will fail, and always informed by and aware of proximal learning capacity).

10. The therapist creates and recognises boundaries, maintaining a level of closeness that fits the needs, capacities, and attachment style of each client.

11. The therapist is attuned to personal feelings that develop as a result of the therapeutic relationship (counter-transference), using these to better understand the client and the therapeutic relationship, guide treatment interventions, and maintain appropriate boundaries.

12. The therapist maintains clear but flexible boundaries, allowing the development of a genuine relationship but able to move in and out of engagement with the client as needed.

13. The therapist helps the client develop the capacity to experience and tolerate difficulty, uncertainty, and doubt.

14. The therapist sensitively dissolves the therapeutic bond when appropriate, so that it will serve as a model for handling separations in life.

Attachment theory teaches us that we develop a view of ourselves and others through early important relationships, and that these early relationships have a remarkable effect throughout our lives. Although attachment theory has weaknesses and leaves many questions unanswered, and the concept of attachment is not well understood past early to middle childhood, we can nevertheless apply a perspective to our work that is informed by attachment theory. For a brief review of attachment theory and its implications for our work with sexually abusive youth, see Rich (2007).

Treatment structure

Therapy is enhanced and facilitated when the process embodies confidence in the client, an expectation of success, and empathic warmth for the client. Beverly James (1994) describes the therapeutic environment as one in which the client feels emotionally safe enough to explore difficult issues, in which the therapeutic alliance is achieved only when the purpose, structure, and methods of treatment are understandable, consistent, and predictable.

However, therapy not only occurs within a relationship, but the relationship itself occurs within a therapeutic structure that provides safety and protection for both client and clinician. Structure provides order and consistency to the therapeutic relationship and process, defines roles, and communicates expectations for both clinician and juvenile (Day and Sparacio, 1989). Therapy, therefore, is enhanced and facilitated when roles are clarified, structure and rules are discussed and understood, and the treatment process is explained, including what the client can expect and what is expected from the client. Recognising that structure cannot substitute for clinician competence, effective therapeutic structure is:

- Flexible and open to modification.
- Guided by a rationale that can be explained, without unnecessary or purposeless rules.
- Clear in rules and expectations for staff and clients.
- Neither over-structured, rigid, nor punitive.
- Shaped by each individual client's need for structure.

- Sensitive to client needs, readiness, tolerance level, and resistance.
- Empathically attuned to and valuing of the client.
- Supportive of and confident in client capacity for change.
- Provided by treatment staff who maintain a professional demeanour.

Functional therapy

Transforming these attributes of the clinician and the treatment environment into practice means envisioning what form therapy might take in the treatment of sexually abusive youth.

Recalling that the common factors model asserts that underlying all technique lie relationship factors, we recognise that a cognitive-behavioural approach devoid of relationships is unlikely to contribute to the development of a therapeutic alliance. Indeed, this was the conclusion of both Castonguay et al. (1996) and Ablon and Jones (1998) who noted that when prescriptive elements of cognitive-behavioural treatment were used without applying the relational skills of clinical work, therapy outcome was negative. Alternatively, there is little to convince us that deeply psychodynamic therapy is of any practical use in the treatment of sexually abusive behaviour. Consequently, the integrated prototype (Figure 16.3) blends elements of both cognitive-behavioural and psychodynamic treatment into a single model, because it appears that both orientations have great values in a well-rounded approach to sex offender specific treatment. Further, this prototype omits the extremes of either form of therapy and instead combines the strengths of both psychodynamic and cognitive-behavioural therapy into a single model of therapeutic interaction.

If the goals of therapy include self-awareness and insight, as well as cognitive and behavioural change, the therapy provided must be built around the integrated prototype, capable of increasing personal and social awareness while providing cognitive-behavioural guidance. Such a therapy must therefore be pragmatic, as the goals are neither increased awareness nor improved self-expression alone, but include the rehabilitation of ideas and behaviours in order to decrease antisocial behaviour. This therapy is not focused on deeply unconscious processes and conflicts, but is instead focused on understanding the roots and effects of *everyday* interactions, and aimed at producing useful information and results in order to change attitudes and behaviours. At the same time, bearing in mind that 85 per cent of therapeutic change is influenced by interpersonal factors, we recognise a therapy that is relationship-oriented and reflects and embodies the alliance between client and clinician.

Accordingly, for the sexually abusive youth, a pragmatic form of therapy will emphasise the counselling relationship and highlight the clinician's role as guide, and, while focusing on the development of insight and awareness, it will place limited emphasis on unconscious ideas that may or may not lie beneath behaviour. Related to therapist attributes, therefore, the clinician's approach (or focus) will be high in interaction, support, direction, and interpretation. With respect to attributes of the therapeutic process, therapy will be high in the discovery of ideas, attitudes, relationships, and motivators that have practical value to the client, and low in exploration of the unconscious. Accordingly, the application of therapy with sexually abusive youth will be interactive and interpersonal, concentrating on building the therapeutic alliance, developing shared goals, and helping clients to recognise how they are affected by their experiences and interactions, and how these shape their cognitions, emotions, and behaviours. From here, the clinician can help sexually abusive youths recognise and more fully experience their impact on others, the nature of their relationships, their values, and their personal goals and how to accomplish them.

The focus, then, is on the more concrete end of the cognitive scale, closer to conscious awareness and immediate recognition where insight and self-awareness have more meaning and more practical value. This emphasis on high relationship and practical application of ideas lends itself to an interpersonal, or client-centred, and functional form of psychodynamic therapy, shown in Figure 16.4, with an emphasis on self-awareness and personal development. This form of high engagement with a focus on practical discovery is described in the upper left quadrant as 'Interpersonal Functional Therapy.'

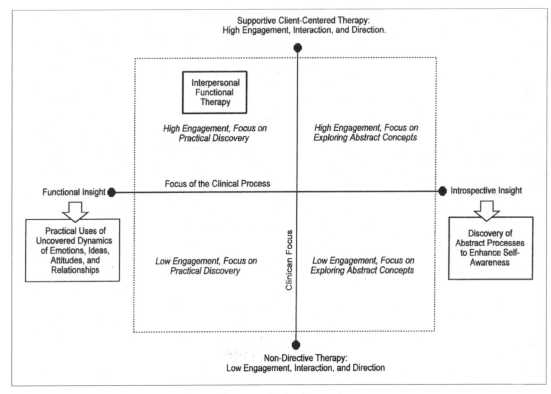

Figure 16.4   Interpersonal functional therapy for sexually abusive youth

How to engage youth in treatment

Responding most directly to the title of the chapter, how do we best engage sexually abusive youth in treatment? The first answer is that, as clinicians, on the twin levels of the therapeutic relationship and the case formulation, we don't treat them any differently than we would any child or adolescent, or adult for that matter, whom we are treating. That is, other than providing specific treatment interventions aimed at the sexually abusive behaviour, in terms of how we conceptualise the case we apply the same level of understanding as we would (or should) in all cases. We try to understand our clients in their totality or 'wholeness,' and not just their sexually abusive behaviour. In terms of our treatment of them, not the application and provision of psycho-educational ideas, we build the same sort of therapeutic relationship as we would (or should) with any client. In this relationship, we are genuine, actively engaged, tuned in to the phenomenological world of the client, strive to experience empathy for the client,

and find ways to genuinely value and care for and about our client, and ensure that our client feels understood, valued, and cared for. And, because this is therapy, and not relationship building per se, we must, at the same time, maintain an all-important clinical distance so that we can remain neutral and objective, despite our engagement.

This kind of therapy is far more difficult and energy consuming than a therapy guided by treatment protocols or workbooks, and requires good training and supervision. This is a therapy of engagement, in which the clinician is a significant conduit for self-realisation and change in the client, and in which the therapeutic relationship becomes a crucible in which growth is fermented and from which change emerges. This *is* an attached relationship, in which the clinician serves as caregiver and the client as the individual receiving (and presumably needing) the care and direction, containing many of the elements expected in attachment relationships, as described by Margaret Parish and Morris Eagle (2003). They found that clients admired and found their therapists emotionally available, sought proximity to their therapists and evoked mental representations of their therapists in the therapist's absence, and experienced their therapists as a source of personal security and confidence outside of therapy.

In fact, if we wish to 'engage' our clients in treatment, they must come to feel we care for and about them, and that we understand them and are acting in their best interests. In order to have them see us in this way, we must *actually* feel this way. The irony here is that, in treating sexually abusive youth, the primary mode of treatment is not sex offender specific at all. We recognise our clients as sexual offenders, yet acknowledge and respond to them as people. Most of the work involves the *universal* work of therapy, embedded in relationships and about discovery, within which we apply the techniques and teach the ideas of sex offender specific treatment.

There are, then, returning to the opening theme of the chapter, two types of sex offender specific treatment. There is the type in which treatment is necessarily sterilised and objectified, reduced into protocols that contain defined techniques and interventions that can be placed into treatment manuals. This model in great part depends on the clinician's adherence to technique, as well as the motivation of the client and the client's adoption of cognitive ideas and behavioural plans.

And there is the type of sex offender specific treatment described here, in which the specific techniques, interventions, and protocols of sex offender specific treatment are embedded within the therapeutic relationship, rather than vice versa. It is not that protocol and techniques are not important (indeed, as noted, they are), or that protocols cannot describe or depend upon the development of the therapeutic relationship and the resulting therapeutic bond and alliance. However, it is difficult to know how exactly to manualise the skills required for a therapeutic relationship. In this second, and increasingly common form of treatment for sexually abusive youth, we return to a model of treatment that delivers specific sexual abuse work within a larger and more holistic treatment environment in which the child is recognised as a whole person. In this model, we recognise that sexually abusive behaviour is, in most cases, an attempt, no matter how distorted, to engage in a social relationship and accomplish desired social goals. For many sexually abusive youth, and even adult sexual offenders, sexually abusive behaviour is a

disturbed way to meet social needs and make social connections.

Twelve tips for engagement

There are many final points to be made about engagement in treatment, most of which have been described in the literature of psychotherapy for decades. However, I have selected 12 points, which seem a fitting way to conclude this chapter, summing up its ideas and pointing the way to engagement in treatment.

Nevertheless, despite our best efforts, there are always going to be clients with whom we cannot engage, and quite probably clients we find it difficult to like, although hopefully this will be the exception rather than the rule. There are also going to be clients who, despite real engagement, seem unable or unwilling (or perhaps not ready) to change. Hence, all of these 'tips' or take home points, are easier said than done. Despite this, they offer the keys to engaging with clients, whether voluntary or involuntary, in treatment.

1. *Formulate the case.* Learn about the client and his or her developmental pathways, and the factors that have contributed to who the child is today and what motivated or led to his or her behaviours, including sexually abusive behaviour. Develop a theory about what makes your client tick, and under what circumstances.
2. *Recognise wholeness.* Your clients are more than simply, or only, sexually abusive youth. They are complete people, who are much more than their behaviour alone. Many life issues and developmental forces come together to produce each individual and the behaviour of each individual. Despite some of their behaviour, most of the children and adolescents with whom we work are not deviant sexual offenders, nor especially bad people. Accordingly, recognise the totality, or the wholeness of your clients, and make sure that they recognise that you see and value them.
3. *Build relationships.* Most of the work is about relationships and rehabilitation, not teaching concepts about sexually abusive behaviour, although this is an essential part of the work.
4. *Work from strengths.* Discover for yourself and help your clients find their strengths, and work to build upon these.

5. *Like your clients*. This goes hand in hand with working from your client's strengths. It is not only important to not judge, dismiss and disrespect clients, but more to the point it is important to actively *like* them. Right to the point, the child psychiatrist Uri Bronfenbrenner commented that all children want someone to be crazy about them.

6. *Authenticity*. Be genuine in your relationships with your clients.

7. *Unlock and demonstrate empathy*. Experience the world that your client lives within, and the way that he or she experiences that world. Your capacity to be empathically attuned to your client may help your client learn to recognise the experiences of and experience empathy for others.

8. *Start where the client is at*. Recognise the developmental, cognitive, and emotional capacities of each client, as well their individual needs, and start treatment at that point. This means designing and employing interventions that match each client's current level.

9. *Maintain the right emotional distance*. Recognise and respond to each client's attachment needs and style. Some clients need to get closer to you, some need to remain more distant. Maintaining your own appropriate boundaries will help you to set the 'right' emotional distance, based on the individual needs and styles of each client.

10. *Pace treatment*. Remember that some things happen later in treatment rather than earlier. Don't expect too much too soon, and think about a logical progression in treatment for each client. In some cases, recognise that the things you want to get at may not emerge until much later in treatment, if at all, such as the 'truth' behind the nature or extent of the sexually abusive behaviour.

11. *Expect regression*. This is the phenomenon of one step forward, two steps back. At different times and under different circumstances, clients will move forward and then appear to fall back in treatment. They usually haven't really fallen back, but have just stepped off to one side or taken a dead end road. They may not be able to move forward, but they almost certainly haven't lost all of the gains previously made.

12. *Change comes slowly*. Recognise that changing means giving up prior ways of behaving that were, more likely than not, adaptive in some way, and that change not only means finding new ways to adapt but comes slowly.

Conclusion

Working with adolescents who engage in sexually abusive behaviour, or, more specifically, *engaging* such youth in treatment, is straightforward to the degree that the work is no different than therapeutic work with any other client population. That is, the workbooks, the relapse prevention plans, and the interventions targeted specifically towards sexually aggressive and inappropriate behaviour are interwoven into a larger treatment programme that is no different than any other kind of broad treatment programme addressed towards troubling and troubled adolescent behaviour. However, the individual practitioner has to decide whether model one or model two is most appropriate, both from a philosophical perspective about treatment and with regard to what constitutes necessary and effective treatment.

Model one is constituted by the 'one-size-fits-all' approach that is technique and technically driven. This model/philosophy is exemplified by Quinsey et al. (1998: 72) who write that 'treatment methods are sufficiently well specified that they can be taught to intelligent laypeople . . . the general conclusion seems to be that clinical intuition, experience, and training . . . are not helpful in either (evaluation) or treatment delivery'. Conversely, model two is that described in this chapter, in which we recognise that our capacity as trained, experienced, and knowledgeable clinicians (in the areas of child and adolescent development, mental health, and forensics) is central to the work.

With respect to this second model, we recall the common factors model in which 40 per cent of therapeutic outcome is dependent upon client variables, or what the client brings into treatment. In this model, it's clear that who the client is, what the client brings into treatment, and the client's attitudes and perspectives about treatment are very much influenced by the therapeutic relationship, which, in turn, has an impact upon the expectancy effect, or the client's belief that things can and will improve through therapy. Accordingly, outcome variables are chiefly moulded by client expectations, therapeutic alliance, and placebo effect that work together. The argument here is straightforward;

it's the therapeutic relationship that makes the difference in the capacity to engage the client in treatment.

From this perspective, engaging involuntary juvenile sexual offenders in treatment is a matter of therapeutic practice and skill, transforming involuntary participants into voluntary participants through, not technique, but clinical skill.

References

Ablon, J.S. and Jones, E.E. (1998.) How Expert Clinicians' Prototypes of an Ideal Treatment Correlate with Outcome in Psychodynamic and Cognitive-Behavioural Therapy. *Psychotherapy Research*, 8, 71–83.

Asay, T.P. and Lambert, M.L. (1999) The Empirical Case for the Common Factors in Therapy: Quantitative Finding. In Hubble, M.A., Duncan, B.L. and Miller, S.D. (Eds.) *The Heart and Soul of Change: What Works in Therapy*. Washington, DC: American Psychological Association.

Bachelor, A. and Horvath, A. (1999) The Therapeutic Relationship. In Hubble, M.A., Duncan, B.L. and Miller, S.D. (Eds.) *The Heart and Soul of Change: What Works in Therapy*. Washington, DC: American Psychological Association.

Blanchard, G.T. (1998) *The Difficult Connection: The Therapeutic Relationship in Sexual Offender Treatment*. Brandon, VT: Safer Society Press.

Bordin, E.S. (1976) The Generalisability of the Psychoanalytical Concept of the Working Alliance. *Psychotherapy: Theory, Research, and Practice*, 16, 252–60.

Castonguay, L.G. et al. (1996) Predicting the Effect of Cognitive Therapy for Depression: A Study of Unique and Common Factors. *Journal of Consulting and Clinical Psychology*, 64, 497–504.

Day, R.W. and Sparacio, R.T. (1989) Structuring the Counselling Process. In Dryden, W. (Ed.) *Key Issues for Counselling in Action* (16–25) London: Sage.

Dryden, W. (1989) The Therapeutic Alliance as an Integrating Framework. In Dryden, W. (Ed.) *Key Issues for Counselling in Action*. London: Sage.

Holmes, J. and Bateman, A. (2002) *Integration In Psychotherapy: Models and Methods*. Oxford: Oxford University Press.

James, B. (1994) *Handbook for Treatment of Attachment-Trauma Problems in Children*. New York: The Free Press.

Keijsers, G.P., Schaap, C.P. and Hoogduin, C.A. (2000) The Impact of Interpersonal Patient and Therapist Behaviour on Outcome in Cognitive-Behaviour Therapy: A Review of Empirical Studies. *Behaviour Modification*, 24, 264–97.

Kirby, D. (2001) Understanding What Works and What Doesn't in Reducing Adolescent Sexual Risk-Taking. *Family Planning Perspectives*, 33, 276–81.

Lambert, M.J. (1992) Implications of Outcome Research for Psychotherapy Integration. In Norcross, J.C. and Goldstein, M.R. (Eds.) *Handbook of Psychotherapy Integration*. New York: Basic Books.

Lambert, M.J. and Bergin, A.E. (1993) The Effectiveness of Psychotherapy. In Bergin, A.E. and Garfield, S.L. (Eds.) *Handbook of Psychotherapy and Behaviour Change*. 4th edn. New York: John Wiley.

Minuchin, S. and Fishman, H.C. (1981) *Family Therapy Techniques*. Cambridge, MA: Harvard University Press.

Norcross, J.C. (2000) Toward the Delineation of Empirically Based Principles in Psychotherapy: Commentary on Beutler (2000) *Prevention and Treatment*. From Http:// Www.Journals.Apa.Org/Prevention/ Volume3/Pre0030028c.Html.

Parish, M. and Eagle, M.N. (2003) Attachment to the Therapist. *Psychoanalytic Psychology*, 20, 271–86.

Quinsey, V.L. et al. (1998) *Violent Offenders: Appraising and Managing Risk*. Washington, DC: American Psychological Association.

Rich, P. (2003) *Understanding Juvenile Sexual Offenders: Assessment, Treatment, and Rehabilitation*. New York, John Wiley.

Rich, P. (2006) *Attachment and Sexual Offending: Understanding and Applying Attachment Theory to the Treatment of Juvenile Sexual Offenders*. Chichester: John Wiley and Son.

Rich, P. (2007) The Implications of Attachment Theory in the Treatment of Sexually Abusive Youth. In Calder, M.C. (Ed.) *Working with Children and Young People who Sexually Abuse: Taking the Field Forward*. Lyme Regis: Russell House Publishing.

Vygotsky, L.S. (1978) *Mind In Society: The Development of Higher Psychological Processes*. Cambridge: Harvard University Press.

CHAPTER 17

Working with Parents for Family Safety where Domestic Violence is a Child Protection Concern

Erica Flegg and Calvin Bell

Mandation of parents for treatment

Our work comprises risk assessment and treatment in two family law contexts: private law, that is, disputed child contact/residence cases, and public law, as in child protection proceedings. In this chapter we examine some of the issues arising from our experience of assessing parents for treatment suitability and delivering treatment in public law cases. Effectively, parents are 'mandated' to participate if treatment is recommended to reduce risk, and the local authority will move to take children into care or proceed to put children for adoption if the parents do not successfully undertake treatment, assuming this position is supported by the court. The court, therefore, does not itself 'order' treatment, although it may order assessment of treatment suitability. Public money is available through legal aid for assessment, but not for treatment, which is at the discretion of the local authority. Moreover, the family law system is adversarial, with different 'players' pursuing their interests through their legal representatives, a system in which we, like others engaged as experts, do not have any legal representation.

Effective mandation will therefore only occur when parents believe, and are advised by their lawyers, that their best chance, or only hope, of family rehabilitation and closure of the case is successful participation in treatment. This can be undermined where the local authority is unconvinced about the need for or likely success of treatment, or the type of treatment recommended, and/or where other experts are appointed who do not support our treatment recommendations or do not accept the results of our suitability assessments. All too frequently, local authorities simply do not commission the recommended work even where parents are deemed suitable, because of shortage of funds; typically, rather than stating that they cannot afford to pay, there is then an unsuccessful attempt to shift responsibility elsewhere such as to primary care trusts. Parents therefore find themselves in a context where they are also 'players' and can make their own assessment of the likely consequences of declining to participate in the recommended treatment.

For this reason, where parents are reluctant to engage with treatment, which is the case with most of our referrals, we are reliant on the support of the local authority, and preferably also the children's guardian, to supply mandation for treatment. With other referrals it may be the case that the parents are ready, willing and able to start treatment, but the local authority does not wish to support or fund it; where the latter are nevertheless pressured into doing so for want of an alternative to progress the case, it can be seen that the question of client mandation and motivation is posed in quite a different way, as is the nature of the therapist-client relationship. In both cases, however, our agency is in a position of power in relation to the client or clients, where both parents are referred, since we are the assessors of risk, of suitability for treatment, and of the level of therapeutic engagement, and ultimately, of risk reduction/success of treatment.

From this outline it can readily be seen that this is a very different context for treatment from that of the criminal justice system. Mandation of clients to reduce the risk of domestic violence, however, is usually thought of in terms of perpetrator programmes for men who have been convicted for assaulting their partner, there being no designated crime of 'domestic violence' per se. Their partners, moreover, are usually offered only some, often quite inadequate, safety support and are not mandated to participate. In this context, women are seen as 'victims', and children, when considered at all, are incidental victims, since the women concerned may or may not be mothers. Practitioners who work in the specialised milieu of domestic violence mainly comprise those trained in the criminal justice field or those who work in the voluntary sector, particularly the women's refuge movement. Both of these contexts are dominated by a perspective derived from 'radical' feminism, in which men are seen as perpetrators and women as victims, even if they are designated as 'survivors' for ideological reasons, and in which the questioning of a mother's 'ability to protect' is generally contested as a form of oppression in which she is held accountable for the consequences of *his* violence.[1]

Social workers find themselves in something of a dilemma since they are charged with a legal duty to protect children, although trained in the same feminist paradigm concerning domestic violence. Moreover, current practice means that they are increasingly impelled towards assessment of parenting and away from intervention to support parental change. The result tends to be that parents who have experienced domestic violence in their relationship are warned that there must be no recurrence in the interest of child protection, and when there is recurrence, as there is likely to be without preventive intervention, the mother is pressurised to choose between her partner and her children. Many vulnerable mothers resist making such a choice or are unable, without support, to 'choose' their children (i.e. to separate). Consequently, many children either continue to be exposed to the harmful effects of exposure to domestic violence or else to the harmful effects of being taken into care. In the absence of specialist services to work for family safety, they will then often move towards being placed for adoption.

Our agency has developed a specialised risk assessment model, the Risk Assessment Framework, which helps the courts and concerned professionals to quantify risk of domestic violence in families by identifying and rating risk and vulnerability factors. We also attempt to help identify those parents most amenable to change within the children's timescale needs for permanency and stability and can offer treatment. Our treatment model is tailored to address the risks identified in our risk assessment, and we have a 'menu' of treatment goals or targets from which we select for the particular case. Mandation of the parents with whom we work, therefore, also takes place within a timeframe that is very circumscribed, and early referral for our services is clearly indicated (though seldom achieved).

Our paradigm and professional ethics

Like other colleagues indicated above, our work has also grown from a feminist perspective on domestic violence, but we attempt to avoid the pitfalls of the binary perpetrator/victim approach where possible, since this poses some difficulties in the risk assessment model which of necessity separates risk and vulnerability factors. We recognise that both men and women can be violent, and that many violent relationships involve abusive behaviour on the part of the primary victim, but we also recognise that men hold more social as well as physical power than women and that parenting roles are unequal. However, we see both socially prescribed gender roles, the 'masculine' and the 'feminine', as containing oppressive elements, and recognise that men's unacknowledged and socially prohibited vulnerability and dependency often underpins their abuse of power in relationships with women and children. We are also aware of the extent to which abusive fathers are likely to be survivors of abuse in childhood, because our risk assessment model draws attention to this as a risk factor.

In terms of responsibility for violence, we never hold victims responsible for the abuse perpetrated against them, but we do hold adult victims (mothers) accountable for their choices that affect their own and their children's safety, and we work with them to increase their psychological autonomy and efficacy, recognising that the language of 'choice' often obscures the fact that clients' behaviour is often not motivated by conscious decision-making. Where mothers are also violent and/or abusive, even if their violence is mainly self-defensive or retaliatory, we work with them to change their behaviour and to avoid escalating the risk of domestic violence. We work with both parents, or care-givers – many of the men we treat are not the biological fathers of some or all of the children in the household – to understand the impact of domestic violence on children and to increase parental capacity for empathy.

Our perspective also differs from the dominant feminist paradigm in that we recognise, and our risk assessment model cites the evidence, that social and environmental factors, particularly adverse childhood experience and poverty, greatly influence the risk and vulnerability factors that sit on top of gender. While it is true that domestic violence cuts across all social classes and subcultures, it is also true that it affects the 'socially excluded' at far higher rates than it affects others; and it also occurs at higher rates in families with children than in childless couples. These realities, while amply supported by empirical evidence, are ignored and obscured by public policy; they are also contested or disregarded by the radical feminist lobby, who focus solely on gender concerns, with the result that those who are most vulnerable to domestic violence remain socially invisible. Resources to combat domestic violence, which are grossly inadequate in any event, are consequently not targeted where they are most needed, i.e. to helping families in the child protection system.

Because we put the safety of children first, as the most vulnerable, we do not see it as problematic that parents be mandated to work for family safety and this therefore presents no ethical dilemmas for us as therapists. We do not feel that our professional practice is compromised, but rather that this context for therapeutic work requires higher levels of skill. Moreover, where parents cannot engage with treatment to prevent domestic violence within the timescales, we feel that it is likely to be best for their children to be placed elsewhere, and so in our hierarchy of successful treatment outcomes (see Table 17.1 below) discovering this earlier rather than later is deemed a successful outcome for the children; we do not advocate for continued treatment no matter what the performance of the parents. Fortunately, in terms of the objective needs of children, we do not have a financial interest in advocating for treatment, since our business resides primarily in risk assessment. However, regrettably, privatisation of services does inevitably entail that some agencies develop a vested interest in advocating for services that they provide. In the case of residential assessments, this can be very expensive to the public purse through the funding by legal aid, and moreover does not provide effective intervention to address longer-term family safety concerns.

Lastly, because our clients are generally the least privileged members of our society, and also the least likely to seek therapy or have the resources to access it, we see the mandate for treatment through the child protection system as a form of social redistribution in which parents who are socially marginalised may be helped to enrich their own and their children's lives, even if reluctant to engage with the process at the outset. Whatever one's values with regard to social justice, this is clearly in the interests of the children most at risk, since many children exposed to domestic violence also present social problems later on, including raised risk of experiencing domestic violence in their adult relationships. Policy to counteract anti-social behaviour in young people fails to take account of the fact that many of them have grown up in violent or abusive families, and that parenting programmes are an inadequate response to this. Many of the parents we see have themselves been failed as children in terms of the public duty to protect them, and this provides an additional reason in favour of the argument that resources should be allocated to help them and their own children before the cycle is repeated.

'Therapy culture' and aspirations of 'personal growth' are not familiar for our client group, but those who most 'need help' may be those least inclined to seek it and those least able to have access to the necessary resources. Therefore we feel that our clients, particularly given their damaged personal histories and social deprivation, 'deserve' help even when they often strongly object and perceive it as thrust upon them. Our most rewarding work is done with clients who eventually feel not only a sense of gratitude for the service they initially rejected, but more importantly, a sense of personal achievement in overcoming their own resistance and playing an active part in the transformation of their lives, becoming, for the first time, drivers of their own destinies.

From an ethical perspective, our difficulty is not so much what we are tasked to do with our clients, as with the fact that our society allocates so few resources to help these families and there is such a dearth of services of the kind we offer. Arguably, working with mandated parents to reduce the risk of domestic violence through the child protection system could be promoted as a more effective way to combat the problem than working through the criminal justice system, whose success rates are unimpressive in terms of recidivism and which does not reach mothers or children. As is well known, mothers frequently do not support prosecution, and mandatory prosecution policies do not adequately address the reasons why they may not perceive prosecution to be in the best interests of the family.[2] Another factor is that in terms of motivation for perpetrators to engage with treatment, fathers seem to be more motivated than men without families.

Table 17.1   Treatment viability indicators

Factors	unsuitable	→			suitable
1	**Understanding of child protection concerns**	No understanding of the child protection concerns	Little understanding of the child protection concerns	Some understanding of the child protection concerns	Understands the concerns and the purpose of treatment	Fully understands the concerns and the purpose of treatment
2	**Attitude to child protection concerns**	Totally rebuts all child protection concerns	Largely rebuts the child protection concerns	Partially accepts the child protection concerns	Accepts the child protection concerns	Fully accepts the child protection concerns
3	**Attitude to treatment goals**	Refusal to address treatment goals	Refusal to address some of the treatment goals	Ambivalent but willing to address the treatment goals	Desire to address all treatment goals	Strong desire to address all treatment goals
4	**Willingness to work collaboratively**	Confrontational stance	Will not collaborate (or is overly compliant)	Some collaboration with the therapist	Collaborates	Collaborates fully
5	**Authenticity of presentation**	Previous deceit; evidence of current deceit	Previous deceit; inauthentic presentation	Previous deceit; evasive	Previous deceit; authentic presentation	No history of deceit; authentic presentation
6	**Motivation to pursue change through treatment**	No motivation	Minimal motivation	Ambivalent	Some motivation	Highly motivated
7	**Insight**	No capacity or desire to self-reflect	Little capacity or desire to self-reflect	Some capacity and desire to self-reflect	Capacity and desire to self-reflect	High capacity and desire to self-reflect
8	**Cognitive distortion**	Frequent and significant cognitive impairment	Distortions of perceptions, attribution, interpretations etc.	Occasional distortions	Some minor distortions	No obvious distortions
9	**Emotional regulation**	Highly reactive to aversive feelings	Reactive to aversive feelings	Some capacity to contain aversive feelings	Capacity to contain aversive feelings	High capacity to contain aversive feelings
10	**Attendance**	Less than 50% attendance	Irregular attendance	Some unacceptable absences	No unacceptable absences	Full attendance and regular punctuality
11	**Substance use**	Frequently arrives for sessions under the influence	Has arrived for session under the influence	Not under the influence but adverse effects from recent use	No adverse effects on treatment from recent substance use	No known substance misuse
12	**Assignments**	Unwilling or unable to complete homework	No homework completed	Some homework completed	Homework completed	All homework completed well

Table 17.1   Continued

Factors	unsuitable		suitable		
Context					
Life circumstances	Life circumstances likely to make treatment unworkable	Life circumstances likely to compromise treatment	Life circumstances unlikely to impact on treatment	Life circumstances likely to support treatment	Life circumstances likely to enhance treatment
Access	Transport/childcare problems likely to make treatment unworkable	Transport/childcare problems likely to compromise attendance	Transport/childcare issues unlikely to impact on attendance	Transport/childcare arrangements likely to facilitate attendance	Transport/childcare arrangements likely to ensure full attendance
The local authority's position	LA position and resourcing likely to make treatment unworkable	LA position and resourcing likely to compromise treatment	LA position and resourcing unlikely to impact on treatment	LA position and resourcing likely to support treatment	LA position and resourcing likely to enhance treatment
Inter-agency functioning	Effect of multi-agency functioning is likely to make treatment unviable	Multi-agency functioning is likely to undermine treatment	Multi-agency functioning is unlikely to impact on treatment	Multi-agency functioning is likely to support treatment	Multi-agency functioning is likely to enhance treatment

Some difficulties of the child protection context for mandation

Our clients, male or female, are all parents, or cohabiters or step-parents in households where there are child protection concerns because of risk of exposure to domestic violence. There may be an established history of domestic violence between the couple concerned or there may be concerns about risk because of the histories of either or both parents. In the latter case, it is typically particularly difficult to persuade the parents that there is a valid concern about the risk of something occurring in future that may not have occurred between them in the past.

Because our work takes place in the context of intervention by social services, there is the particular difficulty of working with people whose personal lives are subject to high levels of scrutiny in the most intimate areas of personal, sexual and family life. The client group is subject to frequent assessment, child protection review meetings and the like in which large numbers of different professionals are involved, including at times foster parents, head teachers, family doctors, health visitors and so on. It is often not sufficiently appreciated, we think, how stressful and intrusive this is for the families concerned; we try to show our clients an empathic awareness of this, without losing the focus on the need to work for safety.

We are all sensitive to having our parenting criticised and examined. Humiliation is a key issue for our clients and it is also a key factor in domestic violence: men behaving aggressively in response to the perception of humiliation and women feeling oppressed by the humiliation of the child protection process on top of prior sensitivity to abuse; this complicates our work. Offenders in the criminal justice system are often able to accept that they have violated a social or moral code: 'thou shalt not kill, steal' etc. The task of intervention is more to induce them to practise and share that code rather than to accept that they have transgressed it. In the family law system, however, parents are required to accept that they have acted against the best interests of their children, and it is contrary to our clients' self-image, as it would be to any parent, to see themselves as 'bad parents'; in this sense we are working against the grain.

We have taken the view that the best context for effective work with our client group is when the local authority concerned gives us mandation and co-operates with us, so that the treatment is harmonised/integrated with their intervention. This is described in more detail below. However, this is often not possible, and sometimes the local authority will be hostile to treatment. Where we believe that the client nevertheless has the potential for change and there is a genuine prospect of working for family/child safety within the timescales, we can find ourselves thrown into a position of potentially 'colluding' with the client to prove to the court that the local authority and/or guardian is wrong about the prospects for rehabilitation.

Such a situation can, of course, provide strong motivation for the client to engage effectively with treatment and to build a working alliance with the therapist. For the therapist, however, there is the danger of being drawn into over-identification with the client and loss of objectivity. Occasionally, difficult feelings towards other professionals and strained professional relationships can result from this situation and we need to process our feelings so that we remain as constructive as possible and preserve important relationships with colleagues with whom we may need to work again on other cases where we may, indeed, find ourselves aligned rather than at odds. This makes particular demands on us because the work with the clients is so taxing in itself and we are likely to be the practitioners with the closest relationship with the parents concerned.

This is one of the reasons that skilled and frequent supervision is necessary for us to manage our work. Another reason for giving importance to supervision is the problems generated by working with both parents, when a male therapist works with the father and a female therapist with the mother, which is our preferred modality when the parental couple is referred. Here again, there is potential for each therapist to identify with their client and to experience tension with the other therapist, or for one or both of the therapists to bring their own gender issues into the way the issues in the case are viewed. Without a commitment to self-critical professional and personal reflection and also openness to honest disclosure of difficulties in a supportive supervisory setting, there is a tendency for the treatment to go off course. We also feel that professional burn-out is predictable if we fail to help each other and enrich our understanding of our work, ourselves and our working relationships with each other. Good supervision, then, is vital; it also provides the main context for professional development in terms of deepening our understanding of domestic violence dynamics and effective ways of intervening.

Because we are human and we are working on a daily basis with disturbing psychic material that is bound to touch upon our own insecurities and any unresolved childhood difficulties, and given that we work within a child protection system that is often frustrating and sometimes dysfunctional in terms of meeting children's needs, it is inevitable that we will suffer stress and not always be aware of our inner conflicts aroused by the work. We try to nurture each other and take care of ourselves. Sometimes we have fits of laughter about terrible things when the absurd takes over; it can feel as if we might seem mad to outsiders at times like this, but allowing ourselves to express our feelings safely helps us to stay sane. By contrast, colleagues who work in social services and probation have little or no opportunity for supervision to process their feelings in response to client material or relations with other professionals, and this likely hinders effective work at times and affects their morale.

'Line management' supervision, which is all that our colleagues usually receive, is of course necessary, but it is not sufficient and tends to increase anxiety in difficult cases, through fear of mistakes and consequences, rather than helping practitioners to manage their own anxiety in the interests of more effective working. Deeper-reaching therapy entails working with uncertainty, and treatment is helped when colleagues join with us in trying to steer a path between erring on the side of caution, such as failure to work to rehabilitate families who might be able to make the necessary changes, or on the side of over-optimism, the failure to mandate parents and allowing unsafe rehabilitation. Clients perceive and often manipulate differences between agencies in terms of attitude to case management, and this is another reason why we strive for effective inter-agency working. Unfortunately, the legal context, or attitudes about it, often seems to obstruct, rather than support, information-sharing and co-operation.

Motivation through child protection

Our work, being focused on the interests of the next generation, is preventive rather than punitive in purpose, but this perception is not typically shared by our clients at the outset. Nevertheless, the desire 'to get social services off our backs and get our children home', can be harnessed to the common end of working towards case closure. We are able to define a common goal with clients in this way and thereby enhance motivation to undertake treatment. Men mandated to attend perpetrator programmes through the criminal justice system may also have a positive motivation, as opposed to the negative one of avoiding further social sanctions for their behaviour, but this is unlikely to be as powerful as the desire to keep their children and prevent the breakup of their families. On the other hand, powerful feelings of anger and shame are likely to be elicited by the intrusion of social services and the courts into family life, which is socially visible in their communities of origin and which carries significant social stigma. This is much more so, it seems, than with involvement in the criminal justice system, where sometimes a criminal history may even carry a certain 'kudos'. Both mothers and fathers frequently manifest strong antipathy to the statutory authority of the child protection system. This anti-authoritarian response poses a challenge to the development of a therapeutic alliance, since we function as part of that system.

In rating clients for suitability for treatment we do assess 'motivation for change' (internal motivation) as one of more than a dozen factors, because our experience is that where clients are able to express a genuine desire for personal change, work is likely to proceed more quickly and a therapeutic alliance is easier to build. However, we also accept external motivation ('if I have to do this to get my children back, I will'), as a sufficient basis to start treatment. We find that clients who start from this basis often develop internal motivation during the course of treatment if they experience the therapist as helpful to them in addressing their distress, frustration and life problems. This is particularly the case when they find that employing new assertiveness skills rather than aggression improves the quality of their inter-personal relationships, not only within the family but also with professionals, leading to progress of their case and a 'positive feedback loop'.

More difficult to help are those clients whose distress is repressed and who are unable to tolerate the anxiety provoked by treatment, because of the necessity to delve below the surface and to open up painful past experiences, often the legacy of childhood trauma, whose lack of resolution contributes to risk and vulnerability. Clients who have little sense of the story of their childhood, and their life in general, poor recollection and poor ability to reflect, can be helped to develop what attachment and narrative therapists would call an 'emotionally coherent narrative history' of their formative experiences, and indeed their difficulties in this respect can be traced to their attachment difficulties in childhood. The therapy then helps the client to make up for their early attachment deficit by learning how to see themselves from the perspective of another and by developing the ability to process their own emotional experience. When the client shows no curiosity about themselves and actively resists exploration of the legacy of past experience, however, the prognosis for significant personal change within the timescales is poor. Treatment goals addressing the relevant issues are in the recommendations from the risk assessment and therefore the client is assessed as to their willingness to address all treatment goals. Where some of the goals are refused, and attempts to shift this inflexibility fail, we are unlikely to rate the parent as suitable for treatment because a successful outcome depends upon the ability to address the identified risk issues.

In this area our treatment approach has at times been undermined by colleagues from other disciplines who do not accept the link we make between identified risk and treatment goals, and object that parents who do not wish to consent to a treatment menu as a package should not be required to do so. The court has sometimes been advised that a 'non-confrontational approach', which usually means 'client-centred', might be more successful with the particular client. While it is of course true that a therapeutic alliance is easier to build when the treatment goals are negotiated with the client, this does not seem to us to meet the needs of child protection because the treatment would begin in an open-ended way with no guarantee that the relationship would be founded on working for family safety or addressing relevant criminogenic need. We accept that therapist style is an important issue and we agree that confrontational approaches to treatment are ineffective because they provoke 'resistance', but the purpose of treatment needs to be clear in our opinion, because the issue is not so much 'Can some form of therapy be found to

engage this client?', but rather 'Can this client engage with therapy to address the risk and/or vulnerability concerns within the children's timescales?' Without the purpose of treatment being clear from the outset, clients cannot really give their informed consent, and they may also be able to sabotage effective treatment by declining to engage with issues brought by the therapist. In addition, without agreed treatment goals addressing safety concerns, how could the progress or success of treatment be measured?

If no negative consequences flow from the client's refusal to engage with a particular treatment goal, i.e. there is no effective mandate, then the safety objective of the work is, in our view, compromised. As stated above, some parents flatly refuse to discuss painful issues from their past or to accept that there is any relationship between past experience and present feelings and behaviour. While it is possible that such resistance might be overcome in the course of therapeutic work, we question the ethics of setting out to work in a short timeframe, typically no more than six months, with such uncertainty, when the needs of children demand that we select those parents most likely to succeed in addressing the relevant risk issues in the time available.

Denial, like motivation, is another contested issue in debates about client suitability for treatment and likely outcome. Again, we feel that treatment success is more likely when denial of risk, or of past behaviour, is not present, but in itself we do not feel denial precludes undertaking treatment, except for those individuals whose denial is a product of self-deception because of narcissistic or psychopathic traits. Participation in treatment can be negotiated on the basis of ensuring future safety even if the parent is unwilling to accept that they have placed their children at risk in the past or are likely to do so in future. This problem, like minimisation, seems to us less fundamental an obstacle to undertaking treatment than rejection of treatment goals.

The question of power in the consulting room

The professional working for behaviour change with a mandated client is by definition working in a context of unequal power relationship. As risk assessors recommending treatment intervention and as practitioners delivering and reporting/evaluating that treatment, we are not offering clients a service that they are free to reject without adverse consequences. As stated above, if this is not clearly the case, our position is weakened, perhaps fatally. Although we are not the decision-makers regarding the future of the children concerned, we do contribute to that process and we are typically perceived by clients as agents of statutory authority. Our choice as therapists is either to try to ally ourselves with the clients to defend their interests in that power system, or to present ourselves as representatives of the system and utilise our power in the consulting room. To attempt to be neutral would be to abrogate our responsibility for child protection, and to fail to make use of the leverage with clients that our position gives us. To most therapists trained to contract with clients on the basis of equality, this is anathema.

By contrast, we believe that the aspiration to equality in the therapeutic relationship is itself misguided and naïve and in some cases, unethical, in that it obscures the reality that troubled and vulnerable people seeking the help of trained professionals are all vulnerable to abuses of power in that relationship, for instance, through sexual impropriety. In our work, because our intervention needs to be guided by children's interests and because the work is mandated by a legal system, we believe the best way of dealing with the reality of the power relationship is not to ignore it and hope that it will not impair the work, but rather to be transparent and accountable in the way we operate. When we do this in a straightforward and non-oppressive way we find that clients tend to welcome it and to accord us more, rather than less, respect.

Accordingly, we:

- Share our criteria for assessment with our clients and invite them to do self-assessment.
- Show clients our feedback to referrers on sessions and invite them to approve our records as accurate.
- Share our concerns with clients and invite them to reflect on the consequences of their possible failure to engage.

It is our experience that this approach reduces hostility and generally works to our advantage in forging a working relationship, since clients are sensitive to power issues and are not 'fooled' by the fiction that we meet as friends or mere helpers; they prefer us to be respectful and professional in our dealings even if our manner is informal and 'friendly'. Similarly, we accept that parents are unlikely to be truthful with us on all occasions, and we do not insist on honesty as a precondition of the work. To do so would be to forge a relationship on a false foundation, since it would indicate our lack of realism to the client and also disallow them from moving to a position in the course of the work where they choose to disclose to us behaviours or deceptions that they have previously kept hidden. Increasing honesty in the relationship is a process that indicates engagement with treatment, in our view, although we often find that other professionals, particularly social workers, will point to evidence of deceit as an invalidation of treatment effectiveness.

Honesty on the part of the client is likely viewed by most psychotherapists as a necessary basis for meaningful work to take place. By contrast, our context for treatment has obliged us to start from the premise that our clients are likely to lie to us, particularly when parents are trying to preserve their relationship with each other. Finding a successful way to build a relationship with the client despite this is 'work in progress' for us. We try to avoid saying to clients that we believe or disbelieve them; rather we convey that we would like them to convince us of their authenticity. In doing so, we believe it is important for them to be able to move to a position where they can own that they have not been truthful in the past without feeling shamed or humiliated. We have worked a case with a mother whose child was eventually successfully rehabilitated despite the local authority having attempted, at great expense, to prove through the court that she was lying about maintaining contact with the father. Because this mother was in fact in the process of engaging with therapy and personal change, she was able finally to break with the father when she saw that colluding with him led to further abuse.

Power itself is a key theme in domestic violence and we believe that in order to confront it as an issue in our clients' personal lives and behaviour we need to be honest and transparent about the way we approach the issue in our own dealings with them, so that they can experience non-abusive ways of using and responding to the exercise of power. Parenting itself is a relationship of power in which children are dependent and vulnerable but needing to be treated with respect, and the way in which the therapist models the respectful and responsible exercise of power is, we believe, an important part of the therapeutic experience for the client.

Working with mothers for family safety

An important distinguishing feature of our risk assessment and treatment model is that we recognise that working with mothers is a vital part of protecting children from exposure to domestic violence. Although this may seem obvious to the outside observer, the fact is that most research and intervention on domestic violence risk and prevention focuses on men. This is true not only in the context of mandated work (criminal justice perpetrator programmes) but also in the women's refuge movement, both of which contexts tend to allocate all responsibility to the man and to see the woman as victim or survivor. Social services, by contrast, tend to perceive women subject to domestic violence as either 'good' or 'bad' mothers. Our work attempts to avoid these binary oppositions and to identify the vulnerabilities of mothers and target them for treatment to enhance a mother's ability to protect herself and her children. Where the mother herself has a tendency to aggression or hostile thinking, we identify this as contributing to risk and as a treatment target. We do this without necessarily shifting the paradigm to treating the woman as 'the perpetrator' and losing a gendered understanding.

Ideally, risk assessments of families where children have been, or are thought at risk of being, exposed to domestic violence, should include both parents, so that treatment intervention targets for each of them, and family safety measures, can be correctly identified. In developing our understanding of family violence and modalities of prevention, we have identified the following vulnerability factors for mothers:

- Co-habitation.[3]
- Being of reproductive age, especially if under 25 years.[4]
- Having low educational attainment.[5]
- Subjection to harsh parenting or abuse as a child.[6]
- Exposure to violence between her parents.[7]
- Previous sexual or physical assault.[8]
- Disability.[9]

- Pregnancy.[10]
- Substance abuse.[11]
- Mental health difficulties.[12]
- Poor health.[13]
- Involvement in prostitution.[14]
- Low family income.[15]
- Financial dependence on a partner and other wage.[16]
- Other power imbalances (e.g. class or educational status).[17]
- Low quality of housing.[18]
- Overcrowding.[19]
- Social isolation.[20]
- Not working outside the home.[21]
- An ethnic minority background.[22]
- Having one or more children in the home (especially of pre-school age).[23]
- Having a child from a prior union in the home.[24]
- Her own use of aggression within the relationship.[25]
- Repeated separations and reconciliations or ongoing conflict (especially about whether the relationship is to continue or not).[26]

To address these circumstances and enhance a mother's ability to protect her children, we have devised a menu of treatment targets for mothers from which we select – and to which we can add – for a particular case. Our recommendations for treatment normally comprise most of the following:

- To raise her awareness of the nature and development of domestic violence and abuse and of the consequences of exposure for both herself and her children.
- To raise her awareness about the risk posed by the father, and to help her appreciate the implications for her own and her children's safety of continued association with him. If the father is unable to evidence an ability to make changes in himself, to provide her with the emotional support needed to separate from him, and to take the steps necessary to protect herself and her children against further violence and abuse.
- To improve her capacity to empathise with her children and to make amends for the past.
- To help her come to terms with the traumas of her childhood.
- To help her address her unmet attachment needs and to develop an improved capacity to be discerning in partner choice.

- To help her develop the capacity to recognise potential abuse in a prospective partner and to develop basic recognition and safety strategies.
- To improve her assertiveness, to differentiate between violence, aggression and expressions of anger, and to develop less destructive ways of managing intense emotions associated with vulnerability and anger.
- To help her fully understand the risk implications of her own use of aggression within intimate relationships.
- To help her to recognise and change her negative or hostile thinking patterns so as to reduce conflict in her relationships, improve co-operation with professionals, improve her social integration and promote the emotional welfare of her children.
- To help her to manage boundaries with professionals and to find ways of improving her working relationship with social services.
- To explore future contraception options and to address her apparently ambivalent attitude to pregnancy, since further pregnancies would significantly increase her vulnerability, raise risk levels for any other children in her care, and detract from her ability to meet her existing children's needs.
- To help her develop a pro-social support network, especially with women, independent of the father.
- To help her review her attitude to education and employment (unemployment, financial dependence upon men and not working outside the home are key vulnerability factors for women's further exposure to domestic violence), and to self-care (poor diet is associated with mood and aggression).

In working with mothers, as with fathers, we need to deploy the concepts of 'responsibility' and 'choice'. If we were to regard abusive fathers as the only parents responsible for the exposure of children to domestic violence, this would mean that mothers could be seen only in the frame of victims, without any agency or choices in their own lives. There would then be no point in mandated work with them. At the same time, it is important, as the feminist lobby argues, not to treat mothers as responsible for the actions of their abusive partners. We approach this difficulty by inviting mothers to take responsibility for their own and their children's safety. We also argue that there is a social responsibility to protect the vulnerable from

abuse. Where resources are provided to protect a mother and her children, but she rejects this protection in order to maintain her relationship with her abuser, we believe it is appropriate to hold her to account for the risk to which she is exposing her children.

Asking a mother to put her children's needs first is a difficult therapeutic task. As the list of vulnerability factors above shows, the mothers most vulnerable to domestic violence have typically suffered emotional deprivation and lack of protection themselves in childhood. They are being required to provide for their children something they have not experienced themselves. In the language of psychotherapy they have little or no 'internal working model' of what it means to be a protective, responsive and nurturing mother. The female therapist working with the mother is likely to have projected onto her at times the client's own bad experiences with her mother, being seen variously as critical, blaming, rejecting, punishing, insensitive, controlling, abandoning or neglectful. Often, the mother will be not only socially isolated, but suspicious and distrustful of relationships with women, and a task of treatment will be to help her address this aspect of her vulnerability to abusive relationships with men by supporting her in forming a more positive view of women and in making female friends. When the mother begins to see her therapist as working to support her autonomy as a woman rather than wishing to instruct or blame her, and when the mother feels her self-esteem improving, the therapist begins to be seen more positively and engagement with treatment starts or deepens.

Attachment difficulties in childhood are known to lead to difficulties in attachment relationships in adult life, and this is the case for women involved in domestically abusive relationships as well as for men. It is well known that male perpetrators of domestic violence tend to be controlling and proprietorial in the conduct of their sexual relationships, but we have found that many mothers are also insecure and jealous and raise the risk to which they are exposed through behaviours such as preventing men from leaving when they try to practise 'time out', or by initiating or escalating abusive conflict. Some mothers can also be violent, and we knew of a mother whose partner was attending a perpetrator programme, who stabbed her partner in the back with a kitchen knife when he left during an argument; because she was not mandated to attend, she could not be effectively challenged about this. This is not to say that domestic violence is a function of attachment problems, but working with the dynamics of abusive relationships is important when treating a parenting couple and we do undertake some couple work.

Couple sessions focus on safety planning and inviting the parents to take responsibility for safety both separately and jointly. In order to put to parents how we assess their response to treatment, we can use indicators such as the following:

Indicators of treatment failing

- Parents continue to deny risk to children and refuse to plan for safety.
- Parents comply but don't engage with treatment.
- Parents collude with each other and prioritise their own relationship over children's needs.
- Parents deceive therapists or social services and can't form working relationships with them.
- Parents won't take responsibility for their own feelings and behaviour and spend most of the time blaming others.

Indicators of treatment succeeding

- Parents comply and engage.
- Parents are concerned about risk (show that they are willing to listen to others' concerns) and agree to plan for safety.
- Parents support each other but also show ability to think and act independently.

- Parents form working relationships with therapists and improve their relationships with the social worker.
- Parents take responsibility for their own feelings and behaviour rather than concentrating on blaming others.
- Work focuses on children's needs.

Couple sessions are held by agreement between the therapists and the parents and involve all four meeting together. These sessions have a number of benefits, including:

- Ensuring that the therapists present a common front to the parents.
- Reducing the tendency for unhelpful fantasies to develop about the partner's therapist and the work the partner is doing.
- Enabling the therapists to gain more insight into the dynamics of the couple's relationship, including their communication difficulties.
- Preventing the therapists' view of treatment progress and the case issues from diverging and working at cross purposes from each other.

Given the attachment problems in most of our clients' relationships and their tendency to veer between collusion with each other and abusive conflict, it is useful to put to them jointly the following hierarchy of treatment outcomes.

Using this table enables us to focus the parents' attention on the need to demonstrate their engagement and the consequences of failing to do so within the time available. From the point of view of couples work, it also enables us to pose to both parents the need for them to think separately about their options as well as jointly. This is particularly helpful in working with a

Table 17.2 Good treatment outcomes for children

Treatment enables the parents to show that together they can keep the children safe.	Family rehabilitation	Preferred outcomes
Treatment enables a safe separation of the parents.	Children are rehabilitated to one of the parents with the support of the other parent	
One parent drops out or fails the treatment.	Children are rehabilitated to the other parent with safeguards in place.	Next best outcomes
Both parents fail the treatment i.e. it is shown that they can't keep the children safe.	The children can be helped to find safe homes without unnecessary delay.	

mother, so that she can think about the consequences of continuing to pursue the relationship with the father if he fails to demonstrate engagement with treatment. She is usually the only parent likely to be considered as a single parent because of the risk the father poses. Because of the anxiety that thinking about separation arouses, it is also useful to be able to put the issue on the table early in the treatment so that the couple can contemplate that failure of the father to engage will result in the mother having to make a choice between her relationship and her children. The father's failure may result in his losing both his relationship and the children. The couple's joint failure may preserve the relationship, but is likely to result in the permanent loss of the children.

The way that Table 17.2 poses the issue enables us to put the children's needs first and invite the parents to join with us in deciding how they wish – as individuals and as a couple – to address those needs. Using this diagram early in the treatment also enables us to work with the issues of separation and intimacy that have become obscured in the couple's relationship. The parents tend to understand 'separation' as having only the meaning of ending the relationship, whereas psychological separation from each other (individuation) is necessary for them to attain intimacy, rather than the enmeshed togetherness they typically experience, which prevents them from understanding themselves or solving their problems. Promoting psychological separation in the couple and the individual exercise of conscious choice is a key objective of treatment, because it is essential to the decision to prioritise safety when emotionally aroused.

The diagram is also very useful in discussing treatment objectives with the local authority at the outset of treatment, because if the local authority would not consider the mother as a single parent, working for safety with the parents, and the mother in particular, is a flawed endeavour. If the mother's decision to prioritise safety by leaving her partner were to mean that she would lose her children anyway, our work with her loses the ground on which it is based.

Despite the many frustrations and stresses of attempting treatment with parents in this setting, our occasional successes in helping parents achieve the safe rehabilitation of their children against the odds demonstrates the value of the undertaking. If preventive intervention were better supported by public policy, substantial shifts could no doubt be made so that family courts could be in a much better position to know than they are today whether all avenues have been exhausted in testing whether the parents are potentially capable of meeting their children's needs before irrevocable decisions are made. Ideally, we would like to be able to help local authorities assess parents for their suitability for treatment in order to identify those candidates who have the best prognosis, so as to target resources effectively.

In terms of developing our understanding of risk, the opportunity of working directly with parents provides invaluable insights, particularly into the functioning of abusive relationships. By comparison with the research literature on perpetrators, relatively little research has been done on vulnerability to abuse in women and on relationship risk factors; the research that has been done on vulnerability is often not linked to risk factors and is not directly comparable. Little useful literature exists on how to work effectively for safety with parents, particularly on working to enhance the mother's 'ability to protect'. We consequently feel that keeping our treatment service going is worthwhile, not only for the benefits it provides to a few families but because it serves to deepen an understanding of the interlinking of risk assessment and risk reduction intervention. Both undertakings need to learn from each other to ensure that family safety is effectively pursued. To learn how people behave and whether they can change, you need to work directly with them.

References

Acierno, R., Resnick, H. and Kilpatrick, D. (1997) Health Impact of Interpersonal Violence: Prevalence Rates, Case Identification and Risk Factors. *Behavioural Medicine*, 23, 53–64.

Aldorado, E. and Sugarman, D.B. (1996) Risk Markers of the Cessation and Persistence of Wife Assault. *Journal of Consulting and Clinical Psychology*, 64: 5, 110–19.

Alpert, E., Cohen, S. and Sege, R. (1997) Family Violence: An Overview. *Academic Medicine Supplement*, 72: 1, 53–6.

Anderson, D. (2003) The Impact on Subsequent Violence of Returning to an Abusive Partner. *Journal of Comparative Family Studies*, 34: 1, 93–112.

Anderson, K. (1997) Gender, Status and Domestic Violence: An Integration of Feminist and Family Violence Approaches. *Journal of Marriage and the Family*, 59: 3, 655–69.

Baird, C. (1988) *Validation Research in CPS Risk Assessment: Three Recent Studies*. Alaska Department of Health and Social Services.

Barnish, M. (2004) *Domestic Violence: A Literature Review*. HM Inspectorate of Probation.

Bassuk, E. et al. (1996) The Characteristics and Needs of Sheltered Homeless and Low-Income Housed Mothers. *Journal of the American Medical Association*, 276, 640–6.

Belsky, J. (1993) Etiology of Child Maltreatment: A Developmental-Ecological Analysis. *Psychological Bulletin*, 114, 413–34.

Bennett, L. (1995) Substance Abuse and the Domestic Assault of Women. *Social Work*, 40, 760–71.

Bennett, L. and Lawson, M. (1994) Barriers to Cooperation between Domestic Violence and Substance Abuse Programs. *Families in Society*, 75, 277–86.

Bohn, D.K. (1990) Domestic Violence and Pregnancy: Implications for Practice. *Journal of Nursing Midwifery*, 35, 86–98.

Bowker, L.H., Arbitell, M. and McFerron, J.R. (1988) The Relationship between Wife Beating and Child Abuse. In Yllo, K. *Feminist Perspectives on Wife Abuse*. Newbury Park, CA: Sage.

Bowker, L.H. and Maurer, L. (1987) The Medical Treatment of Battered Wives. *Women and Health*, 112: 1, 25–45.

Brewer, V. and Paulsen, D.J. (1999) A Comparison of US and Canadian Findings on Uxoricide Risk for Children Sired by Previous Partners. *Homicide Studies*, 3: 4, 317–32.

Browne, K. and Saqi, S. (1988) Approaches to Screening for Child Abuse and Neglect. In Browne, K., Davies, C. and Stratton, P. (Eds.) *Early Prediction and Prevention*.

Burton, S., Regan, L. and Kelly, L. (1998) *Supporting Women and Challenging Men: Lessons from the Domestic Violence Intervention Project*. London: The Policy Press.

Butchart, A., Lerer, L. and Blanche, M. (1994) Imaginary Constructions and Forensic Reconstruction of Fatal Violence against Women: Implications. *Forensic Science International*, 64, 21–34.

Campbell, J.C. (1986) Nursing Assessments for the Risk of Homicide with Battered Women. *Advances in Nursing Science*, 8: 4, 36–51.

Campbell, J.C. et al. (2003) Assessing Risk Factors for Intimate Partner Homicide. *NIJ Journal*, 250, 14–9.

Campbell, J.C. et al. (2003) Risk Factors for Femicide in Abusive Relationships: Results from a Multisite Case Control Study. *American Journal of Public Health*, 93: 7, 1089–97.

Cherpitel, C. (1994) Alcohol and Injuries Resulting from Violence. A Review of Emergency Room Studies. *Addiction*, 89: 2, 157–65.

Cokkinides, V. and Coker, A. (1998) Experiencing Physical Violence during Pregnancy: Prevalence and Correlates. *Family and Community Health*, 20: 4, 19–37.

Coleman, D.H. and Straus, M.A. (1986) Marital Power, Conflict and Violence in a Nationally Representative Sample of American Couples. *Violence and Victims*, 1: 2, 141–57.

Dansky, B.S. et al. (1995) Prevalence of Victimisation and Post-Traumatic Stress Disorder among Women with Substance Abuse. *The International Journal of the Addictions*, 30, 1079–99.

Dekeseredy, W.S. and Schwartz, M.D. (1998) Women Abuse on Campus: Results from the Canadian National Survey. *Canadian National Survey*. CA: Sage.

Dobash et al. (2002) *Homicide in Britain, Research Bulletin*. Department of Applied Social Science, University of Manchester.

Dobash, R.P. and Dobash, R.E. (1979) *Violence against Wives: A Case against the Patriarchy*. New York: Free Press.

Donate-Bartfield, E. and Passman, R.H. (1985) Attentiveness of Mothers and Fathers to their Baby's Cries. *Infant Behaviour and Development*, 8, 385–93.

Downs, W.R. et al. (1992) Long Term Effects of Parent-to-Child Violence for Women. *Journal of Aggression, Maltreatment and Trauma*, 5: 2, 73–104.

Dutton, D.G. and Kerry, G. (1999) Personality Profiles and Modi Operandi of Spousal Homicide Perpetrators. *International Journal of Law and Psychiatry*, 22: 3–4, 287–300.

Dwyer, D.C. et al. (1995) Domestic Violence Research: Theoretical and Practice Implications for Social Work. *Clinical Social Work Journal*, 23: 2, 185–98.

Estrada, F. and Nilsson, A. (2004) Exposure to Threatening and Violent Behaviour among Single Mothers. *British Journal of Criminology*, 44: 2, 168–87.

Farley, M. and Barkan, H. (1998) Prostitution, Violence and Post-Traumatic Stress Disorder. *Women and Health*, 27, 37–49.

Gelles, R.J. (1997) *Intimate Violence*. London: Sage.

Gelles, R.J. (1974) *The Violent Home*. (Updated 1987.) Beverly Hills, CA: Sage.

Gelles, R.J. (1976) Abused Wives: Why do they Stay? *Journal of Marriage and the Family*, 38, 659–68.

Gelles, R.J. and Loseke, D. (Eds.) (1994) *Current Controversies on Family Violence*. London: Sage.

Gelles, R.J. Wolfner, G.D. and Lackner, R. (1994) Men who Batter: The Risk Markers. *Violence Update*, 4, 1ff.

Gielen, A.C. et al. (1994) Interpersonal Conflict and Physical Violence during the Childbearing Years. *Society of Science and Medicine*, 39: 6, 781–7.

Goodman, M.S. and Fallon, B.C. (1995) *Supplement to Pattern Changing for Abuse Women. An Educational Programme*. Sage.

Grayson, J. (1995) Treatment Outcome for Spouses who Batter. *Virginia Child Protection Newsletter*, 50: 1, 3–15.

Grayson, J. (1995) Treatment Outcome for Families who Abuse or Neglect. *Virginia Child Protection Newsletter*, 46, 8–16.

Hampton, R. and Gelles, R. (1994) Violence toward Black Women in a Nationally Representative Sample of Black Families. *Journal of Comparative Family Studies*, 25: 1, 105–19.

Haver, B. (1987) Female Alcoholics: IV: The Relationship between Family Violence and Outcome 3–10 Years after Treatment. *Acta Psychiatrica Scandanavica*, 75, 449–55.

Hedin, L. (2000) Postpartum: Also a Risk Period for Domestic Violence. *European Journal of Obstetrics, Gynaecology and Reproductive Biology*, 89, 41–5.

Hillard, P.J. (1985) Physical Abuse in Pregnancy. *Obstetrics and Gynecology*, 66, 185–90.

Hoffman, K., Demo, D. and Edwards, J. (1994) Physical Wife Abuse in a Non-Western Society: An Integrated Theoretical Approach. *Journal of Marriage and the Family*, 56, 131–46.

Home Office (2004) *British Crime Survey*. London: HMSO.

Hotaling, G.T. and Sugarman, D.B. (1986) Analysis of Risk Markers in Husband to Wife Violence: The Current State of Knowledge. *Violence and Victims*, 1, 101–24.

Howell, M.J. and Pugliesi, K.L. (1988) Husbands who Harm: Predicting Spousal Violence by Men. *Journal of Family Violence*, 3, 15–27.

Hoyle, C. (1998) *Negotiating Domestic Violence, Criminal Justice and Victims*. Oxford: Clarendon Press.

Jacobs, B.S. and Moss, H.A. (1976) Birth Order and Sex of Sibling as Determinants of Mother-Infant Interaction. *Child Development*, 47, 315–22.

Jewkes, R. (2002) Abstract: Preventing Domestic Violence. *BMJ*, 324: 7332, 253–4.

Jewkes, R. (2002) Intimate Partner Violence: Causes and Prevention, Violence against Women III. *The Lancet*, April 20 Internet: Www.Thelancet.Com, 359, 1423–9.

Kalmus, D.S. and Straus, M.A. (1982) Wife's Marital Dependency and Wife Abuse. *Journal of Marriage and the Family*, 44: 2, 277–86.

Keller, L. (1996) Invisible Victims: Battered Women in Psychiatric and Medical Emergency Rooms. *Bulletin of the Menninger Clinic*, 60: 1, 1–21.

Liebschutz, J.M., Mulvey, K.P. and Samet, J.H. (1997) Victimisation among Substance Abusing Women: Work Health Outcomes. *Archives of Internal Medicine*, 157, 1093–7.

Lyon, E. (2000) Welfare, Poverty and Abused Women: New Research and its Implications. In *Building Co.* Harrisburg, PA: National Resource Centre on Domestic Violence.

Magen, R. H. (1999) In the Best Interest of the Battered Women: Reconceptualise Allegations of Failure to Protect. *Child Maltreatment*, 4: 2, 127–35.

Margolin, L. (1990) Fatal Child Neglect. *Child Welfare*, LXIX: 4, 309–19.

Marshall, L.L. and Rose, P. (1990) Premarital Violence: The Impact of Family of Origin Violence, Stress, and Reciprocity. *Journal of Family Violence*, 5, 51–64.

Martin, M. (1997) Double your Trouble: Dual Arrest in Family Violence. *Journal of Family Violence*, 12: 2, 139–57.

McKenry, P.C., Julian, T.W. and Gavazzi, S.M. (1995) Toward a Biopsychosocial Model of Domestic Violence. *Journal of Marriage and the Family*, 57: 2, 301–20.

McNeil, M. (1987) Domestic Violence: The Skeleton in Tarrasoff's Closet. In Sonkin, D.J. (Ed.) *Domestic Violence on Trial: Psychological and Legal Dimensions of Family Violence*. New York: Springer.

Melchior, L.A. et al. (1999) Evaluation of the Effects of Outreach to Women with Multiple Vulnerabilities on Entry into Substance. *Evaluation and Program Planning*, 22, 269–77.

Metropolitan Police (2003) Findings from the Multi-Agency Domestic Violence Murder Reviews in London. Prepared for the ACPO Homicide Working Group. *Racial and Violent Crime Task Force.*

Mezey, G.C. and Bewley, S. (1997) Domestic Violence in Pregnancy. *BMJ*, 314, 1295 and 104, 523–8.

Milner, J.S. (1995) Physical Child Abuse Assessment: Perpetrator Evaluation. *Assessing Dangerousness*, 3.

Mirrlees-Black, C. (1999) *Domestic Violence: Findings from a New British Crime Survey Self-Completion Questionnaire.* Home Office.

Moore, A. (1997) Intimate Violence: Does Socioeconomic Status Matter? In Cardopelli, A.P. (Ed.) *Violence between Intimate Partners: Patterns, Causes, and Effects*, 90–100. Needham Heights, MA: Allyn & Bacon.

Moreno, C.L. et al. (2002) Correlates of Poverty and Partner Abuse among Women on Methadone. *Violence Against Women*, 8: 4, 455–75.

Morley, R. and Mullender, A. (1994) Domestic Violence and Children: What do we know from Research? In Mullender, A. and Morley, R. (Eds.) *Children Living with Domestic Violence.* London: Whiting and Birch.

Nosek, M.A. and Howland, C.A. (1998) Abuse of Women with Disabilities: Policy Implications. *Journal of Disability Policy Studies*, 8, 157–76.

O'Donnell, C., Smith, A. and Madison, J.R. (2002) Using Demographic Risk Factors to Explain Variations in the Incidence of Violence against Women. *Journal of Interpersonal Violence*, 17:(2, 1239–62.

O'Leary, K.D., Malone, J. and Tyree, A. (1994) Physical Aggression in Early Marriage: Pre-relationship and Relationship Effects. *Journal of Consulting and Clinical Psychology*, 62: 3, 594–602.

Osofsky, J.D. (1995) Children who Witness Domestic Violence: The Invisible Victims. *Society for Research in Child Development*, 9: 3.

Parker, B. et al. (1993) Physical and Emotional Abuse in Pregnancy: A Comparison of Adult and Teenage Women. *Nurs. Res.* 42, 173–8.

Parks, K. and Miller, B. (1997) Bar Victimisation of Women. *Psychology of Women Quarterly*, 21: 4, 509–25.

Radford, L. et al. (1997) For the Sake of the Children: The Law, Domestic Violence and Child Contact in England. *Women's Studies International Forum*, 20: 4, 471–82.

Richards, L. (2003) *MPS Domestic Violence Risk Assessment Model.* London: Metropolitan Police and Home Office.

Riggs, D.S., Caulfield, M.B. and Street, A.E. (2000) Risk for Domestic Violence: Factors Associated with Perpetration and Victimisation. *Journal of Clinical Psychology*, 56: 10, 1289–316.

Rodgers, K. (1994) Wife Assault: The Findings of a National Survey. *Juristat Service Bulletin of The Canadian Center for Justice Statistics*, 14: 9, 1–22.

Saunders, A. (1995) *It Hurts Me Too.* London: Childline/Women's Aid Federation of England/NISW.

Saunders, D.G. (1995) Prediction of Wife Assault. In Campbell, J.C. (Ed.) *Assessing Dangerousness: Violence by Sexual Offenders, Batterers and Child Abusers.* New York: Springer.

Scourfield, J.B. (2001) Constructing Men in Child Protection Work. *Men and Masculinities*, 4: 1, 70–89.

Shackelford, T.K., Buss, D.M. and Weekes-Shackelford, V.A. (2003) Wife Killings Committed in the Context of a Lovers Triangle. *Basic and Applied Social Psychology*, 25, 137–43.

Simons, R.L. et al. (1993) Explaining Women's Double Jeopardy: Factors that Meditate the Association between Harsh Treatment. *Journal of Marriage and the Family*, 55, 713–23.

Stanko, E.A. et al. (1998) *Counting the Costs: Estimating the Impact of Domestic Violence in the London Borough of Hackney.* Swindon: Crime Concern.

Straus, M.A. et al. (1980) *Behind Closed Doors: Violence in the American Family.* New York: Garden Press/Anchor Press/Doubleday.

Stuart, G.L. and Holtzworth-Munroe, A. (1995) Identifying Subtypes of Maritally Violent Men: Descriptive Dimensions, Correlates and Causes of Violence. In Stith, S. and Straus, M. (Eds.) *Understanding Partner Violence: Prevalence, Causes, Consequences and Solutions.* Minneapolis, MN: National Council on Family Relations.

Tomison, A.M. and Wise, S. (1999) Community-Based Approaches in Preventing Child Maltreatment: Issues in Child Abuse Prevention. *National Child Protection Clearinghouse Paper.* AIFS, Australia.

Walby, S. and Allen, J. (2004) *Domestic Violence, Sexual Assault and Stalking: Findings from the British Crime Survey.* London: Home Office.

Walby, S. and Myhill, A. (2001) Assessing and Managing Risk. In Taylor-Browne, J. (Ed.) *What Works in Reducing Domestic Violence?* London: Whiting and Birch.

Walby, S. and Myhill, A. (2000) *Reducing Domestic Violence: What Works? Assessing and Managing the Risk of Domestic Violence.* Policing and Reducing Crime Unit, Home Office.

Weaver, T. and Clum, G. (1996) Interpersonal Violence: Expanding the Search for Long-Term Sequelae within a Sample of Battered Women. *Journal of Traumatic Stress,* 9, 783–803.

Wilson, M. (1998) Report of Domestic Violence Conference. *News Letter, British Juvenile and Family Courts Society,* 1–6.

Wilson, M., Daly, M. and Wright, C. (1993) Uxoricide in Canada: Demographic Risk Patterns. *Canadian Journal of Criminology,* 35: 3, 263–91.

Wright, J. and Kariya, A. (1997) Characteristics of Female Victims of Assault Attending a Scottish Accident and Emergency Department. *Journal of Accident and Emergency Medicine,* 4: 6, 375–8.

Wyatt, G.E. et al. (2000) Examining Patterns of Vulnerability to Domestic Violence among African American Women. *Violence Against Women,* 6, 495–514.

YMCA (2002) Hitting Home: Violence and Young Women. *YMCA,* Winter, 4.

Endnotes

1   Magen (1999) underlines the conceptual and practical difficulties with the concept of 'failure to protect', and asserts that the term *ability* implies circumstances that are controllable; in the context of domestic violence, this presupposes that there are actions that a mother can take that would be effective in protecting her children from harm. Yet in some cases, there may be little she can do, particularly where the protection she needs from the community is not afforded. In many cases a woman's legal actions against her violent partner or her attempts to leave can actually increase the risk of harm; thus the decision *not* to act can at times be in the best interests of the child.

   Magen (1999: 129) also points to a *fundamental attribution error* in which the focus of attention becomes the mother's response to domestic violence rather than the perpetrator's actions, or the inadequate response from the police or the courts, or the lack of alternative accommodation. Mothers can thereby be doubly victimised, firstly by the abuser and secondly by the child

protection proceedings. Scourfield (2001) also highlights how the child welfare industry has focused on mothering rather than parenting; he argues that it should not be a mother's 'failure to protect' but a father's violent and abusive behaviour that is the subject of scrutiny. Similarly, Morley and Mullender (1994) point to research that is critical of the current professional orthodoxy in which responsibility for exposing children to harm is assigned to mothers who fail to meet expectations of 'good mothering' rather than to abusive fathers, who often remain invisible in child protection proceedings.

2   It is clear that many women experiencing domestic violence want help for their abusers rather than punishment (Hoyle, 1998; Burton et al., 1998).

3   Research by Wilson and colleagues (1993) found that uxoricide (wife murder) rates increase sharply following a couple's separation but that women who were co-habiting were at far greater risk than women who had been married. Risk also increased as age disparity increased in both married and co-habiting couples. O'Donnell et al. (2002) and Gelles et al. (1994) also found that women who were separated, divorced or co-habiting were statistically at greater risk of domestic violence than those who were married.

4   Smaller scale studies and national surveys invariably find that youth appears as a constant risk factor for victimisation by domestic violence (e.g. O'Donnell et al., 2002; Alpert et al., 1997; Anderson, 1997; Klein et al., 1997; Moffitt and Caspi, 1999; Rodgers, 1994). The British Crime Survey (Walby and Myhill, 2000) for example, found that the percentage of women assaulted by a partner in the previous year was over twice as high as the average (4.2 per cent) for women aged between 16 and 19 (10.1 per cent) and between 20 to 24 (9.2 per cent). Where domestic violence was the cause of a visit to hospital, 16–25 year olds made up nearly half of all attendances (DoH, 2000). Peters et al. (2002) examined nearly 4000 domestic violence cases and found that rates of victimisation decrease as women age and that younger 'reproductive age' women incur nearly ten times the risk of domestic violence when compared with older post-reproductive age women, independent

of their mateship with younger, more violent men. Whilst youth remains a very robust risk marker, other than psychology's evolutionary hypothesis tested by Peters et al. (2002), (which holds that at least one goal of domestic violence is to control female sexuality and to deter infidelity), there is little attempt in the literature to explain it. Walby and Myhill (2001) speculate that youth may be correlated with a lack of financial resources, is related to less maturity and experience and is independently correlated with criminal behaviour. Some researchers have found, however, that women over the age of eighteen years face greater risk of being injured or murdered (Cokkinides and Coker, 1998; Dwyer et al., 1995; Keller, 1996; Hampton and Gelles, 1994; Butchart et al., 1994).

5   According to O'Donnell (2002) women with low educational attainment are at higher risk of exposure to domestic violence.

6   Harsh corporal punishment during childhood has been shown to elevate the probability of women being subjected to domestic violence by a boyfriend or spouse as an adult (Simons et al., 1993; Downs et al., 1992; Marshall and Rose, 1990; Walker, 1984; Haver, 1987). It seems that children who experience maltreatment develop a higher tolerance for such acts when they are committed by others in adulthood. Moreover, Gelles (1976) postulated an 'assortative mating process' whereby women who grew up in an environment of family violence are more likely to associate with and marry men with similar characteristics. In turn, these men are more likely to behave violently to their spouses than men from non-abusive homes.

7   Of the 42 markers considered in their research, Hotaling and Sugarman (1986) found that exposure to violence between one's parents or care-givers was consistently correlated with being a victim of a male partner's violence.

8   Previous sexual or physical assault is associated with a high risk of repeat assault (Bosch, 2002; Dowd et al., 1997; Moffit and Caspi, 1999; Rodgers, 1994; Weaver and Clum, 1996).

9   It is the most isolated and the most marginalised people in society who are most frequently subjected to violence and abuse of all kinds (Tomison and Wise, 1999: 5; Clapton and Fitzgerald, 1996). Although in its infancy, research into the prevalence of domestic violence against women with disabilities suggests that physical, sensory or mental impairment puts women at increased risk of victimisation (Kelley and Moore, 2000; Moffit and Caspi, 1999; Chenoweth, 1997; Rodgers, 1994). Some studies reveal that as many as 40 per cent of disabled women had experienced abuse primarily from a spouse or ex-partner (see Nosek and Howland, 1998).

10   Though many women do find that abuse starts when they become pregnant (Bowker and Maurer, 1987), pregnancy is not regarded in itself as a risk marker for domestic violence by specialist researchers such as Prof. Campbell (John Hopkins University School of Nursing), except where the male partner is convinced that the baby is not his. However, particularly during its advanced stages, pregnancy does leave women very vulnerable and least likely to be able to protect themselves (Mezey, 1997; Browne, 1997). Hedin (2000) and Gielen and colleagues (1994) also found that pregnant *and post-partum* mothers were susceptible to an increase in both the frequency and severity of violence. Research by St. Thomas's and Guy's Hospitals estimated that between 40 per cent and 60 per cent of women who experience domestic abuse are assaulted during pregnancy when physical violence often begins for the first time or escalates where it has already started (Bohn, 1990; Hillard, 1985). Radford et al. (1998) also found that up to 60 per cent of women in refuges had reported abuse during pregnancy. Adolescent mothers also appear to be at particular risk. Two studies found higher rates of domestic violence among pregnant teenagers than among older women (Parker et al., 1993; Gazmararian, 1995).

11   Alcohol and drug use are associated with an increased risk of assault (Melchior et al., 1999; Moffit and Caspi, 1999; Dekeseredy and Schwarz, 1998; Liebschutz et al., 1997; Martin, 1997; Parks and Miller, 1997; Wright and Kariya, 1997; Sorenson et al., 1996; Dansky et al., 1995; Bennett, 1995; Rodgers, 1994; Cherpitel, 1994; Bennett and Lawson, 1994).

12   Women with mental health difficulties are at increased risk of sexual and physical assault (Kelley and Moore, 2000; Moffit and Caspi, 1999; Brown, 1997; Goodman et al., 1995; Acierno et al., 1997; Rodgers, 1994; Jacobson and Richardson, 1987).

13   In the British Crime Survey (Home Office, 2004) women who reported being in poor health also reported suffering domestic violence at more than twice the rate of their healthy counterparts. Swedish researchers found similar results (Estrada and Nilsson, 2004). In their research into Black women in the US, Wyatt et al. (2000) found a strong relationship between positive HIV status and experience of domestic violence and abuse.

14   A study of prostitutes in Bradford found that 42 per cent had been victims of violence from their boyfriend (Streets and Lanes Project). Farley and Barkan (1998) found a strong link between prostitution and sexual abuse.

15   Whilst domestic violence is certainly a cross-cultural phenomenon and one that occurs at all levels of society, it is not equally widespread. Mirrlees-Black (1999) reported that families in financial difficulties were two to three times more at risk of domestic violence than those who were financially secure. Other studies have found that the presence of social or economic stressors are significant in both spouse and child abuse. The British Crime Survey, for example, found that people living in poor and financially insecure households were more likely to suffer from domestic violence (Walby and Myhill, 2001, 2000). US researchers (Moreno et al., 2002; Moore, 1997; Gelles et al., 1994; Hoffman et al., 1994; Campbell, 1986; Hotaling and Sugarman, 1986) found similar results and identified unemployment and low income as strong situational risk markers for domestic violence. Osofsky (1995) found that homes where domestic violence occurred were often characterised by poverty, exposure to chronic community violence, high stress and job and family instability. This concurs with research elsewhere which suggests that women living in poverty are at especially high risk for all types of abuse, particularly for severe and life-threatening violence (O'Donnell et al., 2002; Walby and Myhill, 2000, 2001; Browne, 1997; McKenry et al., 1995). Women who are unemployed or

housewives are also more than twice as likely to face domestic violence than their employed counterparts (Walby and Myhill, 2001; Mirrlees-Black, 1999). One study found that nearly half of the women receiving welfare benefit have experienced physical abuse at some point in their lives (Lyon, 2000). Another study found that 63 per cent of homeless and low-income housed mothers reported experiencing violence from an intimate partner (Bassuk et al., 1996). It does seem that, whilst most deprived families are not families where domestic violence occurs, the stress provided by exposure to poverty when coupled with other risk factors does intensify the likelihood of abuse occurring (Howell and Pugliesi, 1988). Domestic violence can also lead to poverty as it tends to increase ill-health and makes it more difficult for women to maintain stable employment. Lack of economic resources also mean that it is much more difficult to leave a violent partner.

16   An age gap of at least ten years – especially young women married to much older men – appears as a risk factor for lethal domestic violence (Wilson et al., 1993, 1998).

17   Domestic violence is also at its highest in in-egalitarian households. Relative power imbalances (e.g. the couple's class, status or physical strength) and women's dependence have been found to augment considerably the incidence and severity of domestic violence (Walby and Myhill, 2001; Gelles et al., 1994). The woman's greater educational or occupational status also emerges as a risk factor in most studies (Saunders, 1995). In their research, Coleman and Straus (1986) also found that symmetrical households were less likely to succumb to violence when faced with conflict than asymmetrical ones. Kalmus and Straus (1982) argued that the rate of severe violence was nearly three times higher among maritally dependent women (e.g. the women's lack of independent income or where the husband earned more than 75 per cent of the couple's income). Women with young children are also more likely to be at home than older women whose children have reached school age (O'Donnell, 2002). These younger women are therefore more likely to be financially dependent on their partner, accentuating the power imbalance and making it much more

difficult to escape a violent relationship on which they and their children depend for food and shelter (YWCA, 2002).

18   Perhaps linked to poverty, housing tenure also appears as a risk factor for women's exposure to domestic violence. The British Crime Survey (Mirrlees-Black, 1999) revealed that women living as council or housing association tenants were significantly more likely to be at risk than their owner-occupier counterparts.

19   The cumulative effect of other factors and overcrowding (often interpreted as more people in a dwelling than the number of habitable rooms) can lead to substantially increased stress levels and therefore increased risk of domestic violence occurring.

20   Isolation from one's community, extended family and other social support networks can be seen as an aggravating factor in marital conflict as it restricts access to potential resources such as emotional support, information, transport and legal and professional assistance (Stuart and Holtzworth-Munroe, 1995; Dobash and Dobash, 1979; Gelles, 1974). Gelles (1997: 137) proposes that family violence is more common when non-nuclear family members (e.g. friends, relatives, bystanders) are unavailable, unable or unwilling to be part of the daily system of family interaction and thus cannot serve as agents of formal and informal social control. Isolation thus diminishes the likelihood that social sanctions will be meaningfully applied against the abusive partner (Wallace, 1996).

21   According to the Metropolitan Police (2003) women who are unemployed or housewives are also more than twice as likely to face domestic violence than their employed counterparts (Walby and Myhill, 2001; Mirrlees-Black, 1999). The risk of exposure is also regarded as being a function of the *amount* of time spent in the home. Barnish (2004) points to the potential protective quality of working outside the home, especially in an all-female environment: it can provide a source of social support, as well as reduced financial dependence.

22   Where minority women do face increased risk, it often appears to be associated with poverty and isolation (Browne, 1997). Analysis of the British Crime Survey

findings, as well as of many other surveys, also seems to reveal no significant differences in the risk of domestic violence by race or ethnicity (though under-reporting remains a key issue for all groups). Nevertheless, many women from ethnic minorities are likely to face greater difficulty in accessing services because of discrimination among service providers and the barriers provided by language and other cultural differences.

23   According to Walby and Allen's (2004) analysis of the British Crime Survey, the presence of children in the household nearly doubles the risk of domestic violence for women. Stanko et al. (1998) found an even higher association with rates over twice as high for women with children. In their earlier review, Mirrlees-Black (1999) found that for women aged over 30 years, the risk was three times higher than for those without children. Barnish (2004) points to an association between risk and the numbers of children in a household, though Jewkes (2002) suggests that this may be a consequence rather than a cause of domestic violence. Estrada and Nilsson (2004) point to research that highlights the high levels of victimisation by crime, and neighbourhood and domestic violence faced by single mothers compared with other social groups.

Various studies suggest that the presence of children means that women are less likely to save themselves by breaking up a home, are concerned for the disruptive effects on the children, and are more likely to be financially dependent on their partner if they are primary carers (and therefore less able to set up and maintain a new home) (Walby and Allen, 2004; Anderson, 2003; WHO, 2002; Rodgers, 1994).

Moreover, consistent with research that suggests parents tend to be more responsive to the needs of their first-born children than to those born later (Donate-Bartfield and Passman, 1985; Jacobs and Moss, 1976), various studies have found that abuse and neglect is more likely if there is more than one child in the home, especially where there is only a short time (typically less than 18 months) between the birth of the children (Ethier et al., 2004; Milner, 1995; Grayson, 1995; Belsky, 1993; Margolin, 1990; Browne and Saqi, 1988; Starr, 1988; Baird, 1988; Straus et al., 1980). In their research, Bowker et al. (1988) reported that the risk of child abuse increased from 51 per cent with one child to 92 per cent with four or more children.

24   It is commonly understood that stepfamilies generally have more problems to deal with than biological families, especially if the partners are unmarried. Less well known is research which supports evolutionary psychology's perspectives that independent of the direct risks to the child involved, women with children from a prior union are themselves at an increased risk of harm, including homicide (Campbell et al., 2003; Shackleford et al., 2003; Wilson and Daly, 1993; Daly et al., 1997; Daly et al., 1993). Brewer and Paulsen (1999) for example, found that women who were co-resident with young children who were not the natural offspring of their current intimate partners faced a *fourfold risk* of being murdered compared to those women whose children were the man's progeny.

25   Felson and Cares (2004)and Riggs et al. (2000) for example, point to research which highlights aggression on the part of a woman as being positively associated with subsequent violence perpetration on the part of her male partner. It remains unclear whether this link reflects women's use of violence in self-defence or some form of 'mutual combat' but regardless of the dynamics involved, a woman's own use of aggression places her at risk of future victimisation with the relationship. Feld and Straus (1989) found that women who employed severe violence (kicking, biting, threatening with weapon etc) against their non-violent spouse or partner were up to seven times more likely than women who did not use violence to suffer severe victimisation from their partner in the ensuing year.

26   Couples who have a history of separation and reconciliation, ongoing or unresolved marital conflict and verbal aggression have been cited as among the strongest correlates of physical abuse (Aldorado and Sugarman, 1996; McKenry et al., 1995; O'Leary et al., 1994; Wilson and Daly, 1993; O'Leary and Vivian, 1990). High risks of violence have also been identified by some researchers in cases where the woman wants the relationship to end but the man is unwilling to separate, or the man is living apart from his partner but wants to resume co-habitation despite the woman's resistance (Wilson et al., 1993; McNeil, 1987; Sonkin et al., 1985). Men who kill a woman partner often do so at a point when there is a conflict about whether the relationship continues or is ended, or when she wants it to end and he wants it to continue (Dobash et al., 2002; Dutton and Kerry, 1999; Gillespie, 1989). Hotaling and Sugarman (1986) noted the volatile mix that frequently occurs when the man's religious background differs from his partner's. Hotaling and Sugarman's (1990) meta-analysis of factors related to male violence found that high levels of marital conflict and low socio-economic status emerged as the primary predictors of an increased likelihood and severity of wife assault.

CHAPTER 18

Working with Mothers in Situations of Sexual and Domestic Abuse: Reframing Resistance as Restricted Choices

Martin C. Calder and Lynda Regan

Introduction

As our understanding evolves about the dynamics operating within domestic violence cases we are beginning to see the parallels with sexual abuse and this extends beyond the harm to the nature of the professional responses.

Domestic violence, like child sexual abuse, cuts across all boundaries of class, ethnicity, disability, sexuality, religion and age. It can begin at any time in a relationship, go on for many years and continue once the relationship has ended. It can happen to anyone although it is recognised that, in the majority of cases, women are the victims and men the perpetrators. It involves the misuse of power and the exercise of control in a relationship and usually follows a pattern of abuse and intimidation of increasing severity over time. The abuse is often expressed in a number of ways and is commonly manifested in more than one form at the same time. It can have physical, psychological and social consequences, which in turn may impact on a parent's ability to care for his or her children. Domestic violence can include physical injuries, sexual violence, verbal abuse, the withholding of financial support, the control of independence and choice, denial of physical freedom, humiliation, undermining of the victim both as an individual and as a parent, and isolation from family, friends and community.

Hooper (1992) highlighted clearly the inter-connections between woman abuse and child sexual abuse, suggesting that ongoing violence and abuse directed towards women provides the context for men to sexually abuse their children. Moreover, the sexual abuse of children is often intended as a further abuse of mothers. The forced sex aspect of domestic violence is often neglected. Approximately 40–45 per cent of all battered women are forced into sex by their male partners (Campbell, 1989). Forced sex can range from unwanted roughness, painful or particular sexual acts, through threatened violence if sexual demands are not met to actual beatings prior to, during or after sex, or sex with objects (Campbell and Alford, 1989). Browne (1993) reported some similarities between those who physically and sexually abuse their children and those who abuse their wives: a misperception of the victim, low self-esteem, sense of incompetence, social isolation, a lack of support and help, lack of empathy, marital difficulties, depression, poor self-control, and a history of abuse and neglect as a child.

One of the recurring themes in professional responses to domestic violence is that mothers are unfairly dealt with by the professional systems, thus compounding the harm they have already experienced within the violent relationship. Given that most children stay with their mothers after parents separate, it is vital that we rapidly develop a system that allows for the mother's experience and the impact of the abuse to be resolved in a safe way for the children. Mothers have needs and are better able to provide for their children if those needs are acknowledged and built into the systems of response. Regrettably, this is sometimes considered a luxury given the increasing pressures on agencies and the deficits in resources that threaten to dismantle even the existing systems of inter-agency working (Calder, 2003).

Mothers needs on discovery of sexual abuse

For me to be able to heal . . . to recover from my secondary abuse as the non-abusing parent . . . I do not need to be victimised or rescued; nor do I need to be punished for what has happened to my children. Like most non-abusing parents, I have already crucified myself with feelings of guilt for what my children experienced. I do not need to run the gauntlet of suspicion and distrust, or endure aloofness and indifference.

(Brown, 1998: 174)

The evolution of work with mothers in sexually abusing families has been protracted, low key, a low priority and incomplete. There is a need to provide a framework to guide workers to assess a mother's ability to protect, and to join this with the needs of the mothers at each stage of the child protection process, exploring how particular approaches and professional strategies create a pre-determined view of them (such as 'collusive' or as an 'accomplice'). Such approaches **dis**able the mother in her mothering tasks. It also prevents an objective assessment of their ability to protect from taking place (Calder, 2003).

Previous studies have shown that the impact on women finding out about the sexual abuse of their children is serious, long lasting and consistently under-estimated by professionals (Humphreys, 1992). There are multiple losses occurring or threatened as a consequence of the abuse. These can include loss of control over their own and their child's life, loss of trust in the man who abused the child and the loss of a sense of being a good mother (Hooper, 1992). Hooper also records that women from her study felt that the effects were something that would never entirely go away.

There are a number of contextual considerations worthy of note. Professionals are often required to undertake an assessment of a mother's failure/ability or capacity to protect following disclosure by her child. Despite the different terminology and attempts to make it sound more palatable, in essence nothing has changed either in the context of the assessment or in the expectations of the mother.

The words failure, ability and capacity assume that a deficit in the mother's parenting may have existed pre-disclosure, when research tells us that in most cases the mothers had no indication that anything was wrong, that (unknowingly) mothers go through a grooming process alongside the grooming of their child and that sexual abuse is based on power, control and secrecy.

Behroozi (1992) refers to a transactional approach to motivation with involuntary clients. Based on this approach the worker first assesses the person's available motivation and then tries to re-motivate them, including helping them to enhance their level of motivation for the desired change.

Regan's experience of working with mothers in this position over the last eleven years confirms this approach; where there is no judgement made on the mother's initial presentation or stance, but where efforts are made to understand these and then to offer education and discussion around the

processes involved, motivation rarely becomes a prolonged issue. However, this does not fit comfortably with current timescales for investigations.

The concept of failure to protect requires mothers to protect children from fathers who are equally responsible for and available to the children (Magen, 1999). For mothers to avoid allegations of failure to protect requires either leaving the situation and/or taking action against the perpetrator. If they do not, then the problem is defined in terms of what the mother failed to do rather than in terms of the perpetrator's actions. It assumes that leaving is a woman's responsibility that leaving is a solution to the abuse, and that leaving is appropriate and available to all women. Those professionals who ask the question 'Why didn't she leave?' continue to reflect victim-blaming attitudes. This is clearly a blaming and fault approach to child protection (Lyon, 1999). Hill (2001) found that at its most benign women reported a lack of understanding about what they were going through. More seriously in many cases there was a failure to offer any meaningful help and women felt the spotlight was on them as mothers:

> My skills as a parent were being scrutinised and it took me a while to realise what was going on. I had reported this man because of what he had done and all of a sudden I was being questioned about my parenting, I couldn't believe it.

> I'd had help offered from social services and it all made me feel worse, more guilty, more responsible because of their attitude.

A second contextual consideration relates to the socialisation processes that exist within our society. Reid (1989) extensively reviewed the concepts of motherhood. She noted that the idealised mother is boundlessly giving and endlessly available. The sentimentalised nuclear family is believed to be a shelter from the demands of work and a protective environment for children. This ignores the sad reality that the family is probably the most violent group to which women and children belong. Although women may be seen as powerful in the domestic sphere, they do not share equal status with men.

Girls are still socialised to learn their second-class status as they are treated differently from boys, and some may still perceive their mothers as powerless. In the past acceptable behaviours were more distinct for each gender. More recently there has been a trend for girls to grow up believing that they can 'compete' with the boys. This, however, does not promote equality for the girls, it simply masks many of the gender issues under the guise of equality. Girls still grow up constantly learning their nurturing role: to put their own needs second and to be sensitive to others. Girls learn that to earn love and approval, they must be nurturing and giving. They may now receive messages about it being acceptable to take risks, or be assertive, although when put into practice they are quickly labelled as a problem for not conforming to the gender stereotypes that we, as a society, prefer. Wider society supports and perpetrates this view, for example in its organisation and advertising. This can influence a child's perceptions as they grow and develop, and where there are limited resilience factors and support networks available to the child, can lay the foundations for dependant, submissive and self-sacrificing roles in later life, leaving the woman with a dearth of coping skills. They soon learn that whatever goes wrong, they will be blamed and expected to take responsibility, and in this process they often judge themselves more harshly than anyone else, even when they are not at fault.

Unfortunately, social work intervention into families where sexual abuse is a feature often reinforces this socialisation process. Women continue to be seen as disproportionately responsible by social workers for the wellbeing of their children. What is often missing is the contribution of men to the originating problem and worse still, the mothers can be portrayed as being to blame for their partner's actions, for not controlling him or for 'provoking' him. Research tells us that most men only engage in the child protection process until they get their own outcome satisfied; whilst the attendance of men at conferences impacts to lessen the likelihood of registration, unlike mothers who attend alone, and are often not the primary risk.

Mothers are expected to take responsibility for child care and child protection even when it is the man who is responsible for the abuse. Featherstone (1999) has questioned whether this is affected by the status of the man or whether it is a blanket strategy. She identified several relevant issues: fear of men's violence, a general lack of clarity about what should be expected of fathers and constructions of motherhood (see Milner, 1996; Parton et al., 1997). These focus on an analysis of what workers do or do not do, thus analysing one side of the encounter.

A third contextual consideration of relevance is having an understanding about the modus operandi of sexual perpetrators. To understand sexual offending, we need to identify and understand the multi-level influences and possible interactions that may lead to a sexual offence being committed. Finkelhor developed a multi-factor model to explain child sexual abuse by integrating a variety of single factor theories. It incorporates characteristics of the offender, disinhibitors, the environment and the victim (see Figure 18.1). It operates at a high level of generality, thus allowing its use across a wide range of sexual offenders, whilst also encouraging analysis of the relative significance of the different factors in individual cases. It allows individual cases to be examined in detail, moving an offender on from asserting that his behaviour 'just happened', to an understanding of the thoughts, feelings and conscious manipulation of people and events which he undertook before the offence could take place. It thus emphasises that sexual abuse only takes place if the offender already has sexual feelings towards the child, and this firmly locates responsibility with the offender. Finkelhor's model accounts for both familial and extra-familial child sexual abuse, and, although widely used, there remains a paucity of hard evidence to support the model or risk factors.

Finkelhor (1984) argues that all the known factors contributing to child sexual abuse can be grouped into four pre-conditions, which need to be met prior to the instigation of child sexual abuse. The four pre-conditions are: *Motivation:* The potential offender needs to have some motivation to sexually abuse a child. Thus, he will need to find children erotically and sexually desirable. *Internal inhibitions:* The potential offender must overcome internal inhibitions that may act against his motivation to sexually abuse. *External inhibitions:* The potential offender also has to overcome external obstacles and inhibitions prior to sexually abusing the child. *Resistance:* Finally, the potential offender has to overcome the child's possible resistance to being sexually abused.

All four preconditions have to be fulfilled, in a logical, sequential order, for the abuse to commence. The presence of only one condition, such as a lack of maternal protection, social isolation or emotional deprivation is not sufficient to explain abuse.

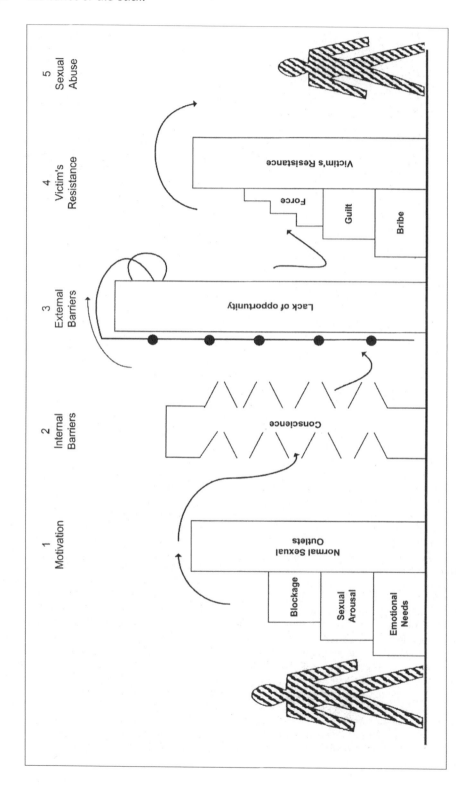

Figure 18.1   Four preconditions of sexual abuse

1. Motivation to sexually abuse

Finkelhor argues that there are three functional components subsumed under the motivation to sexually abuse children:

1. *Emotional congruence*, in which sexual contact with a child satisfies profound emotional needs.
2. *Sexual arousal*, in which the child represents the source of sexual gratification for the abuser.
3. *Blockage*, when alternative sources of sexual gratification are not available or are less satisfying.

As these components are not actual preconditions, not all three need to be present for sexual abuse to occur. They are, however, important in explaining the variety of motivations that offenders may have for sexually abusing children. The three components explain not only the instance of offenders who aren't sexually motivated but enjoy degrading victims by wielding power, but also the paedophile, and the sexually motivated offender who looks towards children for variety, even though he has access to other sources of sexual gratification. In some instances, elements from all three components may be present to account for whether the motivation is strong and persistent, weak and episodic, or whether the focus is primarily on girls or boys, or both.

2. Overcoming internal inhibitors

To sexually abuse, the offender needs not only to be motivated but also to be able to overcome his internal inhibitions against acting on his motivation. No matter how strong the sexual interest in children might be, if the offender is inhibited by taboos then he will not abuse. Arguably, most people do have some inhibitions towards sexually abusing children. Dis-inhibition is not a source of motivation, it merely releases the motivation. Thus an individual who has no inhibitions against child sexual abuse, but who is not motivated, will not abuse. The second precondition aims to isolate the factors that account for how inhibitions are overcome and whether they are temporary or not. The element of dis-inhibition is an integral part of understanding child sexual abuse.

3. Overcoming external inhibitors

While preconditions one and two account for the offender's behaviour, preconditions three and four consider the environment outside the offender and child which control whether and whom he abuses. External inhibitors that may restrain the offenders' actions include family constellation, neighbours, peers, and societal sanctions, as well as the level of supervision that a child receives. Although a child cannot be supervised constantly, a lack of supervision has been shown in the clinical literature to be a contributing factor to sexual abuse, as has physical proximity and opportunity. External inhibitions against committing child sexual abuse may easily be overcome if the offender is left alone with a child who is not supervised.

4. Overcoming the resistance of the child

One limitation of much of the research literature is the failure to recognise that children are able to resist, or avoid abuse. The focus in the clinical literature is on children who have been sexually abused, while ignoring those who although approached were able to avoid it or resist. The feminist argument proposes that insufficient attention is paid to the fact that children do have a capacity to resist. This capacity may operate in a very subtle, covert way, and does not necessarily involve overt protestations. Offenders may sense which children are good potential targets, who can be intimidated, and can be exhorted to keep a secret. Offenders report that they can almost instinctively pick out a vulnerable child on whom to focus their sexual attentions, while ignoring those who might resist. Frequently, these children may not even be aware that they are being sexually approached, or indeed resisting such advances. This framework highlights just how secretive the process of sexual offending is and provides us with an insight into how mothers may be groomed alongside their children. In many senses it can be likened to being put into a straightjacket without knowing it. There are a number of assumptions that can be made about sex offender behaviour:

- Assume the offender's actions were premeditated-it is rarely a spontaneous crime, and develops through a process of establishing and normalising need.

- Assume the offender's role was active and conscious. Offending is a choice at all levels of awareness including conscious, subconscious and unconscious.
- Assume that they rehearsed the offence in fantasy.
- Assume they targeted their victim.
- Assume that they groomed the environment – using seductive techniques, which surprise many workers as to why children ever tell.
- Assume that their offending is repetitive (offender's rarely commit 'one-off' offences).
- Assume that offenders have multiple patterns, offences and victim types.
- Assume that an addictive cycle of behaviour has developed.
- Assume that offending is supported by the dysfunctional lifestyle behaviours (i.e. antisocial, narcissistic) although these will vary in both intensity and strength of pattern.
- Assume they will seek support for their rationalisations from peers, family, victims and professionals, yet assume the rationalisations and excuses may not be what they actually believe-although it is easy to persuade oneself of the truth of one's own rationalisations.
- Assume their motivation to adhere to the assessment will fluctuate.
- Assume they have a long-term risk of re-offending. There is no cure.
- Assume that for every piece of information they reveal, the question arises as to what information they have thereby decided to conceal.
- Assume that their version of events is incorrect and incomplete.
- Assume that their apparent normality is their most striking diagnostic characteristic.
- Assume they will analyse and feed the needs/wants of the worker.
- Assume they know their actions are wrong because they persuade, coerce or threaten children into secrecy.
- Assume they will attempt to manipulate and deceive those making the assessment.
- Assume they have a vested interest in silencing their victims and partners.
- Assume they will portray the child as being responsible for all the above and
- Assume they will deny all the above (Calder, 1999).

The assumptions which professionals make and take into their work with mothers will determine the responses they receive. For example, if they assume the mother should have known about the abuse then the mother's denial will become entrenched, denying them access to much needed support. Alternatively, if workers accept initial denial and disbelief as a 'normal' response to a loss or trauma, then helping them work through this will lead to a more realistic measure of support to the child and will lead them to accessing and utilising the necessary support options. Peake and Fletcher (1997: 18–9) set out four reasons why mothers rarely know at the time of the sexual abuse:

- Children cannot tell about sexual abuse: either because they are too young or don't have the language to tell what is happening to them. They may have been threatened, tricked or bribed into secrecy.
- Society has been slow to recognise the prevalence of child sexual abuse and that the principal perpetrators are those the child knows or trusts, rather than a complete stranger. Even where abuse is recognised, there are powerful obstacles to societal acceptance. Thus, to set mothers up as needing to be more insightful about potential risks is unfair.
- There is little support for prevention programmes to educate people and warn mothers and the children about the problem in advance. Most mothers do concede, with hindsight, that there were indicators that something was wrong, but this is an unfair baseline against which to judge them. Most mothers have no basis on which they could have known.
- Perpetrators are clever. They are meticulous in planning and executing their offences. They often groom the mother as part of the process, and it is often noted that the mother is dependent on the man to have some of her own needs met (there is a variance on the degree of dependency). It is difficult for mothers to perceive that someone they know and trust, such as a friend, relative, or a professional, may be the abuser. The fact that many other people in contact with the child and the family did not identify a problem pre-disclosure also supports the assertion that mothers did not know what was going on.

Workers should thus approach the work with the following assumptions:

- Most mothers will only be learning of the sexual abuse as the professionals do.
- Mothers require professional help to work through the process of disclosure and subsequent activities.
- Mothers have been groomed (by the perpetrator), in a similar way to the child. The mother may also be a victim.
- Most mothers have a considerable amount to lose from the professional intervention.
- Mothers will not respond positively to a professional focus on them as in some way culpable with the perpetrator for the abuse.

Trotter (1996) has argued that mothers of sexually abused children are marginalised and stigmatised by social workers they come into contact with, as well as being discriminated against in a variety of ways. They could not describe their relationship with social workers as a partnership. She argues that the source of these problems is prejudice: families whose children have been sexually abused have been stereotyped and labelled. Two common mistakes are made by social workers: they automatically unite mothers and fathers as 'parents' regarding them as one unit when discussing sexual abuse of children – their connection with the abuse, their responses to it and their views about it are considered uniform; and when it is necessary to distinguish between the two parents, the mother will almost always be more relevant than the father. Workers are often pushed into these mistakes through the legislation (e.g. The Children Act 1989) and child protection procedures (that pull mothers into the system and push fathers into the background).

Plummer and Eastin (2007) identified that the mothers involved in the study they were undertaking felt that they received a negative response from professionals which included, 'being reportedly treated as if they were guilty of something or were simply, 'crazy'. Mothers also reported a sense of helplessness, feeling unprepared for the interventions and the way they were treated, and being incensed about the insensitivity shown to their victimised children.'

Contradictory or ambivalent feelings, thoughts, and behaviours have long been noted in some non-offending parents as they respond to their children's disclosure of sexual abuse. Ambivalence is typically considered an indication of less supportive parents who are unable to consistently protect and support their children. As such, children of ambivalent parents are at

great risk of removal from their homes (Everson et al., 1989).

Approximately one third of non-offending parents are scored across studies as partially supportive or ambivalent toward their sexually abused children after disclosure of the abuse (Bolen, 2002). Even so, ambivalence in support is seldom discussed in the empirical literature. When it is noted, it is most often conceptualised as a middle level of parental support, with ambivalent parents vacillating in actions, thinking, or affect toward the victim and sometimes the perpetrator. Ambivalent parents are those who are inconsistently emotionally supportive, inconsistently believe their child's disclosure, inconsistently make active demonstrations of disapproval against the perpetrator, or a combination of these. Thus, partial support or ambivalence has alternatively been captured as ambivalence toward the child or ambivalence between the child and perpetrator. Not surprisingly, one of the most important predictors of parental support is the closeness of the relationship between the parent and offender, with a closer relationship being related to lesser support (Bolen, 2002).

Bolen and Lamb (2007) examined whether non-offending parents can be both ambivalent and supportive. They hypothesised that non-offending parents can experience ambivalence after disclosure without a dilution of support. More specifically, they hypothesised that parental support and ambivalence are unrelated when parental support and ambivalence are separately captured (i.e., when indicators of ambivalence are not used as indicators of parental support). Their study also considered precursors to ambivalence. The most important finding in this study was that maternal support and ambivalence were unrelated, suggesting the possibility that non-offending parents can be both ambivalent and supportive after disclosure of their child's sexual abuse.

Corcoran (2002) examined the trans-theoretical stages of change model (explained in detail in Chapter 10) and motivational interviewing to enhance the mother's ability to protect and support their children by motivating an ambivalent mother toward the next level of change. At the pre-contemplation level the individual lacks awareness of the problem. Women learning of their children's sexual abuse may accept the perpetrator's denial of the problem and believe that the victim is to blame.

The worker's task in this case is to raise the client's consciousness about sexual abuse dynamics. In the second stage of contemplation, the individual begins to consider that there is a problem. People at this stage think about changing and are more open to information about how to change, but they are not ready for action. They are often ambivalent about the feasibility and costs of changing the behaviour. Women, whose partners have sexually abused their children, may be attached to their partners and dependent on their emotional and financial support; at the same time they may care about their children and do not want child protection workers or systems in their lives. Alongside this is the fact that sexual abuse is perceived as the worst thing that can happen to a child and a view, often compounded by professional intervention, that they should have known or been able to stop it happening. It is difficult for someone who has not been in this position to understand the devastation to their lives, and the high levels of shame and stigma that are experienced by mothers at this time.

Every mother we have worked with, whether they were able to believe from the point of disclosure, whether it took time to get to that position, or whether they chose not to believe at all, have felt paralysed by the investigative process, and the shame of it being in relation to sexual abuse. It is not something that is easily, or readily talked about with family and friends, therefore access to support networks is compromised from the beginning. It is also the case that once the woman does tell her family or friends about what has happened, she cannot guarantee that they will provide the support she requires, as they then also have to manage their own feelings and views about the allegations, and the (alleged) perpetrator. Many families experience a 'splitting' at this point, with some believing the abuse, whilst others feel unable to believe. This then adds a further burden of pressure and feelings of responsibility onto the woman, and to the child.

Women in the pre-contemplation stage are at risk of becoming entrenched in a position of non-support for their children. For this reason, interventions that are aimed at mobilising their support are essential. Motivational interviewing involves the strategic use of questioning to elicit self-motivational statements from clients. The advantages of change are enhanced and the disadvantages of change are lessened by

challenging beliefs that maintain problematic behaviour and by finding more functional alternatives. In the determination stage a decision has been made to take action and change. If a woman decides to leave the man who abused her children, she may use this stage as a time to figure out how she will manage the break and establish independence. She will work out the details of the plan and will build up financial support and emotional resources. The workers efforts at this stage should be around helping the mother identify viable housing options and linking her with the available financial systems. Once the practical issues are resolved attention can be moved to communication skills: to enhance existing support networks, communicate her support to her children to enhance their recovery and to prepare herself for any communication with the perpetrator and his allies. In the action stage, the parent has taken a strong measure of action in support of her child such as leaving the perpetrator and the worker can focus on strengthening the mother-child bond. Consistent change over six months takes individuals into the maintenance stage; however, it is also possible that relapse occurs, meaning the cycle starts all over again.

Corcoran et al. (2005) identified also that the way to achieve the priority of children's safety is to develop a collaborative relationship between the helper and the non-offending parent. A woman's strengths, her coping skills in the midst of a period of intense distress and crisis, and her supportive attitudes and behaviours are amplified through solution-focused techniques as well as motivational interviewing. Engagement of mothers involves listening and validating women's concerns when she learns that her child has been sexually abused. The worker's initial task is to create a supportive atmosphere for the mother by listening to and validating her concerns. Although assessment of maternal belief and protective action begins with the moment of the first contact, problem exploration will take a more targeted approach. Problem exploration first involves assessing and building the mother's level of support by asking the mother questions to elicit self-motivational statements. A more explicit way to discuss the advantages and disadvantages of increasing maternal support is through the decisional balance as well as assessing maternal attributions – who she holds responsible for the abuse. Mothers may assign responsibility to various parties associated with abuse. The mother may partly blame herself, the perpetrator, her child and perhaps others. Using a pie of attribution as an assessment device involves getting the mother to divide up the pie according to how much responsibility she places on each person connected to the abuse (see figure below). This gives the worker and the mother greater clarification when it comes to her thoughts and feelings about the abuse and where further attention is warranted. The main goal of the work at the stage of disclosure is to build maternal supportiveness for the child who has been sexually abused. A secondary goal is to help mothers manage the crisis of disclosure. This is not only to help mothers during this difficult time but also because maternal adjustment affects children's recovery.

Mothers living with domestic violence

The Woman Who Walked into Doors,

Broken nose, loose teeth, cracked ribs,
Ask me . . .
Sometimes I'd think I could escape if
I could get behind the right curtain,
if I was asked the right questions.
  Ask me.

                                    (Roddy Doyle)

Perpetrators of domestic violence share many of the characteristics of sex offenders in that their primary motivating feature is the exercise of power and control. They groom the environment over a period of time to render the potential for disclosure, belief and professional action almost impossible. Children fear the cost of disclosure and their opportunities are often narrowed through perpetrator threat or the systematic undermining of their critical relationship with their mother. Children may fear the costs of disclosure in terms of disruption to their siblings, peer networks and family relationships. Women fear the costs of leaving since they are at elevated risk, physically and emotionally; and fear potential stalking, especially if contact application to their children is granted. Indeed, the number of children killed in court-ordered contact and the risks from domestic violence and related stalking are both high. Figure 18.2 sets out the range of impacts of domestic violence for children.

Many perpetrators restrict their behaviour to specific places or contexts such as the home environment. For example, many hold down professional jobs and externally present as pillars of the community. However, they perpetuate physical, sexual and emotional abuse as well as neglect. Their control of the family is rarely

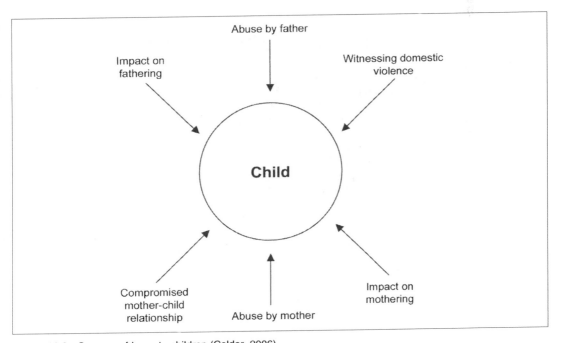

Figure 18.2   Sources of harm to children (Calder, 2006)

restricted to the mother and there is evidence of direct harm to children other than the witnessing or awareness of domestic violence. More actively, they may groom the children to perpetrate harm to their mother, particularly in their absence, to ensure a 24 hour, 7 days-a-week regime of control. This may be coupled with their behaviour towards the mother that has independently drained her of the energies necessary for parenting. Children also expect protection from their mothers and may apportion blame to her for either not leaving the perpetrator or naming and shaming his behaviour.

Any evidence of active parenting from the mother may be witnessed by professionals as physical abuse. There is evidence that mothers may strive to regulate the behaviour of their children for fear of a severe response if witnessed by the perpetrator, and this may result in physical injuries through attempts to physically control. This is not intentional harm, and in fact is driven by a need to protect their children from more severe harm from the perpetrator. The perpetrator of the domestic violence has thus successfully displaced the professional and child focus of blame to the mother rather than seeing the physical injury as a symptom of his abusive and controlling pattern of behaviour. Mothers may also be robbed of energies and so the focus of professional concern is again likely to be the mother since the concerns relate to child neglect. Professionals need to search for the origins of the presenting problem rather than dealing with the symptoms out of context. There is much in domestic violence to support the belief that men are resistant to accepting responsibility for their behaviour, they deploy effective displacement of responsibility strategies, and make effective help-seeking on the part of their victims a dangerous and potentially life-threatening activity. Rather than reflecting much child protection experience that when the going gets tough, the men get going, they stay put and challenge their victims to leave if they dare (Calder, 2006).

The male perpetrator expresses his dominance and asserts his identity through attempting to control and master every aspect of his partner's life. He uses patterns of coercive and violent behaviour to establish control and power over his partner (Dobash and Dobash, 1979; Stark, 2007). Through creating an illusion of omnipotence, his own feelings of inadequacy and helplessness are temporarily alleviated. Such projective

identification is a powerful means of attempting to rid oneself of unacceptable impulses through denying them in oneself and identifying them in another. Their partner becomes the sponge for their feelings of inadequacy and self-contempt. The female often absorbs these feelings, becoming increasingly depressed and he, in turn, loses touch with his own feelings of vulnerability, finding his aggressive and sadistic feelings more acceptable and less frightening to acknowledge. The perpetrator clearly needs the victim to remain alive: the goal is to control and preserve rather than destroy.

Some of the consequences for the perpetrator of the domestic violence include loss of the partner; injury or death at the hands of a partner who decides to retaliate or defend herself; alienation from their children; guilt, shame, and loss of self-esteem; and a range of legal effects, including arrest, trial and incarceration or other penalties.

Like the alcoholic, most perpetrators of domestic violence will not seek help until the situation becomes a crisis and they are mandated to do so, either because their partners have taken their children or they have been processed through the criminal justice system.

The Duluth power and control wheel identifies clearly the range of tactics deployed by men who perpetrate domestic violence (see Figure 18.3)

Traumatic bonding

Trauma bonding is a relationship based on terror. The goals of submission and obedience can be reached almost immediately. Trauma-bonded persons commonly experience their abuser as being in total control and feel their lives are in danger. The relief victims experience when not killed is often expressed as gratitude towards the perpetrator.

(James, 1994)

James reminds us that there are variations in the strength and features of trauma bonds, just as there are variations in the strength and quality of attachments. When observing a child–parent relationship we need to understand the quality and function of the relationship before we make a judgement about its relevance to the child.

Traumatic bonding is a useful theory that tries to explain why abusive relationships are so powerful. Several factors have been identified that must be present for such a bond to form. First, for traumatic bonding to take place, a relationship must contain an imbalance of power. This often takes the form of the abuser controlling

Figure 18.3   Duluth power and control wheel

the key aspects to the relationship, making most of the decisions and controlling the finances. The second factor in traumatic bonding is the sporadic nature of the abusive behaviour. In most abusive relationships the bad times are intermingled with the good times. The abuse is usually preceded and followed by very loving, giving periods. This pattern of on-going off-again abuse and affection is the strongest form of reinforcement. The third factor is denial where the victim makes excuses to make the situation seem better than it really was. The final factor involves finding ways to mask the abuse and can

include self-medicating with alcohol or drugs. These four elements combine to create a traumatic bond with the abuser and once established, becomes difficult to escape from (Dutton and Hock, 2000).

A similar process was described by Roland Summit in relation to sexual abuse, that helps us to understand how children learn to survive and live with their experiences. It is important for professionals to understand these processes when intervening in families where there has been sexual or domestic abuse, as it can easily distort our perception of attachments. For example, a child who appears to be well attached to the parent who has sexually abused them or who has been responsible for domestic abuse in the family, may well simply be ensuring their own survival at that point in time. Conversely, a professional may observe a child who does not seem as strongly attached to the mother as to the perpetrator. In these cases the worker needs to be careful not to make assumptions about what this means, without first placing what they have observed within a framework for understanding the grooming process and the way that both sexual and domestic abusers manipulate relationships, to ensure there is some distance between the child and any person from whom they may seek help, including the mother.

Therefore, making assessments of attachment and speaking to children about issues in relation to their feelings, or about issues of contact needs to be approached with caution. This raises some dilemmas for professionals who are charged with the task of presenting a child's view to courts or conferences, often within short timescales. It is possible to present the child's view, but this must be done within the context of what is known about the process of domestic abuse and trauma bonding. A true picture will only emerge over time once the child feels truly safe.

The Stockholm Syndrome describes a scenario of how 'captured' bond to their captor as a means of surviving a life-threatening situation and this is transferable to domestic violence situations in order to explain the seemingly illogical actions of the victims. Graham and Rawlings (1991) hypothesised that as the abuser traumatises the woman by threatening her physical or psychological survival, she comes to see him as a captor. Then, due to her subsequent isolation and her abuser's small kindnesses, she must turn to him alone for nurturance and sustenance. In this closed system, she learns to keep him happy so that he will let her live. However, in doing so, the woman unconsciously takes on his perspective of the world. This includes her denial of the abuse. Like traumatic bonding it assumes four conditions:

- The victim is threatened with death or great physical harm and perceives the perpetrator capable of acting on these threats.
- The victim sees no means of escape and thus perceives that her life depends on her captor.
- The victim feels isolated and holds little hope of outside intervention by family or friends.

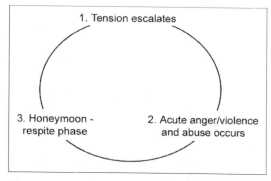

Figure 18.4   Cycle of violence, Walker (1979)

- The victimiser offers kindness along with the violence and thus increases the victim's perception of complete helplessness and dependence on him.

Walker (1979) has described a cycle of events which exist periodically in an abusive relationship (see Figure 18.4). This graphically depicts the cyclic pattern of violence observed by Walker in her interviews with 120 battered women. This cycle is made up of three phases: a tension-building phase, a period of acute violence and a state of reconciliation. Each of these phases vary in time and intensity for the same couple and for different couples. In the tension-building phase the abuser uses one or more of the control tactics defined earlier by Pence and Paymar (1986) in the Duluth power and control wheel. Minor physical assaults were described during this phase, but differed from the acute battering incident, both in the intensity of the attack and in the sense of the control the women reported feeling they still had over the violence. Denial, anger, fear of the anticipated beating, and rationalisation for the abuse were common elements in the women's descriptions of this phase. This phase tended to last from several months to several years. The acute battering incident was described by the women as a psychologically and physically paralysing event where the futility of escape prevailed. This phase can last from two hours to two days or more. After the attack, many of the partners became extremely contrite and loving, tearfully apologised, and promised never to be violent again. A honeymoon-like period followed but inevitably drifted back into a new tension-building phase. Over time, the battering incidents tended to increase in severity and

Mother	Children
Tiredness and lack of energy (or too much energy). Physical ill-health. Impact of abuse during pregnancy.	Aggressive behaviour and demonstrations of anger. Physical injuries. Hyperactivity. Stress-related illnesses such as asthma and bronchitis. Eating problems.

Figure 18.5   Physical effects

frequency and the honeymoon period shortened and then disappeared.

The effect of the domestic violence on the mother is devastating. They live in constant fear, not knowing when the next attack will take place, although they are certain that it will. They are thus on their guard constantly. They are often isolated from family and friends, often imposed on them by the abuser who may even have confiscated their clothes, or is even self-inflicted due to shame and a need to conceal what is going on. This reflects the belief that they are to blame for their situation. Such stresses are compounded if they have children as they also fear for their safety. Bagshaw and Chung (2000) reported on the experiences of mothers of domestic violence that included:

- Abuse of the mother in front of the children ranging from verbal abuse and 'put downs' through to serious physical violence (some involving weapons) sometimes with children being caught in the fray.
- Torture or killing of children's pets by kicking, strangling, hanging or with weapons such as knives and guns, often in front of the children.
- Obsessive control over what the children eat and when they eat, including locking food in the cupboards – some mothers reported that they and their children were regularly starved of food.
- Unreasonable control over children's outings and friendships and rudeness to visitors to the home.

Domestic violence destroys women, it destroys children, and it destroys communities. Women may often keep silent about the extent and severity of their situations in order to minimise the level and speed of this destruction. Women do not leave for all sorts of reasons, and in some cases women do not leave initially because they genuinely want to save the relationship, but they do want the violence and abuse to end. Attempts to seek help are mostly met by inadequate and

inappropriate responses, and in our experience most women stay in or return to a violent relationship because of the inertia that they meet along the way, and the fear that leaving may put them in increased danger. This is a very rational fear because research tells us that the most dangerous time for a woman is at the point of leaving or after she has left, and simple solutions put forward by all agencies fail to grasp the dangerousness of her situation (Rowsell, 2003).

Finally, there are the multiple features of the impact of domestic violence on children, which correlate to the devastating impact of sexual abuse on its victims. The following figures identify some of the common aspects for the mother and for the child.

Mothers also have needs

Recognition by a mother that she has her own needs and priorities is very important for a child's development. If the child is to develop a sense of themselves as a person in their own right, the mother must offer the child the experience of engaging with another autonomous being. A child cannot experience recognition by someone whom he or she controls. Not only should mothers have their own needs met, but it is actually very good for their children that they do so. A mother's safety is linked to her potential to parent and protect. There has been some recognition that parental needs, where unmet, potentially contribute to child abuse. This makes for a complex, sophisticated response from professionals. They may need to '*re-mother*' needy clients, acting as the '*good enough parent*', so that the adult client can then go on to care for their children.

The type of needs experienced by a mother might include:

- Someone to talk to, and to express trust and belief in her, often over weeks or months after the disclosure or identification of abuse.

Mother	Children
Continual and persistent fear.	Introversion and withdrawal.
Feelings of worthlessness and inadequacy.	Advanced maturity.
Lack of confidence.	Feelings of guilt and blame.
Erosion of self-esteem.	Fear and insecurity.
Feeling undermined and blamed.	Secretive and quiet.
Not being allowed to develop.	Being protective of mother and/or siblings.
Inability to maintain meaningful relationships.	Attempting to intervene physically or in other ways.
Isolation from friends, family and community.	Unpredictable behaviour and changes in behaviour.
Feelings that there is no way out of the situation.	Truanting/disruptions in schooling.
	Emotional confusion.
	Sleep disturbances including nightmares and bedwetting.
	Depression, anxiety, low self-esteem.
	Difficulties with concentration.

Figure 18.6   Emotional effects

Mother	Children
Inability to think clearly, make decisions and choices.	All areas of development are affected.
Inability to settle and lack of sleep.	Children may replicate the abusive behaviour.
Reliance on alcohol and or drugs (as a coping mechanism).	
Eating disorders/self-harm/suicide.	
Presence of mental health problems or symptoms.	

Figure 18.7   Effects on behaviour

- Someone to counsel her about the domestic and possible sexual violence perpetrated upon her.
- To know that she is not the first mother this has happened to, that she is not alone, and can possibly meet others and learn from shared feelings.
- To have a break from the perpetrator in order to gain a perspective, consider her feelings about the relationship etc.
- To be treated as a person, to have their feelings listened to seriously, to feel respected, to be acknowledged.
- To regain control of her life and mind, particularly resuming control over day-to-day events and personal thoughts.
- To obtain basic information on survival, to embrace new aspects of her life, such as courts, police, treatment, etc.
- To understand how domestic violence and sexual abuse are related, and to understand that they are separate issues that need to be addressed.
- To make basic life decisions such as to move away, separate or divorce, tell people, etc.
- To know options regarding contact and custody: both in relation to their partner, but also if the child has been removed from home by the local authority.
- To know how the children will react, as everyone will be affected to some degree by the trauma.
- To ensure that this will not happen again. Taking steps to safeguard the child from continued abuse, such as no contact or supervised contact, is important.

The needs of non-abusing parents can be neglected as professional responses focus on the children. In this respect, the professional systems are insensitive to the needs of women. However, these women need the therapeutic opportunity to deal with their feelings about what has happened and to adjust to the major change that has taken place in their lives. These are essential to the women's own emotional survival and growth. They are also vital in assisting those mothers to provide appropriate parenting for their children, thereby reducing the need for their children to be removed from their care, or to be placed outside of their family for the longer term.

Mills (2000) pointed out that child welfare workers hold strong views about battered women's responsibilities; they view the mother as the primary caretaker and often hold her to a higher level of responsibility than her husband or partner to protect her children. This higher standard finds more battered women being held responsible for a 'failure to protect' their children from exposure to domestic violence or from the risk of direct physical abuse by the perpetrator (Davidson, 1995; Davis, 1995; Magen, 1999). Hartley (2004) examined the differences between families in which less or more severe domestic violence and child maltreatment were present compared to families in which only child maltreatment was known to be present. Both child physical abuse and neglect were examined using child maltreatment reports involving parental perpetrators. The study found a higher percentage of neglect, specifically lack of supervision, and less child physical abuse in the more severe domestic violence compared to the child maltreatment only and less severe domestic violence groups. More mothers were found responsible for lack of supervision and fewer fathers were responsible for child physical abuse in the severe domestic violence group. Child protection workers also reported a higher level of concern for cases involving domestic violence. However, a closer examination of the qualitative characteristics of the domestic violence cases revealed that quantitative findings do not accurately present the whole story. Both mothers and fathers engaged in serious acts of physical abuse against their children. In addition, many mothers were held responsible for 'failure to protect' their children from the father's domestic violence.

Responding effectively to the co-occurrence of child maltreatment and domestic violence presents many challenges. The tensions between the 'best interests of the children' and the 'best interests of the mother' are not easily responded to. The strong cultural conceptions of mothers as the primary caretaker also contribute to mothers being judged more harshly by the child protection system than fathers (Mills, 2000). What is needed is a continuing shift from a view of the mother as 'failing to protect' to a view that recognises that to address the child's safety, we need interventions that focus on the circumstances that endanger both mother and child (Aron and Olson, 1997; Davidson, 1995). According to Fleck-Henderson (2000) best practices for families where both children and women are at risk of violence requires service

providers to 'see double'; drawing from the knowledge and values of both perspectives to best meet the needs of these families. 'Seeing double' should apply in all child maltreatment cases involving domestic violence. Child protection workers especially need to 'see double' in cases where mothers have maltreated their children. The presence of domestic violence should not negate a mother's responsibility for the maltreatment when it is clear she physically abused or neglected her child. Conversely, a founded maltreatment incident against the mother should not exclude her from receiving support and services to address the domestic violence, and it should not lead to her being held responsible for failure to protect her children from domestic violence (Magen, 1999). The perpetrator, not the battered woman, should consistently be held responsible for exposing children to his violence against the mother.

One intervention that might prove empowering to battered mothers is motivational interviewing (Hohman, 1997). Motivational interviewing helps clients become more aware of the reality of the situation they are experiencing, addresses the ambivalence or fear they feel about making changes in their lives, and identifies choices they may consider as they begin to move towards change (Hohman, 1997; Miller and Rollnick, 1991). Such techniques might prove particularly useful for child protection investigators when interacting with mothers who are not voluntarily seeking services for domestic violence. In addition to changes in their interactions with abused mothers, child protection systems need to consider policy changes that shift the gender bias in their practices. Typically in child maltreatment cases involving domestic violence, the mother is seen as responsible for following through with service plan even if she is not the identified perpetrator in the case. If the abusive father fails to comply with services, child protection has little leverage against him (Fleck-Henderson, 2000). Child protection can threaten to remove a child from the home, but this action unfairly punishes the non-offending mother and child. Instead, Davidson (1995) argues that child protection systems should seek statutory powers to request protective orders and court-ordered removal of domestic violence perpetrators from the home. Such powers would allow child protection to hold the perpetrators accountable for their abusive behaviour while meeting the safety needs of both the mother and child.

Corcoran and Bell (2005) considered the model of change with women exposed to domestic violence. In the first stage of change, or pre-contemplation, the individual lacks awareness of a problem. A woman in this stage may accept the perpetrator's denial of the problem and her blame. In the contemplation stage the woman thinks about changing her situation. She is more open to information about how to go about changing her situation, how exactly to go about achieving this, but is not yet ready for action. Ambivalent about the feasibility and costs of changing her behaviour, she may remain in contemplation for years. In determination, a decision has been made to take action and change, perhaps within the next month. If a woman decides to leave, she may use this time to figure out how she will manage the break and establish independence. She will work out the details of the plan and build up financial support and emotional resources. Some small steps may be taken to ready her family, such as putting away or borrowing money to leave and exploring alternative places to stay. In the action stage, the woman has undertaken a strong measure of action, such as leaving the perpetrator. Consistent change for six months leads individuals into the maintenance stage; however, it is also possible that relapse occurs and the woman returns to the relationship.

Engaging with women living in a violent relationship involves assessing the safety of the victim, providing empathy and validation and recognising the client's relationship with the change process. Often the worker contact takes place in crisis situations and the safety of the woman is a primary concern. After assessing immediate safety it is important to move into rapport building so that the worker understands what the woman is seeking and what she is motivated to do.

When looking at the attribution of responsibility for child maltreatment when domestic violence is present, evidence supporting advocates' concerns that battered women are being held responsible for failure to protect their children from the perpetrator's violence comes from qualitative interviews with workers (Beeman, Hagemeister and Edleson, 1999) and anecdotal observations of cases (Hartley, 2004). One of the few empirical studies available found that even after domestic violence training, a substantial proportion of child protection workers (40.5 per cent) held women responsible for the child's safety and stopping the perpetrator's violence against them (Saunders and Anderson, 2000). This study did not identify which characteristics of the cases affected workers' attribution of responsibility. More recently, Coohey (in press) found that among the small proportion of child maltreatment incidents involving failure to protect a child from domestic violence, child protection workers were less likely to substantiate an allegation of exposure to domestic violence if the domestic violence victim engaged in protective behaviours that ended contact between the perpetrator and her children. This same study determined that all the perpetrators investigated who were in the caregiver role at the time of exposure to domestic violence were substantiated. These findings, while encouraging, are based on 31 cases in one mid-western county.

Landsman and Hartley (2007) examined factors that influence how child welfare workers attribute responsibility for child maltreatment and child safety in cases involving domestic violence. They found that the presence of domestic violence significantly affected workers' assessments of the attribution of responsibility and concern for child safety, more so than variables related to child maltreatment. Responsibility for exposing a child to domestic violence differed for males and females, with more factors explaining female responsibility. Substance use by either caregiver was significant in attributing responsibility for physical harm, not watching the child closely enough, and concern for child safety, but not for exposure to domestic violence.

Problems with professional intervention involving mothers

There is plenty of evidence that, unless carefully crafted, professional responses can mirror their original experiences of harm, and can escalate the seriousness, frequency and range of behaviours from the perpetrator. In order to try and construct a more victim-friendly intervention, it is important that we try and name those factors that contribute to a professionally dangerous response (for a more detailed discussion of this issue, the reader is referred to Calder, 2008). The first concern relates to the current system of determining eligibility for a social work service. At the present time this is constructed to try and manage crisis or incident-driven situations (see Figure 19.8).

Level	Category	Definition
5	Collapsed	Children looked after or living away from home as a result of actual or likely significant harm or family breakdown.
4	Critical	Families in which there is clear evidence that children are suffering or likely to suffer significant harm. Social work intervention is urgently required in order to prevent family breakdown and avoid the children's removal from home.
3	Compromised	Families who are experiencing substantial difficulties in meeting their children's needs and where some form of intervention is required in order to prevent or delay further deterioration.
2	Vulnerable	Families in which children have acquired or encountered some difficulty which requires additional help if their life chances are to be optimised or the risk of social exclusion is to be averted.
1	Prevention	Selective services targeted at families or sections of the community where research evidence indicates an above average vulnerability to social exclusion.
0	Promotional	Universal services aimed at promoting the welfare of all children in the community.

Figure 18.8 A framework for determining eligibility for service provision (Calder, 2003)

This system will struggle to safely manage domestic violence notifications which are sent from the police, in response to their attendance, to social services or health for follow-up. Like the parallel system for managing 'schedule one offenders' (recently abolished in favour of 'risks to children', see Home Office; 2005), the number of pieces of paper circulating within the system make it difficult to immediately define which cases are in need of careful attention (see risk section chapter for a further discussion on this). The end product is that we have a system driven by a professional need to self-protect and in so doing induces professional paralysis.

What we have to do is to build a system of response that is specific to domestic violence. Like sexual abuse, domestic violence is a process. It is a pattern of behaviour rather than a series of isolated individual events. It also involves the use of power and control: the goal of the perpetrator is to ensure that he is in complete control of his partner and of the relationship. Domestic violence tends to increase in severity and frequency each time the cycle is played out, unless some intervention is made.

As a consequence, we tend to respond after a serious incident in which the mother and children have been physically harmed. This is indefensible when we could have reasonably predicted that the harm would materialise and that it would be significant for the victims. One of the key professional challenges is to construct a response

system that reflects the nature of domestic violence – embracing process as a predictor of likely future harm and assessing/intervening before it materialises. At the present time family experiences of social work responses tends to reinforce their negative view of social services in that when services become involved they are likely to remove the children. Figure 18.9 reflects

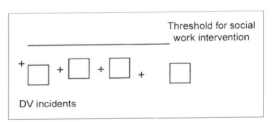

Figure 18.9 Crisis response system

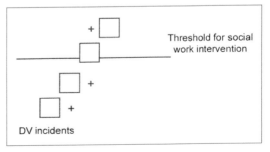

Figure 18.10 Process response system

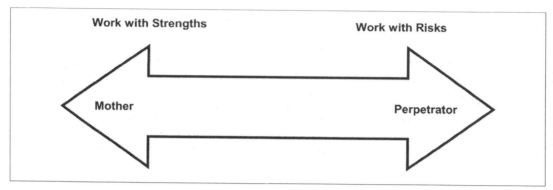

Figure 18.11   Risk-balancing approach in domestic violence (Calder, 2006)

a response system governed by crisis compared to Figure 18.10 which embraces process.

In order to move from a crisis to a process driven system we need to have an agreed risk assessment measurement framework and an agreed outcome-measurement framework, adopted across all the key agencies, to reduce confusion, conflicting responses and alienation of the victims as well as enhancing safety and engagement with those who need it. Since fiscal resources fall short of identified need on a 3:1 ratio currently, this raises key questions about the boundary between children and mothers deemed 'in need' or 'in need of protection'.

A critical element of a safe professional response is for professionals to intervene to help mothers and children in a way that embraces their experiences. In circumstances when a child protection response has been identified, the rigid assessment framework timescales kick in. Since they are linked to key performance indicators in social services, they are the driving force for staff, who need also to ensure that safe decisions are taken – both for themselves as well as the mother and her children. Expecting a mother to take immediate decisions that correspond with the professional preferences is unrealistic because:

- They are often in a state of shock.
- The risks to herself escalate significantly when she has left the home, and the impact of sustained disempowerment and abuse on her over a period of time renders her incapable of making safe or informed choices.

One of the key challenges for child protection is to hold the perpetrator accountable for his behaviour and any knock-on consequences such as displacement of the family, involvement of young people in their controlling strategy, compromised resilience or enhanced risks when they are prosecuted or in receipt of treatment. It is equally challenging for workers to approach mothers as victims rather than perpetrators, as lacking information and choices, to avoid extending or replicating perpetrator control, to facilitate reparation of the perpetrator-initiated impairment of the mother-child relationship, as well as in the transition from victim to survivor.

Research also highlights that professional intervention heightens the risks to women and children in many circumstances. Farmer and Owen (1998) reported that mothers tend to be under-represented in relation to offers of service and over-represented in respect of professional attempts to control them. When professionals intervene they tend to have most contact with the mothers and hold them accountable for the risks to their children, rather than with the men, who tend to stay involved until they achieve their own particular outcome, such as non-prosecution, or deflection of focus on to the mother and her parenting. Mothers also report feeling unable to disclose domestic violence when professionals are making enquiries for other reasons as they fear it will be held against them and their capacity to protect will be questioned and interrogated further. Figure 18.11 offers a more balanced approach from professionals and which is less likely to alienate mothers as well as being more likely to hold the perpetrator culpable and responsible for the multiplicity of harm.

Cammaert (1988) argued that rather than viewing the mother as a secondary perpetrator, it is important to conceptualise that she has strengths. Many mothers struggle to keep the family together; the children are fed, clothed and disciplined. Part of the package of survival skills includes a need to be compliant and to please the powerful male in order to avoid confrontation. Workers thus need to acknowledge that some mothers may not have any resources left to relate emotionally to anyone – after attending to the basic survival needs of the family. It is important that workers build on her survival skills and enlarge her skill repertoire to include the ability to increase her self-worth and independence for herself and skills to heal the mother-daughter relationship. For a detailed discussion on how to conduct strengths-based assessments, the reader is referred to Calder (1999) and Calder, Peake and Rose (2001).

In relation to mothers whose children have been sexually abused it is important that professionals view their work with the mother as a process, rather than waiting for her to give the answers they are wanting to hear. Given the circumstances it is entirely normal for the mother to start at the point of shock and denial. The task is to help them make informed choices, whatever they may be. These choices will then provide direction for intervention, rather than starting with an end point and viewing anything less as a deficit in the woman's parenting.

Engagement considerations

Too many myths still exist about the mother in situations where their child has been sexually abused. These include:

- They knew of the abuse and refused to do anything about it.
- They were indifferent or absent.
- They were weak and submissive.
- They wanted their children to 'mother' their partners.
- They were frigid.

Workers need to be cautious in developing generalisations about mothers in families where sexual abuse has occurred. The responses and circumstances of mothers will vary with the uniqueness of their personalities, needs and life experiences. Such stereotypes provide perpetrators with a ready supply of justifications for their abusive behaviour. The first task of the worker is therefore to assume the mother has not precipitated the abuse in any way. There are now

several useful texts that explore the experiences of women whose daughters have been sexually abused (see Orr, 1995), and by sharing their experiences and feelings, these women resist the stereotypical roles a patriarchal society would have them assume. They can also educate professionals about their job. This is useful as it moves away from the literature that either sets out stereotypes for women, or criticises them.

The workers' intervention is then built on their instinct or intuition, rather than on an objective assessment of the situation. We know that there is a very clear process, which faces individuals confronted with a disclosure of child sexual abuse that mirrors that of bereavement. Here, parents can display very powerful negative emotions such as anger, guilt and despair. They may well be grieving the loss of the victim's innocence, or they may be experiencing other impacts on family functioning, such as expressing confusion about what is happening and responding inappropriately or inconsistently as a result. They may also be traumatised by a feeling they should have known, or that they had not taken some cues or partial disclosures seriously at an earlier date. Parents cannot change overnight, particularly in the absence of any professional help. At this initial stage, therefore, we should be prepared for some response from the mother, and we should anticipate having to deal with their distress. Haase et al. (1990) outlined the stages of emotional response for parents: disbelief and denial that it could be possible; shock and alarm that may immobilise them; anger and rage accompanied by retaliatory urges; guilt and anguish where they blame themselves for the abuse; depression and loss which emerges as a result of emotional exhaustion combined with mourning the loss of a child's innocence; and recovery for the mother.

Featherstone (1999: 58) has noted that 'engaging with mothers who are service users around what they feel, is highly complex, particularly in a context where a child has been hurt. However, they may not be helped by explanations that suggest that they are feeling bad because they have been socialised into a particular maternal role'.

Resistance is a natural response to the fear of change. A worker who understands that resistance is part of the dynamics of a helping relationship will be able to help the client in the process of making the desire to change their own behaviour. Even initially hostile and uncooperative clients prefer openness and honesty and a social worker who shows concern and listens to their point of view. There will always be some families that do not wish to work in partnership with the statutory agencies because they believe they have no problem or because of their hostility towards such bodies. Even with the most resistant of families it should be possible to engage some members in the child protection process and at the very least keep them informed about what is happening and how they could participate more fully. The guiding principle for work that encourages the involvement of and partnership with families must be that the welfare of the child is of paramount importance. Low levels of client resistance are not only easier for the worker but it is also associated with longer-term change. By re-framing resistance as a feature of motivated behaviour, the workers can unlock an opportunity to help the client's change. It is important to identify the individual features of resistance to select a commensurate strategy of intervention, which may include:

Interviewing strategies

- Simple reflection – and acknowledgement of the disagreement, emotion, or perception can permit further exploration rather than defensiveness.
- Amplified reflection – or exaggeration can encourage them to back off a bit and reflect.
- Double-sided reflection – acknowledges what they have said and we then add it to the other side of their ambivalence.
- Shifting focus – away from the stumbling block by bypassing them.
- Agreement with a twist – offer initial agreement, but with a slight change of emphasis that can influence the direction and momentum of change.
- Emphasising personal choice and control – in the end, even where the current freedom of choice is threatened.
- Re-framing – information they offer so you acknowledge it but offer a new meaning of it or interpretation for them.
- Therapeutic paradox – where the resistance is designed with the hope of movement by the client in a beneficial direction.
- Handling missed appointments – seek them out and offer them a new appointment,

regardless of the reasons (adapted from Miller and Rollnick,1991: 104–11).
- Change the style of the worker to either increase or decrease the level of resistance.
- Where the family dispute the findings of the investigation, suggest that a fuller assessment would give them the opportunity to demonstrate evidence for their claims. It is important that any evidence parents produce to support claims or demonstrate strengths and positive qualities is taken seriously and looked at together with evidence that demonstrates problems or confirms concerns, and use any high levels of anxiety to reduce any resistance to any ongoing work, e.g., where clients see their situation as beyond their control. Here, we can often get them to consider alternatives to their resistant behaviour or situation as a prelude to change.

There are several useful mechanisms for eliciting the co-operation of the mother:

- Acknowledge their shock/numbness/shame/humiliation/feelings of failure and powerlessness, and give them space to feel uncertain and vulnerable.
- Give them information on abusing behaviour as well as the procedure and process of response.
- Advise them that they can be very influential in a discovery and recovery process.
- Encourage them to be a part of the assessment.
- Address their denial (if it exists), recognising that it is a common initial response, but becomes maladaptive if sustained. Denial is a block that they currently have about the need to change. The worker then has the task of finding the mechanism that will help the mother confront her worst fears.
- Supervise/monitor the children if remaining at home, or during any contact periods.
- Stress the family strengths.
- Normalise without minimising.
- Watch for signs of depression.
- Identify intra-familial sources of support (excluding the perpetrator's mother), especially other mothers who have shared their experience.
- Despite overt distrust, assume that they are searching for explanations and answers underneath.
- Adopt realistic time-scales.

Boulton and Burnham (1989) suggest that women who have low self-esteem, are poorly nurtured themselves, experience financial and environmental stress and are socially isolated, and inevitably more likely to have a greater need for the support their partners provide. Research into abusers would indicate that it is often families in this position that increase child vulnerability and it is such families which are targeted by abusers. Thus it is not surprising that in being asked to choose, many women opt to continue their relationship with their partner in some way, either overtly or covertly. Rose and Savage (2000) during the course of their work, found professionals attaching negative labels to these women. They have been described as collusive of the abuse, in denial, unfit mothers, minimising of the effects of the abuse, etc.

When professionals fail to recognise the feelings of the women and the context within which they are asked to make a choice, the assumptions about the 'sort' of mothers they are, appears to follow. The perceived hostile responses of professionals to women in this position often serve to strengthen the relationship between the women and their partners (where the women feel needed). The responses of workers to the women commonly took the form of the children's names being placed on the Child Protection Register as well as the initiation of care proceedings. This action supported the concept of these carers as unsafe, and further entrenched the positions of the two: professionals and mothers.

The tasks for the worker, therefore, is to be clear, first of all with themselves, what assumptions they may have already made about the women, based on the information they have. The worker must critically review their own expectations and interventions in the context of those assumptions in order to ensure they do not, in themselves, drive the woman to take a defensive position. In their work together, the woman and the worker need to explore each of the choices available to the woman and the risks for the child attached to each choice. Once this is achieved, the task is to explore how these risks might be managed and minimised. This will make clear what the women are responsible for, where the gaps are and where else safe support may come, both in the immediate and longer term. In working through this process, the worker must ensure that the choices remain open to the woman, and that changing position can be about gaining clarity and confidence rather than defeat.

When the woman has had time and information within which to make some decisions, she should be clear both of the risks to the child in making these decisions and proposed ways of managing that, together with any gaps. The worker should also be clear about why the woman has made those decisions, whether they consider the risks to be manageable and why, and what additional support/work may be needed. Leaving both professional and parental decision open to discussion and exploration together, over time, avoids dictating, distrust, dis-empowerment and ultimately disengagement.

Jones and Ramchandani (1999) explored the question: 'How do professionals manage the dilemma of discovering whether a child is safe, while also not alienating potential carers, who may eventually work in partnership with the professional?' They found that the way in which a case is handled initially could affect the entire subsequent process. Where handled well and sensitively, keeping the non-abusing parent informed and involved, there can be a positive effect on the eventual outcome. Conversely, poorly handled initial contact can alienate both the child and carer, making later work more difficult. The variation in initial approach may reflect a worker's underlying beliefs about the way in which an investigation should be carried out. They found that some professionals approach parents on the basis of supportive acceptance, whilst others require parents to accept responsibility. The majority favour the latter. This has implications in the case of sexual abuse, where the wide range of parental reactions are often difficult to interpret accurately, particularly at the time when they were also considering placement issues. There is thus a wide difference in perspectives between the parents and the professionals. Parents were typically shocked, frightened, or became withdrawn, whereas for the professional this was a 'routine' job. In these circumstances, professionals sometimes misjudged parental capacity to understand allegations or protect their children.

They found that parents retained a strong expectation of help despite the quality of the initial contact, showing that the prospect of working in partnership is not necessarily lost forever, particularly with mothers who remained open and receptive to advice given their predicament. Workers face the difficult task of balancing the need to obtain the non-abusing parent's commitment to help protect the child,

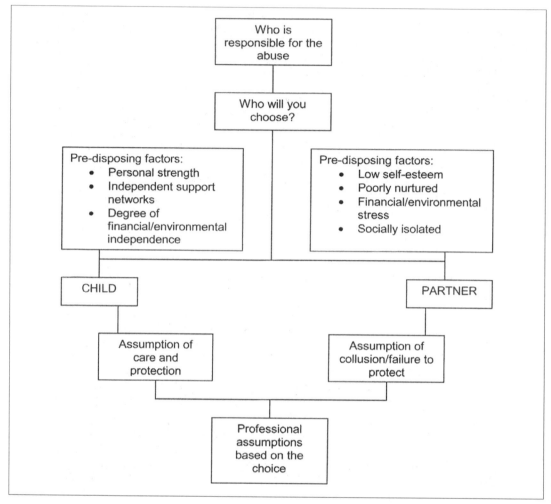

Figure 18.12   Who is responsible for the abuse? (adapted from Bourton and Burnham, 1989 by Rose and Savage, 2000)

while also being responsive to that parent's needs for understanding, information and psychological treatment. Fortunately, many believe it possible to balance a supportive and accepting stance with one of encouraging parental responsibility, seeing them as a tension that can be maintained rather than a dichotomous choice. Regan (2006) provides a clear framework that has a strong emphasis on starting the work focusing on the engagement of the mother, moving onto some educative materials and supporting her in transferring this to her own situation where appropriate. This supports mothers to move to a point of making realistic choices and decisions.

Parents who were not kept well informed were marginalised when they attended the initial child protection conference. They wanted professionals to consider all the family history and not just the sexual abuse in order to take decisions on the way forward. For example, issues of finances, supports, general parenting ability, previous domestic violence with its potential repercussions, were all central to such decisions. Families have broad needs that require services and a focus in the assessment. Farmer (1993) has noted that the conference has an important role in ensuring the mother does not feel blamed, as this can be a block to partnerships later. It has an important role in helping the mother become equal with the professionals.

Once registered, a comprehensive assessment needs to be undertaken as part of a broader child protection plan. If the parents had not been party to its construction, then it is unlikely to be accepted by them. This is unacceptable when you consider that sexual abuse has multiple impacts on the family, and that many professionals missed or overlooked the parents' needs in the process. As Calder (2000) has argued, there has been a fundamental lack of practice guidance for workers undertaking this task, with the effect that it has become a hugely varying task (see Calder, 2007b). Such detailed assessments are the key to successful long-term planning. If there is no assessment and a lack of parental co-operation then it is very difficult to review and amend the plan to accommodate changing circumstances.

Most clients' value courtesy and respect, being treated as equals, as individuals and as people who can make their own decisions; they value workers who are experienced, well informed and reliable, able to explain things clearly without condescension, and who really listen; and they value workers who are able to act effectively and make practical things happen. Workers who deal with their clients in these ways empower them. This can become more difficult in some situations of child protection, where workers have considerable power, which makes the relationship inherently unequal.

Smart (1997) found that the women in her sample generally regarded social work involvement negatively, being perceived as intrusive, unsupportive, and dis-empowering. Despite this, the mothers did note that they were provided with a good understanding of the role of social services in the protection of children, and this facilitated some positive working relationships. This finding is not consistent with the work of Farmer and Owen (1995) who found that parental distrust tends to stem from a lack of information passed on to them. The mother's comments did indicate that in forming alliances with professionals, several aspects of the process needed improvement.

Smart's research explored the women's experiences of social work intervention at each stage of the child protection process to identify areas where services could be improved.

Previous involvement with social services

Farmer and Owen (1995) noted that some parents felt alienated by previous involvement with social services and this clearly made the parents reluctant to engage with social workers. Engaging statutory help is a complex issue for a family who have previous knowledge or past experience of unwanted, or inappropriate intervention, seeing alternative support as preferable.

Initial investigation

> . . . these bodies come and arrive in your home who you've never seen before and I found it quite gruelling because I realise they've got a job to do, but some of the questioning was quite grilling like I was part of it and I know what this is what they're trying to find out, but I felt as though I was being put in the dock, so that side of it I found quite offensive.

Others described social workers as being judgemental and insensitive, and none had prior notification of the social worker's visits. It is clear that workers do need to understand the impact of the news and acknowledge this as a prelude to the mothers' co-operation. The feeling that mothers were not listened to was often expressed as a factor leading to poor alliances at the start of the process.

Many women need a longer period to work through their feelings and make plans for their own and their child's future, than is allowed for in this initial period. However, if we start with the mother's own position, accept the time factors that may be needed in order for her to be clearer about her views and plans, we can get a starting point from which to measure further changes. I would suggest that only if a mother has been directly implicated, or if she has actively undermined her child should she be assessed as being unable or unwilling, to protect. In my experience, it is preferential to begin by accepting that she will find the choices ahead difficult and the role is to support her to make an informed decision, whatever that might be.

It is often the structure and organisation of this material that is most problematic for professionals. However, based on work with parents, Regan (2007) has developed a framework to help professionals make sense of changes that do (or don't) occur and presents a format for evidencing this.

Initial child protection conference

Overall, mothers experienced the conference negatively despite some preparation for it. For a useful discussion of ideas on how to prepare mothers for the conference, the reader is referred to Peake and Fletcher (1997, p34). Some said they had not retained the information or it had gone 'over my head'. This is a symptom of a lot going on at any one time. Whilst mothers did have the opportunity to read the report for the conference in advance, they were shocked when it contained details of the abuse about which they had been unaware. This led to distress and a loss of composure, which meant mothers were unable to function clearly in the meeting. The ways in which the mothers were informed about and invited to the conference influenced their attitudes and the quality of their participation. The issue of the perpetrator's attendance was crucial. Some wanted to speak and attend separately as they had nothing to hide, although the perpetrator's denial can have an effect on the mother and influence professional views of the mother negatively.

Registration

All the children's names were placed on the child protection register, and many women felt this decision punished them for the abuser's behaviour and apportioned some of the blame onto them. Some did not understand the concept of 'high risk' used, even though they themselves accepted there was some risk. Farmer (1993) has stated clearly that the basis of the decision to register needs to be carefully explained to parents – is it because abuse has occurred or is it because there is still an assessed risk based on the information gathered? Several of the women questioned the conference conclusion that they may not be able to protect their child/ren, and this added to their distress. Despite this, most mothers noted that registration would not harm the child/ren further and they understood the professional perspective.

Support from the social worker

Several of the mothers felt unsupported by the social worker, whilst others stated they felt the workers tried but had nothing to offer – this was devastating to those mothers where the social worker was their sole support. Offers of counselling were not successful – either as

mothers could not consider it (brick wall), or they found it only scraped the surface of their problems. It is clear that there are increasing difficulties in accessing resources in the aftermath of abuse and this is crucial when you consider that an important aspect of co-operation is the availability of therapeutic agencies, and of appropriate settings, for parents to be able to do the work and achieve change; and that the requirement of a 'therapeutic life support system' for mothers is a necessary aspect of intervention following child sexual abuse disclosure. Humphreys (1995) explored in detail the issue of counselling and support for mothers (and fathers) of sexually abused children. This is a necessary intervention given that many of a mother's normal avenues of support are unavailable and they have their own needs, which should be met. She found that half of the mothers had been referred for counselling. Unfortunately, the form that such work took usually had more to do with the policy, skills and resources of the counselling agency rather than the needs specified by the worker or the parent.

Some were suspicious of their social worker withholding information from them, such as convictions of the partner, or the partner forming new relationships, and this was a reflection of their level of involvement in the process. They were concerned about this as the children often chose to talk about the abuse in more detail after the crisis and they needed professional guidance and support in managing this effectively. Many mothers felt they would be seen as inadequate parents had they sought assistance for this reason.

Follow up

Despite concerns about what the professionals could offer, many cases remained open some time after the case had reached its conclusion (de-registration, legal proceedings), often to compensate for the lack of other external supports. Others wanted the cases closed and saw this as a relief. There often needs to be a considered discussion on the way forward given that where perpetrators are removed from the home and it was felt mothers could protect their children, social work intervention terminates prematurely and the difficulties for both the mother and the child/ren can then deepen (Farmer and Owen, 1995).

Issues to consider

Rose and Savage (1998) provided us with a useful framework to empower and facilitate women in making informed decisions about their children and their own lives. Practical ways in which this can be achieved include:

- Information: about the cycle of abuse, emotional impact on all family members, practical ways to manage behavioural effects of trauma, how to explain what is going on to the children, how the child protection system works, what the woman's rights are within this, treatment options, tips about survival and stress management etc. The natural progression of understanding these issues will inform their decision-making about their partner's future in the family. If the decision is for him to return, the emphasis will be on practical ways to make themselves and their children safe. This will be how they live with risk.
- Support: formal and informal. The women and children need safe and independent ways of checking out their own understanding of the information workers provide. The women identified a need to be able to make mistakes without this having negative implications for assessment.
- Time-scales: this cannot be determined by a social services need for the women to reach particular decisions. The time-scale is shaped by how the women develop links between an understanding of the risks, which they are able to reflect in practical ways and their own situations. For example, how homes can become safe, whether or not the allegation that was made is believed and why and how this is followed by any form of criminal prosecution.
- Clarity of task: if the focus is not just to assess parenting, it is important to become clear with the women what it is and what is expected of them in the process.

Jones and Ramchandani (1999: 25) set out some useful factors influencing a mother's co-operation with agencies:

- It is important to attempt to work in partnership with parents, especially with mothers who refer many, if not most, cases of suspected sexual abuse.
- Parents, and especially mothers, require clear information in an attempt to work as openly as possible, in order to keep them engaged in the process.
- Informing parents as swiftly and as completely as possible after children have been interviewed is necessary to enable trust to be maintained. Parallel sessions interviewing parents and children in tandem may prove useful.
- If conflict occurs between potentially jeopardising the partnership with parents and on the other hand fully protecting the child from harm, it is clear that the child's needs are paramount.
- Few specialists are currently involved and thus it may be useful to identify cases that need specialist help at an early stage.
- The early planning stage, following the initial referral, would be the most useful point to identify issues of race, culture, or language, which may require addressing.

Defining risk is an important starting point in work with mothers. Wherever social workers 'intervene' with families, they start with a view about why they are there and what the best outcome could be. Achieving these outcomes can be relatively straightforward, i.e. where a child is sexually abused by a stranger, the family believe and are sensitive to the needs of family members. The worker's view of the needs is most likely to be mirrored by the family's view and everybody is agreed about what needs to happen. Alternatively, the perception of the risk may not be immediately shared, e.g. a woman whose partner has offended outside the home, may view her own children to be perfectly safe (Rose and Savage, 2000).

There is also a group of women who do take the decision to remain with their partners, the perpetrators. Whilst they would not be defined as traditional 'safe carers', neither were they the principal risk. They are women who need to learn to 'live with risk'. Rose and Savage helped them to develop an understanding that it is possible for some women to choose to continue their relationship, in some shape or form, with partners who are Schedule One offenders. However, in doing this, they can also remain carers of their children. Their belief remained that, if the 'risk' presented by the continuing relationship between the women and their partners could be managed safely for the children, then this was their choice and needed to be the focus of the work.

The most significant confusion lay in workers failing to define with the women what the risk was, or where the differing responsibilities lay for managing that. The use of the child protection and court system only served to reinforce the position of fight rather than adding clarity to the plan. The final, and additional, task for the worker is to assess whether the suggested management of the risk is safe for the children. If it isn't, where this process has been followed, it should be relatively easy to be clear about why not.

All the women accepted and agreed that putting the children's safety and wellbeing first was the most important thing. Equally, all the women agreed on some level that continuing a relationship with this man posed some risk. Even if women were saying they felt sure he wouldn't re-offend within the family now, the women acknowledged they were often kept awake at night worrying about 'What if?' Once the risk to all family members had been named, the women were able to acknowledge that they were willing to accept this level of risk and move to developing ways of managing this risk.

Even in situations where involvement results in being unable to agree on the presence of a risk, the process of exploring this can enable women to gain some insight and information into why protective action was necessary. Rose and Savage found that the process of defining the risk was resolved much more quickly than they had imagined, with many of the mothers reaching a point by the third session where they were asking for more information and clarification in order to develop ways of managing their households. The conclusion for many was that they were dependent on the honesty of their partners and the focus then became one of developing rules for safe caring within their own situations, based on the assumptions that they would be unlikely to know prior to their partner's re-offending. The enormity of trying to manage this risk was realised when the women began to think about their daily routine. For example, the simple task of bathing the children – the sounds may, for their partner, trigger distorted thinking without being involved in the bathing itself.

Concluding thoughts

It is often difficult for mothers to co-operate closely with agencies whose intervention alienates them and subjects them to prescribed societal expectations. Many mothers have reported the services provided to be inadequate.

For example, those mothers who were sent onto parenting courses were confused as to the reasoning behind this and why the focus was on them. This appeared to be consistent with the view of women's responsibility being to protect the children. Most mothers are willing to co-operate in the necessary assessment and treatment work once they trust that they are not being criticised or labelled for their confused and conflicting feelings.

References

Aron, L.Y. and Olson, K.K. (1997) Efforts by Children Welfare Agencies to Address Domestic Violence. *Public Welfare*, 55, 4–13.

Bagshaw, D. and Chung, D. (2000) *Reshaping Responses to Domestic Violence: The Needs of Children and Young People.* Presentation to 'The Way Forward: Children, Young People and Domestic Violence', Carlton Crest Hotel, Melbourne, 26–27th April.

Beeman, S.K., Hagemeister, A.K. and Edleson, J.L. (1999) Child Protection and Battered Women's Services: From Conflict to Collaboration. *Child Maltreatment*, 4, 116–26.

Bolen, R.M. (2002) Guardian Support of Sexually Abused Children: A Definition in Search of a Construct. *Trauma, Violence and Abuse*, 3: 1, 40–67.

Bolen, R.M. and Lamb, J.L. (2007) Can Non-Offending Mothers of Sexually Abused Children be both Ambivalent and Supportive? *Child Maltreatment*, 12: 191.

Boulton, A. and Burnham, L. (1989) Stand by Your Man: or Your Child? *Social Work Today*, Sep., 20.

Brown, K. (1998) *Surviving Sexual Abuse.* Crowborough: Monarch Books.

Browne, K.D. (1993) Violence in the Family and its Links to Child Abuse. *Bailliere's Clinical Paediatrics*, 1: 1 149–64.

Calder M.C., Peake, A. and Rose, K. (2001) *Mothers of Sexually Abused Children: A Framework for Assessment, Intervention and Support.* Lyme Regis: Russell House Publishing.

Calder, M.C., Harold, G. and Howarth, E. (2004) *Children Living with Domestic Violence: Towards a Framework for Assessment and Intervention.* Lyme Regis: Russell House Publishing.

Calder, M.C. (1999) *Assessing Risk in Adult Males who Sexually Abuse Children: A Practitioners Guide.* Lyme Regis: Russell House Publishing.

Calder, M.C. (2000) *A Complete Guide to Sexual Abuse Assessments.* Lyme Regis: Russell House Publishing.

Calder, M.C. (2003) Child Sexual Abuse and Domestic Violence: Parallel Considerations to Inform Professional Responses. *Seen and Heard,* 12: 4.

Calder, M.C. (2003b) The Assessment Framework: A Critique and Reformulation. In Calder, M.C. and Hackett, S. (Eds.) *Assessment in Child Care: Using and Developing Frameworks for Practice.* Lyme Regis: Russell House Publishing

Calder, M.C. (2006) Domestic Violence and Child Protection: Challenges for Professional Practice. *Context,* 84: 11–14.

Calder, M.C. (2008) *Contemporary Risk Assessment.* Lyme Regis: Russell House Publishing.

Calder, M.C. (2008b) *Sexual Abuse Assessments.* Lyme Regis: Russell House Publishing.

Campbell, J.C. (1989) Women's Responses to Sexual Abuse in Intimate Relationships. *Women's Health Care International,* 8: 335–47.

Campbell, J.C. and Alford, P. (1989) The Dark Consequences of Marital Rape. *American Journal of Nursing,* 89: 946–9.

Cammaert, L. (1988). Non-Offending Mothers: A New Conceptualisation. In Walker, L.E. (Ed.) *Handbook on Sexual Abuse of Children: Assessment and Treatment Issues,* New York: Springer Publishing.

Coohey, C. (In press) What Criteria do Child Protective Services Investigators use to Substantiate Exposure to Domestic Violence? *Child Welfare.*

Corcoran, J. (2002) The Transtheoretical Stages of Change Model and Motivational Interviewing for Building Maternal Supportiveness in Cases of Sexual Abuse. *Journal of Child Sexual Abuse,* 11: 3, 1–17.

Corcoran, J. and Bell, H. (2005) The Strengths and Skills-Building Model: Application to Women in Violent Relationships. In Corcoran, J. (Ed.) *Building Strengths and Skills.* Oxford University Press.

Corcoran, J., Hart, D., Garell, K.A. and Berry-Edwards, J. (2005) Working with Non-Offending Parents of Sexual Abuse Victims. In Corcoran, J. (Ed.) *Building Strengths and Skills.* Oxford University Press.

Davidson, H.A. (1995) Child Abuse and Domestic Violence: Legal Connections and Controversies. *Family Law Quarterly,* 29, 357–73.

Davis, J (1995) Failure to Protect and its Impact on

Battered Mothers. *Courts and Communities Confronting Violence in the Family,* 1, 6–7.

Dobash, R.E. and Dobash, R.P. (1979) *Violence against Wives.* NY: The Free Press.

DoH (2000) *Framework for the Assessment of Children in Need and Their Families.* London: TSO.

Edleson, J.L. (1998) Responsible Mothers and Invisible Men: Child Protection in the Case of Adult Domestic Violence. *Journal of Interpersonal Violence,* 13, 294–8.

Edleson, J.L. (1999) The Overlap between Child Maltreatment and Woman Battering. *Violence Against Women,* 5, 134–54.

Everson, M.D. et al. (1989) Maternal Support following Disclosure of Incest. *American Journal of Orthopsychiatry.* 59: 2, 197–207.

Farmer, E. (1993) The Impact of Child Protection Interventions: The Experiences of Parents and Children. In Waterhouse, L. (Ed.) *Child Abuse and Child Abusers.* London: Jessica Kingsley.

Farmer, E. and Owen, M. (1995) *Child Protection Practice: Private Risks and Public Remedies.* London: HMSO.

Farmer, E. and Owen, M. (1998) Gender and the Child Protection Process. *British Journal of Social Work,* 28: 545–64.

Featherstone, B. (1999) Mothering and the Child Protection System. In Violence against Children Study Group. *Children, Child Abuse and Child Protection: Placing Children Centrally.* Chichester: Wiley and Son.

Finkelhor, D. (1984) *Child Sexual Abuse: New Theory and Research.* NY: The Free Press.

Fleck-Henderson, A. (2000) Domestic Violence in the Child Protection System: Seeing Double. *Children and Youth Services Review,* 22, 333–54.

Giles-Sims, J. (1985) A Longitudinal Study of Battered Children of Battered Wives. *Family Relations,* 34, 205–10.

Graham D.L. and Rawlings, E.I. (1991) Bonding with Abusive Dating Partners: Dynamics of the Stockholm Syndrome. In Levy, B. (Ed.) *Dating Violence: Young Women in Danger.* Seattle: Seal Press.

Grubin, D. (1998) *Sex Offending against Children: Understanding the Risk.* London: Home Office.

Haase, C.C., Kempe, R.S. and Grosz, C.A. (1990) Non-Familial Sexual Abuse: Working with Children and their Families. In Oates, R.K. (Ed.) *Understanding and Managing Child Sexual Abuse.* Marrickville: Harcourt, Brace and Jovanovich.

Hartley, C.C. (2004) Severe Domestic Violence and Child Maltreatment: Considering Child

Physical Abuse, Neglect, and Failure to Protect. *Children and Youth Services Review*, 26: 373–92.

HM Probation Service/National Probation Service (2001) *OASYS*. London: Home Office.

Hohman, M.M. (1997) Motivational Interviewing: An Intervention Tool for Child Welfare Case Workers Working with Substance-Abusing Parents. *Child Welfare*, 77, 275–89.

Home Office (1998) *Guidance to the Probation Service on Working with Sex Offenders*. London: HMSO.

Home Office (2005) *Identification of Individuals who Present a Risk to Children*. London: Home Office.

Hooper, C. (1992) *Mothers Surviving Child Sexual Abuse*. London: Routledge.

Humphreys, C. (1992) Disclosure of Child Sexual Assault: Implications for Mothers. *Australian Social Work*, 45: 3, 27–35.

Humphreys, C. (1995) Counselling and Support Issues for Mothers and Fathers of Sexually Abused Children. *Australian Social Work*, 48: 4, 13–19.

James, B. (1994) *Handbook for the Treatment of Attachment: Trauma Problems in Children*. Lexington Press.

Jones, D.P. and Ramchandani, P. (1999) *Child Sexual Abuse: Informing Practice from Research*. Oxford: Radcliffe Medical Press.

Landsman, M.J. and Hartley, C.C. (2007) Attributing Responsibility for Child Maltreatment when Domestic Violence is Present. *Child Abuse and Neglect*, 1: 445–61.

Lyon, T.D. (1999) Are Battered Women Bad Mothers? Rethinking the Termination of Abused Women's Parental Rights for Failure to Protect. In Dubowitz, H. (Ed.) *Neglected Children: Research, Practice and Policy*. Thousand Oaks: Sage.

Magen, R.H. (1999) In the Best Interests of Battered Women: Reconceptualising Allegations of Failure to Protect. *Child Maltreatment*, 4, 127–35.

Magen, R.H., Conroy, K. and Del Tufo, A. (2000) Domestic Violence in Child Welfare Preventative Services: Results from an Intake Screening Questionnaire. *Children and Youth Services Review*, 22, 251–74.

Mill, L.G. et al. (2000) Child Protection and Domestic Violence: Training, Practice, and Policy Issues. *Children and Youth Services Review*, 22, 315–33.

Miller, W.R. and Rollnick, S. (1991) *Motivational Interviewing*. New York: Guilford.

Mills, L.G. (2000) Woman Abuse and Child Protection: A Tumultuous Marriage. *Children and Youth Services Review*, 22, 199–205.

Milner, J. (1996) Men's Resistance to Social Workers. In Fawcett, B. et al. (Eds.) *Violence and Gender Relations: Theories and Interventions*. London: Sage.

Orr, T. (1995) *No Right Way: The Voices of Mothers of Incest Survivors*. London: Scarlet Press.

Parton, N., Wattam, C. and Thorpe, D. (1997) *Child Protection, Risk and the Moral Order*. London: Macmillan.

Peake, A. and Fletcher, M. (1997) *Strong Mothers: A Resource for Mothers and Carers of Children who have been Sexually Assaulted*. Lyme Regis: Russell House Publishing.

Pence, E. and Paymar, M. (1986) *Power and Control: Tactics of Men who Batter: An Educational Curriculum*. Duluth, Minnesota: Minnesota Program Development.

Plummer, C.A. and Eastin, J.A. (2007) System Intervention Problems in Child Sexual Abuse Investigations. *Journal of Interpersonal Violence*, 22:6, 275–87

Regan, L. (2006) *Helping Mothers Move Forward: A Workbook to Help Provide Assessment and Support to the Safe Carers of Children who have been Sexually Abused*. Lyme Regis: Russell House Publishing.

Reid, C. (1989) *Mothers of Sexually Abused Girls: A Feminist Analysis*. Social Work Monographs. Norwich: University of East Anglia.

Rose, K. and Savage, A. (1998) *Stand by Your Man*. Presentation to A One-Day Conference, 'A Betrayal of Trust: Who Abuses Children and Why' at The Dalmeny Hotel, Lytham St Annes, 21st Jan.

Rose, K. and Savage, A. (2000) Living with Risk. In Wheal, A. (Ed.) *Working in Partnership with Parents*. Lyme Regis: Russell House Publishing.

Rowsell, C. (2003) Domestic Violence and Children: Making a Difference in a Meaningful Way for Women and Children. In Calder, M.C. and Hackett, S. (Eds.) *Assessment in Child Care: Using and Developing Frameworks for Practice*. Lyme Regis: Russell House Publishing.

Smart, P. (1997) *Child Sexual Abuse: Non-Abusing Parents Perspectives of Social Work Intervention*. Unpublished BA Research Project. University College, Salford.

Stark, E. (2007) *Coercive Control: How Men Entrap Women in Personal Life*. NY: Oxford University Press.

Trotter, J. (1996) *Illusive Partnerships: Gender and Sexuality Issues Relating to Child Sexual Abuse and Child Protection Practices*. Presentation to ISPCAN Conference, Dublin, Ireland.

Walker, L.E. (1979) *The Battered Woman*. NY: Harper and Row.

CHAPTER 19

Engaging Substance Misusers through Coercion

Phil Harris

Introduction

The role of coercion had always existed in treatment services. Until, in 1998, the UK Government's strategy *Tackling Drugs to Build a Better Britain* (Cabinet Office, 1998) set new priorities for drug services. Primary amongst these was to increase the number of problem users in active treatment. This was to include problem users in the criminal justice system. Although the links between crime and substance use are complex (Hammersley et al., 1989), criminally involved users were seen as an ideal target group for a number of reasons. Criminal justice services retain a large population of problem users. It can impose legally binding sanctions or rewards in terms of removing liberty or mitigation of prison sentencing and has the resources to track clients over time and wide geographic areas. As individuals within the criminal justice system demand high supervision, the additional costs of providing treatment is minimised. Furthermore, the idea had political appeal in asserting the government's credentials on being tough on anti-social behaviours. Treatment services had been collaborating with criminal justice services on a voluntary basis since the 1980s, but the plethora of government initiatives has now formalised these relationships at every level of criminal involvement. Arrest Referral Schemes, Direct Testing and Treatment Orders, CARAT services have been expanded with Drug Intervention Programmes and the introduction of Tough Choices to increase the legal sanctions on untried offenders to attend assessment. Within the space of a decade, treatment has given way to 'threatment'.

Whilst substance misuse services have been quick to capitalise on new areas of funding, the idea of coercing involuntary substance misusers into treatment remains controversial. Coercion runs in contradiction to the fundamental values of the treatment field. Many contend that treatment cannot work for those who are not internally motivated to engage in it and as such,

funding criminal justice-based interventions is money poorly spent (see Rosenthal, 1988; Platt et al., 1988). Whilst others suggest that few chronic problem users self-elect for treatment and that the criminal justice system has a moral duty to intercept and address problematic consumption (Anglin, 1988; Salmon and Salmon, 1983). This ambivalence can be difficult to reconcile for those tasked with working with people who are sentenced to change. This chapter will explore the idea of coercion in substance abuse treatment. In order to do so, we shall take a wider view of coercion and its role within addiction as it occurs in the natural history of the problem user's life. We will then review the findings of treatment outcomes for involuntary clients in detail to ascertain the value of the approach. Against this theoretical backdrop, key issues in working with coerced clients will then be identified. This will explore working with both formal and informal settings, and how coercion can be entwined in not just treatment entry but the treatment course itself to improve outcomes.

What is coercion?

Coercion is not a crisp variable. Reviewing the literature we find it is a difficult concept to define in pragmatic terms and this has confounded both research and treatment attitudes. We might assume coercion is an external force that compels an individual into treatment against their own will. Coerced clients are often identified in research and treatment populations by referral source, typically legal status. This has created a conceptual bias that coercion is the sole preserve of legal mandates. However, coercion occurs across a wider spectrum. In their study of treatment entry pressures of 415 problematic substance misusers, Marlowe et al. (2001) identified that coercion occurred across several formal and informal domains. Cluster analysis found that they could be characterised into five sub-groups (see Figure 19.1).

Domain	Percentage of sample (n = 415) (%)
Financial and social coercion	17
Financial	16
Legal coercion	6
Medical psychiatric	27
Family	35

Figure 19.1   Reported treatment entry pressures amongst problem drug and alcohol users (Marlowe et al., 2001)

Marlowe et al. (2001: 105) concluded: 'Virtually all participants reported a combination of both negative and positive pressures to enter treatment, and both externally mediated and non-externally mediated pressures. It may be insufficient, therefore, to characterise a particular client as having entered treatment for either negative or positive reasons or because of either internal or external factors. It maybe more useful, rather, to represent motivation for treatment as a multidimensional profile of various treatment entry pressures, with different participants producing relative elevations on different types of pressures.' Similarly, Hartjen et al. (1976) identified that only 5 per cent of clients freely elected to enter treatment purely on their own initiative. As such, coercion is not a discreet preserve of legal sanctions but is multi-factorial, constant and occurs across many domains of the user's life simultaneously.

Even research within the criminal justice system has been confounded by a lack of clarity between key definitions. De Leon (1988) noted that terms such as *legal status*, *legal referral* and *legal pressure* are not adequately separated in the majority of studies. Whilst many in treatment services have a *legal status*, in being involved in the criminal justice system, not all of these clients were legally referred into treatment. *Legal referral* identifies those who have been directed to attend treatment through the criminal justice system. But this can vary on a spectrum from those choosing treatment at arrest, judges offering the client a choice to enter into treatment or prison, probation services directing people to attend treatment, court imposed sanctions or access to prison based treatment services instead. *Legal pressure* refers to the degree of threat felt by the individual as a result of these sanctions. Referral and threat are not synonymous. The threat of the

legal sanction is supposedly the critical element in the intervention, yet research demonstrates that individuals vary widely in whether they experienced discomfort in non-compliance, despite the certainly of imprisonment. Many problem users often perceive prison as a welcome respite from chaotic lives.

It is not surprising that the internal experience of coercion as experienced by involuntary clients varies considerably too. Far from being experienced as an external threat, numerous researchers have noted that coercion is a subjective state rather than an objective imposition. For example, Wild et al.'s (1998) study of perceived coercion amongst people entering treatment identified that 35 per cent of legally mandated clients and 61 per cent of non-mandated clients did not recognise any coercion compelling them into treatment. This was despite the fact that 37 per cent of those who reported self-referral into treatment were in fact coerced into it. Alternatively, Farabee et al. (1998) identified high levels of pre-existent motivation within legally coerced populations. They cite research that identified that 50 per cent of one prison population were interested in participating in drug and alcohol treatment programmes, and 50 per cent of those interested were even prepared to extend their prison stay by three months in order to complete it. Similarly, data from the Drug Abuse Treatment Outcomes Study (NIAAA, 1997), indicated that 42 per cent of clients coerced into treatment indicated that they would have presented anyway. Conversely, voluntary entry into treatment does not always equate with significant gains. For example research has indicated that between 17–25 per cent of voluntary clients do not respond to methadone treatment on any measure (Gossop et al., 1998; Belding et al., 1998). This includes opiate use, adjunct use, offending, injecting or reducing sharing behaviour. Coercion, then, is a composite of both formal and informal pressures, the user's individual sensitivity to threatened sanctions and their current motivation. Theoretically, the taxonomy of coerced client populations could be far broader than assumed (see Figure 19.2).

Coercion and addiction

Coercion, far from being a recent policy direction, appears to be intrinsic to the problematic using experience and change. It is essential that we

	Informal coercion		Formal coercion	
	High internal motivation	Low internal motivation	High internal motivation	Low internal motivations
Sensitive to threat				
Non-sensitive to threat				

Figure 19.2 Possible permutations of coerced client populations by variable

understand the relationship between the individuals desire to use against the external responses to it. This is important to grasp as coercion is only necessitated where disagreement exists between whether a problem exists that needs remedying. Therefore, practitioners working with coerced clients need a clear understanding of the criteria for substance misuse problems and the degree of leverage that coercion can exert upon it. Natural remission studies, where people change with professional assistance, is a particularly fertile area for understanding addiction as these individuals are freed from re-attributing their experience in accordance with treatment ideologies. These studies report that social pressures from loved ones, families, social group and legal sanctions increasingly drove them towards change. For example, Klingemann (1991) reports that his 60 alcohol and heroin remitters identified a wide range of life events were instrumental in changing. The highest incidence of problems that preceded change included internal psychological pressure derived from dependence and feeling out of control. But equally as important, if not in some cases more so, were the reactions and responses of others to their use (see Figure 19.3). Coercion was vivid in their change process.

This study highlights a duality in the nature of problematic substance misuse which can be characterised by two different but often over lapping problems (Harris, 2007). The criterion for

dependence was developed by Edwards and Gross (1976) to identify the specific medical aspects of problematic use of alcohol, but has been applied to a wide range of drug consumption. Clinical dependence can be characterised by the biological action of the substance on the individual. This comprises of the narrowing of focus on consumption, the saliency of the using behaviour over activities, profound tolerance and withdrawal, a subjective compulsion to use and resumption of use after periods of abstinence (see Figure 19.4). Specific physical illnesses may also stem from the repeat long-term exposure.

Of these criteria, only tolerance and withdrawal have been demonstrated as the most consistent (Cottler et al. 1995). Edwards et al. (2003: 59) assert '. . . for clinical purposes it is probably best to restrict the diagnosis of alcohol dependence to patients who have experienced withdrawal symptoms to at least some degree.'

At the same time, many substance misusing clients experience significant problems without chronic tolerance or withdrawal. Their problems stem from their inability to maintain social responsibilities and commitments because of use (see Klingemann and Gmel, 2001). This is where consumption compromises their social as opposed to biological functioning. This includes areas such as marriage, family, housing, finance, employment, social life and crime that were akin to Marlowe's (2001) cluster groups. As such, it is this erosion of relationships that creates the social

Stressful life events	Percentage of alcohol users (n = 30)	Percentage of heroin users (n = 30)
Health problems	73	67
Feelings of helplessness or insecurity	83	70
Job difficulties	40	67
Family tensions	73	60
Fear of trouble with authorities	30	83

Figure 19.3 Top life events predating change in natural remitters (Klingemann 1991)

Criteria	Description
Narrowing of repertoire	Use occurs regardless of context, including time, day of the week or social context.
Salience of drinking	Use is a priority over other sources of satisfaction.
Increased tolerance to alcohol	The individual develops an extremely highly tolerance which allows them to function on doses that would incapacitate others.
Withdrawal	The user experiences profound withdrawal which can incapacitate them.
Relief avoidance of withdrawal symptoms with further drinking	Use occurs to alleviate profound withdrawal symptoms.
Subjective awareness of the compulsion to drink	The user recognises that they are unable to control consumption despite intentions to do so.
Reinstatement after abstinence	Rapid reinstatement occurs where the individual resumes pre-abstinence levels of consumptions after a few days.

Figure 19.4   Diagnostic criteria of dependence (Edwards and Gross, 1976)

exclusion of *addiction*. These relationships inevitably respond with increasing fear, concern and estrangement to the user that are expressed through entries to change. Just as the onset of addictions assumes its own natural life course, this will inevitably be paralleled by others' reaction to it. Coercion is the consequence of relationships under strain leading to coercive attempts to stem use. This is what Weisner (1990: 579) defined as 'a form of institutionalised pressure' to change and restore the previous equilibrium.

Polcin and Weisner's (1999: 67) sample of 987 problem alcohol users presenting for treatment identified that the vast majority of ultimatums to change came from family members first, then legal mandates second. This was true even for those users who were single. And interestingly, the number of ultimatums issued bore no correspondence with the actual severity of dependence. They concluded: 'These findings suggest that for clients entering treatment, severity of alcohol problems per se is not what results in family, friends, or representatives from community institutions to become concerned and pressure them into treatment. Rather, it is the type of alcohol related problem that makes a difference.' Thus it is not consumption itself which may elicit concern but how use impacts on others. This has been found in other studies of wider substance misuse as well (Weisner, 1992; Weisner et al., 1995; Kaskutas et al., 1997). Similar findings were reported by Lawental et al. (1996) in their study of clients coerced into treatment

through the workplace urine surveillance. Levels of coercion did not correlate with levels of use. Coercion resulting from dependence only occurred in medical settings where dependence with severe health consequences occurred. Where the informal sanctions exhaust themselves, fail or are indifferent to consumption, it may then befall the criminal justice services to intercede. These discrepancies are important and may be central in resolving differing perceptions of the need for change and readiness to engage in treatment.

Does 'threatment' work?

In light of the preceding discussion, the question of whether coercion into treatment is effective is difficult to assess and demands caveats. Categorising involuntary clients via criminal justice services is wholly inadequate considering the defuse role that coercion plays in addiction. This is further compounded by the current inequity that exists in the provision for treatment. Heavy investment in funding criminal justice services has led to a disparity in treatment provision. Criminality is now a means of rapid access to prescribing and highly resourced treatment programmes whilst non-offenders confront long waiting lists. 'Treatment entry crime' is common in working practice though not a popular research topic, though some have warned of its potential (see Finch et al., 2003). Finally, many researchers have noted that much of the research conducted on offending populations has been poor. For example, Pearson and Lipton (1999) and Inciardi et al. (2004) raised serious concerns that most published work on treatment outcomes for coerced clients was anecdotal and lacking in methodological rigour. For example, Pearson et al. (2002) found that of 30 criminal justice outcome studies they rated, 14 were 'poor', 15 were rated as 'fair' and only one was 'good'.

Within this, research generally suggests little difference in treatment outcomes between coerced clients and their voluntary peers. The majority of studies suggest that involuntary clients do as well, if not better than voluntary clients. In his broad overview of treatment effectiveness, Lurigo (2000: 514) concluded: 'coerced drug using offenders began treatment sooner and remained in treatment longer than those who entered treatment voluntarily.' This has been confirmed in the largest treatment studies conducted to date. The major US studies of treatment effectiveness, such as the Drug Abuse Reporting Project (DARP), the Treatment Outcome Prospective Study (TOPS), the Drug Abuse Treatment Outcome Study (DATOS), and the National Treatment Improvement and Evaluation Study (NTIES), represent a treatment sample of more than 70,000 problem users. Approximately 40–50 per cent of this treatment population were legally mandated. The two principal findings of these studies were that duration of retention predicted treatment outcome and that the coerced client remained in treatment longer. However, these generalisations are not sufficient to assert that coercion works. Especially as some researchers have found more mixed responses (see Farabee et al., 1998).

As Salmon and Salomon (1983: 17) noted: 'Coercion appears to facilitate treatment success by certain criteria, for certain population groups and certain treatment modalities'. One of the most well proven treatment modalities for legally mandated clients is therapeutic communities, especially those that operate within the prison setting (De Leon, 1988; Hillier et al., 1996). Pearson and Lipton's (1999) meta-analysis suggested that the current research base was only robust enough to substantiate this modality as demonstrably effective. Other approaches had to be studied more rigorously before their value could be ascertained. Pearson et al. (2002) found prison-based treatment that incorporated cognitive behavioural approaches appeared to be superior to standard drug programmes, but they

identified widely discrepant practice in its delivery. A perennial research finding is that prison based treatment outcomes show a sharp decay line without sufficient aftercare in the community.

In terms of methadone maintenance prescribing, Brecht and Anglin (1993), and Anglin et al. (1989), found no difference in outcome between legally coerced and non-legally coerced clients regardless of the level of coercion exerted upon them. Methadone maintenance as a pre-release strategy for those exiting prison services has also shown favourable outcomes compared to non-treatment groups. For example, Kinlock et al. (2002) found that of those inducted onto methadone maintenance pre-release, 95 per cent entered into community treatment, as opposed to 10 per cent of the control group who were merely referred to community services. Although this study did experience methodological problems and was based on a small sample group, its findings were significant.

Research on the outcomes of community based treatment services for offenders does show more modest improvement. One study (Santa Clara County Courts, 1996) compared drug court probationers who were sentenced to treatment with those on standard supervision, enhanced supervision and electronic monitoring. The drug court group had lower illicit use. In a randomised study, Deschenes et al. (1996) also found lower arrests and incarceration in treatment sentenced groups compared to non-participants. Case management approaches in the community are common sentencing options, and again show more modest gains (Hanlon et al., 1999; Martin and Incardi, 1997). A cross comparison of case management treatment in the first UK DTTO research (Finch et al., 2003) found that clients were more likely to complete orders if on methadone maintenance programmes (28 per cent of revoked) than if they were in abstinent programmes (60 per cent of orders revoked). In general, there is a lack of consistent research on community programmes. Community based programmes are idiosyncratic in their structure and often recruit mixed client groups (Polcin, 2001). Small variance could make substantial differences to outcomes. For example, Howard and McCaughrin (1996) found that programmes with 75 per cent or higher legally mandated clients, tended to produce worse outcomes than those with 25 per cent or less legally mandated clients. Outcomes for interventions at arrest show positive outcomes at follow up. Hough's (1996) review of the preliminary research into arrest referral schemes found that of 90 clients who could be contacted six months after being interviewed at arrest, almost a quarter of them had desisted from use and just under half reported that they had refrained from using heroin or stimulants.

Involvement in criminal justice services may in itself increase motivation for change in many users (Gregoire and Burke, 2004). Motivation is an area neglected in the research literature in general. Certainly, eliciting internal motivation for change is suggested as important in treatment retention (Miller, 1989; De Leon and Jainchill, 1986). Motivational interviewing (Miller and Rollnick, 2002), a brief intervention that has demonstrated positive outcomes for initiating change in drinkers, has been widely recommended as an early interception strategy for those at arrest or as a primer for coerced treatment entry. However, very little research has been conducted on its effectiveness with coerced clients. Some studies have found a beneficial effect (Blankenship et al., 1999; Lincourt et al., 2002) whilst others found its impact to be minimal (Harper and Hardy, 2000). Miller and Rollnick (2002: 187) state: '*We believe that unless a current "problem" behaviour is in conflict with something that the person values more highly, there is no basis for motivational interviewing to work* (their italics). This means that clients who do not perceive they have a problem, or are immersed in the identity of the problem user, may not be as susceptible to the approach. This is borne out in research that identifies who is more responsive to coerced interventions.

Whilst the most ideal treatment population for coercion has not been clearly established, in general Salmon and Salmon (1983) identified that older users were more likely to benefit from coerced treatment which has been supported by other research (see Anglin et al., 1996). For the most social excluded user, coercion had little effect (Farabee et al., 2004; Harrell et al., 2004; Hanlon et al., 1999). At the other end of the spectrum, those who had experienced little psychosocial dysfunction resulting from their use were also less likely to do well (Marlowe et al., 2001). Those who readily admit (recognise) problems do better (Simpson, 1998). In terms of informal coercion we see similar results. Those coerced into treatment through employment drug testing demonstrated the same outcomes as those who self-refer (Lawental et al., 1996). And studies have consistently identified that treatment seeking in the wider population of problem users was directly related to pressure from family and friends (see Cunningham et al., 1995; Hingson et al., 1982). Family involvement in treatment has a significant impact on treatment outcomes (Stanton and Shadish, 1997).

Coercion in practice

What is striking in this research is that although coerced clients can do as well as non-coerced clients, therapists expectations of their performance is much lower than for voluntary clients (Marlowe et al., 2001; Goldsmith and Latessa, 2001; Martin and Incardi, 1997). This is of central importance as treatment outcomes are sourced in the quality of the alliance that the worker creates with the client. In his seminal paper, Bordin (1979) identified that treatment outcomes were driven by three inter-related elements. These are the establishment of a bond of mutual respect between worker and the client; identifying goals which are important to the client; and the negotiation of manageable tasks to accomplish these goals. All three aspects are important. For example, a client may bond with their worker but if they have no goal to work towards the relationship will be purposeless. Alternatively, the client with goals that feel unobtainable to them in the normal course of their life will feel disheartened if the tasks to achieve them cannot be established.

It is how efficiently the worker can match the bond, goals and task that feel meaningful to the client that elicits outcomes, regardless of the particular school of treatment they use to do it. Wampold's (2001) meta-analysis of counselling outcomes demonstrated that there was no evidence to support the idea that one treatment style was more effective than another. Differences between styles could only account for one per cent difference in treatment outcomes. Outcomes were predicted by the strength of the alliance. Hovarth (2001) suggests that 50–66 per cent of outcomes variance is attributable to the alliance between the helper and the client. This suggests the alliance contributes 5–10 times more to outcome than the style of therapy. Project MATCH (Project MATCH Research Group, 1997), the largest and most statistically powerful clinical trial in the history of substance misuse, found that only one of 64 possible interactions tested proved significant. This was the alliance between the client and the helper, and was supported at 10-year follow up.

The alliance is thus a central force in addiction treatment. However, in line with the humanistic tradition in the field, workers tend to over-emphasise the bond in working practice as the sole vehicle of change. No client ever stopped using drugs solely because they liked their worker so much. Goals and tasks are as important, as without incentives to work towards and the means to achieve them change does not occur. This is important when it comes to motivation in coerced relationships. But again, motivation is a term that needs clarifying. The concept of motivation often takes two distinct forms in the field (Harris, 2007). We may describe a client as unmotivated if they do not engage with us or alternatively, if the client is not working towards any goals. Willingness to comply with treatment is determined by the bond between the worker and the client, but willingness to work towards change relates to the incentives inherent in the clients goals. Coerced clients may not be particularly interested in engaging with the treatment provider initially, but may be very motivated to avoid the sanction threatened by the coercer. Hence the goal to avoid the negative sanction may be far more pre-eminent than the rapport with the treatment provider. Furthermore, as the legal mandate remains constant over extended periods of time, this may sustain motivation as it is less subject to competing sub-goals, environmental changes or the successful mollification of informal relationships. In discussing assessment for suitability for entry into structured programmes, very often workers tend to select those who engage with them. However, as we have seen, the degree of threat felt through the sanction may be a better indicator of motivation to change.

The realignment in the client who accepts treatment as a forced choice is little understood but important. Clients coerced into treatment must make a transition from being goal orientated in wanting to avoid the sanction towards becoming engaged in the treatment process itself. De Leon's (1988) study of involuntary client's attendance in therapeutic communities identified a three-stage process in the progressive reconciliation to the aims of treatment. The first stage of compliance entailed conforming to the rules and regulations of the treatment provider in order to avoid the negative sanction. This is then followed by conformity to the group norms in order to gain or preserve acceptance from other treatment-group members. Finally comes the commitment to change ones lifestyle. Each of these stages emanates from the preceding one. And although the client may adopt a pro-social disposition, it is not until the commitment to change is made that it is liable to stabilise. This may explain why treatment outcomes are higher in therapeutic communities where the client is totally immersed in a treatment culture. And why treatment outcomes may be diluted in a high ratio of coerced to voluntary clients that would dilute the social pressure to conform. As such, in the early phases of the intervention, whilst involuntary clients may appear to be going through the motions of treatment, the worker must trust the sanction to do the work before the client acclimatises to the treatment group and then the treatment aims. Why people enter treatment and why they are successful in that process may not be related.

Working with formally coerced clients

This demands that practitioners working with involuntary clients should be sensitive to the goals of the client first and foremost and expect the bond to evolve at a slower pace. This may be especially important for the sub-population of coerced clients who do not recognise they either have a problem or need help. This is more likely to occur where the level of coercion feels disproportionate to their subjective awareness of the problem. As we have seen, coercion and problem severity are not necessarily related. But it may also occur where there is a lack of clarity regarding what constitutes problematic use. For example, a cocaine user who is experiencing a chronic erosion of their wider relationships may not deem themselves problematic as they have no physical dependence. Conversely, the alcohol user whose tolerance and withdrawal is chronic but maintains their relationships may not perceive themselves as alcoholics. The fact that substance related problems are not widely understood and occur on a spectrum in two very different domains can give the coerced client the scope to defend their use. De Leon's (1996) research observed that in the early stages of contemplation, problems are more likely to be attributed to external factors first, before the

'Whose idea was it for you to come here today?'

'What makes X think you should be here?'

'What does X want you to be doing differently?'

'Has anyone else said similar things to you?'

'Is this something that you want?'

If the client says yes, proceed to treatment contracting; if they say no, then ask:

'What are the consequences of not coming?'

'What is this worst case scenario?'

If the client backtracks –

'And is that what you want for yourself?'

If the client cannot live with these consequences, proceed to treatment contracting, but if not then terminate warmly.

Figure 19.5   Opening script template for involuntary clients (based on Lipchick, 2002)

client gains insight into how they are contributing to their own circumstances. Hence the user may perceive their use as manageable but the reactions of others as the problem, courts and treatment providers included. This can only be explored systematically with the client where the worker has a clear grasp of the dimension as to what constitutes problem use.

Any direct suggestion that they need treatment may be met with reactance (Brehm and Brehm, 1981). Reactance occurs when we feel a sense of threat or a loss of personal freedom, and the coerced problem user may experience both. In this situation, the individual is liable to form opinions in contradiction to others, and defend or rationalise their use. Reactance can be acerbated by forewarning, where the individual anticipates another persuasive intent to change them (Cialdini and Petty, 1979).

It is important that the practitioner appears to be warm, genuine, concerned and interested in the client in the early stages of contact, even when the client presents as being resistant or disinterested in treatment. It is essential to take a neutral position, as any attempt by the worker to tip the client towards change will cause the client to contradict. Lipchick (2002) demonstrates that a simple way to avoid reactance in this early stage is to begin by focusing on the referral landscape itself and not the client's own subjective estimate of the problem (see Figure 19.5). Who has referred the client? What do they believe is the problem and what do they want the client to be

doing differently? This establishes the context of the client's predicament. This can then be widened out to include any other sources of pressure or ultimatums from others as well. This allows the marshalling of feedback from people close to the client. Has their partner, parents or employers said similar things or expressed such concerns with them? Do they want the client to be doing something differently too? Is everybody wrong to be so concerned about them?

Empathetic listening is important to both ensure an understanding of the situation but also to transmit interest and concern to the client. Once this is established, the client can then be asked whether they feel they need to do something too? If the client says yes, then this can be explored in more detail and the treatment contract agreed. If the client does not have the internal motivation to change and says no, then the practitioner can allow the sanction to do the work. Asking the client what are the consequences of not engaging is helpful in judging the clients sensitivity to the sanction. Getting the client to describe the worst case scenario can crystallise the impact of the consequences. Remember, it is important to focus this question towards both health concerns and any important relationships in the client's life and allow them to state the concerns for themselves. This is a powerful line of questioning for people and will elicit deep anxiety in some. This should be antidoted by offering the client a clear understanding of what they must do in order to overcome this threat, and the more manageable these tasks, the more likely the client will engage. Treatment contracting can then begin.

More resistant clients may articulate their worst fears and then react to their own voice but stating how, even in the worst eventuality, that they would survive adversity or regain lost status and loved ones. Again, empathy can be useful here to let the client articulate this fantasy. Only when it is all talked out, the client can then be asked 'But, is that what you want for yourself?' This will reverse their direction without confrontation. As the fantasy has been fully stated and understood, they cannot return to their original point. The client has nowhere else to go but respond to the negatives of their situation. If, however, the client genuinely believes that they can live with these consequences regardless of their magnitude then terminate warmly. At least they will be clear in terms of what will happen next and the respectful experience of treatment may make them more amenable to professional help next time.

At this stage the client is not facing coercive treatment, but rather a forced choice between treatment or legal sanctions. When it comes to potentially life changing decisions it is important that the worker always anticipates ambivalence. Miller and Rollnick (2002) state that the central problem in change is ambivalence because it paralyises the process. If clients did not have mixed feeling regarding change, then they would change. Committing to change is to both liberate oneself from problems but to also sever familiar attachments, meanings and lifestyles. Therefore, in the early discussions with clients, we should be watchful of mixed feelings, contradictory positions or hesitancy that may indicate ambivalent feelings towards change.

Ambivalence is not resistance, but a cost-benefit analysis that is integral to the change process (Prochaska et al., 1994). We can resolve these feelings by exploring the pros and cons of change with the client in an open manner. However, we do not simply want a list. We want to know what each item means to the client. Clients in lower states of readiness to change may report external pros of change such as getting family, employers or the legal services off their back. Again, workers may anticipate a poor prognosis for these clients and may push them to consider the 'higher' aspirations of self-improvement. For clients that see no benefit in change for themselves, these external forces can be internalised by asking them what difference it would make to their life if these individuals did stop pressuring them. However, at this stage, it may simply be enough that the client wishes to avoid the sanction regardless of their internal motivations. As Goldsmith and Latessa (2001: 663) stated: 'Therapists must recognise that motivation resides outside of the identified individual'. And Miller et al. (2005) have demonstrated positive outcomes by working with the externalised wants of the involuntary client.

Once the client does commit to entering treatment their early experience becomes important. The client who experiences early subjective benefits from treatment is liable to remain engaged. Furthermore, when treatment works it works quickly, with the majority of treatment gains occurring sooner, rather than later (Orlinsky and Howard, 1980). Those who do not experience any improvement within the first three sessions are unlikely to experience any benefit from the treatment process at all (Brown et al., 1999). Early benefits are then essential to induct the formally coerced client into engagement. Instead of forcing the issue of acceptance to change, time should be spent working with the client to achieve practical benefits that improve the quality of their life. This might include housing, prescribing, benefits or charitable applications which can deepen the bond and foster increasing degrees of engagement.

Working with formally coerced clients

An area which has been historically under-addressed in substance misuse treatment services is the nature of the informal coercion that may prompt change. This is surprising, considering that research has continually iterated that informal relationships exert a powerful influence on treatment entry (Orford, 1992; Room et al., 1991). As a result, the established approaches to working with concerned others has been largely based on ideological principles rather than empirical findings. These approaches have relied heavily on confrontation. For example, Al Anon, an off-shoot of the Twelve Step movement, endorses a tough love policy which teaches the concerned others that they are powerless to change their loved ones substance use. Here, concerned others are advised that problem users should be confronted, experience personal growth through challenge or be ostracised until they reach rock bottom. This was the point of complete emotional and physical collapse which the Fellowship advises is a precursor necessary for change. In the Johnson Institute Intervention (Johnson, 1986), the problem user is to be confronted by their network of family, friends and work colleagues in a 'surprise party.' At this gathering, prepared speeches are made that spell out their concerns and implore the user into treatment.

The rationale of these approaches is augmented by the view of the concerned other as suffering from their own form of addiction – to the problem other. Co-dependency originates in the concept that women purposefully partnered problem drinkers to meet a pathological need in themselves, even to the point of sabotaging their husbands change attempts in order to continue to satisfy the need for control (Kalashian, 1959; Futterman, 1953). This idea has now been extended to incorporate *all* family members involved in the problem user's life. Separation is recommended for the concerned others own 'recovery' along with their own specialist therapy.

There are problems with these approaches. There is no evidence to support the idea of a distinct, maladaptive response in the problem user's family (Gierymski and Williams, 1986; Gomberg, 1989; Hands and Dear, 1994). Orford and Edwards (1977) found that wives responded to problematic alcohol consumption in their husbands in a stratified approach. Strategies include purposeful attempts to change the individual through attack, manipulation or constructive help seeking, which if these fail, give way to tolerance and eventual withdrawal that terminates the relationship. Loneck et al. (1996a, 1996b), found that high levels of conflict reduced treatment retention rates and increased relapse rates. Invariably, those close to problem users do suffer psychological collateral damage from use. It is estimated that for every single user, five others are affected. But the idea of co-dependency as a discrete pathological issue is poorly delineated, lacks any empirical evidence and has no clinical utility. It also plays on the self-blame that people often feel for their loved ones substance use. Those working with concerned others should abandon this idea, and consign it to the province of aggressive self-help literature that is popular in the US.

Informal relationships with problem users are important attachments in the concerned others

lives. They are their sons, husbands, wives, daughters and friends. The impulse to protect, defend, control, change or minimise the impact of consumption are natural responses that need not be pathologised. If problem users are not responsive to these demands for change, the concerned others will experience anger, frustration, fear and eventual termination. As a result, the concerned others may show a wide range of hopefulness and motivation to help the loved one. But often they wish to remain in contact with them and make constructive intervention to restore the previous relationship.

Community reinforcement and family training

The Community Reinforcement and Family Therapy Training (CRAFT) has been developed specifically to assist concerned others whose loved ones are experiencing substance misuse problems (Smith and Meyers, 2004). Its central aims are to influence the unmotivated substance misuser to enter treatment or reduce their consumption. Equally, it also aims to reduce the stress and improve the quality of life of the concerned other *regardless of whether the problem user seeks help.* This is important, as those close to the user are liable to experience depression, low self-esteem, anxiety and are more likely to be the victims of domestic violence (Brown et al., 1995; Moos et al., 1982; Black et al., 1986). And, contrary to other family interventions, it also works towards improving the relationship between problem users and their concerned others.

Concerned others often know more about the loved ones' pattern of use than the problem user themselves. They also share the same social environment and therefore they are ideally placed to influence the context of using behaviour. The approach is based upon behaviour therapy which suggests that any given behaviour is maintained or stopped by the consequences that follow its implementation. If the consequences of an activity are rewarding they are likely to be repeated, whilst if the consequences are punishing they are more likely to be reduced. As the more immediate and profound rewards of drug and alcohol use outweigh the longer term consequences, this balance must be re-dressed through restructuring the user's environment. In order to do this, CRAFT makes extensive use of functional

Antecedents		Behaviour	Consequences	
External	Internal		Short-term benefits	Long-term consequence

Figure 19.6 Functional analysis

analysis to help the concerned other chart the function of use (see Figure 19.6). This is done by identifying the external and internal triggers of the loved ones consumption (Antecedents). Careful attention is paid to what people use and for how long (Behaviour). And finally it identifies the short-term benefits experienced by the user and the long-term problems caused by use (Consequences).

Once the function of the problem use is mapped, CRAFT teaches the concerned other the skills to rearrange the rewards and allow natural consequences to occur in the problem users life. It does this through assisting the concerned other to identify other (non-using) rewarding activities the loved one desires that can be scheduled at those times when they are likely to use. These are designed to challenge and interfere with the external and internal triggers that drive use. Simple problem solving skills are taught to generate options and select the most effective solutions that are then refined over time.

The concerned other is also taught to identify enabling behaviours. Enabling is when the concerned other attempts to reduce, minimise or repair the damage generated through the loved ones consumption. Instead, they are taught to allow the natural consequences of use to occur. Rather than making excuses for lateness at work, hiding use from other family members, paying for drugs or helping resolve drug induced crises, the concerned other withdraws and allows the user to confront the difficulties. In this way, they can begin to shift the decisional balance of change by increasing both the pros of change and the cons of use. As the expectations of consumption can vary depending on the situation in which they are used, the functional analysis can be used repeatedly to identify specific patterns and evolve approaches tailored to each eventuality. CRAFT is also unique in conducting functional analysis on non-using activities as well. This allows the concerned other to identify the external and internal triggers that will make the non-using

activity more likely to occur; evaluate how deeply the problem user engages in the activity; review short-term consequences that may be eliminated and long-term benefits the problem user enjoys.

Whilst CRAFT stresses the importance of a warm, therapeutic alliance with the concerned other, it is primarily a skills based programme. Environmental rearrangement is supplemented with specific skills. Primary amongst these are communication skills which are designed to reduce conflict. Conflict is a notable characteristic of these relationships (Wilson and Orford, 1978; Reich et al., 1988). regarding consumption and wider issues. Confrontation, adversarial attitudes and aggression are counter-productive as likely to instil reactance, where the loved one defends their behaviour and increases consumption as substance use can sedate negative mood states. The cause of heavy bouts of use can also be attributed to the concerned other's aggression and lack of understanding. Instead, concerned others are taught to make 'I' statements, as opposed to the accusational 'you' statements; request exactly what is desired from the loved one, as opposed to what they must stop; and delivered with both empathy and offers to support the user to resolve difficulties. This is especially important when the loved one is engaged in consumption, as these communication skills will facilitate the gentle withdrawal of the concerned other at these times. It may also be used to raise the idea of treatment, once the implemented programme begins to take effect. Again, possible hooks into treatment that the loved one is likely to respond to are identified, whether they be conflicts, bad using experiences or comments from others, and the suggestion of treatment is couched carefully. If the client declines, the concerned other simply accepts the loved ones position and waits for the next opportunity. In the meantime, the programme focuses on assessing the concerned others current levels of satisfaction in life and implements practical support to improve it in every domain.

Clinical trials have consistently demonstrated the effectiveness of CRAFT over other family-based interventions (Smith and Meyers, 2004). Miller et al. (1999) randomly assigned concerned others into three different treatment programmes. This inducted 45 people into CRAFT, 45 into Al Anon and 40 with the Johnson Institute intervention. Scheduled over 12 sessions, 89 per cent of the CRAFT group and 95 per cent of the Al Anon programme completed all sessions. In contrast, only 53 per cent completed the Johnson approach, with many families reporting they felt unease at family confrontation. CRAFT assisted 64 per cent of problematic using loved ones into treatment, the Johnson approach managed to get 30 per cent into treatment and Al Anon only achieved 13 per cent success. CRAFT has also consistently demonstrated significant treatment advantages over other interventions, regardless of the configuration of the relationship between the concerned other and identified substance user (see Sisson and Azrin, 1986; Meyers and Smith, 1997; Meyers et al., 1999: 10). In summary, Smith and Meyers (2004) state: 'In a series of studies, CRAFT-trained CSOs [concerned significant others] were able to influence these resistant substance abusers to enter treatment in 64–86 per cent of the cases, and in a relatively brief period of time . . . Furthermore, CRAFT-trained CSOs typically felt better about themselves after treatment, regardless of whether or not their IP [identified patient] entered therapy.' (*My brackets.*)

Treatment in criminal justice settings

One significant challenge in delivering treatment to those legally coerced is that the practitioner must operate in partnership with the criminal justice system. Partnership working is difficult, and this may be especially so where partners share alternative world views and purposes. But the practitioner working with clients in coercive environments must not only maintain a relationship with the client, but also with criminal justice services. This may create tensions and pressures as two very often contrary ideologies must integrate in order to provide effective interventions. This can be difficult because of the value base of these two systems. Whilst it is necessary for the drug worker to 'side' with the offender in order to facilitate change and rehabilitation, the criminal justice worker must 'side' with society in order to uphold the retributive element of the law. Whilst this is a simplistic rendition, it is vital that ideological differences do not undermine the intervention. By Goldsmith and Latessa (2001) have elucidated the principles of effective partnership working in coerced client populations (see Figure 19.7).

Lurigo (2000) has identified the principles of effective treatment in criminal justice services. Good assessment is important to ensure that the client is matched with an appropriate service. This demands that a thorough assessment is conducted which identifies current levels of dependence, the level of social erosion and the client's current level of motivation. Previous treatment history may also provide additional insight into appropriate support. We must recognise that treatment works best when the treatment philosophy makes sense to the client. Whilst this sounds obvious, very often clients in criminal justice programmes receive treatment based on where the treatment services wants the client to be, rather than that which meets their

---

Guidelines of collaboration (based on Goldsmith and Latessa, 2001

Treatment personnel must understand the intent of the sentencing.

Formal and regular contact must be maintained by the criminal justice service to sustain the imminence of the sanctions.

The scope and the responsibilities of both providers must be clarified at the outset.

Both substance misuse services and the criminal justice services must develop a clear understanding of each other, their working practices and their values.

It is essential to establish which system will prevail in which circumstances.

Communication is essential when criminal justice and treatment services work in parallel to each other.

Figure 19.7   Partnerships in criminal justice system

needs. For example, a group on dealing with cravings will have little resonance for clients in early contemplation. This situation can be worsened by the increasing use of manualised approaches in criminal justice settings, which tend to decrease outcomes. The alliance is more important than the method of treatment, and rigid programmes can comprise its integrity.

Length of participation is essential in drugs misuse services. The longer the client is retained in treatment, the better the outcomes (see Collins and Allison 1983). The optimum period is a minimum of 90 days, with clients who drop out prior to this period being more susceptible to return to use. High quality programmes with a strong emphasis on the alliance therefore become important for good outcomes. However, time in treatment is not a crisp variable because it does not account for the quality, frequency and intensity of the programmes. As Fletcher et al. (1997: 223) observed: 'time itself is a surrogate measure that might represent, for example, motivation, willingness to adhere to treatment, a process of behavioural change, or the ability of the practitioner to engage the patient'. Treatment outcomes may be related to time because motivated clients simply stay longer.

Coercion within treatment

For many clients, coercion is a forced choice to enter treatment. However, coercion many constitute elements of the actual treatment itself. Each programme should combine high structure with flexibility. This sounds like a contradiction. But programmes must set clear boundaries that are policed, along with regular urine testing, in order to establish that behavioural change is sustained. Whilst involuntary clients are likely to do as well as voluntary clients, both groups are likely to experience lapses and setbacks. Responding to slips in use with expulsion from the programme can be counter-productive, and fails to account for the recovery process as it occurs in this population. Therefore, flexible but clear boundaries need to be established in a microclimate of sanctions and rewards for treatment compliance. The benefits of compliance and the consequences of use should be made explicit to the client at the outset of treatment in the contracting stage and should be enforced consistently for all clients. Positive rewards for compliance should always be married to negative consequences for non-compliance. Whilst abrupt and negative sanctions such as removal from programmes often exhibit higher drop-out rates, they increase the outcomes for programme survivors (see Kidorf and Stitzer, 1993; Dolon et al., 1985).

The motivated stepped care approach has proven to be very effective in increasing client compliance in substance misuse services. This has been piloted with great effect in non-responsive methadone treatment clients (Brooner and Kidorf, 2002) and alcohol users (see Sobell and Sobell, 1993; 2000). Following entry to treatment, further therapeutic interventions are based upon the client's treatment performance. When clients do not respond to treatment, its intensity is increased. In methadone prescribing, clients are inducted to treatment with standard case working, urine testing, and daily pick-up of prescriptions. If clients engage in their programme and routinely return clear urine samples, they may be offered treatment privileges, less contact time and even mentoring roles. Alternatively, for those individuals who fail to produce clean samples or attend, they will be placed on more intensive contact periods for a set period of weeks. This might include additional group or one-to-one sessions to support them to make these changes. If they complete this stratum of intensive treatment they then return to the standard programme. If they fail, a second level of even more intensive contact time can be introduced where greater attendance is required, again for a set period of time, which if completed returns the client to the next level. This allows unresponsive clients the opportunity and rewards for working toward greater compliance. Where clients fail to achieve these goals, people can be placed on rapid reduction scripts or revoked. Motivated stepped care has demonstrated superior retention and treatment outcomes to standard treatment (Brooner et al., 2004). Research by Griffith et al. (2000) demonstrated that reinforcement procedures have the biggest impact on the most unresponsive clients.

Motivated stepped care has proved very useful in increasing retention rates to over 90 per cent with chaotic opiate using populations. This is important, as these clients are the least likely to remain in treatment. However, the idea of staged interventions that create a microclimate of rewards and consequences could be adopted more widely. For example, Kleiman (1996)

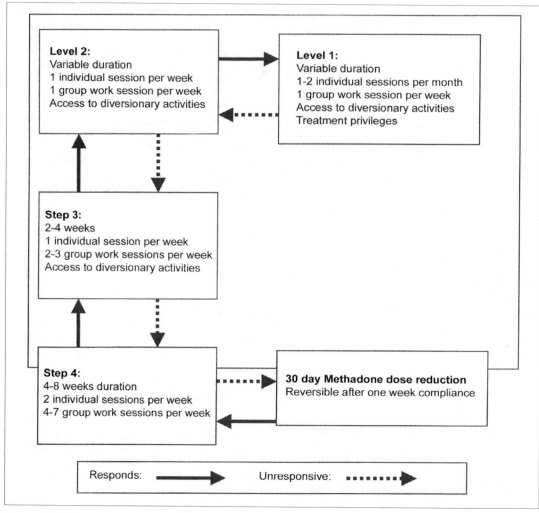

Figure 19.8   An example of motivated stepped care for opiate users (based on Brooner and Kidorf 2002)

proposed an abstinence based programme with regular testing and small sanctions, such as two days in prison for failure to comply, with offenders. Several similar pilot programmes in the criminal justice system have shown extremely promising results compared to those on standard probation schemes (see Boyum and Kleiman, 2002; Harrell et al., 1999). Harrell et al. (2004), in a large scale study of 2,075 clients across three cities, found superior outcomes for the micro-sanction group than the probation clients. Methodological issues of low follow-up rates (67–70 per cent), that were confined to the more stable users did compromise the findings of this study. But it has highlighted a promising area for further development.

It is also important to recognise that problem users in the criminal justice services are likely to have broader range of more complex needs than individuals who are in the community. They may exhibit higher incidence of antisocial personality disorder (Messina et al., 1990). Heighten impulsivity can have a detrimental effect on the implementation of cognitive skills. Therefore, more highly controlled treatments may be necessary to establish new patterns of behaviour. Furthermore, high levels of exclusion, coupled long-term prison incarceration can foster developmental delay and considerable skills gaps (see Harris, 2005). Therefore, programmes need to be expansive and address a wide range of social, medical, psychiatric and vocational support. 'In short, criminal addicts should be treated holistically, and their various problems should be addressed simultaneously, not sequentially' (Lurigo, 2000: 517).

Aftercare: beyond coercion

Finally, there is need for aftercare on treatment completion. This appears particularly salient for those leaving prison settings and returning to the community (Lipton, 1995; Peters, 1993). Addictions are a chronic relapse condition. A prisoner may be particularly prone to relapse for several reasons. Firstly, when the sanctions that entered them into treatment cease there may be little incentive to continue their recovery. Once again, the importance of desirable goals remains pertinent to drive the recovery process. Secondly, offending histories may create additional obstacles to the reintegration into pro-social groups and employment, factors that are essential to the recovery process (Harris, 2007). And thirdly, the paucity of relapse prevention programmes nationally may break the continuity of care. Numerous studies have identified that those prison leavers who continue to engage in aftercare do better than those who exit treatment without aftercare. Specifically, treatment interventions such as the Community Reinforcement Approach, that systematically work to increase levels of satisfaction across the users lives, including employment, family, vocational and social and recreational life, have demonstrated superior outcomes to standard drug counselling for coerced clients (Azrin et al., 1994.) As Kidorf et al. (2006: 136) stated in their review of counselling services for opiate users: 'One particularly important goal is for patients to become more involved in drug free social support outside the clinic. Research showing a strong association between positive social support and reduced risk for relapse to opioid use and other substances supports the aggressive pursuit of this goal.'

Certainly one area which has not been explored is the purposeful combination of formal and informal approaches. For example, families of criminally involved substance abusers who wish to maintain contact with their loved one could provide informal support to maintain formal treatment gains through CRAFT and other family based approaches. Similar methods have been adopted in network therapy (Galanter, 1993), in the treatment of a wider range of substance abuse problems. Here, significant others become involved in the therapy process itself in 'network sessions' and continue to augment treatment gains in the client's social environment, even whilst the identified patient is not present. Strengthening the informal social network and increasing their capacity to influence the user would provide a significant safety net to catch those that drop out of formal treatment. Whilst professionals often believe that these additional support measures may not be applicable to the most estranged of problem opiate users, research suggests that 85 per cent of clients could identify and involve significant others in treatment when it was contingent on their involvement (Kidorf et al., 1997).

Ethical issues

The ethical issues concerning coercing clients into treatment has not been discussed in the wider clinical research to any great extent. However, there are four key issues to be considered, only one of which has received attention. Collins and Allison (1983) suggest that as coercion appears to work, ethical debates regarding coercion are irrelevant. However, the issue of ethics is not confined to the justification of investment in 'effective' coercive treatment. Even relatively small gains with high tariff offenders would pay for itself in savings from the elimination of the wider social cost. It does remain an issue that the inequity of investment in coerced treatment has directed funds away from mainstream services where non-offending individuals experience long waiting lists and less well resourced treatment. This encourages offending as a means to treatment and normalises the substance misuse equals crime equation which is far from a universal experience. This issue of inequity will not be resolved until comparable funding is invested in creating accessible services available in the community for all people experiencing difficulty. This in itself may alleviate pressure on criminal justice services, as effective generic drug treatment can reduce crime as a by-product of its treatment agenda (see Gossop et al. 1998).

A second issue is that formal coercion may undermine the integrity of mainstream treatment programmes. Those who do not comply with treatment protocols in open access services and are discharged, can simply resort to criminality and be fast tracked back into the very treatment service that they failed to comply with via the criminal justice system. Thirdly, the long-term effect of short treatment exposure is currently not known. For the high consuming and most socially excluded clients who are least likely to respond to coercive treatment, brief engagement with treatment will not impact on their use. But, it may inoculate them to subsequent treatment effects by increasing forewarning of its action through familiarity.

Finally, a more thorny area is a second imbalance, and which is widely neglected, that of the disparity between the support structures for problematically using offenders in contrast to that of the victims of their crime. Whilst it could be argued that the impact of treatment to break the use, crime and re-incarceration cycle does serve the greater public good, those individually affected by crime remain a minority voice in the criminal justice system. Whilst the experience of crime for many has become normalised as a nuisance, for others, the impact of crime can have profound and enduring effects. And support services for those individuals are not resourced to the same level as those for the offender.

Conclusion

Whilst new policy initiatives have raised the profile of coercion in substance misuse services, it holds a ubiquitous role in addictions. A social problem characterised by the disintegration in both private and public relationships is inevitably challenged by those whom are affected. Whether this is motivated by the desire to restore once loving relationships or for the wider public interest, coercion may serve as a functional mechanism to regulate deviant behaviours. The formalisation and expansion of criminal justice responses has stimulated deeper study, but the current research base has failed to develop shared frames of reference, identify salient variables and establish common definitions that make convergence difficult to establish. As a result, its findings must be generalised across the treatment field with caution. Within this, there is sufficient evidence to suggest that coercive responses can impact on both substance use and criminality. This demands a shift in attitude in the criminal

justice systems to appreciate the value of 'soft disciplines' in addressing offending. Equally, it demands that substance misuse services revise their assumptions of both addiction and the delivery of treatment. Treatment outcomes will only endure if services can not only bond with the most excluded users, but capture their individual aspirations and cultivate their resources to achieve them. Likewise, informal relationships should be recognised as an unmet need and as a potent resource for change. This potential should not be therapised with unsubstantiated judgments, but supported in the attainment of mutually shared goals of restoring cherished relationships. This means that in both the formal and informal domains, coercion should not replace engagement as the central force in change. Problematic users should not refrain from consumption simply because to do so has become entirely hostile, but because they have come to value a new life more highly. Coercion may provide the means but it can never be the end.

References

Anglin, M.D. (1988) The Efficacy of Civil Commitment in Treating Narcotics Addiction. *Journal of Drug Issues*, 18: 527–45.

Anglin, M.D., Brecht, M.L. and Maddahian, E. (1989) Pretreatment Characteristics of Treatment Performance of Legally Coerced Versus Voluntary Methadone Maintenance Admissions. *Criminology*, 27: 3, 537–57.

Anglin, M.D. et al. (1996) *Studies of the Functioning and Effectiveness of Treatment Alternatives to Street Crime Programs.* University of Los Angeles, Los Angeles Drug Abuse Research Centre.

Azrin, N.H. et al. (1994) Behaviour Therapy for Drug Abuse; A Controlled Treatment Outcome Study. *Behaviour, Research and Therapy*, 32: 857–66.

Belding, M. et al. (1998) Characterising 'Nonresponsive' Patients. *Journal of Substance Abuse Treatment*, 15: 485–92.

Black, C., Bucky, S.F. and Wilder-Padilla, S. (1986) The Interpersonal and Emotional Consequences of Being an Adult Child of an Alcoholic. *International Journal of Addictions*, 21: 213–321.

Blankenship, J., Dansereau, D.F. and Simpson, D.D. (1999) Cognitive Enhancements of

Readiness for Corrections-Based Treatment or Drug Abuse. *The Prison Journal*, 79: 432–45.

Bordin, E.S. (1979) The Generalisability of the Psychoanalytic Concept of the Working Alliance. *Psychotherapy: Theory, Research and Practice*, 16: 3, 252–60.

Boyum, D.A. and Kleiman, M.A. (2002) Substance Abuse Policy from a Crime-Control Perspective. In Wilson, J.Q. and Petersila, J. (Eds) *Crime*. ICS Press.

Brecht, M. and Anglin, M.D. (1993) Treatment Effectiveness for Legal Coerced Versus Voluntary Methadone Maintenance Admissions Clients. *American Journal of Drug and Alcohol Abuse*, 19:1, 89–106.

Brehm, S.S. and Brehm, J.W. (1981) *Psychological Reactance: A Theory of Freedom and Control*. Academic Press.

Brooner, R.K. and Kidorf, M.S. (2002) Using Behaviour Reinforcement to Improve Methadone Treatment Participation. *Science and Practice Perspectives*, 1: 38–48.

Brooner, R.K. et al. (2004) Behavioural Contingencies Improve Counselling Attendance in an Adaptive Treatment Model. *Journal of Substance Abuse Treatment*, 27: 223–32.

Brown, J., Dries, S. and Nace, D.K. (1999) What Really Makes a Difference in Psychotherapy Outcome? Why Does Managed Care Want to Know? In Hubble, M.A., Duncan, B.L. and Miller, S.D. (Eds). *The Heart and Soul of Change: What Works in Therapy*. American Psychological Association Press.

Brown, T.G. et al. (1995) The Role of Spouse of Substance Abusers in Treatment: Gender Differences. *Journal of Psychoactive Drugs*, 27: 223–9.

Cabinet Office (1998) *Tackling Drugs to Build a Better Britain: The Government's Ten-Year Strategy for Tackling Substance Misuse*. April. Cabinet Office.

Cialdini, R.B. and Petty, R.E. (1979) Anticipatory Opinion Effects. In Petty, R., Ostrom, T. and Brock, T. (Eds.) *Cognitive Responses in Persuasion*. New York: Lawrence Erlbaum.

Collins, J.J. and Allison, M. (1983) Legal Coercion and Retention in Drug Abuse Treatment. *Hospital and Community Psychiatry*, 34: 12, 1145–9.

Cottler L.B., Phelps, D.L. and Compton, W.M. (1995) Narrowing of the Drinking Repertoire Criterion: Should it be Dropped from ICD 10? *Journal of Studies on Alcohol*, 56: 173–6.

Cunningham, J.A. et al. (1995) Resolution from Alcohol Treatment Problems with and without Treatment: Reasons for Change. *Journal of Substance Abuse*, 7: 365–72.

De Leon, G. (1988) Legal Pressures in Therapeutic Communities. *Journal of Drug Issues*, 18: 4, 625–40.

De Leon, G. (1996) Integrative Recovery: A Stage Paradigm. *Substance Abuse*, 175: 1–63.

De Leon, G. and Jainchill, N. (1986) Circumstances, Motivation, Readiness and Suitability as Correlates of Treatment Tenure. *Journal of Psychoactive Drugs*, 18: 203–8.

Deschenes, E.P. (1996) *An Experimental Evaluation of Drug Testing and Treatment Interventions for Probationers in Maricopa County, Arizona*. Santa Monica, CA: Rand Corporation.

Dolon, M.P. et al. (1985) Contracting for Treatment Termination to Reduce Illicit Drug Use Among Methadone Maintenance Treatment Failures. *Journal of Consulting and Clinical Psychology*, 55: 549–51.

Edwards, G. and Gross, M. (1976) Alcohol Dependence: Provisional Description of a Clinical Syndrome. *British Medical Journal*, 1: 1058–61.

Edwards, G., Marshall, E.J. and Cook, C.C. (2003) *The Clinical Management of Alcohol Problems*. Cambridge University Press.

Farabee, D. et al. (2004) Recidivism among an Early Cohort of California's Proposition 36 Offenders. *Criminology and Public Policy*, 3: 563–84.

Farabee, D., Prendergst, M. and Anglin, D. (1998) The Effectiveness of Coerced Treatment for the Drug-Abusing Offender. *Federal Probation*, 62: 1, 3–10.

Finch, E. et al. (2003) Sentenced to Treatment: Early Experience of Drug Treatment and Testing Orders in England. *European Addiction Research*, 9: 131–7.

Fletcher, B.W., Tims, F.M. and Brown, B.S. (1997) The Drug Abuse Treatment Outcomes Study: Treatment Evaluation Research in the United States. *Psychology of Addictive Behaviours*, 11: 216–29.

Futterman, S. (1953) Personality Trends in Wives of Alcoholics. *Journal of Psychiatric Social Work*, 23: 34–41.

Galanter, M. (1993) *Network Therapy for Drug and Alcohol Abuse*. New York: Guildford Press.

Gierymski, T. and Williams, T. (1986) Co-Dependency. *Journal of Psychoactive Active Drugs*, 18: 1, 7–13.

Goldsmith, R.J. and Latessa, E. (2001) Coerced Treatment of Addictions in the Criminal Justice System. *Psychiatric Annals*, 31: 11, 657–63.

Gomberg, E. (1989) On Terms Used and Abused: The Concept of Co-Dependency. *Drugs and Society*, 3: 113–32.

Gossop, M. et al. (1998) Substance Use, Health and Social Problems of Clients at 54 Drug Treatment Agencies: Intake Data from the National Treatment Outcomes Research Study. *British Journal of Psychiatry*, 173: 166–71.

Gregoire, T.K. and Burke, A.C. (2004) The Relationship of Legal Coercion to Readiness to Change among Adults with Alcohol and other Drug Problems. *Journal of Substance Abuse Treatment*, 26: 35–41.

Griffith, J.D. et al. (2000) Contingency Management in Outpatient Methadone Treatment: A Meta-Analysis. *Drug and Alcohol Dependence*, 58: 55–66.

Hammersley, R. et al. (1989) The Relationship between Crime and Opiate Use. *British Journal of Addictions*, 84: 1029–43.

Hands, M. and Dear, G. (1994) Co-Dependency: A Critical Review. *Drug and Alcohol Review*, 13: 4, 437–45.

Hanlon, T.E. et al. (1999) The Relative Effects of Three Approaches to the Parole Supervision of Narcotic Addicts and Cocaine Abusers. *The Prison Journal*, 79: 163–81.

Harper, R. and Hardy, S. (2000) An Evaluation of Motivational Interviewing as a Method of Intervention with Clients in a Probation Setting. *British Journal of Social Work*, 30: 393–400.

Harrell, A., Cavannaugh, S. and Roman, J. (1999) *Final Report: Findings from the Evaluation of the DC Superior Court Drug Intervention Programme*. National Institute of Justice, Bureau of Justice Statistics.

Harrell, A. et al. (2004) *Evaluation of Breaking the Cycle*. The National Institute of Justice.

Harris, P. (2005) *Drug Induced: Addiction and Treatment in Perspective*. Lyme Regis: Russell House Publishing.

Harris, P. (2007) *Empathy for the Devil: How to Help People Overcome Drug and Alcohol Problems*. Lyme Regis: Russell House Publishing.

Hillier, M.L. et al. (1996) Postreatment Outcomes for Substance Abusing Probationers Mandated in Residential Treatment. *Journal of Psychoactive Drugs*, 28: 3, 291–6.

Hingson, R. et al. (1982) Seeking Help for Drinking Problems: A Study in the Boston Metropolitan Area. *Journal of Studies on Alcohol*, 43: 271–88.

Hough, M. (1996) *Drug Misuse and the Criminal Justice System: A Review of the Literature*. Home Office.

Hovarth, A.O. (2001) The Alliance. *Psychotherapy*, 38: 365–72.

Howard, D.L. and McCaughrin, W.C. (1996) The Treatment Effectiveness of Outpatient Substance Misuse Organisation between Court Mandated and Voluntary Clients. *Substance Use and Misuse*, 31: 7, 895–926.

Inciardi, J.A., Martin, S.S. and Butzin, C.A. (2004) Five-Year Outcomes of Therapeutic Community Treatment of Drug Involved Offenders after Release from Prison. *Crime and Delinquency*, 50: 88–107.

Johnson, V. (1986) *Intervention: How to Help Someone who Does Not Want Help*. Johnson Institute.

Kalashian, M.M. (1959) Working with the Wives of Alcoholics in an Outpatient Clinic Setting. *Marriage and Family*, 21: 130–3.

Kaskutas, L., Weisner, C. and Caetano, R. (1997) Predictors of Help Seeking among Longitudinal Sample of General Population, 1984–1992. *Journal of Studies on Alcoholism*, 58:155–61.

Kidorf, M., Brooner, R.K. and King, V.L. (1997) Motivating Methadone Patients to Include Drug-Free Significant Others in Treatment: A Behavioural Intervention. *Journal of Substance Abuse Treatment*, 14, 23–8.

Kidorf, M. and Stitzer, M.L. (1993) Contingent Access to Methadone Maintenance Treatment: Effects of Cocaine Use of Opiate-Cocaine Users. *Experimental Clinical Psychopharmacology*, 1: 200–6.

Kidorf, M., Van, L. and King, M.D. (2006) Counselling and Psychosocial Services. In Strain, E.C. and Stitzer, M.L. (Eds.) *The Treatment of Opioid Dependence*. Johns Hopkins.

Kinlock, T.W, Battjes, R.J. and Schwartz, R.P. (2002) A Novel Opioid Maintenance Program for Prisoners: Preliminary Findings. *Journal of Substance Abuse Treatment*, 22: 141–7.

Kleiman, M.A. (1996) Coerced Abstinence for Drug-Involved Offenders on Probation and Parole: A Proposed Experiment. *On Balance*, Spring: 4–6.

Klingemann, H.K. (1991) The Motivation to Change from Problem Alcohol and Heroin Use. *British Journal of Addiction*, 86: 23–5.

Klingeman, H. and Gmel, G. (Eds.) (2001) *Mapping the Social Consequences of Alcohol Consumption*. Kluwer Academic Publishers.

Lawental, E. et al. (1996) Coerced Treatment for Substance Abuse Problems Detected through Workplace Urine Surveillance: Is It Effective? *Journal of Substance Abuse*, 8: 1, 115–28.

Lincourt, P., Kuettel, T. and Bombardier, C. (2002) Motivational Interviewing in Group Setting With Mandated Clients: A Pilot Study. *Addictive Behaviours*, 27, 381–91.

Lipchick, E.D (2002) *Beyond Technique in Solution Focused Therapy*. New York: Guildford Press.

Lipton, D.S. (1995) *The Effectiveness of Treatment for Drug Abusers under Criminal Justice Supervision*. National Institute of Justice.

Loneck, B., Garret, J. and Banks, S.A. (1996a) Comparison of the Johnson Intervention to Four Other Methods of Referral to Outpatient Treatment. *American Journal of Drugs and Alcohol Abuse*, 22: 233–46.

Loneck, B., Garret, J. and Banks, S.A. (1996b) The Johnson Intervention and Relapse during Outpatient Treatment. *American Journal of Drug and Alcohol Abuse*, 22: 233–46.

Lurigo, A.J. (2001) Drug Treatment Availability and Effectiveness: Studies of the General and Criminal Justice Populations. *Criminal Justice and Behaviour*, 27: 4, 495–528.

Marlowe, D. B. et al. (2001) Multidimensional Assessment of Perceived Treatment-Entry Pressures Among Substance Abusers. *Psychology of Addictive Behaviours*, 15: 2, 97–108.

Martin, S.S. and Incardi, J.A. (1997) A Case Management Treatment Program for Drug Involved Prison Releasees. *The Prison Journal*, 73: 319–31.

Messina, N.P., Wish, E.D. and Nemes, S. (1999) Therapeutic Community Treatment for Substance Abusers with Antisocial Personality Disorder. *Journal of Substance Abuse Treatment*, 17: 1–2, 121–8.

Meyers, R.J. et al. (1999) Community Reinforcement and Family Training: Engaging Unmotivated Drug Users in Treatment. *Journal of Substance Abuse*, 10: 291–308.

Meyers, R.J. and Smith, J.C. (1997) Getting off the Fence: Procedures to Engage Treatment-Resistant Drinkers. *Journal of Substance Abuse Treatment*, 14: 467–72.

Miller, S.D. et al. (2005) Making Treatment Count: Client Directed, Outcome Informed Clinical Work with Problem Drinkers. *Psychotherapy in Australia*, 11: 4, 42–56.

Miller, W.R. (1989) Increasing Motivation for Change. In Hester, R.K. and Miller, W.R. (Eds.) *Handbook of Alcoholism Treatment Approaches*. Pergamon Press.

Miller, W.R., Meyers, R.J. and Tonigan, J.S. (1999) Engaging The Unmotivated in Treatment for Alcohol Problems: A Comparison of Three Intervention Strategies. *Journal of Consulting and Clinical Psychology*, 67: 5, 688–97.

Miller, W.R. and Rollnick, S. (2002) *Motivational Interviewing: Preparing People for Change*. New York: Guildford Press.

Moos, R.H., Finney, J.W. and Gamble, W. (1982) The Process of Recovery from Alcoholism: II. Comparing Spouses of Alcoholic Patients and Matched Community Controls. *Journal of Studies on Alcohol*, 43: 88–90.

National Institute on Alcohol Abuse and Alcoholism (1997) *Improving the Delivery of Alcohol Treatment and Prevention Services: Executive Summary*. NIH Publication No. 97-4224.

Orford, J. (1992) Control, Confront, Collude: How Family Members and Society Respond to Excessive Drinking. *British Journal of Addictions*, 87: 1513–25.

Orford, J. and Edwards, G. (1977) *Alcoholism: A Comparison of Treatment Advice, with a Study of the Influence of Marriage*. Maudsley Monograph, 26, Oxford University Press.

Orlinsky, D.E. and Howard, K.I. (1980) Gender and Psychotherapeutic Outcome. In Brodksy, A.M. and Hare-Mustin, R.T. (Eds.) *Women and Psychotherpay*. New York: Guildford Press.

Pearson, F.S. and Lipton, D.S. (1999) Meta-Analytic Review of the Effectiveness of Corrections-Based Treatment for Drug Abuse. *The Prison Journal*, 79: 384–410.

Pearson, F.S. et al. (2002) The Effects of Behaviour, Cognitive Behavioural Programs on Recidivism. *Crime and Delinquency*, 48: 476–96.

Peters, R.H. (1993) Drug Treatment in Jails and Detention Settings. In Inciardi, J.A. (Ed.) *Drug Treatment and the Criminal Justice System*. Sage.

Platt, J.J. et al. (1988) The Prospects and Limitations of Compulsory Treatment for Drug Addiction. *Journal of Drug Issues*, 18: 505–25.

Polcin, D.L. (2001) Drug and Alcohol Offenders Coerced into Treatment: A Review of Modalities and Suggestions for Research on Social Model Programs. *Substance Use and Misuse*, 36: 5, 589–608.

Polcin, D.L and Weisner, C. (1999) Factors Associated with Coercion in Entering Treatment for Alcohol Problems. *Drug and Alcohol Dependence*, 54: 63–8.

Prochaska, J.O., Norcross, J.C. and DiClemente, C.C. (1994) *Changing for Good*. William Morrow.

Project MATCH Research Group (1997) Matching Alcohol Treatments to Client Heterogeneity: Project MATCH Post-Treatment Drinking Outcomes. *Journal of Studies on Alcohol*, 58: 7–29.

Reich, W., Earls, E. and Powell, J. (1988) A Comparison of the Home and Social Environments of Children with Alcoholic Parents. *British Journal of Addiction*, 83: 831–9.

Room, R. Greenfield, T.K. and Weisner, C. (1991) People who might have Liked You to Drink Less. Changing Responses to Drinking by US Family Member and Friends, 1979–1990. *Contemporary Drug Problems*, 18: 573–95.

Rosenthal, M.P. (1988) The Constitutionality of Involuntary Civil Commitments of Opiate Addicts. *Journal of Drug Issues*, 18: 641–61.

Salmon, R.W. and Salmon, R.J. (1983) The Role of Coercion on Rehabilitation of Drug Abusers. *International Journal of Addictions*, 18: 9–21.

Santa Clara County Courts (1996) *Drug Treatment Second Progress Report.*

Simpson, D.D. (1998) *Patient Engagement and Duration of Treatment.* Paper Presented to the Office of National Drug Control Policy's Conference of Scholars and Policy Makers.

Sisson, R.W. and Azrin, N.H. (1986) Family-Member Involvement to Initiate and Promote Treatment of Problem Drinkers. *Journal of Behaviour Therapy and Experimental Psychiatry*, 17: 15–21.

Smith, J.E. and Meyers, R.J. (2004) *Motivating Substance Abusers to Enter Treatment: Working with Family Members.* New York: Guildford Press.

Sobell. M.B. and Sobell, L.C. (1993) Treatment for Problem Drinkers: A Public Health Priority. In Baer, J.S., Marlatt, G.A. and Mcmahon, R.J. (Eds.) *Addictive Behaviours across the Lifespan: Prevention, Treatment and Policy Issues.* Sage.

Sobell. M.B. and Sobell, L.C. (2000) Stepped Care as a Heuristic Approach to the Treatment of Alcohol Problems. *Journal of Consulting and Clinical Psychology*, 68: 573–9.

Stanton, M.D. and Shadish, W.R. (1997) Outcome, Attrition and Family-Couples Treatment for Drug Abuse: A Meta-Analysis and Review of the Controlled and Comparative Studies. *Psychological Bulletin*, 122: 170–91.

Wampold, B.E. (2001) *The Great Psychotherapy Debate: Models, Methods and Findings.* London: Erlbaum.

Weisner, C. (1990) Coercion in Alcohol Treatment. In Institute of Medicine (Ed.) *Broadening the Base of Treatment for Alcohol Problems.* National Academy Press.

Weisner, C. (1992) A Comparison of Alcohol and Drug Treatment Clients: Are they the Same Population? *American Journal of Drug and Alcohol Abuse*, 18: 4, 429–44.

Weisner, C., Greenfield, T. and Room, R. (1995) Trends in the Treatment of Alcohol Problems in the US General Population, 1979 Through 1990. *American Journal of Public Health*, 85: 1, 55–60.

Wild, T.C., Newton-Taylor, B. and Alletto, R. (1998) Perceived Coercion among Clients Entering Substance Abuse Treatment; Structural and Psychological Determinants. *Addictive Behaviours*, 23: 1, 81–95.

Wilson, C. and Orford, J. (1978) Children of Alcoholics: Report of a Preliminary Study and Comments on the Literature. *Quarterly Journal of Studies on Alcohol*, 39: 121–42.

Russell House Publishing Ltd

We publish a wide range of professional, reference and educational books including:

Safeguarding children and young people: A guide to integrated practice
By Steven Walker and Christina Thurston   ISBN 978-1-903855-90-4

Developing collaborative relationships in interagency child protection work
By Michael Murphy   ISBN 978-1-903855-48-5

Child exploitation and communication technologies
By Alisdair A. Gillespie   ISBN 978-1-905541-23-2

Children living with domestic violence: Towards a framework for assessment and intervention
Edited by Martin C. Calder   ISBN 978-1-903855-45-4

Secret lives: growing with substance - working with children and young people affected by familial substance misuse
Edited by Fiona Harbin and Michael Murphy   ISBN 978-1-903855-66-9

Preventing breakdown: A manual for childcare professionals working with high risk families
By Mark Hamer   ISBN 978-1-903855-61-4

Contemporary Risk Assessment in Safeguarding Children
Edited by Martin C. Calder   ISBN 978-1-905541-20-1

For more details, please visit our website: www.russellhouse.co.uk

Parents' anger management: The PAMP programme
By Gerry Heery   ISBN 978-1-905541-04-1

**The child and family in context: Developing ecological
practice in disadvantaged communities**
By Owen Gill and Gordon Jack   ISBN 978-1-905541-15-7

**Parental alienation: How to understand and address
parental alienation resulting from acrimonious
divorce or separation**
By L. F. Lowenstein   ISBN 978-1-905541-10-2

**Assessment in child care: Using and developing
frameworks for practice**
Edited by Martin C. Calder and Simon Hackett   ISBN 978-1-903855-14-0

Complete guide to sexual abuse assessments
By Martin C. Calder et al.   ISBN 978-1-898924-76-0

**Juveniles and children who sexually abuse:
Frameworks for assessment. Second Edition**
By Martin C. Calder et al.   ISBN 978-1-898924-95-1

For more details, please visit our website: *www.russellhouse.co.uk*

Or we can send you our catalogue if you contact us at:

Russell House Publishing Ltd,
4 St George's House, Uplyme Road Business Park,
Lyme Regis DT7 3LS, England,
Tel: 01297 443948
Fax: 01297 442722
Email: help@russellhouse.co.uk